HMH SOCIAL STUDIES

HMH

UNITED STATES HISTORY

CIVIL WAR TO THE PRESENT

HISTORY.

Educational Advisory Panel

The following educators provided ongoing review during the development of prototypes and key elements of this program.

Contents

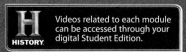

Videos related to each module can be accessed through your digital Student Edition.

Prologue

★

Module 1

★

Module 2

Module 3

Module 4

⭐

Module 5

⭐

Module 6

⭐

Module 7

⭐

Module 8

⭐

Module 9

⭐

Module 10

Module 11

Module 12

⭐

Module 13

⭐

Module 14

⭐

Module 15

Module 16

References

Available Online

Reading Like a Historian

Historic Documents

Biographical Dictionary

Close-Read Screencasts

Facts About the States

Presidents of the United States

Supreme Court Decisions

Economics Handbook

Geography and Map Skills Handbook

Skillbuilder Handbook

 Multimedia Connections

HISTORY.

These online lessons feature award-winning content and include short video segments, maps and visual materials, primary source documents, and more.

Days of Darkness: The Gettysburg Civilians

Lewis and Clark

Henry Ford

Ellis Island

Dear Home: Letters from World War I

Memories of World War II

October Fury: The Cuban Missile Crisis

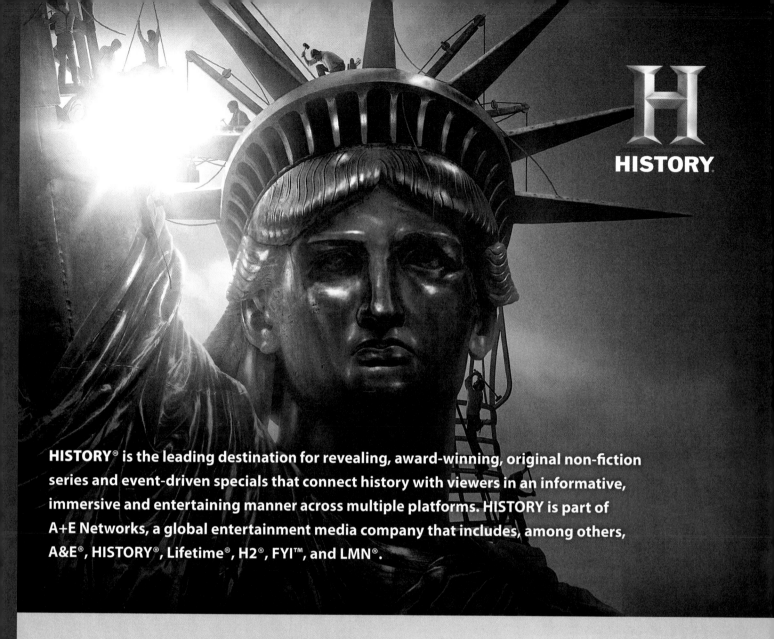

HISTORY® is the leading destination for revealing, award-winning, original non-fiction series and event-driven specials that connect history with viewers in an informative, immersive and entertaining manner across multiple platforms. HISTORY is part of A+E Networks, a global entertainment media company that includes, among others, A&E®, HISTORY®, Lifetime®, H2®, FYI™, and LMN®.

HISTORY programming greatly appeals to educators and young people who are drawn into the visual stories our documentaries tell. Our Education Department has a long-standing record in providing teachers and students with curriculum resources that bring the past to life in the classroom. Our content covers a diverse variety of subjects, including American and world history, government, economics, the natural and applied sciences, arts, literature and the humanities, health and guidance, and even pop culture.

The HISTORY website, located at **www.history.com**, is the definitive historical online source that delivers entertaining and informative content featuring broadband video, interactive timelines, maps, games, podcasts and more.

"We strive to engage, inspire and encourage the love of learning..."

Since its founding in 1995, HISTORY has demonstrated a commitment to providing the highest quality resources for educators. We develop multimedia resources for K–12 schools, two- and four-year colleges, government agencies, and other organizations by drawing on the award-winning documentary programming of A&E Television Networks. We strive to engage, inspire and encourage the love of learning by connecting with students in an informative and compelling manner. To help achieve this goal, we have formed a partnership with Houghton Mifflin Harcourt.

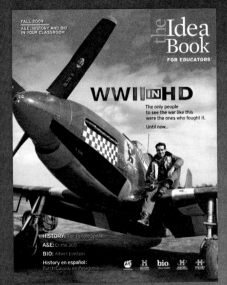
The Idea Book for Educators

Classroom resources that bring the past to life

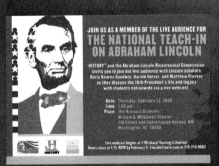
Live webcasts

HISTORY Take a Veteran to School Day

In addition to premium video-based resources, **HISTORY** has extensive offerings for teachers, parents, and students to use in the classroom and in their in-home educational activities, including:

- *The Idea Book for Educators* is a biannual teacher's magazine, featuring guides and info on the latest happenings in history education to help keep teachers on the cutting edge.

- **HISTORY** Classroom (www.history.com/classroom) is an interactive website that serves as a portal for history educators nationwide. Streaming videos on topics ranging from the Roman aqueducts to the civil rights movement connect with classroom curricula.

- **HISTORY** email newsletters feature updates and supplements to our award-winning programming relevant to the classroom with links to teaching guides and video clips on a variety of topics, special offers, and more.

- **Live webcasts** are featured each year as schools tune in via streaming video.

- **HISTORY** Take a Veteran to School Day connects veterans with young people in our schools and communities nationwide.

In addition to **Houghton Mifflin Harcourt**, our partners include the *Library of Congress,* the *Smithsonian Institution, National History Day, The Gilder Lehrman Institute of American History,* the Organization of American Historians, and many more. HISTORY video is also featured in museums throughout America and in over 70 other historic sites worldwide.

Reading Social Studies

Did you ever think you would begin reading your social studies book by reading about reading? Actually, it makes better sense than you might think. You would probably make sure you learned soccer skills and strategies before playing in a game. Similarly, you need to learn reading skills and strategies before reading your social studies book. In other words, you need to make sure you know whatever you need to know in order to read this book successfully.

Tip #1

Use the Reading Social Studies Pages

Take advantage of the two pages on reading at the beginning of every module. Those pages introduce the module themes, explain a reading skill or strategy, and identify key terms and people.

Themes

Why are themes important? They help our minds organize facts and information. For example, when we talk about baseball, we may talk about types of pitches. When we talk about movies, we may discuss animation.

Historians are no different. When they discuss history or social studies, they tend to think about some common themes: Economics, Geography, Religion, Politics, Society and Culture, and Science and Technology.

Reading Skill or Strategy

Good readers use a number of skills and strategies to make sure they understand what they are reading. These lessons will give you the tools you need to read and understand social studies.

Key Terms and People

Before you read the module, review these words and think about them. Have you heard the word before? What do you already know about the people? Then watch for these words and their meanings as you read the module.

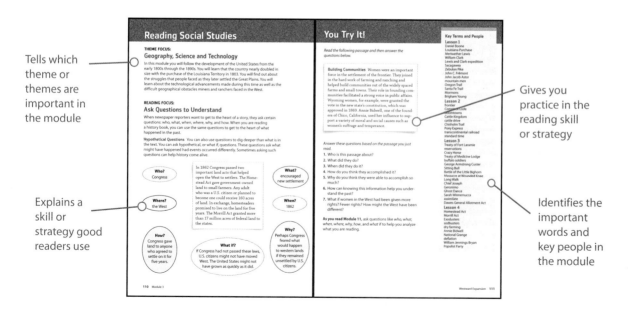

Tells which theme or themes are important in the module

Explains a skill or strategy good readers use

Gives you practice in the reading skill or strategy

Identifies the important words and key people in the module

Tip #2

Read like a Skilled Reader

You will never get better at reading your social studies book—or any book for that matter—unless you spend some time thinking about how to be a better reader.

Skilled readers do the following:

- They preview what they are supposed to read before they actually begin reading. They look for vocabulary words, titles of lessons, information in the margin, or maps or charts they should study.

- They divide their notebook paper into two columns. They title one column "Notes from the Lesson" and the other column "Questions or Comments I Have."

- They take notes in both columns as they read.

- They read like **active readers**. The Active Reading list below shows you what that means.

- They use clues in the text to help them figure out where the text is going. The best clues are called signal words.

    Chronological Order Signal Words: *first, second, third, before, after, later, next, following that, earlier, finally*

    Cause and Effect Signal Words: *because of, due to, as a result of, the reason for, therefore, consequently*

    Comparison/Contrast Signal Words: *likewise, also, as well as, similarly, on the other hand*

Active Reading

Successful readers are **active readers**. These readers know that it is up to them to figure out what the text means. Here are some steps you can take to become an active, and successful, reader.

Predict what will happen next based on what has already happened. When your predictions don't match what happens in the text, reread the confusing parts.

Question what is happening as you read. Constantly ask yourself why things have happened, what things mean, and what caused certain events.

Summarize what you are reading frequently. Do not try to summarize the entire module! Read a bit and then summarize it. Then read on.

Connect what is happening in the part you're reading to what you have already read.

Clarify your understanding. Stop occasionally to ask yourself whether you are confused by anything. You may need to reread to clarify, or you may need to read further and collect more information before you can understand.

Visualize what is happening in the text. Try to see the events or places in your mind by drawing maps, making charts, or jotting down notes about what you are reading.

Tip #3

Pay Attention to Vocabulary

It is no fun to read something when you don't know what the words mean, but you can't learn new words if you use or read only the words you already know. In this book, we know we probably have used some words you don't know. But, we have followed a pattern as we have used more difficult words.

Key Terms and People

At the beginning of each lesson you will find a list of key terms and people that you will need to know. Be on the lookout for those words as you read through the lesson.

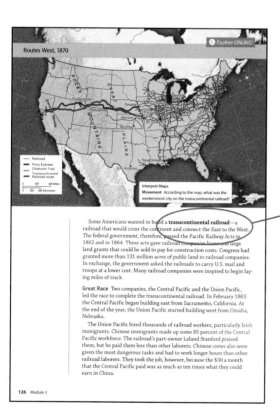

Academic Vocabulary
facilitate to make easier

Academic Vocabulary

When the text uses a word that is important in all classes, not just social studies, we define it in the margin under the heading Academic Vocabulary. You will run into these academic words in other textbooks, so you should learn what they mean while reading this book.

Academic and Social Studies Words

As you read this social studies textbook, you will be more successful if you know or learn the meanings of the words on this page. Academic words are important in all classes, not just social studies. Social studies words are special to the study of U.S. history and other social studies topics.

Academic Words

abstract expressing a quality or idea without reference to an actual thing

acquire to get

advocate to plead in favor of

affect to change or influence

agreement a decision reached by two or more people or groups

aspects parts

authority power, right to rule

cause the reason something happens

circumstances surrounding situations

classical referring to the cultures of ancient Greece or Rome

complex difficult, not simple

concrete specific, real

consequences the effects of a particular event or events

contemporary existing at the same time

contract a binding legal agreement

criteria rules for defining

develop/development 1. the process of growing or improving; 2. creation

distinct separate

distribute to divide among a group of people

effect the result of an action or decision

efficient/efficiency productive and not wasteful

element part

execute to perform, carry out

explicit fully revealed without vagueness

facilitate to bring about

factor cause

features characteristics

function use or purpose

impact effect, result

implement to put in place

implications effects of a decision

implicit understood though not clearly put into words

incentive something that leads people to follow a certain course of action

influence change or have an effect on

innovation a new idea or way of doing something

logic/logical 1. reasoned, well thought out; 2. well thought out idea

motive a reason for doing something

neutral unbiased, not favoring either side in a conflict

policy rule, course of action

primary main, most important

principle basic belief, rule, or law

procedure a series of steps taken to accomplish a task

process a series of steps by which a task is accomplished

reaction a response

role 1. a part or function; 2. assigned behavior

strategy a plan for fighting a battle or war

structure the way something is set up or organized

traditional customary, time-honored

values ideas that people hold dear and try to live by

vary/various 1. to be different; 2. of many types

Social Studies Words

AD refers to dates after the birth of Jesus of Nazareth

BC refers to dates before the birth of Jesus

BCE refers to "Before Common Era," dates before the birth of Jesus

CE refers to "Common Era," dates after the birth of Jesus

century a period of 100 years

civilization the culture of a particular time or place

climate the weather conditions in a certain area over a long period of time

culture the knowledge, beliefs, customs, and values of a group of people

custom a repeated practice, tradition

democracy governmental rule by the people, usually on a majority rule principle

economy the system in which people make and exchange goods and services

geography the study of the earth's physical and cultural features

independence freedom from forceful rule

monarchy governmental rule by one person, a king or queen

North the region of the United States sometimes defined by the states that did not secede from the Union during the Civil War

rebellion an organized resistance to the established government

society a group of people who share common traditions

South the region of the United States sometimes defined by the states that seceded from the Union to form the Confederate States of America

Using This Book

Studying U.S. history will be easy for you using this textbook. Take a few minutes to become familiar with the easy-to-use structure and special features of this history book. See how this U.S. history textbook will make history come alive for you!

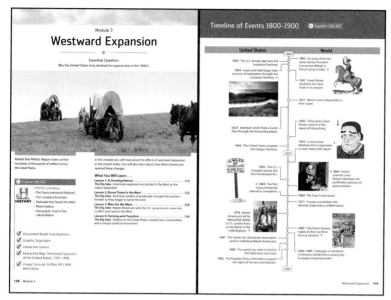

Module

Each module begins with an Essential Question and a Timeline of Events showing important dates in U.S. and world history, and ends with a Module Assessment.

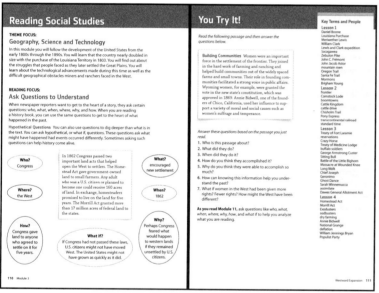

Reading Social Studies

These reading lessons teach you skills and provide opportunities for practice to help you read the textbook more successfully. There are questions in the Module Assessment to make sure you understand the reading skill.

Social Studies Skills

The Social Studies Skills lessons give you an opportunity to learn and use a skill you will most likely use again while in school. You will also be given a chance to make sure that you understand each skill by answering related questions in the Module Assessment activity.

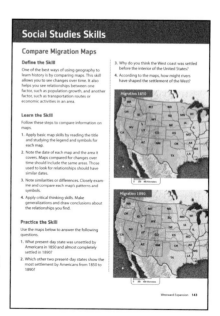

Lesson

The lesson opener includes an overarching Big Idea statement, Main Ideas, and Key Terms and People.

If YOU were there . . . introductions begin each lesson with a situation for you to respond to, placing you in the time period and in a situation related to the content you will be studying in the lesson.

Headings and subheadings organize the information into manageable chunks of text that will help you learn and understand the lesson's main ideas.

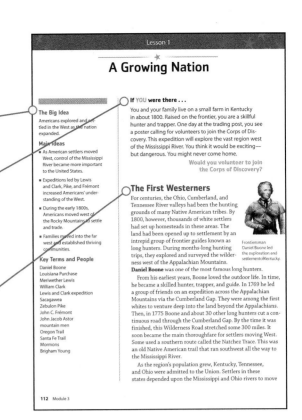

A Growing Nation

The Big Idea
Americans explored and settled in the West as the nation expanded.

Main Ideas
- As American settlers moved West, control of the Mississippi River became more important to the United States.
- Expeditions led by Lewis and Clark, Pike, and Frémont increased Americans' understanding of the West.
- During the early 1800s, Americans moved west of the Rocky Mountains to settle and trade.
- Families moved into the far west and established thriving communities.

Key Terms and People
Daniel Boone
Louisiana Purchase
Meriwether Lewis
William Clark
Lewis and Clark expedition
Sacagawea
Zebulon Pike
John C. Frémont
John Jacob Astor
mountain men
Oregon Trail
Santa Fe Trail
Mormons
Brigham Young

If YOU were there . . .
You and your family live on a small farm in Kentucky in about 1800. Raised on the frontier, you are a skillful hunter and trapper. One day at the trading post, you see a poster calling for volunteers to join the Corps of Discovery. This expedition will explore the vast region west of the Mississippi River. You think it would be exciting—but dangerous. You might never come home.

Would you volunteer to join the Corps of Discovery?

The First Westerners
For centuries, the Ohio, Cumberland, and Tennessee River valleys had been the hunting grounds of many Native American tribes. By 1800, however, thousands of white settlers had set up homesteads in these areas. The land had been opened up to settlement by an intrepid group of frontier guides known as long hunters. During months-long hunting trips, they explored and surveyed the wilderness west of the Appalachian Mountains. **Daniel Boone** was one of the most famous long hunters.

From his earliest years, Boone loved the outdoor life. In time, he became a skilled hunter, trapper, and guide. In 1769 he led a group of friends on an expedition across the Appalachian Mountains via the Cumberland Gap. They were among the first whites to venture deep into the land beyond the Appalachians. Then, in 1775 Boone and about 30 other long hunters cut a continuous road through the Cumberland Gap. By the time it was finished, this Wilderness Road stretched some 300 miles. It soon became the main thoroughfare for settlers moving West. Some used a southern route called the Natchez Trace. This was an old Native American trail that ran southwest all the way to the Mississippi River.

As the region's population grew, Kentucky, Tennessee, and Ohio were admitted to the Union. Settlers in these states depended upon the Mississippi and Ohio rivers to move

Frontiersman Daniel Boone led the exploration and settlement of Kentucky.

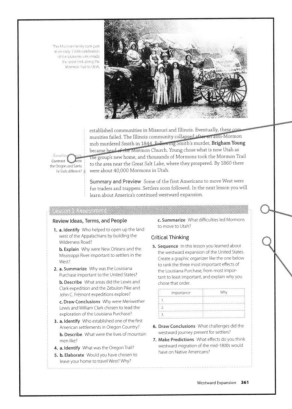

This Mormon family took part in an early-1900s celebration of the pioneers who made the great trek along the Mormon Trail to Utah.

established communities in Missouri and Illinois. Eventually, these communities failed. The Illinois community collapsed after an anti-Mormon mob murdered Smith in 1844. Following Smith's murder, **Brigham Young** became head of the Mormon Church. Young chose what is now Utah as the group's new home, and thousands of Mormons took the Mormon Trail to the area near the Great Salt Lake, where they prospered. By 1860 there were about 40,000 Mormons in Utah.

Reading Check
Contrast How were the Oregon and Santa Fe Trails different?

Summary and Preview Some of the first Americans to move West were fur traders and trappers. Settlers soon followed. In the next lesson you will learn about America's continued westward expansion.

Lesson 1 Assessment

Review Ideas, Terms, and People
1. **a. Identify** Who helped to open up the land west of the Appalachians by building the Wilderness Road?
   b. Explain Why were New Orleans and the Mississippi River important to settlers in the West?
2. **a. Summarize** Why was the Louisiana Purchase important to the United States?
   b. Describe What areas did the Lewis and Clark expedition and the Zebulon Pike and John C. Frémont expeditions explore?
   c. Draw Conclusions Why were Meriwether Lewis and William Clark chosen to lead the exploration of the Louisiana Purchase?
3. **a. Identify** Who established one of the first American settlements in Oregon Country?
   b. Describe What were the lives of mountain men like?
4. **a. Identify** What was the Oregon Trail?
5. **b. Elaborate** Would you have chosen to leave your home to travel West? Why?

c. Summarize What difficulties led Mormons to move to Utah?

Critical Thinking
5. **Sequence** In this lesson you learned about the westward expansion of the United States. Create a graphic organizer like the one below to rank the three most important effects of the Louisiana Purchase, from most important to least important, and explain why you chose that order.

Importance	Why
1	
2	
3	

6. **Draw Conclusions** What challenges did the westward journey present for settlers?
7. **Make Predictions** What effects do you think westward migration of the mid-1800s would have on Native Americans?

Reading Check questions are at the end of each main heading so you can test whether or not you understand what you have just studied.

Summary and Preview statements connect what you have just studied in the lesson to what you will study in the next lesson.

Lesson Assessment boxes provide an opportunity for you to make sure you understand the main ideas of the lesson.

HMH Social Studies
Dashboard

Designed for today's digital natives, **HMH® Social Studies** offers you an informative and exciting online experience.

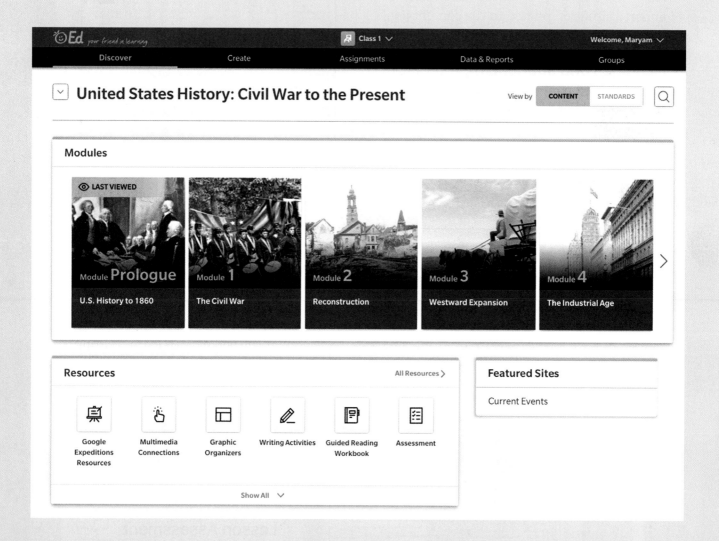

Your personalized Dashboard is organized into three main sections:

1. **Discover**—Quickly access content and search program resources

2. **Assignments**—Review your assignments and check your progress on them

3. **Data & Reports**—Monitor your progress on the course

Explore Online ▷
to **Experience** the **Power** of
United States History
Civil War to the Present

Houghton Mifflin Harcourt™ is **changing** the way you **experience** social studies.

By delivering an immersive experience through compelling narratives enriched with media, we're connecting you to history through experiences that are energizing, inspiring, and memorable. The following pages highlight some digital tools and instructional support that will help you approach history through active inquiry, so you can connect to the past while becoming active and informed citizens for the future.

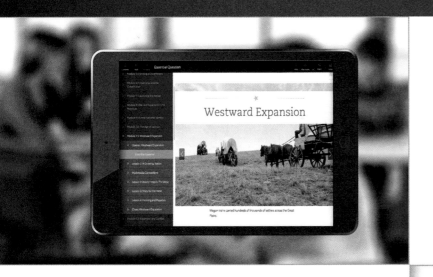

The Student eBook is the primary learning portal.

More than just the digital version of a textbook, the Student eBook serves as the primary learning portal for you. The narrative is supported by a wealth of multimedia and learning resources to bring history to life and give you the tools you need to succeed.

Bringing Content to Life

HISTORY® videos and Multimedia Connections bring content to life through primary source footage, dramatic storytelling, and expert testimonials.

In-Depth Understanding

Close Read Screencasts model an analytical conversation about primary sources.

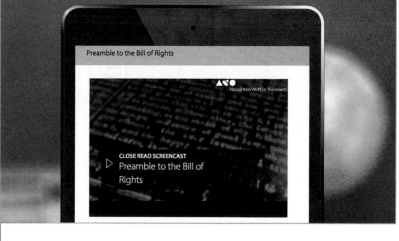

Content in a Fun Way

Interactive Features, Maps, and **Games** provide quick, entertaining activities and assessments that present important content in a fun way.

Investigate Like a Historian

Document-Based Investigations in every lesson build to end-of-module DBI performance tasks so you can examine and assess primary sources as historians do.

Full-Text Audio Support

You can listen while you read.

Skills Support

Point-of-use support is just a click away, providing instruction on critical reading and social studies skills.

Personalized Annotations

My Notes encourages you to take notes while you read and allows you to customize them to your study preferences. You can easily access them to review later as you prepare for exams.

Interactive Lesson Graphic Organizers

Graphic organizers help you process, summarize, and keep track of your learning for end-of-module performance tasks.

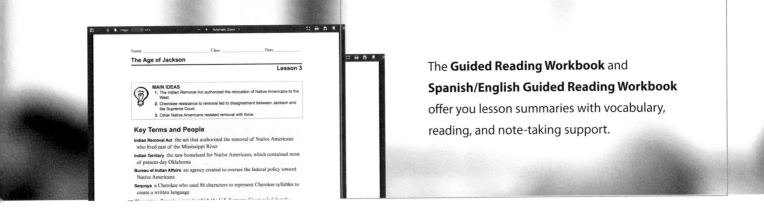

The **Guided Reading Workbook** and **Spanish/English Guided Reading Workbook** offer you lesson summaries with vocabulary, reading, and note-taking support.

Current Events features trustworthy articles on today's news that connect what you learn in class to the world around you.

No Wi-Fi®? No problem!

HMH Social Studies United States History: Civil War to the Present will allow you to connect to content and resources by downloading them when online and accessing them when offline.

Prologue

U.S. History to 1860

★

Essential Question
What historical forces were most important in shaping the United States before 1860?

About the Photo: On July 4, 1776, American colonial leaders approved the Declaration of Independence, breaking all ties to Great Britain.

▷ *Explore ONLINE!*

HISTORY.

VIDEOS, including...
- American Revolution: One Word
- Columbus Sails West
- Jefferson Writes the Declaration of Independence
- The Mexican-American War

☑ Document-Based Investigations

☑ Graphic Organizers

☑ Interactive Map: Migrations of Early People

☑ Image with Hotspots: The First Cabinet

☑ Image Carousel: Images of Slavery

In this module you will learn about the key events and people in U.S. history from the nation's beginnings to the outbreak of the Civil War.

What You Will Learn

United States

1492

1492 Christopher Columbus and his crew reach the Americas on October 12. ⟩

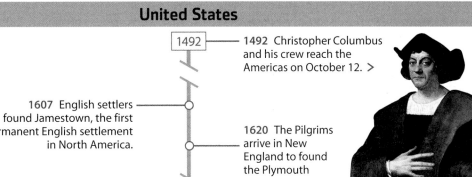

1607 English settlers found Jamestown, the first permanent English settlement in North America.

1620 The Pilgrims arrive in New England to found the Plymouth Colony.

⟨ **1765** Great Britain's Parliament passes the Stamp Act, establishing new taxes for the American colonists.

1776 On July 4, the 13 colonies issue the Declaration of Independence and break away from Great Britain. ⟩

1775 The Revolutionary War begins with the fighting at Lexington and Concord.

1787 On May 14, state delegates begin to arrive at the Constitutional Convention in Philadelphia.

1791 The Constitution's first ten amendments, which form the Bill of Rights, are ratified on December 15.

⟨ **1804** Lewis and Clark begin their journey westward.

1831 Nat Turner leads a slave rebellion in Virginia.

∧ **1838** The Trail of Tears begins when U.S. troops remove the Cherokee from Georgia.

1846 The United States declares war against Mexico.

1860 Abraham Lincoln wins the U.S. presidential election.

1850 California enters the Union as a free state.

1860

Reading Social Studies

THEME FOCUS:
Politics, Society and Culture

This module provides an overview of United States history before 1860. You will learn about the people and cultures that contributed to the founding and growth of the United States. You will also read about important events that led the nation to expand westward and gain new territory. Throughout the module, you will also read about key social and political forces that united and divided the nation.

READING FOCUS:
Specialized Vocabulary of Social Studies

If you flipped through the pages of this book, would you expect to see anything about square roots or formulas? How about petri dishes or hypotheses? Of course you wouldn't. Those are terms you see only in math and science books.

Specialized Vocabulary Like most subjects, social studies has its own specialized vocabulary. Included in it are words and phrases you will see over and over as you read social studies materials. The charts below list some terms you will encounter as you read this book.

Terms about Time	
decade	a period of 10 years
century	a period of 100 years
era	a long period marked by great events, developments, or figures
BC	a term used to identify dates that occurred long ago, before the birth of Jesus Christ, on whose teachings Christianity was founded; it means "before Christ." BC dates get smaller as time passes, so the larger the number, the earlier the date.
AD	a term used to identify dates that occurred after Jesus's birth; it comes from a Latin phrase that means "in the year of our Lord." Unlike BC dates, AD dates get larger as time passes, so the larger the number, the later the date.

Terms about Government, Society and Culture	
society	a group of people that shares a culture
colony	a territory settled and controlled by a country
politics	the art of creating government policies
economics	the study of the creation and use of goods and services
movement	a series of actions that bring about or try to bring about a change in society
campaign	an effort to win a political office, or a series of military actions

You Try It!

The following passage shows you how some specialized vocabulary is defined in context.

The Earliest Americans Many historians agree that **Paleo-Indians**, the first people to live in North America, came from Asia sometime between 38,000 and 10,000 BC. One theory proposes that people walked across a thin strip of land called the Bering Land Bridge that once connected northeastern Asia to present-day Alaska. Another theory suggests that people from East Asia may have traveled to the Americas by boat. As they spread through the Americas, these early Native Americans created many societies—groups that share a culture, or a set of common values and traditions.

Use the clues to understand meaning.

1. In the first sentence, find the term *Paleo-Indians*. Notice that the term is **highlighted** in yellow. Highlighted terms appear in a list under Key Terms and People on the first page of each lesson. Why do you think some specialized vocabulary terms are highlighted, while others are not?

2. Again, find the word *Paleo-Indians*. The phrase after the comma is the definition. Specialized vocabulary words are often defined after a comma or dash. So be on the lookout for commas and dashes.

3. The word *societies* is defined in the last sentence. The clue to finding this definition is the dash. In this case, the definition of societies is "groups that share a culture."

4. The word *culture* is also defined in the final sentence. The clue to finding this definition is the comma followed by the word **or**. Commas followed by words such as **called** or **known as** are also often clues that a definition is coming up. So be on the lookout for commas followed by *or*, *called*, and *known as*.

As you read the Prologue, keep track of the specialized vocabulary that you learn.

Key Terms and People

Lesson 1
Paleo-Indians
Christopher Columbus
Jamestown
Puritans
Great Awakening
Declaration of Independence
Patriots
Treaty of Paris of 1783

Lesson 2
Articles of Confederation
Shays's Rebellion
Constitutional Convention
Three-Fifths Compromise
Antifederalists
Federalists
federalism
George Washington

Lesson 3
Thomas Jefferson
Alien and Sedition Acts
Louisiana Purchase
Lewis and Clark expedition
Monroe Doctrine
Erie Canal
Missouri Compromise
Jacksonian Democracy

Lesson 4
Trail of Tears
Oregon Trail
manifest destiny
Eli Whitney
abolition movement
Frederick Douglass
temperance movement
Elizabeth Cady Stanton

Lesson 5
Free-Soil Party
Compromise of 1850
Fugitive Slave Act
Kansas-Nebraska Act
Harriet Beecher Stowe
Dred Scott
Abraham Lincoln
Confederate States of America

★ Our Colonial Heritage

The Big Idea
The English founded thirteen colonies along the east coast of North America.

Main Ideas
- Christopher Columbus sailed across the Atlantic Ocean and reached a continent with cultures previously unknown to Europeans.
- Despite a difficult beginning, the English colonies soon flourished.
- After more than a hundred years, American colonists risked their lives for independence.

Key Terms and People
Paleo-Indians
Christopher Columbus
Jamestown
Puritans
Great Awakening
Declaration of Independence
Patriots
Treaty of Paris of 1783

If YOU were there . . .

A year ago, in 1609, you moved to the colony of Virginia. Life here has been hard. During the winter many people died of cold or sickness. Food is always scarce. Now it is spring, and a ship has come from England bringing supplies. In a week it will sail home. Some of your neighbors are giving up and returning to England. They ask you to come, too.

Would you take the ship back to England?

American Beginnings

The Earliest Americans Many historians agree that **Paleo-Indians**, the first people to live in North America, came from Asia sometime between 38,000 and 10,000 BC. One theory proposes that people walked across a thin strip of land called the Bering Land Bridge that once connected northeastern Asia to present-day Alaska. Another theory suggests that people from East Asia may have traveled to the Americas by boat. As they spread through the Americas, these early Native Americans created many societies— groups that share a culture, or a set of common values and traditions.

Land and climate had a dramatic impact on these early societies. Some places were good for farming or had a rich supply of wild animals and plants. In these areas large groups of people lived in villages. This was true in the Pacific Coast and parts of the East and Southwest. Other parts of North America had less game and were too dry and cold for farming. In these regions Native Americans lived in smaller groups and had to move often to find food. Farther south, in modern-day Mexico and Peru, Native Americans called the Aztec, Maya, and the Inca each built powerful empires.

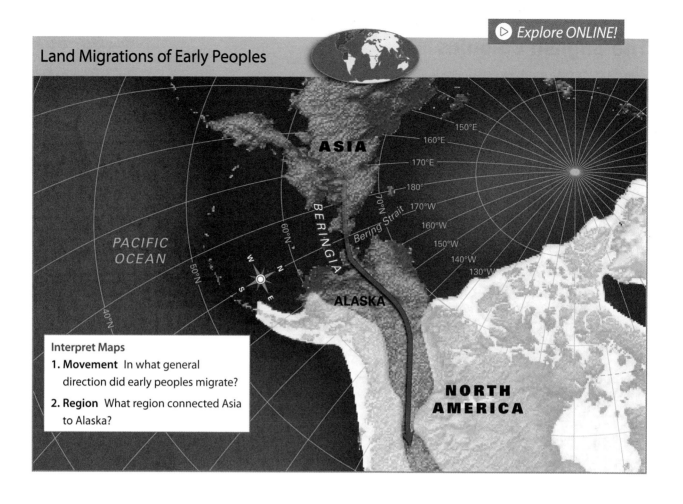

Land Migrations of Early Peoples

▶ Explore ONLINE!

ASIA

150°E
160°E
170°E
180°
70°N
170°W
160°W
150°W
140°W
130°W
60°N
50°N
40°N

BERINGIA

Bering Strait

PACIFIC OCEAN

ALASKA

NORTH AMERICA

Interpret Maps

1. **Movement** In what general direction did early peoples migrate?

2. **Region** What region connected Asia to Alaska?

Reading Check
Identify Points of View
Why did Columbus want to sail across the Atlantic?

European Exploration and Colonies The Atlantic and Pacific Oceans kept the Americas isolated from the rest of the world for many years. By the AD 1400s, however, Europeans were exploring the seas. They wanted to find overseas routes to the valuable Asian silk and spice trade. Portuguese sailors traveled east around the southern tip of Africa to reach Asia. **Christopher Columbus**, a sailor from Genoa, Italy, convinced the king and queen of Spain to support his search for a western sea route. In 1492 Columbus's small fleet crossed the Atlantic Ocean. The ships landed not in Asia, as Columbus believed, but on an island in the Bahamas.

Other Europeans soon came to the Americas. Spanish soldiers called conquistadors conquered the Aztec and Inca and claimed their lands, encouraging Spain to carve out an empire in the Americas. Spain's success led countries such as France, the Netherlands, Sweden, and England to form their own colonies in North America.

Two years after landing on the Caribbean island of Hispaniola, Christopher Columbus wrote a letter to the Spanish king and queen outlining his ideas for its colonization.

The English Colonies

The first permanent English settlement in North America was **Jamestown**, in what is now Virginia. In time, England founded thirteen colonies in North America, in three general regions, each with its own unique characteristics.

The Jamestown colonists came seeking wealth and opportunity. Other English colonists, such as the Pilgrims and the English Catholics who founded Maryland, came seeking religious freedom. All found many challenges and opportunities awaiting them in a new land.

The Southern Colonies Virginia, Maryland, Georgia, and North and South Carolina made up the southern colonies. Like later colonists in New England, the early Virginia settlers relied on the aid of local Native Americans to survive the harsh conditions they faced. The southern economy depended upon growing cash crops such as tobacco and rice. The biggest farms were called plantations. At first indentured servants did much of the work on these plantations. By the 1700s, however, enslaved Africans had replaced indentured servants as the main source of labor. The southern colonies used harsh laws called slave codes to control and punish slaves.

The New England Colonies New England consisted of Massachusetts, Connecticut, New Hampshire, and Rhode Island. Puritans seeking religious freedom founded colonies in New England. The **Puritans** were English Protestants who wanted to reform the Church of England but were persecuted for their beliefs. In 1620 a group of Puritans called Pilgrims became the first English

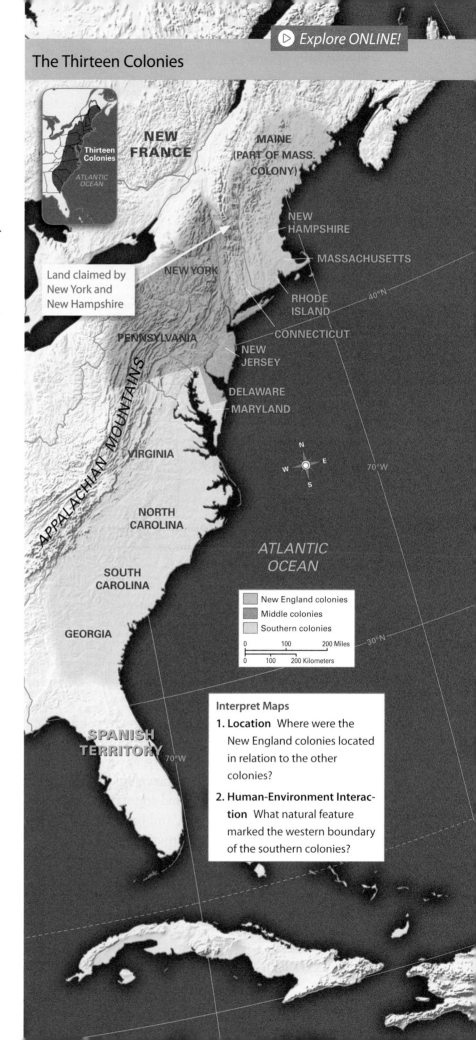

▶ Explore ONLINE!

The Thirteen Colonies

Thirteen Colonies

ATLANTIC OCEAN

NEW FRANCE

MAINE (PART OF MASS. COLONY)

NEW HAMPSHIRE

MASSACHUSETTS

NEW YORK

RHODE ISLAND

40°N

CONNECTICUT

Land claimed by New York and New Hampshire

PENNSYLVANIA

NEW JERSEY

DELAWARE

MARYLAND

APPALACHIAN MOUNTAINS

VIRGINIA

70°W

NORTH CAROLINA

ATLANTIC OCEAN

SOUTH CAROLINA

New England colonies
Middle colonies
Southern colonies

GEORGIA

0   100   200 Miles
0 100 200 Kilometers

30°N

SPANISH TERRITORY

70°W

Interpret Maps

1. **Location** Where were the New England colonies located in relation to the other colonies?

2. **Human-Environment Interaction** What natural feature marked the western boundary of the southern colonies?

The Mayflower Compact

In November 1620 Pilgrim leaders aboard the *Mayflower* drafted the Mayflower Compact. This excerpt from the Mayflower Compact describes the principles of the Pilgrim colony's government.

> "We whose names are underwritten . . . having undertaken, for the glory of God, and advancement of the Christian faith, and the honour of our King and country, a voyage to plant the first colony in the northern parts of Virginia, do by these **presents**[1] solemnly and mutually in the presence of God, and one of another, **covenant**[2] and combine ourselves together into a civil body **politic**[3] for our better ordering and preservation and furtherance of the ends **aforesaid**[4]; and by **virtue**[5] hereof, to enact, constitute, and frame such just and equal laws, **ordinances**[6], acts, constitutions, and offices . . . as shall be thought most **meet**[7] and convenient for the general good of the colony unto which we promise all due . . . obedience."

The Pilgrims describe the reasons they want to form a colony in North America.

The Pilgrims promise to obey laws that help the whole colony.

[1] *by these presents:* by this document
[2] *covenant:* promise
[3] *civil body politic:* group organized to govern
[4] *aforesaid:* mentioned above
[5] *virtue:* authority
[6] *ordinances:* regulations
[7] *meet:* fitting

Analyze Historical Sources
Why do you think the colonists felt the need to establish a government for themselves?

settlers in Massachusetts. From the start, the Pilgrims tested out new forms of government. Before landing at Plymouth Rock in present-day Massachusetts, the male passengers on board the *Mayflower* signed the Mayflower Compact. The Compact established a self-governing colony based on the majority rule of male church members.

Settlers in New England built a diverse economy based on shipping, fishing, farming, and manufacturing. Puritan families valued education and built schools for their children. Politics and religion were closely connected, with only church members allowed to vote or hold office. The center of politics was the town meeting, where people met to discuss local issues. Conflict over religious beliefs led Puritan leaders to banish people like Anne Hutchinson and Roger Williams from Massachusetts.

The Middle Colonies The middle colonies included New York, New Jersey, Pennsylvania, and Delaware. They combined qualities of the New England and southern colonies. Like New England, they had many towns and were centers of trade with Britain and the West Indies. Like the southern colonies, the middle colonies grew large amounts of crops, mainly wheat, barley, and oats. Indentured servants and, to a lesser degree, slaves did much of the labor.

Reading Check
Find Main Ideas
What were some of the reasons colonists came to the English colonies?

Creating a Nation

Two historical events, the Great Awakening and the French and Indian War, helped unite colonists living in very different areas. In the 1730s and 1740s, a Christian religious movement called the **Great Awakening** swept the colonies. It drew people from all walks of life to hear sermons about spiritual equality and social issues.

In 1754 the French and Indian War began, pitting the British colonists against French colonists and their Indian allies. The British won the war in 1763. This victory encouraged colonists to settle farther west.

Road to War To pay for the war, Parliament passed new taxes on colonial goods, such as sugar, paper products, and tea. Many colonists saw this as "taxation without representation," because they had no officials representing them in Parliament. They responded by boycotting, or refusing to buy, British goods. Tensions rose. When British troops fired on a Boston mob in 1770, colonists were outraged. Colonists called the shootings the Boston Massacre. Paul Revere created an elaborate color print titled "The Bloody Massacre perpetrated in King Street."

When colonists dumped British tea into the Boston Harbor in 1773, Parliament was furious. Soon British troops occupied Boston and closed its harbor.

DOCUMENT-BASED INVESTIGATION   Historical Source

The Boston Massacre

An account of the Boston Massacre appeared in the *Boston Gazette and Country Journal* soon after the event.

Analyze Historical Sources
Why do you think the people described were not intimidated by the soldiers?

"The People were immediately alarmed with the Report of this horrid Massacre, the Bells were set a Ringing, and great Numbers soon assembled at the Place where this tragical Scene had been acted; their Feelings may be better conceived than expressed; and while some were taking Care of the Dead and Wounded, the Rest were in Consultation what to do in these dreadful Circumstances.

But so little intimidated were they [Bostonians], notwithstanding their being within a few Yards of the Main Guard, and seeing the 29th Regiment under Arms, and drawn up in King street; that they kept their Station and appeared, as an Officer of Rank expressed it, ready to run upon the very Muzzles of their Muskets."

—*Boston Gazette and Country Journal*, March 12, 1770

The American Revolution Colonial delegates met at the First Continental Congress and decided to prepare for war. When British troops tried to destroy a supply of weapons at Lexington and Concord, Massachusetts, colonial minutemen fought back, beginning the Revolutionary War. At the Second Continental Congress, delegates put George Washington in charge of the Continental Army.

A widely read pamphlet by Thomas Paine called *Common Sense* argued that the colonies should declare independence, and that the people, not kings, should make the laws. On July 4, 1776, the United States of America was born when the Continental Congress approved the **Declaration of Independence**.

The **Patriots**, or supporters of independence, lacked a well-trained army, but they knew the land on which they fought. They had few victories until defeating the British in the Battle of Saratoga. This win convinced France and Spain to become their allies. After a brutal winter at Valley Forge and a shift to fighting in the South, the Patriots finally won the decisive victory at Yorktown in 1781. Great Britain recognized U.S. independence in the **Treaty of Paris of 1783**.

Summary and Preview In this lesson you learned about U.S. history from its earliest days through the Revolutionary War. In the next lesson, you will learn about the founding and early days of the United States.

Reading Check
Summarize
How did the Patriots turn the tide of the war?

Lesson 1 Assessment

Review Ideas, Terms, and People

1. a. Define Who were the Paleo-Indians?

b. Contrast How did Columbus's plan to reach Asia differ from that of other European explorers?

c. Summarize What impact did Spanish conquistadors have on the Americas?

2. a. Recall What was the significance of Jamestown?

b. Contrast How did the economies of the southern, New England, and middle colonies differ?

c. Predict How might the Mayflower Compact have influenced later colonial governments?

3. a. Describe What was the Great Awakening and why did it appeal to colonists?

b. Sequence What events led to the Boston Massacre?

c. Draw Conclusions Why might rulers in Europe have viewed the Declaration of Independence as a dangerous document?

Critical Thinking

4. Categorize Review your notes on U.S. history before the Revolutionary War. In a chart like the one below, identify the key people, places, and events that shaped the U.S. history from its earliest beginnings through colonial times and the Revolutionary War.

Era	People	Places	Events
American Beginnings			
The English Colonies			
Creating a Nation			

A New Nation

The Big Idea

In its early days, the United States faced challenges and took measures to grow strong.

Main Ideas

- The American people explored and tested many ideas to strengthen their government.
- A new Constitution provided a framework for a stronger national government.
- George Washington and members of Congress established a new national government.

Key Terms and People

Articles of Confederation
Shays's Rebellion
Constitutional Convention
Three-Fifths Compromise
Antifederalists
Federalists
federalism
George Washington

Quick Facts

Weaknesses of the Articles of Confederation

- Most power held by states
- One branch of government
- Legislative branch has few powers
- No executive branch
- No judicial system
- No system of checks and balances

If YOU were there . . .

You live in a town in New England during the 1770s. In the town meeting, people are hotly debating about who will have the right to vote. Most think that only men who own property should be able to vote. Some think that all property owners—men and women—should have that right. A few others want all free men to have the vote. Now it is time for the meeting to decide.

How would you have voted on this issue?

Forming a Government

Ideas about Government The new United States needed a government to lead it. American political ideas were shaped by European and colonial models. English examples included Magna Carta and the English Bill of Rights. Magna Carta had made the king subject to law, while the Bill of Rights gave Parliament greater power. Enlightenment philosophers also influenced American political ideas. John Locke claimed that rulers and their people were bound by a social contract. Baron de Montesquieu called for the separation of government powers. Americans also had their own models of self-government, such as town meetings, the Mayflower Compact, and the principles set forth in the Declaration of Independence.

The Second Continental Congress drafted the **Articles of Confederation**, the document that outlined the first national government for the United States. The Articles created a Congress with limited powers. There was no executive branch or judicial system. To organize western settlement, Congress passed the Northwest Ordinance of 1787, creating the Northwest Territory. The law allowed new territories to join the Union as equal states.

National Challenges The weakness of the Articles of Confederation and the new Congress caused many problems, especially with the economy. Great Britain and Spain cut American merchants off from trade and made them pay high taxes on imports and exports. Trade laws also varied from state to state, hurting businesses. In an effort to pay high war debts, some states printed too much paper money. This money soon became worthless, causing inflation. When poor farmers in Massachusetts faced high taxes, they joined **Shays's Rebellion** against the state courts. Although the rebellion failed, to many people it was a sign that a change in the government was needed.

The Constitutional Convention The states held a **Constitutional Convention** in 1787 to improve the Articles of Confederation. Instead of rewriting the Articles, however, the convention drafted a new document. Delegates included Benjamin Franklin, Alexander Hamilton, James Madison, and George Washington.

The delegates debated many issues. The Great Compromise created a two-house Congress where each state has an equal voice in the Senate and larger states have more representation in the House of Representatives. The **Three-Fifths Compromise** counted three-fifths of the slave population when determining representation. These compromises settled disputes between large and small states and northern and southern states.

Opponents of the new Constitution, called **Antifederalists**, objected to the plan for a stronger central government. Supporters of the Constitution, called **Federalists**, won the public debate by convincing people that the new government would not only provide security but also protect their rights.

Reading Check
Recall
Why did the states call for a Constitutional Convention in 1787?

Historical Source

Compromise and the Slave Trade

At the Constitutional Convention, the issue of slavery highlighted differences between the North and the South. Gouverneur Morris, representing Pennsylvania, spoke with much emotion against the Three-Fifths Compromise. Also, the idea of banning the foreign slave trade prompted southerners such as John Rutledge of South Carolina to defend the practice.

"If the Convention thinks that North Carolina, South Carolina, and Georgia will ever agree to the plan [to prohibit the slave trade], unless their right to import slaves be untouched, the expectation is vain [useless]."

—John Rutledge, quoted in *The Atlantic Monthly*, February 1891, by Frank Gaylord Cook

"The admission of slaves into the Representation . . . comes to this: that the inhabitant of [a state] who goes to the coast of Africa and . . . tears away his fellow creatures from their dearest connections and damns them to the most cruel bondage [slavery], shall have more votes in a Government [established] for protection of the rights of mankind."

—Gouverneur Morris, quoted in *The Constitution: A Pro-Slavery Compact*, edited by Wendell Phillips

Analyze Historical Sources
How did these two views of slavery differ?

Separation of Powers

U.S. Constitution

Legislative Branch
(Congress)

- Writes the laws
- Confirms presidential appointments
- Approves treaties
- Grants money
- Declares war

Executive Branch
(President)

- Proposes laws
- Administers the laws
- Commands armed forces
- Appoints ambassadors and other officials
- Conducts foreign policy
- Makes treaties

Judicial Branch
(Supreme Court)

- Interprets the Constitution and other laws
- Reviews lower-court decisions

The Constitution

The system of government established by the Constitution is called federalism. Under **federalism** powers are divided between the states and the federal, or national, government. States keep control over many issues, such as local government and local laws. The sharing of power between the national and state governments is one of the strengths of Constitution.

Separation of Powers The power of the federal government is divided among three branches. The legislative branch, or Congress, passes laws. The executive branch, made up of the president and many departments, makes sure the laws are carried out. The judicial branch, consisting of the national courts, interprets laws and punishes criminals.

A system of checks and balances keeps any one branch from becoming too powerful. For example, the president can veto a law passed by Congress. The Constitution also allows the people to ratify amendments that change the document to adjust to changing times. Citizens have not only rights but also responsibilities under federalism. Fulfilling these duties helps the system work fairly and effectively for all Americans.

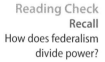

Reading Check
Recall
How does federalism divide power?

Washington's Presidency

Americans believed in **George Washington**. They saw him as an honest leader and hero of the Revolution. In 1789, Washington was elected as the first U.S. president. The First Congress created departments in the executive branch for different areas of national policy. Washington met with the department heads, or cabinet members, who advised him.

Secretary of State Thomas Jefferson and Secretary of the Treasury Alexander Hamilton disagreed on many important issues, including the size and purpose of government, financing the government, and interpreting the Constitution. Their disagreements helped shape the young nation.

George Washington

The First Cabinet

Washington's cabinet members kept him informed on political matters and debated important issues with one another. Each of the men chosen had experience that made him a wise choice to advise the nation's first president. By 1792 cabinet meetings were a common practice.

1 Henry Knox, secretary of war
2 Thomas Jefferson, secretary of state
3 Edmund Randolph, attorney general
4 Alexander Hamilton, secretary of the treasury
5 George Washington, president

Foreign and domestic conflicts disrupted the peace during Washington's administration. The United States tried to remain neutral in European conflicts, but the U.S. Army did go to war with Native American forces in the Northwest Territory. The government faced angry farmers when Congress passed a tax on American whiskey. Washington led an army to end the so-called Whiskey Rebellion.

Washington decided not to run for reelection in 1796 after two terms in office. In his farewell address, Washington advised future leaders to maintain U.S. neutrality in foreign affairs and to avoid the dangers of political parties. Political divisions between followers of Jefferson and Hamilton contributed to the growth of political parties, however.

Reading Check
Explain
Why did Americans choose George Washington to be president?

Summary and Preview In this lesson you learned how the Constitution established a framework for national government. In the next lesson you will learn about events that brought the nation closer together and more people into the political process.

Lesson 2 Assessment

Review Ideas, Terms, and People

1. **a. Recall** What was the chief purpose of the Articles of Confederation?

   b. Summarize What major compromises were made at the Constitutional Convention?

   c. Contrast How did the views of Antifederalists and Federalists differ?

2. **a. Define** What is federalism?

   b. Summarize How did the system of government established under the Constitution resolve the weaknesses of the Constitution?

   c. Explain Why is a system of checks and balances important?

3. **a. Explain** Which qualities helped George Washington win the presidency?

   b. Summarize What challenges did Washington face as president?

   c. Describe What advice did George Washington offer in his Farewell Address?

Critical Thinking

4. **Summarize** Copy the chart below. Use it to summarize details about the key people, ideas, and events discussed in this lesson.

Era	Details
Forming a Government	
The Constitution	
Washington's President	

History and Geography

Origins of the Constitution

The U.S. Constitution created a republican form of government based on the consent of the people. The framers of the Constitution blended ideas and examples from both the American colonies and England to write this lasting document.

THE MAYFLOWER COMPACT, 1620

The *Mayflower*, shown here in an illustration, sailed to America in 1620. Aboard the ship, 41 men signed the Mayflower Compact, the first document in the colonies to establish guidelines for self-government. The signers agreed that they and their families would combine to form a "civil body politic," or community.

COLONIAL ASSEMBLIES

The British Parliament's two-chamber structure also influenced colonial governments. In Article I, Section 1, of the Constitution, the framers continued the practice of a two-chamber legislature.

"All legislative powers . . . shall be vested in a Congress of the United States, which shall consist of a Senate and House of Representatives."

—Article I, Section 1, U.S. Constitution

VIRGINIA STATUTE FOR RELIGIOUS FREEDOM, 1786

Classical liberal principles, such as the written protection of citizens' personal liberties, were reflected in the addition of the Bill of Rights. The First Amendment's freedom of religion clauses were based on Thomas Jefferson's Virginia Statute for Religious Freedom. The document, which was accepted by the Virginia legislature in 1786, ensured the separation of church and state in Virginia.

"Congress shall make no law respecting an establishment of religion, or prohibiting the free exercise thereof . . . "

—First Amendment, U.S. Constitution

American colonies

MAGNA CARTA, 1215

In this painting, King John of England is signing the Magna Carta, or the Great Charter, which established that the king was subject to the law just like everyone else. It also declared that people could not be deprived of their lives, liberty, or property "except by the lawful judgment of [their] peers, or by the law of the land." Compare this language to that of the Fifth Amendment to the Constitution.

"No person shall be . . . deprived of life, liberty, or property, without due process of law . . . "

—Fifth Amendment, U.S. Constitution

THE ENGLISH BILL OF RIGHTS, 1689

This painting shows King William and Queen Mary of England. Before taking the throne, William and Mary had to accept the English Bill of Rights. The English Bill of Rights took even more power away from the monarch than did the Magna Carta. It also protected the rights of English citizens. These ideas would later influence the U.S. Constitution.

"Excessive bail ought not be required, nor excessive fines imposed; nor cruel and unusual punishments inflicted."

—English Bill of Rights

THE ENLIGHTENMENT, 1700s

Enlightenment thinkers such as English philosopher John Locke supported the movement toward self-government. Locke argued in his writings that government could exist only with "the consent of the governed." The framers of the Constitution looked to Locke for inspiration when writing the Constitution, as you can see from its very first words.

"We the people of the United States, . . . "

—Preamble, U.S. Constitution

Analyze Information

1. What documents did the framers look to when writing the Constitution?

2. How did the English Parliamentary system affect the kind of government the framers created?

England

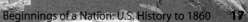

The New Republic

The Big Idea

Early presidents of the United States held differing ideas about the role of the federal government.

Main Ideas

- The election of 1796 saw the rise of political parties and began a new era in U.S. politics.

- Success in war contributed to a growing sense of American nationalism.

- Jacksonian democracy was marked by an expansion of voting rights and a strong executive branch.

Key Terms and People

Thomas Jefferson
Alien and Sedition Acts
Louisiana Purchase
Lewis and Clark expedition
Monroe Doctrine
Erie Canal
Missouri Compromise
Jacksonian Democracy

If YOU were there . . .

You are a newspaper editor in Virginia in 1798. You've joined Jefferson's political party, which opposes the new president. In fact, your paper has printed many articles that criticize him, calling him greedy and foolish. You believe that's your right in a free country. But now Congress has passed a law that makes it illegal to criticize the government. You could be arrested for your articles!

Would you stop criticizing the government? Why?

The American Republic

Federalist John Adams defeated Democratic-Republican **Thomas Jefferson** in the 1796 presidential election. During Adams's term, the United States nearly went to war with France. When Democratic-Republicans who supported France criticized the Federalists for their actions toward France, Congress passed the **Alien and Sedition Acts**. These laws limited freedom of speech and the press. Jefferson and others called these acts unconstitutional.

The election of 1800 pitted Adams and Jefferson against each other again. Jefferson won the election after a bitter campaign. This victory marked the first peaceful change of power from one political party to another in U.S. history.

Jefferson's Era During Jefferson's presidency the Supreme Court increased its power with the case *Marbury* v. *Madison*. Chief Justice John Marshall's ruling established the power of judicial review, which allows the Court to declare an act of Congress unconstitutional.

One of Jefferson's biggest achievements as president was agreeing to the **Louisiana Purchase**, which nearly doubled the size of the United States. He then sent the **Lewis and Clark expedition**, a journey of discovery led by Meriwether Lewis and William Clark, to explore and map this vast new territory.

Lewis and Clark kept detailed journals. They mapped new lands and recorded the natural wonders, people, and animals they encountered on their way to the Pacific Ocean and back.

The Election of 1800

John Adams and the Federalists
- Rule by wealthy class
- Strong federal government
- Emphasis on manufacturing
- Loose interpretation of the Constitution
- British alliance

Thomas Jefferson and the Democratic-Republicans
- Rule by the people
- Strong state governments
- Emphasis on agriculture
- Strict interpretation of the Constitution
- French alliance

Adams receives 65 votes and Pinckney receives 64 votes.

Election Results

Jefferson and running mate Burr receive 73 votes each.

- Peaceful change of political power from one party to another
- The tied race led to the Twelfth Amendment (1804), which created a separate ballot for president and vice president.

War and Peace Jefferson tried unsuccessfully to protect American neutrality with France and Great Britain. Both countries captured U.S. ships trading with the enemy. Efforts to ban trade with these countries only hurt Americans. The British also supported Native Americans who opposed American settlement in the West. As a result, President James Madison called for war against Britain. During the War of 1812, neither side gained any territory.

Reading Check
Find Main Ideas
How did the election of 1796 change the nature of politics in the United States?

Growing Nationalism

A positive outcome of the war was that it boosted American patriotism and confidence. President James Monroe issued the **Monroe Doctrine**, warning Europeans not to interfere in the Western Hemisphere.

Political conflict declined from 1815 to 1825, called the Era of Good Feelings. States built new roads and canals to link distant regions together. For example, the **Erie Canal**, completed in 1825, ran all the way from Albany to Buffalo, New York. Writers such as Washington Irving

The Monroe Doctrine

President James Monroe established the foundation for U.S. foreign policy in Latin America in the Monroe Doctrine of 1823.

In this phrase, Monroe warns European nations against trying to influence events in the Western Hemisphere.

Monroe notes here the difference between existing colonies and newly independent countries.

Analyze Historical Sources
What warning did President Monroe give to European powers in the Monroe Doctrine?

The occasion has been judged proper for asserting . . . that the American continents . . . are henceforth not to be considered as subjects for future colonization by any European powers . . .
The political system of the allied powers is essentially different . . . from that of America. We . . . declare that we should consider any attempt on their part to extend their system to any portion of this hemisphere as dangerous to our peace and safety . . .
With the existing colonies . . . we have not interfered and shall not interfere. But with the governments who have declared their independence and maintained it, and whose independence we have . . . acknowledged, we could not view any **interposition**[1] *for the purpose of oppressing them . . . by any European power in any other light than as the* **manifestation**[2] *of an unfriendly* **disposition**[3] *toward the United States.*

[1] *interposition:* interference
[2] *manifestation:* evidence
[3] *disposition:* attitude

Reading Check
Summarize What events contributed to a growing sense of nationalism among Americans in the early 1800s?

and painters like the members of the Hudson River school created new American styles of art.

Yet one threat to unity remained. Northern and southern states disagreed about whether to let slavery expand westward. The **Missouri Compromise** of 1820 tried to keep the balance between the number of slave and free states. It was only a temporary solution, however.

The Age of Jackson

By 1828 many states had passed laws increasing suffrage for white men. This led to an era of a rise in popular politics, which became known as **Jacksonian Democracy**, after politician Andrew Jackson. Jackson's defeat in 1824 led his supporters to create the Democratic Party. Many saw his victory in the 1828 presidential election as a win for the common people.

Jackson faced a major crisis when South Carolina threatened to leave the Union if Congress did not lower taxes on imports. Jackson opposed the view that states could reject, or nullify, laws of Congress and the crisis ended.

Reading Check
Analyze Why did Jackson oppose the Second Bank of the United States?

Jackson did not always support federal authority, however. He opposed the Second Bank of the United States because he felt it favored the rich. The Supreme Court had declared the Bank to be constitutional in *McCulloch* v. *Maryland*. Still, Jackson was able to kill public support for the Bank. After he left office, the loss of the Bank helped cause the economic depression called the Panic of 1837. This crisis hurt the Democratic Party and helped the Whig Party win the presidential election of 1840.

Andrew Jackson 1767–1845

Jackson was born in Waxhaw, a region along the border of the North and South Carolina colonies. In 1788 he moved to Nashville, Tennessee, which was still a part of North Carolina. There he built a mansion called the Hermitage. He lived in Washington as president, then retired to the Hermitage, where he died.

Jackson had no formal education, but he taught himself law and became a successful lawyer. He became Tennessee's first representative to the U.S. Congress and also served in the Senate. Jackson became a national hero when his forces defeated the Creek and Seminole Indians. He went on to battle the British in the Battle of New Orleans during the War of 1812. Jackson was elected as the nation's seventh president in 1828 and served until 1837.

The power of the office became more powerful during Jackson's presidency. His belief in a strong presidency made him both loved and hated. He vetoed as many bills as the six previous presidents combined. Jackson also believed in a strong Union. When South Carolina tried to nullify, or reject, a federal tariff, he threatened to send troops into the state to force it to obey.

Identify Cause and Effect
Why did Jackson gain loyal friends and fierce enemies?

Summary and Preview In this lesson you learned about events that helped the nation grow and unite, as well as about the contributions of Andrew Jackson. In the next lesson you will learn about the westward growth of the nation, growing differences between North and South, and efforts to reform issues in American society.

Lesson 3 Assessment

Review Ideas, Terms, and People

1. **a. Identify Cause and Effect** How did the Louisiana Purchase contribute to the growth of the United States?

   b. Explain Why did Jefferson oppose the Alien and Sedition Acts?

   c. Summarize How did *Marbury* v. *Madison* increase the power of the Supreme Court?

2. **a. Summarize** What did the Monroe Doctrine state?

   b. Make Generalizations Why were roads and canals important to the growth of the nation?

   c. Identify Main Ideas What issue threatened national unity in the early 1800s?

3. **a. Recall** What was Jacksonian Democracy?

   b. Explain Why did Jackson oppose the Second Bank of the United States?

   c. Identify Cause and Effect What caused the Panic of 1837?

Critical Thinking

4. **Identify Main Ideas and Details** Review your notes on this lesson. Then copy the chart below and use it to identify the main ideas and details covered in each section of this lesson.

Era	Main Ideas	Details
The American Republic		
Growing Nationalism		
The Age of Jackson		

The Nation Expands

The Big Idea

As Americans settled in the West, the nation expanded.

Main Ideas

■ Westward expansion transformed the nation.

■ The Industrial Revolution transformed life in the northern states.

■ The Southern economy and society centered on agriculture.

■ In the mid-1800s, social reformers aimed to improve lives of Americans.

Key Terms and People

Trail of Tears
Oregon Trail
manifest destiny
Eli Whitney
abolition movement
Frederick Douglass
temperance movement
Elizabeth Cady Stanton

If YOU were there . . .

You are a cowboy in Texas in 1875. You love life on the open range, the quiet nights, and the freedom. You even like the hard work of the long cattle drives to Kansas. But you know that times are changing. Homesteaders are moving in and fencing off their lands. Some of the older cowboys say it's time to settle down and buy a small ranch. You hope that they're not right.

What would make you give up a cowboy's life?

Expanding West

As America's population grew, settlers looked for more territory. In the 1800s, Americans pushed steadily westward, moving beyond and pushing out the boundaries of the United States.

Indian Removal In 1830 Congress passed the Indian Removal Act with the support of President Jackson. This law allowed the removal of Native Americans living east of the Mississippi to western land known as Indian Territory. Groups such as the Cherokee protested the law. Not even a Supreme Court ruling in their favor could save them, however. In 1838 several thousand Cherokee died on the march west known as the **Trail of Tears**.

Indian Removal

In his painting, *The Trail of Tears,* Robert Lindneux captured the anguish of the thousands of Cherokee forced to move west into what today is Oklahoma.

Trails Leading West

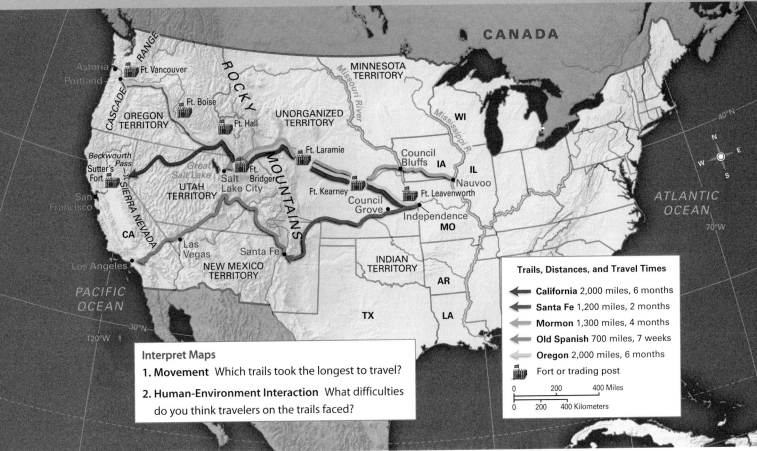

Trails, Distances, and Travel Times

- **California** 2,000 miles, 6 months
- **Santa Fe** 1,200 miles, 2 months
- **Mormon** 1,300 miles, 4 months
- **Old Spanish** 700 miles, 7 weeks
- **Oregon** 2,000 miles, 6 months
- Fort or trading post

Interpret Maps

1. **Movement** Which trails took the longest to travel?

2. **Human-Environment Interaction** What difficulties do you think travelers on the trails faced?

Manifest Destiny Indian removal did not stop more Americans from pushing even farther westward. Fur trappers were some of the first Americans to reach the Rockies. Later, thousands of pioneers followed the 2,000-mile-long **Oregon Trail** to the Pacific Northwest.

Thousands more settled in the Mexican province of Texas. The Mexican government grew worried that these Americans were disobeying Mexican laws. When Mexico banned further American settlement, tempers flared. In 1836 Texas rebelled against Mexico and won its independence.

Many Americans began to believe that America had a **manifest destiny**, or obvious fate, to settle all the way to the Pacific Ocean. Soon there were calls to annex Texas and Oregon. President James K. Polk gained Oregon peacefully by treaty with Great Britain. But the conflict over Texas led to the Mexican-American War.

The overwhelming U.S. victory in that war led Mexico to grant huge pieces of land to the United States. This so-called Mexican Cession included California and most of the present-day American Southwest.

The discovery of gold in California brought a rush of miners from all over the world. These included some of the first Chinese immigrants to America. California's population and economy boomed as a result of this Gold Rush. By 1850 California had become the 31st state.

Reading Check
Define
What is manifest destiny?

Elements of Industrialization

Eli Whitney developed the idea of using interchangeable parts. Interchangeable parts are identical parts. Rather than being custom-made by hand, interchangeable parts are made using machine tools like the one shown below (left). Whitney's idea laid the groundwork for mass production, a method for producing large quantities of goods quickly using low-skilled workers who perform specific tasks, like those here.

The Industrial North

As pioneers headed west, new industries grew in the Northeast. The first American factories used water-powered machines to make cloth. Inventor **Eli Whitney** later came up with the idea of interchangeable parts, which helped make possible mass production and less expensive goods.

Factories employed men, women, and children to run the machinery. Workers toiled long hours in difficult conditions, often for little pay. Labor reform efforts had little success. Some workers formed unions and used strikes to demand better treatment.

The Transportation Revolution Steamboats and steam-powered trains made transportation faster and cheaper than ever before. By 1860 the United States had more than 400 steamboats in operation and nearly 30,000 miles of railroad tracks.

Communication also improved with the invention of the telegraph, which carried messages across wires. These changes helped fuel economic growth.

Immigration and City Life Steam power also allowed factories to move from the countryside to the cities. City populations boomed, thanks to new jobs and the arrival of several million immigrants. Most of these people came from Ireland and Germany, fleeing famine or political troubles. Many immigrants faced prejudice from other Americans.

Mississippi River Steamboats

Deckhands load a Mississippi River steamboat in Memphis, Tennessee. By the mid-1800s, hundreds of steamboats traveled up and down American rivers. Steamboats enabled Americans to ship more goods farther, faster, and for less money than ever before.

Reading Check
Draw Conclusions
How did the Industrial Revolution affect the lives of city dwellers?

Industry and city growth helped create a new middle class of managers and skilled workers. The downsides of city growth were overcrowding, crime, disease, and the threat of fires.

The Agricultural South

Compared to the North, the South had less industry and fewer big cities. As a result, fewer immigrants settled in the region. Instead, the South remained rural and agricultural, relying on cash crops for its wealth.

The Cotton Boom The first southern cash crops were tobacco, rice, and indigo. Eli Whitney's invention of the cotton gin in 1793 made cotton the South's biggest crop. The gin quickly removed seeds from cotton fibers.

The demand for cotton boomed as textile mills in the American North and in Great Britain grew. The South became a major player in world trade and was sometimes called the Cotton Kingdom.

Cotton Gin

Before the cotton gin, cotton seeds had to be removed by hand, a slow and laborious process.

The Slave System Cotton brought wealth but also increased the demand for slave labor to grow and process the crop. Only about one-third of white southerners had slaves. Yeomen farmers and poor whites owned few or no slaves, but most defended the slave system. Many slaves lived on the small number of large plantations owned by wealthy planters.

Enslaved African Americans usually lived in small cabins with dirt floors.

Reading Check
Draw Conclusions
How did the cotton gin change life in the South?

On big plantations most slaves worked in the fields, while some had specific skilled jobs like carpentry. Slaves' living conditions were poor and the punishments they faced harsh. Slave codes limited slaves' right to travel and banned them from schools. Still, enslaved people kept alive African customs and expressed themselves through folktales and spirituals. Some slaves even led rebellions, though these were rare and severely punished.

New Movements in Society

Some Americans formed the **abolition movement** to oppose slavery. Former slaves **Frederick Douglass** and Sojourner Truth were two leading abolitionists. Abolitionists used speeches and newspapers to spread their antislavery messages. They based many speeches and articles on the ideas of equality found in the Declaration of Independence. Abolitionists fought against laws that protected slavery, including laws that made it illegal to help runaway slaves.

After escaping slavery, Frederick Douglass became a leader in the abolitionist movement.

Sojourner Truth was a leader in both the abolitionist and women's rights movements.

Abolition was just one of the many reform movements that arose in the United States. The religious revival called the Second Great Awakening triggered a wave of reform efforts. Some people supported the **temperance movement**, which tried to stop alcohol abuse. They blamed alcohol for problems of society such as crime and poverty.

Others called for prison and education reform, such as better treatment for prisoners and more public schools for children. Reformers helped spread education to African Americans and women by opening schools that would accept them.

Women who took part in the abolition movement, like **Elizabeth Cady Stanton**, began to demand more rights for women as well. Stanton and other reformers called for women's suffrage, or the right to vote. Some claimed that women did not have an obligation to follow the laws of a nation that did not let them vote. These were just the first steps toward gaining equal rights for many Americans.

Reading Check
Recall
How did abolitionists get their message out?

DOCUMENT-BASED INVESTIGATION   Historical Source

Family Temperance Pledge

The temperance movement, an effort to convince people to avoid drinking alcohol, promoted abstinence with posters like the one shown here.

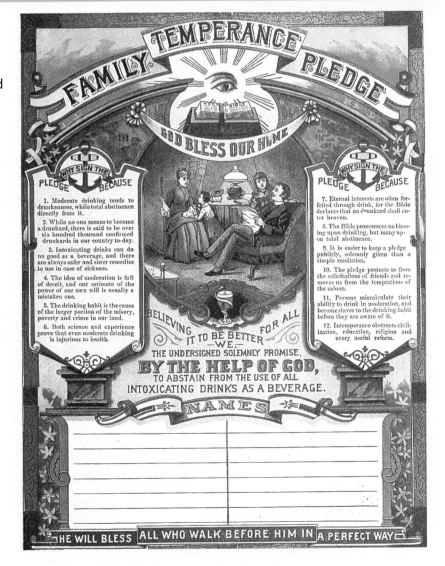

Analyze Historical Sources
What point is the illustrator of this poster making about alcohol and family life?

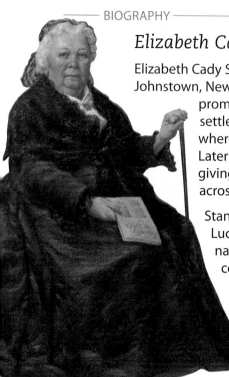

BIOGRAPHY

Elizabeth Cady Stanton 1815–1902

Elizabeth Cady Stanton was born in Johnstown, New York. She married a prominent abolitionist and settled in Seneca Falls, New York, where she had seven children. Later in life she traveled widely, giving lectures and speeches across the country.

Stanton and fellow activist Lucretia Mott organized the nation's first women's rights convention, at Seneca Falls in 1848. She and Susan B. Anthony founded the National Woman Suffrage Association in 1869. For nearly six decades, she spoke and wrote passionately about women's rights.

Stanton helped author the Declaration of Sentiments, which demanded equal rights for women, including the right to vote. A brilliant speaker and debater, Stanton spoke out against laws that kept married women from owning property, earning wages, and keeping custody of their children.

Find Main Ideas
What problems did Stanton try to correct? What problems did she face in accomplishing her goals?

Summary and Preview In this lesson you learned about westward expansion, differences between North and South, and reform movements. In the next lesson you will learn about how tensions over slavery threatened to tear the United States apart.

Lesson 4 Assessment

Review Ideas, Terms, and People

1. a. Draw Conclusions What lessons might be learned from the Trail of Tears?

b. Sequence What events led to the Mexican-American War?

c. Evaluate How would you assess the importance of manifest destiny on the expansion of the United States? Explain.

2. a. Explain How did Eli Whitney contribute to the economies of the North and the South?

b. Summarize What advancements in transportation and communication happened in the early 1800s?

c. Identify Cause and Effect How did the Industrial Revolution affect cities in the North?

3. a. Define What was the cotton gin?

b. Describe What type of work did enslaved people perform on plantations?

c. Compare How did the economy of the North compare to the economy of the South?

4. a. Recall What types of laws did abolitionists oppose?

b. Summarize How did Frederick Douglas and Elizabeth Cady Stanton contribute to reform movements in the mid-1800s?

c. Identify Main Ideas Why did supporters of the temperance movement oppose alcohol?

Critical Thinking

5. Identify Cause and Effect Review your notes on this lesson. Then use a graphic organizer like the one below to take notes on the causes and effects related to westward expansion, industrialization in the North, agriculture in the South, and the rise of reform movements.

Topic	Causes	Effects
Westward Expansion		
Industrialization in the North		
Agriculture in the South		
Reform Movements		

The Nation Breaks Apart

The Big Idea

The acquisition of new lands and antislavery literature intensified the debate over slavery.

Main Ideas

- By the mid-1800s, the nation was deeply divided by the issue of slavery.

- Political division and judicial decisions increased the debate over slavery.

Key Terms and People

Free-Soil Party
Compromise of 1850
Fugitive Slave Act
Kansas-Nebraska Act
Harriet Beecher Stowe
Dred Scott
Abraham Lincoln
Confederate States of America

If YOU were there . . .

You live in a crowded neighborhood in New York City in 1854. Your apartment building is home to a variety of people—long-time residents, Irish immigrants, free African Americans. One day, federal marshals knock on your door. They claim that one of your neighbors is a fugitive slave. The marshals say you must help them find her. If you don't, you will be fined or even sent to jail.

What would you tell the federal marshals?

Deepening Divisions

By 1850 the North and South had grown apart in many ways. The regions had different economies, different societies, and different goals. People in one region knew fairly little about their fellow citizens in another part of the country. As both regions pushed westward, their differences led to conflict.

Many northerners did not want slavery to spread to the West. Some opposed it for moral reasons, while others felt it would take jobs from white workers. After the Mexican-American War, Representative David Wilmot said that slavery should be banned in the new lands gained by the United States. Southerners strongly opposed this idea. In the North, the **Free-Soil Party** arose to oppose the spread of slavery.

Failed Compromises The addition of California as a state threatened to upset the political balance between slave and free states in the Union. An unequal balance would affect the political make up of the Senate. The North already had an edge in the House of Representatives. Henry Clay offered the **Compromise of 1850** to keep the peace. According to the compromise, California would

This engraving offers a dignified portrayal of the debate in the Senate over the Compromise of 1850. Henry Clay stands at the center of the image, addressing the senators.

The Missouri Compromise, 1820

Under the Missouri Compromise of 1820, there are an equal number of free states (orange) and slave states (green).

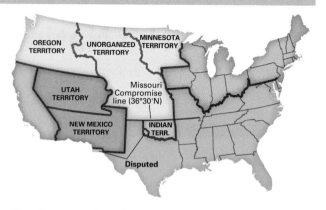

The Compromise of 1850

The Compromise of 1850 allowed for one more free state (California) than slave state but also passed a strict fugitive slave law.

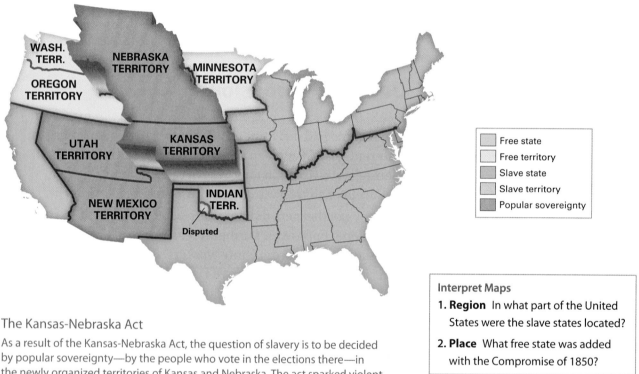

	Free state
	Free territory
	Slave state
	Slave territory
	Popular sovereignty

The Kansas-Nebraska Act

As a result of the Kansas-Nebraska Act, the question of slavery is to be decided by popular sovereignty—by the people who vote in the elections there—in the newly organized territories of Kansas and Nebraska. The act sparked violent conflict between pro-slavery and antislavery groups.

Interpret Maps

1. **Region** In what part of the United States were the slave states located?

2. **Place** What free state was added with the Compromise of 1850?

join the Union as a free state, but other territories in the Southwest would be allowed to choose whether to allow slavery.

Bleeding Kansas The Compromise of 1850 introduced a law called the **Fugitive Slave Act**. This act made it easier to capture runaway slaves hiding in the North. The law angered many northerners. Those opposed to slavery were equally upset when the **Kansas-Nebraska Act** opened the door to the spread of slavery in the Midwest. The Missouri Compromise had once banned slavery in that region. **Harriet Beecher Stowe's** popular antislavery novel *Uncle Tom's Cabin* fanned these flames by upsetting many southerners.

So when the Kansas Territory was opened, both proslavery and anti-slavery settlers rushed in. Each side was determined to control the territory. The result was a series of attacks and killings by both groups that shocked the nation.

Reading Check
Summarize
How did the addition of new lands intensify the debate over slavery?

Prelude to War

Northerners received another shock when the Supreme Court reviewed and decided a complex case involving an enslaved man named **Dred Scott**. In this case, the Court ruled that African Americans could not be U.S. citizens and that Congress could not ban slavery in any of the territories. This decision boosted support for the new Republican Party, which opposed the spread of slavery to the West.

Abolitionist John Brown stunned the South when he attacked Harpers Ferry, Virginia, trying to start a slave rebellion. Many northerners called Brown a hero. The presidential election of 1860 took place in this bitter atmosphere. Republican **Abraham Lincoln** won the election without winning a single electoral vote from the South, upsetting southern leaders.

Southern leaders feared that Lincoln would ban slavery. Such a move would destroy the South's economy and change its society. South Carolina, Mississippi, Florida, Alabama, Georgia, Louisiana, and Texas responded to Lincoln's win by withdrawing from the Union. They formed the **Confederate States of America**, or the Confederacy. Lincoln insisted that the Confederate states could not simply leave the

---

DOCUMENT-BASED INVESTIGATION   **Historical Source**

A House Divided

In 1858 Abraham Lincoln gave a passionate speech to Illinois Republicans about the dangers of the disagreement over slavery. Some considered it a call for war.

This line is a paraphrase of a line in the Bible.

Lincoln expresses confidence that the Union will survive.

"In my opinion, it [disagreement over slavery] will not cease [stop], until a crisis shall have been reached and passed. "A house divided against itself cannot stand." I believe this government cannot endure permanently half slave and half free. I do not expect the Union to be dissolved—I do not expect the house to fall—but I do expect it will cease to be divided."

—Abraham Lincoln, quoted in *Speeches and Letters of Abraham Lincoln 1832–1865*, edited by Merwin Roe

Analyze Sources
What do you think Lincoln meant by "crisis"?

Election of 1860

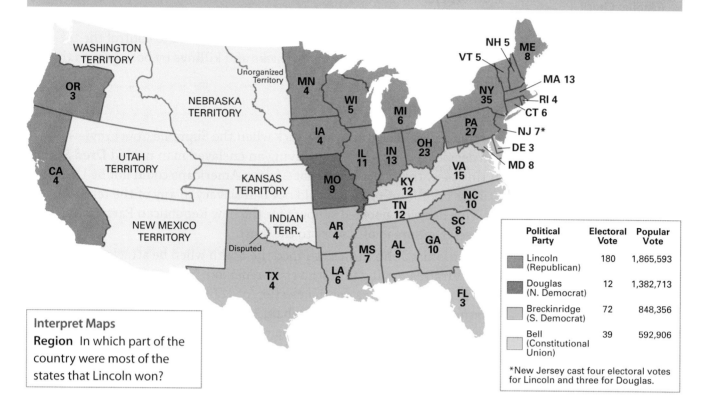

WASHINGTON TERRITORY

OR 3

Unorganized Territory

NEBRASKA TERRITORY

UTAH TERRITORY

CA 4

NEW MEXICO TERRITORY

Disputed

KANSAS TERRITORY

INDIAN TERR.

MN 4

WI 5

IA 4

MO 9

AR 4

TX 4

LA 6

MS 7

IL 11

IN 13

KY 12

TN 12

AL 9

GA 10

FL 3

MI 6

OH 23

VA 15

NC 10

SC 8

NH 5

VT 5

ME 8

MA 13

NY 35

RI 4

CT 6

PA 27

NJ 7*

DE 3

MD 8

Political Party	Electoral Vote	Popular Vote
Lincoln (Republican)	180	1,865,593
Douglas (N. Democrat)	12	1,382,713
Breckinridge (S. Democrat)	72	848,356
Bell (Constitutional Union)	39	592,906

*New Jersey cast four electoral votes for Lincoln and three for Douglas.

Interpret Maps

Region In which part of the country were most of the states that Lincoln won?

Reading Check
Summarize
Why did southern leaders form the Confederate States of America?

Union or keep the federal property within their borders. The stage was set for a terrible conflict pitting North against South.

America had developed from a collection of loose-knit colonies to an independent and united country to a nation divided over issues such as slavery. Now the nation faced the terrible prospect of a civil war that would threaten its very existence.

Summary and Preview In this lesson you learned how disagreements over the issue of slavery increasingly divided the nation. In the next module, you will learn about the Civil War.

Lesson 5 Assessment

Review Ideas, Terms, and People

1. **a. Describe** What were the terms of the Compromise of 1850?

   b. Explain How did the Fugitive Slave Act and the Kansas-Nebraska Act add to tensions over slavery?

   c. Sequence What events led up to violence erupting in Kansas over slavery?

2. **a. Identify Cause and Effect** How did the Supreme Court's decision in the Dred Scott case affect the debate over slavery?

   b. Identify Main Ideas Why were southerners unhappy with the election of Abraham Lincoln?

   c. Recall What states formed the Confederate States of America?

Critical Thinking

3. **Sequence** Review your notes on this lesson. Then create a graphic organizer like the one below to show the significant events that led the southern states to withdraw from the Union and form the Confederate States of America.

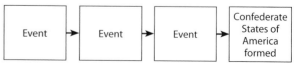

Event → Event → Event → Confederate States of America formed

Social Studies Skill

Interpret Timelines

Define the Skill

Knowing the sequence, or order, in which historical events took place is important to understanding these events. Timelines visually display the sequence of events during a particular period of time. They also let you easily see time spans between events, such as how long after one event a related event took place—and what events occurred in between. In addition, comparing timelines for different places makes relationships between distant events easier to identify and understand.

Learn the Skill

Follow these guidelines to read, interpret, and compare timelines.

1. Determine each timeline's framework. Note the years it covers and the periods of time into which it is divided. Be aware that a pair of timelines may not have the same framework.

2. Study the order of events on each timeline. Note the length of time between events. Compare what was taking place on different timelines around the same time period.

3. Look for relationships between events. Pay particular attention to how an event on one timeline might relate to an event on another.

Practice the Skill

Interpret the timelines below to answer the following questions.

1. What is each timeline's framework?

2. In what year did the conflict between Britain and the colonists turn violent?

3. What event caused colonists to dump British tea in Boston Harbor?

4. The Revolutionary War began in 1775 when fighting broke out between British soldiers and a colonial militia in Lexington, Massachusetts. What does the timeline suggest about the years leading up to this event?

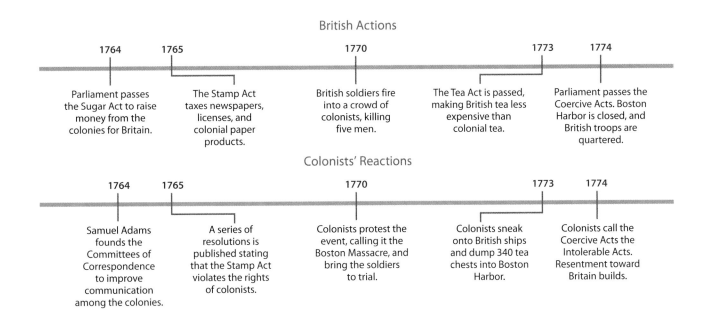

British Actions

| 1764 | 1765 | 1770 | 1773 | 1774 |

Parliament passes the Sugar Act to raise money from the colonies for Britain.

The Stamp Act taxes newspapers, licenses, and colonial paper products.

British soldiers fire into a crowd of colonists, killing five men.

The Tea Act is passed, making British tea less expensive than colonial tea.

Parliament passes the Coercive Acts. Boston Harbor is closed, and British troops are quartered.

Colonists' Reactions

| 1764 | 1765 | 1770 | 1773 | 1774 |

Samuel Adams founds the Committees of Correspondence to improve communication among the colonies.

A series of resolutions is published stating that the Stamp Act violates the rights of colonists.

Colonists protest the event, calling it the Boston Massacre, and bring the soldiers to trial.

Colonists sneak onto British ships and dump 340 tea chests into Boston Harbor.

Colonists call the Coercive Acts the Intolerable Acts. Resentment toward Britain builds.

Module Assessment

Review Vocabulary, Terms, and People

Identify the correct term or person from the chapter that best fits each of the following descriptions.

1. first permanent English settlement in North America
2. supporters of independence from Great Britain
3. meeting held by the states in 1787 to improve the Articles of Confederation
4. people who opposed ratification of the Constitution
5. main author of the Declaration of Independence and the third president of the United States
6. purchase of French land between the Mississippi River and the Rocky Mountains that doubled the size of the United States
7. belief shared by many Americans in the 1800s that the United States should settle all the way to the Pacific Ocean
8. inventor of the cotton gin and interchangeable parts
9. act that made it easier to capture run-away slaves hiding in northern states
10. author of the famous antislavery novel, *Uncle Tom's Cabin*

Comprehension and Critical Thinking

Lesson 1

11. a. **Explain** Why did the Puritans leave Europe for the Americas?
     b. **Compare** How did the colonists fill the demand for agricultural labor in the southern, middle, and New England colonies?
     c. **Predict** What might have happened if the Patriots had lost the Revolutionary War?

Lesson 2

12. a. **Recall** What was the Three-Fifths Compromise?
     b. **Draw Conclusions** Why is it significant that the Constitution gives the president the power to command the armed forces and Congress the power to declare war?
     c. **Summarize** What issues did Washington's cabinet disagree about?

Lesson 3

13. a. **Identify Main Ideas** Why did Jefferson sponsor the Lewis and Clark expedition?
     b. **Infer** How do you think European nations reacted to the Monroe Doctrine?
     c. **Draw Conclusions** Who do you think were Andrew Jackson's strongest supporters in the 1828 presidential election?

Lesson 4

14. a. **Identify Cause and Effect** How did the discovery of gold affect California and the United States?
     b. **Describe** What factors changed cities in the North in the early 1800s?
     c. **Draw Conclusions** What effects might strengthening slave codes have had on slaves?
     d. **Develop** What arguments might you use to counter the arguments of a person opposed to the abolition movement?

Lesson 5

15. a. **Evaluate** Was the Compromise of 1850 a good solution to the conflict over slavery? Explain why or why not.
     b. **Sequence** What events led to the creation of the Confederate States of America?

Module Assessment, continued

Reviewing Themes

16. **Politics** For each term, write a sentence explaining its significance to the foundation of U.S. government: Declaration of Independence, Articles of Confederation, Constitutional Convention, federalism.

17. **Society and Culture** What goals did the major social reform movements of the early 1800s have?

Reading Skills

Specialized Vocabulary of Social Studies *Use the reading skills taught in this chapter to answer the question about the reading selection below.*

Many historians agree that **Paleo-Indians**, the first people to live in North America, came from Asia sometime between 38,000 and 10,000 BC.

18. What is the definition of the word *Paleo-Indians* in the sentence above?

Social Studies Skills

Interpret Timelines *Use the skills and timeline on the Social Studies Skills page in this module to answer the questions below.*

19. How did colonists react to the passage of the Stamp Act?

20. How many years after the passage of the Stamp Act did Parliament pass the Coercive Acts?

Focus on Speaking

21. **Prepare an Oral Report** In this module, you learned about great events, courageous deeds, and heroic people in U.S. history before 1860. Prepare for your oral report by identifying one or two important ideas, events, or people for each lesson in this module. Next, write a one-sentence introduction to your talk. Then write a sentence or two for each lesson in this module. Write a concluding sentence that makes a quick connection between the history of the United States before 1860 and our lives today. Practice your talk until you can give it with only a glance or two at your notes.

The Civil War

★

Essential Question
How did the Civil War transform the nation?

About the Photo: Among those who marched off to war were these drummer boys of the Union army.

In this module you will learn how the resources of the North enabled it to defeat the South in the Civil War.

What You Will Learn . . .

▶ *Explore ONLINE!*

HISTORY.

VIDEOS, including...
• Emancipation Proclamation
• Battle of Antietam
• 54th Regiment
• The Civil War: Gettysburg
• Sherman's March to the Sea

✓ Document-Based Investigations

✓ Graphic Organizers

✓ Interactive Games

✓ Animation: Ironclad Technology

✓ Image with Hotspots: Copperhead Political Cartoon

✓ Image Carousel: Civil War Families

Timeline of Events 1860–1866

▶ *Explore ONLINE!*

United States		World
	1860	

1861 Confederate guns open fire on Fort Sumter on April 12. Confederates win the first battle of the Civil War on July 21 at Bull Run in Virginia. — **1861**

1861 Great Britain and France decide to buy cotton from Egypt instead of from the Confederacy.

1862 The *Monitor* fights the *Virginia* on March 9. — **1862**

1862 An imperial decree expels foreigners from Japan.

1863 The Emancipation Proclamation is issued on January 1. ∨ — **1863**

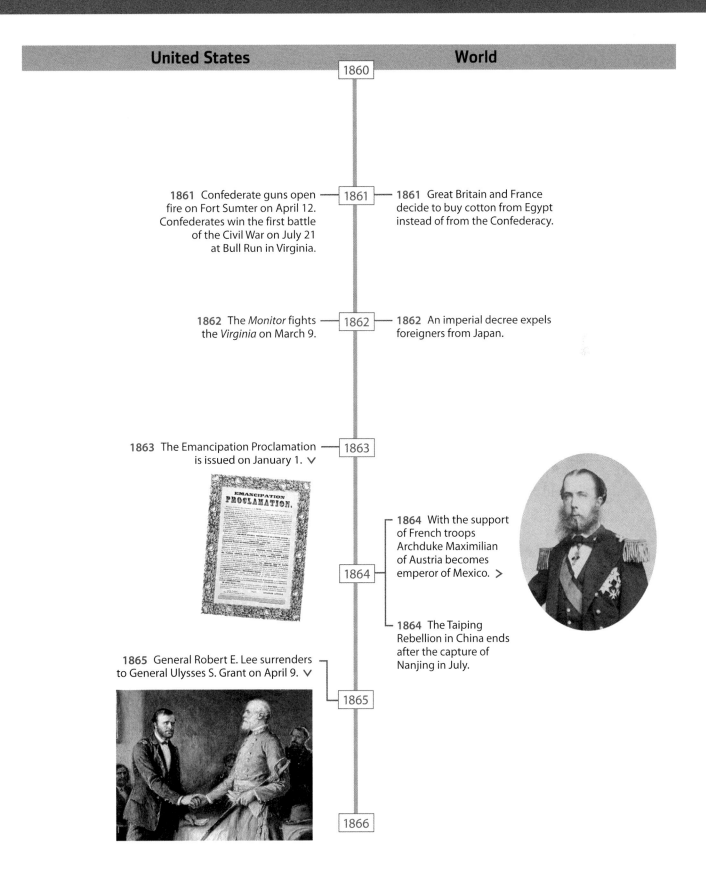

1864 With the support of French troops Archduke Maximilian of Austria becomes emperor of Mexico. >

— **1864**

1864 The Taiping Rebellion in China ends after the capture of Nanjing in July.

1865 General Robert E. Lee surrenders to General Ulysses S. Grant on April 9. ∨ — **1865**

1866

Reading Social Studies

THEME FOCUS:

Politics, Society and Culture

As you read this module about the Civil War, you will see that this was a time in our history dominated by two major concerns: politics and society and culture. You will not only read about the political decisions made during this war, but also you will see how the war affected all of American society. You will read about the causes and the key events during the war and the many consequences of this war. This module tells of one of the most important events in our history.

READING FOCUS:

Supporting Facts and Details

Main ideas and big ideas are just that, ideas. How do we know what those ideas really mean?

Understand Ideas and Their Support A main idea or big idea may be a kind of summary statement or it may be a statement of the author's opinion. Either way, a good reader looks to see what support—facts and various kinds of details—the writer provides. If the writer doesn't provide good support, the ideas may not be trustworthy.

Notice how the passage below uses facts and details to support the main idea.

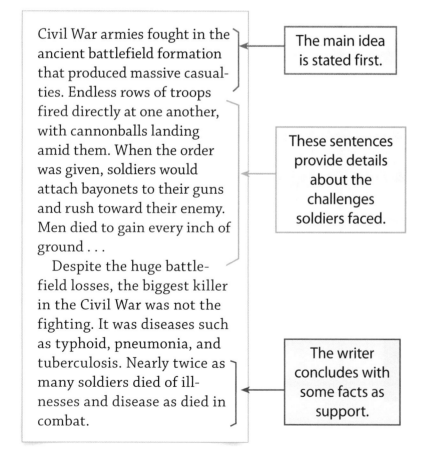

Civil War armies fought in the ancient battlefield formation that produced massive casualties. Endless rows of troops fired directly at one another, with cannonballs landing amid them. When the order was given, soldiers would attach bayonets to their guns and rush toward their enemy. Men died to gain every inch of ground . . .

Despite the huge battlefield losses, the biggest killer in the Civil War was not the fighting. It was diseases such as typhoid, pneumonia, and tuberculosis. Nearly twice as many soldiers died of illnesses and disease as died in combat.

The main idea is stated first.

These sentences provide details about the challenges soldiers faced.

The writer concludes with some facts as support.

Writers support propositions with . . .

1. **Facts and statistics**—statements that can be proved; facts in number form
2. **Examples**—specific instances that illustrate the facts
3. **Anecdotes**—brief stories that help explain the facts
4. **Definitions**—explanation of unusual terms or words
5. **Comments from the experts or eyewitnesses**—statements from reliable sources

You Try It!

The following passage is from the module you are about to read. As you read it, look for the writer's main idea and support.

In February 1862 Grant led an assault force into Tennessee. With help from navy gunboats, Grant's Army of the Tennessee took two outposts on key rivers in the West. On February 6 he captured Fort Henry on the Tennessee River. Several days later he took Fort Donelson on the Cumberland River.

Fort Donelson's commander asked for the terms of surrender. Grant replied, "No terms except an unconditional and immediate surrender can be accepted." The fort surrendered. The North gave a new name to Grant's initials: "Unconditional Surrender" Grant.

After you read the passage, answer the following questions.

1. Which sentence best states the writer's main idea?
   a. The fort surrendered.
   b. In February 1862 Grant led an assault force into Tennessee.
   c. Fort Donelson's commander asked for the terms of surrender.

2. Which method of support is not used to support the main idea?
   a. facts
   b. comments from experts or eyewitnesses
   c. anecdotes

3. Which sentence in this passage provides a comment from an expert or eyewitness?

As you read Module 1, pay attention to the details that the writers have chosen to support their main ideas.

The War Begins

The Big Idea
Civil war broke out between the North and the South in 1861.

Main Ideas
- Following the outbreak of war at Fort Sumter, Americans chose sides.
- The Union and the Confederacy prepared for war.

Key Terms and People
Fort Sumter
border states
Winfield Scott
cotton diplomacy

If YOU were there . . .

You are a college student in Charleston in early 1861. Seven southern states have left the Union and formed their own government. All-out war seems unavoidable. Your friends have begun to volunteer for either the Union or the Confederate forces. You are torn between loyalty to your home state and to the United States.

Would you join the Union or the Confederate army?

Americans Choose Sides

Furious at Lincoln's election and fearing a federal invasion, seven southern states had seceded. The new Commander in Chief tried desperately to save the Union.

In his inaugural address, Lincoln promised not to end slavery where it existed. The federal government "will not assail [attack] you. You can have no conflict without being yourselves the aggressors," he said, trying to calm southerners' fears. However, Lincoln also stated his intention to preserve the Union. He believed that saving the Union would help to save democracy. If the Union and its government failed, then monarchs could say that people were unable to rule themselves. As a result, Lincoln refused to recognize secession, declaring the Union to be "unbroken."

In fact, after decades of painful compromises, the Union was badly broken. From the Lower South, a battle cry was arising, born out of fear, rage—and excitement. Confederate officials began seizing branches of the federal mint, arsenals, and military outposts. In a last-ditch effort to avoid war between the states, Secretary of State Seward suggested a united effort of threatening war against Spain and France for interfering in Mexico and the Caribbean. In the highly charged atmosphere, it would take only a spark to unleash the heat of war.

In 1861 that spark occurred at **Fort Sumter**, a federal outpost in Charleston, South Carolina, that was attacked by

Charleston

In Charleston all activity came to a complete stop. Citizens crowded rooftops to watch the battle.

Castle Pinckney

The first shot fired on Fort Sumter was fired from Fort Johnson.

Charleston Harbor

Shots fired at the ironclad battery did little damage.

Fort Johnson

Fort Sumter

Fort Sumter was strategically placed to control Charleston Harbor.

Fort Moultrie

Cummings Point

Atlantic Ocean

Charleston

ATLANTIC OCEAN

Fort Sumter

The first shots of the Civil War were fired at Fort Sumter, South Carolina. Although no one was killed there, the bloodiest war in the country's history had begun.

Interpret Maps

1. **Human-Environment Interaction** Why would the Union army need to resupply Fort Sumter?

2. **Place** What advantages would a floating battery have?

Confederate troops, beginning the Civil War. Determined to seize the fortress—which controlled the entrance to Charleston Harbor—the Confederates ringed the harbor with heavy guns. Instead of surrendering the fort, Lincoln decided to send in ships to provide badly needed supplies to defend the fort. Confederate officials demanded that the federal troops evacuate. The fort's commander, Major Robert Anderson, refused.

Now it was Jefferson Davis who faced a dilemma. If he did nothing, he would damage the image of the Confederacy as a sovereign, independent nation. On the other hand, if Davis ordered an attack on Fort Sumter, he would turn peaceful secession into war. Davis chose war. Before sunrise on April 12, 1861, Confederate guns opened fire on Fort Sumter. A witness wrote that the first shots brought "every soldier in the harbor to his feet, and every man, woman, and child in the city of Charleston from their beds." The Civil War had begun.

The fort, although massive, stood little chance. Its heavy guns faced the Atlantic Ocean, not the shore. After 34 hours of cannon blasts, Fort Sumter surrendered. "The last ray of hope for preserving the Union has expired at the assault upon Fort Sumter . . ." Lincoln wrote.

Reaction to Lincoln's Call The fall of Fort Sumter stunned the North. Lincoln declared the South to be in a state of rebellion and asked state governors for 75,000 militiamen to put down the rebellion. States now had to choose: Would they secede, or would they stay in the Union? Democratic senator Stephen Douglas, speaking in support of Lincoln's call for troops, declared, "There can be no neutrals in this war, *only patriots*—or *traitors*."

Volunteers Wanted!

NO COMPROMISE

WITH TRAITORS, and No Argument but the Cannon's Mouth.

PENNSYLVANIA SHARP SHOOTERS,

COL. J. F. STAUNTON.

HEAD QUARTERS.

Company

RECRUITS WILL BE MUSTERED AND SENT TO CAMP

AT ONCE!

Recruitment posters like this one made use of eye-catching symbols and colors to entice Pennsylvanians to fight for the Union.

Pennsylvania, New Jersey, and the states north of them rallied to the president's call. The crucial slave states of the Upper South—North Carolina, Tennessee, Virginia, and Arkansas—seceded and joined the Confederate States of Texas, Louisiana, Mississippi, Alabama, Georgia, Florida, and South Carolina. The slave states of the Upper South provided soldiers and supplies to the rest of the South. The western territories were disputed between the Union and the Confederacy. Mary Boykin Chesnut, whose husband became a Confederate congressman, wrote in her diary:

"I did not know that one could live in such days of excitement. . . . Everybody tells you half of something, and then rushes off . . . to hear the last news."

—Mary Boykin Chesnut, quoted in *Mary Chesnut's Civil War*, edited by C. Vann Woodward

Wedged between the North and the South were the key **border states** of Delaware, Kentucky, Maryland, and Missouri—slave states that did not join the Confederacy. Kentucky and Missouri controlled parts of important rivers. Maryland separated the Union capital, Washington, DC, from the North.

People in the border states were deeply divided on the war. The president's own wife, Mary Todd Lincoln, had four brothers from Kentucky who fought for the Confederacy. Lincoln sent federal troops into the border states to help keep them in the Union. He also sent soldiers into western Virginia, where Union loyalties were strong. West Virginia set up its own state government in 1863.

Northern Resources Numbers tell an important story about the Civil War. Consider the North's advantages. It could draw soldiers and workers from a population of 22 million. The South had only 5.5 million people to draw from. One of the greatest advantages in the North was the region's network of roads, canals, and railroads. Some 22,000 miles of railroad track could move soldiers and supplies throughout the North. The South had only about 9,000 miles of track.

In the North, the Civil War stimulated economic growth. To supply the military, the production of coal, iron, wheat, and wool increased. Also, the export of corn, wheat, beef, and pork to Europe doubled. In the South, the export of resources decreased because of the Union blockade.

▶ Explore ONLINE!

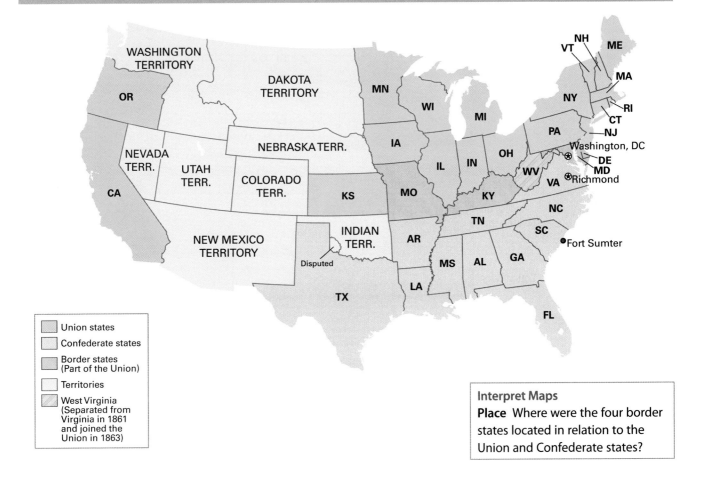

Legend:
- Union states
- Confederate states
- Border states (Part of the Union)
- Territories
- West Virginia (Separated from Virginia in 1861 and joined the Union in 1863)

Interpret Maps
Place Where were the four border states located in relation to the Union and Confederate states?

Finally, the Union had money. It had a more developed economy, banking system, and a currency called greenbacks. The South had to start printing its own Confederate dollars. Some states printed their own money, too. This led to financial chaos.

Taking advantage of the Union's strengths, General **Winfield Scott** developed a two-part strategy: (1) destroy the South's economy with a naval blockade of southern ports; (2) gain control of the Mississippi River to divide the South. Other leaders urged an attack on Richmond, Virginia, the Confederate capital.

Southern Resources The Confederacy had advantages as well. With its strong military tradition, the South put many brilliant officers into battle. Southern farms provided food for its armies. The South's best advantage, however, was strategic. It needed only to defend itself until the North grew tired of fighting.

The North had to invade and control the South. To accomplish this, the Union army had to travel huge distances. For example, the distance from northern Virginia to central Georgia is about the length of Scotland and England combined. Because of distances such as this, the North had to maintain long supply lines.

Resources of the North and South

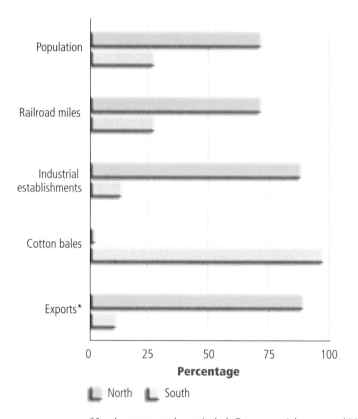

Percentage

North   South

*Southern exports do not include Tennessee, Arkansas, and Mississippi.

Analyze Visuals
1. Do you think the North or the South could maintain better supply lines for their troops? Explain.
2. Do you think the North or the South could provide more weapons for their troops? Explain.

In addition, wilderness covered much of the South. Armies found this land difficult to cross. Also, in Virginia many of the rivers ran from east to west. Because of this, they formed a natural defense against an army that attacked from the north to the south. As a result, northern generals were often forced to attack Confederate troops from the side rather than from the front. Furthermore, because southerners fought mostly on their home soil, they were often familiar with the area.

The South hoped to wear down the North and to capture Washington, DC. Confederate president Jefferson Davis also tried to win foreign allies through **cotton diplomacy**. This was the idea that Great Britain would support the Confederacy because it needed the South's raw cotton to supply its booming textile industry. Cotton diplomacy did not work as the South had hoped. Britain had large supplies of cotton, and it got more from India and Egypt.

**Reading Check
Compare** What advantages did the North and South have leading up to the war?

Union and Confederate Soldiers

Early in the war, uniforms differed greatly, especially in the Confederate army. Uniforms became simpler and more standard as the war dragged on.

The soldiers carried food, extra ammunition, and other items in their haversacks.

Each soldier was armed with a bayonet, a knife that can be attached to the barrel of a rifle. The bayonets were stored in scabbards on their belts.

Confederate Soldier

Both soldiers were also armed with single-shot, muzzle-loading rifles.

Union Soldier

Analyze Visuals
How are the Union and Confederate uniforms and equipment similar and different?

Preparing for War

The North and the South now rushed to war. Neither side was prepared for the tragedy to come.

Volunteer Armies Volunteer militias had sparked the revolution that created the United States. Now they would battle for its future. At the start of the war, the Union army had only 16,000 soldiers. Within months that number had swelled to a half million soldiers. Southern men rose up to defend their land and their ways of life. Virginian Thomas Webber came to fight "against the invading foe [enemy] who now pollute the sacred soil of my beloved native state." When Union soldiers asked one captured rebel why he was fighting, he replied, "I'm fighting because you're down here."

Helping the Troops Civilians on both sides helped those in uniform. They raised money, provided aid for soldiers and their families, and ran emergency hospitals. Dr. Elizabeth Blackwell, the first woman to receive a license to practice medicine, organized a group that pressured President Lincoln to form the U.S. Sanitary Commission in June 1861. The Sanitary, as it was called, was run by clergyman Henry Bellows. Tens of thousands of volunteers worked with the U.S. Sanitary Commission to send bandages, medicines, and food to Union army camps and hospitals. Some 3,000 women served as nurses in the Union army.

Training the Soldiers Both the Union and Confederate armies faced shortages of clothing, food, and even rifles. While the U.S. Army troops had standard issue uniforms, volunteer militias frequently had their own uniforms and individual volunteers often simply wore their own clothes. Eventually, each side chose a color for their uniforms. The Union chose blue. The Confederates wore gray.

The problem with volunteers was that many of them had no idea how to fight. Schoolteachers, farmers, and laborers all had to learn the combat basics of marching, shooting, and using bayonets.

Days in camp were long and boring. They typically began at 5 a.m. in summer and 6 a.m. in winter. After breakfast, the men took part in up to five daily drills. During these two-hour sessions they learned and practiced battlefield maneuvers. Between drills, the troops cleaned the camp, gathered firewood, wrote letters home, and played games. With visions of glory and action, many young soldiers were eager to fight. They would not have to wait long.

Discipline and drill were used to turn raw volunteers into an efficient fighting machine. During a battle, the success or failure of a regiment often depended on its discipline—how well it responded to orders.

Volunteers also learned how to use rifles. Eventually, soldiers were expected to be able to load, aim, and fire their rifles three times in one minute. The quality of the weapons provided varied greatly. Most soldiers favored the Springfield and Enfield rifles for their accuracy. On the other hand, soldiers often complained about their Austrian and Belgian rifles. A soldier remarked, "I don't believe one could hit the broadside of a barn with them."

Reading Check
Summarize
How did soldiers and civilians prepare for war?

On average, soldiers spent about 75 percent of their time in camp. In wet weather, camps were a sea of mud. In dry weather, they were filled with clouds of dust. The Union army provided the infantry with two-person tents. However, soldiers often discarded these tents in favor of more portable ones. The Confederate army did not usually issue tents. Instead, Confederates often used tents that were captured from the Union army.

Summary and Preview As citizens chose sides in the Civil War, civilians and soldiers alike became involved in the war effort. In the next lesson you will learn about some early battles in the war, both on land and at sea.

Lesson 1 Assessment

Review Ideas, Terms, and People

1. **a. Identify** What event triggered the war between the Union and the Confederacy?

   b. Contrast How did the Union's strategy differ from that of the Confederacy?

   c. Evaluate Which side do you believe was better prepared for war? Explain your answer.

2. **a. Describe** How did women take part in the war?

   b. Summarize In what ways were the armies of the North and South unprepared for war?

   c. Elaborate Why did men volunteer to fight in the war?

Critical Thinking

3. **Compare and Contrast** In this lesson you learned about the preparations for war by the North and the South. Create a chart similar to the one below and use it to show the strengths and weaknesses of each side in the war.

	Union	Confederacy
Strengths		
Weaknesses		

★
The War in the East

The Big Idea

Confederate and Union forces faced off in Virginia and at sea.

Main Ideas

- Union and Confederate forces fought for control of the war in Virginia.
- The Battle of Antietam gave the North a slight advantage.
- The Confederacy attempted to break the Union naval blockade.

Key Terms and People

Thomas "Stonewall" Jackson
First Battle of Bull Run
George B. McClellan
Robert E. Lee
Seven Days' Battles
Second Battle of Bull Run
Battle of Antietam
ironclads

If YOU were there . . .

You live in Washington, DC, in July 1861. You and your friends are on your way to Manassas, near Washington, to watch the battle there. Everyone expects a quick Union victory. Your wagon is loaded with food for a picnic, and people are in a holiday mood. You see some members of Congress riding toward Manassas, too. Maybe this battle will end the war!

Why would you want to watch this battle?

War in Virginia

The troops that met in the first major battle of the Civil War found that it was no picnic. In July 1861 Lincoln ordered General Irvin McDowell to lead his 35,000-man army from the Union capital, Washington, to the Confederate capital, Richmond. The soldiers were barely trained. McDowell complained that they "stopped every moment to pick blackberries or get water; they would not keep in the ranks." The first day's march covered only five miles.

Bull Run/Manassas McDowell's army was headed to Manassas, Virginia, an important railroad junction. If McDowell could seize Manassas, he would control the best route to the Confederate capital. Some 22,000 Confederate troops under the command of General Pierre G. T. Beauregard were waiting for McDowell and his troops along a creek called Bull Run. For two days Union troops tried to find a way around the Confederates. During that time, Beauregard requested assistance, and General Joseph E. Johnston headed toward Manassas with another 10,000 Confederate troops. By July 21, 1861, they had all arrived.

In this painting of the First Battle of Bull Run, Confederate general Thomas "Stonewall" Jackson looks over the battlefield.

That morning, Union troops managed to cross the creek and drive back the left side of the Confederate line. Yet one unit held firmly in place.

"There is Jackson standing like a stone wall!" cried one southern officer. "Rally behind the Virginians!" At that moment General **Thomas "Stonewall" Jackson** earned his famous nickname.

A steady stream of Virginia volunteers arrived to counter the attack. The Confederates surged forward. One eyewitness described the scene.

> "There is smoke, dust, wild talking, shouting; hissings, howlings, explosions. It is a new, strange, unanticipated experience to the soldiers of both armies, far different from what they thought it would be."
> —Charles Coffin, quoted in *Voices of the Civil War* by Richard Wheeler

The battle raged through the day, with rebel soldiers still arriving. Finally, the weary Union troops gave out. They tried to make an orderly retreat back across the creek, but the roads were clogged with the fancy carriages of panicked spectators. The Union army scattered in the chaos.

The Confederates lacked the strength to push north and capture Washington, DC. But clearly, the rebels had won the day. The **First Battle of Bull Run** was the first major battle of the Civil War and the Confederates' victory. The battle is also known as the First Battle of Manassas. It shattered the North's hopes of winning the war quickly.

More Battles in Virginia The shock at Bull Run persuaded Lincoln of the need for a better-trained army. He put his hopes in General **George B. McClellan**. The general assembled a highly disciplined force of 100,000 soldiers called the Army of the Potomac. The careful McClellan spent

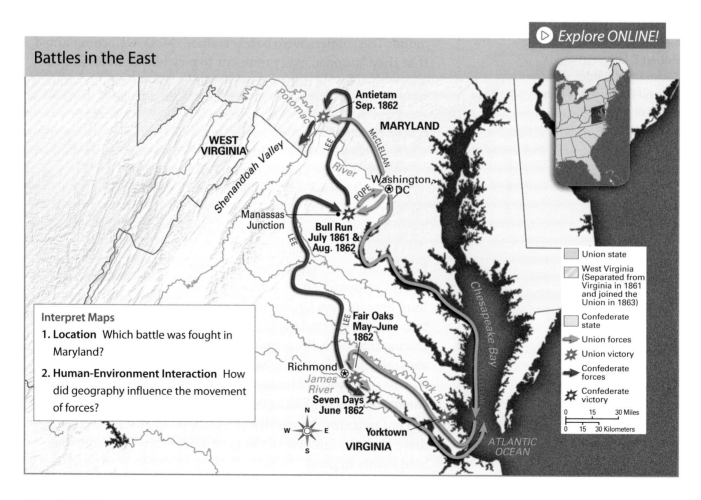

Battles in the East

▶ *Explore ONLINE!*

Interpret Maps

1. **Location** Which battle was fought in Maryland?

2. **Human-Environment Interaction** How did geography influence the movement of forces?

Union state

West Virginia (Separated from Virginia in 1861 and joined the Union in 1863)

Confederate state

→ Union forces

✴ Union victory

→ Confederate forces

✴ Confederate victory

0   15   30 Miles

0   15   30 Kilometers

Robert E. Lee 1807–1870

Robert E. Lee was born into a wealthy Virginia family and graduated second in his class from West Point, the U.S. military academy. He fought in the Mexican-American War of 1846, helping to capture Veracruz. When the Civil War began, President Lincoln asked Lee to lead the Union army. Although Lee opposed secession, he declined Lincoln's offer and resigned from the U.S. Army to become a general in the Confederate army. As a general, Lee was brilliant, but a lack of supplies from civilian leaders weakened his position. His soldiers—some of whom called him Uncle Robert—almost worshiped him because he insisted on sharing their hardships. After the war ended, Lee became president of Washington College in Virginia, now known as Washington and Lee University. Lee swore renewed allegiance to the United States, but Congress accidentally neglected to restore his citizenship. Still, Lee never spoke bitterly of northerners or the Union, and many southerners saw Lee as a war hero.

Draw Conclusions
How did Lee's choice reflect the division of the states?

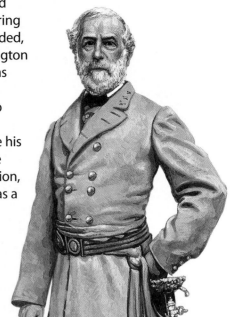

months training. However, because he overestimated the size of the Confederate army, McClellan hesitated to attack. Lincoln grew impatient. Finally, in the spring of 1862 McClellan launched an effort to capture Richmond, called the "Peninsular Campaign." Instead of marching south for a direct assault, McClellan slowly brought his force through the peninsula between the James and York rivers. More time slipped away.

The South feared that McClellan would receive reinforcements from Washington. To prevent this, Stonewall Jackson launched an attack toward Washington. Although the attack was pushed back, it prevented the Union from sending reinforcements to McClellan.

In June 1862, with McClellan's force poised outside Richmond, the Confederate army in Virginia came under the command of General **Robert E. Lee**. A graduate of the U.S. Military Academy at West Point, Lee had served in the Mexican War and had led federal troops at Harpers Ferry. Lee was willing to take risks and make unpredictable moves to throw Union forces off balance.

During the summer of 1862, Lee strengthened his positions. On June 26 he launched a series of clashes known as the **Seven Days' Battles** that forced the Union army to retreat from near Richmond. Confederate general D. H. Hill described one failed attack. "It was not war—it was murder," he said. Lee saved Richmond and forced McClellan to retreat. A frustrated Lincoln ordered General John Pope to march directly on Richmond.

Jackson wanted to defeat Pope's army before it could join up with McClellan's larger Army of the Potomac. Jackson's troops met Pope's Union forces on the battlefield in August 1862. The three-day battle became known as the **Second Battle of Bull Run**, or the Second Battle of Manassas.

The first day's fighting was savage. Captain George Fairfield of the 7th Wisconsin regiment later recalled, "What a slaughter! No one appeared to know the object of the fight, and there we stood for one hour, the men falling all around." The fighting ended in a stalemate.

On the second day, Pope found Jackson's troops along an unfinished railroad grade. Pope hurled his men against the Confederates. But the attacks were pushed back with heavy casualties on both sides.

On the third day, the Confederates crushed the Union army's assault and forced it to retreat in defeat. The Confederates had won a major victory, and General Robert E. Lee decided it was time to take the war to the North.

Reading Check
Sequence List in order the events that forced Union troops out of Virginia.

Battle of Antietam

Confederate leaders hoped to follow up Lee's successes in Virginia with a major victory on northern soil. On September 4, 1862, some 40,000 Confederate soldiers began crossing into Maryland. General Robert E. Lee decided to divide his army. He sent about half of his troops, under the command of Stonewall Jackson, to Harpers Ferry. There they defeated a Union force and captured the town. Meanwhile, Lee arrived in the town of Frederick and issued a Proclamation to the People of Maryland, urging them to join the Confederates. However, his words would not be enough to convince Marylanders to abandon the Union. Union soldiers, however, found a copy of Lee's battle plan, which had been left at an abandoned Confederate camp. General McClellan learned that Lee had divided his army in order to attack Harpers Ferry. However, McClellan hesitated to attack. As a result, the Confederates had time to reunite.

The two armies met along Antietam Creek in Maryland on September 17, 1862. The battle lasted for hours. By the end of the day, the Union had

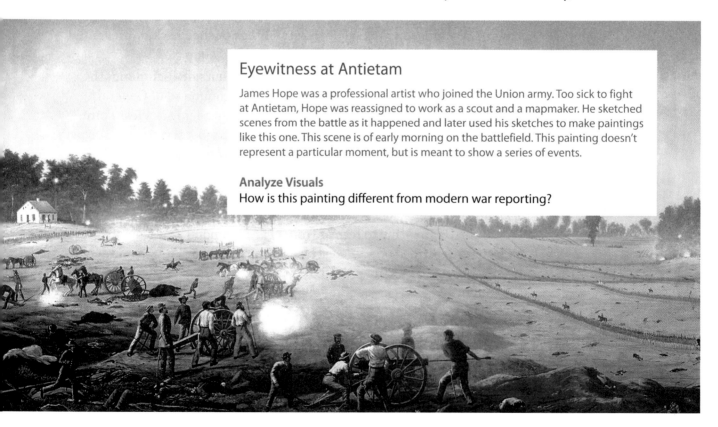

Eyewitness at Antietam

James Hope was a professional artist who joined the Union army. Too sick to fight at Antietam, Hope was reassigned to work as a scout and a mapmaker. He sketched scenes from the battle as it happened and later used his sketches to make paintings like this one. This scene is of early morning on the battlefield. This painting doesn't represent a particular moment, but is meant to show a series of events.

Analyze Visuals
How is this painting different from modern war reporting?

suffered more than 12,000 casualties. The Confederates endured more than 13,000 casualties. Union officer A. H. Nickerson later recalled, "It seemed that everybody near me was killed." The **Battle of Antietam**, also known as the Battle of Sharpsburg, was the bloodiest single-day battle of the Civil War—and of U.S. history. More soldiers were killed and wounded at the Battle of Antietam than the deaths of all Americans in the American Revolution, War of 1812, and Mexican-American War combined.

During the battle, McClellan kept four divisions of soldiers in reserve and refused to use them to attack Lee's devastated army. McClellan was convinced that Lee was massing reserves for a counterattack. Those reserves did not exist. Despite this blunder, Antietam was an important victory. Lee's northward advance had been stopped.

Reading Check
Analyze Why was the Battle of Antietam significant?

Breaking the Union's Blockade

While the two armies fought for control of the land, the Union navy controlled the sea. The North had most of the U.S. Navy's small fleet, and many experienced naval officers had remained loyal to the Union. The North also had enough industry to build more ships. The Confederacy turned to British companies for new ships.

The Union's Naval Strategy The Union navy quickly mobilized to set up a blockade of southern ports. The blockade largely prevented the South from selling or receiving goods, and it seriously damaged the southern economy.

The blockade was hard to maintain because the Union navy had to patrol thousands of miles of coastline from Virginia to Texas. The South used small, fast ships to outrun the larger Union warships. Most of these blockade runners traveled to the Bahamas or Nassau to buy supplies for the Confederacy. These ships, however, could not make up for the South's

Historical Source

Anaconda Plan

This cartoon shows visually the North's plan to cut off supplies to the South through naval blockades, a strategy called the Anaconda Plan.

> Why is the snake's head red, white, and blue?

> How does the cartoonist show what the snake represents?

Analyze Historical Sources
Why do you think the plan was called the Anaconda Plan?

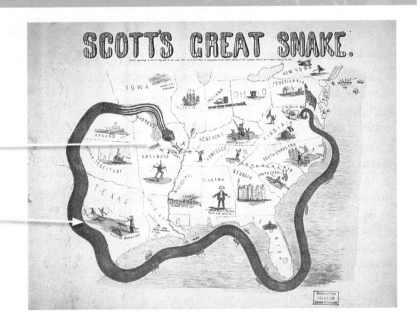

loss of trade. The Union blockade reduced the number of ships entering southern ports from 6,000 to 800 per year.

Clash of the Ironclads Hoping to take away the Union's advantage at sea, the Confederacy turned to a new type of warship—**ironclads**, or ships heavily armored with iron. The British government neglected to stop these ships from being delivered, in violation of its pledge of neutrality. The Confederates had captured a Union steamship, the *Merrimack*, and turned it into an ironclad, renamed the *Virginia*. One Union sailor described the **innovation** as "a huge half-submerged crocodile." In early March 1862 the ironclad sailed into Hampton Roads, Virginia, an important waterway guarded by Union ships. Before nightfall, the *Virginia* easily sank two of the Union's wooden warships, while it received minor damage.

The Union navy had already built its own ironclad, the *Monitor*, designed by Swedish-born engineer John Ericsson. Ericsson's ship had unusual new features, such as a revolving gun tower. One Confederate soldier called the *Monitor* "a tin can on a shingle!" Although small, the *Monitor* carried powerful guns and had thick plating.

When the *Virginia* returned to Hampton Roads later that month, the *Monitor* was waiting. After several hours of fighting, neither ship was seriously damaged, but the *Monitor* forced the *Virginia* to withdraw. This success saved the Union fleet and continued the blockade. The clash of the ironclads also signaled a revolution in naval warfare. The days of wooden warships powered by wind and sails were drawing to a close.

The *Monitor* sank in North Carolina in the winter of 1862. Scientists located the shipwreck in 1973, and remains of the ship are part of the exhibit at the USS *Monitor* Center, which opened in 2007.

Summary and Preview The early battles of the Civil War were centered in the East. In the next lesson you will read about battles in the West.

Academic Vocabulary
innovation a new idea or way of doing something

Reading Check
Evaluate How effective was the Union blockade?

Lesson 2 Assessment

Review Ideas, Terms, and People

1. **a. Identify** List the early battles in the East and the outcome of each battle.
   b. Elaborate Why do you think the Union lost the First Battle of Bull Run?
2. **a. Describe** What costly mistake did the Confederacy make before the Battle of Antietam?
   b. Analyze What was the outcome of the Battle of Antietam, and what effect did it have on both the North and the South?
   c. Elaborate Why do you think General George B. McClellan did not finish off General Robert E. Lee's troops when he had the chance?

3. **a. Describe** What was the Union's strategy in the war at sea?
   b. Draw Conclusions Why were ironclads more successful than older, wooden ships?

Critical Thinking

4. **Support a Point of View** In this lesson you learned about the Civil War battles in the East and at sea. Create a chart similar to the one below and use it to show which three conflicts you think were the most significant and why.

Most Significant	Why

The War in the West

The Big Idea

Fighting in the Civil War spread to the western United States.

Main Ideas

- Union strategy in the West centered on control of the Mississippi River.

- Confederate and Union troops struggled for dominance in the Far West.

Key Terms and People

Ulysses S. Grant
Battle of Shiloh
David Farragut
Siege of Vicksburg

If YOU were there . . .

You live in the city of Vicksburg, set on high bluffs above the Mississippi River. Vicksburg is vital to the control of the river, and Confederate defenses are strong. But the Union general is determined to take the town. For weeks you have been surrounded and besieged. Cannon shells burst overhead, day and night. Some have fallen on nearby homes. Supplies of food are running low.

How would you survive this siege?

Union Strategy in the West

While Lincoln fumed over the cautious, hesitant General McClellan, he had no such problems with **Ulysses S. Grant**. Bold and restless, Grant grew impatient when he was asked to lead defensive military maneuvers. He wanted to be on the attack. As a commander of forces in the Union's western campaign, he would get his wish.

The western campaign focused on taking control of the Mississippi River. This strategy would cut off the eastern part of the Confederacy from sources of food production in Arkansas, Louisiana, and Texas. From bases on the Mississippi, the Union army could attack southern communication and transportation networks.

In February 1862 Grant led an assault force into Tennessee. With help from navy gunboats, Grant's Army of the Tennessee took two outposts on key rivers in the West. On February 6 he captured Fort Henry on the Tennessee River. Several days later he took Fort Donelson on the Cumberland River.

Fort Donelson's commander asked for the terms of surrender. Grant replied, "No terms except an unconditional and immediate surrender can be accepted." The fort surrendered. The North gave a new name to Grant's initials: "Unconditional Surrender" Grant.

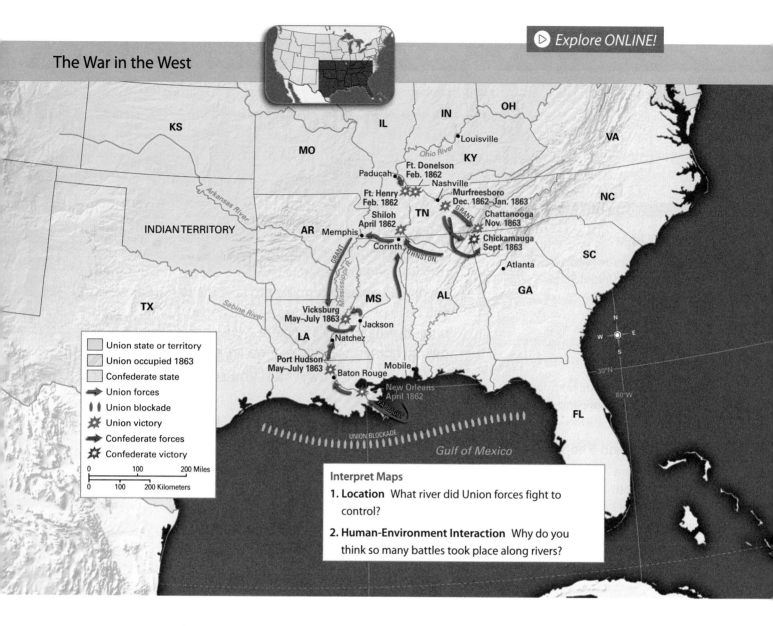

Explore ONLINE!

Interpret Maps

1. **Location** What river did Union forces fight to control?

2. **Human-Environment Interaction** Why do you think so many battles took place along rivers?

Advancing south in Tennessee, General Grant paused near Shiloh Church to await the arrival of the Army of the Ohio. Grant knew that the large rebel army of General A. S. Johnston was nearby in Corinth, Mississippi, but he did not expect an attack. Instead of setting up defenses, he worked on drilling his new recruits.

In the early morning of April 6, 1862, the rebels sprang on Grant's sleepy camp. This began the **Battle of Shiloh**, in which the Union army gained greater control of the Mississippi River valley.

During the bloody two-day battle, each side gained and lost ground. Johnston was killed on the first day. The arrival of the Ohio force helped Grant regain territory and push the enemy back into Mississippi. The armies finally gave out, each with about 10,000 casualties. Both sides claimed victory, but, in fact, the victor was Grant.

The Fall of New Orleans As Grant battled his way down the Mississippi, the Union navy prepared to blast its way upriver to meet him. The first obstacle was the port of New Orleans, the largest city in the Confederacy and the gateway to the Mississippi River.

David Farragut 1801–1870

David Farragut was born in Tennessee to a Spanish father and an American mother. At age seven Farragut was adopted by a family friend who agreed to train the young boy for the navy. Farragut received his first navy position—midshipman at large—at age nine and commanded his first vessel at 12. He spent the rest of his life in the U.S. Navy. Farragut helped the war effort of the North by leading key attacks on the southern ports of Vicksburg and New Orleans.

Draw Inferences
How did Farragut help the war effort of the North?

With 18 ships and 700 men, Admiral **David Farragut** approached the two forts that guarded the entrance to New Orleans from the Gulf of Mexico. Unable to destroy the forts, Farragut decided to race past them.

The risky operation would take place at night. Farragut had his wooden ships wrapped in heavy chains to protect them like ironclads. Sailors slapped Mississippi mud on the ships' hulls to make them hard to see. Trees were tied to the masts to make the ships look like the forested shore.

Before dawn on April 24, 1862, the warships made their daring dash. The Confederates fired at Farragut's ships from the shore and from gunboats. They launched burning rafts, one of which scorched Farragut's own ship. But his fleet slipped by the twin forts and made it to New Orleans. The city fell on April 29.

Farragut sailed up the Mississippi River, taking Baton Rouge, Louisiana, and Natchez, Mississippi. He then approached the city of Vicksburg, Mississippi.

The Siege of Vicksburg Vicksburg's geography made invasion all but impossible. Perched on 200-foot-high cliffs above the Mississippi River, the city could rain down firepower on enemy ships or on soldiers trying to scale the cliffs. Deep gorges surrounded the city, turning back land assaults. Nevertheless, Farragut ordered Vicksburg to surrender.

> "Mississippians don't know, and refuse to learn, how to surrender . . . If Commodore Farragut . . . can teach them, let [him] come and try."
> —Colonel James L. Autry, military commander of Vicksburg

Farragut's guns had trouble reaching the city above. It was up to General Grant. His solution was to starve the city into surrender.

General Grant's troops began the **Siege of Vicksburg** in mid-May 1863, cutting off the city and shelling it repeatedly. As food ran out, residents and soldiers survived by eating horses, dogs, and rats. "We are utterly cut off from the world, surrounded by a circle of fire," wrote one woman. "People do nothing but eat what they can get, sleep when they can, and dodge the shells."

The Confederate soldiers were also sick and hungry. In late June a group of soldiers sent their commander a warning.

"If you can't feed us, you had better surrender us, horrible as the idea is. . . . This army is now ripe for mutiny [rebellion], unless it can be fed."

—Confederate soldiers at Vicksburg to General John C. Pemberton, 1863

Reading Check
Summarize
How did the Union gain control of the Mississippi River?

On July 4 Pemberton surrendered. Grant immediately sent food to the soldiers and civilians. He later claimed that "the fate of the Confederacy was sealed when Vicksburg fell."

Struggle for the Far West

Early on in the war, the Union halted several attempts by Confederate armies to control lands west of the Mississippi. In August 1861 a Union detachment from Colorado turned back a Confederate force at Glorieta Pass. Union volunteers also defeated rebel forces at Arizona's Pichaco Pass.

Confederate attempts to take the border state of Missouri also collapsed. Failing to seize the federal arsenal at St. Louis in mid-1861, the rebels fell back to Pea Ridge in northwest Arkansas. There, in March 1862 they attacked again, aided by some 800 Cherokee. The Union defense of Missouri held.

The Union navy played an important part in the Civil War. Besides blockading and raiding southern ports, the navy joined battles along the Mississippi River, as in this painting of Vicksburg.

DOCUMENT-BASED INVESTIGATION
Historical Source

Response to Farragut

The mayor of New Orleans considered the surrender of the city to the Union navy:

"We yield to physical force alone and maintain allegiance to the Confederate States; beyond this, a due respect for our dignity, our rights and the flag of our country does not, I think, permit us to go."

—Mayor John T. Monroe quoted in *Confederate Military History*, Vol. 10

Analyze Historical Sources
How does Monroe's statement reveal his attitude about surrender?

Although the Union army won the battle, Indian troops commanded by Cherokee leader Stand Watie fought bravely. Watie was later promoted to general, the only Native American on either side to hold this rank in the war.

More than 10,000 Native Americans took part in the Civil War. Many Cherokee fought for the Confederacy, but the war bitterly divided the Cherokee—and other nations as well—over issues of loyalty and slavery.

Some nations saw the transfer of soldiers from western forts to eastern battlefields as a chance to take back land they had lost. The Indians also hoped the Confederates would give them greater freedom. In addition, slavery was legal in Indian Territory, and some Native Americans who were slaveholders supported the Confederacy. Pro-Confederate forces remained active in the region throughout the war. They attacked Union forts and raided towns in Missouri and Kansas, forcing Union commanders to keep valuable troops stationed in the area.

Summary and Preview The North and the South continued their struggle with battles in the West. A number of key battles took place in the Western theater, and several important Union leaders emerged from these battles. One, Ulysses S. Grant, would soon become even more important to the Union army. In the next lesson you will learn about the lives of civilians, enslaved African Americans, and soldiers during the war.

Reading Check
Analyze What was the importance of the fighting in the Far West?

Lesson 3 Assessment

Review Ideas, Terms, and People

1. **a. Identify** What role did Ulysses S. Grant play in the war in the West?

   b. Explain Why was the Battle of Shiloh important?

   c. Elaborate Do you think President Lincoln would have approved of Grant's actions in the West? Why or why not?

2. **a. Describe** How did the Union take New Orleans, and why was it an important victory?

   b. Draw Conclusions How were civilians affected by the Siege of Vicksburg?

   c. Predict What might be some possible results of the Union victory at Vicksburg?

Critical Thinking

3. **Identify Cause and Effect** In this lesson you learned about the Union's military strategy in the West. Create a graphic organizer similar to the one below and use it to show the causes and effects of each battle.

The Vicksburg Strategy

"Vicksburg is the key!"

President Abraham Lincoln declared. "The war can never be brought to a close until that key is in our pocket." Vicksburg was so important because of its location on the Mississippi River, a vital trade route and supply line. Union ships couldn't get past the Confederate guns mounted on the high bluffs of Vicksburg. Capturing Vicksburg would give the Union control of the Mississippi, stealing a vital supply line and splitting the Confederacy in two. The task fell to General Ulysses S. Grant.

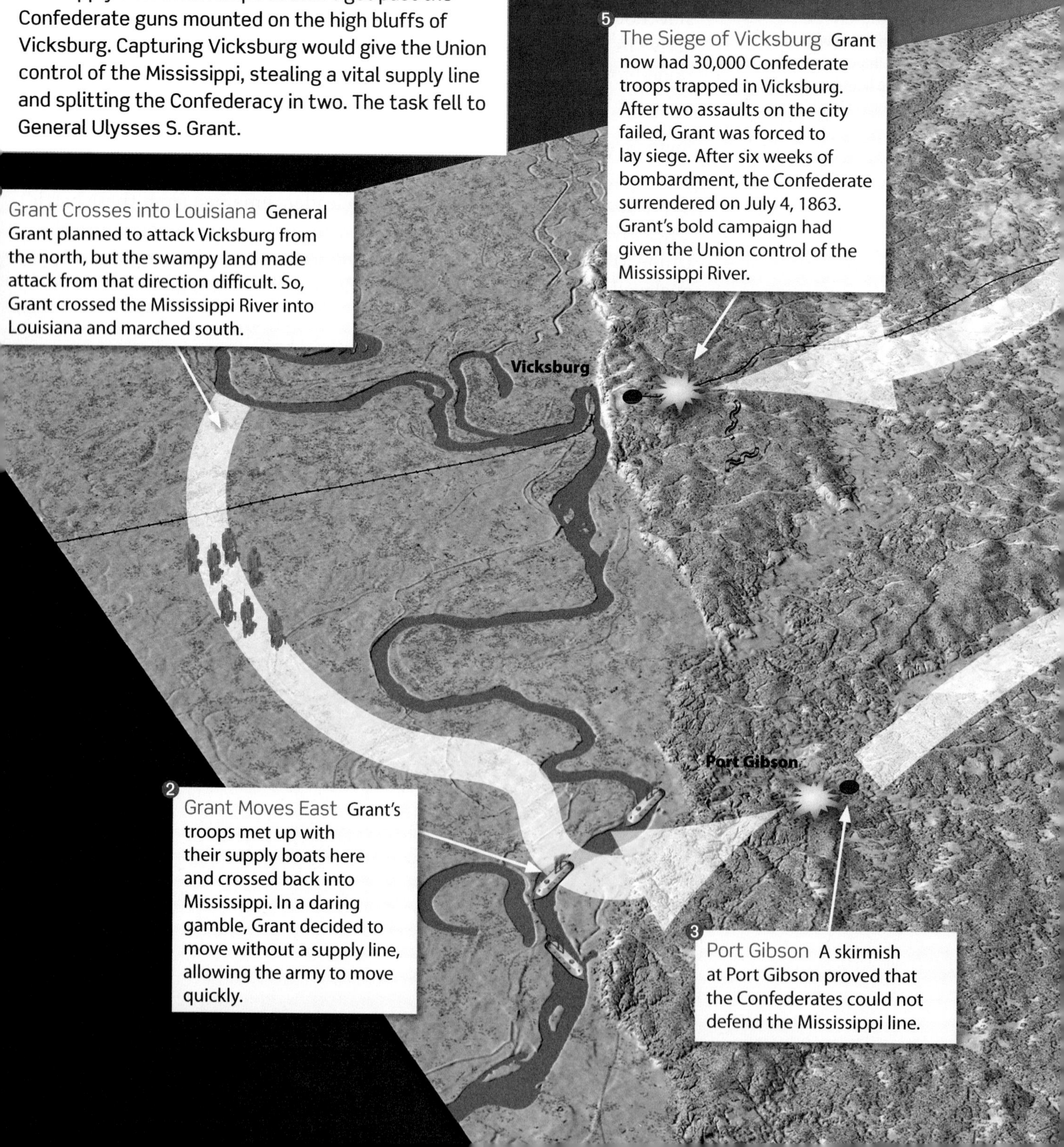

Grant Crosses into Louisiana General Grant planned to attack Vicksburg from the north, but the swampy land made attack from that direction difficult. So, Grant crossed the Mississippi River into Louisiana and marched south.

5 The Siege of Vicksburg Grant now had 30,000 Confederate troops trapped in Vicksburg. After two assaults on the city failed, Grant was forced to lay siege. After six weeks of bombardment, the Confederate surrendered on July 4, 1863. Grant's bold campaign had given the Union control of the Mississippi River.

Vicksburg

Port Gibson

2 Grant Moves East Grant's troops met up with their supply boats here and crossed back into Mississippi. In a daring gamble, Grant decided to move without a supply line, allowing the army to move quickly.

3 Port Gibson A skirmish at Port Gibson proved that the Confederates could not defend the Mississippi line.

UNION
CONTROL

CONFEDERATE
CONTROL

Missouri
Kentucky
Virginia
North Carolina
Arkansas
Tennessee
South Carolina
Alabama
Georgia
VICKSBURG
Mississippi
Louisiana
GULF OF MEXICO

Jackson

4 The Battle of Jackson Grant defeated a Confederate army at Jackson and then moved on to Vicksburg. This prevented Confederate forces from reinforcing Vicksburg.

Ironclads Union ironclads were vital to the Vicksburg campaign. These gunboats protected Grant's troops when they crossed the Mississippi. Later, they bombarded Vicksburg during the siege of the city.

— BIOGRAPHY —

Ulysses S. Grant 1822–1885

Ulysses S. Grant was born in April 1822 in Ohio. Grant attended West Point in New York and fought in the Mexican-American War. He resigned in 1854 and worked at various jobs in farming, real estate, and retail. When the Civil War started, he joined the Union army and was quickly promoted to general. After the Civil War, Grant rode a wave of popularity to become president of the United States.

Interpret Maps

1. Location Why was Vicksburg's location so important?

2. Place What natural features made Vicksburg difficult to attack?

Daily Life during the War

The Big Idea

The lives of many Americans were affected by the Civil War.

Main Ideas

- The Emancipation Proclamation freed slaves in Confederate states.

- African Americans participated in the war in a variety of ways.

- President Lincoln faced opposition to the war.

- Life was difficult for soldiers and civilians alike.

Key Terms and People

emancipation
Emancipation Proclamation
contrabands
54th Massachusetts Infantry
Copperheads
habeas corpus
Clara Barton

If YOU were there . . .

You live in Maryland in 1864. Your father and brothers are in the Union army, and you want to do your part in the war. You hear that a woman in Washington, DC, is supplying medicines and caring for wounded soldiers on the battlefield. She is looking for volunteers. You know the work will be dangerous, for you'll be in the line of fire. You might be shot or even killed.

Would you join the nurses on the battlefield?

Emancipation Proclamation

At the heart of the nation's bloody struggle were millions of enslaved African Americans. Abolitionists urged President Lincoln to free them.

In an 1858 speech, Lincoln declared, "There is no reason in the world why the negro is not entitled to all the natural rights numerated in the Declaration of Independence—the right to life, liberty, and the pursuit of happiness." Yet as president, Lincoln found **emancipation**, or the freeing of slaves, to be a difficult issue. He did not believe he had the constitutional power. He also worried about the effects of emancipation.

Lincoln Issues the Proclamation Northerners had a range of opinions about abolishing slavery.

- The Democratic Party, which included many laborers, opposed emancipation. Laborers feared that freed slaves would come north and take their jobs at lower wages.
- Abolitionists argued that the war was pointless if it did not win freedom for African Americans. They warned that the Union would remain divided until the problem was resolved.

- Lincoln worried about losing support for the war. Previous wartime Confiscation Acts that had attempted to free the slaves had been unpopular in the border states.
- Others, including Secretary of War Edwin Stanton, agreed with Lincoln that the use of slave labor was helping the Confederacy make war. Therefore, as commander in chief, the president could free the slaves in all rebellious states. Freed African Americans could then be recruited into the Union army.

For several weeks in 1862, Lincoln worked intensely, thinking, writing, and rewriting. He finally wrote the **Emancipation Proclamation**, the order to free the Confederate slaves. The proclamation declared that:

"... all persons held as slaves within any State or designated part of a State the people whereof shall then be in rebellion against the United States shall be then, thenceforward, and forever free."

—Emancipation Proclamation, 1862

Confederates reacted to the Proclamation with outrage. Jefferson Davis called it the "most execrable [hateful] measure recorded in the history of guilty man." As some northern Democrats had predicted, the Proclamation had made the Confederacy more determined than ever to fight to preserve its way of life.

The Emancipation Proclamation was a military order that freed slaves only in areas controlled by the Confederacy. In fact, the proclamation had little immediate effect. It was impossible for the federal government to enforce the proclamation in the areas where it actually applied—the states in rebellion that were not under federal control. The proclamation did not

▶ *Explore ONLINE!*

Emancipation Proclamation

Legend:
- Union state
- Confederate state
- Border state
- Area of legal slaveholding
- Area in which slavery was abolished by the Emancipation Proclamation

Interpret Maps

Place In which places was slavery still legal after the Emancipation Proclamation?

stop slavery in the border states, where the federal government would have had the power to enforce it. The words written in the Emancipation Proclamation were powerful, but the impact of the document was more symbolic than real. It defined what the Union was fighting against and discouraged Britain from aiding the Confederacy.

Lincoln wanted to be in a strong position in the war before announcing his plan. The Battle of Antietam gave him the victory he needed. He issued the Emancipation Proclamation on September 22, 1862. The proclamation went into effect on January 1, 1863. As one of the first civil rights documents in United States history, the Emancipation Proclamation continues to impact Americans today as a symbol of equal rights for all Americans. The historic document paved the way for future civil rights legislation, which gave minorities and women more equal rights.

Reaction to the Proclamation New Year's Eve, December 31, 1862: In "night watch" meetings at many African American churches, worshippers prayed, sang, and gave thanks. When the clocks struck midnight, millions were free. Abolitionists rejoiced. Frederick Douglass called January 1, 1863, "the great day which is to determine the destiny not only of the American Republic, but that of the American Continent."

William Lloyd Garrison was quick to note, however, that "slavery, as a system" continued to exist in the loyal slave states. Yet where slavery

---

BIOGRAPHY

Abraham Lincoln 1809–1865

Abraham Lincoln is one of the great symbols of American democracy. He was born in a log cabin to a poor family in Kentucky and grew-up in Kentucky and Illinois. Lincoln went to school for less than a year, but taught himself law and settled in Springfield, where he practiced law and politics. The issue of slavery defined Lincoln's entire political career. He was not an abolitionist, but he strongly opposed extending slavery into the territories. In a series of famous political debates against Senator Stephen Douglas of Illinois, Lincoln championed his views on slavery and made a brilliant defense of democracy and the Union. "A house divided against itself cannot stand," he declared in a debate with Douglas.

Elected president in 1860, Lincoln led the nation through the Civil War and worked constantly to preserve a unified nation. In 1863, he issued the Emancipation Proclamation. His address to commemorate the bloody battlefield at Gettysburg is considered to be one of the best political speeches in American history. Only days after the Civil War ended, John Wilkes Booth assassinated Lincoln on April 14, 1865.

Summarize
Why is Lincoln such an important figure in American history?

remained, the proclamation encouraged many enslaved African Americans to escape when the Union troops came near. They flocked to the Union camps and followed them for protection. The loss of slaves crippled the South's ability to wage war.

African Americans Participate in the War

As the war casualties climbed, the Union needed even more troops. African Americans were ready to volunteer. Not all white northerners were ready to accept them, but eventually they had to. Frederick Douglass believed that military service would help African Americans gain rights.

> "Once let the black man get upon his person the brass letters, U.S.; . . . and a musket on his shoulder and bullets in his pocket, and there is no power on earth which can deny that he has earned the right to citizenship."
>
> —Frederick Douglass, quoted in *The Life and Writings of Frederick Douglass, Vol. 3*

Congress began allowing the army to sign up African American volunteers as laborers in July 1862. The War Department also gave **contrabands**, or escaped slaves, the right to join the Union army in South Carolina. Free African Americans in Louisiana and Kansas also formed their own units in the Union army. By the spring of 1863, African American army units were proving themselves in combat. They took part in a Union attack on Port Hudson, Louisiana, in May.

One unit stood out above the others. The **54th Massachusetts Infantry** consisted mostly of free African Americans. In July 1863 this regiment led a heroic charge on South Carolina's Fort Wagner. The 54th took heavy fire and suffered huge casualties in the failed operation. About half the regiment was killed, wounded, or captured. Edward L. Pierce, a

Reading Check
Find Main Ideas
How did northerners view the Emancipation Proclamation?

DOCUMENT-BASED INVESTIGATION   Historical Source

Letter from a Union Soldier

On June 23, 1863, Joseph E. Williams, an African American soldier and recruiter from Pennsylvania, wrote this letter describing why African Americans fought for the Union.

"*We are now determined to hold every step that has been offered to us as citizens of the United States for our elevation [benefit], which represent justice, the purity, the truth, the aspiration [hope] of heaven. We must learn deeply to realize the duty, the moral and practical necessity for the benefit of our race . . . Every consideration of honor, of interest, and of duty to God and man, requires that we should be true to our trust.*"

—quoted in *A Grand Army of Black Men,* edited by Edwin S. Redkey

Analyze Historical Sources
Why did Williams think being soldiers was so important for African Americans?

New Soldiers

African American soldiers, such as the 54th Massachusetts Infantry and Company E of the 4th U.S. Colored Infantry, shown here, fought proudly and bravely in the Civil War. At right is a flyer used to recruit African American soldiers.

NOW IN CAMP AT READVILLE!

54th REGIMENT!

MASS. VOLUNTEERS, composed of men of

AFRICAN DESCENT

Col. ROBERT G. SHAW.

Colored Men, Rally 'Round the Flag of Freedom!

BOUNTY $100!

AT THE EXPIRATION OF THE TERM OF SERVICE.

Pay, $13 a Month!

Good Food & Clothing!

State Aid to Families!

RECRUITING OFFICE.

COR. CAMBRIDGE & NORTH RUSSELL STS.,

BOSTON.

Lieut. J. W. M. APPLETON, Recruiting Officer.

correspondent for the *New York Tribune,* wrote, "The Fifty-fourth did well and nobly . . . They moved up as gallantly as any troops could, and with their enthusiasm they deserved a better fate." The bravery of the 54th regiment made it the most celebrated African American unit of the war.

About 180,000 African Americans served with the Union army. They initially received $10 a month, while white soldiers got $13. In June 1864 Congress passed a bill granting African American soldiers equal pay.

African Americans faced special horrors on the battlefield. Confederates often killed their black captives or sold them into slavery. In the 1864 election, Lincoln suggested rewarding African American soldiers by giving them the right to vote.

Reading Check
Analyze Information How did African Americans support the Union?

Growing Opposition

The deepening shadows in Lincoln's face reflected the huge responsibilities he carried. Besides running the war, he had to deal with growing tensions in the North.

Copperheads As the months rolled on and the number of dead continued to increase, a group of northern Democrats began speaking out against

The Copperheads
This political cartoon pokes fun at Copperhead northerners who want peace. The cartoon implies that the Copperheads' plan is to bore the Confederate states into rejoining the Union.

the war. Led by U.S. representative Clement L. Vallandigham of Ohio, they called themselves Peace Democrats. Their enemies called them Copperheads, comparing them to a poisonous snake. The name stuck.

Many **Copperheads** were midwesterners who sympathized with the South and opposed abolition. They believed the war was not necessary and called for its end. Vallandigham asked what the war had gained and then said, "Let the dead at Fredericksburg and Vicksburg answer."

Lincoln saw the Copperheads as a threat to support of the war effort. To silence them, he suspended the right of habeas corpus. **Habeas corpus** is a constitutional protection against unlawful imprisonment. Ignoring this protection, Union officials jailed their enemies, including some Copperheads, without evidence or trial. Lincoln's action greatly angered Democrats and some Republicans.

Northern Draft In March 1863 war critics erupted again when Congress approved a draft, or forced military service. For $300, men were allowed to buy their way out of military service. For an unskilled laborer, however, that was nearly a year's wages. Critics of the draft called the Civil War a "rich man's war and a poor man's fight."

In July 1863 riots broke out when African Americans were brought into New York City to replace striking Irish dockworkers. The city happened to be holding a war draft at the same time. The two events enraged rioters, who attacked African Americans and draft offices. More than 100 people died.

In this tense situation, the northern Democrats nominated former general George McClellan for president in 1864. They called for an immediate end to the war. Lincoln defeated McClellan in the popular vote, winning by about 400,000 votes out of 4 million cast. The electoral vote was not even close. Lincoln won 212 to 21.

Reading Check
Identify Cause and Effect Who opposed the war, and how did Lincoln respond to the conflict?

Life for Soldiers and Civilians

Young, fresh recruits in both armies were generally eager to fight. Experienced troops, however, knew better.

On the Battlefield Civil War armies fought in the ancient battlefield formation that produced massive casualties. Endless rows of troops fired directly at one another, with cannonballs landing amid them. When the order was given, soldiers would attach bayonets to their guns and rush toward their enemy. Men died to gain every inch of ground.

Doctors and nurses in the field saved many lives. Yet they had no medicines to stop infections that developed after soldiers were wounded. Many soldiers endured the horror of having infected legs and arms amputated without painkillers. Infections from minor injuries caused many deaths.

Despite the huge battlefield losses, the biggest killer in the Civil War was not the fighting. It was diseases such as typhoid, pneumonia, and tuberculosis. Nearly twice as many soldiers died of illnesses and disease as died in combat.

Infantry Family
While wealthy civilians could avoid military service, poorer men were drafted to serve in the Union army. This member of the 31st Pennsylvania Infantry brought his family along with him. His wife probably helped the soldier with many of the daily chores such as cooking and laundry.

Why would soldiers bring their families to live with them in camp?

Prisoners of War As hard as army life was, conditions for prisoners of war were much worse. At first, neither North nor South kept large numbers of captured soldiers. Many prisoners were released if they promised to go home instead of back to their army. Others were exchanged for prisoners held by the other side. Military prisoners on both sides lived in unimaginable misery. In prison camps, such as Andersonville, Georgia, and Elmira, New York, soldiers were packed into camps designed to hold only a fraction of their number. Soldiers had little shelter, food, or clothing. Starvation and disease killed thousands of prisoners.

Life as a Civilian The war effort involved all levels of society. Women as well as people too young or too old for military service worked in factories and on farms. Economy in the North boomed as production and prices soared. The lack of workers caused wages to rise by 43 percent between 1860 and 1865.

Women were the backbone of civilian life and took over farms, plantations, stores, and other businesses while their fathers, husbands, and sons served in armies. On the farms, women and children performed the daily chores usually done by men. One visitor to Iowa in 1862 reported that he "met more women . . . at work in the fields than men." Southern women also managed farms and plantations.

The need for clothes, shoes, and other supplies created about 100,000 jobs for women in northern factories. Women also worked in the South's few factories, and women on both sides performed dangerous work making ammunition for the troops.

Many women found new occupations. Hundreds were hired by the Union government as clerks. They became the first women to hold federal government jobs. Women also staffed government offices in the South. Like clerical work, nursing was a man's job before the war. During the war, however, about 3,000 women served the Union army as paid nurses.

One woman brought strength and comfort to countless wounded Union soldiers. Volunteer **Clara Barton** organized the collection of medicine and supplies for delivery to the battlefield. At the field hospitals, the "angel of the battlefield" soothed the wounded and dying and assisted doctors as bullets flew around her. Barton's work formed the basis for the future American Red Cross.

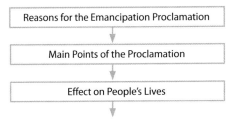

Clara Barton founded the American Red Cross.

In the South, Sally Louisa Tompkins established a small hospital in Richmond, Virginia. By the end of the war, it had grown into a major army hospital. Jefferson Davis recognized her value to the war effort by making her a captain in the Confederate army.

Reading Check
Analyze How did women help the war effort on both sides?

Summary and Preview Many lives were changed by the war. In the next lesson you will learn about the end of the war.

Lesson 4 Assessment

Review Ideas, Terms, and People

1. a. Recall Why did some Americans want to end slavery?

b. Contrast How did reactions to the Emancipation Proclamation differ?

c. Elaborate How and why does the Emancipation Proclamation continue to impact American life? Explain your answer.

2. a. Recall Why did some northerners want to recruit African Americans into the Union army?

b. Contrast In what ways did African American soldiers face more difficulties than white soldiers did?

3. a. Identify Who were Copperheads, and why did they oppose the war?

b. Evaluate Should President Lincoln have suspended the right to habeas corpus? Why?

4. a. Describe What were conditions like in military camps?

b. Draw Conclusions How did the war change life on the home front?

Critical Thinking

5. Identify Effects In this lesson you learned about the Emancipation Proclamation. Create a chart similar to the one below and use it to summarize the reasons for the Emancipation Proclamation, its main points, and its effects on different people.

Reasons for the Emancipation Proclamation

↓

Main Points of the Proclamation

↓

Effect on People's Lives

↓

The Tide of War Turns

The Big Idea

Union victories in 1863, 1864, and 1865 ended the Civil War.

Main Ideas

- The Union tried to divide the Confederate army at Fredericksburg, but the attempt failed.

- The Battle of Gettysburg in 1863 was a major turning point in the war.

- During 1864, Union campaigns in the East and South dealt crippling blows to the Confederacy.

- Union troops forced the South to surrender in 1865, ending the Civil War.

Key Terms and People

Battle of Gettysburg
George Pickett
Pickett's Charge
Gettysburg Address
Wilderness Campaign
William Tecumseh Sherman
total war
Appomattox Courthouse

If YOU were there . . .

You live in southern Pennsylvania in 1863, near a battlefield where thousands died. Now people have come from miles around to dedicate a cemetery here. You are near the front of the crowd. The first speaker impresses everyone with two hours of dramatic words and gestures. Then President Lincoln speaks—just a few minutes of simple words. Many people are disappointed.

Why do you think the president's speech was so short?

Fredericksburg and Chancellorsville

Frustrated by McClellan's lack of aggression, Lincoln replaced him with General Ambrose E. Burnside as leader of the Army of the Potomac. Burnside favored a swift, decisive attack on Richmond by way of Fredericksburg. In November 1862 he set out with 120,000 troops.

Burnside's tactics surprised General Lee. The Confederate commander had divided his force of 78,000 men. Neither section of the Confederate army was in a good position to defend Fredericksburg. However, Burnside's army experienced delays in crossing the Rappahannock River. These delays allowed Lee's army to reunite and entrench themselves around Fredericksburg. Finally, the Union army crossed the Rappahannock and launched a series of charges. These attacks had heavy casualties and failed to break the Confederate line. Eventually, after suffering about 12,600 casualties, Burnside ordered a retreat. The Confederates had about 5,300 casualties.

Soon Burnside stepped down from his position. Lincoln made General Joseph Hooker the commander of the Army of the Potomac. At the end of April 1863, Hooker and his army of about 138,000 men launched a frontal attack on Fredericksburg. Then Hooker ordered about 115,000 of his troops to split off and approach the Confederate's flank, or side. Hooker's strategy seemed about to work. But for some reason he hesitated and had his flanking troops take a defensive position at Chancellorsville. This town was located a few miles west of Fredericksburg.

The following day, Lee used most of his army (about 60,000 men) to attack Hooker's troops at Chancellorsville. Stonewall Jackson led an attack on Hooker's flank while Lee commanded an assault on the Union front. The Union army was almost cut in two. They managed to form a defensive line, which they held for three days. Then Hooker ordered a retreat.

Reading Check
Compare What did generals McClellan, Burnside, and Hooker have in common?

Lee's army won a major victory. But this victory had severe casualties. During the battle, Lee's trusted general, Stonewall Jackson, was accidentally shot by his own troops. He died a few days later.

Battle of Gettysburg

General Lee launched more attacks within Union territory. As before, his goal was to break the North's will to fight. He also hoped that a victory would convince other nations to recognize the Confederacy. The three-day battle at Gettysburg was the largest and bloodiest battle of the Civil War. In three days, more than 51,000 soldiers were killed, wounded, captured, or went missing. It was an important victory for the Union, and it stopped Lee's plan of invading the North.

First Day In early June 1863 Lee cut across northern Maryland into southern Pennsylvania. His forces gathered west of a small town called Gettysburg. Lee was unaware that Union soldiers were encamped closer to town. He had been suffering from a lack of enemy information for three days because his cavalry chief "Jeb" Stuart was not performing his duties. Stuart and his cavalry had gone off on their own raiding party, disobeying Lee's orders.

Day One:
July 1, 1863
Artillery played a key role in the Battle of Gettysburg on July 1, 1863.

Another Confederate raiding party went to Gettysburg for boots and other supplies. There, Lee's troops ran right into Union general George G. Meade's cavalry, triggering the **Battle of Gettysburg**, a key battle that finally turned the tide against the Confederates. The battle began on July 1, 1863, when the Confederate raiding party and the Union forces began exchanging fire. The larger Confederate forces began to push the Union troops back through Gettysburg.

The Union soldiers regrouped along the high ground of Cemetery Ridge and Culp's Hill. General Lee wanted to prevent the Union forces from entrenching themselves. He therefore ordered General Ewell to attack immediately. However, Ewell hesitated and thereby gave the Federals time to establish an excellent defensive position.

In fact, Confederate general James Longstreet thought that the Union position was almost impossible to overrun. Instead of attacking, he felt that the Confederate army should move east, take a strong defensive position, and wait for the Union forces to attack them. However, General Lee was not convinced. He believed that his troops were invincible.

The Confederates camped at Seminary Ridge, which ran parallel to the Union forces. Both camps called for their main forces to reinforce them and prepare for combat the next day.

Second Day On July 2, Lee ordered an attack on the left side of the Union line. Lee knew that he could win the battle if his troops captured Little Round Top from the Union forces. From this hill, Lee's troops could easily fire down on the line of Union forces. Union forces and Confederate troops fought viciously for control of Little Round Top. The fighting was particularly fierce on the south side of the hill. There, the 20th Maine led by Colonel Joshua Chamberlain battled the 15th Alabama led by Colonel

Day Two: July 2, 1863, 10 a.m.

Union soldiers desperately defended Little Round Top from a fierce Confederate charge.

William Oates. Later, when describing the conflict, Oates said, "The blood stood in puddles in some places in the rocks." Eventually, the Union soldiers forced the Confederates to pull back from Little Round Top.

Then, the Confederates attacked Cemetery Hill and Culp's Hill. The fighting lasted until nightfall. The assault on Cemetery Hill was unsuccessful. The Confederates did manage to take a few trenches on Culp's Hill. Even so, the Union forces still held a strong defensive position by the day's end.

Pickett's Charge On the third day of battle, Longstreet again tried to convince Lee not to attack. But Lee thought that the Union forces were severely battered and ready to break. Because of this, he planned to attack the center of the Union line on Cemetery Ridge. Such a tactic, he felt, would not be expected. Indeed, General Meade left only about 5,750 troops to defend the center.

For over an hour, the Confederates shelled Cemetery Ridge with cannon fire. For a while, the Union cannons fired back. Then they slacked off. The Confederates assumed that they had seriously damaged the Union artillery. In reality, the Confederate barrage did little damage.

The task of charging the Union center fell to three divisions of Confederate soldiers. General **George Pickett** commanded the largest unit. In late afternoon nearly 15,000 men took part in **Pickett's Charge**. For one mile the Confederates marched slowly up toward Cemetery Ridge.

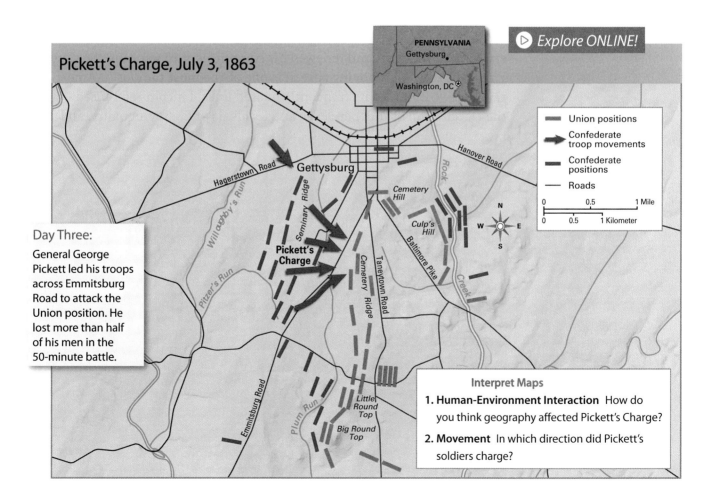

Pickett's Charge, July 3, 1863

PENNSYLVANIA
Gettysburg
Washington, DC

Explore ONLINE!

Union positions
Confederate troop movements
Confederate positions
Roads

Hanover Road
Hagerstown Road
Gettysburg
Seminary Ridge
Willoughby's Run
Pitzer's Run
Cemetery Hill
Culp's Hill
Pickett's Charge
Cemetery Ridge
Taneytown Road
Baltimore Pike
Rock Creek
Emmitsburg Road
Plum Run
Little Round Top
Big Round Top

Day Three:
General George Pickett led his troops across Emmitsburg Road to attack the Union position. He lost more than half of his men in the 50-minute battle.

Interpret Maps
1. **Human-Environment Interaction** How do you think geography affected Pickett's Charge?
2. **Movement** In which direction did Pickett's soldiers charge?

Showered with cannon and rifle fire, they suffered severe losses. But eventually, some of them almost reached their destination. Then Union reinforcements added to the barrage on the rebels. Soon the Confederates retreated, leaving about 7,500 casualties on the field of battle. Distressed by this defeat, General Lee rode among the survivors and told them, "It is all my fault."

On the fourth day, Lee began to retreat to Virginia. In all, nearly 75,000 Confederate soldiers and 90,000 Union troops had fought during the Battle of Gettysburg.

General Meade decided not to follow Lee's army. This decision angered Lincoln. He felt that Meade had missed an opportunity to crush the Confederates and possibly end the war.

Aftermath of Gettysburg Gettysburg was a turning point in the war. Lee's troops would never again launch an attack in the North. The Union victory at Gettysburg took place on the day before Grant's capture of Vicksburg, Mississippi. These victories made northerners believe that the war could be won.

In addition, the Union win at Gettysburg helped to end the South's search for foreign influence in the war. After Gettysburg, Great Britain and France refused to provide aid to the Confederacy. The South's attempt at cotton diplomacy failed.

The Gettysburg Address On November 19, 1863, at the dedicating ceremony of the Gettysburg battlefield cemetery, President Lincoln gave a speech called the **Gettysburg Address**, in which he praised the bravery of Union soldiers and renewed his commitment to winning the Civil War. This short but moving speech is one of the most famous in American history. In one of its frequently quoted lines, Lincoln referenced the Declaration of Independence and its ideals of liberty, equality, and

Lincoln's address at the dedication of the Gettysburg National Cemetery

Reading Check
Analyze Why was Gettysburg a turning point?

democracy—ideals that still impact Americans today. He reminded listeners that the war was being fought for those reasons.

Lincoln rededicated himself to winning the war and preserving the Union. A difficult road still lay ahead.

Union Campaigns Cripple the Confederacy

Lincoln had been impressed with General Grant's successes in capturing Vicksburg. He transferred Grant to the East and gave him command of the Union army. In early 1864 Grant forced Lee to fight a series of battles in Virginia that stretched Confederate soldiers and supplies to their limits.

Wilderness Campaign in the East From May through June, the armies fought in northern and central Virginia. Union troops launched the **Wilderness Campaign**—a series of battles designed to capture the Confederate capital at Richmond, Virginia. The first battle took place in early May, in woods about 50 miles outside of Richmond. Grant then ordered General Meade to Spotsylvania, where the fighting raged for five days.

Over the next month Union soldiers moved the Confederate troops back toward Richmond. However, Grant experienced his worst defeat at the Battle of Cold Harbor in early June, just 10 miles northeast of Richmond. In only a few hours the Union army suffered 7,000 casualties. The battle delayed Grant's plans to take the Confederate capital.

Union forces had suffered twice as many casualties as the Confederates had, yet Grant continued his strategy. He knew he would be getting additional soldiers, and Lee could not. Grant slowly but surely advanced his troops through Virginia. He told another officer, "I propose to fight it out on this line if it takes all summer."

After Cold Harbor, General Grant moved south of Richmond. He had hoped to take control of the key railroad junction at Petersburg, Virginia. Lee's army, however, formed a solid defense, and Grant could not **execute** his attack. Grant was winning the war, but he still had not captured Richmond. Facing re-election, Lincoln was especially discouraged by this failure.

Academic Vocabulary
execute to perform, carry out

Sherman Strikes the South Lincoln needed a victory for the Union army to help him win re-election in 1864. The bold campaign of General **William Tecumseh Sherman** provided this key victory. Sherman carried out the Union plan to destroy southern railroads and industries.

In the spring of 1864 Sherman marched south from Tennessee with 100,000 troops. His goal was to take Atlanta, Georgia, and knock out an important railroad link. From May through August, Sherman's army moved steadily through the Appalachians toward Atlanta. Several times, Sherman avoided defenses set up by Confederate general Joseph Johnston.

In July Sherman was within sight of Atlanta. Confederate president Jefferson Davis gave General John Hood command of Confederate forces in the region. Hood repeatedly attacked Sherman in a final attempt to save Atlanta, but the Union troops proved stronger. The Confederate troops retreated as Sherman held Atlanta under siege.

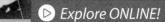

Explore ONLINE!

Map labels:

IA, IL, IN, OH, NJ, MD, DE, Washington, DC, WV, Richmond, VA, KS, MO, KY, Ohio River, Appalachian Mts., KY

Nashville Dec. 15–16, 1864, TN, Raleigh April 13, 1865, NC, Hood

OK, AR, Atlanta Sept. 2, 1864, SC, Sherman, Wilmington Feb. 22, 1865

MS, AL, GA, Sherman, Savannah Dec. 21, 1864

LA, TX, Pensacola

ATLANTIC OCEAN, 30°N, 70°W, 80°W, Gulf of Mexico, FL

Inset map: PA, Gettysburg, July 1–3, 1863, MD, Washington, DC, WV, The Wilderness, May 5–7, 1864, Chancellorsville, May 1–5, 1863, Grant, Lee, VA, Spotsylvania Courthouse, May 8–19, 1864, Richmond, Cold Harbor, June 3, 1864, Appomattox Courthouse, Apr. 9, 1865—Lee surrenders to Grant, Grant, Petersburg, June 1864–April 1865

Legend:
- Union state
- Union occupied, 1865
- Confederate state
- Union forces
- Union victory
- Confederate forces
- Confederate victory

0   100   200 Miles
0   100   200 Kilometers

N W E S

Interpret Maps

1. **Movement** About how long was Sherman's March to the Sea from Atlanta to Savannah?

2. **Movement** What challenges do you think Sherman faced on his southern attacks?

Atlanta fell to Sherman's troops on September 2, 1864. Much of the city was destroyed by artillery and fire. Sherman ordered the residents who still remained to leave. Responding to his critics, Sherman later wrote, "War is war, and not popularity-seeking." The loss of Atlanta cost the South an important railroad link and its center of industry.

Many people in the North had been upset with the length of the war. However, the capture of Atlanta showed that progress was being made in defeating the South. This success helped to convince Union voters to re-elect Lincoln in a landslide.

Sherman did not wait long to begin his next campaign. His goal was the port city of Savannah, Georgia. In mid-November 1864, Sherman left Atlanta with a force of about 60,000 men. He said he would "make Georgia howl!"

During his March to the Sea, Sherman practiced **total war**—destroying civilian and economic resources. Sherman believed that total war would ruin the South's economy and its ability to fight. He ordered his troops to destroy railways, bridges, crops, livestock, and other resources. They burned plantations and freed slaves.

Reading Check
Draw Conclusions
How did Sherman hope to help the Union with his total-war strategy?

Sherman's army reached Savannah on December 10, 1864. They left behind a path of destruction 60 miles wide. Sherman believed that this march would speed the end of the war. He wanted to break the South's will to fight by marching Union troops through the heart of the Confederacy. In the end Sherman's destruction of the South led to anger and resentment toward the people of the North that would last for generations.

The South Surrenders

In early April Sherman closed in on the last Confederate defenders in North Carolina. At the same time, Grant finally broke through the Confederate defenses at Petersburg. On April 2 Lee was forced to retreat from Richmond.

Fighting Ends By the second week of April 1865, Grant had surrounded Lee's army and demanded the soldiers' surrender. Lee hoped to join other Confederates in fighting in North Carolina, but Grant cut off his escape just west of Richmond. Lee tried some last-minute attacks but could not break the Union line. Lee's forces were running low on supplies. General James Longstreet told about the condition of Confederate troops. "Many weary soldiers were picked up . . . some with, many without, arms [weapons],—all asking for food."

Trapped by the Union army, Lee recognized that the situation was hopeless. "There is nothing left for me to do but go and see General Grant," Lee said, "and I would rather die a thousand deaths."

On April 9, 1865, the Union and Confederate leaders met at a home in the small town of **Appomattox Courthouse** where Lee surrendered to Grant, thus ending the Civil War.

During the meeting, Grant assured Lee that his troops would be fed and allowed to keep their horses, and they would not be tried for treason. Then

Surrender at Appomattox

Union general Grant rose to shake hands with Confederate general Lee after the surrender. Grant allowed Lee to keep his sword and Lee's men to keep their horses.

Was it important for Grant and Lee to shake hands? Why or why not?

Causes and Effects of the Civil War

Causes

- Disagreement over the institution of slavery
- Economic differences
- Political differences

Effects

- Slavery ends
- 620,000 Americans killed
- Military districts created
- Southern economy in ruins

Interpret Charts
How important was slavery to the Civil War?

Reading Check
Predict What problems might the Union face following the Civil War?

Lee signed the surrender documents. The long, bloody war had finally ended. Grant later wrote that he found the scene at Appomattox Courthouse more tragic than joyful.

"I felt . . . sad and depressed at the downfall of a foe [enemy] who had fought so long and valiantly [bravely], and had suffered so much for a cause, though that cause was, I believe, one of the worst for which a people ever fought."

—Ulysses S. Grant, *Battle Cry of Freedom*

As General Lee returned to his troops, General Grant stopped Union forces from cheering their victory. "The war is over," Grant said with relief. "The rebels are our countrymen again."

The Civil War had deep and long-lasting effects. Almost 620,000 Americans lost their lives during the four years of fighting.

The defeat of the South ended slavery there. The majority of former slaves, however, had no homes or jobs. The southern economy was in ruins. A tremendous amount of hostility remained, even after the fighting had ceased. The war was over, but the question remained: How could the United States be united once more?

Summary and Preview After four long years of battles, the Civil War ended with General Lee's surrender at Appomattox Courthouse. In the next module you will read about the consequences of the war in the South.

Lesson 5 Assessment

Review Ideas, Terms, and People

1. **a. Identify** What Confederate general died from his wounds at Chancellorsville?
   b. Draw Conclusions Why was the Union army defeated at Chancellorsville?
2. **a. Identify** What was the Gettysburg Address?
   b. Analyze Why was geography important to the outcome of the Battle of Gettysburg?
3. **a. Recall** What was the purpose of the Wilderness Campaign?
   b. Draw Conclusions In what way was the capture of Atlanta an important victory for President Lincoln?

4. **a. Identify** What events led to Lee's surrender at Appomattox Courthouse?
   b. Summarize How did the military conflict of the Civil War impact the United States?

Critical Thinking

5. **Support a Point of View** In this lesson you learned about the end of the Civil War. Create a similar triangle to the one below and use it to show the three events in this lesson that you think contributed most to the end of the Civil War and explain why.

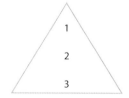

Social Studies Skills

Interpret Political Cartoons

Define the Skill

Political cartoons are drawings that express views on important issues. They have been used throughout history to influence public opinion. The ability to interpret political cartoons will help you understand issues and people's attitudes about them.

Learn the Skill

Political cartoons use both words and images to convey their message. They often contain caricatures or symbolism. A caricature is a drawing that exaggerates the features of a person or object. Symbolism is the use of one thing to represent something else. Cartoonists use these techniques to help make their point clear. They also use titles, labels, and captions to get their message across.

Use these steps to interpret political cartoons.

1. Read any title, labels, and caption to identify the cartoon's general topic.

2. Identify the people and objects. Determine if they are exaggerated and, if so, why. Identify any symbols and analyze their meaning.

3. Draw conclusions about the message the cartoonist is trying to convey.

The following cartoon was published in the North in 1863. The cartoonist has used symbols to make his point. Lady Liberty, representing the Union, is being threatened by the Copperheads. The cartoonist has expressed his opinion of these people by drawing them as the poisonous snake for which they were named. This cartoon clearly supports the Union's continuing to fight the war.

Practice the Skill

Apply the guidelines to interpret the cartoon below and answer the questions that follow.

1. What do the two men on either side of Lincoln represent?

2. What message do you think the artist was trying to convey?

LINCOLN'S TWO DIFFICULTIES.
Lis. "WHAT? NO MONEY! NO MEN!"

Module 1 Assessment

Review Vocabulary, Terms, and People

Match the numbered definitions with the correct terms from the list below.

a. contrabands
b. cotton diplomacy
c. Second Battle of Bull Run
d. Siege of Vicksburg
e. Thomas "Stonewall" Jackson

1. Attack by Union general Ulysses S. Grant that gave the North control of the Mississippi River
2. Confederate general who held off Union attacks and helped the South win the First Battle of Bull Run
3. Important Confederate victory in which General Robert E. Lee defeated Union troops and pushed into Union territory for the first time
4. Southern strategy of using cotton exports to gain Britain's support in the Civil War
5. Term given to escaped slaves from the South

Comprehension and Critical Thinking

Lesson 1

6. **a. Identify** When and where did fighting in the U.S. Civil War begin?
   b. Analyze How did civilians help the war effort in both the North and the South?
   c. Elaborate Why do you think the border states chose to remain in the Union despite their support of slavery?

Lesson 2

7. **a. Identify** What was the first major battle of the war? What was the outcome of the battle?
   b. Analyze What was the Union army hoping to accomplish when it marched into Virginia at the start of the war?
   c. Evaluate Was the Union's naval blockade of the South successful? Why or why not?

Lesson 3

8. **a. Identify** Which side did the Cherokee support in the fighting at Pea Ridge? Why?
   b. Draw Conclusions What progress did Union leaders make in the war in the West?
   c. Evaluate Which victory in the West was most valuable to the Union? Why?

Lesson 4

9. **a. Describe** What responsibilities did women take on during the war?
   b. Analyze What opposition to the war did President Lincoln face, and how did he deal with that opposition?
   c. Predict What might be some possible problems that the newly freed slaves in the South might face?

Lesson 5

10. **a. Recall** When and where did the war finally end?
    b. Compare and Contrast How were the efforts of generals Grant and Sherman at the end of the war similar and different?
    c. Elaborate What do you think led to the South's defeat in the Civil War? Explain.

Social Studies Skills

Interpret Political Cartoons *Use the Social Studies Skills taught in this module to answer the question about the political cartoon below.*

11. What do you think the artist is saying about politicians with this cartoon?

Reading Skills

Supporting Facts and Details *Use the Reading Skills taught in this module to answer the question about the reading selection below.*

> Lee was unaware that Union soldiers were encamped closer to town. He had been suffering from a lack of enemy information for three days because his cavalry chief "Jeb" Stuart was not performing his duties. Stuart and his cavalry had gone off on their own raiding party, disobeying Lee's orders.

12. What is the main idea of the reading selection?
   a. "Jeb" Stuart was not performing his duties.
   b. Stuart and his cavalry had gone off on their own.
   c. Stuart and his cavalry disobeyed Lee's orders.
   d. Lee was suffering from a lack of enemy information.

Review Themes

13. **Society and Culture** What effects did the Civil War have on American society?

14. **Politics** What political difficulties did the Emancipation Proclamation cause for President Lincoln?

Focus on Writing

15. **Write a Newspaper Article** Consider all the Civil War events discussed in this module. Then choose one of those events to write about in a newspaper article. Write an attention-grabbing headline. Then write the news article, describing the event and giving as many facts as possible about the event. Be sure to use proper grammar, punctuation, spelling, and capitalization.

DAYS OF DARKNESS:
THE GETTYSBURG CIVILIANS

Gettysburg, Pennsylvania, was a sleepy agricultural town of about 2,400 residents when the Civil War arrived on its doorstep in the early summer of 1863. Many of the town's men were elsewhere, either fighting in the war or guarding their livestock in the countryside. This left mostly women and children to endure the battle. For three terrifying days, they hid in basements or in tightly shuttered houses. Even after the battle finally ended, the horrors continued, as the Gettysburg civilians emerged to find a scene of unimaginable death and destruction.

Explore some of the personal stories and recollections of the Gettysburg civilians online. You can find a wealth of information, video clips, primary sources, activities, and more through your online textbook.

> *"I had scarcely reached the front door, when, on looking up the street, I saw some of the men on horseback. . . .*
> *What a horrible sight! . . .*
> *I was fully persuaded that the Rebels had actually come at last. What they would do with us was a fearful question to my young mind. . . ."*
>
> —Tillie Pierce, age 15

 A Young Woman's Account

Read the document to witness the arrival of Confederate troops through the eyes of a Gettysburg teenager.

A Citizen-Soldier

Watch the video to meet John Burns, the man who would come to be called the "Citizen Hero of Gettysburg."

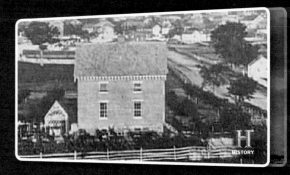

A Family's Story

Watch the video to discover the story of courage and commitment exhibited by one Gettysburg family.

The National Cemetery

Watch the video to learn about the Soldiers' National Cemetery and the speech President Lincoln gave there.

Reconstruction

★

Essential Question
To what extent did Reconstruction achieve its goals?

About the Photo: The ruins of this southern plantation stand as a bleak reminder of the changes brought to the South by the Civil War.

▷ *Explore ONLINE!*

HISTORY

VIDEOS, including...
- Lincoln's Legacy
- The Fall of Richmond
- After the Assassination
- Johnson's Impeachment

☑ Document-Based Investigations

☑ Graphic Organizers

☑ Interactive Games

☑ Image Carousel: Testing Freedoms

☑ Image with Hotspots: *The First Vote*

In this module you will learn about the challenges that faced the nation after the Civil War and the attempts to meet those challenges.

What You Will Learn . . .

United States	World

1860

∧ **1865** Abraham Lincoln is assassinated. ——○—— **1865** Black Jamaicans rebel against the wealthy planter class.

1868 President Andrew Johnson is impeached and almost removed from office. ∨ ——○—— **1868** The Meiji dynasty returns to power in Japan.

——○—— **1869** The Suez Canal opens, linking the Mediterranean and Red seas. ∨

1870

1870 Hiram Revels becomes the first African American to serve in the U.S. Senate. ∨

1871 Otto von Bismarck and Wilhelm I unite Germany. ∨

1877 The Compromise of 1877 ends Reconstruction. ——○

1880

THEME FOCUS:

Politics, Society and Culture

In this module you will read about the time immediately after the Civil War. You will see how the government tried to rebuild the South and you will learn about how life changed for African Americans after slavery was declared illegal.

You will read about the political conflicts that emerged as southern leadership worked to gain control of Reconstruction efforts. Throughout the module you will read how the culture of the South changed after the war.

READING FOCUS:

Analyze Historical Information

History books are full of information. As you read, you are confronted with names, dates, places, terms, and descriptions on every page. You don't want to have to deal with anything unimportant or untrue.

Identify Relevant and Essential Information Information in a history book should be relevant to the topic you're studying. It should also be essential to understanding the topic and should be verifiable. Anything else distracts from the material you are studying.

The first passage below includes several pieces of irrelevant and nonessential information. In the revised passage this information has been removed. Note how much easier the revised passage is to understand.

First Passage
President Abraham Lincoln, who was very tall, wanted to reunite the nation as quickly and painlessly as possible. He had proposed a plan for readmitting the southern states even before the war ended, which happened on a Sunday. Called the Ten Percent Plan, it offered southerners amnesty, or official pardon, for all illegal acts supporting the rebellion. Today a group called Amnesty International works to protect the rights of prisoners. Lincoln's plan certainly would have worked if it would have been implemented.

Lincoln's appearance and the day on which the war ended are not essential facts.

Amnesty International is not relevant to this topic.

There is no way to prove the accuracy of the last sentence.

Revised Passage
President Abraham Lincoln wanted to reunite the nation as quickly and painlessly as possible. He had proposed a plan for readmitting the southern states even before the war ended. Called the Ten Percent Plan, it offered southerners amnesty, or official pardon, for all illegal acts supporting the rebellion.

You Try It!

The following passage is adapted from the module you are about to read. As you read the passage, look for irrelevant, nonessential, or unverifiable information.

Freedmen's Bureau In 1865 Congress established the Freedmen's Bureau, an agency providing relief for freedpeople and certain poor people in the South. The Bureau had a difficult job. It may have been one of the most difficult jobs ever. At its high point, about 900 agents served the entire South. All 900 people could fit into one hotel ballroom today. Bureau commissioner Oliver O. Howard eventually decided to use the Bureau's limited budget to distribute food to the poor and to provide education and legal help for freedpeople. One common food in the South at that time was salted meat. The Bureau also helped African American war veterans. Today the Department of Veterans' Affairs assists American war veterans.

After you read the passage, answer the following questions.

1. Which sentence in this passage is unverifiable and should be cut?

2. Find two sentences in this passage that are irrelevant to the discussion of the Freedmen's Bureau. What makes those sentences irrelevant?

3. Look at the last sentence of the passage. Do you think this sentence is essential to the discussion? Why or why not?

As you read Module 2, ask yourself what makes the information you are reading essential to a study of Reconstruction.

Key Terms and People

Lesson 1
Reconstruction
Ten Percent Plan
Thirteenth Amendment
Freedmen's Bureau
Andrew Johnson

Lesson 2
Black Codes
Radical Republicans
Civil Rights Act of 1866
Fourteenth Amendment
Reconstruction Acts
impeachment
Fifteenth Amendment

Lesson 3
Hiram Revels
Ku Klux Klan
Enforcement Acts
Compromise of 1877
poll tax
segregation
Jim Crow laws
Plessy v. *Ferguson*
sharecropping

Rebuilding the South

The Big Idea

The nation faced many problems in rebuilding the Union.

Main Ideas

- President Lincoln and Congress differed in their views as Reconstruction began.

- The end of the Civil War meant freedom for African Americans in the South.

- President Johnson's plan began the process of Reconstruction.

Key Terms and People

Reconstruction
Ten Percent Plan
Thirteenth Amendment
Freedmen's Bureau
Andrew Johnson

If YOU were there . . .

You are a young soldier who has been fighting in the Civil War for many months. Now that the war is over, you are on your way home. During your journey, you pass plantation manor homes, houses, and barns that have been burned down. No one is doing spring planting in the fields. As you near your family's farm, you see that fences and sheds have been destroyed. You wonder what is left of your home and family.

What would you think your future on the farm would be like?

Reconstruction Begins

After the Civil War ended in 1865, the U.S. government faced the problem of dealing with the defeated southern states. The challenges of **Reconstruction**, the process of readmitting the former Confederate states to the Union, lasted from 1865 to 1877.

Damaged South Tired southern soldiers returned home to find that the world they had known before the war was gone. Cities, towns, and farms had been ruined. Because of high food prices and widespread crop failures, many southerners faced starvation. The Confederate money most southerners held was now worthless. Banks failed, and merchants had gone bankrupt because people could not pay their debts.

Former Confederate general Braxton Bragg was one of many southerners who faced economic hardship. He found that "*all, all* was lost, except my debts." In South Carolina, Mary Boykin Chesnut wrote in her diary about the isolation she experienced after the war. "We are shut in here. . . . All RR's [railroads] destroyed—bridges gone. We are cut off from the world."

Lincoln's Plan President Abraham Lincoln wanted to reunite the nation as quickly and painlessly as possible. He had proposed a plan for readmitting the southern states even before the war ended. Called the **Ten Percent Plan**, it offered southerners amnesty, or official pardon, for all illegal acts supporting the rebellion. To receive amnesty, southerners had to do two things. They had to swear an oath of loyalty to the United States. They also had to agree that slavery was illegal. Once 10 percent of voters in a state made these pledges, they could form a new government. The state then could be readmitted to the Union.

Louisiana quickly elected a new state legislature under the Ten Percent Plan. Other southern states that had been occupied by Union troops soon followed Louisiana back into the United States.

Wade-Davis Bill Some politicians argued that Congress, not the president, should control the southern states' return to the Union. They believed that Congress had the power to admit new states. Also, many Republican members of Congress thought the Ten Percent Plan did not go far enough. A senator from Michigan expressed their views.

> "The people of the North are not such fools as to . . . turn around and say to the traitors, 'all you have to do [to return] is . . . take an oath that henceforth you will be true to the Government.'"
>
> —Senator Jacob Howard, quoted in *Reconstruction: America's Unfinished Revolution, 1863–1877*, by Eric Foner

Academic Vocabulary
procedure a series of steps taken to accomplish a task

Two Republicans—Senator Benjamin Wade and Representative Henry Davis—had an alternative to Lincoln's plan. Following <u>procedures</u> of the Wade-Davis bill, a state had to meet two conditions before it could rejoin the Union. First, it had to ban slavery. Second, a majority of adult males in the state had to take the loyalty oath.

Under the Wade-Davis bill, only southerners who swore that they had never supported the Confederacy could vote or hold office. In general, the bill was much stricter than the Ten Percent Plan. Its provisions would make it harder for southern states to rejoin the Union quickly.

Reading Check
Contrast How was the Ten Percent Plan different from the Wade-Davis bill?

President Lincoln therefore refused to sign the bill into law. He thought that few southern states would agree to meet its requirements. He believed that his plan would help restore order more quickly.

Freedom for African Americans

One thing Republicans agreed on was abolishing slavery. The Emancipation Proclamation had freed slaves only in areas that had not been occupied by Union forces, not in the border states. Many people feared that the federal courts might someday declare the proclamation unconstitutional.

Slavery Ends On January 31, 1865, at President Lincoln's urging, Congress proposed the **Thirteenth Amendment**. This amendment made slavery illegal throughout the United States.

The amendment was ratified and took effect on December 18, 1865. When abolitionist William Lloyd Garrison heard the news, he declared that his work was now finished. He called for the American Anti-Slavery Society to break up. Not all abolitionists agreed that their work was done,

These freedpeople have packed their household belongings and are leaving Richmond. Many people traveled in search of relatives. Others placed newspaper advertisements looking for long-lost relatives.

In what ways did former slaves react to freedom?

however. Frederick Douglass insisted that "slavery is not abolished until the black man has the ballot [vote]."

Freedom brought important changes to newly freed slaves. Many couples held ceremonies to legalize marriages that had not been recognized under slavery. Many freedpeople searched for relatives who had been sold away from their families years earlier. Others placed newspaper ads seeking information about their children. Many women began to work at home instead of in the fields. Still others adopted children of dead relatives to keep families together. Church members established voluntary associations and mutual-aid societies to help those in need.

Now that they could travel without a pass, many freedpeople moved from mostly white counties to places with more African Americans. Other freedpeople traveled simply to test their new freedom of movement. Northern migration, while not as extensive as the coming World War I Great Migration beginning in 1910, significantly increased the urban black population of the North. Detroit's African American population, for instance, more than doubled during the 1860s with the vast majority of its new arrivals coming from the South. A South Carolina woman explained this need. "I must go, if I stay here I'll never know I'm free."

For this couple, freedom brought the right to marry.

For most former slaves, freedom to travel was just the first step on a long road toward equal rights and new ways of life. Adults took new last names and began to insist on being called Mr. or Mrs. as a sign of respect, rather than by their first names or by nicknames. Freedpeople began to demand the same economic and political rights as white citizens. Henry Adams, a former slave, argued that "if I cannot do like a white man I am not free."

Forty Acres to Farm? Many former slaves wanted their own land to farm. Near the end of the Civil War, Union general William Tecumseh Sherman had issued an order to break up plantations in coastal South Carolina and Georgia. He wanted to divide the land into 40-acre plots and give them to former slaves as compensation for their forced labor before the war.

Many white planters refused to surrender their land. Some freedpeople pointed out that it was only fair that they receive some of this land because their labor had made the plantations prosper. In the end, the U.S. government returned the land to its original owners. At this time, many freedpeople were unsure about where they would live, what kind of work they would do, and what rights they had. Freedoms that were theirs by law were difficult to enforce.

Freedmen's Bureau In 1865 Congress established the **Freedmen's Bureau**, an agency providing relief for freedpeople and certain poor people in the South. The Bureau had a difficult job. At its high point, about 900 agents served the entire South. Bureau commissioner Oliver O. Howard eventually decided to use the Bureau's limited budget to distribute food to the poor and to provide education and legal help for freedpeople. The Bureau also helped African American war veterans.

The Freedmen's Bureau played an important role in establishing more schools in the South. Laws against educating slaves meant that most freedpeople had never learned to read or write. Before the war ended, however, northern groups, such as the American Missionary Association, began providing books and teachers to African Americans. The teachers were mostly women who were committed to helping freedpeople. One teacher said of her students, "I never before saw children so eager to learn. . . . It is wonderful how [they] . . . can have so great a desire for knowledge, and such a capacity for attaining [reaching] it."

After the war, some freedpeople organized their own education efforts. For example, Freedmen's Bureau agents found that some African Americans had opened schools in abandoned buildings. Many white southerners continued to believe that African Americans should not be educated. Despite

African American students and teachers outside the Freedmen's Bureau school in Beaufort, South Carolina

Reading Check
Analyze How did the Freedmen's Bureau help reform education in the South?

opposition, by 1869 more than 150,000 African American students were attending more than 3,000 schools. The Freedmen's Bureau also helped establish a number of universities for African Americans, including Howard and Fisk universities.

Students quickly filled the new classrooms. Working adults attended classes in the evening. African Americans hoped that education would help them to understand and protect their rights and to enable them to find better jobs. Both black and white southerners benefited from the effort to provide greater access to education in the South.

Helping the Freedpeople

Congress created the Freedmen's Bureau to help freedpeople and poor southerners recover from the Civil War. The Bureau assisted people by:

- providing supplies and medical services.
- establishing schools.
- supervising contracts between freedpeople and employers.
- taking care of lands abandoned or captured during the war.

What role did the Freedmen's Bureau play during Reconstruction?

President Johnson's Reconstruction Plan

While the Freedmen's Bureau was helping African Americans, the issue of how the South would politically rejoin the Union remained unresolved. Soon, however, a tragic event ended Lincoln's dream of peacefully reuniting the country.

A New President On the evening of April 14, 1865, President Lincoln and his wife attended a play at Ford's Theater in Washington, DC. During the play, John Wilkes Booth, a southerner who opposed Lincoln's policies, sneaked into the president's theater box and shot him. Lincoln was rushed to a boardinghouse across the street, where he died early the next morning. Lincoln, his leadership remembered for its honesty, deep intelligence, and high morals, became a symbol for the nation of the struggle of the Civil War.

Vice President **Andrew Johnson** was sworn into office quickly. Reconstruction had now become his responsibility. He would have to win the trust of a nation shocked at its leader's death. Johnson's plan for bringing southern states back into the Union was similar to Lincoln's plan. However, he decided that wealthy southerners and former Confederate officials would need a presidential pardon to receive amnesty. Johnson shocked Radical Republicans by eventually pardoning more than 7,000 people by 1866.

New State Governments Johnson was a Democrat whom Republicans had put on the ticket in 1864 to appeal to the border states. A former slaveholder, he was a stubborn man who would soon face a hostile Congress.

Johnson offered a mild program for setting up new southern state governments. First, he appointed a temporary governor for each state. Then, he required that the states revise their constitutions. Next, voters elected state and federal representatives. The new state government had to declare that secession was illegal. It also had to ratify the Thirteenth Amendment and refuse to pay Confederate debts.

By the end of 1865, all the southern states except Texas had created new governments. Johnson approved them all and declared that the United States was restored. Newly elected representatives came to Washington from each reconstructed southern state. However, Republicans complained that many new representatives had been leaders of the Confederacy. Congress therefore refused to readmit the southern states into the Union. Clearly, the nation was still divided.

Reading Check
Summarize What was President Johnson's plan for Reconstruction?

Summary and Preview In this lesson you learned about early plans for Reconstruction. In the next lesson you will learn that disagreements about Reconstruction became so serious that the president was almost removed from office.

Lesson 1 Assessment

Review Ideas, Terms, and People

1. **a. Identify** What does Reconstruction mean?
   b. Summarize What was President Lincoln's plan for Reconstruction?
2. **a. Recall** What is the Thirteenth Amendment?
   b. Elaborate In your opinion, what was the most important accomplishment of the Freedmen's Bureau? Explain.
3. **a. Recall** Why was President Lincoln killed?
   b. Analyze Why did some Americans oppose President Johnson's Reconstruction plan?

Critical Thinking

4. **Summarize** In this lesson you learned about Reconstruction. Create a graphic organizer similar to the one below and show how African Americans were affected by the end of the war.

African Americans and Reconstruction — Marriages are legalized.

The Fight over Reconstruction

The Big Idea

The return to power of the pre-war southern leadership led Republicans in Congress to take control of Reconstruction.

Main Ideas

- Black Codes led to opposition to President Johnson's plan for Reconstruction.

- The Fourteenth Amendment ensured citizenship for African Americans.

- Radical Republicans in Congress took charge of Reconstruction.

- The Fifteenth Amendment gave African Americans the right to vote.

Key Terms and People

Black Codes
Radical Republicans
Civil Rights Act of 1866
Fourteenth Amendment
Reconstruction Acts
impeachment
Fifteenth Amendment

If YOU were there . . .

A member of Congress, you belong to the same political party as the president. But you strongly disagree with his ideas about Reconstruction and civil rights for African Americans. Now some of the president's opponents are trying to remove him from office. You do not think he is a good president. On the other hand, you think removing him would be bad for the unity of the country.

Will you vote to remove the president?

Opposition to President Johnson

In 1866 Congress continued to debate the rules for restoring the Union. Meanwhile, new state legislatures approved by President Johnson had already begun passing laws to deny African Americans' civil rights. "This is a white man's government, and intended for white men only," declared Governor Benjamin F. Perry of South Carolina.

Black Codes Soon, every southern state passed **Black Codes**, or laws that greatly limited the freedom of African Americans. They required African Americans to sign work contracts, creating working conditions similar to those under slavery. In most southern states, any African Americans who could not prove they were employed could be arrested. Their punishment might be one year of work without pay. African Americans were also prevented from owning guns. In addition, they were not allowed to rent property except in cities.

Black Codes in Mississippi and South Carolina also included Apprentice Laws. These laws required law enforcement officials to semiannually report to the Probate Court orphaned children or children of parents deemed unfit. The Probate Court was then required to find work for the minor as an apprentice. The former owner had priority in choosing the minor as his apprentice.

"Provided, that said apprentice shall be bound by indenture, in case of males until they are twenty-one years old, and in case of females until they are eighteen years old."

—Laws of the State of Mississippi, Passed at a Regular Session of the Mississippi Legislature, Jackson, 1865

Masters had the right to inflict moderate punishment on their apprentices and to recapture runaways. But the codes also required masters to provide food and clothing to their apprentices, teach them a trade, and send them to school.

The Black Codes alarmed many Americans. As one Civil War veteran asked, "If you call this freedom, what do you call slavery?" African Americans organized to oppose the codes. One group sent a petition to officials in South Carolina.

"We simply ask . . . that the same laws which govern *white men* shall govern *black men* . . . that, in short, we be dealt with as others are—in equity [equality] and justice."

—Petition from an African American convention held in South Carolina, quoted in *There Is a River: The Black Struggle for Freedom in America* by Vincent Harding

Radical Republicans The Black Codes angered many Republicans. They thought the South was returning to its old ways. Most Republicans were moderates who wanted the South to have loyal state governments. They also believed that African Americans should have rights as citizens. They

---

DOCUMENT-BASED INVESTIGATION Historical Source

Johnson vs. Stevens

President **Andrew Johnson**, a southern Democrat from Tennessee and former slaveholder, argued that the South should not be placed under military control.

Thaddeus Stevens, a Pennsylvanian Radical Republican and champion of equal rights for African Americans, believed that Congress had the power to treat the South as conquered territory.

Analyze Historical Sources
How did Johnson's and Stevens's views on the South differ? What role do you think their personal backgrounds played in shaping their views?

"*Military governments . . . established for an indefinite period, would have divided the people into the vanquishers and the vanquished, and would have envenomed [made poisonous] hatred rather than have restored affection.*"

—Andrew Johnson

"*The future condition of the conquered power depends on the will of the conqueror. They must come in as new states or remain as conquered provinces. Congress . . . is the only power that can act in the matter.*"

—Thaddeus Stevens

hoped that the government would not have to force the South to follow federal laws.

Radical Republicans, on the other hand, took a harsher stance. They wanted the federal government to force change in the South. Like the moderates, they thought the Black Codes were cruel and unjust. The Radicals, however, wanted the federal government to be much more involved in Reconstruction. They feared that too many southern leaders remained loyal to the former Confederacy and would not enforce the new laws. Thaddeus Stevens of Pennsylvania and Charles Sumner of Massachusetts were the leaders of the Radical Republicans.

A harsh critic of President Johnson, Stevens was known for his honesty and sharp tongue. He wanted economic and political justice for both African Americans and poor white southerners. Sumner had been a strong opponent of slavery before the Civil War. He continued to argue tirelessly for African Americans' civil rights, including the right to vote and the right to fair laws.

Both Stevens and Sumner believed that, like Lincoln's proposed Ten Percent Plan, President Johnson's Reconstruction plan was too lenient toward the South, thereby making it a failure. Although the Radicals did not control Congress, they began to gain support among moderates when President Johnson ignored criticism of the Black Codes. Stevens believed the federal government could not allow racial inequality to survive.

Reading Check
Compare and Contrast How were Radical Republicans and moderate Republicans similar and different?

Fourteenth Amendment

Urged on by the Radicals in 1866, Congress proposed a new bill. It would give the Freedmen's Bureau more powers. The law would allow the Freedmen's Bureau to use military courts to try people accused of violating African Americans' rights. The bill's supporters hoped that these courts would be fairer than local courts in the South.

Johnson versus Congress Surprising many members of Congress, Johnson vetoed the Freedmen's Bureau bill. He insisted that Congress could not pass any new laws until the southern states were represented in Congress. Johnson also argued that the Freedmen's Bureau was unconstitutional.

Republicans responded with the **Civil Rights Act of 1866**. This act provided African Americans with the same legal rights as white Americans. President Johnson once again used his veto power. He argued that the act gave too much power to the federal government. He also rejected the **principle** of equal rights for African Americans. Congress, however, overrode Johnson's veto.

Many Republicans worried about what would happen when the southern states were readmitted. Fearing that the Civil Rights Act might be overturned, the Republicans proposed the **Fourteenth Amendment** in the summer of 1866. The Fourteenth Amendment included the following provisions:

1. It defined all people born or naturalized within the United States, except Native Americans, as citizens.

Academic Vocabulary
principle basic belief, rule, or law

2. It guaranteed citizens the equal protection of the laws.
3. It said that states could not "deprive any person of life, liberty, or property, without due process of law."
4. It banned many former Confederate officials from holding state or federal offices.
5. It made state laws subject to federal court review.
6. It gave Congress the power to pass any laws needed to enforce it.

1866 Elections President Johnson and most Democrats opposed the Fourteenth Amendment. As a result, civil rights for African Americans became a key issue in the 1866 congressional elections. To help the Democrats, Johnson traveled around the country defending his Reconstruction plan. Johnson's speaking tour was a disaster. It did little to win votes for the Democratic Party. Johnson even got into arguments with people in the audiences of some of his speaking engagements.

Two major riots in the South also hurt Johnson's campaign. On May 1, 1866, a dispute in Memphis, Tennessee, took place between local police and black Union soldiers. The dispute turned into a three-day wave of violence against African Americans. About three months later, another riot took place during a political demonstration in New Orleans. During that dispute, 34 African Americans and three white Republicans were killed.

Reading Check
Summarize What issue did the Fourteenth Amendment address, and how did it affect the congressional elections of 1866?

Congress Takes Control of Reconstruction

The 1866 elections gave the Republican Party a commanding two-thirds majority in both the House and the Senate. This majority gave the Republicans the power to override any presidential veto. In addition, the Republicans became united as the moderates joined with the Radicals. Together, they called for a new form of Reconstruction.

Reconstruction Acts In March 1867, Congress passed the first of several **Reconstruction Acts**. These laws divided the South into five districts. A U.S. military commander controlled each district.

The military would remain in control of the South until the southern states rejoined the Union. To be readmitted, a state had to write a new state constitution supporting the Fourteenth Amendment. Finally, the state had to give African American men the right to vote.

Thaddeus Stevens was one of the new Reconstruction Acts' most enthusiastic supporters. He spoke in Congress to defend the acts.

"Have not loyal blacks quite as good a right to choose rulers and make laws as rebel whites? Every man, no matter what his race or color . . . has an equal right to justice, honesty, and fair play with every other man; and the law should secure him those rights."

–Thaddeus Stevens, quoted in *Sources of the American Republic*, edited by Marvin Meyers et al.

President on Trial President Johnson strongly disagreed with Stevens. He argued that African Americans did not deserve the same treatment as white people. The Reconstruction Acts, he said, used "powers not granted

The Reconstruction Amendments

Thirteenth Amendment (1865)

"Neither slavery nor involuntary servitude, except as a punishment for crime whereof the party shall have been duly convicted, shall exist within the United States, or any place subject to their jurisdiction."

This amendment legally banned slavery throughout the United States but it was not without fault. A loophole, or an ambiguity of a law, existed. "Involuntary servitude," according to this amendment, could be enforced as punishment for a crime. The amendment also failed to specify what the legal status of freedpeople would be or if they would be fully entitled to the rights of American citizens.

How might the loophole in the Thirteenth Amendment have been exploited by opponents of the amendment's ratification?

Fourteenth Amendment (1868)

"All persons born or naturalized in the United States, and subject to the jurisdiction thereof, are citizens of the United States and the State wherein they reside. No State shall make or enforce any law which shall abridge the privileges or immunities of citizens of the United States; nor shall any State deprive any person of life, liberty, or property, without due process of law; nor deny to any person within its jurisdiction the equal protection of the laws."

Most notably, this amendment overturned the *Dred Scott* case by granting citizenship to all people born in the United States (except for Native Americans).

What role do you think Black Codes played in the drafting of this amendment?

Fifteenth Amendment (1870)

"The right of citizens of the United States to vote shall not be denied or abridged by the United States or by any State on account of race, color, or previous condition of servitude."

This amendment, for all intents and purposes, gave African American men the right to vote.

According to the language of this amendment, what group of citizens was not granted voting rights? How would you change the language to include all citizens?

---

to the federal government or any one of its branches." Knowing that Johnson did not support its Reconstruction policies, Congress passed a law limiting his power. This law prevented the president from removing cabinet officials without Senate approval. Johnson quickly broke the law by firing Edwin Stanton, the secretary of war.

For the first time in United States history, the House of Representatives responded by voting to impeach the president. **Impeachment** is the process used by a legislative body to bring charges of wrongdoing against a public official. The next step, under Article I of the Constitution, was a trial in the Senate. A two-thirds majority was required to find Johnson guilty and remove him from office.

Although Johnson was unpopular with Republicans, some of them believed he was being judged unfairly. Others did not trust the president

This Reconstruction-era painting shows African American men voting after passage of the Fifteenth Amendment.

What right did the Fifteenth Amendment protect?

pro tempore of the Senate, Benjamin Wade. He would become president if Johnson were removed from office. By a single vote, Senate Republicans failed to convict Johnson. Even so, the trial weakened his power as president.

Election of 1868 Johnson did not run for another term in 1868. The Democrats chose former New York governor Horatio Seymour as their presidential candidate. The Republicans chose Ulysses S. Grant. As a war hero, Grant appealed to many northern voters. He had no political experience but supported the congressional Reconstruction plan. He ran under the slogan "Let Us Have Peace."

Shortly after Grant was nominated, Congress readmitted seven southern states—Alabama, Arkansas, Florida, Georgia, Louisiana, North Carolina, and South Carolina. (Tennessee had already been readmitted in 1866.) Under the terms of readmission, these seven states approved the Fourteenth Amendment. They also agreed to let African American men vote. However, white southerners used violence to try to keep African Americans away from the polls.

Despite such tactics, thousands of African Americans voted for Grant and the "party of Lincoln." The *New Orleans Tribune* reported that many former slaves "see clearly enough that the Republican party [is] their political life boat." African American votes helped Grant to win a narrow victory.

Reading Check
Analyze Information
To which voters did Grant appeal in the presidential election of 1868?

Fifteenth Amendment

After Grant's victory, Congressional Republicans wanted to protect their Reconstruction plan. They worried that the southern states might try to keep black voters from the polls in future elections. Also, some Radical Republicans argued that it was not fair that many northern states still had laws preventing African Americans from voting. After all, every southern state was required to grant suffrage to African American men.

In 1869 Congress proposed the **Fifteenth Amendment**, which gave African American men the right to vote. Abolitionist William Lloyd Garrison praised what he saw as "this wonderful, quiet, sudden transformation of four millions of human beings from . . . the auction block to the ballot-box." The amendment went into effect in 1870 as one of the last Reconstruction laws passed at the federal level.

The Fifteenth Amendment did not please every reformer, however. Many women were angry because the amendment did not also grant them the right to vote.

Summary and Preview In this lesson you learned that Congress took control of Reconstruction and took steps to protect the rights of African Americans. In the next lesson you will learn about increasing opposition to Reconstruction.

Reading Check
Find Main Ideas
How did Radical Republicans take control of Reconstruction?

Lesson 2 Assessment

Review Ideas, Terms, and People

1. **a. Describe** What were Black Codes?
   b. Make Inferences Why did Republicans think Johnson's Reconstruction plan was a failure?
2. **a. Recall** What was the Civil Rights Act of 1866?
   b. Summarize Why was the Fourteenth Amendment important?
3. **a. Recall** Why was President Johnson impeached?
   b. Evaluate Which element of the Reconstruction Acts do you believe was most important? Why?
4. **a. Recall** What does the Fifteenth Amendment state?
   b. Elaborate Do you think that women should have been included in the Fifteenth Amendment? Explain.

Critical Thinking

5. **Identify** In this lesson you learned about the issues that led Republicans to take over Reconstruction. Create a graphic organizer similar to the one below and identify the main provisions of the Fourteenth Amendment and their effects.

Provisions	Effects

Reconstruction in the South

The Big Idea

As Reconstruction ended, African Americans faced new hurdles and the South attempted to rebuild.

Main Ideas

- Reconstruction governments helped reform the South.

- The Ku Klux Klan was organized as African Americans moved into positions of power.

- As Reconstruction ended, the rights of African Americans were restricted.

- Southern business leaders relied on industry to rebuild the South.

Key Terms and People

Hiram Revels
Ku Klux Klan
Enforcement Acts
Compromise of 1877
poll tax
segregation
Jim Crow laws
Plessy v. *Ferguson*
sharecropping

If YOU were there . . .

You live on a farm in the South in the 1870s. Times are hard because you do not own your farm. Instead, you and your family work in a landowner's cotton fields. You never seem to earn enough to buy land of your own. Some of your neighbors have decided to give up farming and move to the city. Others are going to work in the textile mills. But you have always been a farmer.

Will you decide to change your way of life?

Reconstruction Governments

After Grant became president in 1869, the Republicans seemed stronger than ever. They controlled most southern governments, partly because of the support of African American voters. However, most of the Republican officeholders were unpopular with white southerners.

Carpetbaggers and Scalawags Some of these office-holders were northern-born Republicans who had moved to the South after the war. Many white southerners called them carpetbaggers. Supposedly, they had rushed there carrying all their possessions in bags made from carpeting. Many southerners resented these northerners, accusing them—often unfairly—of trying to profit from Reconstruction. Because the South needed both physical and economic rebuilding, there were many business opportunities. Northerners who had not been devastated by the war had more money to invest and could therefore profit from these opportunities.

Southern Democrats cared even less for white southern Republicans. They referred to them as scalawags, or greedy rascals. Democrats believed that these southerners had betrayed the South by voting for the Republican Party. Many southern Republicans were small farmers who had supported the Union during the war. Others, like Mississippi governor James Alcorn, were former members of the Whig Party. They preferred to become Republicans rather than join the Democrats.

Clergyman and educator Hiram Revels was the first African American elected to the U.S. Senate in 1870.

African American Leaders African Americans were the largest group of southern Republican voters. During Reconstruction, more than 600 African Americans won election to state legislatures. Some 16 of these politicians were elected to Congress. Other African Americans held local offices in counties throughout the South.

African American politicians came from many backgrounds. **Hiram Revels** was born free in North Carolina and went to college in Illinois. He became a Methodist minister and served as a chaplain in the Union army. In 1870 Revels became the first African American in the U.S. Senate. He took over the seat previously held by Confederate president Jefferson Davis. Revels held a moderate view of the readmission of former Confederates. Education and employment for African Americans were two of his top priorities. Revels exemplified the ability of African Americans to take part in governing. After completing his term, he became the first president of Alcorn University.

Unlike Revels, Blanche K. Bruce grew up in slavery in Virginia. Bruce became an important Republican in Mississippi and served one term as a U.S. senator. He worked to integrate the military while in office.

State Governments Change Direction The new Reconstruction state governments made policies that increased civil and voting rights for African Americans. They passed laws that ensured African Americans were allowed to vote in every community. In many places, however, there was still resistance by whites. Because former Confederates usually could not vote, they struggled to maintain political influence.

Reconstruction governments provided money for many new programs and organizations in the South. They helped to establish some of the first state-funded public school systems in the South. They also built new hospitals, prisons, and orphanages and passed laws prohibiting discrimination against African Americans. Many of these programs improved the lives of African Americans and whites in the South and gave people economic opportunities and access to political offices. However, racism and the dramatically different culture of groups led to conflicting expectations, and sometimes tensions led to violence.

Southern states under Republican control spent large amounts of money. They aided the construction of railroads, bridges, and public buildings. These improvements were intended to help the southern economy recover from the war. To get the money for these projects, the Reconstruction governments raised taxes and issued bonds. Although some people protested the increased taxes, the improved infrastructure helped the South to increase its trade and production capabilities.

Reading Check
Summarize What reforms did Reconstruction state governments carry out?

Ku Klux Klan

As more African Americans took office, resistance to Reconstruction increased among white southerners. Democrats claimed that the Reconstruction governments were corrupt, illegal, and unjust. They also disliked having federal soldiers stationed in their states. Many white southerners disapproved of African American officeholders. One Democrat

The Ku Klux Klan

Members of the Ku Klux Klan often attacked under cover of darkness to hide their identities. This Klan member, shown on the left, even disguised his horse.

Why do you think Klan members disguised themselves?

noted, "'A white man's government' [is] the most popular rallying cry we have." In 1866 a group of white southerners in Tennessee created the **Ku Klux Klan**. This secret society opposed civil rights, particularly suffrage, for African Americans. The Klan used violence and terror against African Americans. The group's membership grew rapidly as it spread throughout the South. Klan members wore robes and disguises to hide their identities. They attacked—and even murdered—African Americans, white Republican voters, and public officials, usually at night.

Local governments did little to stop the violence. Many officials feared the Klan or were sympathetic to its activities. In 1870 and 1871 the federal government took action. In an affirmation of federal authority, Congress passed laws, called the **Enforcement Acts**, that made it a federal crime to interfere with elections or to deny citizens equal protection under the law.

Within a few years, the Klan was no longer an organized threat. But groups of white vigilantes, including the White League in Louisiana and the Red Shirts in Mississippi, North and South Carolina, continued to assault African Americans and Republicans throughout the 1870s. Unlike the Ku Klux Klan, the White League and the Red Shirts operated openly.

Reading Check
Draw Conclusions
Why did southerners join the Ku Klux Klan or other vigilante groups?

Reconstruction Ends

The violence of the Ku Klux Klan was not the only challenge to Reconstruction. Republicans slowly lost control of southern state governments to the Democratic Party. The General Amnesty Act of 1872 allowed former Confederates, except those who had held high ranks, to serve in public office. Many of these former Confederates, most of whom were Democrats, were soon elected to southern governments.

The Republican Party also began losing its power in the North. Although President Grant was re-elected in 1872, financial and political scandals in his administration upset voters. In his first term, a gold-buying scheme involving Grant's cousin led to a brief crisis on the stock market called Black Friday. During his second term, his personal secretary was involved in the Whiskey Ring scandal, in which whiskey distillers and public officials worked together to steal liquor taxes from the federal government. Also, people blamed Republican policies for the Panic of 1873.

Panic of 1873 This severe economic downturn began in September 1873 when Jay Cooke and Company, a major investor in railroads and the largest financier of the Union's Civil War effort, declared bankruptcy. The company had lied about the value of land along the side of the Northern Pacific Railroad that it owned and was trying to sell. When the truth leaked out, the company failed.

The failure of such an important business sent panic through the stock market, and investors began selling shares of stock more rapidly than people wanted to buy them. Soon, 89 of the nation's 364 railroads had failed as well. The failure of almost 18,000 other businesses followed within two years. By 1876 unemployment had risen to 14 percent, with an estimated two million people out of work. The high unemployment rate set off numerous strikes and protests, many involving railroad workers. In 1874 the Democrats gained control of the House of Representatives. Northerners were becoming less concerned about southern racism and more concerned about their financial well-being.

Election of 1876 Republicans could tell that northern support for Reconstruction was fading. Voters' attention was shifting to economic problems. In 1874 the Republican Party lost control of the House of Representatives to the Democrats. The Republicans in Congress managed to pass one last civil rights law. The Civil Rights Act of 1875 guaranteed African Americans equal rights in public places, such as theaters and public transportation. But as Americans became increasingly worried about economic problems and government corruption, the Republican Party began to abandon Reconstruction.

Republicans selected Ohio governor Rutherford B. Hayes as their 1876 presidential candidate. He believed in ending federal support of the Reconstruction governments. The Democrats nominated New York governor Samuel J. Tilden. During the election, Democrats in the South again used violence at the polls to keep Republican voters away.

The election between Hayes and Tilden was close. Tilden appeared to have won. Republicans challenged the electoral votes in Oregon and three southern states. A special commission of members of Congress and Supreme Court justices was appointed to settle the issue.

The commission narrowly decided to give all the disputed votes to Hayes. Hayes thus won the presidency by one electoral vote. In the **Compromise of 1877**, the Democrats agreed to accept Hayes's victory. In return, they wanted all remaining federal troops removed from the South. They also asked for funding for internal improvements in the South and the appointment of a southern Democrat to the president's cabinet. Shortly after he took office in 1877, President Hayes removed the last of the federal troops from the South.

Redeemers Gradually, Democrats regained control of state governments in the South. In each state, they moved quickly to get rid of the Reconstruction reforms.

Democrats who brought their party back to power in the South were called Redeemers. They came from a variety of backgrounds. For instance, U.S. senator John T. Morgan of Alabama was a former general in the Confederate army. Newspaper editor Henry Grady of Georgia was interested in promoting southern industry.

Redeemers wanted to reduce the size of state government and limit the rights of African Americans. They lowered state budgets and got rid of a variety of social programs. The Redeemers cut property taxes and cut public funding for schools. They also succeeded in limiting African Americans' civil rights.

Jim Crow Laws
This 1913 illustration shows the segregation of society caused by Jim Crow laws. After Reconstruction ended, the U.S. court system upheld legalized segregation for nearly eighty years. The Civil Rights Act of 1964 finally put an end to all state and local laws requiring segregation.

African Americans' Rights Restricted Redeemers set up the poll tax in an effort to deny the vote to African Americans. The **poll tax** was a special tax people had to pay before they could vote.

Some states also targeted African American voters by requiring them to pass a literacy test. A so-called grandfather clause written into law affected men whose fathers or grandfathers could vote before 1867. In those cases, a voter did not have to pay a poll tax or pass a literacy test. As a result, almost every white man could escape the voting restrictions.

Redeemer governments also introduced legal **segregation**, the forced separation of whites and African Americans in public places. **Jim Crow laws**—laws that enforced segregation—became common in southern states in the 1880s.

African Americans challenged Jim Crow laws in court. In 1883, however, the U.S. Supreme Court ruled that the Civil Rights Act of 1875 was unconstitutional. The Court also ruled that the Fourteenth Amendment applied only to the actions of state governments. This ruling allowed private individuals and businesses to practice segregation.

Plessy v. Ferguson In 1896 the U.S. Supreme Court returned to the issue of segregation. When Homer Plessy, an African American, refused to leave the whites-only Louisiana train car he was riding on, he was arrested and accused of breaking Louisiana's Separate Car Act of 1890. This Jim Crow law stated that:

> "all railway companies carrying passengers in their coaches in this state, shall provide equal but separate accommodations for the white, and colored races, by providing two or more passenger coaches for each passenger train, or by dividing the passenger coaches by a partition so as to secure separate accommodations. . . ."
>
> —Separate Car Act of 1890, Louisiana state law

Plessy sued the railroad company and lost. His lawyers argued that the law violated his right to equal treatment under the Fourteenth Amendment. He then appealed to the U.S. Supreme Court. The Supreme Court ruled against Plessy in *Plessy v. Ferguson.* Segregation was allowed, said the Court, if "separate-but-equal" facilities were provided. Among the justices, only John Marshall Harlan disagreed with the Court's decision.

Segregation became widespread across the country. African Americans were forced to use separate public schools, libraries, and parks. When they existed, these facilities were usually of poorer quality than those created for whites. In practice, these so-called separate-but-equal facilities were separate and unequal. Neither Congress nor the president would make significant actions to overturn the doctrine until the 1900s.

Farming in the South Few African Americans in the South could afford to buy or even rent farms. Many African Americans therefore remained on plantations. Others tried to make a living in the cities.

African Americans who stayed on plantations often became part of a system known as **sharecropping**, or sharing the crop. Landowners provided the land, tools, and supplies, and sharecroppers provided the labor. At harvest time, the sharecropper usually had to give most of the crop to the landowner. Whatever remained belonged to the sharecropper. In theory, "croppers" who saved a little might even rent land for cash and keep their full harvest in a system known as tenant farming.

Instead, most sharecroppers lived in a cycle of debt. When they needed food, clothing, or supplies, most families had to buy goods on credit because they had little cash. When sharecroppers sold their crops, they hoped to be able to pay off these debts. However, bad weather, poor harvests, or low crop prices often made this dream impossible.

Sharecroppers usually grew cotton, one of the South's most important cash crops. When too many farmers planted cotton, however, the supply became excessive. As a result, the price per bale of cotton dropped. Many farmers understood the drawbacks of planting cotton. However, farmers felt pressure from banks and others to keep raising cotton.

Reading Check
Find Main Ideas How were African Americans' rights restricted?

Rebuilding Southern Industry

The southern economy suffered through cycles of good and bad years as cotton prices went up and down. Some business leaders hoped industry would strengthen the southern economy and create a New South.

Southern Industry Henry Grady, an Atlanta newspaper editor, was a leader of the New South movement. Grady and his supporters felt that with its cheap and abundant labor, the South could build factories and provide a workforce for them.

The most successful industrial development in the South involved textile production. Businesspeople built textile mills in many small towns to produce cotton fabric. Many people from rural areas came to work in the mills, but African Americans were not allowed to work in most of them.

Southern Mill Life Work in the cotton mills appealed to farm families who had trouble making ends meet. Recruiters sent out by the mills promised good wages and steady work. Mills employed large numbers of women and children. Women did most of the spinning and were valued workers. However, few women had the opportunity to advance within the company.

The New South

Atlanta rebuilt quickly after the war, becoming a leading railroad and industrial center. Newspaper editor Henry Grady gave stirring speeches about the need for industry in the South. He became one of the best-known spokesmen of the "New South."

Why might Grady point to Atlanta as a model for economic change?

"The New South . . . is stirred with the breath of a new life."

—Henry Grady

Reading Check
Find Main Ideas
What did southern business leaders hope industry would do?

Many mill workers were proud of the skills they used, but they did not enjoy their work. Workers often labored 12 hours a day, six days a week. Cotton dust and lint filled the air, causing asthma and an illness known as brown-lung disease. Fast-moving machinery caused injuries and even deaths. Despite the long hours and dangerous working conditions, wages remained low. However, mill work did offer an alternative to farming.

Reconstruction in the North

Although most federal Reconstruction policies were designed to reform the South, they affected groups in the North as well. There were many groups that worked to advance their own rights and interests during this time.

Women and Northern African Americans The Radical Republicans passed many federal laws that required southern states to allow African American men to vote. They based their cause on the ideal of equality found in the Declaration of Independence and the Constitution. Women's suffragists began using these same arguments to support their own suffrage. Wyoming and Utah granted women the vote in 1869, but their motivations were not just to ensure equal rights for women. Wyoming leaders hoped to attract more women residents, while Utahans hoped to counteract the rising number of non-Mormon voters.

African Americans in the North faced less social discrimination than they did in the South but still faced racism and segregation. In response, some state governments passed laws that made segregation illegal. Some integrated their school systems. Still, most states upheld the principle of separate-but-equal facilities.

A Changing Economy During the war and Reconstruction, the economy of the North and the West grew rapidly. Manufacturing, commerce, and rail transportation generated tremendous fortunes. Large companies grew by buying smaller companies, and railroads made huge profits transporting goods and people. Tax revenue increased as well, and governments were able to provide more services and make more investments.

Between 1865 and 1873, more than 2 million immigrants arrived in the United States. They provided a new pool of labor for the growing industrial economy. The number of labor unions increased, and they began to push for policies that protected workers. Reformers pressed for eight-hour-workday and fair-pay laws. In addition, the increase in commercial and trading businesses led to a shift in the makeup of the working class. It now included a majority of professionals and white-collar workers.

Eventually the focus of the Republican Party began to move away from civil rights for African Americans and toward reducing government corruption. The acceptance of the Compromise of 1877 signaled the end of the Republican focus on reforming racial politics in the South.

Summary and Preview In this lesson you learned about the end of Reconstruction. In the years that followed, the South continued to rebuild, but the gains made by African Americans were reversed.

Reading Check
Compare and Contrast How was Reconstruction in the North similar to and different from Reconstruction in the South?

Lesson 3 Assessment

Review Ideas, Terms, and People

1. a. Identify Who were some prominent African American leaders during Reconstruction? Why was the election of Hiram Revels significant?

b. Evaluate What do you think was the most important change made by Reconstruction state governments? Explain your answer.

2. a. Recall For what reasons did some local governments not stop the Ku Klux Klan?

b. Draw Conclusions How did the Ku Klux Klan's use of terror interfere with elections in the South?

3. a. Summarize What was the Compromise of 1877?

b. Evaluate How did *Plessy* v. *Ferguson* affect life in the United States?

c. Explain What was the relationship between Jim Crow laws and segregation?

4. a. Identify Who was Henry Grady, and why was he important?

b. Predict What are some possible results of the rise of the "New South"?

Critical Thinking

5. Identify Causes and Effects In this lesson you learned about Reconstruction governments. Create a graphic organizer similar to the one below and show why Reconstruction ended, as well as the results of its end.

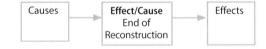

Causes → Effect/Cause End of Reconstruction → Effects

Social Studies Skills

Chance, Oversight, and Error in History

Understand the Skill

Sometimes, history can seem very routine. One event leads to others which, in turn, lead to still others. You learn to look for cause-and-effect relationships among events. You learn how point of view and bias can influence decisions and actions. These approaches to the study of history imply that the events of the past are orderly and predictable.

In fact, many of the events of the past *are* orderly and predictable. They may seem even more so since they're over and done with, and we know how things turned out. Yet, predictable patterns of behavior *do* exist throughout history. Recognizing them is one of the great values and rewards of studying the past. As the philosopher George Santayana once famously said, "Those who cannot remember the past are condemned to repeat it."

At its most basic level, however, history is people, and people are "human." They make mistakes. Unexpected things happen to them, both good things and bad. This is the unpredictable element of history. The current phrase "stuff happens" is just as true of the past as it is today. Mistakes, oversights, and just plain "dumb luck" have shaped the course of history—and have helped to make the study of it so exciting.

Learn the Skill

California merchant John Sutter decided to build a sawmill along a nearby American river in 1848. He planned to sell the lumber it produced to settlers who were moving into the area. Sutter put James W. Marshall to work building the mill. To install the large waterwheel that would power the saw, Marshall first had to deepen the riverbed next to the mill. During his digging, he noticed some shiny bits of yellow metal in the water. The result of this accidental find was the California gold rush, which sent thousands of Americans to California, and speeded settlement of the West.

In 1863 the army of Confederate general Robert E. Lee invaded Maryland. The Civil War had been going well for the South. Lee hoped a southern victory on Union soil would convince the British to aid the South in the war. However, a Confederate officer forgot his cigars as his unit left its camp in the Maryland countryside. Wrapped around the cigars was a copy of Lee's battle plans. When a Union soldier came upon the abandoned camp, he spotted the cigars. This chance discovery enabled the Union army to defeat Lee at the Battle of Antietam. The Union victory helped keep the British out of the war. More importantly, it allowed President Lincoln to issue the Emancipation Proclamation and begin the process of ending slavery in the United States.

Practice the Skill

In April 1865 President Lincoln was assassinated while attending the theater in Washington, DC. Bodyguard John Parker was stationed outside the door of the president's box. However, Parker left his post to find a seat from which he could watch the play. This allowed the killer to enter the box and shoot the unprotected president.

Write an essay about how this chance event altered the course of history. How might Reconstruction, North–South relations, and African Americans' struggle for equality have been different had Lincoln lived?

Module 2 Assessment

Review Vocabulary, Terms, and People

Complete each sentence by filling in the blank with the correct term or person from the module.

1. _____ were laws that allowed racial segregation in public places.

2. The Radical Republicans were led by _____, a member of Congress from Pennsylvania.

3. The period from 1865 to 1877 that focused on reuniting the nation is known as _____.

4. Following the Civil War, many African Americans in the South made a living by participating in the _____ system.

5. After opposing Congress, Andrew Johnson became the first president to face _____ proceedings.

6. The _____ Amendment made slavery in the United States illegal.

7. In 1870 _____ became the first African American to serve in the U.S. Senate.

Comprehension and Critical Thinking

Lesson 1

8. a. **Describe** How did the lives of African Americans change after the Civil War?

   b. **Compare and Contrast** How was President Johnson's Reconstruction plan similar and different from President Lincoln's Ten Percent Plan?

   c. **Evaluate** Which of the three Reconstruction plans that were originally proposed do you think would have been the most successful? Why?

Lesson 2

9. a. **Identify** Who were the Radical Republicans, and how did they change Reconstruction?

   b. **Analyze** How did the debate over the Fourteenth Amendment affect the election of 1866?

   c. **Elaborate** Do you think Congress was right to impeach President Andrew Johnson? Explain.

Lesson 3

10. a. **Describe** What reforms did Reconstruction governments in the South support?

    b. **Draw Conclusions** In what ways did southern governments attempt to reverse the accomplishments of Reconstruction?

    c. **Evaluate** Do you think the South was successful or unsuccessful in its rebuilding efforts? Explain your answer.

Module 2 Assessment, continued

Review Themes

11. **Politics** Explain the political struggles that took place during Reconstruction.

12. **Society and Culture** How were the lives of ordinary southerners affected in the years after Reconstruction?

Reading Skills

Analyze Historical Information *Use the Reading Skills taught in this module to answer the question about the reading selection below.*

> Radical Republicans, on the other hand, took a harsher stance. They wanted the federal government to force change in the South. Like the moderates, they thought the Black Codes were cruel and unjust.

13. Which of the following is relevant information for the passage above?
    a. Thaddeus Stevens was a Radical Republican.
    b. Andrew Johnson was a Democrat.
    c. Radical Republicans wanted the federal government to make major changes in the South.
    d. Radical Republicans were eventually removed from power.

Social Studies Skills

Chance, Oversight, and Error in History *Use the Social Studies Skills taught in this module to answer the question about the reading selection below.*

> Johnson's speaking tour was a disaster. It did little to win votes for the Democratic Party. Johnson even got into arguments with people in the audiences of some of his speaking engagements.

14. Which of the following is an example of chance, oversight, or error that affected history?
    a. Johnson got into arguments with audiences.
    b. The tour was a disaster.
    c. The tour did not win votes.
    d. Johnson spoke for the Democratic Party.

Focus on Writing

15. **Write a Job History** In this module you read about the changing job scene during Reconstruction. Put yourself in the shoes of a person living then. It could be anyone—a returning soldier, a shopkeeper, a schoolteacher, or a politician. What jobs would that person seek? Why would he or she leave one job for another? Write a brief job history for that person during Reconstruction. Include at least four jobs. Make each job description two to four sentences long. End each one with a sentence or two about why the person left that job. Add one sentence explaining why he or she took the next job. Be sure to include specific historical details.

Westward Expansion

Essential Question

Was the United States truly destined to expand west in the 1800s?

About the Photo: Wagon trains carried hundreds of thousands of settlers across the Great Plains.

In this module you will read about the effects of westward expansion in the United States. You will also learn about how Native Americans resisted these changes.

What You Will Learn . . .

▷ *Explore ONLINE!*

HISTORY

VIDEOS, including...
- The Transcontinental Railroad
- The Louisiana Purchase
- Railroads that Tamed the West
- Plains Indians
- Sitting Bull: Chief of the Lakota Nation

☑ Document-Based Investigations

☑ Graphic Organizers

☑ Interactive Games

☑ Interactive Map: Territorial Expansion of the United States, 1783–1898

☑ Image Carousel: Buffalo Bill's Wild West Show

Timeline of Events 1800–1900 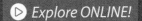 ▷ *Explore ONLINE!*

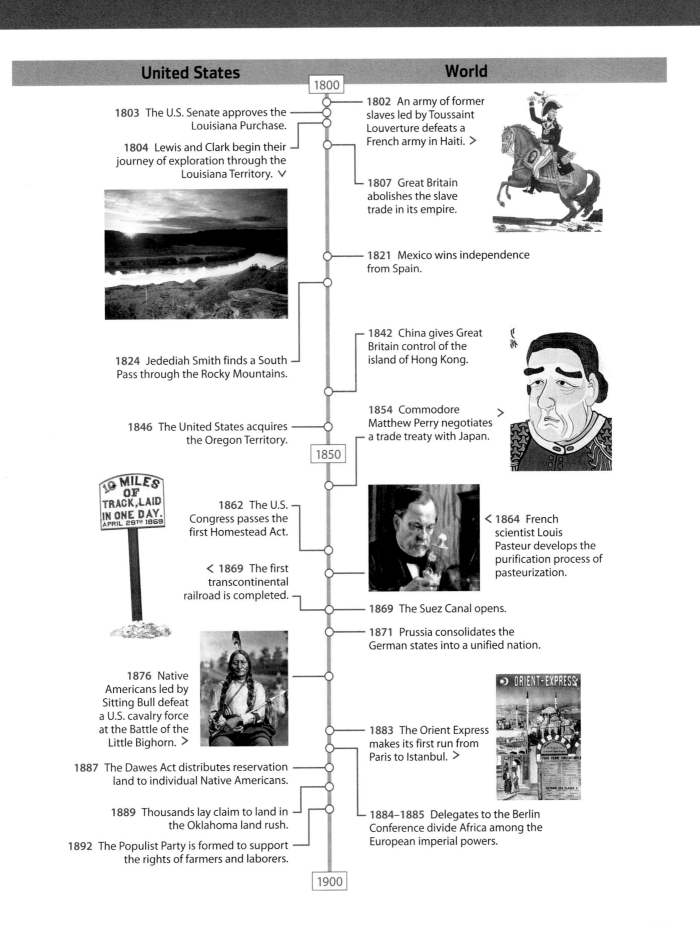

United States

World

1800

1803 The U.S. Senate approves the Louisiana Purchase.

1804 Lewis and Clark begin their journey of exploration through the Louisiana Territory. ∨

1824 Jedediah Smith finds a South Pass through the Rocky Mountains.

1846 The United States acquires the Oregon Territory.

1850

1862 The U.S. Congress passes the first Homestead Act.

< 1869 The first transcontinental railroad is completed.

1876 Native Americans led by Sitting Bull defeat a U.S. cavalry force at the Battle of the Little Bighorn. >

1887 The Dawes Act distributes reservation land to individual Native Americans.

1889 Thousands lay claim to land in the Oklahoma land rush.

1892 The Populist Party is formed to support the rights of farmers and laborers.

1802 An army of former slaves led by Toussaint Louverture defeats a French army in Haiti. >

1807 Great Britain abolishes the slave trade in its empire.

1821 Mexico wins independence from Spain.

1842 China gives Great Britain control of the island of Hong Kong.

1854 Commodore Matthew Perry negotiates a trade treaty with Japan.

< 1864 French scientist Louis Pasteur develops the purification process of pasteurization.

1869 The Suez Canal opens.

1871 Prussia consolidates the German states into a unified nation.

1883 The Orient Express makes its first run from Paris to Istanbul. >

1884–1885 Delegates to the Berlin Conference divide Africa among the European imperial powers.

1900

Reading Social Studies

Geography, Science and Technology

In this module you will follow the development of the United States from the early 1800s through the 1890s. You will learn that the country nearly doubled in size with the purchase of the Louisiana Territory in 1803. You will find out about the struggles that people faced as they later settled the Great Plains. You will learn about the technological advancements made during this time as well as the difficult geographical obstacles miners and ranchers faced in the West.

READING FOCUS:

Ask Questions to Understand

When newspaper reporters want to get to the heart of a story, they ask certain questions: who, what, when, where, why, and how. When you are reading a history book, you can use the same questions to get to the heart of what happened in the past.

Hypothetical Questions You can also use questions to dig deeper than what is in the text. You can ask hypothetical, or what if, questions. These questions ask what might have happened had events occurred differently. Sometimes asking such questions can help history come alive.

Who?
Congress

Where?
the West

How?
Congress gave land to anyone who agreed to settle on it for five years.

In 1862 Congress passed two important land acts that helped open the West to settlers. The Home-stead Act gave government-owned land to small farmers. Any adult who was a U.S. citizen or planned to become one could receive 160 acres of land. In exchange, homesteaders promised to live on the land for five years. The Morrill Act granted more than 17 million acres of federal land to the states.

What?
encouraged new settlement

When?
1862

What if?
If Congress had not passed these laws, U.S. citizens might not have moved West. The United States might not have grown as quickly as it did.

Why?
Perhaps Congress feared what would happen to western lands if they remained unsettled by U.S. citizens.

You Try It!

Read the following passage and then answer the questions below.

Building Communities Women were an important force in the settlement of the frontier. They joined in the hard work of farming and ranching and helped build communities out of the widely spaced farms and small towns. Their role in founding communities facilitated a strong voice in public affairs. Wyoming women, for example, were granted the vote in the new state's constitution, which was approved in 1869. Annie Bidwell, one of the founders of Chico, California, used her influence to support a variety of moral and social causes such as women's suffrage and temperance.

Answer these questions based on the passage you just read.

1. Who is this passage about?
2. What did they do?
3. When did they do it?
4. How do you think they accomplished it?
5. Why do you think they were able to accomplish so much?
6. How can knowing this information help you understand the past?
7. What if women in the West had been given more rights? Fewer rights? How might the West have been different?

As you read Module 3, ask questions like *who, what, when, where, why, how,* and *what* if to help you analyze what you are reading.

A Growing Nation

The Big Idea

Americans explored and settled in the West as the nation expanded.

Main Ideas

- As American settlers moved West, control of the Mississippi River became more important to the United States.

- Expeditions led by Lewis and Clark, Pike, and Frémont increased Americans' understanding of the West.

- During the early 1800s, Americans moved west of the Rocky Mountains to settle and trade.

- Families moved into the far west and established thriving communities.

Key Terms and People

Daniel Boone
Louisiana Purchase
Meriwether Lewis
William Clark
Lewis and Clark expedition
Sacagawea
Zebulon Pike
John C. Frémont
John Jacob Astor
mountain men
Oregon Trail
Santa Fe Trail
Mormons
Brigham Young

If YOU were there . . .

You and your family live on a small farm in Kentucky in about 1800. Raised on the frontier, you are a skillful hunter and trapper. One day at the trading post, you see a poster calling for volunteers to join the Corps of Discovery. This expedition will explore the vast region west of the Mississippi River. You think it would be exciting—but dangerous. You might never come home.

Would you volunteer to join the Corps of Discovery?

The First Westerners

For centuries, the Ohio, Cumberland, and Tennessee River valleys had been the hunting grounds of many Native American tribes. By 1800, however, thousands of white settlers had set up homesteads in these areas. The land had been opened up to settlement by an intrepid group of frontier guides known as long hunters. During months-long hunting trips, they explored and surveyed the wilderness west of the Appalachian Mountains.

Frontiersman Daniel Boone led the exploration and settlement of Kentucky.

Daniel Boone was one of the most famous long hunters.

From his earliest years, Boone loved the outdoor life. In time, he became a skilled hunter, trapper, and guide. In 1769 he led a group of friends on an expedition across the Appalachian Mountains via the Cumberland Gap. They were among the first whites to venture deep into the land beyond the Appalachians. Then, in 1775 Boone and about 30 other long hunters cut a continuous road through the Cumberland Gap. By the time it was finished, this Wilderness Road stretched some 300 miles. It soon became the main thoroughfare for settlers moving West. Some used a southern route called the Natchez Trace. This was an old Native American trail that ran southwest all the way to the Mississippi River.

As the region's population grew, Kentucky, Tennessee, and Ohio were admitted to the Union. Settlers in these states depended upon the Mississippi and Ohio rivers to move their products to eastern markets. New Orleans, located at the mouth of the Mississippi, was a very important port. Its busy docks were filled with settlers' farm products and valuable furs bought from American Indians. Many of these cargoes were then sent to Europe. At the same time, manufactured goods passed through the port on their way upriver. As American dependence on the river grew, President Thomas Jefferson began to worry that a foreign power might shut down access to New Orleans.

Spain controlled both New Orleans and the Louisiana Territory. This region stretched west from the Mississippi River to the Rocky Mountains. Although Spain owned Louisiana, Spanish officials found it impossible to keep Americans out of the territory. "You can't put doors on open country," the foreign minister said in despair. Years of effort failed to improve Spain's position. Under a secret treaty, Spain agreed to trade Louisiana to France, passing the problem on to someone else. One Spanish officer expressed his relief. "I can hardly wait to leave them [the Americans] behind me," he said.

Reading Check
Analyze Information
Why was New Orleans important to settlers in the western regions of the United States?

▷ *Explore ONLINE!*

The Louisiana Purchase and Western Expeditions

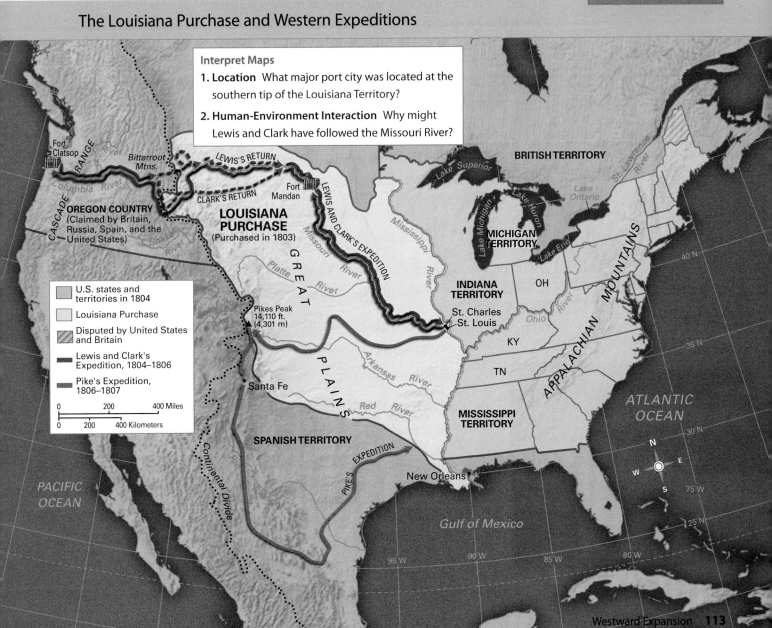

Interpret Maps

1. **Location** What major port city was located at the southern tip of the Louisiana Territory?

2. **Human-Environment Interaction** Why might Lewis and Clark have followed the Missouri River?

Legend:
- U.S. states and territories in 1804
- Louisiana Purchase
- Disputed by United States and Britain
- Lewis and Clark's Expedition, 1804–1806
- Pike's Expedition, 1806–1807

0   200   400 Miles
0   200   400 Kilometers

Louisiana and Western Explorers

In 1802, just before handing over Louisiana to France, Spain closed New Orleans to American shipping. Angry farmers worried about what this would do to the economy. President Jefferson asked the U.S. ambassador to France, Robert R. Livingston, to try to buy New Orleans. Jefferson sent James Monroe to help Livingston.

Napoléon and Louisiana France was led by Napoléon (nuh-POH-lay-uhn) Bonaparte, a powerful ruler who had conquered most of Europe. He wished to rebuild France's empire in North America. Napoléon's strategy was to use the French colony of Haiti, in the Caribbean, as a supply base. From there he could send troops to Louisiana. However, in the 1790s enslaved Africans, led by Toussaint Louverture (too-SAN loo-vehr-TOOR), revolted and freed themselves from French rule. Napoléon sent troops to try to regain control of the island, but they were defeated in 1802. This defeat ended his hopes of rebuilding a North American empire.

Jefferson Buys Louisiana Livingston and Monroe got a surprising offer during their negotiations with French foreign minister Charles Talleyrand. When the Americans tried to buy New Orleans, Talleyrand offered to sell all of Louisiana. With his hopes for a North American empire dashed, Napoléon had turned his attention back to Europe. France was at war with Great Britain, and Napoléon needed money for military supplies. He also hoped that a larger United States would challenge British power.

Livingston and Monroe knew a bargain when they saw one. They quickly accepted the French offer to sell Louisiana for $15 million, and Jefferson agreed to the purchase. On October 20, 1803, the Senate approved the **Louisiana Purchase** agreement, which roughly doubled the size of the United States.

Explorers Head West President Jefferson wanted to learn more about the West and the Native Americans who lived there. He also wanted to see if there was a river route that could be taken to the Pacific Ocean. So, in 1803 Jefferson asked Congress to fund an expedition to explore the West. To lead it, he chose former army captain **Meriwether Lewis**. Lewis then chose his friend Lieutenant **William Clark** to be the co-leader of the expedition. With Clark, Lewis carefully selected about 50 skilled frontiersmen to join the Corps of Discovery, as they called their group.

In May 1804 the **Lewis and Clark expedition** began its long journey to explore the Louisiana Purchase. Lewis and Clark used the Missouri River as their highway through the unknown lands. By late October the Corps of Discovery had pushed more than 1,600 miles upriver. They spent the winter among the Mandan people. At this time, the Corps also came into contact with British and Canadian trappers and traders, who were not happy to see them. The traders feared American competition in the trade in beaver fur—and they would be proved right.

The Lewis and Clark expedition followed the Missouri River for most of the journey across the Great Plains.

Meriwether Lewis's Journal Entry

On September 17, 1804, while traveling across the Great Plains, Meriwether Lewis marveled at the richness of the land.

"The shortness . . . of grass gave the plain the appearance throughout its whole extent of beautiful bowling-green in fine order . . . this scenery, already rich, pleasing, and beautiful was still farther heightened by immense herds of Buffaloe, deer Elk and Antelopes which we saw in every direction feeding on the hills and plains. I do not think I exaggerate when I estimate the number of Buffalo which could be compre[hend]ed at one view to amount to 3000."

—Meriwether Lewis, quoted in *Original Journals of the Lewis and Clark Expedition*, edited by Reuben Bold Theraites

Analyze Historical Sources
What did Lewis find so impressive about the Great Plains?

Sacagawea, whose name is believed to mean "bird woman," contributed greatly to the success of the Lewis and Clark expedition.

In the spring of 1805, the expedition set out again. They were joined by **Sacagawea** (sak-uh-guh-WEE-uh), a Shoshone from the Rocky Mountains. Her language skills—she knew several Native American languages—and her knowledge of the geography of the region proved very useful to Lewis and Clark. Sacagawea also helped the expedition by naming plants and by gathering edible fruits and vegetables for the group. At one point, the group met with Sacagawea's brother, who provided horses and a guide to lead the expedition across the mountains.

After crossing the Rockies, Lewis and Clark followed the Columbia River. Along the way they met the powerful Nez Percé. Like the Shoshone, the Nez Percé provided the expedition with supplies. At last, in November 1805 Lewis and Clark reached the Pacific Ocean. The explorers stayed in the Pacific Northwest during the rough winter. In March 1806 Lewis and Clark set out on the long trip home.

Lewis and Clark had not found a river route across the West to the Pacific Ocean. But they had learned much about western lands and paths across the Rockies. They used this knowledge to produce the first accurate maps of the Louisiana Territory. The explorers also established contact with many Native American groups and collected much valuable information about western plants and animals.

Other Explorations In 1806 a young army officer named **Zebulon Pike** was sent on another mission to the West. He was ordered to find the starting point of the Red River. This was important because the United States considered the Red River to be a part of the Louisiana Territory's western border with New Spain.

Heading into the Rocky Mountains, in present-day Colorado, Pike tried to reach the summit of the mountain now known as Pikes Peak. In 1807 he traveled into Spanish-held lands until Spanish cavalry arrested him. They suspected Pike of being a spy. When he was finally released, he returned to the United States and reported on his trip. This report offered many Americans their first description of the Southwest. Not all of Pike's information was accurate, however. For example, he described the treeless Great Plains as a desert. This led many Americans to believe, mistakenly, that the Plains region was useless for farming.

Another explorer, **John C. Frémont**, led an expedition to the Rocky Mountains in May 1842. Upon his return, Frémont compiled a report of his journey, which became a guide for future travelers to the West. It detailed the geology, botany, and climate of the region. It also crushed the mistaken belief that the West was a vast desert, attracting more settlers as a result. Buoyed by the success of his first effort, Frémont led several more surveys of the American West in the 1840s and 1850s.

Mountain Men Go West

In the early 1800s, Americans pushed steadily westward, moving even beyond the territory of the United States. They traveled by canoe and flatboat, on horseback, and by wagon train. Some even walked much of the way.

The rush to the West occurred, in part, because of a hat. The "high hat," made of water-repellent beaver fur, was popular in the United States and Europe. While acquiring fur for the hats, French, British, and American companies gradually killed off the beaver population in the East. Companies moved West in search of more beavers. Most of the first non-Native Americans who traveled to the Rocky Mountains and the Pacific Northwest were fur traders and trappers.

American merchant **John Jacob Astor** created one of the largest fur businesses, the American Fur Company. His company bought skins from western fur traders and trappers, who became known as **mountain men**. These adventurers were among the first to explore the Rocky Mountains and lands west of them. The knowledge they acquired helped settlers who made the westward journey. Mountain men lived lonely and often dangerous lives. They trapped animals on their own, far from towns and settlements. Mountain men such as Jedediah Smith, Manuel Lisa, Jim Bridger, and Jim Beckwourth survived many hardships during their search for wealth and adventure. To survive on the frontier, mountain men adopted Native American customs and clothing. In addition, they often married Native American women. The Indian wives of trappers often worked hard to contribute to their success.

Pioneer William Ashley saw that frequently bringing furs out of the Rocky Mountains was expensive. He asked his traders to stay in the mountains and meet once a year to trade and socialize. This practice helped make the fur trade more profitable. The yearly meeting was known as the rendezvous. At the rendezvous, mountain men and Native American trappers sold their fur to fur-company agents. One trapper described the people at a typical rendezvous in 1837. He saw Americans, Canadian French, some Europeans, and "Indians, of nearly every tribe in the Rocky Mountains." The rendezvous was filled with celebrating and storytelling. At the same time, the meeting was also about conducting business.

Reading Check
Compare What did the expeditions of Lewis and Clark, Pike, and Frémont reveal about the West?

Jim Beckwourth was an African American fur trapper and explorer of the West in the early 1800s.

In 1811 John Jacob Astor founded a fur-trading post called Astoria at the mouth of the Columbia River. Astoria was one of the first American settlements in what became known as Oregon Country. American Indians occupied the region, which was rich in forests, rivers, and wildlife. However, Britain, Russia, Spain, and the United States all claimed the land. Recognizing the huge economic value of the Pacific Northwest, the United States made treaties in which Spain and Russia gave up their claims to various areas. The United States also signed treaties with Britain allowing both countries to occupy Oregon Country, the Columbia River, and its surrounding lands.

By the 1840s the era of American fur trading in the Pacific Northwest was drawing to a close. The demand for beaver furs had fallen because fashions had changed. Too much trapping had also greatly reduced the number of beavers. Some mountain men gave up their work and moved back East. Their daring stories, however, along with the treaties made by the U.S. government, fired the imagination of many Americans.

Reading Check
Draw Conclusions
How did the mountain men help to open up the West for future settlement?

Settling the West

The success of early pioneers convinced thousands of families and individuals to make the dangerous journey west. They traveled along a series of routes that led to New Mexico, Oregon, and Utah. Once in these places, the new pioneers claimed the land and established settlements.

The Oregon Trail Many settlers moving to Oregon Country and other western areas followed the 2,000-mile-long **Oregon Trail**, which stretched from places such as Independence, Missouri, and Council Bluffs, Iowa, west into Oregon Country. The trail followed the Platte and Sweetwater Rivers over the Plains. After it crossed the Rocky Mountains, the trail forked. The northern branch led to the Willamette Valley in Oregon. The other branch went to California and became known as the California Trail.

Traveling the trail challenged the strength and determination of pioneer families. The journey usually began after the rainy season ended in late spring and lasted about six months. The cost, about $600 for a family of four, was high at a time when a typical worker usually made about $1.50 per day. Young families made up most groups of settlers. They gathered in wagon trains for the trip. There could be as few as ten wagons or as many as several dozen in a wagon train. Some pioneers brought small herds of cattle with them on the trail.

Oxen, mules, or horses pulled the wagons. Pioneers often walked to save their animals' strength. They kept up a tiring pace, traveling from dawn until dusk. They faced severe hardships, including shortages of food, supplies, and water. Rough weather and geographic barriers, such as rivers and mountains, sometimes forced large numbers of pioneers to abandon their wagons. In the early days of the Oregon Trail, many Native Americans helped the pioneers, acting as guides. They also traded goods for food. Although newspapers sometimes reported Native American "massacres" of pioneers, few settlers died from Indian attacks. The settlers who arrived safely in Oregon and California found generally healthy and pleasant climates. By 1845 some 5,000 settlers occupied the Willamette Valley.

▶ *Explore ONLINE!*

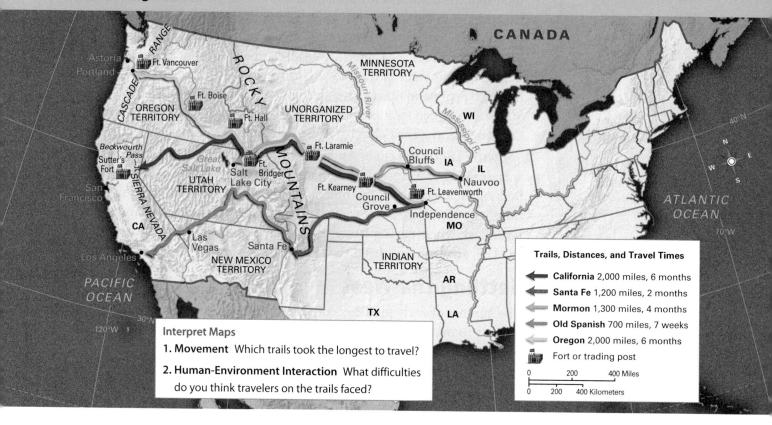

Interpret Maps

1. **Movement** Which trails took the longest to travel?

2. **Human-Environment Interaction** What difficulties do you think travelers on the trails faced?

Trails, Distances, and Travel Times

- **California** 2,000 miles, 6 months
- **Santa Fe** 1,200 miles, 2 months
- **Mormon** 1,300 miles, 4 months
- **Old Spanish** 700 miles, 7 weeks
- **Oregon** 2,000 miles, 6 months
- Fort or trading post

The Santa Fe Trail The **Santa Fe Trail** was another important path west. It led from Independence, Missouri, to Santa Fe, New Mexico. It followed an ancient trading route first used by Native Americans. American traders loaded their wagon trains with cloth and other manufactured goods to exchange for horses, mules, and silver from Mexican traders in Santa Fe.

The long trip across blazing deserts and rough mountains was dangerous. But the lure of high profits encouraged traders to take to the trail. One trader reported a 2,000 percent profit on his cargo. The U.S. government helped protect traders by sending troops to ensure that Native Americans were not a threat.

Mormons Travel West One large group of settlers traveled to the West in search of religious freedom. In 1830 a young man named Joseph Smith founded the Church of Jesus Christ of Latter-day Saints in western New York. The members of his church became known as **Mormons**. Smith told his followers that he had found and translated a set of golden tablets containing religious teachings. The writings were called the *Book of Mormon.*

Church membership grew rapidly, but certain beliefs and practices caused Mormons to be persecuted. For example, beginning in the 1850s some Mormon men practiced polygamy—a practice in which one man is married to several women at the same time. The church outlawed this practice in 1890.

In the early 1830s Smith and his growing number of converts left New York. Many traveled on the recently completed Erie Canal and Lake Erie to Ohio, where they set up new communities. Later, they moved on and

This Mormon family took part in an early-1900s celebration of the pioneers who made the great trek along the Mormon Trail to Utah.

established communities in Missouri and Illinois. Eventually, these communities failed. The Illinois community collapsed after an anti-Mormon mob murdered Smith in 1844. Following Smith's murder, **Brigham Young** became head of the Mormon Church. Young chose what is now Utah as the group's new home, and thousands of Mormons took the Mormon Trail to the area near the Great Salt Lake, where they prospered. By 1860 there were about 40,000 Mormons in Utah.

Summary and Preview Some of the first Americans to move West were fur traders and trappers. Settlers soon followed. In the next lesson you will learn about America's continued westward expansion.

Reading Check
Summarize How did settlers travel west, and what challenges did they face on their journey?

Lesson 1 Assessment

Review Ideas, Terms, and People

1. **a. Identify** Who helped to open up the land west of the Appalachians by building the Wilderness Road?

   b. Explain Why were New Orleans and the Mississippi River important to settlers in the West?

2. **a. Summarize** Why was the Louisiana Purchase important to the United States?

   b. Describe What areas did the Lewis and Clark expedition and the Zebulon Pike and John C. Frémont expeditions explore?

   c. Draw Conclusions Why were Meriwether Lewis and William Clark chosen to lead the exploration of the Louisiana Purchase?

3. **a. Identify** Who established one of the first American settlements in Oregon Country?

   b. Describe What were the lives of mountain men like?

4. **a. Identify** What was the Oregon Trail?

   b. Elaborate Would you have chosen to leave your home to travel West? Why?

c. Summarize What difficulties led Mormons to move to Utah?

Critical Thinking

5. **Sequence** In this lesson you learned about the westward expansion of the United States. Create a graphic organizer like the one below to rank the three most important effects of the Louisiana Purchase, from most important to least important, and explain why you chose that order.

Importance	Why
1.	
2.	
3.	

6. **Draw Conclusions** What challenges did the westward journey present for settlers?

7. **Make Predictions** What effects do you think westward migration of the mid-1800s would have on Native Americans?

History and Geography

America's Growth by 1820

In 1803 the United States made the biggest land purchase in its history—the Louisiana Purchase. With this purchase, the country stretched west all the way to the Rocky Mountains. In 1819 the United States acquired Florida from Spain, gaining even more new territory. By 1820 the young American republic had roughly doubled in size, as you can see on the map. Explorers, traders, and settlers began to pour into the new lands in search of wealth, land, and a place to call home.

— 50°N

British Territory

Claimed by United States, ceded to Great Britain in 1818

49th Parallel

Oregon Country Both the United States and Great Britain claimed Oregon Country.

Oregon Country

R O C K Y   M O U N T A I N S

42nd Parallel

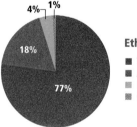

America's Population, 1820: 10.1 million

1%
4%
18%
77%

Ethnic Groups, 1820
- ■ White/European
- ■ African American
- ■ Native American
- ■ Other

— 30°N

PACIFIC OCEAN

Spanish Territory

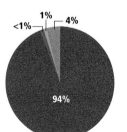

1%
<1%
4%
94%

Religions, 1820
- ■ Protestant
- ■ Jewish
- ■ Catholic
- ■ Other

Louisiana Purchase, 1803

Claimed by United States and Great Britain, 1818

Convention of 1818

From Britain to United States, 1818

Adams-Onís Treaty of 1819

From Spain to United States, 1819

| 0 | 150 | 300 Miles |
| 0 | 150 | 300 Kilometers |

130°W   120°W   110°W

Early Traders Soon after Lewis and Clark explored the Louisiana Territory, American fur traders and trappers began setting up trading posts there. Many of these posts later became towns as more settlers arrived.

Through the Gaps Settlers crossed the Appalachians through valleys called gaps. In time, roads were built through the gaps, making it easier for settlers to head West.

Unorganized Territory

Missouri River

Missouri Territory

Arkansas Territory

Red River

Mississippi River

Delaware Gap

APPALACHIAN MTS

Cumberland Gap

ATLANTIC OCEAN

40°N

N
W   E
S

The Mighty Mississippi The Mississippi River was the great highway of the United States. Americans west of the Appalachians shipped farm goods and supplies up and down the Mississippi and to its major port, New Orleans.

Louisiana   New Orleans

Gulf of Mexico

Unorganized Territory (Florida)

70°W

Interpret Maps

1. **Movement** In which directions did the United States expand before 1820?

2. **Region** Based on the map, why do you think the United States was interested in claiming Oregon Country?

Boom Times in the West

The Big Idea

American settlers dramatically changed the western frontier as they began to tame the land.

Main Ideas

- Valuable deposits of gold and silver in the West created opportunities for wealth and brought more settlers to the region.
- The cattle industry thrived on the Great Plains, supplying beef to the East.
- The transcontinental railroad succeeded in linking the eastern and western United States.

Key Terms

frontier
Comstock Lode
boomtowns
Cattle Kingdom
cattle drive
Chisholm Trail
Pony Express
transcontinental railroad
standard time

If YOU were there . . .

You are a cowboy in Texas in 1875. You love life on the open range, the quiet nights, and the freedom. You even like the hard work of the long cattle drives to Kansas. But you know that times are changing. Homesteaders are moving in and fencing off their lands. Some of the older cowboys say it's time to settle down and buy a small ranch. You hope that they're not right.

What would make you give up a cowboy's life?

Mining Boom Brings Growth

During the years surrounding the Civil War, most Americans had thought of the Great Plains and other western lands as the Great American Desert. In the years following the Civil War, Americans witnessed the rapid growth of the U.S. population and the spread of settlements throughout the West. With the admission of the state of California to the Union in 1850, the western boundary of the American **frontier**—an undeveloped area—had reached the Pacific Ocean.

The frontier changed dramatically as more and more people moved westward. Settlers built homes, fenced off land, and laid out ranches and farms. Miners, ranchers, and farmers remade the landscape of the West as they adapted to their new surroundings. The geography of the West was further changed by the development and expansion of a large and successful railroad industry that moved the West's natural resources to

Hydraulic Mining
Miners used high-powered water jets to blast earth from a hillside in order to expose the gold in the rock.

eastern markets. Gold and silver were the most valuable natural resources, and mining companies used the growing railroad network to bring these precious metals to the East.

Big Business Most of the precious metals were located in western Nevada. In 1859 miner Henry Comstock discovered a huge deposit of gold and silver in Nevada that became called the **Comstock Lode**. The deposit was incredibly rich

Posters like this one were designed to persuade people to move West.

and deep. In just the first year after its discovery, the Comstock Lode lured thousands of California miners to Nevada. Over the next 20 years, the Comstock Lode produced more than $500 million worth of gold and silver.

Expensive equipment was needed to remove the silver and gold that were trapped within quartz rock. Larger mining companies bought up land claims from miners who could not afford this machinery. As a result, mining became a big business in the West.

As companies dug bigger and deeper mines, the work became more dangerous. Miners had to use unsafe equipment, such as elevator platforms without protective walls. They worked in dark tunnels and breathed hot, stuffy air. They suffered from lung disease caused by dusty air. Miners often were injured or killed by poorly planned explosions or by cave-ins. Fire was also a great danger. Mining was therefore one of the most dangerous jobs in the country. In the West, worries about safety and pay led miners to form several unions in the 1860s.

Settlers People from all over the world came to work in the western mines. Some miners came from the eastern United States. Others emigrated from Europe, Central and South America, and Asia. Many Mexican immigrants and Mexican Americans were experienced miners. They were skilled in assaying, or testing, the contents of valuable ore. One newspaper reporter wrote, "Here were congregated the most varied elements of humanity . . . belonging to almost every nationality and every status of life."

New Towns Mining booms also produced **boomtowns**, communities that grew suddenly when a mine opened. They disappeared just as quickly when the mine closed. The California town of Bodie, located just southeast of Lake Tahoe, provides a vivid illustration of a mining boomtown. In the early 1870s it was a mining camp with just a handful of inhabitants. The discovery of a rich vein of gold in the late 1870s drew thousands. Within months, Bodie had become a bustling town of some 8,000 people. It had a railroad station, a school, two banks, three newspapers, two churches, and dozens of saloons. Once the gold in the mine was worked out, however, Bodie went into an equally rapid decline. By 1900 the population was less than 1,000.

Few women or families lived in even the most bustling boomtowns. "I was never so lonely and homesick in all my life," wrote one young woman. The women who did settle there washed, cooked, made clothes, and chopped wood. They also raised families, established schools, and wrote for newspapers. Their work helped turn some boomtowns into successful, permanent towns.

Reading Check
Summarize What risks did miners face?

Cattle Ranching in the West

The cattle industry was another area of rapid growth. Following the Civil War, a growing economy and population created a greater demand for beef in the East. Cattle worth $3 to $6 each in Texas could be sold for $38 each in Kansas. In New York, they could be sold for $80 each. The most popular breed of cattle was the longhorn. The longhorn breed spread quickly throughout western Texas. Because these animals needed very little water and could survive harsh weather, they were well suited to the dry, desert-like environment of western Texas. But how could Texas ranchers move the longhorns to eastern markets?

In 1867 businessman Joseph McCoy discovered a solution. He built pens for cattle in the small town of Abilene, Kansas. The Kansas Pacific Railroad line went through Abilene. As a result, cattle could be shipped by rail from there. Soon, countless Texas ranchers were making the trip north to Abilene to sell their herds of cattle.

Around the same time, cattle ranching began to expand in the Midwest. The vast open range of the Great Plains from Texas to Canada, where many ranchers raised cattle in the late 1800s, became known as the **Cattle Kingdom**. Ranchers grazed huge herds on public land called the open range. The land had once been occupied by Plains Indians and buffalo herds.

Importance of Cowboys The workers who took care of the ranchers' cattle were known as cowhands or cowboys. They adopted many techniques and tools from vaqueros (bah-KER-ohs), Mexican ranch hands who cared for cattle and horses. From vaqueros came the western saddle and the lariat, a rope used for lassoing cattle. The cowboys also borrowed the vaqueros' boot. Its narrow toe fit easily into the riding stirrup, and the high heel hooked the stirrup for stability. Cowboys adopted and changed the vaqueros' broad felt hat, turning it into the familiar high-peaked cowboy hat.

One of the cowboy's most important and dangerous duties was the **cattle drive**. On these long journeys, cowboys herded cattle to the market or to the northern Plains for grazing. These long drives usually lasted several months and covered hundreds of miles. Workdays on the drive were long—often up to 15 hours—and sometimes very dull. Excitement came with events such as stampedes. Frightened by a sudden noise such as a thunderclap, the whole herd would take off running wildly. Bringing the herd under control was dangerous and hard work. The **Chisholm Trail**, which ran from San Antonio, Texas, to the cattle town of Abilene, Kansas, was one of the earliest and most popular routes for cattle drives. It was blazed, or marked, by Texas cowboy Jesse Chisholm in the late 1860s.

At times, rowdy cowboys made life in cattle towns rough and violent. There were rarely shoot-outs in the street, but there often was disorderly behavior. Law officials such as Wyatt Earp became famous for keeping the peace in cattle towns.

End of the Open Range As the cattle business boomed, ranchers faced more competition for use of the open range. Farmers began to buy range

Myth and Reality in the Wild West

No episode in American history has given rise to as many myths as the Wild West. Writers of dime novels, popular in the East, helped create the myths in the years after the Civil War. Even today, popular books, television shows, and movies continue to portray the West in ways that are more myth than reality.

Myth: The cowboy was a free-spirited individual.

Reality: Most cowboys were employees. Many joined labor unions and even went on strike.

Myth: Western cow towns were wild places where cowboys had gunfights, and there was little law and order.

Reality: Most were orderly places with active law enforcement. Showdowns rarely, if ever, occurred.

Myth: Almost all cowboys were Anglo Americans.

Reality: About 25 percent of cowboys were African Americans, and 12 percent were Hispanic. Some Native Americans also worked as cowhands.

African American cowboy Nat Love (above); Marshal Wyatt Earp (left)

land on the Great Plains, where cattle had once grazed. Small ranchers also began competing with large ranchers for land. Then in 1874, Joseph Glidden's invention of barbed wire allowed westerners to fence off large amounts of land cheaply. The competition between farmers, large ranchers, and small ranchers increased. This competition led to range wars, or fights for access to land.

Making matters worse, in 1885 and 1886, disaster struck the Cattle Kingdom. The huge cattle herds on the Plains had eaten most of the prairie grass. Unusually severe winters in both years made the ranching situation even worse. Thousands of cattle died, and many ranchers were ruined financially. The Cattle Kingdom had come to an end.

The Transcontinental Railroad

As more Americans began moving West, the need to send goods and information between the East and West increased. Americans searched for ways to improve communication and travel across the country.

In 1860 a system of messengers on horseback called the **Pony Express** began to carry the mail West. The Pony Express operated from St. Joseph, Missouri, to Sacramento, California, a route of almost 2,000 miles. The business purchased over 400 horses, and riders used a relay system, switching horses at stations 10 to 15 miles apart. The Pony Express cut mail delivery time in half, from three weeks to ten days. The completion of a telegraph line to California in 1861, which sent messages much faster, quickly put the Pony Express out of business.

Reading Check
Draw Conclusions
Why did the Cattle Kingdom come to an end?

The Pony Express mail system helped speed up communication across the United States.

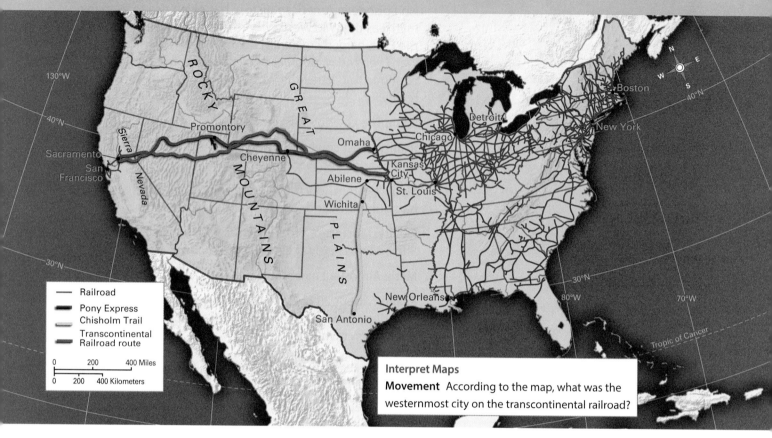

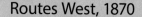

Explore ONLINE!

Interpret Maps

Movement According to the map, what was the westernmost city on the transcontinental railroad?

Some Americans wanted to build a **transcontinental railroad**—a railroad that would cross the continent and connect the East to the West. The federal government, therefore, passed the Pacific Railway Acts in 1862 and in 1864. These acts gave railroad companies loans and large land grants that could be sold to pay for construction costs. Congress had granted more than 131 million acres of public land to railroad companies. In exchange, the government asked the railroads to carry U.S. mail and troops at a lower cost. Many railroad companies were inspired to begin laying miles of track.

Great Race Two companies, the Central Pacific and the Union Pacific, led the race to complete the transcontinental railroad. In February 1863 the Central Pacific began building east from Sacramento, California. At the end of the year, the Union Pacific started building west from Omaha, Nebraska.

The Union Pacific hired thousands of railroad workers, particularly Irish immigrants. Chinese immigrants made up some 85 percent of the Central Pacific workforce. The railroad's part-owner Leland Stanford praised them, but he paid them less than other laborers. Chinese crews also were given the most dangerous tasks and had to work longer hours than other railroad laborers. They took the job, however, because the $30 a month that the Central Pacific paid was as much as ten times what they could earn in China.

Railroad companies faced many geographic challenges. For example, workers for Central Pacific struggled to cross the Sierra Nevada mountain range in California. Breaking apart its rock formations required setting carefully controlled explosions using large amounts of blasting powder and the explosive nitroglycerin. And in the winter of 1866, snowdrifts more than 60 feet high trapped and killed dozens of workers. Faced with these obstacles, the Central Pacific took four years to lay the first 115 miles of track.

Meanwhile, Union Pacific workers faced harsh weather on the Great Plains. In addition, the company pressured them to work at a rapid pace—at times laying 250 miles of track in six months.

For both railroad companies, providing food and supplies for workers was vital. This job became more difficult in remote areas. The railroad companies consequently often relied on local resources. Professional hunters, such as William "Buffalo Bill" Cody, shot thousands of buffalo to feed Union Pacific workers.

Golden Spike Congress required the two completed rail lines to connect at Promontory, Utah. On May 10, 1869, a golden spike was used to connect the railroad tie joining the two tracks. Alexander Toponce witnessed the event.

> "Governor Stanford, president of the Central Pacific, took the sledge [hammer], and the first time he struck he missed the spike and hit the rail. What a howl went up! Irish, Chinese, Mexicans, and everybody yelled with delight. 'He missed it' . . . Then Stanford tried it again and tapped the spike."
>
> —Alexander Toponce, from *Reminiscences of Alexander Toponce, Written by Himself*

The railroad companies were not finished, though. Following completion of the transcontinental railroad, they continued building railroads until the West was crisscrossed with rail lines.

The Central Pacific and Union Pacific connected their tracks at Promontory, Utah, in 1869, completing the transcontinental railroad.

Results of the Railroad The transcontinental railroad increased both economic growth and the population in the West. Railroad companies provided better transportation for people and goods. They also sold land to settlers, which encouraged people to move West. The development of the West brought about the railroad; however, it also would prove to be the beginning of the end of the Plains Indians' way of life.

New railroads helped businesses. Western timber companies, miners, ranchers, and farmers shipped wood, metals, meat, and grain East by railroad. In exchange, eastern businesses shipped manufactured goods to the West. As trade between regions increased, the idea that the U.S. economy was interdependent became more widespread.

Even perceptions of time became more formal as railroad schedules began to unite areas that before had existed under different times. Before the railroads, each community determined its own time, based on calculations about the sun's travels. This system, called "solar time," caused problems for people who scheduled trains crossing a long distance. The railroad companies addressed the issue by setting up **standard time**. This system divided the United States into four time zones.

Railroad companies encouraged people to invest in the railroads, which they did—sometimes unwisely. Speculation and the collapse of railroad owner Jay Cooke's banking firm helped start the Panic of 1873. Despite such setbacks, Americans remained interested in railroad investments. By 1890 there were about 164,000 more miles of track than in 1865. Railroads had become one of the biggest industries in the United States.

Reading Check
Find Main Ideas
How did the railroad affect the development of the West?

Summary and Preview In this lesson you learned about the increased settlement of the West. In the next lesson you will learn about conflicts with Native Americans.

Lesson 2 Assessment

Review Ideas, Terms, and People

1. **a. Recall** Why did Americans move West in the years following the Civil War?

   b. Draw Conclusions What effect did the discovery of the Comstock Lode have on the West?

   c. Evaluate Do you think women were important to the success of mining towns? Why or why not?

2. **a. Recall** What led to the cattle boom in the West?

   b. Analyze Why was there competition between ranchers and farmers to settle in the Great Plains?

   c. Evaluate What played the biggest role in ending the Cattle Kingdom? Why?

3. **a. Recall** When and where did the Union Pacific and Central Pacific lines meet?

   b. Describe What role did Irish and Chinese immigrants play in opening up the West?

   c. Make Generalizations How do you think the transcontinental railroad improved people's lives?

Critical Thinking

4. **Identify Cause and Effect** In this lesson you learned about the kinds of economic opportunities that people found in the West. Create a graphic organizer similar to the one below to list these opportunities and their effects.

Opportunity	Effect

Wars for the West

The Big Idea

Native Americans and the U.S. government came into conflict over land in the West.

Main Ideas

- As settlers moved to the Great Plains, they encountered the Plains Indians.

- Native Americans attempted to keep their lands through treaties with the U.S. government.

- Continued pressure from white settlement and government legislation brought the Plains Indians' traditional way of life to an end.

Key Terms and People

Treaty of Fort Laramie
reservations
Crazy Horse
Treaty of Medicine Lodge
buffalo soldiers
George Armstrong Custer
Sitting Bull
Battle of the Little Bighorn
Massacre at Wounded Knee
Long Walk
Chief Joseph
Geronimo
Ghost Dance
Sarah Winnemucca
assimilate
Dawes General Allotment Act

If YOU were there . . .

You are a member of the Sioux nation, living in Dakota Territory in 1875. These lands are sacred to your people, and the U.S. government has promised them to you. But now gold has been found here, and the government has ordered you to give up your land. Some Sioux leaders want to fight. Others say that it is of no use, that the soldiers will win.

Would you fight to keep your lands? Why?

Settlers Encounter the Plains Indians

As miners and settlers began crossing the Great Plains in the mid-1800s, they pressured the federal government for more access to western lands. To protect these travelers, U.S. officials sent agents to negotiate treaties with the Plains Indians.

Crazy Horse (Tashunka Witco) was a Sioux chief who fought to defend his people's way of life and resisted attempts to force the Sioux onto reservations.

The Plains Indians lived in the Great Plains, which stretch north into Canada and south into Texas. Indian groups such as the Apache and the Comanche lived in and around Texas and what is now Oklahoma. The Cheyenne and the Arapaho lived in different regions across the central Plains. The Pawnee lived in parts of Nebraska. To the north were the Sioux. These groups spoke many different languages. However, they used a common sign language to communicate and they shared a similar lifestyle.

Hunting Buffalo For survival, the Plains Indians depended on two animals—the horse and the buffalo. The Spanish brought horses to America in the 1500s. The Plains Indians learned to ride horses, and hunters used them to follow buffalo herds year-round. While on horseback, most Plains Indian hunters used a short bow and arrows to shoot buffalo from close range.

The Plains Indians used buffalo for food, shelter, clothing, utensils, and tools. Women dried buffalo meat to make

The Plains Indians depended on two animals—the horse and the buffalo.

jerky. They made tepees and clothing from buffalo hides, and cups and tools from buffalo horns. As one Sioux explained, "When our people killed a buffalo, all of the animal was utilized [used] in some manner; nothing was wasted." The Plains Indians prospered. By 1850 some 75,000 Native Americans lived on the Plains.

Struggle to Keep Land Miners and settlers were also increasing in numbers—and they wanted the Indians' land. The U.S. government tried to avoid disputes by negotiating the **Treaty of Fort Laramie**, the first major treaty between the U.S. government and Plains Indians. Two years later, several southern Plains nations signed a treaty at Fort Atkinson in Nebraska. These treaties recognized Indian claims to most of the Great Plains. They also allowed the United States to build forts and roads and to travel across Indian homelands. The U.S. government promised to pay for any damages to Indian lands.

The treaties did not keep the peace for long. In 1858 the discovery of gold in what is now Colorado brought thousands of miners to the West. They soon clashed with the Cheyenne and the Arapaho. In 1861 the U.S. government negotiated new treaties with Plains Indians. These treaties created **reservations**, areas of federal land set aside for Native Americans. The government expected Indians to stay on the reservations, which made hunting buffalo almost impossible.

Pioneers and miners continued to cross the Great Plains. Many miners used the Bozeman Trail. To protect them, the U.S. Army built forts along the trail, which ran through favored Sioux hunting grounds. The Sioux responded with war. In late 1866 a group led by **Crazy Horse**, an Oglala Sioux chief, ambushed and killed 81 cavalry troops.

In 1868 under the Second Treaty of Fort Laramie, the U.S. government agreed to close the Bozeman Trail and abandon the forts, and forced some of the Sioux onto reservations. The U.S. government also forced

Reading Check
Summarize What
was the federal policy
toward the Plains
Indians in the 1860s
and 1870s?

some of the southern Plains Indians to move off their land. In the 1867 **Treaty of Medicine Lodge**, most southern Plains Indians agreed to live on reservations. However, many Indians did not want to give up their hunting grounds. Fighting soon broke out between the Comanche and Texans. The U.S. Army and the Texas Rangers were unable to defeat the Comanche, so they cut off the Comanche's access to food and water. In 1875 the last of the Comanche war leaders surrendered.

Fighting on the Plains

In the northern Plains, Southwest, and Far West, Native Americans continued to resist being moved to and confined on reservations. The U.S. government sent troops into the area to force the Indians to leave. These troops included African American cavalry, who the Indians called **buffalo soldiers**—a term of honor, inspired by their short, curly hair, that compared their fighting spirit to that of the buffalo.

Battles on the Northern Plains As fighting on the southern Plains came to an end, new trouble started in the north. In 1874 Lieutenant Colonel

▶ Explore ONLINE!

Native American Land Loss in the West, 1850–1890

	1850–1870
	1870–1890
	Reservations in 1890
UTE	Native American group

0   200   400 Miles
0   200   400 Kilometers

Battles and Treaties of the Indian Wars

1 Treaties at Fort Laramie, 1851 and 1868

2 Treaty at Fort Atkinson, 1853

3 Sand Creek Massacre, 1864

4 Fetterman Massacre, 1866

5 Treaty of Medicine Lodge, 1867

6 Battle of the Little Bighorn, 1876

7 Battle of the Rosebud, 1876

8 Wounded Knee Massacre, 1890

Interpret Maps
Region In what regions did Native Americans lose land in the late 1800s?

The Native Americans are shown surrounding a small force of U.S. soldiers.

Custer is shown standing among his men as he fires.

The U.S. Army is shown on horseback in this drawing.

These horses have been captured by the Native Americans.

Two Views of a Historic Battle

Art historians have identified about 1,000 paintings of the Battle of the Little Bighorn. The painting at the top was painted in 1899. The drawing below it is one of the many colored-pencil drawings of the battle done by Amos Bad Heart Buffalo, who based his drawing on memories from Sioux warriors who participated in the battle.

Analyze Visuals
How do these paintings show the influences of different cultures?

George Armstrong Custer's soldiers discovered gold in the Black Hills of the Dakotas. **Sitting Bull**, a leader of the Lakota Sioux, protested U.S. demands for the land.

> "What treaty that the whites have kept has the red man broken? Not one. What treaty that the white man ever made with us have they kept? Not one."
>
> —Sitting Bull, quoted in *Life of Sitting Bull and the History of the Indian Wars of 1890–1891* by W. Fletcher Johnson

Apache leader Geronimo fought settlers on his land for more than 25 years—all the while avoiding permanent capture.

Other Sioux leaders listened to Sitting Bull and refused to give up land. During late 1875 and early 1876, many Sioux and Cheyenne warriors left their reservations. They united under the leadership of Sitting Bull and Crazy Horse. Their plan was to drive the intruders from the Black Hills. Custer was sent to force the Native Americans back onto their reservations.

On June 25, 1876, Custer's scouts found a large Sioux camp along the Little Bighorn River in Montana Territory. Leading about 200 of his soldiers, Custer raced ahead without waiting for any supporting forces. In the **Battle of the Little Bighorn**, Sioux and Cheyenne forces led by Crazy Horse surrounded and defeated Custer and his troops. Newspapers called the battle "Custer's Last Stand" because his entire command was killed. It was the worst defeat the U.S. Army suffered in the West. The Battle of the Little Bighorn was also the Sioux's last major victory in the Sioux Wars.

In 1881 Sitting Bull and a few followers returned from Canada where they had fled after Little Bighorn. They had run out of food during the hard winter. They joined the Sioux on Standing Rock Reservation in Dakota Territory.

Almost a decade later, in 1890, while following orders to arrest Sitting Bull, reservation police killed him. Many Sioux left the reservation in protest. Later that year, the U.S. Army shot and killed about 150 Sioux men, women, and children near Wounded Knee Creek in South Dakota. This **Massacre at Wounded Knee** was the last major military incident on the Great Plains.

Southwest The Navajo lived in what became Arizona and New Mexico. In 1863 the Navajo refused to settle on a reservation. In response, U.S. troops made raids on the Navajo's fields, homes, and livestock.

When the Navajo ran out of food and shelter, they started surrendering to the U.S. Army. In 1864 the army led Navajo captives on the **Long Walk**. On this brutal 300-mile march, the Navajo were forced to walk across the desert to a reservation in Bosque Redondo, New Mexico. Along the way, countless Navajo died.

Far West The United States had promised to let the peaceful Nez Percé keep their land in Oregon. Within a few years, however, the government ordered the Nez Percé to a reservation in what is now Idaho. A group of Nez Percé led by **Chief Joseph** resisted, and in 1877 left to seek refuge in Canada. For four months, they crossed more than 1,000 miles with army troops in pursuit. Near the border, U.S. troops overtook them and sent them to a reservation in what is now Oklahoma.

Final Battles By the 1880s, most Native Americans had stopped fighting. The Apache of the Southwest, however, continued to battle the U.S. Army. A Chiricahua Apache named **Geronimo** and his band led raids on both sides of the Arizona–Mexico border, avoiding capture for many years. In September 1886 Geronimo surrendered and was sent to an Apache internment camp in Florida. This ended the Apache armed resistance in the Southwest.

Reading Check
Contrast How did the Apache resistance differ from that of the Navajo?

A Way of Life Ends

By the 1870s many Native Americans lived on reservations, where land was usually not useful for farming or buffalo hunting. Many were starving.

A Paiute Indian named Wovoka began a religious movement, the **Ghost Dance**, that predicted the arrival of paradise for Native Americans. In this paradise, the buffalo herds would return and the settlers would disappear.

U.S. officials did not understand the meaning of the Ghost Dance. They feared it would lead to rebellion, so they tried to end the movement, which had spread to other groups, including the Sioux. After the massacre in 1890 at Wounded Knee, the Ghost Dance movement gradually died out.

In the late 1870s a Paiute Indian named **Sarah Winnemucca** called for reform—particularly of the reservation system. A writer, educator, and interpreter, she toured the country speaking on behalf of Native Americans. Her 1883 autobiography *Life Among the Paiutes* is one of the

---

BIOGRAPHY

Chief Joseph c. 1840–1904

Chief Joseph became leader of the Nez Percé in 1871. He led his people in an effort to hold onto their homeland and to avoid war with the United States. In 1877, when the U.S. government ordered the Nez Percé to relocate

to a reservation, Chief Joseph at first agreed, but then was forced to flee. He attempted to escape into Canada with about 750 of his people. On a courageous journey across Idaho, Montana, Oregon, and Washington, they defeated pursuing troops who greatly outnumbered them. Traveling with families, and low on supplies, the Nez Percé managed to evade the U.S. Army for four months. Ultimately though, Chief Joseph saw that resistance was futile. Upon his surrender, he gave a speech that has become one of the most famous in American history.

"I am tired of fighting. Our chiefs are killed. . . . The old men are all dead. . . . It is cold, and we have no blankets. The little children are freezing to death. My people, some of them, have run away to the hills, and have no blankets, no food. No one knows where they are—perhaps freezing to death. I want to have time to look for my children, and see how many of them I can find. Maybe I shall find them among the dead. Hear me, my chiefs! I am tired. My heart is sick and sad. From where the sun now stands I will fight no more forever."

—Chief Joseph, October 5, 1877

Identify Cause and Effect
What brought suffering to Chief Joseph and his people?

Sarah Winnemucca spoke out for the fair treatment of her people.

Reading Check
Summarize
How did reformers try to influence Native Americans' lives?

most significant accounts of traditional Native American culture. Writer Helen Hunt Jackson published a book in 1881 that pushed for reform of U.S. Indian policy. Titled *A Century of Dishonor,* it described the mistreatment of many Native American groups in an attempt to force the government to establish fairer policies.

Some reformers believed that Native Americans should **assimilate** by giving up traditional ways and adopting Anglo-American gender and family roles, cultural and social practices, and language. The **Dawes General Allotment Act** of 1887 tried to lessen traditional influences on Indian society by making land ownership private for male-headed households rather than shared communally. The act also promised—but failed to deliver—U.S. citizenship to Native Americans. After breaking up reservation land, the government sold the acreage remaining. The act took about two-thirds of Indian land.

The U.S. government also sent many Native American children to boarding schools in an effort to "Americanize" them. The children were dressed in European-style clothes, learned English, and often spent part of the day farming or doing other work. They were discouraged from practicing their own culture or speaking their own language. Many were separated from their families for years at a time.

Summary and Preview In this lesson you read about conflict in the settlement of the West. In the next lesson you will learn more about Great Plains settlers.

Lesson 3 Assessment

Review Ideas, Terms, and People

1. a. **Describe** What animals did Plains Indians depend on, and how did they use those animals?
   b. **Analyze** How did U.S. policy toward the Plains Indians change in the late 1850s?
   c. **Elaborate** Would you have agreed to move to a reservation? Why or why not?
2. a. **Describe** What events led to the Battle of the Little Bighorn?
   b. **Elaborate** Why do you think most Indian groups eventually stopped resisting the United States?
3. a. **Describe** How did the Dawes General Allotment Act affect American Indians?

b. **Predict** What effect do you think the Massacre at Wounded Knee would have on relations between Plains Indians and the United States?

Critical Thinking

4. **Sequence** In this lesson you learned about the major events surrounding the loss of land rights of Native Americans. Create a timeline similar to the one below to organize the events in sequence.

1851   1864 1867   1887

★
Farming and Populism

The Big Idea

Settlers on the Great Plains created new communities and a unique political movement.

Main Ideas

- Many Americans started new lives on the Great Plains.
- Economic challenges led to the creation of farmers' political groups.
- By the 1890s the western frontier had come to an end.

Key Terms and People

Homestead Act
Morrill Act
Exodusters
sodbusters
dry farming
Annie Bidwell
National Grange
deflation
William Jennings Bryan
Populist Party

If YOU were there . . .

You are a female schoolteacher in Wisconsin in 1880. You live and teach in a small town, but you grew up on a farm and are used to hard work. Now you are thinking about moving West to claim free land from the government. You could teach in a school there, too. You think it would be an exciting adventure, but your family is horrified that a single woman would move West on her own.

Would you decide to become a homesteader?

New Lives on the Plains

In 1862 Congress passed two important land grant acts that helped open the West to settlers. The **Homestead Act** gave government-owned land to small farmers. Any adult who was a U.S. citizen or planned to become one could receive 160 acres of land. In exchange, homesteaders promised to live on the land for five years. The **Morrill Act** granted more than 17 million acres of federal land to the states. The act required each state to sell this land and to use the money to build colleges to teach agriculture and engineering.

Pioneers like this family often lived in houses made of sod because there were few trees for lumber on the Plains.

This family of African Americans moved to the West in order to build new lives after the Civil War.

Settling the Plains People from all over the country moved West. Many farming families moved from areas where farmland was becoming scarce or expensive, such as New England. Many single women moved West. The Homestead Act granted land to unmarried women, which was unusual for the time.

In the late 1870s, large numbers of African Americans began to move West. Some fled the South because of violence and repression. The end of Reconstruction in 1877 led to harsh new segregation laws. Also, the withdrawal of federal troops left African Americans unprotected from attacks by such groups as the Ku Klux Klan. Benjamin "Pap" Singleton, a former slave from Tennessee, inspired others. Born in Nashville in 1809, Singleton fled slavery several times. Eventually he got to the North and settled in Detroit. There, he helped runaway slaves escape to Canada. After the Civil War, he returned to Tennessee. He wanted to help freed African Americans buy farmland. However, white landowners refused to sell. So he urged African Americans to leave the South and build their own communities in Kansas and elsewhere in the West.

By 1879 some 20,000 southern African Americans had moved to Kansas. Many others settled in Missouri, Indiana, and Illinois. These African American migrants were known as **Exodusters** because they had made a mass exodus, or departure, from the South.

The promise of free land also drew thousands of Europeans to the West. Scandinavians from Norway, Sweden, Denmark, and Finland came to the northern Great Plains in the 1870s. Many Irish who had helped to build the railroads decided to settle on the Plains. Russians also came to the Plains, bringing with them their experience of farming on the vast steppes, or grasslands, of their homeland. Germans and Czechs created many small farming communities on the Plains, especially in Texas.

Letter from the Plains, 1863

In a letter to her family in Norway, immigrant Gro Svendsen describes her new life as a farmer on the plains of Iowa.

> *"I remember I used to wonder when I heard that it would be impossible to keep the milk here as we did at home. Now I have learned that it is indeed impossible because of the heat here in the summertime . . . It's difficult, too, to preserve the butter. One must pour brine [salt water] over it or salt it.*
>
> *   The thunderstorms are so violent that one might think it was the end of the world . . . Quite often the lightning strikes down both cattle and people, damages property, and splinters sturdy oak trees into many pieces."*
>
> —quoted in *Frontier Mother: The Letters of Gro Svendsen*

Analyze Historical Sources
What might be some of the differences between Norway and Svendsen's new home in Iowa?

Laura Ingalls Wilder (right) wrote the *Little House on the Prairie* series based on her childhood in a settler family.

Farming the Plains Plains farmers had many unique challenges. The seasons were extreme. Weather could be harsh. Also, the root-filled sod, or dirt, beneath the Plains grass was very tough. The hard work of breaking up the sod earned Plains farmers the nickname **sodbusters**.

In the 1890s western Plains farmers began **dry farming**, a new method of farming that shifted the focus away from water-dependent crops such as corn. Instead, farmers grew more hardy crops like red wheat. In addition, new inventions helped Plains farmers meet some of the challenges of frontier life. A steel plow invented by John Deere in 1837 and improved upon by James Oliver in 1868 sliced through the tough sod of the prairie. Windmills adapted to the Plains pumped water from deep wells to the surface. Barbed wire allowed farmers to fence in land and livestock. Reapers made the harvesting of crops much easier, and threshers helped farmers to separate grain or seed from straw.

These inventions also made farm work more efficient. During the late 1800s, farmers greatly increased their crop production. They shipped their harvest east by train. From there, crops were shipped overseas. The Great Plains soon became known as the breadbasket of the world.

Building Communities Women were an important force in the settlement of the frontier. They joined in the hard work of farming and ranching and helped build communities out of the widely spaced farms and small towns. Their role in founding communities **facilitated** a strong voice in public affairs. Wyoming women, for example, were granted the vote in the new state's constitution, which was approved in 1869. **Annie Bidwell**, one of the founders of Chico, California, used her influence to support a variety of moral and social causes such as women's suffrage and temperance.

Academic Vocabulary
facilitate to make easier

Reading Check
Compare and
Contrast How were
settlers' lives alike and
different from their
lives in the East?

Many early settlers found life on their remote farms to be extremely difficult. Farmers formed communities so that they could assist one another in times of need. One of the first things that many pioneer communities did was establish a local church and school.

Children helped with many chores around the farm. Author Laura Ingalls Wilder was one of four children in a pioneer family. Wilder's books about settlers' lives on the prairie are still popular today.

Farmers' Political Groups

From 1860 to 1900, the U.S. population more than doubled. To feed this growing population, the number of farms tripled. With modern machines, farmers in 1900 could harvest a bushel of wheat almost 20 times faster than they could in 1830.

Farm Incomes Fall The combination of more farms and greater productivity, however, led to overproduction. Overproduction resulted in lower prices for crops. As their incomes decreased, many farmers found it difficult to pay bills. Farmers who could not make their mortgage payments lost their farms and homes. Many of these homeless farmers became tenant farmers who worked land owned by others. By 1880 one-fourth of all farms were rented by tenants, and the number continued to grow.

The National Grange Many farmers blamed businesspeople—wholesalers, brokers, grain buyers, and especially railroad owners—for making money at their expense. As economic conditions worsened, farmers began to follow the example of other workers. They formed associations to protect and help their interests.

Agricultural Supply and Demand

Connect to Economics The amount of goods available for sale is the supply. The willingness and ability of consumers to buy goods is called demand. The law of supply and demand says that when supply increases or demand decreases, prices fall. By contrast, when supply decreases or demand rises, prices rise.

What happened to the price of wheat as the supply increased?

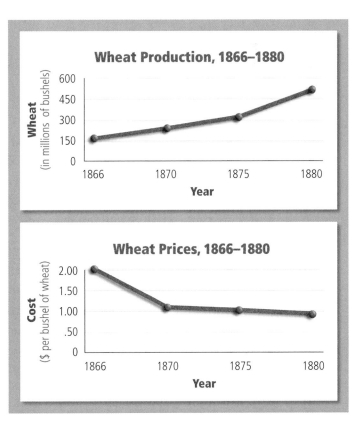

One such organization was founded by Oliver Hudson Kelley, who toured the South in 1866 for the U.S. Department of Agriculture. Kelley saw firsthand how the country's farmers suffered. Afterward, Kelley and several government clerks formed the National Grange of the Patrons of Husbandry in 1867. The **National Grange** was a social and educational organization for farmers. (*Grange* is an old word for "granary.") Local chapters were quickly founded, and membership grew rapidly.

After the founding of the National Grange, other groups, including the Farmers' Alliance, formed to advance the interests of farmers.

The Grange campaigned for political candidates who supported farmers' goals. The organization also called for laws that regulated rates charged by railroads. The U.S. Supreme Court ruled in 1877 that the government could regulate railroads because they affected the public interest. In 1886 the Court said that the federal government could only regulate companies doing business across state lines. Rate regulation for railroad lines within states fell to the state governments.

In February 1887 Congress passed the Interstate Commerce Act, providing national regulations over trade between states and creating the Interstate Commerce Commission to ensure fair railroad rates. However, the commission lacked power to enforce its regulations.

Free Silver Debate Money issues also caused problems for farmers. Many farmers hoped that help would come from new laws affecting the money supply.

Since 1873 the United States had been on the gold standard, meaning that all paper money had to be backed by gold in the treasury. As a result, the money supply grew more slowly than the nation's population and led to **deflation**—a decrease in the money supply and overall lower prices. One solution was to allow the unlimited coining of silver and to back paper currency with silver. This was the position of those in the Free Silver movement.

During the late 1870s, there was a great deal of support for the Free Silver movement. Many farmers began backing political candidates who favored free silver coinage. One such candidate was **William Jennings Bryan** of Nebraska.

The two major political parties, however, largely ignored the money issue. After the election of 1888, the Republican-controlled Congress passed the Sherman Silver Purchase Act. The act increased the amount of silver purchased for coinage. However, this did not help farmers as much as they had hoped.

Populist Party To have greater power, many farmers organized to elect candidates who would help them. These political organizations became known as the Farmers' Alliances.

In the 1890 elections the Alliances were a strong political force. State and local wins raised farmers' political hopes. At a conference in Cincinnati, Ohio, in 1891, Alliance leaders met with labor and reform groups. Then, at a convention in St. Louis in February 1892, the Alliances formed a new national political party.

William Jennings Bryan
1860–1925

William Jennings Bryan was born in Illinois but moved to Nebraska when he finished law school. He was elected Nebraska's first Democratic Congress member in 1890. Through his political campaigns and work as a newspaper editor, he became one of the best-known supporters of Populist ideas. After a dramatic speech at the 1896 Democratic National Convention, Bryan was nominated for the presidency. He was the youngest presidential candidate up to that time. Although he lost the election, he continued to be an influential speaker and political leader. Many of the reforms that he fought for in the late 1800s, such as an eight-hour workday and woman suffrage, later became law.

Make Inferences
Why was Bryan's support of Populist ideas important?

The new party was called the **Populist Party**, and it called for the government to own railroads and telephone and telegraph systems. It also favored the "free and unlimited coinage of silver." To gain the votes of workers, the Populists backed an eight-hour workday and limits on immigration.

The concerns of the Populists were soon put in the national spotlight. During the Panic of 1893, the U.S. economy experienced a crisis that some critics blamed on the shortage of gold. The failure of several major railroad companies also contributed to the economic problems.

The Panic of 1893 led more people to back the Populist call for economic reform. In 1896 the Republicans nominated William McKinley for president. McKinley was firmly against free coinage of silver. The Democrats nominated William Jennings Bryan, a strong supporter of the Free Silver movement.

The Populists had to decide between running their own candidate, and thus splitting the silver vote, or supporting Bryan. They decided to support Bryan. The Republicans had a well-financed campaign, and they won the election. McKinley's victory in 1896 marked the end of both the Populist Party and the Farmers' Alliances.

Reading Check
Summarize Why did farmers, laborers, and reformers join to form the Populist Party?

End of the Frontier

By 1870 only small portions of the Great Plains remained unsettled. For most of the next two decades, this land remained open range.

In March 1889, government officials announced that homesteaders could file claims on land in what is now the state of Oklahoma. This land had belonged to Creek and Seminole Indians. Within a month, about 50,000 people rushed to Oklahoma to stake their claims.

In all, settlers claimed more than 11 million acres of former Indian land in the famous Oklahoma land rush. This huge wave of pioneers was the

Oklahoma Land Rush

- The rush began at noon on April 22, 1889.
- Some witnesses said they could feel the ground shake as 50,000 people raced to claim land.
- Single women and widows could claim land on an equal basis with men.
- Many settlers were dismayed to find some people had claimed land before the rush legally began. These people were called *sooners*.

Guthrie, Oklahoma

Reading Check
Find Main Ideas
What event signaled the closing of the frontier?

last chapter of the westward movement. From the time it began gathering information, the U.S. Census Bureau had mapped a "frontier line" along the edge of western population. The 1890 census showed that more than 20 million people lived between the Mississippi River and the Pacific coast. "There can hardly be said to be a frontier line," a Bureau report stated. The disappearance of the "line" is considered the closing of the frontier.

Summary and Preview In this lesson you read about the challenges settlers in the West faced. Despite these difficulties, the promise of open land and a fresh start continued to lure Americans westward.

Lesson 4 Assessment

Review Ideas, Terms, and People

1. **a. Describe** What groups settled in the Great Plains?

   b. Explain How did the U.S. government make lands available to western settlers?

   c. Elaborate Would you have chosen to settle on the frontier? Why or why not?

2. **a. Recall** What was the goal of the National Grange?

   b. Make Inferences Why did the Populist Party want the government to own railroads and telegraph and telephone systems?

   c. Evaluate Do you think farmers were successful in bringing about economic and political change? Explain.

3. **a. Recall** What was the Oklahoma land rush?

   b. Explain Why did the frontier cease to exist in the United States?

Critical Thinking

4. **Compare and Contrast** In this lesson you learned about the reasons for the rise of populism in the United States. Create a table similar to the one below to explain why Populists sought the changes they did.

Change sought	Reason why

Social Studies Skills

Compare Migration Maps

Define the Skill

One of the best ways of using geography to learn history is by comparing maps. This skill allows you to see changes over time. It also helps you see relationships between one factor, such as population growth, and another factor, such as transportation routes or economic activities in an area.

Learn the Skill

Follow these steps to compare information on maps.

1. Apply basic map skills by reading the title and studying the legend and symbols for each map.

2. Note the date of each map and the area it covers. Maps compared for changes over time should include the same areas. Those used to look for relationships should have similar dates.

3. Note similarities or differences. Closely examine and compare each map's patterns and symbols.

4. Apply critical thinking skills. Make generalizations and draw conclusions about the relationships you find.

Practice the Skill

Use the maps below to answer the following questions.

1. What present-day state was unsettled by Americans in 1850 and almost completely settled in 1890?

2. Which other two present-day states show the most settlement by Americans from 1850 to 1890?

3. Why do you think the West coast was settled before the interior of the United States?

4. According to the maps, how might rivers have shaped the settlement of the West?

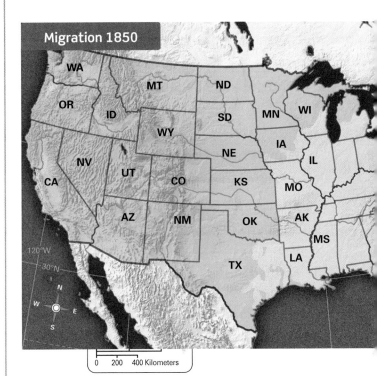

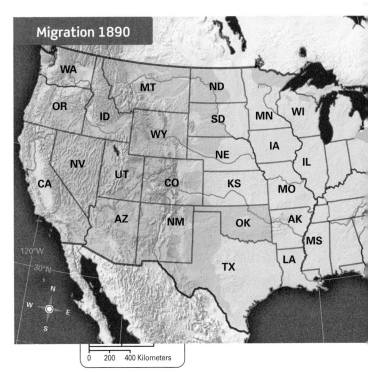

Module 3 Assessment

Review Vocabulary, Terms, and People

Complete each sentence by filling in the blank with the correct term or person.

1. In 1803 Congress approved the _____, which added former French territory in the West to the United States.

2. Members of the Church of Jesus Christ of Latter-day Saints were known as _____.

3. _____ were fur traders and trappers who lived west of the Rocky Mountains and in the Pacific Northwest.

4. The _____ Trail, which ran from Missouri to New Mexico, was an important route for trade between American and Mexican merchants

5. _____ lead the 7th Cavalry in the Battle of the Little Bighorn.

6. The _____ gave government-owned land to small farmers. In return the farmers had to live on the land for at least five years.

7. A Paiute Indian named _____ worked hard to reform the reservation system.

8. The _____ Trail was one of the most popular routes for cattle drives.

9. The huge deposit of gold and silver found in Nevada in 1859 was known as the _____.

10. Formed in 1867, the _____ was a social and educational organization for farmers.

Comprehension and Critical Thinking

Lesson 1

11. **a. Identify** Which routes did settlers use to move into the land west of the Appalachians?

   b. Draw Conclusions What are three ways in which the United States benefited from the Louisiana Purchase?

   c. Evaluate Do you think that Napoléon made a wise decision when he sold Louisiana to the United States? Explain your answer.

Lesson 2

12. **a. Recall** Why were many Americans eager to move to the western frontier?

   b. Analyze How did railroads and ranching change the landscape of the West?

   c. Elaborate In your opinion, which made the greatest changes to the West—mining, ranching, or railroads? Explain your answer.

Lesson 3

13. **a. Describe** What was life like for the Plains Indians before and after the arrival of large numbers of American settlers?

   b. Draw Conclusions Why did the spread of the Ghost Dance movement cause concern for U.S. officials?

   c. Elaborate What do you think about the reservation system established by the United States?

Lesson 4

14. **a. Identify** What political organizations did western farmers create? Why did farmers create these organizations?

   b. Analyze How did women participate in the settling of the American frontier?

   c. Predict How might the end of the frontier in the United States affect the nation?

Review Themes

15. **Geography** Through what geographic regions did the Lewis and Clark expedition travel?

16. **Geography** What geographic obstacles did miners, ranchers, and railroad workers face in the West?

17. **Science and Technology** What types of technology did farmers on the Great Plains use, and how did it benefit them?

Reading Skills

Ask Questions to Understand *Use the Reading Skills taught in this module to answer the question about the reading selection below.*

For survival, Plains Indians depended on two animals—the horse and the buffalo. The Spanish brought horses to America in the 1500s. Plains Indians learned to ride horses, and hunters used them to follow buffalo herds year-round.

18. Write two or three questions you have about the information in the passage above. Remember to use the five Ws—Who? What? When? Where? and Why?

Social Studies Skills

Compare Migration Maps *Use the Social Studies Skills taught in this module to answer the question about the map below.*

19. According to the map above, for what reasons did settlers migrate to the West?
    a. for mining, ranching, and farming
    b. for jobs in manufacturing
    c. for the homes in the major cities there
    d. for the fishing industry

Focus on Writing

20. **Write a Job Description** Write a job description for a cowboy. Note the skills required for the job and the equipment needed. Also outline a typical workday for a cowboy. To add interest to your description, include appropriate visual materials.

Lewis and Clark

In 1804, Meriwether Lewis, William Clark, and the 33-man Corps of Discovery began an 8,000-mile journey across uncharted territory. Under orders from President Thomas Jefferson, the expedition mapped a route across the Louisiana Purchase to the Pacific Ocean. From St. Louis, Missouri, they traveled west up the Missouri River, then across the Rocky Mountains, and to the Pacific. They met Native American peoples and cataloged geography, plants, and animals. Not only was their mission one of history's greatest explorations; it also secured an American claim to the Pacific coast and helped inspire millions to migrate west.

Explore entries from Lewis's journal and other primary sources online. You can find a wealth of information, video clips, activities, and more through your online textbook.

". . . the Indian woman recognized the point of a high plain to our right which she informed us was not very distant from the summer retreat of her nation on a river beyond the mountains which runs to the west."

— Meriwether Lewis

"Lewis's Journal, Entry 1"
Read an excerpt from Meriwether Lewis's journal that details Sacagawea's assistance during the journey.

Underway on the Missouri
Watch the video to see how the Corps of Discovery sailed up the Missouri River to begin their expedition.

Making Friends Upriver
Watch the video to see which Native American peoples the Corps met and traded with as they made their journey west.

The Shores of the Pacific
Watch the video to see how the Corps tried to adapt to a different climate and the new peoples that they met along the Pacific coast.

Module 4

The Industrial Age

★

Essential Question
How revolutionary was the Second Industrial Revolution?

About the Photo: Technological advances changed city life in the United States.

In this module you will learn about the new inventions of the late 1800s. You will also read about how life and business changed because of these inventions.

What You Will Learn . . .

▶ *Explore ONLINE!*

VIDEOS, including...
- Skyscrapers
- The Steel Industry
- Henry Ford and the Model T
- The Wright Brothers Controversy
- John D. Rockefeller: The Standard Oil Trust
- Homestead Strike

☑ Document-Based Investigations

☑ Graphic Organizers

☑ Interactive Games

☑ Animation: Early Refrigerated Railroad Cars

☑ Image Carousel: The Age of Inventions

☑ Interactive Map: Major Labor Strikes, Late 1800s

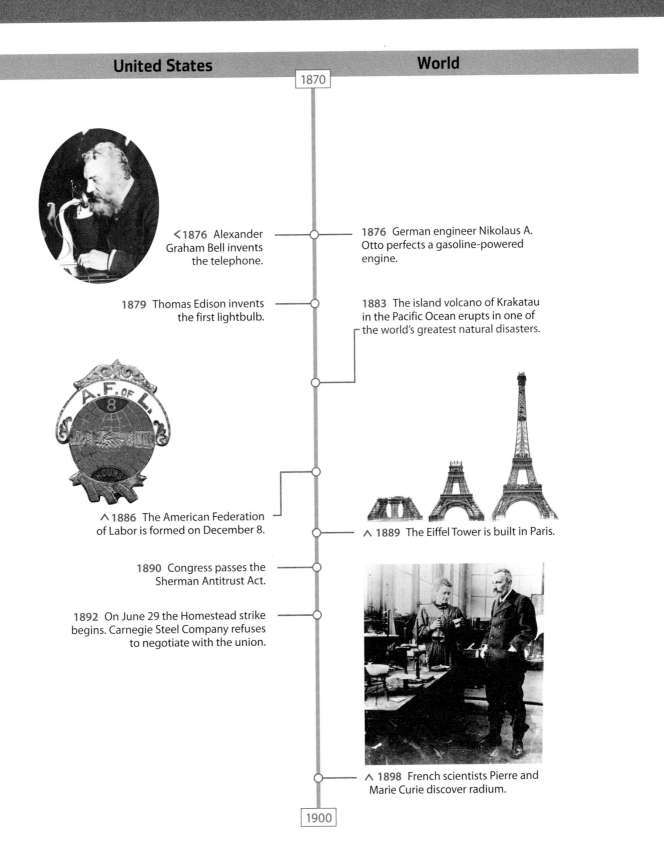

United States

World

1870

<1876 Alexander Graham Bell invents the telephone.

1876 German engineer Nikolaus A. Otto perfects a gasoline-powered engine.

1879 Thomas Edison invents the first lightbulb.

1883 The island volcano of Krakatau in the Pacific Ocean erupts in one of the world's greatest natural disasters.

∧**1886** The American Federation of Labor is formed on December 8.

∧ **1889** The Eiffel Tower is built in Paris.

1890 Congress passes the Sherman Antitrust Act.

1892 On June 29 the Homestead strike begins. Carnegie Steel Company refuses to negotiate with the union.

∧ **1898** French scientists Pierre and Marie Curie discover radium.

1900

Reading Social Studies

Economics, Society and Culture

In this module you will read about the advancements in transportation and communication made during what is called the Second Industrial Revolution. You will learn about the rise of powerful corporations. You will also read about the workers who organized in the late 1800s and will see what happened as unions began demanding better treatment for workers. Throughout the module you will see how society was affected by the changing economy.

READING FOCUS:

Identify Patterns of Organization

How are clothes organized in a department store? How are files arranged in a file cabinet? Clear organization helps us find the product we need, and it also helps us find facts and information.

Understand Structural Patterns Writers use structural patterns to organize information in sentences or paragraphs. What's a structural pattern? It's simply a way of organizing information. Learning to recognize those patterns will make it easier for you to read and understand social studies texts.

Patterns of Organization		
Pattern	**Clue Words**	**Graphic Organizer**
Cause-effect shows how one thing leads to another.	as a result, therefore, because, this led to	Cause → Effect, Effect, Effect
Chronological order shows the sequence of events or actions.	after, before, first, then, not long after, finally	First → Next → Last
Comparison-contrast points out similarities and/or differences.	although, but, however, on the other hand, similarly, also	Differences / Similarities
Listing presents information in categories such as size, location, or importance.	also, most important, for example, in fact	Category • Fact • Fact • Fact

To use text structure to improve your understanding, follow these steps:

1. Look for the main idea of the passage you are reading.
2. Then look for clues that signal a specific pattern.
3. Look for other important ideas and think about how the ideas connect. Is there any obvious pattern?
4. Use a graphic organizer to map the relationships among the facts and details.

You Try It!

The following passages are from the module you are about to read. As you read each set of sentences, ask yourself what structural pattern the writer used to organize the information.

(A) Great advances in communication technologies took place in the late 1800s. By 1861 telegraph wires connected the East and West coasts. Five years later, a telegraph cable on the floor of the Atlantic Ocean connected the United States and Great Britain.

(B) Many business leaders justified their business methods through their belief in social Darwinism. . . . Other business leaders, however, believed that the rich had a duty to aid the poor.

(C) During the late 1800s, several factors led to a decline in the quality of working conditions. Machines run by unskilled workers were eliminating the jobs of many skilled craftspeople. These low-paid workers could be replaced easily.

After you read the passages, answer the following questions:

1. Re-read passage A. What structural pattern did the writer use to organize this information? How can you tell?

2. Re-read passage B. What structural pattern did the writer use to organize this information? How can you tell? Why do you think the writer chose this pattern?

3. Re-read passage C. What structural pattern did the writer use to organize this information? How can you tell? Why do you think the writer chose this pattern?

As you read Module 4, think about the organization of the ideas. Ask yourself why the writer chose to organize the information in this way.

The Second Industrial Revolution

The Big Idea

The Second Industrial Revolution led to new sources of power and advances in transportation and communication.

Main Ideas

- Breakthroughs in steel processing led to a boom in railroad construction.
- Advances in the use of oil and electricity improved communication and transportation.
- A rush of inventions changed Americans' lives.

Key Terms and People

Second Industrial Revolution
Bessemer process
Thomas Edison
patents
Alexander Graham Bell
Henry Ford
moving assembly line
Wilbur and Orville Wright

If YOU were there . . .

You live in a small town but are visiting an aunt in the city in the 1890s. You are amazed when your aunt pushes a button on the wall to turn on electric lights. At home you still use kerosene lamps. You hear a clatter outside and see an electric streetcar traveling down the street. You are shocked when a telephone rings and your aunt speaks to someone miles away!

Which of these inventions would you find most amazing?

Breakthroughs Fuel Industrialization

In the late 1800s, new technologies helped industry grow at a staggering pace. Electrical power replaced steam and water power. Factories became larger and produced more and more goods. Faster transportation helped move people and goods more cheaply. These advances and others fueled the **Second Industrial Revolution**, a period of rapid growth in U.S. manufacturing in the late 1800s. By the mid-1890s the United States had become the world's industrial leader.

Bessemer Steel Process Some of the most important advances in technology happened in the steel industry. Steel is iron that has been made stronger by heat and the addition of other metals. In the mid-1850s Henry Bessemer invented the **Bessemer process**, a way to manufacture steel quickly and cheaply by blasting hot air through melted iron to quickly remove impurities. Before, turning several tons of iron ore into steel took a day or more. The Bessemer process took only 10 to 20 minutes.

New Use for Steel The Bessemer process cut the time and the cost required to produce steel. Factories began to make many products out of steel, including barbed wire, nails, and beams for buildings. To meet demand for these products, the nation's steel production rose dramatically, from 77,000 tons in 1870 to more than 1 million tons in 1879.

Steel made innovative construction possible. One of the most remarkable structures was the Brooklyn Bridge. Completed in 1883 it spanned 1,595 feet across the East River in New York City. Not only was it the longest suspension bridge in the world, it was the first to use steel cables.

Riding the Rails Steel was also used for rails to expand the railroads. As steel prices dropped, so too did the cost of railroad construction. Companies built thousands of miles of new steel track. The design of elegant passenger and sleeping cars improved passenger service. Manufacturers and farmers sent products to market faster than ever by rail in newly invented refrigerated shipping cars. Cities where major rail lines crossed, such as Chicago, grew rapidly. Railroads also increased western growth by offering free tickets to settlers. Finally, as rail travel and shipping increased, railroads and related industries began employing more people.

Reading Check
Identify Cause and Effect
How did steel processing change in the 1850s, and how did this affect the United States?

Use of Oil and Electricity

The Second Industrial Revolution was characterized by dramatic developments in the use and distribution of oil and electricity. These power sources fueled other changes.

Oil as a Power Source Other important technological breakthroughs in the late 1800s led to the widespread use of petroleum, or oil, as a power

Homestead Steel Mill

Steel mills like this one in Homestead, Pennsylvania, were the center of the new steel industry that led to advancements in rail travel. Workers used the Bessemer process to make steel more quickly.

How do you think mills like this one affected the surrounding area?

Quick Facts

Factors Affecting Industrial Growth

- Greater ability to use natural resources
- A growing population
- Transportation advances
- Rising immigration
- Inventions and innovations
- Increasing business investment
- Government policies assisting business, such as protective tariffs

source. In the 1850s scientists discovered an inexpensive way to convert crude, or unprocessed, oil into a fuel called kerosene that could be used to light lamps. Because kerosene was so affordable, people quickly put it to good use lighting their homes and businesses.

Not surprisingly, demand for oil skyrocketed and companies set out to discover new oil sources. Until this time, people had collected oil from seeps, places where oil naturally oozes from the ground. However, oil from seeps couldn't keep up with demand. One company hired Edwin L. Drake, who believed he could access oil by drilling into the ground in Pennsylvania. At first people mocked Drake's drilling efforts as "Drake's Folly." Then, in 1859 his crew hit an underground spring deep in the rock. The next day, oil seeped up and the crew scrambled to collect it in buckets, tubs, and barrels. Edwin Drake had drilled the first commercial oil well. He was soon steadily pumping "black gold" to the surface.

The output from Drake's well was modest, but it drew plenty of wild-catters, or oil prospectors, to Ohio, Pennsylvania, and West Virginia. Oil became a big business as these states began producing millions of barrels per year. Oil companies built refineries to turn the crude oil into finished products like kerosene. One oil company supervisor referred to oil workers as "men who are supplying light for the world."

Electricity Spreads In addition to kerosene, electricity became a critical source of light and power during the Second Industrial Revolution. The possible uses of electricity interested inventors like **Thomas Edison**. His

Timeline: The Spirit of Innovation

Improvements in steel production and the use of oil and electricity as power sources led to inventions that changed the ways Americans communicated, traveled, worked, and lived.

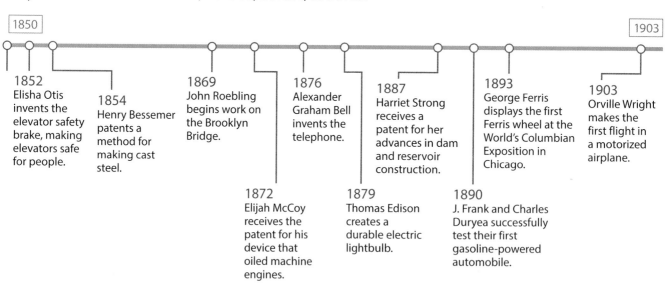

1850

1903

1852 Elisha Otis invents the elevator safety brake, making elevators safe for people.

1854 Henry Bessemer patents a method for making cast steel.

1869 John Roebling begins work on the Brooklyn Bridge.

1876 Alexander Graham Bell invents the telephone.

1887 Harriet Strong receives a patent for her advances in dam and reservoir construction.

1893 George Ferris displays the first Ferris wheel at the World's Columbian Exposition in Chicago.

1903 Orville Wright makes the first flight in a motorized airplane.

1872 Elijah McCoy receives the patent for his device that oiled machine engines.

1879 Thomas Edison creates a durable electric lightbulb.

1890 J. Frank and Charles Duryea successfully test their first gasoline-powered automobile.

Analyze Timelines
Which inventions improved transportation and communication?

research center in Menlo Park, New Jersey, was called an invention factory. Edison explained his practical approach to science.

"I do not regard myself as a pure scientist, as so many persons have insisted that I am. I do not search for the laws of nature . . . for the purpose of learning truth. I am only a professional inventor . . . with the object [goal] of inventing that which will have commercial utility [use]."

—Thomas Edison, quoted in *Scientific American*, July 8, 1893

Edison eventually held more than 1,000 **patents**, exclusive rights to make or sell inventions. Patents allowed inventors to protect their inventions from being manufactured by others.

In 1878 Edison announced that he would soon invent a practical electric light. By the end of 1879 Edison and his team of inventors had created the electric lightbulb. The public was excited. However, Edison had a problem. At the time, few homes or businesses could get electricity. Edison therefore built a power plant that began supplying electricity to dozens of New York City buildings in September 1882. The *New York Times* reported that with electric lighting in the newspaper offices, "it seemed almost like writing by daylight." However, Edison's equipment could not send electricity over long distances. As a result, his power company, Edison Electric, provided electricity mainly to central cities.

In the late 1880s George Westinghouse built a power system that could send electricity across many miles. As Edison and Westinghouse competed, the use of electricity spread rapidly in the nation's cities. After a while, electricity soon lit homes and businesses and powered city factories. Electricity also was used to power streetcars in cities across the nation.

Reading Check
Draw Conclusions
Why did people begin to pump oil from the ground?

Rush of Inventions

In the late 1800s inventors focused on finding solutions to practical problems. Communication and transportation took the lead.

Advances in Communication Great advances in communication technologies took place in the late 1800s. By 1861 telegraph wires connected the East and West coasts. Five years later, a telegraph cable on the floor of the Atlantic Ocean connected the United States and Great Britain.

However, the telegraph carried only written messages and was difficult for untrained people to use. These problems were solved in March 1876, when inventor **Alexander Graham Bell** patented the telephone. Bell was a Scottish-born speech teacher who studied the science of sound. He called the telephone a "talking telegraph."

Companies quickly found telephones to be an essential business tool. People wanted them in their homes, too. Telephone companies raced to lay thousands of miles of phone lines. By 1880 there were about 55,000 telephones

Alexander Graham Bell opened the telephone line that connected New York and Chicago in 1892.

J. Frank and Charles Duryea designed and invented the first gasoline-powered automobile in America.

Academic Vocabulary
implement to put in place

in the United States. By 1900 about 1.5 million telephones had been installed in homes and offices across the nation.

Automobiles and Planes In 1876 a German engineer invented an engine powered by gasoline, another fuel made from oil. In 1893 two brothers, Charles and J. Frank Duryea, used a gasoline engine to build the first practical motorcar in the United States. By the early 1900s, thousands of cars were being built in the United States.

At first, cars were luxury items that only the wealthy could buy. That changed when a young entrepreneur, **Henry Ford**, introduced the Model T in 1908. Ford aimed to make "a motor car for the great multitude." At first, Ford's mechanics built Model Ts one car at a time, but this soon changed.

Ford started by simplifying his design and making all of his cars identical. This brought the cost down, but not enough to make cars affordable to ordinary people. So Ford studied manufacturing processes that would reduce costs by increasing productivity and efficiency, such as using interchangeable parts and the assembly line.

Ford became the first to **implement** a large-scale **moving assembly line** to make cars. On Ford's assembly line, each car that was being built moved along a conveyor belt to workers at various workstations. The work of building the car was broken down into 84 steps. Each worker was trained to do just one job, requiring simple skills and interchangeable parts. This process allowed Ford to produce more cars at a lower cost. In its first year, the Ford assembly line produced a car every hour and a half. The cars sold for under $500, about half the cost of the first Model Ts and a price that many people could afford.

New engine technology helped make another breakthrough in transportation possible—air flight. Brothers **Wilbur and Orville Wright** built a lightweight airplane that used a small, gas-powered engine. On December 17, 1903, the Wright brothers tried out their airplane at Kitty Hawk, North Carolina. In freezing temperatures and a strong wind, Orville climbed into the pilot's seat and the plane took off across the beach. It flew just inches above the ground and landed 120 feet from where it had started. This short trip—12 seconds in all—was the first true flight in an airplane. The Wright brothers quickly followed this success with even longer flights.

Airplanes would soon give Americans another transportation option. Passenger airlines first flew through American skies in the 1920s. Early flights offered little comfort—some passengers wore goggles and helmets for protection. Moreover, planes couldn't fly over mountains or at night. In

Wilbur and Orville Wright invented the first power-driven airplane in 1903.

Reading Check
Compare What new inventions excited the public in the 1800s, and how were they used?

fact, for cross-country travel, trains were more comfortable, faster, and less expensive option. Still, for a handful of Americans, the thrill of air travel outweighed the early discomfort.

Summary and Preview The Second Industrial Revolution led to advances in energy sources, communication, and transportation. In the next lesson you will learn about the growth of big business.

Lesson 1 Assessment

Review Ideas, Terms, and People

1. a. **Describe** What was the Bessemer process?

   b. **Summarize** How did improvements to railroads affect the economy and transportation in the United States?

   c. **Elaborate** What was the most important effect of the Bessemer process? Why?

2. a. **Describe** How does the paragraph about Edwin L. Drake and oil drilling show the cause and effect structure?

   b. **Describe** Using technology related to oil production, explain how technological innovations impact how people modify the physical environment.

   c. **Explain** What problem did Thomas Edison face regarding the use of electricity, and how did he solve it?

3. a. **Recall** What contribution did Wilbur and Orville Wright make to transportation?

   b. **Draw Conclusions** How did Alexander Graham Bell's invention improve life in the United States?

   c. **Elaborate** Why do you think there was a rush of inventions in the late 1800s?

Critical Thinking

4. **Analyze** In this lesson you learned about inventors. Complete a table like the one below about inventors, their inventions, and their impact on Americans.

Inventor	Invention	Impact

Big Business

The Big Idea

The growth of big business in the late 1800s led to the creation of monopolies.

Main Ideas

- The rise of corporations and powerful business leaders led to the dominance of big business in the United States.

- People and the government began to question the methods of big business.

Key Terms and People

corporations
Andrew Carnegie
vertical integration
John D. Rockefeller
horizontal integration
trust
Leland Stanford
social Darwinism
monopoly
Sherman Antitrust Act

If YOU were there . . .

It is 1895, and your town is home to a large corporation. The company's founder and owner, a wealthy man, lives in a mansion on a hill. He is a fair employer but not especially generous. Many townspeople work in his factory. You and other town leaders feel that he should contribute more to local charities and community organizations.

How could this business leader help the town more?

Dominance of Big Business

In the late 1800s many entrepreneurs formed their businesses as **corporations**, or businesses that sell portions of ownership called stock shares. The leaders of these corporations were some of the richest and most influential members of American society in the late 1800s. Political leaders praised prosperous businesspeople as examples of American hard work, talent, and success.

Corporations Generate Wealth Successful corporations reward not only the people who found them but also investors who hold stock. Stockholders in a corporation typically get a percentage of profits based on the amount of stock they own. Although stockholders actually own the corporation, they do not run its day-to-day business. Instead, they elect a board of directors that chooses the corporation's main leaders, such as the president.

New sales techniques like those taught by John H. Patterson helped change business practices.

The Rise of Investing

Investors purchased stock in corporations in record numbers in the late 1800s. They received stock certificates, like the one shown here, to document their part ownership in corporations. Corporations used the money raised by selling stocks to expand. Standard Oil Company financed the building of this refinery in Richmond, California, by selling stock.

Why did investors buy stock?

Corporations provided several important advantages over earlier business forms. Stockholders in a corporation are not responsible for business debts. If a corporation fails financially, the stockholders lose only the money that they invested. Stockholders are also usually free to sell their stock to whomever they want, whenever they want. As a result, corporations encouraged more investment in businesses. By 1900 more than 100 million shares per year were being traded on the New York Stock Exchange.

Business Leaders Some business leaders became wealthy, powerful, and famous because of the business boom. **Andrew Carnegie** was one of the most admired businesspeople of the time. Born in Scotland, Carnegie came to the United States as a poor immigrant. As a teenager he took a job with a railroad company and quickly worked his way up to the position of railroad superintendent.

In 1873 he focused his efforts on steelmaking. Carnegie expanded his business by buying out competitors when steel prices were low. By 1901 Carnegie's mills were producing more steel than all of Great Britain's mills combined. Carnegie's businesses succeeded largely through **vertical integration**, or ownership of businesses involved in each step of a manufacturing process. For example, to lower production costs, Carnegie **acquired** the iron ore mines, coalfields, and railroads needed to supply and support his steel mills.

John D. Rockefeller was also successful in consolidating, or combining, businesses. By age 21, while a partner in a wholesale business, he decided to start an oil-refining company. In only ten years Rockefeller's Standard Oil Company was the country's largest oil refiner. Like Carnegie, Rockefeller used vertical integration. For example, the company controlled most of the pipelines it used.

Rockefeller's company also developed **horizontal integration**, or owning all businesses in a certain field. By 1880 Rockefeller's companies controlled about 90 percent of the oil refining business in the United States. Rockefeller also formed a **trust**, a legal arrangement grouping together a number of companies under a single board of directors. To earn more money, trusts often tried to get rid of competition and to control production.

Leland Stanford was another important business leader of the late 1800s. He made a fortune selling equipment to miners. While governor of California, he became one of the founders of the state's Central Pacific Railroad. He also founded Stanford University. Late in life, Stanford argued that industries should be owned and managed cooperatively by workers. He believed this would be the fulfillment of democracy.

Leland Stanford moved to California during the Gold Rush and made his fortune in the railroad industry.

Reading Check
Compare and Contrast Why did Andrew Carnegie use vertical integration?

Questioning the Methods of Big Business

In the late 1800s many Americans admired business tycoons as natural leaders and "captains of industry." However, other people and the government began to see the tough tactics of big business as a problem.

Social Darwinism Many business leaders justified their business methods through their belief in **social Darwinism**, a view of society based on scientist Charles Darwin's theory of natural selection. Social Darwinists thought that Darwin's "survival of the fittest" theory decided which human beings would succeed in business and in life in general.

Other business leaders, however, believed that the rich had a duty to aid the poor. These leaders tried to help the less fortunate through philanthropy, or giving money to charities. Carnegie, Rockefeller, Stanford, and other business leaders gave away large sums. Carnegie gave away more than $350 million to charities, about $60 million of which went to fund public libraries to expand access to books. By the late 1800s various charities had received millions of dollars from philanthropists.

The Antitrust Movement Critics of big business said that many business leaders earned their fortunes through unfair business practices. These criticisms grew stronger in the 1880s as corporations became more powerful. Large corporations often used their size and strength to drive smaller competitors out of business. Carnegie and Rockefeller, for example, pressured railroads to charge their companies lower shipping rates. Powerful trusts also arranged to sell goods and services below market value. Smaller competitors went out of business trying to match those prices. Then the trusts raised prices again.

Some people became concerned when a trust gained a **monopoly**, or total ownership of a product or service. Critics argued that monopolies reduced necessary competition. They believed competition in a free market economy kept prices low and the quality of goods and services high.

Some Americans also worried about the political power of wealthy trusts. Many citizens and small businesses wanted the government to help control monopolies and trusts. People who favored trusts responded that trusts were more efficient and gave the consumer dependable products or services.

"What a Funny Little Government"

This 1899 cartoon of John D. Rockefeller expressed a fear shared by many Americans—trusts, such as Standard Oil, had grown too powerful.

What do you think the smokestacks on the Capitol represent?

What does the position of the White House suggest?

Analyze Historical Sources
How does the cartoonist show Rockefeller's power?

Reading Check
Analyze How did concerns about trusts lead to the Sherman Antitrust Act?

Many members of Congress favored big business. However, elected officials could not ignore the concerns of voters. In July 1890 Congress passed the **Sherman Antitrust Act**, a law that made it illegal to create monopolies or trusts that restrained trade. It stated that any "attempt to monopolize . . . any part of the trade or commerce among the several States" was a crime. However, the act did not clearly define a trust in legal terms. The antitrust laws were therefore difficult to enforce. Corporations and trusts kept growing in size and power.

Summary and Preview In this lesson you learned how, in the late 1800s, some corporations became monopolies that dominated entire industries, such as oil. In the next lesson you will learn about how industrial workers organized to improve working conditions.

Lesson 2 Assessment

Review Ideas, Terms, and People

1. a. **Identify** What are horizontal and vertical integration?
   b. **Explain** What are the benefits of investing in corporations?
   c. **Evaluate** What do you think about the business methods of Carnegie, Rockefeller, and Stanford?
2. a. **Describe** What is social Darwinism?
   b. **Summarize** What concerns did critics of big business have regarding trusts?
   c. **Evaluate** Was the Sherman Antitrust Act successful? Why or why not?

Critical Thinking

3. **Contrast** In this lesson you learned about new business practices. Create a graphic organizer like the one below and identify examples of these new business practices.

New Practices	Example

Industrial Workers

The Big Idea

Changes in the workplace led to a rise in labor unions and workers' strikes.

Main Ideas

- The desire to maximize profits and become more efficient led to poor working conditions.

- Workers began to organize and demand improvements in working conditions and pay.

- Labor strikes often turned violent and failed to accomplish their goals.

Key Terms and People

Frederick W. Taylor
collective bargaining
Knights of Labor
Terence V. Powderly
American Federation of Labor (AFL)
Samuel Gompers
Mary Harris Jones
Haymarket Riot
Homestead strike
Pullman strike

Reading Check
Identify Cause and Effect Why did companies begin to use scientific management, and how did it affect workers?

If YOU were there . . .

You run a button machine in a clothing factory in the 1890s. You work from 7:00 in the morning until 6:00 at night, every day except Sunday. Your only break is 15 minutes for lunch. Now you hear about a movement to start a workers' union to bargain with your employer. Union members will ask for an eight-hour workday. But you think your employer might fire you if you join.

Would you join the union?

Maximizing Profits and Efficiency

During the late 1800s several factors led to a decline in the quality of working conditions. Skilled craftspeople found themselves replaced by machines operated by unskilled workers, who were low-paid and easily replaced. This was an unfortunate side effect of new technologies and increasing labor specialization, or the splitting of work into smaller and more specific tasks.

For workers, specialization often meant having to perform the same small task over and over again. This made workers tired, bored, and more likely to be injured. But, for factories, specialization reduced costs and greatly increased production. For example, specialization along Ford's moving assembly line sped the production and lowered the cost of making automobiles. As a result, automobiles became affordable to a wider segment of the population than ever before.

In 1909 **Frederick W. Taylor**, an efficiency engineer, published a popular book called *The Principles of Scientific Management*. He encouraged managers to view workers as interchangeable parts of the production process. In factories, managers influenced by Taylor paid less attention to working conditions. Injuries increased, and as conditions grew worse, workers looked for ways to bring about change.

Poor Working Conditions

Small, crowded rooms. Stuffy air. Unsafe workplaces. Long hours. Low pay. No job security. These were the facts of working life for millions of Americans during the Second Industrial Revolution.

What does this photograph suggest about working conditions?

Workers Organize

By the late 1800s working conditions and pay were so poor that workers began to join labor unions to improve their lot. By joining forces with others, they hoped to pressure employers into paying better wages and improving working conditions. With **collective bargaining**—all workers acting collectively, or together—workers had a much greater chance of success in negotiating with management. Most employers opposed collective bargaining. One company president said, "I shall never give in. I would rather go out of business."

Tailors who wanted to protect their interests founded the first national labor union, the **Knights of Labor**, in Philadelphia in 1869 as a secret society. In the 1880s, under the leadership of **Terence V. Powderly**, the Knights ended its policy of secrecy. It also began to accept unskilled workers, women, and African Americans as members. By 1886 the group had more than 700,000 members.

With the motto "An injury to one is a concern of all," the Knights of Labor campaigned for many reforms. It pushed for an eight-hour workday, equal pay for equal work, and an end to child labor. Union members also wanted the government to regulate trusts. In its early years, the Knights

Samuel Gompers 1850–1924

Samuel Gompers was born to Jewish parents in London. He immigrated to the United States with his parents in 1863 at age 13. He worked as a cigar maker and joined a local union, eventually becoming its president. In time, the cigar-makers' union was reorganized and later joined the American Federation of Labor. Gompers became the AFL's first president and remained so, except for the year 1895, until his death. He campaigned for basic trade-union rights, such as the right to picket and to organize boycotts and strikes. His efforts on behalf of workers helped organized labor to gain respect.

Summarize
How did Samuel Gompers help the labor movement?

discouraged strikes, preferring tactics such as boycotts and negotiations. Yet soon enough, strikes would become commonplace.

Another early labor union was the **American Federation of Labor (AFL)**, led by **Samuel Gompers**. The AFL was founded by members of craft unions who were unhappy with how the Knights of Labor represented their interests. While the Knights organized individual workers, the AFL organized unions, such as the mineworkers' and steelworkers' unions. The AFL also limited its membership to skilled workers. This gave the union great bargaining power but left out most workers. The AFL tried to get better wages, hours, and working conditions for laborers. By 1890 the AFL's membership was larger than that of the Knights. Using strikes and other tactics, the AFL won wage increases and shorter workweeks.

Many women took active roles in unions. For example, **Mary Harris Jones**, an Irish immigrant, dedicated herself to improving the lives of workers. "Mother Jones," as she was affectionately called, was a fiery speaker, who used her abilities to organize strikes and educate workers.

Reading Check
Contrast How did the Knights of Labor and the AFL differ?

Labor Strikes

By the late 1800s other unions were gaining strength. Major workers' strikes swept the country and included miners in Colorado, steelworkers in Pennsylvania, and railroad workers in Illinois and California. Some strikes involved violent clashes with police. One of the worst confrontations occurred in Chicago in 1886.

In May 1886 thousands of union members in Chicago went on strike because they wanted an eight-hour workday. Two strikers were killed in a fight with police. The next night, workers met at Haymarket Square to protest the killings. In what became known as the **Haymarket Riot**, an unidentified person threw a dynamite bomb at police, who were trying to

Major Labor Strikes, Late 1800s

▶ Explore ONLINE!

① Haymarket Riot In May 1886 the Haymarket Riot erupted between protesters and police in Chicago. It resulted in the decline of the Knights of Labor.

② Homestead Strike In 1892 a strike occurred in the Carnegie Steel Company in Homestead, Pennsylvania. The resulting fight left several workers and Pinkerton guards dead.

③ Colorado Miners' Strike In the summer of 1893, gold miners at Cripple Creek, Colorado, went on strike for higher wages and a shorter workday.

④ Pullman Strike The Pullman strike of 1894 began with workers who made Pullman train cars. It soon spread to workers who worked on trains pulling the sleeper cars.

⑤ California Railroad Strike In 1894 railroad workers in Oakland went on strike in the Bay Area's first major strike. Supporting Chicago Pullman workers, they halted passenger, freight, and mail trains for months.

Union Membership, 1880–1900

(Haymarket Riot) (Pullman Strike)

Number of workers (in thousands)

1,000
800
600
400
200
0

1880 1885 1890 1895 1900

Year

— Knights of Labor
— American Railway Union
— AFL (Organized in 1886)

Analyze Information
How did conflicts between striking workers and authorities affect union membership?

---

break up the crowd. The police panicked and fired into the crowd. Before the situation calmed down, seven police officers and four workers were killed. More than 100 others suffered injuries.

Police arrested numerous suspects and eventually charged eight people with conspiracy and murder. No evidence existed to connect these men to the crime. In fact, five of them were not even in Haymarket Square when the bomb went off. Still, all eight were convicted and sentenced to death. Four were hanged and one killed himself in prison. In 1893 the new governor of Illinois pardoned the last three. He believed that their guilt had not been proven.

Sometimes, business owners succeeded in breaking up unions. In 1892 a violent strike called the **Homestead strike** took place at Andrew Carnegie's Homestead steel factory in Pennsylvania. Union members there protested a plan to buy new machinery and cut jobs. The company refused to negotiate with the union and locked workers out of the plant, hiring

The Pullman Strike

On July 6, 1894, during the Pullman Strike, a mob of frustrated strikers toppled and set fire to hundreds of railcars in South Chicago.

strikebreakers to perform their jobs. The workers responded by seizing control of the plant. Gunfire erupted on July 6, when Pinkerton detectives hired by the company tried to enter the plant. A fierce battle raged for 14 hours, leaving 16 people dead. The governor called out the state militia to restore order. Continuing for four more months, the union was eventually defeated.

Another major strike happened at George Pullman's Pullman Palace Car Company in the company town of Pullman, Illinois. Most of the company workers lived there, paying high rents. During a financial depression that began in 1893, Pullman laid off about half of the workers and cut pay for those who were left, without lowering their rents. On May 11, 1894, workers began the **Pullman strike**, which stopped traffic on many railroad lines until federal courts ordered the workers to return to their jobs. President Grover Cleveland sent federal troops to Chicago to stop the strike. Such defeats seriously damaged the labor movement for years.

Reading Check
Analyze What were the effects of early major strikes on workers?

Summary and Preview Workers formed unions to fight for better conditions and to keep their jobs. In the next module you will learn about a new wave of immigrants in the late 1800s.

Lesson 3 Assessment

Review Ideas, Terms, and People

1. **a. Recall** Why did conditions in factories begin to decline?

   b. Draw Conclusions How were workers affected by specialization and scientific management?

   c. Evaluate Do you think scientific management made businesses more successful? Explain.

2. **a. Identify** What role did Mary Harris Jones play in the labor movement?

   b. Analyze Why did workers use collective bargaining, and why did business owners oppose it?

   c. Explain What were the origins and accomplishments of the Knights of Labor and the American Federation of Labor?

   d. Elaborate Do you think the demands made by labor unions were reasonable?

3. **a. Describe** What major labor strikes took place in the late 1800s?

   b. Evaluate Do you think President Cleveland was right to use federal troops to end the Pullman strike? Explain.

Critical Thinking

4. **Analyze** In this lesson you learned about the problems workers faced. Create a table like the one below and show how workers tried to solve the problems they faced.

Problem	Solution

Social Studies Skills

Analyze Costs and Benefits

Define the Skill

Everything you do has both costs and benefits connected to it. *Benefits* are things that you gain from something. *Costs* are what you give up to obtain benefits. For example, if you buy a video game, the benefits of your action include the game itself and the enjoyment of playing it. The most clear cost is what you pay for the game. However, there are other costs that do not involve money. One is the time you spend playing the game. This is a cost because you give up something else, such as doing your homework or watching a TV show, when you choose to play the game.

The ability to analyze costs and benefits is a valuable life skill as well as a useful tool in the study of history. Weighing an action's benefits against its costs can help you decide whether or not to take it.

Learn the Skill

Analyzing the costs and benefits of historical events will help you to better understand and evaluate them. Follow these guidelines to do a cost-benefit analysis of an action or decision in history.

1. First determine what the action or decision was trying to accomplish. This step is needed in order to determine which of its effects were benefits and which were costs.

2. Then look for the positive or successful results of the action or decision. These are its benefits.

3. Consider the negative or unsuccessful effects of the action or decision. Also think about what positive things would have happened if it had *not* occurred. All these things are its costs.

4. Making a chart of the costs and benefits can be useful. By comparing the list of benefits to the list of costs, you can better understand the action or decision and evaluate it.

For example, you learned in Module 20 about the Second Industrial Revolution and its effects on the American economy. A cost-benefit analysis of the changes in American businesses might produce a chart like this one:

Benefits	Costs
New inventions made life easier.	New business methods ran smaller companies out of business.
Communication became easier with new technologies.	Workers received lower wages.
Efficient management reduced costs of products.	Strikes resulted in violence and deaths.
Workers began to organize for better conditions.	

Based on this chart, one might conclude that the Second Industrial Revolution was beneficial to the nation's economy.

Practice the Skill

Among the changes that occurred in the early 1900s was an increase in specialization and efficiency in the workplace. Use information from the module and the guidelines above to do a cost-benefit analysis of this development. Then write a paragraph explaining whether or not it was a wise one.

Module 4 Assessment

Review Vocabulary, Terms, and People

Identify the descriptions below with the correct term or person from the module.

1. Labor organization that represented both skilled and unskilled laborers and was the first national labor union in the United States

2. Inventor who patented the telephone in 1876

3. A way of making steel quickly and cheaply by blasting hot air through melted iron to quickly remove waste

4. A system of business in which one company owns businesses in each step of the manufacturing process

5. Powerful business leader who helped to found the Central Pacific Railroad

6. Union speaker who worked to better the lives of mine workers

7. A method of negotiating for better wages or working conditions in which all workers act together to ensure a better chance for success

Comprehension and Critical Thinking

Lesson 1

8.
  a. **Identify** What was the Second Industrial Revolution?

  b. **Draw Conclusions** Why were advances in transportation and communication important to the Second Industrial Revolution?

  c. **Elaborate** Which invention do you think had the greatest effect on people's lives in the late 1800s? Explain your answer.

Lesson 2

9.
  a. **Recall** What criticisms were made of business leaders and trusts?

  b. **Analyze** How did the rise of corporations and powerful business leaders lead to the growth of big business?

  c. **Evaluate** Do you think the growth of big business helped or hurt ordinary Americans? Explain your answer.

Lesson 3

10.
  a. **Recall** What led to poor working conditions in factories during the Second Industrial Revolution?

  b. **Make Inferences** Why did labor unions have a better chance of improving working conditions than laborers did on their own?

  c. **Evaluate** Did the strikes of the 1880s and 1890s hurt or help the labor movement in the long run? Explain your answer.

Module 4 Assessment, continued

Review Themes

11. Economics How did the rise of big business affect consumers in the United States?

12. Society and Culture What changes in society were brought about by the organization of labor?

Reading Skills

Identify Patterns of Organization *Use the Reading Skills taught in this module to answer the question about the reading selection below.*

> Corporations provided several important advantages over earlier business forms. Stockholders in a corporation are not responsible for business debts. If a corporation fails financially, the stockholders lose only the money that they invested. Stockholders are also usually free to sell their stock to whomever they want, whenever they want.

13. By which structural pattern is the above passage organized?

    a. Listing

    b. Cause-effect

    c. Chronological order

    d. Comparison-contrast

Social Studies Skills

Analyze Costs and Benefits *Use the Social Studies Skills taught in this module to answer the question below.*

14. Write two costs and two benefits of the Pullman strike from the point of view of the workers who participated.

Focus on Writing

15. Write a Business Plan Consider what you learned in this module and determine a good product to sell during the late 1800s. Decide which business practices you would use and which you would not. Consider how you would encourage investors to support your plan. Write two or three paragraphs in which you explain why your product would sell, which business practices you can use to make your product, and how to avoid conflicts with workers. Remember to explain to the investors why your plan will work.

Henry Ford

Henry Ford was a brilliant inventor and industrialist and founder of the Ford Motor Company. He helped bring about a time of rapid growth and progress that forever changed how people worked and lived. Henry Ford grew up on his family's farm near Dearborn, Michigan. As a child, he disliked life on the farm. He found the clicks and whirs of machinery much more exciting. When Ford was 16, he went to nearby Detroit to work in a machine shop. From there, he turned his ideas for how to make affordable and well-built cars into one of the world's largest automobile companies.

Explore the amazing life and career of Henry Ford online. You can find a wealth of information, video clips, primary sources, activities, and more through your online textbook.

> "My 'gasoline buggy' was the first and for a long time the only automobile in Detroit. It was considered . . . a nuisance, for it made a racket and it scared horses."
>
> —Henry Ford

 My Life and Work
Read the document to learn more about Henry Ford's life and career in his own words.

Big Plans
Watch the video to learn more about Henry Ford's early career.

Taking the Low Road
Watch the video to explore Henry Ford's vision for his car company.

The Assembly Line
Watch the video to see how Henry Ford used the assembly line to produce cars more efficiently and cheaply.

Module 5
Immigrants and Urban Life

★

Essential Question
How did immigration and rapid urban growth shape life in the United States?

About the Photo: These immigrants to the United States entered through Ellis Island.

In this module you will learn about immigration and its effects on U.S. cities. You will also read about some of the challenges faced by these cities.

What You Will Learn . . .

▶ *Explore ONLINE!*

HISTORY.

VIDEOS, including...
- Arrival at Ellis Island
- Angel Island: Ellis Island of the West
- Chicago Fire
- Jacob Riis

☑ Document-Based Investigations

☑ Graphic Organizers

☑ Interactive Games

☑ Image Carousel: Coming to America

☑ Image with Hotspots: Steel Beam Skyscrapers

▶ *Explore ONLINE!*

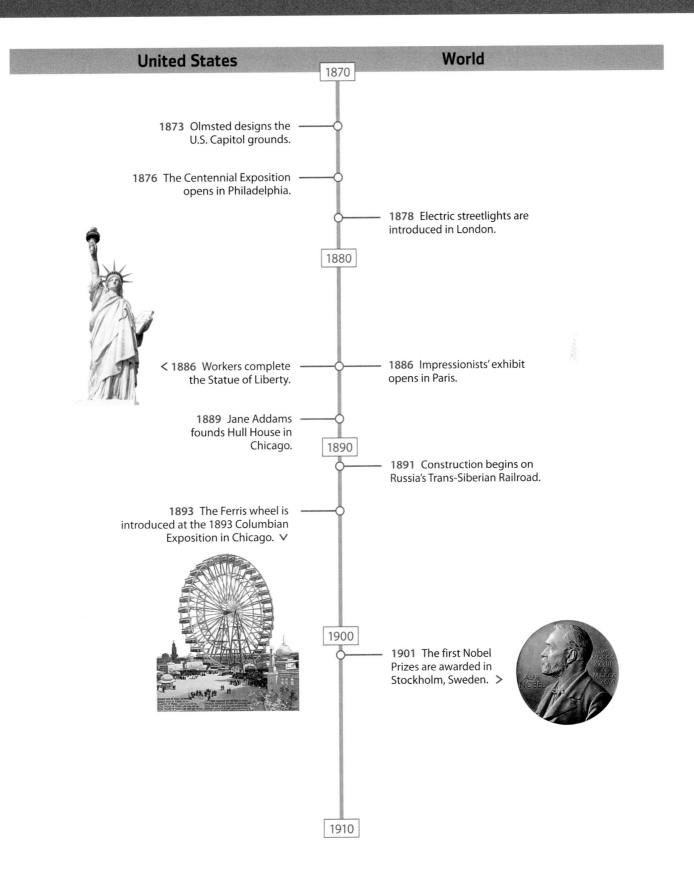

United States | 1870 | **World**

1873 Olmsted designs the U.S. Capitol grounds.

1876 The Centennial Exposition opens in Philadelphia.

1878 Electric streetlights are introduced in London.

1880

< **1886** Workers complete the Statue of Liberty.

1886 Impressionists' exhibit opens in Paris.

1889 Jane Addams founds Hull House in Chicago.

1890

1891 Construction begins on Russia's Trans-Siberian Railroad.

1893 The Ferris wheel is introduced at the 1893 Columbian Exposition in Chicago. ∨

1900

1901 The first Nobel Prizes are awarded in Stockholm, Sweden. >

1910

Reading Social Studies

THEME FOCUS:

Economics, Society and Culture

In this module you will read about the changes in society and culture in the late 1800s. Among these changes was an increase in immigration. New immigrants to America found a society full of economic opportunities and hardships. Immigration and technology combined to change the way of life in cities.

READING FOCUS:

Understand Historical Fact versus Historical Fiction

When you read a book like *The Red Badge of Courage* or see a movie about World War II, do you ever wonder how much is fiction and how much is fact?

Distinguish Fact from Fiction Historical fiction gives readers a chance to meet real historical people and real historical events in the framework of a made-up story. Some of what you read in historical fiction could be verified in an encyclopedia, but other parts existed only in the author's mind until he or she put it on paper. As a good reader of history, you should know the difference between facts, which can be proved or verified, and fiction.

Notice how one reader determined which details could be verified or proved.

> That was a *woman filling her pail by the hydrant* you just bumped against. The *sinks are in the hallway*, that all the tenants may have access—and all be poisoned alike by their summer stenches. Hear the pump squeak! It is the lullaby of tenement house babes. In summer, when *a thousand thirsty throats pant of a cooling drink in this block*, it is worked in vain . . .
>
> —from *How the Other Half Lives*, by Jacob Riis

The woman filling her pail isn't a fact I can check. He's just using her as an example of what women did.

We could probably check city records to see whether the buildings really had sinks in the hallways.

The writer is generalizing here. We probably can't prove 1,000 thirsty throats. We could find out whether the city's water pumps actually went dry in the summer. That's verifiable.

You Try It!

The following passage is from How the Other Half Lives *by Jacob Riis, a journalist and photographer who documented New York tenement life in the late 1800s. After you read it, answer the questions below.*

This gap between dingy brick-walls is the yard. That strip of smoke-colored sky up there is the heaven of these people. Do you wonder the name does not attract them to the churches? That baby's parents live in the rear tenement here. She is at least as clean as the steps we are now climbing. There are plenty of houses with half a hundred such in. The tenement is much like the one in front we just left, only fouler, closer, darker— we will not say more cheerless. The word is a mockery. A hundred thousand people lived in rear tenements in New York last year. Here is a room neater than the rest. The woman, a stout matron with hard lines of care in her face, is at the wash-tub. "I try to keep the childer clean," she says, apologetically, but with a hopeless glance around.
—Jacob Riis, *How the Other Half Lives*

1. Which facts from the paragraph above can be confirmed?
2. What sources might you check to confirm some of these facts?
3. List two things from the passage that could not be confirmed.
4. Why are these two things not able to be confirmed?

As you read Module 5, notice which facts you could easily confirm.

A New Wave of Immigration

The Big Idea

A new wave of immigration in the late 1800s brought large numbers of immigrants to the United States.

Main Ideas

- U.S. immigration patterns changed during the late 1800s as new immigrants arrived from Europe, Asia, and Mexico.

- Immigrants worked hard to adjust to life in the United States.

- Some Americans opposed immigration and worked to restrict it.

Key Terms and People

old immigrants
new immigrants
steerage
benevolent societies
tenements
sweatshops
Chinese Exclusion Act

If YOU were there . . .

You live with your family on a small farm in Italy in the 1890s. You want to earn some money to help your parents, but there are not many jobs nearby. You have heard that jobs are easy to find in the booming factories of the United States. But you speak no English and know no one in America.

Would you travel to the United States in search of new opportunities?

Changing Patterns of Immigration

Millions of immigrants came to the United States from northern Europe in the mid-1800s. They came mainly from Great Britain, Germany, Ireland, and the countries of Scandinavia. Except for the Irish, who were Roman Catholics, most were Protestants. Many were skilled workers. Others settled in rural areas and became farmers. By the late 1800s immigrants from northern Europe were known as **old immigrants**. A newer and larger wave of immigration—from different parts of the world—was arriving in the United States.

New Immigrants During the 1880s more than 5 million immigrants arrived in the United States—about the same number of people as had arrived during the six decades from 1800 to 1860 combined. The majority of these **new immigrants** were from southern and eastern Europe. Thousands of Czechs, Greeks, Hungarians, Italians, Poles, Russians, and Slovaks came to the United States to find new opportunities and better lives. A young woman from Russia spoke for many of her fellow immigrants when she said she hoped "for all manner of miracles in a strange, wonderful land!"

New immigrants came from many different cultural and religious backgrounds. They included Orthodox Christians, Roman Catholics, and Jews. Some were escaping political or religious persecution. They were eager for the job opportunities created by the U.S. industrial boom of the late 1800s.

Immigrants often arrived at Ellis Island with few belongings. This Italian family is looking for lost baggage.

Arriving in a New Land Immigrants usually faced a difficult journey by ship to America. Most traveled in **steerage**—an area below a ship's deck where steering mechanisms were located. Steerage tickets were inexpensive, but the cabins were hot, cramped, and foul-smelling. Many passengers were seasick for the entire journey. Some even died of diseases contracted along the way.

Once in the United States, new arrivals were processed through government-run immigration centers. The busiest center on the East Coast was Ellis Island, which opened in New York Harbor in 1892. The first immigrant processed through Ellis Island was Annie Moore Schayer, a 14-year-old from Ireland. Over the next 40 years, millions of European immigrants came through Ellis Island.

At immigration centers officials interviewed and examined immigrants to decide whether to let them enter the country. People with contagious diseases or legal problems could be turned away. "There was this terrible anxiety that one of us might be rejected," remembered one immigrant traveling with his family. "And if one of us was, what would the rest of the family do?" This rarely happened, however. Less than 2 percent of the people who arrived at Ellis Island were not allowed into the country.

On the West Coast, many Chinese immigrants entered the United States through Angel Island, which opened near San Francisco in 1910. Because laws limited immigration from China, only people whose fathers were U.S. citizens were allowed into the country. Chinese immigrants were often kept at Angel Island for weeks or months while officials investigated their families.

Mexican immigrants also came to the United States in large numbers in the late 1800s. The main processing center for immigrants from Mexico was in El Paso, Texas. Most settled in the Southwest. They found work in construction, steel mills, and mines, and on large commercial farms.

Reading Check
Contrast How was the experience of immigrants at Ellis Island different from that of immigrants at Angel Island?

Adjusting to a New Life

Once they entered the United States, immigrants began the hard work of adjusting to life in a new country. They needed to find homes and jobs. They had to learn a new language and get used to new customs. This was all part of building a new life.

Immigrant Neighborhoods Many immigrants moved into neighborhoods with others from the same country. In these neighborhoods, they could speak their native language and eat foods that reminded them of home. Immigrants could also practice the customs that their families had passed down from generation to generation. An Italian immigrant remembered that in his new neighborhood, "cheeses from Italy, sausage, salamis were all hanging in the window."

In their newly adopted neighborhoods, many immigrant groups published newspapers in their own languages. They founded schools, clubs,

Coming to America

During the late 1800s the places people came from began to change. The charts below show the percentages of people who moved from different places. The total number of immigrants reached a peak in the 1880s, when about 5 million people came to the United States.

By how much did the percentage of immigrants from northern and western Europe change from 1840 to 1900?

Swedish immigrant Swan August Swanson followed his father to Wisconsin to help with the family farm. Like many new Americans, he married within the immigrant community. ∨

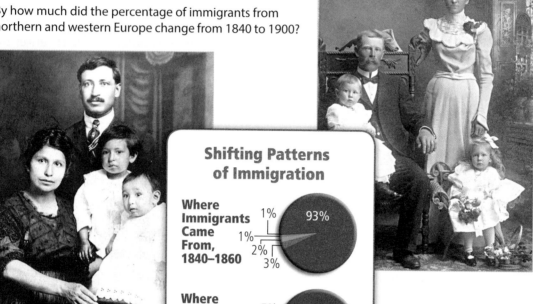

Shifting Patterns of Immigration

Where Immigrants Came From, 1840–1860
1%
1%
2%
3%
93%

Where Immigrants Came From, 1880–1900
.5%
1.5%
6%
61%
31%

- ■ Northern and western Europe
- ■ Eastern and southern Europe
- ■ North and South America
- ■ Asia
- ■ All other areas

∧ Augustin and Maria Lozano and their two children are shown after moving from Mexico to California. Many Mexican immigrants moved into the Southwest.

The son of Italian immigrants, Amadeo Peter Giannini founded the Bank of Italy in San Francisco in 1904. Due to his guidance and perseverance, it became the largest privately owned bank in the world. ∨

∧ In this photo, Japanese men and Chinese women leave the detention center on Angel Island in San Francisco Bay. Angel Island was the processing center for many immigrants from Asia.

and places of worship to help preserve their customs. In New York City, for example, Jewish immigrants founded a theater that gave performances in Yiddish—the language spoken by Jews from central and eastern Europe.

Immigrants often opened local shops and small neighborhood banks. Business owners helped new arrivals by offering credit and giving small loans. Such aid was important for newcomers because there were few commercial banks in immigrant neighborhoods. In 1904 Italian immigrant Amadeo Peter Giannini started the Bank of Italy in San Francisco. This bank later grew and became the Bank of America.

Some immigrant communities formed **benevolent societies**. These aid organizations offered immigrants help in cases of sickness, unemployment, or death. At that time, few national government agencies provided such aid.

Even with neighborhood support, however, immigrants often found city life difficult. Many immigrants lived in **tenements**. These were poorly built, overcrowded apartment buildings. Lacking adequate light, ventilation, and sanitation, tenements were very unhealthy places to live. Disease spread rapidly in the crowded conditions.

The plight of tenement dwellers sparked preliminary efforts at reform. In some cities, local boards of health were established to set sanitation rules. Enforcement was often uneven, however, and the poorer neighborhoods received less attention than richer ones.

Immigrants worked hard to adjust to their new country. Children often learned American customs more quickly than their parents. In public schools, immigrant children learned English from McGuffey's Readers. The Readers were illustrated textbooks that taught reading and writing.

Finding Work Many new immigrants had worked on farms in their homelands. Few could afford to buy land in the United States, however. Instead, they found jobs in cities, where most of the country's manufacturing took place.

Having come from rural areas, few new immigrants were skilled in modern manufacturing or industrial work. They often had no choice but to take low-paying, unskilled jobs. They often worked in garment factories, steel mills, or construction. Long hours were common.

Not all industrial labor took place in large factories. Some immigrants worked for little pay in small shops or mills located in their own neighborhoods. Often associated with the clothing industry, these workplaces were called **sweatshops** because of long hours and hot, unhealthy working conditions. One young immigrant worker remembered:

"When the shirtwaists were finished at the machine . . . we were given scissors to cut the threads off. It wasn't heavy work, but it was monotonous [boring], because you did the same thing from seven-thirty in the morning till nine at night."

—Pauline Newman, quoted in *American Mosaic: The Immigrant Experience in the Words of Those Who Lived It*, by Joan Morrison and Charlotte Fox Zabusky

Asian Americans Today

Today, almost 15 million people in the United States are of Asian origin. They account for about 5 percent of the U.S. population—or about 1 in 20 Americans. Asian Americans trace their roots to various countries, including China, India, the Philippines, and, like this family, Vietnam. Many of these people left their homeland to escape oppression. They sought a life of freedom in the United States. Most Asian Americans live in the West. California has by far the largest Asian American population of any state.

Analyze Information
What push-pull factors do you think caused so many people to move to the United States?

Reading Check
Summarize
How did new immigrants help themselves and others to try to make successful lives in the United States?

Immigrants with skills that were in demand sometimes found work outside factories and sweatshops. Some worked as bakers, carpenters, masons, or skilled machinists. Others saved or borrowed money to open small businesses such as laundries, barbershops, or street vending carts. New immigrants often opened the same types of businesses in which other immigrants from the same country were already succeeding. They worked hard for long hours to become successful themselves.

Opposition to Immigration

Some Americans welcomed new immigrants. Many business leaders, for example, wanted immigrant workers who were willing to work for low pay. In general, however, anti-immigrant feelings grew as immigration increased in the late 1800s. Some labor unions opposed immigration because their members believed immigrants would take jobs away from native-born Americans.

Other Americans called nativists also feared that too many new immigrants were being allowed into the country. Many nativists held racial and ethnic prejudices. They thought that the new immigrants would not learn American customs, which might harm American society.

Academic Vocabulary
advocate to plead in favor of

Some nativists were violent toward immigrants. Others **advocated** laws and policies to stop or limit immigration. For example, in 1880 about 105,000 Chinese immigrants lived in the United States. Two years later, Congress passed the **Chinese Exclusion Act**. This law banned new immigrants to the United States from China for ten years. This was the first time a nationality was banned from entering the country. Although the law violated treaties with China, Congress continued to renew it for several decades. Other immigration policies included another law passed in 1892 that restricted convicts, immigrants with certain diseases, and those likely to need public assistance from entering the country.

Despite such opposition, immigrants continued to arrive in large numbers. They worked for low pay in factories. They built buildings, highways, and railroads. Their labor helped power the continuing industrial growth of the late 1800s and early 1900s. They did not always achieve their dreams as quickly as they had hoped. But most immigrants remained confident about the future for themselves and their families in the United States. An immigrant from Russia named Abraham Hyman expressed this idea, saying, "Your feeling is that a better time is coming, if not for yourself, for your families, for your children."

**Reading Check
Analyze** Why did nativists oppose immigration?

Summary and Preview Immigrants helped build the nation's economy and cities, but they met resistance from some native-born Americans. In the next lesson you will learn about what life was like in urban America.

Lesson 1 Assessment

Review Ideas, Terms, and People

1. **a. Identify** What was Ellis Island?

   b. Contrast What differences existed between the old immigrants and the new immigrants?

2. **a. Identify** What job opportunities were available to new immigrants?

   b. Summarize How did immigrants attempt to adapt to their new lives in the United States?

   c. Elaborate Why do you think many immigrants tolerated difficult living and working conditions?

3. **a. Recall** What was the purpose of the Chinese Exclusion Act?

   b. Explain Why did some labor unions oppose immigration?

   c. Predict How might the growing opposition to immigration lead to problems in the United States?

Critical Thinking

4. **Categorize** In this lesson you learned about the benefits and challenges new U.S. immigrants faced. Create a graphic organizer similar to the one below and categorize the challenges immigrants faced in different areas of life.

Education:

Work:

Challenges faced by new immigrants

Culture:

Living Conditions:

The Growth of Cities

The Big Idea

American cities experienced dramatic expansion and change in the late 1800s.

Main Ideas

- Both immigrants and native-born Americans moved to growing urban areas in record numbers in the late 1800s and early 1900s.

- New technology and ideas helped cities change and adapt to rapid population growth.

Key Terms and People

mass transit
suburbs
mass culture
Joseph Pulitzer
William Randolph Hearst
department stores
Frederick Law Olmsted

If YOU were there . . .

The year is 1905 and you have just come to the city of Chicago from the small town where you grew up. People rush past as you stop to stare up at the skyscrapers. Elevated trains roar overhead, and electric streetcars clatter along streets already crowded with pushcarts and horse-drawn wagons.

Will you stay and look for work in this big city?

Growth of Urban Areas

In 1850 New York City was the only U.S. city with a population of more than 500,000. By 1900 New York City, Chicago, Philadelphia, St. Louis, Boston, and Baltimore all had more than half a million residents. More than 35 U.S. cities had populations greater than 100,000. About 40 percent of Americans now lived in urban areas.

As you have read, new immigrants were responsible for a lot of this urban growth. So were families from rural areas in the United States. As farm equipment replaced workers in the countryside, large numbers of rural residents moved to the cities in search of work in manufacturing and related fields. This fundamental shift in the economy had far-reaching social effects. Previously, most Americans had worked on farms. People worked for themselves, kept the profits they earned, and made much of what they needed.

Americans who worked in factories faced a far different economic situation. They were wage earners. That is, instead of earning income from their own work, they were paid a set amount by business owners. Instead of making the things they needed, they had to buy them—using limited wages—from merchants in the city where they lived.

African Americans from the rural South also began moving to northern cities in the 1890s. They hoped to escape discrimination and find better educational and economic opportunities. Cities such as Chicago; Cleveland,

Ohio; Detroit, Michigan; and New York City saw large increases in their African American populations during the late 1800s and early 1900s.

Perhaps the most dramatic example of urban growth was the rise of Chicago. The city's population exploded from 30,000 in 1850 to 1.7 million in 1900. Chicago passed St. Louis as the biggest city in the Midwest. Along with the large numbers of African Americans moving to the city, many of Chicago's new residents were immigrants from southern and eastern Europe. In 1900 immigrants and their children made up three-quarters of Chicago's population.

Chicago's location was another **factor** in its rapid growth. Many of the new railroad lines connecting the East and West coasts ran through Chicago. This put Chicago at the heart of the nation's trade in lumber, grain, and meat. Thousands of new Chicago residents found work in the city's huge slaughterhouses and meatpacking plants. Here, meat from the West and Midwest was packed into refrigerated train cars and shipped to growing eastern cities, where it could be sold in shops to customers.

Changing Cities

American cities such as Chicago were ill-prepared for the rapid urban growth of the late 1800s and early 1900s. Where was everyone going to live? How were people going to get from home to work on crowded city streets? Several new technologies helped cities meet these challenges. These technologies forever changed the look and function of U.S. cities.

Building Skyscrapers With so many people moving to urban areas, cities quickly ran out of building space in downtown areas. One solution would be to build taller buildings. Typical city buildings in the mid-1800s were only five stories tall, but taller structures were impossible to construct because the building materials available were either too weak or too heavy.

This changed with the rise of the American steel industry in the late 1800s. Mills began producing tons of strong and inexpensive steel. Soon, architects such as Louis Sullivan of Chicago began designing multistory buildings called skyscrapers. Architects used steel beams to make sturdy frames that could support the weight of tall buildings. This allowed builders to use limited city space more efficiently.

The safety elevator, patented by Elisha Otis in the 1850s, helped make skyscrapers practical. Previous elevators had been unsafe because they would crash to the ground if the elevator cable snapped. Otis's safety elevator included a device to hold the elevator in place if the cable broke.

Getting Around Taller buildings made it possible for more people to live and work in city centers. This increased the need for **mass transit**, or public transportation designed to move many people. By the late 1860s New York City had elevated trains running on tracks above the streets. Chicago followed in the 1890s.

Some cities built underground railroads, known as subways. In 1897 the first subway in the United States opened in Boston. In 1904 the first line of the New York City subway system began operation. Cable cars and

Academic Vocabulary
factor cause

Reading Check
Identify Cause and Effect
What factors led to massive population growth in urban areas during the late 1800s and early 1900s?

In the late 1800s, cities like Chicago took bold steps to alleviate crowding by testing new forms of construction and transportation.

Frederick Law Olmsted

Connect to the Arts Frederick Law Olmsted designed Central Park to serve as a place where New York City residents could relax, exercise, and enjoy nature. Olmsted included areas for horseback riding, ice-skating, boating, and baseball. The Children's District was designed as a place where parents could bring children to stay cool in the summer.

Why do you think a city dweller might be attracted to Central Park?

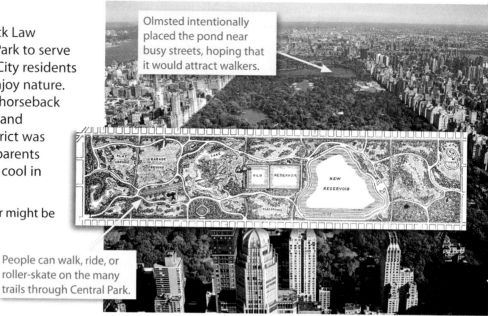

Olmsted intentionally placed the pond near busy streets, hoping that it would attract walkers.

People can walk, ride, or roller-skate on the many trails through Central Park.

electric trolleys also became common. These streetcars cheaply and quickly carried people in the cities to and from work.

Many Americans who could afford it moved to **suburbs**, residential neighborhoods outside of downtown areas that had begun springing up before the Civil War. Mass transit networks made such moves possible. People could live in the suburbs and take trolleys, subways, or trains into the cities.

New Ideas In the late 1800s the United States also began to develop forms of **mass culture**, or leisure and cultural activities shared by many people. One factor contributing to mass culture was a boom in publishing. The invention of the Linotype, an automatic typesetting machine, greatly reduced the time and cost of printing. In 1850 there were fewer than 300 daily newspapers in the country. Because of the use of Linotype machines, by 1900 there were more than 2,000 newspapers.

Big cities often had many newspapers, so publishers had to compete for readers. In 1896 **Joseph Pulitzer** added a color comic to his *New York World* newspaper. More people started buying Pulitzer's paper. **William Randolph Hearst** was publisher of the *New York Journal*. He saw that comics helped sell newspapers. So he added a color comic strip to his paper. Soon, newspapers across the country were adding comic strips.

Mass culture affected how people shopped as well. Giant retail shops, or **department stores**, appeared in some cities during the late 1800s. One of the earliest was Marshall Field in Chicago. Field's offered low prices and large quantities of products. It also was the first department store to offer its customers a restaurant where they could eat while shopping. Newspaper and magazine advertising was used to bring in customers. Advertisers realized that women made most purchasing decisions about household goods, so they targeted their messages to them. The public was also attracted by fancy window displays.

Advertisers also tried new approaches to win customers. Food companies often used wholesome farm images to convey a sense of purity. Some companies came up with clever brand names, such as Uneeda Biscuit crackers, to help customers remember their products.

Rural dwellers did not have access to urban department stores. But they could purchase a huge variety of goods from mail-order companies. In 1897 Sears, Roebuck and Company produced a 507-page catalog. It offered everything from slippers to stoves to saddles. Mail-order customers simply made their selections, sent in their payments, and waited for the merchandise they ordered to arrive by rail or post.

World fairs were another example of mass culture. Fairs brought merchants together, which sometimes resulted in new ideas and products. At the 1904 St. Louis World's Fair, for example, a Syrian food vendor began making cones for a nearby ice cream vendor who had run out of dishes. Ice cream cones became popular throughout the country.

The demand for public entertainment also led to the creation of amusement parks, such as New York's Coney Island. The inexpensive entry tickets made Coney Island a favorite destination for children and families. For a nickel, visitors could ride a new invention called the Switchback Railway—the country's first roller coaster.

As cities grew, people became aware of the need for open public space. Landscape architect **Frederick Law Olmsted** became nationally famous. He designed Central Park in New York City, as well as many state and national parks. Some of his other well-known projects include Prospect Park in Brooklyn, New York, and the U.S. Capitol grounds, which he worked on between 1874 and 1895.

Reading Check
Summarize
What forms of mass culture were available in urban areas?

Summary and Preview Immigration and new technology helped cities grow in the late 1800s. In the next lesson you will learn about some of the problems caused by rapid urban growth.

Lesson 2 Assessment

Review Ideas, Terms, and People

1. a. **Identify** What groups of people began moving to cities in the late 1800s?
   b. **Explain** Why did African Americans begin to move to northern cities in the 1890s?
   c. **Predict** Do you think cities such as Chicago continued to grow in the 1900s? Why or why not?

2. a. **Define** What is mass transit? What made mass transit necessary?
   b. **Explain** How did new inventions make it possible for people to build skyscrapers?
   c. **Evaluate** Which improvement to urban living do you think had the greatest impact on people's lives? Explain your answer.

Critical Thinking

3. **Identify Cause and Effect** In this lesson you learned about the causes for the growth of cities. Create a graphic organizer similar to the one below and identify the effects of city growth. You may need to add more circles.

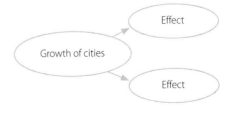

Growth of cities → Effect
Growth of cities → Effect

City Life

The Big Idea

The rapid growth of cities in the late 1800s created both challenges and opportunities.

Main Ideas

- Crowded urban areas faced a variety of social problems.

- People worked to improve the quality of life in U.S. cities.

Key Terms and People

Jacob Riis
settlement houses
Jane Addams
Hull House
assimilation
Florence Kelley

If YOU were there . . .

You live in a fast-growing city in 1895. When you walk the streets, you meet families who are packed into run-down apartments in crowded, filthy neighborhoods. You meet immigrants who want to study English but have no money for classes. You are determined to help these city residents improve their lives.

What would you do to help improve life in your city?

Urban Problems

In cities of the late 1800s and early 1900s, there was a shortage of affordable housing. This forced many poor families to squeeze into tiny tenement apartments, which were frequently unsafe and unsanitary. Journalist and photographer **Jacob Riis** became famous for exposing the horrible conditions in New York City tenements. Riis wrote about one typical tenement family:

> "There were nine in the family: husband, wife, an aged grandmother, and six children . . . All nine lived in two rooms, one about ten feet square that served as parlor, bedroom, and eating-room, the other a small hall-room made into a kitchen."
>
> —Jacob Riis, *How the Other Half Lives*

Overcrowding caused sanitation problems. Most cities did not have a good system for collecting trash, so garbage often piled up outside apartment buildings. An article in the *New York Tribune* described the garbage in front of one tenement as a "mass of air poisoning, death-breeding filth, reeking in the fierce sunshine."

Unsafe conditions were also common in tenements. Before 1900 most cities did not have laws requiring landlords to fix their tenements or to maintain safety standards. A fire on one floor could easily spread, and fire escapes were often blocked or broken.

Overcrowded city tenements caused problems such as disease, fire, and crime.

Tenement Life

Causes
- Overcrowding
- Unsafe buildings
- Unsanitary conditions
- Scarce running water
- Poor ventilation

Effects
- Diseases such as tuberculosis and cholera
- High child death rates
- Fire
- Crime

Tenement rooms had few or no windows to let in fresh air and sunshine. Comfort was also scarce, with so many people crowded into such small spaces. Running water and indoor plumbing were also scarce. So was clean water. Cities often dumped garbage into local rivers that were used for drinking water.

Disease-causing bacteria grew easily in these conditions. Diseases such as cholera, typhoid, influenza, and tuberculosis spread quickly in crowded neighborhoods. Children were the most vulnerable to these diseases. For example, babies born in Chicago in 1870 had only a 50 percent chance of living to the age of five.

Air pollution was also a serious environmental problem in many growing cities. This was a time when many business leaders were building huge oil refineries, steel mills, and other factories. The steel mills of Andrew Carnegie, for example, helped make Pittsburgh the nation's steel-making center in the late 1800s. Steel mills brought jobs and wealth to Pittsburgh. But they also caused some of the nation's worst environmental issues. "Every street appears to end in a huge, black cloud," said one writer. "Pittsburgh is smoke, smoke, smoke—everywhere smoke." The air was so polluted at times that the city had to turn on outdoor lighting during the day.

The work of many city governments slowly helped to lessen some of these urban problems. By the late 1800s new sewage and water purification systems improved city sanitation. Many major cities began hiring

Reading Check
Summarize
What challenges did many city residents face in the late 1800s?

full-time firefighters and police officers. Police officers in cities were typically placed in one neighborhood. They knew the local residents and were frequently involved in local activities. They could spot local problems and, in many cases, provide help to immigrants.

Improving City Life

Jacob Riis hoped his book *How the Other Half Lives* would shock many Americans—and it did. A reformer named Lawrence Veiller helped lead the effort to improve conditions in tenements. Describing the effects of tenement living on children, he wrote:

> "A child living its early years in dark rooms, without sunlight or fresh air, does not grow up to be a normal, healthy person . . . It is not of such material that strong nations are made."
>
> —Lawrence Veiller, quoted in *Readings in American History, Vol. 2*

Veiller worked with an organization called the Charity Organization Society (COS) to get changes made to New York laws. In 1900 he and the COS sponsored an exhibit of photographs and maps graphically showing the conditions of New York tenements. More than 10,000 people visited the exhibit, and they were shocked by what they saw. The work of Veiller and the COS helped pass the 1901 New York State Tenement House Act. This law required new buildings to have better ventilation and running water. It became a model for housing reform in other states.

Because there was little government aid available in the 1800s, private organizations generally took on the task of helping the urban poor. Some individuals set up **settlement houses**, or neighborhood centers in poor areas that offered education, recreation, and social activities.

Hull House

Neighborhood children attended kindergarten at Hull House. Their parents typically had low-paying jobs, and many were children of immigrants. Children like these had few other options for education.

How did Hull House try to improve the lives of children?

Jane Addams 1860–1935

Jane Addams was born in Cedarville, Illinois. Like many upper-class women of the era, she received a college education but found few jobs open to her. In 1888, on a visit to England with classmate Ellen Gates Starr, she visited a London settlement house. On their return to the United States, Addams and Starr opened a settlement house in Chicago. They started a kindergarten and a public playground. Addams also became involved in housing safety and sanitation issues, factory inspection, and immigrants' rights. In 1931 she shared the Nobel Peace Prize for her work with the Women's International League for Peace and Freedom.

Summarize
How did Jane Addams try to improve the lives of workers?

Settlement houses were staffed by professionals and volunteers. Many were educated women who came from wealthy families. In 1886 Charles B. Stover and Stanton Coit established the first settlement house in the United States. It was called Neighborhood Guild and was located on the Lower East Side in New York City. In 1889 **Jane Addams** and Ellen Gates Starr moved into a run-down building in a poor Chicago neighborhood and turned it into **Hull House**, the most famous settlement house of the period.

The Hull House staff focused on the needs of immigrant families. By 1893 Hull House was serving 2,000 people a week. Some families went through a process of **assimilation**, in which they adopted some American beliefs and aspects of American culture. The Hull House staff helped to assimilate the immigrants by providing English classes, day care, and cooking and sewing classes. Children and adults took part in club meetings, art classes, plays, and learned American sports.

Jane Addams and the staff at Hull House also worked for reforms. They studied the problems facing immigrants and poor city dwellers, then searched for ways to improve conditions. **Florence Kelley** was one important reformer at Hull House. She visited sweatshops and wrote about the problems there. Her work helped convince lawmakers to take action. Illinois passed a law in 1893 to limit working hours for women and to prevent child labor.

Kelley became the state's chief factory inspector and helped enforce the law. Although she believed more reforms were needed, she did report some improvements:

"Previous to the passage of the factory law of 1893, it was the rule of [a candy] factory to work the children . . . from 7 A.M. to 9 P.M., with twenty minutes for lunch, and no supper, a working week of eighty-two hours . . . Since the enactment of the factory law, their working week has consisted of six days of eight hours each, a reduction of thirty-four hours a week."

– Florence Kelley and Alzina P. Stevens, from *Hull House Maps and Papers*

Reading Check
Draw Conclusions
How did Hull House help improve city life?

As Hull House gained recognition, the settlement house movement spread to other cities. Most settlement houses continued to provide programs and services for city dwellers through the early 1900s. Some, such as Germantown Settlement in Pennsylvania, remain active today.

Summary and Preview Reformers in the late 1800s worked to solve urban problems. In the next module you will learn how Progressives pushed for further reforms.

Lesson 3 Assessment

Review Ideas, Terms, and People

1. a. Describe What were conditions like in tenements?

b. Summarize What problems resulted from the rapid growth of cities?

c. Draw Conclusions Why do you think people lived in tenements?

2. a. Define What is a settlement house?

b. Explain How did settlement houses help city dwellers?

c. Evaluate Do you think settlement houses were successful? Why or why not?

Critical Thinking

3. Categorize In this lesson you learned about urban problems. Create a chart similar to the one below and identify the responses to those problems.

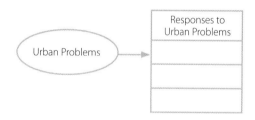

Social Studies Skills

Make Comparisons

Define the Skill

Understanding similarities is important when studying history. Comparing two or more people, things, events, or ideas highlights the similarities between them. Making comparisons can help clarify larger historical issues. This is true when comparing different time periods or when comparing different things from the same time period. Making comparisons is important in identifying historical connections.

Learn the Skill

When you encounter similar people, things, events, or ideas in history, use the following guidelines to make comparisons.

1. Identify who or what you are going to compare.

2. Look for similarities between them. Find examples of what makes them alike. Note any differences as well.

3. Use comparison words such as "like," "both," and "similar" to point out similarities.

In this module you have learned about several reformers, including Lawrence Veiller and Florence Kelley. Veiller helped lead the effort to improve conditions in tenements. Kelley was a reformer who worked at Hull House.

Lawrence Veiller and Florence Kelley were alike in many ways. Although Veiller focused on tenements and Kelley concentrated on factory work, both were concerned with problems that affected children. Both did research about their issues. Both then wrote about the poor conditions they found.

Both Veiller and Kelley worked successfully for laws that would improve those conditions. Kelley's work helped convince Illinois lawmakers to pass a law to limit child labor. Similarly, Veiller helped to get the 1901 New York State Tenement House Act passed.

Practice the Skill

Review the module to find two people, things, events, or ideas that are similar. Then apply the guidelines to answer the following questions.

1. Which people, things, events, or ideas will you compare? Why is each of them important?

2. How are they alike? How are they different?

Module 5 Assessment

Review Vocabulary, Terms, and People

Identify the descriptions below with the correct term or person from the module.

1. Public transportation systems built to move many people and ease traffic in crowded cities

2. Founded Hull House with Ellen Gates Starr in 1889

3. Organizations created by immigrants to help each other in times of sickness, unemployment, or other troubles

4. Law banning Chinese people from moving to the United States

5. Neighborhood centers in poor urban areas that offered education, recreation, and social activities

6. Landscape architect who designed New York City's Central Park

7. Small shops or mills where immigrants worked for long hours in hot, unhealthy conditions

---

Comprehension and Critical Thinking

Lesson 1

8. a. **Identify** From what parts of the world did the wave of new immigrants come?

   b. **Analyze** In what ways did immigration patterns in the United States change in the late 1800s?

   c. **Elaborate** In your opinion, were the difficulties that immigrants faced worth the benefits of life in the United States? Explain.

Lesson 2

9. a. **Recall** Why did U.S. cities experience such rapid growth in the late 1800s?

   b. **Analyze** How did new technologies help cities deal with population growth?

   c. **Elaborate** Would you have preferred to live in a city or in a suburb? Why?

Lesson 3

10. a. **Recall** What were conditions like in tenements in the late 1800s?

    b. **Make Inferences** Why did rapid population growth cause problems in cities?

    c. **Elaborate** Why do you think the settlement house movement grew in the late 1800s and early 1900s?

Review Themes

11. **Economics** What role did economics play in the growth of cities?

12. **Society and Culture** How did the lives of city dwellers change with the rise of mass culture?

Reading Skills

Understand Historical Fact versus Historical Fiction *Use the Reading Skills taught in this module to answer the question about the reading selection below.*

> Mass culture affected how people shopped as well. Giant retail shops, or department stores, appeared in some cities during the late 1800s. One of the earliest was Marshall Field in Chicago. Field's offered low prices and large quantities of products. It also was the first department store to offer its customers a restaurant where they could eat while shopping. Newspaper and magazine advertising was used to bring in customers. Advertisers realized that women made most purchasing decisions about household goods. The public was also attracted by fancy window displays.

13. Which facts above can be verified? Where would you look to verify them?

Social Studies Skills

Make Comparisons *Use the Social Studies Skills taught in this module to complete the activity below.*

14. Choose two reforms that were discussed in this module. Make a comparison between the two.

Focus on Writing

15. **Write a Memo** In this module you learned about the people, places, and events of the late 1800s. Suppose you are a writer at a television network developing a story idea for a drama series set in this time period. Decide which people, places, and events you will include in your television drama series. Then draft a one- or two-paragraph memo to your boss describing the series. Remember to describe the basic plot, setting, and characters.

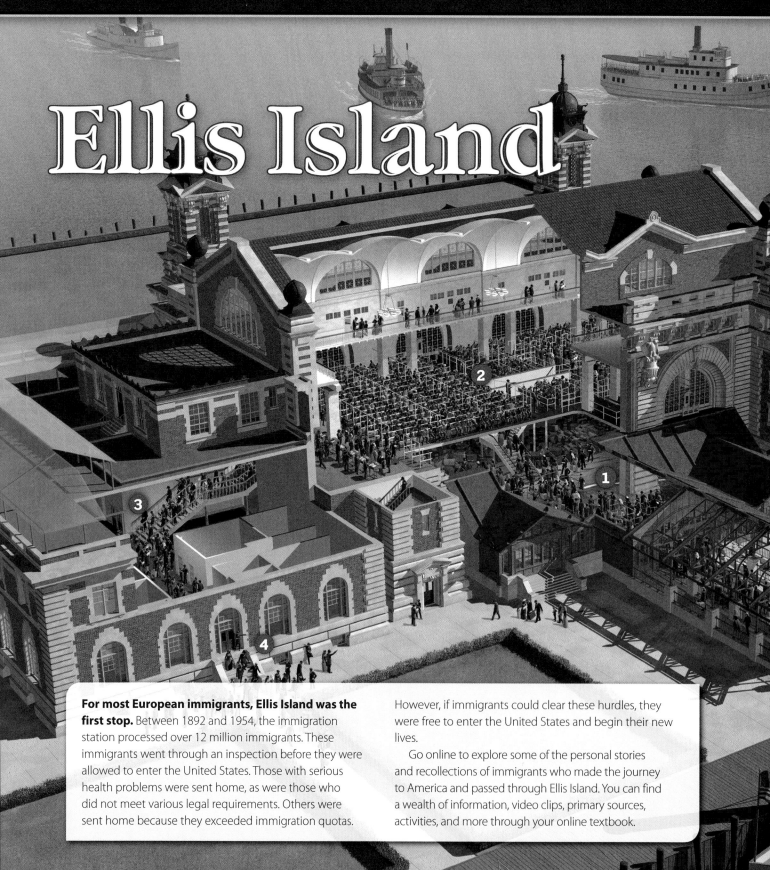

Ellis Island

For most European immigrants, Ellis Island was the first stop. Between 1892 and 1954, the immigration station processed over 12 million immigrants. These immigrants went through an inspection before they were allowed to enter the United States. Those with serious health problems were sent home, as were those who did not meet various legal requirements. Others were sent home because they exceeded immigration quotas.

However, if immigrants could clear these hurdles, they were free to enter the United States and begin their new lives.

Go online to explore some of the personal stories and recollections of immigrants who made the journey to America and passed through Ellis Island. You can find a wealth of information, video clips, primary sources, activities, and more through your online textbook.

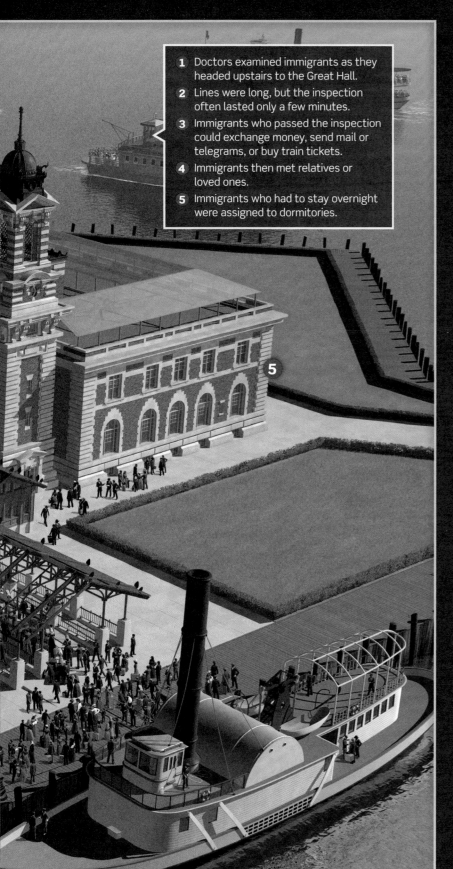

1 Doctors examined immigrants as they headed upstairs to the Great Hall.

2 Lines were long, but the inspection often lasted only a few minutes.

3 Immigrants who passed the inspection could exchange money, send mail or telegrams, or buy train tickets.

4 Immigrants then met relatives or loved ones.

5 Immigrants who had to stay overnight were assigned to dormitories.

The Golden Door

Watch the video to see how and why immigrants traveled to the United States.

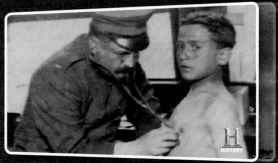

Examination

Watch the video to see the physical examination that immigrants experienced at Ellis Island.

Quotas

Watch the video to see how immigration quotas affected immigrants trying to come to the United States.

Module 6
The Progressive Spirit of Reform

Essential Question
How progressive were the Progressives?

About the Photo: The reform movements of the late 1800s and early 1900s were led by ordinary citizens such as these women, calling for their right to vote.

▶ *Explore ONLINE!*

HISTORY

VIDEOS, including...
- Teddy Roosevelt vs. Corporate America
- James Garfield
- Triangle Shirtwaist Fire
- W.E.B. Du Bois

☑ Document-Based Investigations

☑ Graphic Organizers

☑ Interactive Games

☑ Image Carousel: Gilded Age Presidents

☑ Image with Hotspots: The Other Half

☑ Image with Hotspots: Working Conditions for Children, Early 1900s

In this module you will learn about the reform movements that swept across the United States in the late 1800s and early 1900s.

What You Will Learn . . .

Timeline of Events 1865–1925

▶ *Explore ONLINE!*

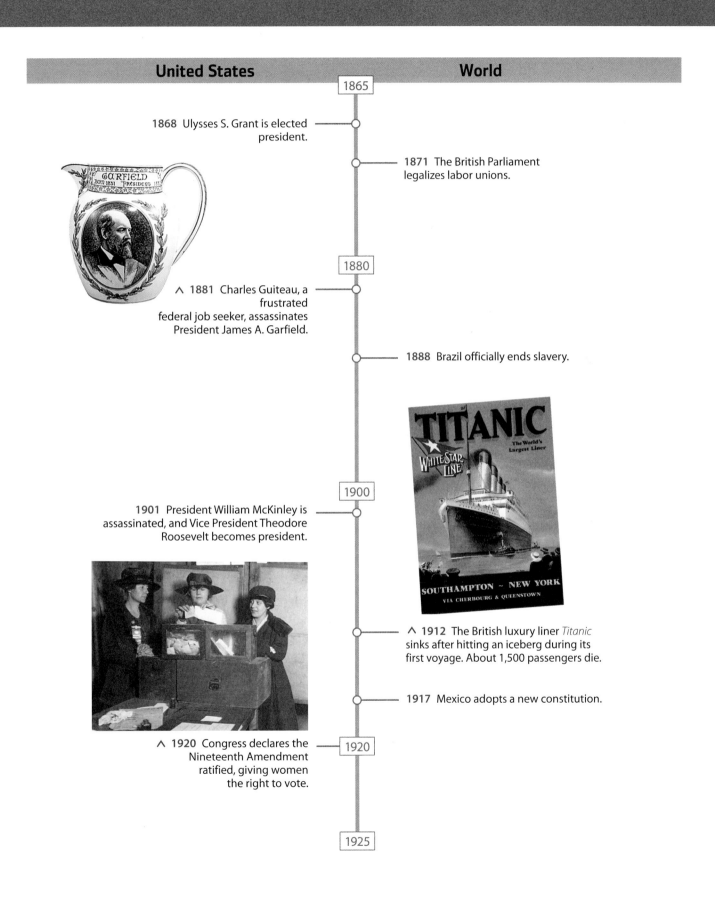

United States | World

1865

1868 Ulysses S. Grant is elected president.

1871 The British Parliament legalizes labor unions.

1880

∧ **1881** Charles Guiteau, a frustrated federal job seeker, assassinates President James A. Garfield.

1888 Brazil officially ends slavery.

1900

1901 President William McKinley is assassinated, and Vice President Theodore Roosevelt becomes president.

∧ **1912** The British luxury liner *Titanic* sinks after hitting an iceberg during its first voyage. About 1,500 passengers die.

1917 Mexico adopts a new constitution.

∧ **1920** Congress declares the Nineteenth Amendment ratified, giving women the right to vote.

1920

1925

Reading Social Studies

THEME FOCUS:

Politics, Society and Culture

In this module you will read about the corrupt politics of the Gilded Age, a time marked by attempts at reform. You will learn how society and culture reacted and responded to the problems of corruption and inequality. Finally, you will read about several presidents of the early 1900s who supported ideas and initiatives that promoted social reform.

READING FOCUS:

Evaluate Sources

Historical texts and current history books are good sources of information about the past. However, some sources can be more reliable than others to learn the truth.

Evaluate Texts Sometimes people write texts with a specific purpose or viewpoint in mind. Determining what the author's goal was in writing a passage can help you evaluate whether to believe all of the text, or merely some of it. Knowing which parts you can believe and which you cannot will help you understand what really happened in history.

Notice how one reader evaluated the source below.

> The man, therefore, who as the owner of newspapers, <u>would corrupt public opinion</u> is the most danger-ous enemy of the State. We may talk about the perils incident [dangers attached] to the <u>concentration of wealth</u>, about the perils flowing from a <u>disregard of fiduciary</u> [finan-cial] responsibility, about <u>abuses of privilege</u>, about <u>exploiting the government for private advantage</u>; but all of these menaces, great as they are, are nothing compared with a deliberate, persistent, artful, purchased endeavor to [change and direct] the public judgment.
>
> —*Harper's Weekly*, October 20, 1906

The author is using strong words to describe his viewpoint. Maybe he isn't being as objective as he should be.

The article lists several ideas that the author seems to think are bad. Are these things really bad? Can that help me determine the author's viewpoint?

This magazine was widely read when the article appeared. I think that makes the article a good source for some viewpoints of the time.

You Try It!

Read the passage below and evaluate whether you would use it as a source for a paper.

> Space is no intervention now between communication. [N]ot only do the wires of copper bind the world together in closer communication, but with the telephone it is possible to converse [talk] with friends a thousand miles away, hearing distinctly every word and recognizing the individual voice. Closer acquaintance has thus wrought [created] vast changes in public opinions and policies. The entire civilized world has been drawn more closely together, old ideas and prejudices have been wiped out.
>
> —*Cincinnati Times-Star,* January 1, 1900, quoted in *Yellow Journalism* by W. Joseph Campbell

1. What viewpoint of new technology is the author taking in this article? How can you tell?
2. Do you believe that the telephone brought about "changes in public opinions and policies"? Why or why not? Why might the author say this?
3. Can you trust the author when he says that "old ideas and prejudices have been wiped out"? Why or why not? Why might the author say this?
4. Did this article appear in a well-known newspaper? Does this make it more trustworthy or less?
5. Would you use this article as a source for writing a paper about how new inventions affected life in the early 1900s? Explain your answer.

As you read Module 6, evaluate the primary sources for their usefulness in understanding history.

Key Terms and People

Lesson 1
political machines
Progressives
muckrakers
Seventeenth Amendment
recall
initiative
referendum
Robert M. La Follette

Lesson 2
Triangle Shirtwaist Fire
workers' compensation laws
capitalism
socialism
William "Big Bill" Haywood
Industrial Workers of the World

Lesson 3
Eighteenth Amendment
National American Woman
   Suffrage Association
Alice Paul
Nineteenth Amendment
Booker T. Washington
Ida B. Wells
W. E. B. Du Bois
National Association for
   the Advancement of
   Colored People

Lesson 4
Theodore Roosevelt
Pure Food and Drug Act
conservation
William Howard Taft
Progressive Party
Woodrow Wilson
Sixteenth Amendment

The Gilded Age and the Progressive Movement

The Big Idea

From the late 1800s through the early 1900s, the Progressive movement addressed problems in American society.

Main Ideas

- Political corruption was common during the Gilded Age.

- Progressives pushed for reforms to improve living conditions.

- Progressive reforms expanded the voting power of citizens.

Key Terms and People

political machines
Progressives
muckrakers
Seventeenth Amendment
recall
initiative
referendum
Robert M. La Follette

If YOU were there . . .

You live in a big-city neighborhood in the 1890s. You and your brother are both looking for jobs. You know that the man down the street is the "ward boss." He can always get city jobs for his friends and neighbors. But in return you'll have to promise to vote the way he tells you to in the upcoming election.

Would you ask the ward boss for a job?
Why or why not?

Political Corruption

The late 1800s in the United States are often called the Gilded Age. The term came from a novel by that name. *The Gilded Age* highlighted the inequality between wealthy business owners, who profited from the Industrial Revolution, and workers, who often labored under terrible conditions for little pay. Many people began to believe that the government should help fix this inequality. The first step was to get rid of corruption in politics.

Political Machines In the late 1800s **political machines** were powerful organizations of professional politicians that dominated city and county politics. Political machines sorted out some of the biggest urban issues of the time. However, they often resorted to corrupt methods.

For example, political machines were notorious for election fraud. Not only did they pay people to vote for their candidates, they also stuffed ballot boxes with extra votes for their candidates and bribed vote counters. Some political machines even hired men called "repeaters" to cast several votes in the same election. To avoid being caught, repeaters would change their coats and shave off their beards between votes. Hence the old Chicago saying "Vote early and vote often."

Political machines were run by leaders called bosses, who used their position to gain money and power. The boss

"Who Stole the People's Money? 'Twas Him"

This 1871 political cartoon shows "Boss" Tweed (bottom left) standing in a ring of corrupt politicians known as Tammany Hall. The cartoonist shows each person blaming the one next to him for government corruption. The labels on the men's backs show that they represent different interests.

The men have labels on their backs that show they represent different interests.

Analyze Historical Sources
Why do you think the men are shown standing in a circle?

would demand bribes and payoffs in exchange for contracts and jobs, as did other machine politicians. They also frequently traded favors for votes. For example, the boss might hand out city jobs to unqualified people in exchange for their political support.

New York City's political machine, Tammany Hall, was one of the most notorious political machines. After winning city elections in 1888, members of Tammany Hall rewarded their supporters with about 12,000 jobs. The leader of Tammany Hall was William Marcy Tweed. Along with his greedy friends, "Boss" Tweed stole enormous amounts of money—up to $200 million—from the city.

Despite such corruption, political machines did a number of good things. They built parks, sewers, schools, and roads in many cities. They also provided key social services, such as orphanages and fire brigades.

Machine politicians made a special effort to reach out to immigrants and poor families. They helped newcomers find jobs and homes, supplied coal in winter, and provided turkeys for holiday suppers. As one Boston politician said, the role of the machine boss was "to be . . . somebody that any bloke [man] can come to . . . and get help." In return, many poor families and immigrants gratefully supported political bosses and machines.

Cleaning Up Political Corruption Corruption was also a problem to the federal government. Many people thought that the corruption extended to the administration of President Ulysses S. Grant. During Grant's second term, federal officials were jailed for taking bribes from whiskey makers in exchange for allowing them to avoid paying taxes. Another scandal involved members of Congress who had taken bribes to allow the Union Pacific Railway to receive government funds. These scandals and others caused many Americans to question the honesty of national leaders.

Gilded Age Presidents

Rutherford B. Hayes

Republican; in office: 1877–1881
Hayes promised to reform the government with "thorough, radical, and complete" changes.

James A. Garfield

Republican; in office: 1881
Garfield attempted reforms before he was assassinated.

Chester A. Arthur

Republican; in office: 1881–1885
Arthur supported a system for awarding federal jobs based on merit, not party loyalty.

Grover Cleveland

Democrat; in office: 1885–1889, 1893–1897
Cleveland was known for his honesty and for getting involved in the day-to-day details of government.

Benjamin Harrison

Republican; in office: 1889–1893
Harrison supported the Sherman Antitrust Act, which regulated business monopolies.

William McKinley

Republican; in office: 1897–1901
McKinley avoided scandals and helped win public trust in the government.

In response, Americans began calling for changes in the civil service, the government job system. They disliked the spoils system, the practice of giving jobs to the winning candidates' supporters. Thomas Jefferson was the first to reward supporters with jobs. After his administration, each time a new party took power, it replaced many government officials. Many new employees were unqualified and untrained.

By the late 1800s government corruption was widespread. Reformers demanded that only qualified people be given government jobs. In response, President Rutherford B. Hayes made minor reforms, such as firing a powerful member of the New York Republican political machine. President James A. Garfield also attempted reforms. But on July 2, 1881, Garfield was attacked and shot twice by a mentally unstable federal job seeker named Charles Guiteau. The president later died from his wounds. Vice President Chester A. Arthur became president.

Arthur continued the push for reforms by backing the Pendleton Civil Service Act, which was passed in 1883. This law set up a merit system for awarding federal jobs. Under the Pendleton Act, more than 10 percent of government job applicants had to pass an exam before they could be hired. It was a start to reforming other government practices.

Reading Check
Analyze Information
What factors led to civil-service reform?

Progressives Push for Reforms

A group of reformers known as **Progressives** also worked to improve society in the late 1800s. Progressives tried to solve problems caused by rapid industrial and urban growth. They wanted to eliminate the causes of problems such as crime, disease, and poverty. They fought for reforms ranging from better working conditions to education programs in poor neighborhoods.

Muckrakers at Work Some journalists urged Progressives to action by writing stories that vividly described problems in society. These journalists were nicknamed **muckrakers** because they "raked up" and exposed the muck, or filth, of society. Muckrakers wrote about troubling issues such as

Historical Source

The Other Half

In 1890 Jacob Riis published *How the Other Half Lives*. The book was a collection of photographs of residents and workers in New York City tenement buildings, including families and immigrants. Sweatshops, such as the one here, were located in tenements to avoid the labor laws that affected factories. Workers crowded into the small, stuffy spaces. The conditions of life that Riis showed in his photographs, like this one, shocked many wealthier Americans.

Sweatshops turned out large amounts of clothing at low prices.

This 12-year-old boy said he was 16 in order to keep his job of pulling threads.

Analyze Historical Sources
How might this photograph encourage people to become reformers?

child labor, racial discrimination, living conditions in housing slums, and corruption in business and politics.

In 1902 and 1903 Lincoln Steffens wrote a series of articles in *McClure's Magazine* exposing corruption in city government. In one article, he described how government officials in St. Louis, Missouri, used their positions to earn extra money illegally:

> "Men empowered to issue peddlers' licenses and permits to citizens who wished to erect awnings or use a portion of the sidewalk for storage purposes charged an amount in excess of the prices stipulated [set] by law, and pocketed the difference."
> —Lincoln Steffens, *The Shame of the Cities*

Another muckraker, Ida B. Tarbell, wrote articles criticizing the unfair business practices of the Standard Oil Company. Upton Sinclair exposed unsanitary practices in the meat-processing industry in his novel *The Jungle*.

Although such writing angered many politicians and business leaders, it also helped to unite Progressives. Muckrakers influenced voters, causing them to pressure politicians into backing reforms.

Reform Successes A major goal of Progressive reformers was to help the urban poor. You have read about the work of housing reformers, which led to the 1901 New York State Tenement House Act. Other Progressives started settlement houses similar to Jane Addams's Hull House. People usually started settlement houses in poor areas in order to improve education, housing, and sanitation there.

The movement for urban reform also led to new professions. City planners helped design safer building codes and opened new public parks. Civil engineers improved transportation by paving streets and building bridges. Sanitation engineers tried to solve problems concerning pollution, waste disposal, and impure water supplies. Death rates dropped dramatically in areas where planners and engineers addressed these problems.

Progressives also believed that improving education would lead to a better society. In response to their demands, states passed laws requiring all children to attend school. Some Progressives started kindergarten programs to help young city children learn basic social skills. In 1873 reformer Susan Blow opened the first American public kindergarten in St. Louis. By 1898 more than 4,000 kindergartens had opened in the United States.

John Dewey was a key supporter of early childhood education. His **motive** was to help children learn problem-solving skills, not just memorize facts. He thought this would help them in everyday life. Dewey's teaching methods became a model for progressive education across the country.

Progressives also worked to improve the education of doctors and nurses. In the late 1800s there were not enough well-trained and professionally organized doctors. Researchers knew the causes of diseases such

Academic Vocabulary
motive a reason for doing something

as pneumonia and tuberculosis. However, there were few medical organizations that could help spread this knowledge.

Under the leadership of Joseph McCormack, the American Medical Association (AMA) brought together local medical organizations in 1901. The AMA supported laws designed to protect public health and showed how Progressives could organize to help improve society. Other organizations followed the AMA's lead.

Reading Check
Find Main Ideas
How did progressive reforms improve society?

Expansion of Voting Power

Some Progressives worked to reduce the power of political machines in state and local governments. In many places, reformers replaced corrupt ballots that listed only one party's candidates with ballots prepared by the government that listed all candidates. Under pressure from reformers, many states adopted secret ballots. This ensured privacy for every voter.

Voting Reforms Progressives thought officials would be more responsive to voters if voters were directly involved in government. To help make this happen, reformers worked to expand voting power. For example, they favored the **Seventeenth Amendment**, which allowed Americans to vote directly for U.S. senators. Before the constitutional amendment was passed in 1913, state legislatures had elected senators.

Reformers also favored the direct primary, an election in which voters choose candidates to run for public office directly. In 1903 Wisconsin became the first state to have a direct primary. Previously, party leaders had selected which candidates would run for office.

Other reform measures allowed voters to take action against corrupt politicians. Some states and cities gave unhappy voters the right to sign a petition asking for a special vote. The purpose of that vote was to **recall**, or remove, an official before the end of his or her term. If enough voters signed the petition, the vote took place. The official could then be removed from office if there was a majority of recall votes.

─────── BIOGRAPHY ───────────────────────────────────

Robert M. La Follette 1855–1925

Born in rural Wisconsin in 1855, Robert M. La Follette began his political career at a young age. He was elected to the U.S. House of Representatives in 1884, becoming the youngest member of Congress. He soon earned the nickname "Fighting Bob" for his energetic speaking style and his active support for progressive reforms.

After serving as Wisconsin's governor and as U.S. senator, La Follette ran for president as the Progressive Party candidate in 1924. He won his home state and received about 16 percent of the popular vote.

Draw Conclusions
Why might La Follette have been proud of the nickname "Fighting Bob"?

In California, Oregon, and states in the Midwest, Progressives worked on reforms to give voters direct influence over new laws. A procedure called the **initiative** allowed voters to propose a new law by collecting signatures on a petition. If enough signatures were collected, the proposed law was voted on at the next election. Another measure was called the **referendum**. It permitted voters to approve or reject a law that had already been proposed or passed by a government body. This process gave voters a chance to overrule laws that they opposed.

Government Reforms Progressives also tried to change the way city government operated. Some reformers wanted city government to be run like a business. As a result of their efforts, several cities changed to council-manager governments. Under this system, voters elect a city council. The council then appoints a professional manager to run the city. Other business-minded reformers supported the commission form of government. Under this system, the city is headed by a group of elected officials. Each official manages a major city agency, such as housing or transportation.

One of the leaders of the effort to reform state government was Wisconsin's Republican governor **Robert M. La Follette**. La Follette decreased the power of political machines. He used university professors and other experts to help write new laws and work in state agencies. He also made information on how politicians voted available to the public. That way, voters would know if leaders had kept their campaign promises. Called the Wisconsin Idea, La Follette's plan became a model for progressive reforms in other states.

Summary and Preview Progressives worked to reform government and improve city life. In the next lesson you will learn about reforms in working conditions.

Reading Check
Summarize
How did Progressives work to change voting procedures?

Lesson 1 Assessment

Review Ideas, Terms, and People

1. **a. Recall** What was the main goal of political machines during the Gilded Age?
   b. Draw Conclusions Why do you think some immigrants supported political machines?
   c. Predict Do you think the system of testing government job applicants created by the Pendleton Civil Service Act would work to reduce corruption in the spoils system? Why or why not?
2. **a. Identify** Who were muckrakers, and what effect did they have on reform?
   b. Explain How did Progressives try to improve education?
   c. Evaluate Which progressive reform do you think was most important? Why?

3. **a. Describe** What new ideas and practices were introduced to give voters more power?
   b. Draw Conclusions How did progressive reforms limit the power of political machines?

Critical Thinking

4. **Categorize** In this lesson you learned about key progressive reforms and the problems they addressed. Create a chart similar to the one below and use it to categorize the various progressive reforms.

Progressive Reforms		
Social	Political	Urban

Literature in History

Reform Literature

Word Help

cuffs punches
utter complete
close stuffy
sole only
access right to use
stenches bad smells
in vain without success
galling causing pain; irritating
fetters chains
heaves rises and falls
avail help

❶ The writer wants you to imagine that he is taking you on a tour of the building. *Why do you think he chooses this way to describe the place?*

❷ Find one detail that appeals to each sense: sight, sound, smell, taste, and touch. *How would you sum up, in one sentence, the place that Riis describes?*

About the Reading *How the Other Half Lives* describes the tenement houses where immigrants lived in New York City. Its author, Jacob Riis, was a newspaper reporter. His nonfiction book made Americans aware of the extremes of poverty suffered by working people. Riis believed that every human being deserved a decent, safe place to live. *How the Other Half Lives* led to reforms and new laws that improved housing conditions.

As You Read Look for details that help you see, hear, and smell Cherry Street.

From *How the Other Half Lives*
by Jacob Riis (1849–1914)

Cherry Street. Be a little careful, please! ❶ The hall is dark and you might stumble over the children pitching pennies back there. Not that it would hurt them; kicks and cuffs are their daily diet. They have little else. Here where the hall turns and dives into utter darkness is a step, and another, another. A flight of stairs. You can feel your way, if you cannot see it. Close? Yes! What would you have? All the fresh air that ever enters these stairs comes from the hall door that is forever slamming, and from the windows of dark bedrooms that in turn receive from the stairs their sole supply of the elements God meant to be free . . . That was a woman filling her pail by the hydrant you just bumped against. The sinks are in the hallway, that all the tenants may have access—and all be poisoned alike by their summer stenches. Hear the pump squeak! It is the lullaby of tenement house babes. In summer, when a thousand thirsty throats pant for a cooling drink in this block, it is worked in vain. . . . ❷

The sea of a mighty population, held in galling fetters, heaves uneasily in the tenements. . . . If it rise once more, no human power may avail to check it. The gap between the classes in which it surges, unseen, unsuspected by the thoughtless, is widening day by day. . . . I know of but one bridge that will carry us over safe, a bridge founded upon justice and built of human hearts.

Word Help

borax white powder used in manufacturing and cleaning

glycerine sweet, sticky liquid

hoppers containers

consumption to eat or drink

consumption tuberculosis, a lung disease that was fatal at that time

ladled added with a large spoon

❶ *What overall effect or mood does Sinclair create?*

❷ *Based on the details in this passage, what were the packers most concerned about?*

❸ *Why do you think rats were considered nuisances?*

❹ *Find details that reveal how one improvement in working conditions might have resulted in healthier sausage.*

About the Reading *The Jungle* focused the nation's attention on immigrant workers in the meatpacking industry. Upton Sinclair's novel showed bosses forcing human beings to live and work like animals. He also described, in shocking detail, how meat was handled. Sinclair published his book in 1906. Later that same year, the U.S. government passed the Pure Food and Drug Act and the Meat Inspection Act. Many Americans even gave up eating meat for a while.

As You Read Look for details that create one overwhelming effect.

From *The Jungle*
by Upton Sinclair (1878–1968)

There was never the least attention paid to what was cut up for sausage; there would come back from Europe old sausage that had been rejected, and that was mouldy and white—it would be dosed with borax and glycerine, and dumped into hoppers, and made over again for home consumption. There would be meat that had tumbled out on the floor, in the dirt and sawdust, where the workers had tramped and spit uncounted billions of consumption germs. ❶ There would be meat stored in great piles in rooms and the water from leaky roofs would drip over it, and thousands of rats would race about on it. It was too dark in these storage places to see well, but a man would run his hand over these piles of meat and sweep off handfuls of the dried dung of rats. ❷ These rats were nuisances, and the packers would put poisoned bread out for them; they would die, and then rats, bread, and meat would go into the hoppers together. . . . ❸ There was no place for the men to wash their hands before they ate their dinner, and so they made a practice of washing them in the water that was to be ladled into the sausage. ❹

Connect Literature to History

1. **Identify Cause and Effect** Jacob Riis and Upton Sinclair were both muckraking journalists. Why do you think so much muck existed in the tenements and in the meatpacking business? Why had people ignored those conditions for so long?

2. **Identify Cause and Effect** Both Riis and Sinclair believed that improving conditions for immigrants would benefit all of society. Explain how one specific change in the tenements might have a favorable effect on everyone. Then explain how one specific change in meat handling might affect everyone.

3. **Compare and Contrast** Both *How the Other Half Lives* and *The Jungle* inspired Progressives to work for reform. Which work do you think had the greater effect on its readers? Use details from each passage to explain your answer.

Reforming the Workplace

The Big Idea

In the early 1900s Progressives and other reformers focused on improving conditions for American workers.

Main Ideas

- Reformers attempted to improve conditions for child laborers.

- Unions and reformers took steps to improve safety in the workplace and to limit working hours.

Key Terms and People

Triangle Shirtwaist Fire
workers' compensation laws
capitalism
socialism
William "Big Bill" Haywood
Industrial Workers of the World

If YOU were there . . .

You have been working in a hat factory since 1900, when you were eight years old. Now you are experienced enough to run one of the sewing machines. You don't earn as much as older workers, but your family needs every penny you bring home. Still, the long hours make you very tired. One day you hear that people are trying to stop children from doing factory work. They think that children should be at school or playing.

Would you be for or against this social reform? Why?

Improving Conditions for Children

In the early 1900s a reformer named Marie Van Vorst took a series of jobs in factories and clothing mills around the country. She wanted to investigate working conditions for children by living and working alongside them. In a South Carolina textile mill, Van Vorst met children as young as seven years old. She described working with one young child:

> "Through the looms I catch sight of . . . my landlord's little child. She is seven; so small that they have a box for her to stand on. . . . I can see only her fingers as they clutch at the flying spools."
> —Marie Van Vorst, *The Woman Who Toils: Being the Experiences of Two Ladies as Factory Girls*

This girl—and other children like her—provided cheap labor for manufacturers. Some children were paid as little as 40 cents per day. Marie Van Vorst helped focus attention on the problem of child labor. Eliminating the problems of child labor became a major issue for Progressives and other reformers.

Children at Work Children did many jobs in the late 1800s. Boys sold newspapers and shined shoes on the streets. Girls often cooked or cleaned for boarders staying with their families. Girls also worked at home with their mothers, sewing clothes or making handicrafts.

Like the child Van Vorst encountered, many children worked in industry. In 1900 more than 1.75 million children age 15 and under worked in factories, mines, and mills, earning very low wages.

Calls for Reform As reporters published shocking accounts of working conditions for children, more people became aware of the problem. Progressives began to call for new reforms. You have read about Florence Kelley's work against child labor in Illinois. Kelley also served as a board member of the National Consumers' League, the major lobbying group for women's and children's labor issues. A lobbying group works to influence legislators in favor of a cause.

During the early 1900s, reformers finally succeeded in getting some laws passed to ease the conditions of child laborers. In 1912 the state of Massachusetts passed the first minimum wage law, and a commission was created to establish rates for child workers.

In 1916 and 1919 Congress passed federal child labor laws. The laws banned products made with child labor from being shipped from one state to another. The Supreme Court, however, ruled that the laws were unconstitutional. The Court argued that the laws went beyond the federal government's legal power to regulate interstate commerce.

In any case, laws alone could not end child labor. Some parents ignored child labor laws so that their children could continue contributing to the family income. Children were often instructed to lie about their age to government inspectors and tell them they were older than they really were.

Reading Check
Find Main Ideas
How did reformers try to improve child labor conditions?

Child Labor

Young children did much of the work in the American factories of the late 1800s. They were paid less than adult workers.

Working Conditions for Children, Early 1900s

This illustration shows some of the jobs that children did in glass factories in the early 1900s. You can see that there were many ways for young workers to be injured on the job.

Hot air blew from the glass ovens into the working space.

Adult workers closely supervised child workers.

Workers wore no protection against the fires and machinery.

Temperatures in the ovens used to make glass were more than 2,000° Fahrenheit.

Bending and lifting often left young workers tired and sore after their long day's work.

Analyze Visuals
Using the illustration, what can you tell about the life and work of these boys?

Safety and Working Conditions

Child labor reform was only part of the progressive effort to help American workers. Many Progressives also favored laws to ensure workers' safety, limit working hours, and protect workers' rights.

Workplace Safety Workplace accidents were common in the 1800s and early 1900s. In 1900 some 35,000 people were killed in industrial accidents. About 500,000 suffered injuries. One child described how her sister was injured using a machine in a string factory. "You see you mustn't talk or look off a minute," she explained. "My sister was like me. She forgot and talked, and just that minute her finger was off, and she didn't even cry till she picked it up."

Accidents like this were not big news in the early 1900s, but in 1911 a much greater workplace tragedy shocked the nation. It took place at the Triangle Shirtwaist Company, a New York City clothing factory that employed mostly Jewish and Italian teenage immigrant women. On the afternoon of March 25, a fire started on the eighth floor of the factory. Workers tried to escape, but factory owners had locked the exit doors—to reduce theft of materials, they said.

Within moments, the eighth floor was ablaze. The fire spread quickly to two other floors. With the doors locked, escape was nearly impossible. The

DOCUMENT-BASED INVESTIGATION   Historical Source

Triangle Shirtwaist Fire

Ethel Monick was one of the teenage factory workers at the Triangle Shirtwaist Company. In the trial that followed the disaster, she described her experience in the fire. New York City firefighters, pictured at right, train their hoses on the multistory building.

I seen the fire and then I seen all the girls rushing down to the place to escape. So I tried to go through the Greene Street door, and there were quick girls there and I seen I can't get out there, so I went to the elevator, and then I heard the elevator fall down, so I ran through to the Washington Place side. . . . I tried the door and I could not open it, so I thought I was not strong enough to open it, so I hollered girls here is a door, and they all rushed over and they tried to open it, but it was locked and they hollered "the door is locked and we can't open it!"

—Testimony of Ethel Monick, age 16

Analyze Historical Sources
According to Monick, what is the feeling in the factory?

building's only fire escape collapsed under the weight of panic-stricken workers, sending them tumbling to their deaths. With flames at their backs, dozens of other workers leaped from the windows.

By the time firefighters brought the fire under control, 146 workers had died. At a memorial service for the victims, union leader Rose Schneiderman called for action. "It is up to the working people to save themselves," she said. The **Triangle Shirtwaist Fire** and similar accidents led to the passage of laws improving factory safety standards.

Labor leaders and reformers also fought for **workers' compensation laws**, which guaranteed a portion of lost wages to workers injured on the job. In 1902 Maryland became the first state to pass such a law. However, new laws were not always strictly enforced. Working conditions remained poor in many places.

The Courts and Labor

Not everyone supported the new workplace regulations. Some business leaders believed that the economy should operate without any government interference. They went to court to block new labor laws.

One important case began in New York in 1897, after the state passed a law limiting bakers to a ten-hour workday. Joseph Lochner, a bakery owner, challenged the law. The case eventually went to the U.S. Supreme Court in 1905. In *Lochner* v. *New York*, the Court ruled that states could not restrict the rights of employers and workers to enter into any type of labor agreement. The New York law was declared unconstitutional.

The Supreme Court did uphold some limits on working hours for women and children. In the 1908 *Muller* v. *Oregon* case, the Court upheld laws restricting women's work hours. The justices stated that such laws protected women's health, which was of public concern.

Workers faced long hours of grueling work after the Supreme Court struck down a New York law limiting bakery employee workdays to 10 hours a day and 60 hours a week.

Labor Unions

Throughout the Progressive Era, labor unions were a strong force for improving working conditions. During this time, union membership grew, rising from about 800,000 in 1900 to about 5 million in 1920.

Founded in 1896 and led by Samuel Gompers, the American Federation of Labor (AFL) continued to be one of the strongest labor unions. The AFL focused on better working conditions and pay for skilled workers. Gompers supported the American economic system of **capitalism**, in which private businesses run most industries and competition determines the price of goods. Still, using strikes and other methods, the AFL won wage increases and shorter workweeks.

Workers also joined energetic new labor unions to fight for reforms. The International Ladies' Garment Workers' Union (ILGWU) was founded in 1900. Unlike the AFL, which allowed only skilled workers, the ILGWU organized unskilled laborers. In 1909 the garment workers called for a mass strike known as the "Uprising of the 20,000." The strikers won a shorter workweek and higher wages. They also attracted thousands of workers to the union.

Some union members, however, believed in **socialism**—a system in which the government owns and operates a country's means of production. Socialists, led by Eugene V. Debs, hoped that the government would protect workers.

In 1905 a group of socialists and union leaders founded a union that welcomed immigrants, women, African Americans, and others not welcome in the AFL. Led by **William "Big Bill" Haywood**, this socialist union was called the **Industrial Workers of the World** (IWW). Its goal was to organize all workers into one large union that would overthrow capitalism. Known as "Wobblies," IWW members used strikes and boycotts to advance their cause, as well as more radical strategies, such as industrial sabotage.

At the height of its strength in 1912, the IWW led about 20,000 textile workers on strike in Lawrence, Massachusetts, to protest pay cuts. After a bitter, well-publicized ten-week strike, the mill owners gave in and raised wages. The IWW's success, however, was short-lived. Several of their strikes were terrible failures. Fearing the union's revolutionary goals, the government cracked down on the IWW's activities. Strong opposition led to its decline by 1920.

Summary and Preview Progressive reformers fought to improve working conditions. In the next lesson you will learn about how women and minorities struggled for their rights.

Reading Check
Analyze Information
How did reforms change the workplace?

Lesson 2 Assessment

Review Ideas, Terms, and People

1. **a. Recall** What jobs did child laborers often hold?

   b. Explain Why did businesses employ children in factories?

   c. Elaborate Why do you think reformers began to demand improvements to child labor conditions?

2. **a. Identify** What events led to the movement to improve workplace safety?

   b. Make Inferences Why did the Industrial Workers of the World frighten some people?

   c. Predict What conflicts might arise between supporters of capitalism and socialism?

Critical Thinking

3. **Analyze** In this lesson you learned about important labor problems in the 1800s and the workers they affected. Create a graphic organizer similar to the one below to give specific examples of how Progressives tried to reform child labor, women's labor, and workplace conditions.

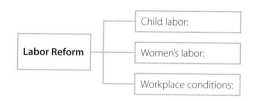

Labor Reform — Child labor: / Women's labor: / Workplace conditions:

The Rights of Women and Minorities

The Big Idea

The Progressive movement made advances for the rights of women and some minorities.

Main Ideas

- Women fought for temperance and the right to vote.
- African American reformers challenged discrimination and called for equality.
- Progressive reforms failed to benefit all minorities.

Key Terms and People

Eighteenth Amendment
National American Woman Suffrage Association
Alice Paul
Nineteenth Amendment
Booker T. Washington
Ida B. Wells
W. E. B. Du Bois
National Association for the Advancement of Colored People

If YOU were there . . .

You are a member of the class of 1912 graduating from an excellent women's college. You have always been interested in science, especially biology. You would like to be a doctor, but you know that medical schools accept very few women. One career path for you is to go into social work. Yet that's not what you really want to do.

How would you want to use your education?

Women Fight for Temperance and Voting Rights

New educational opportunities drew more women into the Progressive movement. In the late 1800s women began attending women's colleges, such as Smith College in Massachusetts and Vassar College in New York, in record numbers. In 1870 only about 20 percent of college students were women. By 1910 that number had doubled. The goal of female students was "to develop as fully as may be the powers of womanhood," said Sophia Smith, founder of Smith College.

Many female graduates entered fields such as social work and teaching. They found it much harder to enter professions such as law and medicine, which were dominated by men. Denied access to such professions, women often put their education to use by becoming active in reform. Women's clubs campaigned for causes such as temperance, women's suffrage, child welfare, and political reform.

The Temperance Movement In the mid-1800s many of these reformers blamed social problems such as family violence and criminal behavior on a number of factors, including urbanization and immigration. They also blamed problems on alcohol consumption. As a result, many groups took up the cause of temperance, or avoidance of alcohol.

In 1874 reformers from many different backgrounds formed the Woman's Christian Temperance Union (WCTU), which fought for adoption of local and state laws restricting the sale of alcohol. Under the leadership of Frances Willard, the organization started 10,000 branches. More than 1,000 saloons were forced to shut down as a result of temperance supporters' efforts.

One especially radical temperance fighter chose more dramatic tactics to fight for her cause. In the 1890s Carry Nation became famous for storming into saloons with a hatchet and smashing liquor bottles. Nation described destroying a Kansas saloon with bricks and rocks:

> "I threw as hard, and as fast as I could, smashing mirrors and bottles and glasses and it was astonishing how quickly this was done."
>
> —Carry Nation, *The Use and Need of the Life of Carry A. Nation, 1909*

Tall and strong, Nation was often arrested for her protest actions. Still, the temperance movement was effective. In 1919 its efforts led to the passage of the **Eighteenth Amendment**, banning the production, sale, and transportation of alcoholic beverages throughout the United States.

The Right to Vote Women reformers also fought for suffrage, or the right to vote. Many people at this time opposed giving women the vote. Political bosses, for instance, worried about the anticorruption efforts of women. Some business leaders worried that women voters would support minimum wage and child labor laws. Other people believed that women should only be homemakers and mothers and not politically active citizens.

In spite of such opposition, the women's suffrage movement began to gain national support in the 1890s. Elizabeth Cady Stanton and Susan B. Anthony founded the **National American Woman Suffrage Association** (NAWSA) in 1890 to promote the cause of women's suffrage. That same year, women won the right to vote in Wyoming. Colorado, Idaho, and Utah soon followed.

In several western states, women had the right to vote. However, it did not become a national right until the ratification of the Nineteenth Amendment in 1920.

The Nineteenth Amendment

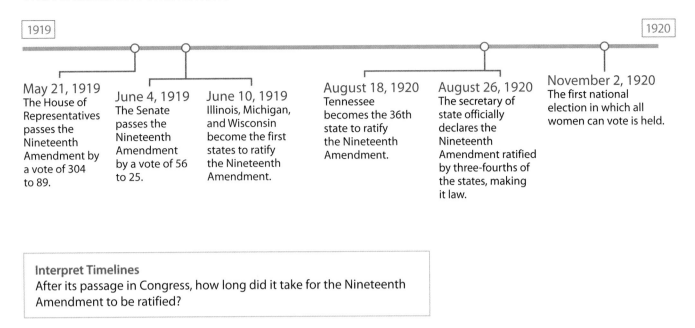

1919

May 21, 1919
The House of Representatives passes the Nineteenth Amendment by a vote of 304 to 89.

June 4, 1919
The Senate passes the Nineteenth Amendment by a vote of 56 to 25.

June 10, 1919
Illinois, Michigan, and Wisconsin become the first states to ratify the Nineteenth Amendment.

August 18, 1920
Tennessee becomes the 36th state to ratify the Nineteenth Amendment.

August 26, 1920
The secretary of state officially declares the Nineteenth Amendment ratified by three-fourths of the states, making it law.

November 2, 1920
The first national election in which all women can vote is held.

1920

Interpret Timelines
After its passage in Congress, how long did it take for the Nineteenth Amendment to be ratified?

Carrie Chapman Catt became president of NAWSA in 1900. Catt mobilized more than 1 million volunteers for the movement. She argued that women should have a voice in creating laws that affected them. "We women demand an equal voice," she said. "We shall accept nothing less."

Some women believed that NAWSA did not go far enough. In 1913 **Alice Paul** founded what would become the National Woman's Party (NWP). The NWP used parades, public demonstrations, picketing, hunger strikes, and other means to draw attention to the suffrage cause. Paul even organized picketing in front of the White House. Paul and other NWP leaders were jailed for their actions.

Suffragists finally succeeded in gaining the vote. In 1919 the U.S. Congress passed the **Nineteenth Amendment**, granting American women the right to vote. The Nineteenth Amendment was ratified by the states the following year, making it law.

African Americans Challenge Discrimination

White reformers often overlooked issues such as racial discrimination and segregation. African American reformers found such issues inescapable. They took the lead in addressing these problems.

One of the most important African American leaders was **Booker T. Washington**. Born into slavery, Washington believed that African Americans should not openly challenge segregation. He thought that whites and blacks could work together yet live separate social lives. Over time, Washington believed that African Americans could gain equal social standing by becoming self-sufficient and economically secure. In 1881 he founded the Tuskegee Institute in Alabama to help African Americans learn trades as well as skills for self-sufficiency.

Reading Check
Analyze Information
How did reformers draw attention to the temperance and women's suffrage movements?

Other African Americans spoke out more directly against racial segregation, discrimination, and violence. Journalist **Ida B. Wells** wrote articles about the unequal education for African American children. In her Memphis newspaper *Free Speech*, Wells also drew attention to the lynching of African Americans. During lynchings people were murdered by mobs instead of receiving a trial. People were lynched after being accused of a crime or even for breaking social codes. More than 3,000 African Americans were lynched between 1885 and 1915.

After three of her friends were lynched in 1892, Wells started an anti-lynching campaign in her newspaper. Death threats forced Wells to move to the North. But she continued campaigning against lynching. In 1900 she wrote:

> "Our country's national crime is lynching . . . In fact, for all kinds of offenses—and, for no offenses—from murders to misdemeanors, men and women are put to death without judge or jury."
>
> —Ida B. Wells, from her article "Lynch Law in America"

Historical Source

Fighting Discrimination

Booker T. Washington and W. E. B. Du Bois had very different views on how African Americans could improve their social and economic standing.

> "Our greatest danger is that in the great leap from slavery to freedom we may overlook the fact that the masses of us are to live by the productions of our hands, and fail to keep in mind that we shall prosper in proportion as we learn to dignify and glorify common labour and put brains and skill into the common occupations of life. . . . It is at the bottom of life we must begin, and not at the top."
>
> —Booker T. Washington

> "Is it possible, and probable, that nine millions of men can make effective progress in economic lines if they are deprived of political rights, made a servile caste,[1] and allowed only the most meager chance for developing their exceptional men? If history and reason give any distinct answer to these questions, it is an emphatic No."
>
> —W. E. B. Du Bois

[1] *caste* lower social rank

Analyze Historical Sources
How do the views of Washington and Du Bois differ?

Like Wells, **W. E. B. Du Bois** took a direct approach to fighting racial injustice. Born in Massachusetts, Du Bois was an educator and civil rights activist. He earned a doctorate from Harvard University. As part of his research, he studied and publicized cases of racial prejudice.

Du Bois believed that African Americans should openly protest unjust treatment and demand equal rights immediately. He also promoted higher education for the most capable African Americans, who he called the "Talented Tenth." These were the teachers, ministers, and professionals that Du Bois believed should lead the struggle for equal rights.

Founding members of the Niagara Movement, including W.E.B. Du Bois (center), sat for this portrait in 1905.

In 1905 Du Bois launched the Niagara Movement to protest discrimination. Four years later, in 1909, he helped found an even more influential organization, **National Association for the Advancement of Colored People** (NAACP). Still active today, the NAACP is a civil rights organization that supports economic and educational equality for African Americans. In its early years, the NAACP worked to secure for African Americans the rights guaranteed by the Thirteenth, Fourteenth, and Fifteenth Amendments to the U.S. Constitution. These rights included equal protection under the law and voting rights for all adult men.

The NAACP fought discrimination against African Americans by using the courts. In 1915 it won the important case of *Guinn* v. *United States*, which made grandfather clauses illegal. These laws were used in the South to keep African Americans from voting. Grandfather clauses imposed strict qualifications on voters unless their grandfathers had been allowed to vote. Many white voters met this requirement and were automatically permitted to vote in elections. However, most African Americans' grandfathers had been enslaved and could not vote.

Another important organization was the National Urban League. It was formed in 1911 by Dr. George Edmund Haynes. This organization aided many African Americans moving from the South by helping them find jobs and housing in northern cities. The Urban League addressed many of the same problems faced by other Progressives, such as health, sanitation, and education.

Reading Check
Find Main Ideas
What was the purpose of the NAACP?

Limits of Reform

The Progressive movement achieved some remarkable successes. But Progressive efforts at reform had limits. In addition to overlooking the challenges faced by African Americans, white reformers also overlooked the discrimination faced by other ethnic groups. Native Americans, for example, were largely left behind by the Progressive movement. Some reformers tried to improve conditions for Native Americans by culturally **assimilating** them into, or having them adopt, white American culture. Unfortunately, these efforts often came at a high cost to Native American culture, religion, and language.

In 1911 two Native American Progressives, Dr. Carlos Montezuma and Dr. Charles Eastman, founded the Society of American Indians. It was the first national organization that aimed to unite diverse Native American groups in an effort to promote American Indian rights. Many of its early

Academic Vocabulary
assimilation adoption of another culture's way of life

leaders believed that integration into white society would help end Native American poverty. Many other Native Americans, however, wanted to preserve their traditional culture. They resisted the movement to adopt white culture and worked to preserve Native American culture.

Immigrants from non-European countries also formed groups to help support their members. Chinese immigrants, for example, organized associations in the communities in which they lived. District associations, cultural groups, churches, and temples provided public services that white reformers ignored. San Francisco's Chinese Hospital was built in 1925 by such a group. Anti-Chinese riots in some western towns and cities caused Chinese immigration to drop, however.

Immigrants from Mexico increased during this time. The borders between the United States and its neighbors were fairly easy to cross. Many Mexican immigrants moved to the South and Southwest. They became an important part of the societies and economies of these regions. Many Mexican immigrants found jobs in the mining and railroad industries. Others became farmers or migrant workers. Progressive labor laws and factory reforms did nothing to improve the poor living and working conditions of migrant farm workers.

Reading Check
Summarize What were the limitations of progressive reforms?

Summary and Preview Many U.S. citizens worked for progressive reforms. In the next lesson you will read about presidents who also worked for progressive goals.

Lesson 3 Assessment

Review Ideas, Terms, and People

1. **a. Identify** What did the Eighteenth and Nineteenth Amendments accomplish?

   b. Summarize How did Alice Paul and the National Woman's Party try to draw attention to the issue of women's suffrage?

2. **a. Identify** What role did Ida B. Wells play in reform efforts for African Americans?

   b. Contrast How did Booker T. Washington differ from other African American leaders?

   c. Evaluate Do you think the National Association for the Advancement of Colored People was successful in fighting discrimination? Explain.

3. **a. Describe** What discrimination did Chinese Americans face?

   b. Summarize How were some minority groups overlooked by the Progressive movement?

Critical Thinking

4. **Analyze** In this lesson you learned about the causes supported by different groups of progressive reformers. Create a graphic organizer similar to the one below to identify the progressive reforms introduced by the temperance movement, the women's suffrage movement, and African Americans.

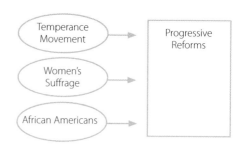

The Progressive Presidents

The Big Idea

American presidents in the early 1900s did a great deal to promote progressive reforms.

Main Ideas

- Theodore Roosevelt's progressive reforms tried to balance the interests of business, consumers, and laborers.

- William Howard Taft angered Progressives with his cautious reforms, while Woodrow Wilson enacted far-reaching banking and antitrust reforms.

Key Terms and People

Theodore Roosevelt
Pure Food and Drug Act
conservation
William Howard Taft
Progressive Party
Woodrow Wilson
Sixteenth Amendment

If YOU were there . . .

It is 1912 and you're voting in your first presidential election. This election is unusual—there are three major candidates. One is the popular former president Theodore Roosevelt, who is running as a third-party candidate. He thinks the Republican candidate will not make enough progressive reforms. But the Democratic candidate is a progressive reformer, too.

How will you decide which candidate to support?

Roosevelt's Progressive Reforms

During a summer tour after his second inauguration in 1901, President William McKinley met a friendly crowd in Buffalo, New York. Suddenly, anarchist Leon Czolgosz stepped forward and shot the president. A little more than a week later, McKinley died. Vice President **Theodore Roosevelt** took office.

Roosevelt's Square Deal Roosevelt believed that the interests of businesspeople, laborers, and consumers should be balanced for the public good. He called this policy the Square Deal. He put the policy to the test in 1902 when faced by a coal miners' strike. Roosevelt knew the strike might leave the country without heating fuel for the coming winter. He threatened to take over the mines unless managers and strikers agreed to arbitration—a formal process to settle disputes. He felt this was the only fair way to protect Americans.

> "The labor unions shall have a square deal, and the corporations shall have a square deal, and in addition all private citizens shall have a square deal."
>
> —President Theodore Roosevelt, quoted in *The Presidency of Theodore Roosevelt*, by Lewis L. Gould

Regulating Big Business Roosevelt made regulating big business a top goal of his administration. Muckrakers helped build support for this regulation. The public was shocked, for instance, after reading Upton Sinclair's description of the meatpacking industry in *The Jungle*. Roosevelt opened an investigation and later convinced Congress to pass a meat inspection law.

In 1906 Congress passed the **Pure Food and Drug Act**. This law prohibited the manufacture, sale, and transport of mislabeled or contaminated food and drugs. Roosevelt also was the first president to successfully use the 1890 Sherman Antitrust Act to break up a monopoly. He persuaded Congress to regulate railroad-shipping rates. The public largely supported this expansion of federal regulatory powers.

Conservation Roosevelt's love of the outdoors inspired him to join other Progressives in supporting **conservation**, or the protection of nature and its resources. Roosevelt was the first president to consider conservation an important national priority.

People believed in conservation for various reasons. Preservationists such as John Muir thought that nature should be left untouched so that people could enjoy its beauty:

> "Thousands of tired, nerve-shaken, over-civilized people are
>   beginning to find out that going to the mountains is going
>   home; that wildness is a necessity; and that mountain parks
>   and reservations are useful not only as fountains of timber and
>   irrigating rivers, but as fountains of life."
>
> —John Muir, *Our National Parks*

Other conservationists wanted to make sure the nation used its natural resources efficiently. Gifford Pinchot, the first head of the newly created

President Theodore Roosevelt and conservationist John Muir in Yosemite National Park in California

Forest Service, valued forests for the resources they provided to build "prosperous homes." The disagreement between the two ideals of conservation eventually widened.

While Roosevelt was in office, the Forest Service gained control of nearly 150 million acres of public land. Roosevelt doubled the number of national parks, created 18 national monuments, and started 51 bird sanctuaries.

Reading Check
Summarize What reforms did Roosevelt support?

Reforms of Taft and Wilson

Theodore Roosevelt hoped that his secretary of war, **William Howard Taft**, would take his place as president in 1908. Like Roosevelt, Taft favored business regulation and opposed socialism. With Roosevelt's assistance, Taft defeated William Jennings Bryan in the election of 1908.

Taft Angers Progressives Despite their friendship, Roosevelt and Taft held different ideas about how a president should act. Taft thought Roosevelt had claimed more power than was constitutional.

As president, therefore, Taft moved cautiously with reform and regulation. This upset Roosevelt and **various** Progressives, who supported stricter regulation of big business. Taft's administration started twice as many antitrust lawsuits as Roosevelt's had. But Progressives were not satisfied.

Academic Vocabulary
various of many types

Taft angered Progressives further by signing the Payne-Aldrich Tariff of 1909. This tariff reduced some rates on imported goods, but it raised others. Progressives wanted all tariffs to be lowered, in order to lower prices for consumers.

Furious with Taft, Roosevelt decided to run for president again in 1912. After Taft won the Republican nomination, Roosevelt and his followers formed the **Progressive Party**. It was nicknamed the Bull Moose Party because Roosevelt said he was "as strong as a bull moose." The split between Taft and Roosevelt divided the Republican vote, and Democratic candidate **Woodrow Wilson** won the electoral vote by a wide margin.

Wilson's Reforms In his inaugural address, Wilson spoke of the terrible social conditions of many working-class Americans. "We have been proud of our industrial achievements," he said, "but we have not hitherto [yet] stopped thoughtfully enough to count the human cost." Passing reform legislation was Wilson's top goal. He pushed for two measures soon after taking office: tariff revision and banking reform.

Wilson backed the Underwood Tariff Act of 1913, which lowered tariffs. The act also introduced a version of the modern income tax. The new tax was made possible in 1913 by the ratification of the **Sixteenth Amendment**. This amendment allows the federal government to impose direct taxes on citizens' incomes.

President Wilson next addressed banking reform. The 1913 Federal Reserve Act created the modern banking system. The Federal Reserve Board (the "Fed") oversees 12 regional Federal Reserve Banks. It makes sure that money is distributed where it is most needed. These are bankers'

The Progressive Amendments, 1909–1920

Number	Description	Proposed by Congress	Ratified by States
16th	Federal income tax	1909	1913
17th	Senators elected by the people rather than state legislatures	1912	1913
18th	Manufacture, sale, and transport of alcohol prohibited	1917	1919
19th	Women's suffrage	1919	1920

banks that serve consumer banks. The Federal Reserve Act created a more flexible currency system by allowing consumer banks to have more control over the money supply. To raise money, the Fed lowers the interest rate that it charges member banks. These banks then borrow more from the Fed, and thus have more money to lend to people and businesses.

Wilson also pushed for laws to regulate big business. The Clayton Antitrust Act of 1914 strengthened federal laws against monopolies. The Federal Trade Commission, created in 1914, had the power to investigate and punish unfair trade practices. Wilson's success in guiding reform programs through Congress helped him to win re-election in 1916.

Reading Check
Analyze Information
Why did Wilson win the election of 1912?

Summary and Preview The progressive presidents tried to change American society for the better. In the next module you will learn how they also helped the United States become a world power.

Lesson 4 Assessment

Review Ideas, Terms, and People

1. a. Describe How did Theodore Roosevelt support progressive reforms?

b. Analyze Why did many Americans support conservation?

c. Evaluate Do you think Roosevelt's reforms benefited the nation? Why or why not?

2. a. Identify What was the Progressive Party? Why was it created?

b. Compare and Contrast How were the administrations of William Howard Taft and Roosevelt similar, and how were they different?

c. Evaluate Which president do you think had the biggest influence on progressive reform—Roosevelt, Taft, or Woodrow Wilson? Explain your choice.

Critical Thinking

3. Compare and Contrast In this lesson you learned about the achievements of each of the progressive presidents. Create a Venn diagram similar to the one below and compare and contrast the reforms of the progressive presidents.

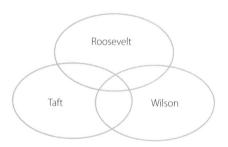

Short- and Long-term Causal Relationships

Define the Skill

Most historical events are the result of other events. When something happens as a result of other things that occur, it is an effect of those things. Some events take place soon after the things that cause them. Such events are called *short-term effects*. In contrast, *long-term effects* can occur years, decades, or even hundreds of years after the events that caused them. Being able to recognize short-term and long-term cause-and-effect relationships will help you to better understand historical events.

Learn the Skill

Clue words can sometimes reveal a cause-and-effect relationship between events. Often, however, such language clues may not be present. Therefore, when you study history, you should always look for other clues that might explain why an action or event occurred.

Short-term effects are usually fairly easy to identify. In historical writing they are often closely linked to the event that caused them. For example, consider this passage from Module 22.

"Some Progressives worked to change state and local governments in order to reduce the power of political machines. In many places, reformers replaced corrupt ballots that listed only one party's candidates with government-prepared ballots that listed all candidates. Under pressure from reformers, many states adopted secret ballots, giving every voter a private vote."

This passage contains no clue words. Yet it is clear that cause-and-effect relationships exist. The power of political machines created corrupt voting practices. Reformers wanted to change this. One effect of this situation was the government-prepared ballot, and another was the secret ballot.

Recognizing long-term causal relationships is often more difficult. Since long-term effects take place well after the event that caused them, they may not be discussed at the same time as their cause. This is why you should always question why an event occurred as you learn about it. For example, in 1971 Congress passed the first federal law to protect the health and safety of all workers. This law was a long-term result of efforts begun years earlier by the Progressives you read about in this module.

Many long-term effects result from major forces running through history that make things happen. They include economics, science and technology, expansion, conflict and cooperation among people, cultural clashes and differences, and moral and religious issues. Ask yourself if one of these forces is involved in the event being studied. If so, the event may have long-term effects that you should be on the lookout for when studying later events.

Practice the Skill

Review the information in Module 22 and answer these questions to practice recognizing short- and long-term causal relationships.

1. All packaged food today must have its contents listed on the container. This requirement is a long-term effect of what progressive reform?

2. Write a paragraph explaining the effects of the muckrakers on the news media today.

Module 6 Assessment

Review Vocabulary, Terms, and People

Complete each sentence by filling in the blank with the correct term or person from the module.

1. Some Americans supported a(n) _____ system, which proposed government ownership of the country's means of production.

2. Republican _____ began a program to reform state politics in Wisconsin.

3. The _____ granted women in the United States the right to vote.

4. The _____ prohibited the manufacture, sale, and transport of mislabeled or contaminated food and drugs.

5. During the Gilded Age, _____ often dominated local politics and used corruption to get their candidates elected.

6. _____ were journalists who wrote about troubling issues such as child labor, tenement housing, and political corruption.

Comprehension and Critical Thinking

Lesson 1

7. a. **Describe** What tactics did bosses and political machines use to gain control of local governments?

    b. **Analyze** What changes did Progressives make to city life?

    c. **Elaborate** Which progressive reform do you think had the greatest effect on Americans?

Lesson 2

8. a. **Identify** What reforms were made to improve working conditions, and who was affected by these reforms?

    b. **Contrast** What are the differences between capitalism and socialism?

    c. **Elaborate** If you were a business owner, would you have supported the progressive workplace reforms? Explain your answer.

Lesson 3

9. a. **Recall** What minority groups were overlooked by progressive reform efforts?

    b. **Analyze** How did women's involvement in the Progressive movement lead to constitutional change?

    c. **Elaborate** Do you agree with Booker T. Washington's approach to improving life for African Americans? Explain your answer.

Lesson 4

10. a. **Describe** How did William Howard Taft disappoint Progressives?

    b. **Compare** In what ways were the reforms of presidents Roosevelt, Taft, and Wilson similar?

    c. **Elaborate** Would you have supported Wilson's progressive reforms? Explain your answer.

Module 6 Assessment, continued

Review Themes

11. **Politics** What role did political machines play in local politics during the Gilded Age?

12. **Society and Culture** How did the movement for workplace reforms affect children?

13. **Economics** How did the Federal Reserve influence the American economy?

Reading Skills

Evaluate Sources *Use the Reading Skills taught in this module to answer the question about the reading selection below.*

> The next day Rose went to town [Chicago] alone. The wind had veered [turned] to the south, the dust blew, and the whole terrifying panorama [view] of life in the street seemed some way blurred together, and forms of men and animals were like figures in tapestry. The grind and clang and clatter and hiss and howl of the traffic was all about her . . .
>
> —Hamlin Garland, from his novel *The Rose of Dutcher's Coolly*, 1895

14. Is this a good source for understanding the experiences of Chicago in the late 1800s? Why or why not?

Social Studies Skills

Short- and Long-Term Causal Relationships *Use the Social Studies Skills taught in this module to answer the question about the reading selection below.*

> Despite their friendship, Roosevelt and Taft held different ideas about how a president should act. Taft thought Roosevelt had claimed more power than was constitutional.
> As president, therefore, Taft moved cautiously with reform and regulation.

15. According to the passage above, what was a long-term cause of Taft's cautious reforms?

Focus on Speaking

16. **Share Your Campaign Promises** Serious problems face the nation, and you must convince voters that you should be the one to tackle those problems. Create a list of campaign promises that you would make if you were a progressive politician running for office in the United States in the late 1800s or early 1900s. Which promises will be most helpful in getting you elected? Look at your promises to see whether they focus on issues important to voters. Then write a speech including your campaign promises that you can deliver to your class.

Essential Question

Why did the United States turn to empire in the late 1800s?

About the Photo: Through a combination of economic strength, military might, and aggressive foreign policy, the United States made its presence known in many parts of the world. One such place was Panama, where the United States built the Panama Canal, shown here.

▷ *Explore ONLINE!*

HISTORY

VIDEOS, including...
- Panama Canal Locks
- China: The Boxer Uprising
- The Battle of San Juan Hill
- Theodore Roosevelt: Big Stick Foreign Policies

☑ Document-Based Investigations

☑ Graphic Organizers

☑ Interactive Games

☑ Image with Hotspots: Perry Arrives in Japan

☑ Interactive Map: War in the Caribbean

☑ Animation: The Panama Canal

In this module you will learn about how the United States became a world power in the late 1800s and early 1900s.

What You Will Learn . . .

Timeline of Events 1860–1920

▶ *Explore ONLINE!*

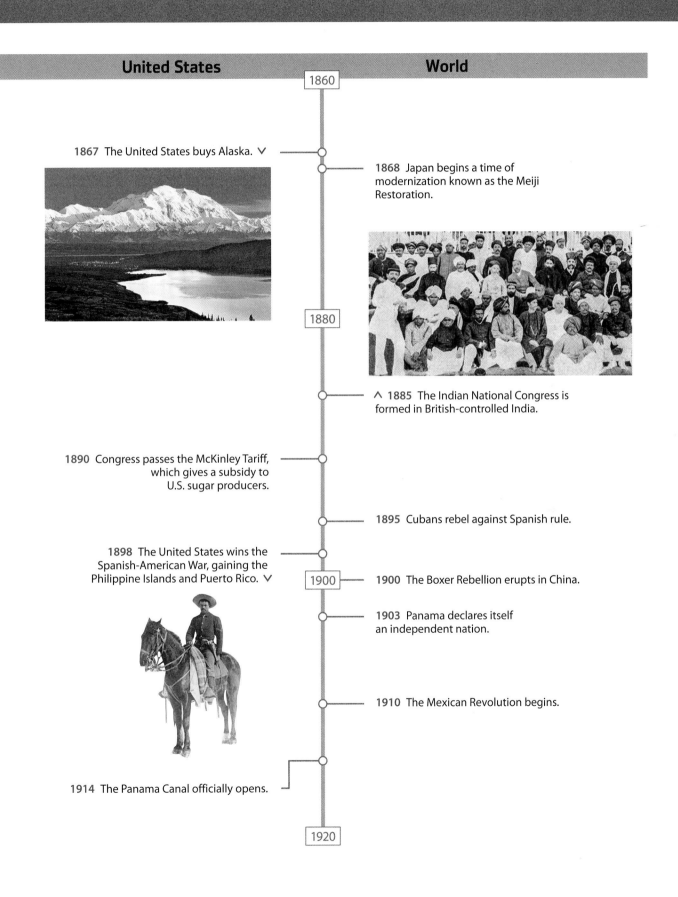

United States		World
	1860	
1867 The United States buys Alaska. ∨		
		1868 Japan begins a time of modernization known as the Meiji Restoration.
	1880	
		∧ **1885** The Indian National Congress is formed in British-controlled India.
1890 Congress passes the McKinley Tariff, which gives a subsidy to U.S. sugar producers.		
		1895 Cubans rebel against Spanish rule.
1898 The United States wins the Spanish-American War, gaining the Philippine Islands and Puerto Rico. ∨		
	1900	**1900** The Boxer Rebellion erupts in China.
		1903 Panama declares itself an independent nation.
		1910 The Mexican Revolution begins.
1914 The Panama Canal officially opens.		
	1920	

Reading Social Studies

Geography and Politics

In this module you will learn about how the political geography of the United States changed as it acquired overseas territories. You will also read about how national and international politics affected foreign policy and brought new responsibilities to the government of the United States.

READING FOCUS:

Compare Historical Texts

A good way to learn what people in the past thought is to read what they wrote. However, most documents will only tell you one side of the story. By comparing writings by different people, you can learn a great deal about various sides of a historical issue or debate.

Compare Texts When you compare historical texts, you should consider two things: who wrote the documents and what the documents were meant to achieve. To do this, you need to find the writers' main point or points.

Document 1

"We have cherished the policy of noninterference with affairs of foreign governments wisely inaugurated [begun] by Washington, keeping ourselves free from entanglement, either as allies or foes, content to leave undisturbed with them the settlement of their own domestic concerns."

—President William McKinley,
First Inaugural Address, 1897

Document 2

"Therefore, Mr. President, here is a war with terrible characteristics flagrant [obvious] at our very doors [in Cuba]. We have the power to bring it to an end. I believe that the whole American people would welcome steps in that direction."

—Senator Henry Cabot Lodge, Speech in
Congress, 1896

Document 1	Document 2
Writer	
President William McKinley	Senator Henry Cabot Lodge
Main Point	
The United States should not involve itself in the affairs of other countries.	The United States should go to war in Cuba.
Both Sides of the Issue	
Americans were torn over the war in Cuba. Some thought the United States should remain uninvolved as it always had. Others thought it was time for a change in foreign policy.	

You Try It!

Read the following passages, both taken from presidential addresses to Congress. As you read, look for the main point each president makes in his address.

Foreign Policy

In treating of our foreign policy and of the attitude that this great Nation should assume in the world at large, it is absolutely necessary to consider the Army and the Navy, and the Congress, through which the thought of the Nation finds its expression, should keep ever vividly in mind the fundamental fact that it is impossible to treat our foreign policy, whether this policy takes shape in the effort to secure justice for others or justice for ourselves, save as conditioned upon the attitude we are willing to take toward our Army, and especially toward our Navy.

—President Theodore Roosevelt, Message to Congress, 1904

The diplomacy of the present administration has sought to respond to modern ideas of commercial intercourse [involvement]. This policy has been characterized as substituting dollars for bullets. It is one that appeals alike to idealistic humanitarian sentiments [feelings], to the dictates [rules] of sound policy and strategy, and to legitimate [make real] commercial aims.

—President William Howard Taft, Message to Congress, 1912

After you read the passages, answer the following questions.

1. What was the main point Roosevelt made in his address?

2. What was the main point Taft made in his address?

3. How can a comparison of Roosevelt's and Taft's addresses to Congress help you understand the issues that shaped U.S. foreign policy in the early 1900s?

As you read Module 7, organize your notes to help you point out the similarities and differences among events or policies.

Key Terms and People

Lesson 1
imperialism
isolationism
William H. Seward
Liliuokalani
spheres of influence
Open Door Policy
Boxer Rebellion

Lesson 2
yellow journalism
Teller Amendment
Emilio Aguinaldo
Anti-Imperialist League
Platt Amendment

Lesson 3
Panama Canal
Roosevelt Corollary
dollar diplomacy
Mexican Revolution
John J. Pershing
Francisco "Pancho" Villa

The United States Gains Overseas Territories

The Big Idea

In the last half of the 1800s, the United States joined the race for control of overseas territories.

Main Ideas

- The United States ended its policy of isolationism and began imperial expansion.

- Hawaii became a U.S. territory in 1898.

- The United States sought trade with Japan and China.

Key Terms and People

imperialism
isolationism
William H. Seward
Liliuokalani
spheres of influence
Open Door Policy
Boxer Rebellion

If YOU were there . . .

You are a Hawaiian living on Maui, one of the Hawaiian Islands, in 1890. Your parents work in a sugar mill owned by American planters. Although the mill supplies jobs, you don't trust the sugar planters. They have already made your king sign a treaty that gives them a lot of power in the islands. You are afraid they will take over the government.

What would you do if the planters took over your islands?

End of Isolation

In the 1800s powerful Western nations were busy building naval bases to protect their shipping routes around the world. This was an aspect of **imperialism**—building an empire by founding colonies or conquering other nations. Between 1870 and 1914, Europeans used this foreign policy to extend their colonial empires until they controlled most of Africa and Southeast Asia.

Roots of Imperialism Several forces drove this wave of European imperialism. Countries wanted sources of raw materials—such as copper, rubber, and tin—to fuel industrial growth. Businesspeople wanted new markets for their manufactured goods. And many Europeans saw colonies as a source of power and national pride.

In contrast, the United States followed a limited foreign policy of **isolationism**—avoiding involvement in the affairs of other countries. In 1789 President George Washington had warned Americans "to steer clear of permanent alliances" with other countries. American leaders tried to follow this advice by staying out of overseas conflicts.

By the late 1800s, however, some American leaders believed the United States needed to expand to keep its economy strong. They sought new sources for raw materials and new places to sell goods. To do so, they wanted the United

States to expand beyond North America and establish territories overseas. In 1890 Alfred T. Mahan wrote *The Influence of Sea Power upon History*. In this book he argued that the United States needed a strong navy to protect its economic interests. Such a navy would need overseas bases and coaling stations—places for ships to take on coal for fuel.

Mahan and others argued that it was in the nation's interest to shift its foreign policy. They supported imperial expansionism. This is a policy of gaining power by taking control of other lands. For the United States this meant acquiring new lands as U.S. territories. Advocates of expansionism claimed that it would increase the nation's financial prosperity, strengthen the nation's military, and help spread democratic ideals. In the late 1800s the U.S. foreign policy did indeed shift from isolationism to imperialism.

Seward's Folly The United States took its first steps in becoming a world power by acquiring Alaska. In 1867 the United States greatly expanded its North American territory. Secretary of State **William H. Seward** arranged the purchase of Alaska from Russia for $7.2 million. Some people thought Alaska was a frozen wasteland, calling the deal "Seward's Folly" [foolish act]. But Seward had purchased an area more than twice the size of Texas for two cents an acre. And as he had hoped, Alaska became a source of valuable natural resources such as fur, timber, and minerals. Gold was found in Alaska in the 1890s, bringing miners and settlers to the area.

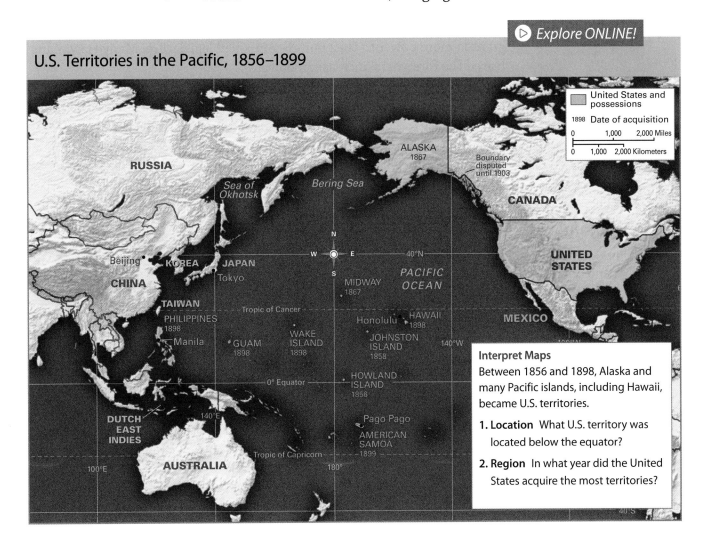

U.S. Territories in the Pacific, 1856–1899

▶ *Explore ONLINE!*

Interpret Maps
Between 1856 and 1898, Alaska and many Pacific islands, including Hawaii, became U.S. territories.

1. **Location** What U.S. territory was located below the equator?

2. **Region** In what year did the United States acquire the most territories?

Reading Check
Analyze Why did U.S. leaders end isolationist policies in the late 1800s?

Based on Seward's belief that the United States "must continue to move on westward," the nation also annexed the Midway Islands in 1867. The islands' location about halfway between the U.S. West Coast and Japan made Midway an excellent coaling station for the U.S. Navy.

The United States wanted the island group of Samoa for similar reasons. The United States and Germany agreed to divide Samoa in 1899.

Hawaii Becomes a Territory

Even more appealing than Samoa were the Hawaiian Islands. The islands provided an economic opportunity for the United States and a chance to gain even more world power. Hawaiians first saw Europeans in 1778. Trading and whaling ships in the Pacific soon began stopping in Hawaii. In the early 1800s American missionaries came and attempted to convert Hawaiians to Christianity. Missionaries opened businesses and raised crops, such as sugarcane. Some Americans became rich sugar planters.

By the 1840s most shops and shipyards in Hawaii were owned by Americans. Sugar became a leading export of the Hawaiian economy. An 1875 treaty allowed Hawaiian sugar to be shipped duty-free to the United States. (A duty is a tax on imported items.) This agreement helped the Hawaiian sugar industry prosper.

The American planters used their power to force the Hawaiian king to sign a new constitution in 1887. It became known as the Bayonet Constitution because the king was forced to sign it at gunpoint. The constitution granted more power to the planter-controlled legislature. Many Hawaiians feared the foreigners' increase in power.

In 1891 the king died, and his sister, **Liliuokalani** (li-LEE-uh-woh-kuh-LAHN-ee), became queen. She proposed a new constitution that would return power to the monarchy. American planters in Hawaii saw these plans as threats to their political and economic interests. The planters

--- BIOGRAPHY ---

Liliuokalani (1838–1917)

Born in Honolulu, Queen Liliuokalani was the first and only queen of Hawaii. She was a defender of Hawaiian traditions and territory. Even after being driven from power in 1893, she continued speaking out on behalf of native-born Hawaiians. In 1897 she traveled to Washington, DC. She met with President Grover Cleveland to argue against the annexation of Hawaii by the United States. Today her reign is a proud reminder of the islands' history as an independent nation.

Draw Conclusions

Why do you think Liliuokalani was a symbol of Hawaiian pride?

revolted. John L. Stevens, U.S. minister to Hawaii, called 150 marines ashore to support the revolt. It succeeded without a battle. The planters formed a new government. They asked the U.S. government to annex Hawaii to become part of the United States.

U.S. leaders already understood the value of the islands. It was in their interest to gain control. In 1887 they had negotiated with Hawaii's king to allow a U.S. base at Pearl Harbor. It was one of the best natural harbors in the eastern Pacific. The base became an important refueling station for American merchant and military ships bound for Asia. This helped the United States continue to gain world political power.

Congress voted to annex the Hawaiian Islands in 1898. Hawaii officially changed from an independent country to an American territory. As a territory, Hawaii would fall under the control of the United States.

With American territory now stretching between two oceans, America was well placed to extend its influence in the Pacific. Through purchase and annexation, the nation began expanding beyond its shores and becoming a world power.

Reading Check
Identify Cause and Effect Why did American planters in Hawaii stage a revolt?

United States Seeks Trade with Japan and China

Economic interest also drew the United States to Japan and China. The United States wanted to open and secure trade markets in both of these Asian countries.

Opening Trade with Japan By the mid-1800s European powers had formed strong trade ties with most East Asian countries. However, the island nation of Japan had isolated itself from the rest of the world for hundreds of years.

The United States wanted to open up trade with Japan before Europeans arrived. President Millard Fillmore sent Commodore Matthew Perry to Japan to secure "friendship, commerce, [and] a supply of coal and provisions." Perry attempted a peaceful alliance in 1853 to influence economic change, but he was not successful.

Perry returned to Japan in 1854 with seven warships. He gave Japanese leaders gifts and tried to show some of the benefits that Japanese-American trade would have. For instance, Perry presented them with a telegraph transmitter and a model train. This effort—and the presence of U.S. naval power—persuaded Japanese officials to open trade with the United States. The two countries signed a trade agreement in 1858.

Some Japanese leaders welcomed trade with the United States. In 1868 people who favored the industrialization **process** came to power in Japan. This began a 40-year period of modernization. By the 1890s Japan was becoming a major imperial power. It defeated China in the Sino-Japanese War from 1894 to 1895. As a result, Japan gained new territory and enjoyed the same trading privileges in China as European countries. In 1904 Japan attacked Russian forces stationed in China. President Theodore Roosevelt helped to negotiate a peace treaty to end the Russo-

Academic Vocabulary
process a series of steps by which a task is accomplished

Perry Arrives in Japan

Connect to the Arts This painting from 1854 shows Commodore Perry landing at Yokohama, Japan. He staged a parade to disembark and meet the imperial commissioners who represented the emperor. This meeting was the first official meeting between an agent of the United States and officials from Japan.

What impression do you think Commodore Perry intended to make?

How might the Japanese have felt seeing these ships arrive?

Japanese War a year later. Japan gained control of Korea, a lease on Port Arthur in China, and other rights. Japan had become a world power.

Foreign Powers in China After Japan defeated China, other countries took advantage of China's weakness. They did this by seizing **spheres of influence**—areas where foreign nations claimed special rights and economic privileges. Germany, Great Britain, France, Japan, and Russia all took control of areas within China.

Some U.S. leaders feared that the United States would be closed out of Chinese markets and resources. To promote its national interests, the United States took action. In 1899 Secretary of State John Hay sent notes to Japan and many European countries announcing the **Open Door Policy**. This policy stated that all nations should have equal access to trade in China. The policy was neither rejected nor accepted by European powers and Japan, but it made U.S. intentions clear.

As a result, many Chinese resented the power and control held by foreign nations. This hostility sparked the **Boxer Rebellion**. The Boxers were Chinese nationalists who were angered by foreign involvement in China. In their language, the group was called the Fists of Righteous Harmony. Westerners called them Boxers because they used a clenched fist as their symbol. Although officially denounced, they were secretly supported by the Chinese government.

In June 1900 the Boxers took to the streets of Beijing, China's capital. They laid siege to the walled settlement where foreigners lived. They killed more than 200 people.

The siege continued for two months. Foreign military forces, including United States Marines, fought their way from the port of Tianjin to Beijing. There they invaded the Forbidden City, the imperial palace complex. The Boxers were soon defeated. China was forced to make a cash payment of $333 million to foreign governments, $25 million of which went to the United States. Secretary of State Hay then sent another Open Door note to Japan and the European nations. The Open Door Policy remained in effect until World War II again closed China's borders to foreign influence.

Foreign forces engage Chinese nationalists in battle at Tianjin, China, in this illustration of China's Boxer Rebellion.

Reading Check
Identify Cause and Effect What factors led to the Boxer Rebellion, and what was the result?

Summary and Preview The United States greatly expanded its territory and influence in the Pacific. In the next lesson you will learn about the causes and effects of the Spanish-American War.

Lesson 1 Assessment

Review Ideas, Terms, and People

1. **a. Describe** What policy had the United States followed regarding other countries before the late 1800s?

   b. Analyze Why did the United States expand to Alaska and to islands in the Pacific?

   c. Evaluate Why did the United States change its foreign policy from one of isolationism to imperialism?

2. **a. Sequence** What events led to Hawaii's annexation as a U.S. territory?

   b. Elaborate Explain why the planters revolted against Queen Liliuokalani.

   c. Compare and Contrast In what way did Hawaii change when it became a territory of the United States?

3. **a. Describe** What was the purpose of the Open Door Policy?

   b. Contrast How was the U.S. experience establishing trade with China different from U.S. attempts to open trade with Japan?

   c. Evaluate Do you think Japan made the right decision in agreeing to open trade with the United States? Explain your answer.

Critical Thinking

4. **Generalize** In this lesson you learned about the areas or trade rights gained by the United States. Create a chart similar to the one below and identify the benefits of these areas and trade rights. Describe how these helped the United States become a world power.

American Expansion	
Areas or Trade Rights Gained	Benefits for United States

The Spanish-American War

The Big Idea

As a result of the Spanish-American War, the United States expanded its reach into new parts of the world.

Main Ideas

- In 1898 the United States went to war with Spain in the Spanish-American War.

- The United States gained territories in the Caribbean and Pacific.

Key Terms and People

yellow journalism
Teller Amendment
Emilio Aguinaldo
Anti-Imperialist League
Platt Amendment

If YOU were there . . .

You live in New York City in 1898. Newspaper headlines are screaming about the start of war in Cuba. You hear that Theodore Roosevelt wants volunteers for a cavalry troop called the Rough Riders. You know how to ride a horse, and you've admired Roosevelt ever since he was New York's police commissioner. You know it will be dangerous, but it also sounds like a great adventure.

Would you join the Rough Riders? Why?

War with Spain

You read earlier that newspaper publishers Joseph Pulitzer and William Randolph Hearst were in a fierce competition for readers. In the late 1890s their newspapers published stories from Cuba, where Cuban rebels were fighting for independence from Spain. To attract readers, Pulitzer and Hearst printed sensational, often exaggerated, news stories. This technique is called **yellow journalism**. Vivid stories about Spanish brutality in Cuba convinced many Americans that the U.S. military should support the Cuban rebels.

Newspapers such as this one used yellow journalism to encourage Americans to seek war with Spain.

Despite growing support for military action in Cuba, President Grover Cleveland was opposed to U.S. involvement. In 1896 William McKinley, a supporter of Cuban independence, was elected president. At first, he was against war, but American public opinion forced him to take action. Several events soon led to war.

In February 1898, Hearst's newspaper published a letter written by the Spanish minister to the United States, Enrique Dupuy de Lôme. In it, de Lôme called McKinley "weak and a bidder for the admiration of the crowd." Many Americans were outraged.

In January 1898, even before de Lôme's letter became public, the United States sent the battleship USS *Maine* to Havana Harbor. Riots had broken out in Havana, the Cuban capital. The *Maine*'s mission was to protect U.S. citizens and economic interests in Cuba from the violence. On February 15 the *Maine* exploded and sank, with a loss of 266 men. Although the cause of the explosion was unclear, the American press immediately blamed Spain. "Remember the *Maine*!" became a rallying cry for angry Americans.

President McKinley requested $50 million to prepare for war. Congress approved the money. Although Cuba was not a U.S. territory, Congress issued a resolution on April 20 declaring Cuba independent and demanding that Spain leave the island within three days. Attached to the resolution was the **Teller Amendment**, which stated that the United States had no interest in taking control of Cuba. In response to the resolution, Spain declared war on the United States. The next day, Congress passed, and McKinley signed, a declaration of war against Spain.

"Remember the *Maine*!"

Most of the men aboard the USS *Maine* were sleeping when a terrible explosion demolished the forward third of the ship at 9:40 p.m. on February 15, 1898. The rest of the ship sank quickly. Some 266 men were killed.

How do you think such images of the Maine *might have affected Americans?*

War in the Philippines While attention was focused on Cuba, the U.S. Navy won a quick victory nearly halfway around the world in the Philippines, a Spanish colony in the Pacific. Filipinos, like Cubans, were rebelling against Spanish rule.

As soon as the Spanish-American War began, American commodore George Dewey raced to the Philippines with four large warships and two small gunboats. On May 1, ignoring reports that mines beneath the water barred his way, Dewey sailed into Manila Bay and destroyed the Spanish Pacific fleet stationed there. Dewey's forces sank or captured ten ships. The Spanish lost 381 lives, but none of Dewey's men were killed.

Dewey had defeated the Spanish, but he did not have enough troops to occupy and secure the Philippines. Troops eventually arrived, and on August 13, U.S. troops and Filipino rebels led by **Emilio Aguinaldo** (ahg-ee-NAHL-doh) took control of the Philippine capital, Manila.

War in the Caribbean In contrast to the navy, the U.S. Army was unprepared for war. At the start of the Spanish-American War, the entire U.S. Army had only 28,000 soldiers. New volunteers raised that figure to more than 280,000 within months. The army did not have enough rifles or bullets for these soldiers. It did not even have appropriate clothing for the troops. Many soldiers received warm woolen uniforms even though Cuba had a warm, tropical climate.

The soldiers faced harsh living conditions in Cuba. They ate canned meat that one general called "embalmed beef." Many were stricken with yellow fever and other deadly diseases. More than 2,000 Americans died from diseases they contracted in Cuba. Fewer than 400 were killed in battle.

— BIOGRAPHY —

Theodore Roosevelt 1858–1919

Theodore Roosevelt was born into a wealthy family in New York City. As a young man, following the tragic deaths of his mother and wife, Roosevelt set out for a new life in the Dakota Territory. For two years he lived as a cattle rancher and cowboy. In 1886 he returned to New York to pursue politics.

In 1898 Roosevelt became a national hero for leading the Rough Riders in the Spanish-American War. Soon after, he was elected governor of New York. In 1901, while Roosevelt was serving as vice president, President McKinley was assassinated. At age 42, Roosevelt was the youngest man in U.S. history to assume the presidency. As president, Roosevelt fought for progressive reforms and set aside millions of acres as national parks and forests. Roosevelt's aggressive foreign policy expanded American power in the world.

Draw Conclusions
What characteristics made Theodore Roosevelt a successful leader?

The most colorful group of U.S. soldiers was the 1st Volunteer Cavalry, nicknamed the Rough Riders. Second in command of this group was Lieutenant Colonel Theodore Roosevelt. Roosevelt had organized the Rough Riders to fight in Cuba. Volunteers included Native Americans, college athletes, cowboys, miners, and ranchers. Newspaper stories of their heroism earned the Rough Riders Americans' admiration. Four privates of the African American 10th Cavalry, who served with the Rough Riders, received the Congressional Medal of Honor.

Landing on June 22, 1898, the U.S. troops captured the hills around the main Spanish forces at Santiago. At the village of El Caney on July 1, some 7,000 U.S. soldiers, aided by Cuban rebels, overwhelmed about 600 Spanish defenders.

The main U.S. force then attacked and captured San Juan Hill. The Rough Riders and the African American 9th and 10th cavalries captured nearby Kettle Hill. The many accounts of the battle became popular with the American public back home. A journalist on the scene described the soldiers' charge:

> "It was a miracle of self-sacrifice, a triumph of bulldog courage. . . .
> The fire of the Spanish riflemen . . . doubled and trebled [tripled] in
> fierceness, the crests of the hills crackled and burst in amazed roars
> and rippled with waves of tiny flame. But the blue line [of United
> States soldiers] crept steadily up and on."
>
> —Richard Harding Davis, quoted in *The American Reader*, edited by Paul M. Angle

On July 3 the commander of the Spanish fleet decided to try breaking through the U.S. blockade. Though every Spanish ship was destroyed in the battle, American forces suffered only two casualties. Santiago surrendered two weeks later. President McKinley began peace negotiations with Spain, which was assured of defeat. A few days later, U.S. troops invaded Spanish-held Puerto Rico, which surrendered with little resistance. Spain signed a cease-fire agreement on August 12, 1898.

Reading Check
Compare How was fighting in the Pacific and the Caribbean similar?

United States Gains Territories

Although Americans had declared war to secure Cuba's independence, U.S. leaders began demanding that Spain also give up other colonies. As a result of the Spanish-American War, the peace treaty placed Cuba, Guam, Puerto Rico, and the Philippines under U.S. control. The United States was developing as a strong world political power.

In reaction, some Americans formed the **Anti-Imperialist League**. This group opposed the treaty and the creation of an American colonial empire. They argued that the treaty threatened democracy because it denied self-government to the people living in the newly acquired territories. The Senate approved the peace treaty by a vote of 57 to 27—just one vote more than the two-thirds majority needed to ratify treaties.

Cuba The Teller Amendment had declared that the United States would not annex Cuba and it would have independence. However, McKinley wanted to create stability and increase U.S. economic activity there. He set

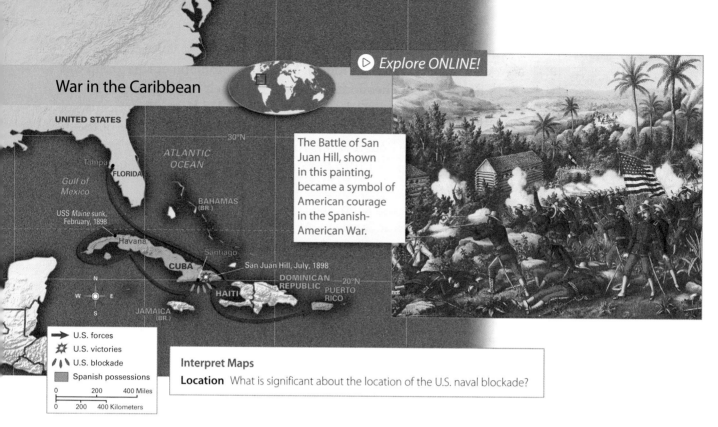

Explore ONLINE!

UNITED STATES

30°N

ATLANTIC OCEAN

Tampa

FLORIDA

Gulf of Mexico

BAHAMAS (BR.)

USS *Maine* sunk, February, 1898

Havana

Santiago

CUBA

San Juan Hill, July, 1898

DOMINICAN REPUBLIC

HAITI

PUERTO RICO

20°N

JAMAICA (BR.)

The Battle of San Juan Hill, shown in this painting, became a symbol of American courage in the Spanish-American War.

N W E S

→ U.S. forces
✳ U.S. victories
⁄⁍\ U.S. blockade
▮ Spanish possessions

0   200   400 Miles
0   200   400 Kilometers

Interpret Maps

Location What is significant about the location of the U.S. naval blockade?

up a military government—a government controlled by the U.S. military. He appointed Leonard Wood, who had commanded the Rough Riders during the war, as governor. Wood quickly began building schools and a sanitation system.

Even with the new sanitation system, disease remained a major problem. Dr. Walter Reed, head of the army's Yellow Fever Commission, was sent to Cuba in 1900 to help fight the disease. He and his volunteers conducted experiments, including allowing themselves to be bitten by infected insects. They soon proved that yellow fever was transmitted by mosquitoes. Getting rid of the standing water where mosquitoes lived helped health officials to control the disease.

Governor Wood also oversaw the writing of a Cuban constitution. The document included the **Platt Amendment**. This amendment limited Cuba's right to make treaties and allowed the United States to intervene in Cuban affairs. It also required Cuba to sell or lease land to the United States. Cuban leaders compared the Platt Amendment to "handing over the keys to our house so that they [the Americans] can enter it at any time, whenever the desire seizes them." The Cubans reluctantly accepted the amendment, and U.S. troops withdrew. The amendment remained in force until 1934. The U.S. government stayed actively involved in Cuban affairs until the late 1950s.

Puerto Rico Like Cubans, Puerto Ricans had hoped for independence after the war. Instead, the U.S. government made the island an American territory. The United States set up a government and appointed top officials. Puerto Ricans were allowed little say in their own affairs. On April 12, 1900, the Foraker Act established a civil government in Puerto Rico. It was headed by a governor and included a two-house legislature.

A debate over the new territory soon arose. People who lived in Puerto Rico were considered citizens of the island but not of the United States. In 1917 the Jones Act gave Puerto Ricans U.S. citizenship and made Puerto Rico a self-governing territory. This act allowed Puerto Ricans to elect both houses of the legislature. However, another 30 years passed before Puerto Ricans could elect their own governor. Today the island has its own constitution and elected officials. However, it remains associated with the United States as a commonwealth under U.S. control.

The Philippines Spain had surrendered the Philippines in return for a $20 million payment from the United States. Americans agreed with President McKinley, who said that the United States would benefit from the islands' naval and commercial value. He also said that annexing the islands would keep Europeans from seizing them.

This 1901 illustration shows the capture of Filipino rebel leader, Emilio Aguinaldo.

Reading Check
Summarize What areas did the United States control as a result of the war?

Filipino rebels, however, had expected to gain independence after the war. They had helped U.S. forces to capture Manila. When the United States decided instead to keep the islands, war broke out. Rebels led by Emilio Aguinaldo started a guerrilla war against the American forces. More than 4,200 U.S. soldiers and hundreds of thousands of Filipinos died before the conflict ended in 1902.

That same year, Congress passed the Philippine Government Act. It provided that an appointed governor and a two-house legislature would rule the Philippines. In 1946 the United States granted full independence to the Philippines.

Summary and Preview The United States fought a war with Spain and gained new territories in the Pacific and Caribbean regions. In the next lesson you will learn about U.S. interests in Latin America.

Lesson 2 Assessment

Review Ideas, Terms, and People

1. **a. Recall** What was the cause of the conflict between Cuba and Spain?
   b. Analyze How did yellow journalism affect public support for U.S. military action in Cuba?
   c. Elaborate In what way did the sinking of the USS *Maine* help cause the Spanish-American War?

2. **a. Identify** What territories did the United States gain as a result of the war?
   b. Analyze Why did some Americans oppose the annexation of the Philippines?
   c. Elaborate Explain how the Spanish-American War affected the relations between the United States and other countries.

Critical Thinking

3. **Categorize** Review your notes on the results of the Spanish-American War. Then copy the graphic organizer shown below. Use your notes to identify arguments for and against taking control of foreign territories.

Arguments against Imperialism		Arguments for Imperialism
	vs.	

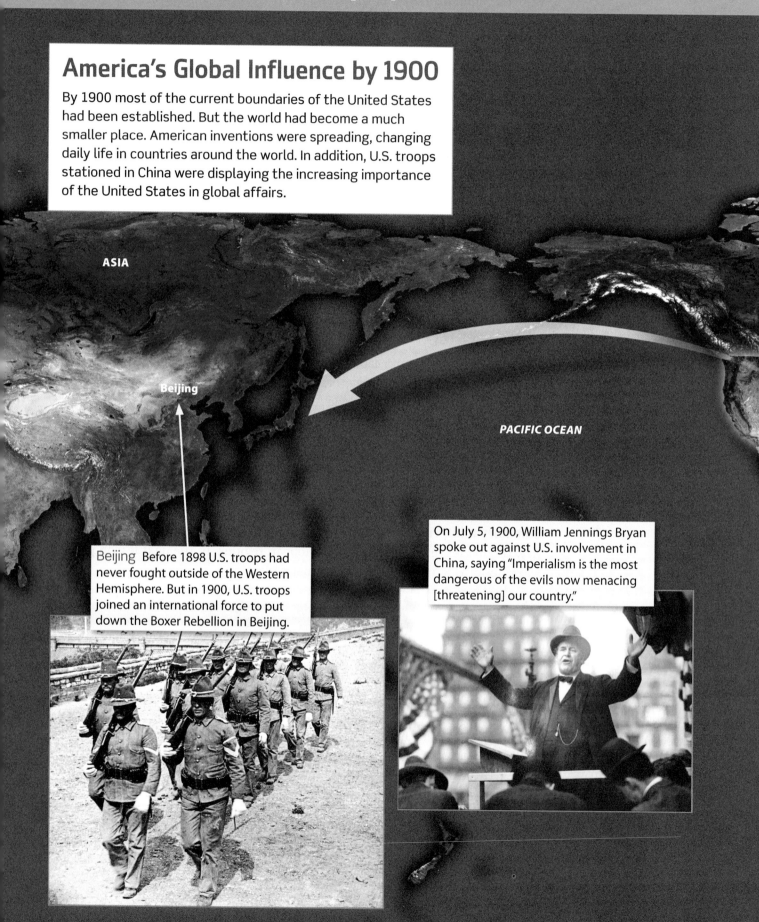

America's Global Influence by 1900

By 1900 most of the current boundaries of the United States had been established. But the world had become a much smaller place. American inventions were spreading, changing daily life in countries around the world. In addition, U.S. troops stationed in China were displaying the increasing importance of the United States in global affairs.

ASIA

Beijing

PACIFIC OCEAN

Beijing Before 1898 U.S. troops had never fought outside of the Western Hemisphere. But in 1900, U.S. troops joined an international force to put down the Boxer Rebellion in Beijing.

On July 5, 1900, William Jennings Bryan spoke out against U.S. involvement in China, saying "Imperialism is the most dangerous of the evils now menacing [threatening] our country."

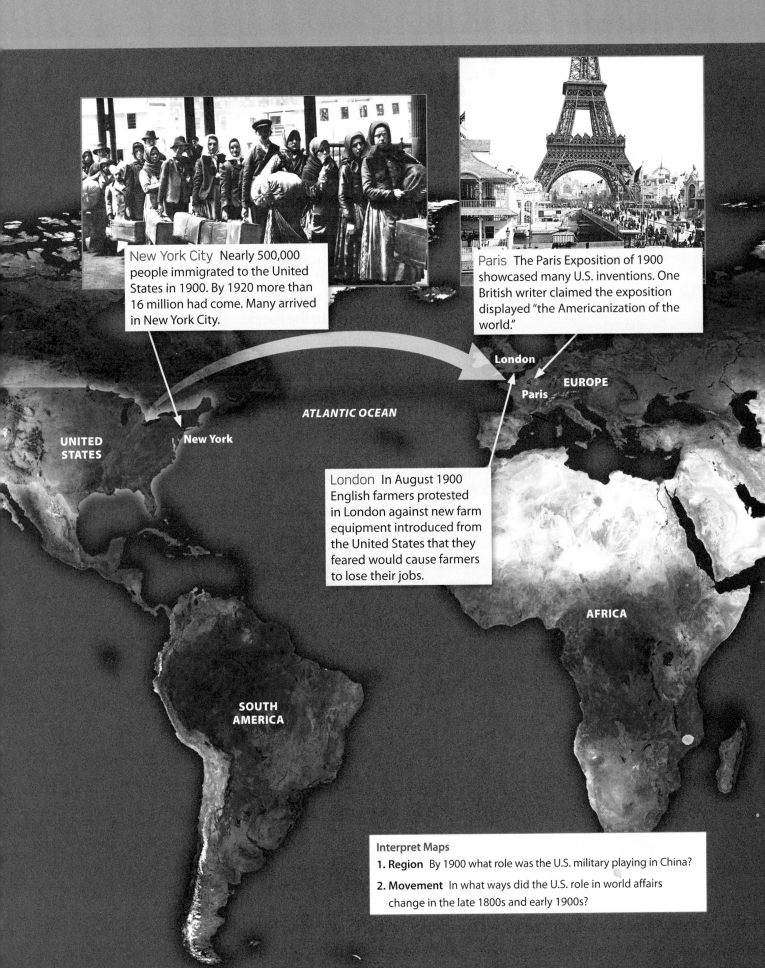

New York City Nearly 500,000 people immigrated to the United States in 1900. By 1920 more than 16 million had come. Many arrived in New York City.

Paris The Paris Exposition of 1900 showcased many U.S. inventions. One British writer claimed the exposition displayed "the Americanization of the world."

London In August 1900 English farmers protested in London against new farm equipment introduced from the United States that they feared would cause farmers to lose their jobs.

London

Paris

EUROPE

ATLANTIC OCEAN

New York

UNITED STATES

SOUTH AMERICA

AFRICA

Interpret Maps

1. **Region** By 1900 what role was the U.S. military playing in China?

2. **Movement** In what ways did the U.S. role in world affairs change in the late 1800s and early 1900s?

The United States and Latin America

The Big Idea

The United States expanded its role in Latin America in the early 1900s with new foreign policy.

Main Ideas

- The United States built the Panama Canal in the early 1900s.

- Theodore Roosevelt changed U.S. foreign policy toward Latin America.

- Presidents Taft and Wilson promoted U.S. interests in Latin America.

Key Terms and People

Panama Canal
Roosevelt Corollary
dollar diplomacy
Mexican Revolution
John J. Pershing
Francisco "Pancho" Villa

If YOU were there . . .

You are an engineer, and you've been working on the Panama Canal for almost eight years. Your work crews used huge steam shovels to slice through a ridge of mountains and built a large artificial lake. You planned a system to move ships through different water levels. Now your work is done. You can watch massive ships travel from the Atlantic to the Pacific.

Which part of the work on the canal was the most challenging?

Building the Panama Canal

A canal across the narrow neck of Central America would link the Atlantic and Pacific oceans and cut some 8,000 miles off the voyage by ship from the West to the East coasts of the United States. It would also allow the U.S. Navy to link its Atlantic and Pacific naval fleets quickly.

Revolution in Panama No one was a stronger supporter of a Central American canal than President Theodore Roosevelt. He knew it made good economic and political sense to build the canal. It would reduce travel time for commercial and military transport. The Spanish-American War, fought in both oceans, also made clear the need for such a shortcut.

Roosevelt knew that the best spot for the canal was the Isthmus of Panama. At the time, this area was part of the nation of Colombia. Roosevelt was unable to convince the Colombian senate to lease a strip of land across Panama to the United States.

Roosevelt considered other ways to gain control of the land. He learned that Panamanian revolutionaries were planning a revolt against Colombia. On November 2, 1903, a U.S. warship arrived outside Colón, Panama. The next day the revolt began. Blocked by the U.S. warship, Colombian forces could not reach Panama to stop the rebellion. Panama declared itself an independent country. The United States then recognized the new nation.

The new government of Panama supported the idea of a canal across its land. The United States agreed to pay Panama $10 million plus $250,000 a year for a 99-year lease on a ten-mile-wide strip of land across the isthmus.

Building the Canal Canal construction began in 1904. Building the canal was a huge challenge. The first obstacle to overcome was tropical disease. The canal route ran through 51 miles of forests and swamps filled with mosquitoes, many of which carried the deadly diseases malaria and yellow fever.

Dr. William C. Gorgas, who had helped Dr. Walter Reed stamp out yellow fever in Cuba, organized a successful effort to rid the canal route of disease-carrying mosquitoes. If Gorgas had not been successful, the canal's construction would have taken much longer. It also would have cost much more in terms of both lives and money.

Even with the reduced risk of disease, the work was very dangerous. Most of the canal had to be blasted out of solid rock with explosives. Workers used dozens of steam shovels to cut a narrow, eight-mile-long channel through the mountains of central Panama. Sometimes workers died when their shovels struck explosive charges. "The flesh of men flew in the air like birds every day," recalled one worker from the West Indies.

More than 44,000 workers, including many black West Indians, labored on the canal. Some 6,000 lives were lost during the American construction of the **Panama Canal**. It was finally opened to ships on August 15, 1914, linking the Atlantic and Pacific oceans. An opening ceremony was held the next year. It had taken ten years to complete, and the cost was $375 million. It was probably the most expensive construction project in the world at that time. In the end, however, the world had its "highway between the oceans." Building the canal also began to change the relationship between the United States and Latin American nations.

Reading Check
Draw Conclusions
Why did building the canal cost so many lives?

The massive Gatun Locks, shown here under construction in 1914, raise ships 85 feet onto Gatun Lake, an inland waterway on the Panama Canal.

The Panama Canal

▶ Explore ONLINE!

NORTH AMERICA

UNITED STATES

San Francisco

New York City

Gulf of Mexico

5,200 Miles

CENTRAL AMERICA

Caribbean Sea

Panama Canal

13,000 Miles

PACIFIC OCEAN

ATLANTIC OCEAN

SOUTH AMERICA

Increasing Exports The Panama Canal did not just increase trade between the East and West coasts of the United States. By shortening the trip from many U.S. ports to other parts of the world, the canal also led to increased exports of agricultural and manufactured goods. It helped the U.S. economy continue to grow.

By how many miles did the Panama Canal shorten the shipping distance between New York City and San Francisco?

Inset map

Colón
Cristobal
Caribbean Sea
Gatun Locks
Gatun Lake
Gaillard Cut
Pedro Miguel Locks
Panama City
Miraflores Locks
Balboa
Bay of Panama
PANAMA

Legend:
- Canal zone
- Canal route
- Railroad
- Locks

0 10 20 Miles
0 10 20 Kilometers

0 400 800 Miles
0 400 800 Kilometers

Interpret Maps

1. **Place** Why was Panama chosen as the site for a canal?

2. **Movement** How many locks did ships have to travel through from Balboa to Colón?

U.S. Policy Toward Latin America

As president, Theodore Roosevelt actively pursued progressive reforms at home. He also believed the United States should play a more active role in the Western Hemisphere. In 1900 Roosevelt said, "I have always been fond of the West African proverb: 'Speak softly and carry a big stick; you will go far.'" Roosevelt wanted everyone to know he would use a "big stick"—meaning U.S. military force—to protect economic and strategic interests of the United States in Latin America.

Roosevelt's foreign policy was a change from the policies of previous presidents. In the 1823 Monroe Doctrine, President James Monroe had warned European nations not to interfere in the Western Hemisphere. And, while the Monroe Doctrine became a major principle of U.S. foreign policy, the United States did not have the military strength to enforce it. By the time of Roosevelt's presidency, this situation was changing. The United States was growing stronger and expanding its influence as a world power.

How should the United States use its new power in Latin America? This question came up often in the early 1900s. In the late 1800s Europeans and Americans had invested large sums of money in Latin America. Much of this investment had come in the form of bank loans. Venezuela, for example, fell deeply in debt to British and German lenders. In 1902 Venezuela refused to repay these debts. A similar situation arose in the Caribbean nation of the Dominican Republic in 1904. European powers prepared to use military force to collect the debts.

Roosevelt insisted the countries repay their debts. But he did not want to allow Europeans to intervene in Latin America. The presence of

Historical Source

Roosevelt's Imperialism

Theodore Roosevelt's foreign policy is shown visually in this cartoon. Roosevelt is the giant leading a group of ships that represent debt collection. The U.S. president is patrolling the Caribbean Sea and Latin American countries, trying to enforce the payment of debts to European countries.

What do you think this stick represents?

Why are these vessels warships?

Analyze Historical Sources
What is the cartoonist trying to tell viewers about the Roosevelt Corollary?

European forces there would violate the Monroe Doctrine and threaten U.S. power in the region.

Roosevelt knew that U.S. officials would have to force debtor nations to repay their loans in order to keep European nations from directly intervening in Latin America. In December 1904 he announced what became known as the **Roosevelt Corollary** to the Monroe Doctrine. This addition warned that in cases of "wrongdoing" by Latin American countries, the United States might exercise "international police power." The Roosevelt Corollary expanded the Monroe Doctrine and increased United States involvement in the affairs of Latin America.

The Roosevelt Corollary asserted a new **role** for the United States as an "international police power" in the Western Hemisphere. Roosevelt actively enforced the corollary throughout the rest of his presidency. This led to great resentment from Latin American countries.

Academic Vocabulary
role assigned behavior

Reading Check
Find Main Ideas
Why did Roosevelt announce the Roosevelt Corollary?

The United States in Latin America

Explore ONLINE!

Guantánamo Bay The United States maintains a naval base on the island of Cuba.

Puerto Rico The island remains a commonwealth of the United States.

Panama Canal The United States turned the canal over to Panama in 1979 but kept the right to defend it.

United States and possessions

U.S. protectorates

Bombarded by U.S. forces

1898 Date of bombardment or occupation

Route of Pershing's U.S. Expeditionary Force

Boundary line negotiated by United States

0   300   600 Miles
0   300   600 Kilometers

Interpret Maps

1. **Region** What parts of this region does the United States still control?

2. **Place** Which country was a U.S. protectorate for the longest period of time?

U.S. Foreign Policy

Departing from the example set by the nation's first president, George Washington, future presidents increased U.S. involvement around the world, particularly in Latin America.

Washington's Farewell Address

The United States will not become involved in European affairs.

Monroe Doctrine

The United States will defend its interests in the Western Hemisphere and keep European powers out.

Roosevelt Corollary

The United States will police wrongdoing by nations in the Western Hemisphere.

Taft's Dollar Diplomacy

The United States will use economic means to aid its interests in Latin America.

Wilson and Democracy

The United States will promote and protect democracy in the Western Hemisphere.

U.S. Interests in Latin America

William Howard Taft, who became president in 1909, also acted to protect U.S. economic interests in Latin America. Taft used a foreign policy called **dollar diplomacy**—influencing governments through economic, not military, intervention.

President Taft described dollar diplomacy as "substituting dollars for bullets. It is . . . directed to the increase of American trade." He wanted to encourage stability and keep Europeans out of Latin America by expanding U.S. business interests there.

For example, in 1911 Nicaragua failed to repay a loan from British investors. American bankers lent Nicaragua $1.5 billion in return for control of the National Bank of Nicaragua and the government-owned railway. When local anger over this deal led to revolt in Nicaragua, Taft sent U.S. Marines to protect American interests.

When President Woodrow Wilson took office in 1913, he rejected Taft's dollar diplomacy. He believed the United States had a moral obligation to promote democracy in Latin America. This, he believed, would advance American interests abroad. Nonetheless, Wilson was willing to use military force to protect U.S. interests. When civil unrest shook Haiti in 1915 and the Dominican Republic in 1916, Wilson sent in military troops. In both cases, U.S. Marines occupied the countries for years.

In 1910 many Mexicans revolted against the harsh rule of Mexican dictator Porfirio Díaz. This was the start of the **Mexican Revolution**, a long, violent struggle for power in Mexico. The war affected U.S. interests because Americans had invested more than $1 billion in Mexican land, mining, oil, and railways. American business leaders feared they would lose their investments.

Though U.S. troops pursued Mexican revolutionary Pancho Villa (above) for nearly a year, they were unable to capture him.

Reading Check
Summarize How did Wilson respond to events in Mexico?

In 1914 President Wilson learned that a German ship carrying weapons was headed to the port of Veracruz, Mexico. To keep the weapons from reaching the rebels, Wilson ordered the navy to seize Veracruz. Wilson acted again in 1916, sending General **John J. Pershing** and 15,000 U.S. soldiers into Mexico. Pershing's mission was to catch the rebel leader **Francisco "Pancho" Villa**, who had killed 17 Americans in New Mexico. The farther Pershing pushed into Mexico, the more the Mexicans resented the Americans. After 11 months of searching, Pershing failed to capture Villa and Wilson recalled the troops. For the rest of Wilson's presidency, relations between the United States and Mexico remained tense.

In 1917 a new constitution promised to bring order to Mexico. The constitution contained ideas of Mexico's revolutionary leaders, and it protected the liberties and rights of citizens. Despite the new constitution, however, fighting continued. Mexico's economy suffered terribly. Agriculture was disrupted, mines were abandoned, and factories were destroyed. Many Mexican men and women immigrated to the United States in search of work and a more stable life.

Summary and Review In the early 1900s the United States changed its foreign policy and expanded its involvement in Latin America in order to secure its strategic and economic interests.

Lesson 3 Assessment

Review Ideas, Terms, and People

1. a. **Recall** Why did the United States want to build a canal?

   b. **Analyze** What challenges did the builders of the Panama Canal face, and how did they overcome them?

   c. **Explain** How did Roosevelt's efforts to build the Panama Canal affect the economy of the United States?

2. a. **Describe** What problem was causing conflict between European and Latin American nations?

   b. **Summarize** How and why did Theodore Roosevelt change U.S. policy toward Latin America?

   c. **Evaluate** How did the Roosevelt Corollary affect the relationship between the United States and Latin American nations?

3. a. **Recall** What did Woodrow Wilson believe was the United States's obligation to Latin America?

   b. **Compare and Contrast** How were the foreign policies of Taft and Wilson toward Latin America similar, and how were they different?

Critical Thinking

4. **Categorize** Review your notes on U.S. policies toward Latin America. Then copy the web diagram below. Use it to analyze how national interest influenced American policies toward Latin America.

Monroe — U.S. Foreign Policy — Taft — Roosevelt — Wilson

Social Studies Skills

Understand Continuity and Change

Define the Skill

A well-known saying claims that "the more things change, the more they stay the same." Nowhere does this observation apply better than to the study of history. Any examination of the past will show many changes—nations expanding or shrinking, empires rising and falling, changes in leadership, or people on the move, for example.

The reasons for change have not changed, however. The same general forces have driven the actions of people and nations across time. These forces are the threads that run through history and give it continuity, or connectedness. They are the "sameness" in a world of continuous change.

Learn the Skill

You can find the causes of all events of the past in one or more of these major forces or themes that connect all history.

1. **Cooperation and Conflict** Throughout time, people and groups have worked together to achieve goals. They have also opposed others who stood in the way of their goals.

2. **Cultural Invention and Interaction** The values and ideas expressed in peoples' art, literature, customs, and religion have enriched the world. But the spread of cultures and their contact with other cultures have produced conflict as well.

3. **Geography and Environment** Physical environment and natural resources have shaped how people live. Efforts to gain, protect, or make good use of land and resources have been major causes of cooperation and conflict in history.

4. **Science and Technology** *Technology,* or the development and use of tools, has helped humans across time make better use of their environment. Science has changed their knowledge of the world, and changed their lives, too.

5. **Economic Opportunity and Development** From hunting and gathering to herding, farming, manufacturing, and trade, people have tried to make the most of their resources. The desire for a better life has also been a major reason people have moved from one place to another.

6. **The Impact of Individuals** Political, religious, military, business, and other leaders have been a major influence in history. The actions of many ordinary people have also shaped history.

7. **Nationalism and Imperialism** *Nationalism* is the desire of a people to have their own country. *Imperialism* is the desire of a nation to influence or control other nations. Both have existed across time.

8. **Political and Social Systems** People have always been part of groups—families, villages, nations, or religious groups, for example. The groups to which people belong shape how they relate to others around them.

Practice the Skill

Check your understanding of continuity and change in history by answering the following questions.

1. What forces of history are illustrated by the events in the module you just studied? Explain with examples.

2. How do the events in this module show continuity with earlier periods in U.S. history?

Module 7 Assessment

Review Vocabulary, Terms, and People

1. In which of the following did the United States declare that it had no interest in taking control of Cuba?
   a. Roosevelt Corollary
   b. Monroe Doctrine
   c. Open Door Policy
   d. Teller Amendment

2. Which leader upset sugar planters in Hawaii by proposing a plan to return power to the monarchy?
   a. Liliuokalani
   b. John L. Stevens
   c. Millard Fillmore
   d. Woodrow Wilson

3. Which president supported Panama's revolt against Colombia in 1903?
   a. Woodrow Wilson
   b. William McKinley
   c. William Howard Taft
   d. Theodore Roosevelt

4. Who led U.S. forces into Mexico after attacks against U.S. citizens by Mexican rebels?
   a. John Hay
   b. William H. Seward
   c. John J. Pershing
   d. Theodore Roosevelt

Comprehension and Critical Thinking

Lesson 1

5. a. **Identify** Into what areas did the United States expand in the late 1800s?
   b. **Draw Conclusions** How did the United States benefit from contact with foreign nations and territories?
   c. **Elaborate** Which policy would you have supported—isolationism or imperialism? Explain your answer.

Lesson 2

6. a. **Describe** What events led the United States to declare war on Spain?
   b. **Draw Conclusions** How did winning the Spanish-American War help the U.S. develop as a world power?
   c. **Predict** How might foreign countries have viewed the actions of the United States in the Spanish-American War?

Lesson 3

7. a. **Identify** In what ways did the United States become involved in Latin American affairs?
   b. **Draw Conclusions** Why did the United States expand its role in Latin America in the early 1900s?
   c. **Evaluate** Do you think the United States should have been as actively involved in Latin America as it was? Explain your answer.

Review Themes

8. **Geography** How did the geography of the United States change after the end of its policy of isolationism?

9. **Politics** How did the policy of imperialism affect American politics in the late 1800s and early 1900s?

Reading Skills

Compare Historical Texts *Use the Reading Skills taught in this module to answer the question about the reading selections below.*

> A. "Sad to say, this most precious and sublime feature of the Yosemite National Park (Hetch Hetchy Valley), one of the greatest of all our natural resources for the uplifting joy and peace and health of the people, is in danger of being dammed and made into a reservoir to help supply San Francisco with water and light. . . ."
>
> —John Muir, *The Yosemite*, 1912
>
> B. "As we all know, there is no use of water that is higher than the domestic use. Then, if there is, as the engineers tell us, no other source of supply that is anything like so reasonably available as this one; if this is the best, and, within reasonable limits of cost, the only means of supplying San Francisco with water, we come straight to the question of whether the advantage of leaving this valley in a state of nature is greater than the advantage of using it for the benefit of the city of San Francisco."
>
> —Gifford Pinchot, address to Congress, 1913

10. How do the two men quoted above differ on the issue of building a dam in the Hetch Hetchy Valley?

Social Studies Skills

Understand Continuity and Change *Use the Social Studies Skills taught in this module to complete the activity below.*

11. Pick three of the themes listed in the Social Studies Skills. Then, using the building of the Panama Canal as a case study, identify instances of continuity and change for each theme. Summarize your findings in a paragraph.

Focus on Writing

12. **Write a List of Pros and Cons** In this module you learned how the United States increased its role in international affairs. Create a list of the pros and cons of U.S. involvement with other nations in the late 1800s and early 1900s. Decide whether you want to include in your lists only facts, only opinions, or some of each. Consider how your analysis of history can help guide U.S. foreign policy in the future. When you have finished your list, use it as the basis for a paragraph recommending either that the United States continue to involve itself in the affairs of other nations or that it pull back from such involvement.

Module 8

World War I

★

Essential Question

How did World War I impact America and transform Europe?

About the Photo: Soldiers faced terrible conditions as they fought the enemy from their trench positions.

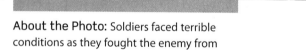

Explore ONLINE!

HISTORY

VIDEOS, including...
- The Challenge
- Armistice
- The Flu
- Wilson Works for Peace

☑ Document-Based Investigations

☑ Graphic Organizers

☑ Interactive Games

☑ Image with Hotspots: Trench Warfare

☑ Image Carousel: The United States Mobilizes for War

☑ Interactive Map: World War I, 1914–1918

In this module you will learn how an assassination in Europe sparked the deadliest war the world had ever seen. You will find out how the United States was drawn into the war and will read about new battle strategies.

What You Will Learn . . .

Timeline of Events 1914–1920

▶ *Explore ONLINE!*

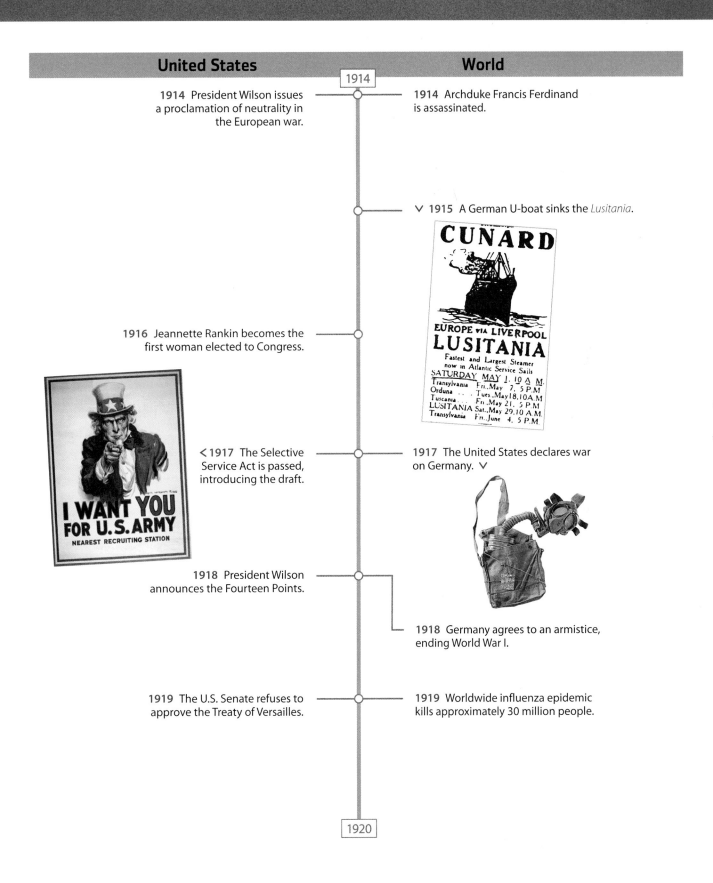

United States	1914	World
1914 President Wilson issues a proclamation of neutrality in the European war.		**1914** Archduke Francis Ferdinand is assassinated.
		∨ **1915** A German U-boat sinks the *Lusitania*.
1916 Jeannette Rankin becomes the first woman elected to Congress.		
‹ **1917** The Selective Service Act is passed, introducing the draft.		**1917** The United States declares war on Germany. ∨
1918 President Wilson announces the Fourteen Points.		
		1918 Germany agrees to an armistice, ending World War I.
1919 The U.S. Senate refuses to approve the Treaty of Versailles.		**1919** Worldwide influenza epidemic kills approximately 30 million people.
	1920	

Reading Social Studies

Politics and Economics

In this module you will read about World War I and the changes it brought to the United States and the world. Many of the political tensions that led to the war were caused by the rise of nationalism in European countries. You will read about how the war devastated European economies and how peace affected European countries.

READING FOCUS:

Recognize Fallacies in Reasoning

As part of evaluating a historical argument, you can judge whether the reasoning is sound. A *fallacy* is a false or mistaken idea.

Recognize Fallacies As you identify a main idea, judge its soundness. Look for cause-and-effect relationships that support the idea. Decide whether you think the argument is logical.

Notice how a reader explained the logical reasoning behind the main idea in the following paragraph.

> Three main factors led to a shortage of labor in the United States during the war. First, American factories were working nonstop to produce weapons and supplies for the Allied forces. Factories needed new workers to meet this huge demand. Second, the war almost completely cut off immigration. As you know, immigrants had provided a steady source of labor to American industry. And third, many of the young men who would normally take factory jobs were off fighting in Europe.

If factories were working overtime, they would need more workers. This supports the main idea of a labor shortage.

If factories were used to having immigrants to hire, and there were fewer immigrants, it would make sense that there was a labor shortage.

Here's a third reason for a labor shortage: many men became soldiers. It makes sense that there was a labor shortage during the war.

You Try It!

The man who assassinated Archduke Francis Ferdinand was a Serb.

↓

All Serbians wanted war with Austria-Hungary.

Wilson wanted to establish the League of Nations.

↓

because he thought it would help ensure peace.

Trench warfare was a new kind of warfare.

↓

Therefore, trench warfare was more horrible than any other kind of warfare.

1. Is the first conclusion reasonable? Why or why not? How can you tell?
2. Do you think the second conclusion is logical or illogical? What makes you think so?
3. Is the third conclusion a fallacy of reason? What reasonable conclusions can you draw from the statement?

As you read Module 8, notice how the authors use logical reasoning to support their main ideas.

The Road to War

The Big Idea

In 1914 tensions in Europe exploded into the deadliest war the world had ever seen.

Main Ideas

- Many factors contributed to the outbreak of World War I.
- European nations suffered massive casualties in the war's early battles.

Key Terms and People

militarism
Archduke Francis Ferdinand
mobilize
Central powers
Allied powers
trench warfare
stalemate
U-boats

If YOU were there . . .

You are walking past a newspaper stand when a headline catches your eye: "Austria-Hungary's Archduke Francis Ferdinand Assassinated in Sarajevo." Your first thought is, "Who's he?" You pick up the paper and read about the archduke and about the rising tensions in Europe related to his death. The article makes it sound like Europe is about to explode into war.

At this point, do you think the assassination will affect the United States? Why or why not?

Outbreak of War

Though Europe was at peace in the early 1900s, relations between European nations were not necessarily friendly. In fact, feelings of fear and distrust were growing among European powers such as Germany, France, Great Britain, Russia, and Austria-Hungary. This dangerous tension had several important causes.

Tensions in Europe One cause of tension was the rise of nationalism in the 1800s. Nationalism is a strong sense of pride and loyalty to one's nation or culture. Nationalism inspired people who shared a language or culture to want to unite politically. In 1871, for example, Chancellor Otto von Bismarck and Kaiser Wilhelm I brought together several German states to form the nation of Germany.

While nationalism helped bring stability to Germany, it caused instability in other places. The empire of Austria-Hungary included people from many different cultural groups. One of these groups was the Slavs. Slavic nationalists wanted to break away from Austria-Hungary and join the independent Slavic country of Serbia on the Balkan Peninsula. Leaders of Austria-Hungary reacted angrily, seeing this movement as a threat to their empire.

Another source of tension in Europe was imperialism. Britain's huge empire, stretching from Africa to Asia, brought it wealth and power. Eager to share in such benefits, other European powers competed for control of overseas territories. Fierce competition for territory took place within Europe as well. For example, Germany had taken the Alsace-Lorraine region from France in the Franco-Prussian War in 1871. France wanted it back.

In this competitive atmosphere, nations focused their resources on **militarism**—the aggressive strengthening of armed forces. European nations raced to build armies and navies that were larger than ever before.

As nations became more powerful, they sought to protect themselves by forming new alliances. Germany formed an alliance with Austria-Hungary in 1879. In this alliance system, each promised to defend the other in case of enemy attack. Concerned with Germany's growing power, France and Russia created their own alliance in 1893. Britain joined France and Russia in 1907.

The assassination of Archduke Francis Ferdinand and his wife, Sophie, by a Serb nationalist sparked the beginning of World War I.

The Spark With so much hostility dividing the nations of Europe, a German general felt that "a European war is bound to come sooner or later." All that was needed was a spark to set Europe on fire. That spark flew from the Balkan province of Bosnia and Herzegovina.

Bosnia and Herzegovina had gained independence from Turkish rule in 1878. In 1908, however, Austria-Hungary annexed the province. Slavic nationalists resisted violently—they wanted the region to be part of Serbia.

On June 28, 1914, **Archduke Francis Ferdinand**, heir to the throne of Austria-Hungary, visited the province's capital of Sarajevo with his wife, Sophie. While riding through the streets, they were shot and killed by a 19-year-old Serb nationalist named Gavrilo Princip.

The assassination shattered Europe's fragile peace. Determined to crush Serbia and the Slavic nationalists, Austria-Hungary declared war on Serbia. Very quickly, other countries were pulled into the fighting. Russia had promised to support Serbia in case of war. It began to **mobilize**, or prepare its military for war. On August 1 Germany, Austria-Hungary's ally, declared war on Russia. Two days later, Germany also declared war on France, Russia's ally. To reach France quickly, the German army marched into Belgium on August 4. Britain, which had promised to support Belgium, then declared war on Germany.

As the fighting started, the alliance between Austria-Hungary and Germany came to be known as the **Central powers**. Bulgaria and the Ottoman Empire later sided with the Central Powers. France, Russia, and Britain were known as the **Allied powers**. Italy joined them in 1915. Over the next several years, soldiers from 30 nations and six continents would fight in what was then called the Great War. The conflict later became known as World War I.

Reading Check
Identify Cause and Effect How did nationalism contribute to political tensions in Europe?

Early Battles of the War

Both sides expected the war to be over in a few months. German leaders planned to defeat France quickly, before Russia could join the fighting. But as the Germans marched toward France, they met fierce resistance from Belgian soldiers. This gave Britain and France time to mobilize their own troops. New military technologies changed military strategy and resulted in an unprecedented number of casualties.

The First Battle of the Marne Belgian resistance slowed the German advance but could not stop it. On September 3 the German army was just 25 miles from Paris, the capital of France. The French army blocked the German advance at the Marne River, east of Paris. The First Battle of the Marne raged for several days before the Germans were pushed back.

By mid-September French and German troops faced each other along a long battle line called the western front. The western front stretched from the North Sea all the way to Switzerland. Meanwhile, the Russian and German armies were struggling back and forth along the eastern front. The eastern front reached from the Black Sea to the Baltic Sea. It quickly became clear that this war would be longer and deadlier than anyone had expected.

A New Kind of War Part of what made World War I so long and deadly was a new technique called **trench warfare**. In trench warfare soldiers defended a position by fighting from the protection of deep ditches. When the French defeated the Germans in the First Battle of the Marne, the Germans did not retreat far. Instead, they dug trenches nearby. Opposite them, the French dug their own trenches. A 400-mile-long network of trenches soon stretched across the western front.

Trench Warfare

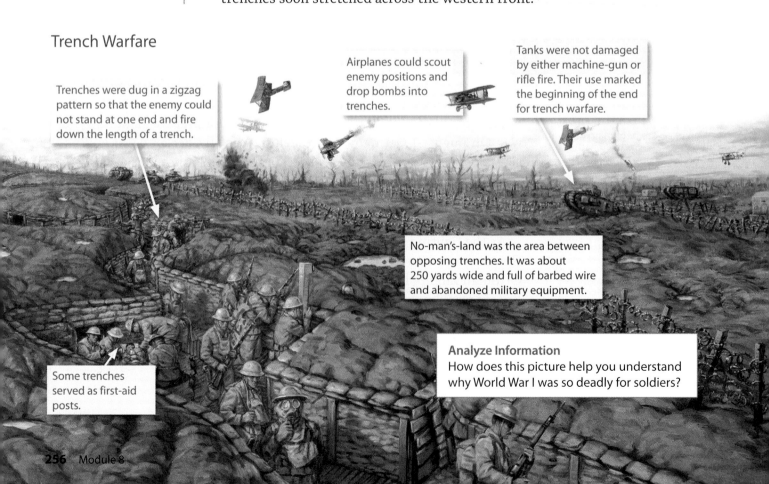

Trenches were dug in a zigzag pattern so that the enemy could not stand at one end and fire down the length of a trench.

Airplanes could scout enemy positions and drop bombs into trenches.

Tanks were not damaged by either machine-gun or rifle fire. Their use marked the beginning of the end for trench warfare.

No-man's-land was the area between opposing trenches. It was about 250 yards wide and full of barbed wire and abandoned military equipment.

Analyze Information
How does this picture help you understand why World War I was so deadly for soldiers?

Some trenches served as first-aid posts.

Soldiers fought in these cold, wet, and muddy ditches, sometimes for months at a time. The filthy trenches were perfect breeding grounds for germs. Soldiers on both sides died from disease. An American in the French army described life in the trenches:

"The impossibility of the simplest kind of personal cleanliness makes vermin [bugs] a universal ill, against which there is no remedy. Cold, dirt, discomfort, are the ever present conditions, and the soldier's life comes to mean . . . the most misery that the human organism [body] can support."

—Alan Seeger, *Letters and Diary of Alan Seeger*

The empty patch of ground between enemy trenches came to be known as "no-man's-land." This area was quickly stripped of trees and blasted full of holes by artillery shells. Anyone who ventured into no-man's-land was likely to be killed by enemy fire.

Another factor that made World War I deadlier than previous wars was the use of modern technology. New machine guns, for example, could fire 400 to 600 bullets a minute. Enormous artillery guns fired shells over the trenches. The shells exploded and sent speeding scraps of metal onto the soldiers below. Other shells spread poisonous gases. If soldiers were not wearing gas masks, the gas destroyed their lungs, causing slow, painful deaths. Poisonous gases were originally banned but came back into use by both sides by the end of the war. This was called chemical warfare.

Other new weapons included tanks and aircraft, including airplanes. Tanks are armored combat vehicles that can cause heavy damage but cannot be destroyed easily. Airplanes were used to fire down on soldiers in trenches and to gather information about enemy locations. Airplanes also battled each other in fights called "dogfights."

Many of the weapons first used in World War I, such as tanks and airplanes, are still used in warfare today. The use of poison gas, however, has been outlawed by international treaties.

This image shows British soldiers firing a machine gun and wearing early gas masks to protect against a gas attack.

Land and Sea Battles After a year of vicious fighting, the war had become a **stalemate**—a situation in which neither side can win a decisive victory. Determined to break the stalemate, both sides launched massive attacks in 1916. In February 1916 the Germans attacked the French city of Verdun, at the southern end of the western front. That summer, the Allies staged an attack along the Somme River, in northeastern France. Both battles raged for months, as the armies attacked and counterattacked.

By the end of the year, the Germans had failed to take Verdun. At the Somme River, the Allies had advanced just seven miles. Almost nothing had changed on the western front. But nearly 1 million men had been killed at Verdun and the Somme River.

As the stalemate on land dragged on, sea battles in the Atlantic Ocean and the North Sea became even more important. The powerful British navy blockaded the ports of the Central powers. They also laid explosive mines in the North Sea. These could blow a huge hole in a ship, sinking

German U-boats

Germany developed small submarines called U-boats as part of its war strategy. U-boats could strike Allied ships without being seen. They destroyed around 10 million tons of Allied and neutral ships and cargo from 1914 to 1918.

Academic Vocabulary

neutral unbiased, not favoring either side in a conflict

Reading Check

Categorize What new technologies did armies in World War I use?

it in minutes. The tactic effectively stopped ships from reaching German ports with needed supplies.

The Germans responded by using submarines called **U-boats**. U-boats launched torpedoes against Allied supply ships, causing heavy losses. The Germans also attacked ships belonging to **neutral** countries they believed were helping the Allies. This would soon pull the United States into World War I.

Summary and Preview World War I became a stalemate by 1916 as countries battled for control. In the next lesson you will find out why the United States decided to join the fighting.

Lesson 1 Assessment

Review Ideas, Terms, and People

1. **a. Describe** What factors contributed to the outbreak of World War I?

   b. Contrast How did nationalism affect Germany and Austria-Hungary differently?

   c. Predict What might have happened if Russia had not honored its agreement to defend Serbia?

   d. Evaluate What were the impacts of changes in military technologies used during World War I?

2. **a. Identify** What were the outcomes of the early battles of the war?

   b. Explain How did Belgian resistance affect the German war plan?

   c. Evaluate How successful was trench warfare as a strategy?

Critical Thinking

3. **Identify Cause and Effect** In this lesson you learned about major battles of World War I. Create a graphic organizer similar to the one below and use it to show the outcomes of these early battles and how they affected the war.

Battle	Outcome	Results

Americans Prepare for War

Everywhere you go, people are talking about the war in Europe. The United States has just joined the fighting on the side of the Allied powers. Many young men you know are volunteering to fight. Women are signing up to drive ambulances or work as nurses. You know that the situation in Europe is dangerous, but you want to serve your country.

Will you volunteer for service in World War I?

The Big Idea

After entering World War I in 1917, Americans began the massive effort of preparing for war.

Main Ideas

- The United States entered the war after repeated crises with Germany.

- The United States mobilized for war by training troops and stepping up production of supplies.

- Labor shortages created new wartime opportunities for women and other Americans.

Key Terms and People

Lusitania
Zimmermann Note
Selective Service Act
Liberty bonds
National War Labor Board

The United States Enters World War I

Millions of Americans at this time were immigrants or children of immigrants. Many came from countries belonging to the Allied or Central powers. They naturally sympathized with their former homelands. This did not change the fact that most Americans viewed World War I as a European conflict. They did not want American soldiers sent to the bloody battlefields of Europe. Shortly after World War I began, President Woodrow Wilson announced that the United States would remain neutral. Most Americans agreed that America should stay out of the war. However, international, economic, and military developments swayed opinion in the United States siding with the Allies and entering World War I.

American Neutrality Threatened Although the United States had a policy of neutrality, its merchants continued to trade with European nations. American ships carried supplies and war materials to the Allies. U.S. banks invested $2 billion in European war bonds, nearly all of it in Allied countries.

The Germans used U-boat attacks to try to stop supplies from reaching the Allies. Sometimes they attacked ships without warning. In May 1915 a German U-boat sank the *Lusitania*, a British passenger liner. Nearly 1,200 people, including 128 Americans, were killed. The incident

Sinking of the *Lusitania*

In 1915 German U-boats sank the *Lusitania*, an event that pushed the United States toward entry into World War I. Newspapers quickly spread news of the disaster.

The ship was treated as an enemy warship.

The ship sank before enough rescue ships could arrive.

"The accounts which have so far been received are fragmentary, and give no clear idea of the disaster. There is, however, no doubt that two torpedoes were fired without warning into the starboard side of the ship soon after 2 o'clock yesterday afternoon. There were conflicting accounts of the period during which the Lusitania remained afloat, but the Cunard Company states that she sunk 40 minutes after being struck."

—*The Register*, quoted in the *Times of London*

Analyze Historical Sources
How might this disaster draw the United States into war with Germany?

fueled anti-German feeling in the United States. Throughout the coming war, German Americans faced nativist attacks, including anti-German speeches, discrimination, and physical attacks.

Secretary of State William Jennings Bryan resigned over President Wilson's handling of the affair. Bryan thought that Wilson's protest note to the Germans was designed to bring the United States into the war.

In March 1916 a German U-boat attacked the *Sussex*, a French passenger ship. Several of the 80 casualties were Americans. Wilson demanded that the Germans stop attacking nonmilitary ships. German leaders responded with the Sussex pledge, agreeing not to attack merchant ships without warning.

Congress Declares War When Wilson ran for reelection in 1916, the promise to remain neutral helped him win the election. Nearly a year after the Sussex pledge, however, the Germans again began launching attacks on ships, including American vessels. In response, Wilson broke off diplomatic relations with Germany.

The United States stepped closer to war when Americans found out about the **Zimmermann Note**, sometimes called the Zimmermann telegram. This secret telegram to Mexico sent by the German foreign minister, Arthur Zimmermann, was decoded and then published by American newspapers in March 1917. In the note, Zimmermann proposed an alliance against the United States. He promised that Germany would help Mexico recapture areas that Mexico had lost during the Mexican-American War.

The American public was outraged by the telegram. President Wilson asked Congress to declare war on Germany. "The world must be made safe for democracy," he proclaimed. Congress declared war on April 6, 1917. The American entrance into this military conflict influenced the development of the United States.

Mobilizing for War

In order to persuade the public to support the war effort, President Wilson formed the Committee on Public Information (CPI). The CPI organized rallies and parades. They published posters and pamphlets. Speakers known as "four-minute men" gave short patriotic speeches delivered in movie theaters and churches.

The U.S. government's war effort also involved limiting some freedoms in the United States. The Espionage Act of 1917 and the Sedition Act of 1918 restricted free speech and allowed the government to arrest opponents of the war. Antiwar mail was prohibited and seized. About 900 opponents of the war were jailed for violating these laws. The Sedition Act was later repealed, but the Espionage Act is still in effect today.

Shortly after the U.S. entered the war, illustrator James Montgomery Flagg created this famous recruitment poster featuring Uncle Sam. More than four million copies were printed.

To prepare the U.S. military, Congress passed the **Selective Service Act** in 1917. The act required men between the ages of 21 and 30 to register to be drafted. Almost 3 million Americans were drafted into service in World War I. A number of the draftees were African Americans. Altogether, about 400,000 African Americans served in the war. Their units were segregated from white forces and were commanded by white officers. Eventually, African Americans were trained as officers. During World War I, however, they were never placed in command of white troops.

Preparations for war were very expensive. Troops had to be trained, supplied, transported, and fed. Ships and airplanes had to be built and fueled. The government raised taxes and issued war bonds. Money from the sale of these **Liberty bonds** provided billions of dollars in loans to the Allies.

The government took other actions to supply the troops. The War Industries Board (WIB) oversaw the production and distribution of steel, copper, cement, and rubber. The Food Administration worked to increase food supplies and distribution for the troops. It guaranteed farmers high prices for their crops. To conserve food at home, citizens were encouraged to practice "meatless Mondays" and "wheatless Wednesdays." Many people also grew their own vegetables in "victory gardens" at home.

Another proposal to conserve food supplies was a prohibition, or ban, on alcoholic beverages. Most alcoholic beverages are made with food crops such as grapes and wheat. Soon after the United States entered the war, Congress granted the president powers to limit the alcohol content of wine and beer so that these crops could be used for food production instead. Some tried to discourage Americans from drinking beer by linking German Americans to the brewing industry. These people hoped that anti-German feelings would lead Americans to stop drinking beer.

In addition, the Fuel Administration was established to set production goals and prices for fuels. Its purpose was to make sure that fuel

Schenck v. United States (1919)

Background of the Case

Charles Schenck was arrested for violating the Espionage Act. He had printed and distributed pamphlets urging resistance to the draft. Schenck argued that the First Amendment, which guarantees freedom of speech and freedom of the press, gave him the right to criticize the government.

The Court's Ruling

The Supreme Court ruled that the pamphlet was not protected by the First Amendment and that the Espionage Act was constitutional.

The Court's Reasoning

The Supreme Court decided that under certain circumstances, such as a state of war, Congress could limit free speech. The Court created a test to distinguish between protected and unprotected speech. Unprotected speech would have to present "a clear and present danger" to national security. For example, the First Amendment would not protect a person who created a panic by yelling "Fire!" in a crowded theater.

Why It Matters

Schenck v. *United States* was important because it was the first case in which the Supreme Court interpreted the First Amendment. The Court concluded that certain constitutional rights, such as free speech, could be limited under extraordinary conditions, such as war. Later rulings by the Court narrowed the test of "clear and present danger" to speech advocating violence. The nonviolent expression of ideas and opinions— however unpopular—was thereby protected.

Analyze Information

1. According to the Supreme Court, when could free speech be limited?

2. How do you think this case affected other people who opposed the war?

Reading Check
Analyze Information How did the U.S. government gain public support for the war?

distribution needs for the military could always be met. To encourage fuel conservation, daylight saving time was introduced in March 1918 to extend daylight hours for those who worked long shifts in factories. Fuel conservation was promoted in other ways, such as through publicity campaigns calling for "gasless Sundays."

New Wartime Opportunities

Three main factors led to a shortage of labor in the United States during the war. First, American factories were working nonstop to produce weapons and supplies for the Allied forces. Factories needed new workers to meet this huge demand. Second, the war almost completely cut off immigration. As you know, immigrants had provided a steady source of labor to American industry. And third, many of the young men who would normally take factory jobs were off fighting in Europe.

Women's War Efforts This labor shortage created new opportunities for many workers. American women took on new roles to help the war effort. Some 1 million women joined the U.S. workforce during the war years. Women replaced male workers in steel mills, ammunition factories, and assembly lines. Women served as street car conductors and elevator operators. For many, this was their first experience working outside the home.

Women also worked for the war effort in Europe. About 25,000 American women worked as nurses, telephone operators, signalers, typists, and interpreters in France. Many women worked as volunteers, serving at Red Cross facilities and encouraging the sale of bonds and planting of victory gardens. Women were not given jobs in combat, but they braved gunfire at the front lines as nurses and ambulance drivers.

Other women, meanwhile, spoke out against U.S. participation in the war. Social reformer Jane Addams was against U.S. entry into the war. Jeannette Rankin of Montana, the first female member of Congress, was 1 of 50 House members to cast a vote against declaring war in 1917. "I want to stand by my country," she said, "but I cannot vote for war."

Labor and the War Even with so many women joining the workforce, factories needed additional workers. New job opportunities encouraged Mexican Americans from the West and African Americans from the South to move to northern industrial cities.

Because labor was scarce, workers were in a good position to demand better wages and conditions. Union membership increased. More than 4 million unionized workers went on strike during the war. Because factory owners could not easily replace workers, they often agreed to demands.

President Wilson set up the **National War Labor Board** in April 1918. The board helped workers and management avoid strikes and reach agreements. The board settled more than 1,000 labor disputes. Its members were generally sympathetic to workers. They helped establish a minimum wage and limited work hours. They also required fair pay for women.

Winning Support Many Americans had been in favor of the U.S. position of neutrality. Now, Americans had to be convinced that it was their duty

In World War I, women drove ambulances and entered the battlefield as nurses and medics. Red Cross volunteers were often responsible for the first stage of treatment of the wounded.

Patriotic Posters

Posters like this one encouraged American citizens to participate in the effort to provide weapons and food to soldiers fighting in World War I.

Analyze Visuals
How does this poster inspire patriotism?

TEAMWORK WINS
UNITED STATES SHIPPING BOARD EMERGENCY FLEET CORPORATION

Reading Check
Find Main Ideas
How did war mobilization benefit American workers?

to support the war. A nationwide campaign of propaganda, or posters, newspaper stories, speeches, and other materials, was started to influence people's opinions. Popular movie stars were hired to speak on behalf of the war effort. Artists were hired to create patriotic posters and pamphlets. Propaganda helped build American support for the war.

Summary and Preview The war effort created new opportunities for women and other Americans. In the next lesson you will learn about what life was like for soldiers overseas.

Lesson 2 Assessment

Review Ideas, Terms, and People

1. **a. Explain** Why did the United States enter World War I?
   b. Evaluate Do you think the United States was right to stay neutral for so long? Why or why not?

2. **a. Recall** What was the purpose of the Committee on Public Information?
   b. Explain How did the United States prepare for war?
   c. Summarize How did the government exercise control over the economy during the war?

3. **a. Describe** How did women help the war effort abroad?
   b. Explain How do you think the end of the war affected labor unions? Explain your answer.
   c. Analyze How was daily life in the United States affected by World War I?

Critical Thinking

4. **Problem Solving** In this lesson you learned about new laws and government programs during World War I. Create a graphic organizer similar to the one below and use it to identify the challenges the United States faced when mobilizing for World War I. List which new laws, government programs, and other changes responded to those challenges.

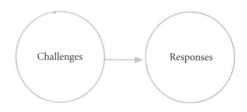

Challenges → Responses

Americans in World War I

The Big Idea

American troops helped the Allies achieve victory in World War I.

Main Ideas

- American soldiers started to arrive in Europe in 1917.
- The Americans helped the Allies win the war.
- Germany agreed to an armistice after suffering heavy losses.

Key Terms and People

American Expeditionary Force
Communists
armistice

If YOU were there . . .

It is April 1918. You are marching into Paris with your army unit on your way to the front lines. Women and children throw flowers from windows and balconies as you pass through the city. You want to do whatever it takes to defend this city and its residents. You know that defeating Germany will be difficult and very dangerous.

Do you think American forces can help the Allies win the war?

American Soldiers Arrive

By the time U.S. troops started to arrive in Europe in 1917, the Allies were dangerously near defeat. German forces were advancing in France, once again driving toward Paris. The German navy was destroying Allied ships at sea. And on the eastern front, the Russians were desperately struggling to hold back the Germans.

Joining the Fight French and British generals called for immediate help on the front lines. They wanted the U.S. troops, known as the **American Expeditionary Force** (AEF), to join French and British units. But General John J. Pershing, leader of the American troops, insisted that the Americans join the fight as a separate force. He refused to have the AEF "scattered among the Allied forces where it will not be an American army at all."

Pershing also demanded that his troops be thoroughly trained for combat before rushing to the front lines. The AEF included many well-trained regular army and National Guard troops. But it also included a large number of inexperienced volunteers and draftees. Pershing gave the men three months of intense training in army discipline and trench warfare. He believed that taking the time to train his soldiers would help the Allies achieve victory.

World War I U.S. Soldier

You can learn a lot about what life was like for a U.S. soldier in World War I by studying the clothing and equipment that was used. Historians evaluate artifacts, such as these, to learn about U.S. history.

The appearance of the Springfield rifles fooled the Germans into thinking the Americans had machine guns.

Gas masks were carried in a pouch around the neck.

Soldiers carried a pack called a haversack, which held food, personal items, and extra socks.

A wool tunic was worn over a wool shirt and wool breeches.

A blanket could be carried at the bottom of the haversack with a special attachment.

Wool cloth strips called puttees were wrapped around the legs and tops of shoes for protection.

Analyze Historical Sources
What can you learn about life for U.S. soldiers by studying these artifacts?

Russia Leaves the War While Pershing trained his troops, the Allies' position became even more dangerous. In November 1917 a group of Russians called the Bolsheviks overthrew the Russian government and seized power. The Bolsheviks were **Communists**—people who favor the equal distribution of wealth and the end of all forms of private property.

Led by Vladimir Lenin, the new Russian government faced a desperate situation. Around 8 million Russians had been killed or wounded during the war. Soldiers were deserting from the eastern front, and sailors were leaving naval bases. Food riots raged in the cities. The Russians could not keep fighting under these conditions. In March 1918 Russia signed the Treaty of Brest-Litovsk, a peace agreement with the Central powers. A civil war then broke out in Russia between the Communists and forces loyal to the czar (ZAHR), Russia's emperor. The United States and other Allied countries sent aid to the czarist forces. Russia, however, one of the main Allied powers, was out of World War I.

Reading Check
Make Inferences
Why do you think General Pershing refused to put American troops in foreign units?

Winning the War

With Russia out of the fighting, German generals saw a chance to win the war. In the spring of 1918 Germany transferred many of its divisions of troops from the eastern front to the western front. Germany planned to smash the stalemate.

The Final Battles At the same time, American soldiers arrived. Even training had not prepared them for the realities of war. The troops lived on dried beef, hard biscuits, and canned emergency rations. The men shared the trenches with rats, lice, and sometimes the bodies of dead soldiers. A soldiers' song of the time described the situation:

> "Sing me to sleep where bullets fall,
> Let me forget the war and all;
> Damp is my dug-out [trench], cold my feet,
> Nothing but bully [canned meat] and biscuits to eat."
>
> —Quoted in *Great Push: An Episode of the Great War*, by Patrick MacGill

On March 21, 1918, the Germans began blasting more than 6,000 heavy guns at Allied troops along the Somme River in northern France. The German advance, helped by a morning fog, surprised the Allies. German forces drove 40 miles into Allied lines before the advance stalled. Some 250,000 Germans had been killed or wounded. British and French casualties totaled 133,000.

The Germans then attacked farther south, advancing to the Marne River and pushing the French line back toward Paris. At this critical moment, General Pershing promised Allied commander Ferdinand Foch: "Infantry, artillery, aviation—all that we have . . . The American people would be proud to be engaged in the greatest battle of history." Two divisions of the AEF joined French forces.

The Germans were unprepared for the fresh energy and fighting skills of the Americans. The U.S. soldiers succeeded in stopping the German advance less than 50 miles from Paris. Then, at Belleau Wood, the Allies attacked and gradually drove the Germans back.

The German generals became desperate. In July 1918 they launched their final offensive—one last attempt to cross the Marne River. Terrible losses on the German side during this push stopped the German offensive. These losses also protected Paris from invasion. Although American troops suffered about 12,000 casualties, they had helped force a major turning point in the war.

Driving the Germans Back Now the Allies drove toward victory. There were more than 1 million U.S. troops in France, and they played a key role in the later battles of the war. In September 1918 Allied forces attacked and defeated the Germans at the town of Saint-Mihiel on the border of France and Germany. Along the Meuse River and in the Argonne Forest, near the French-Belgian border, American and Allied troops again attacked German forces.

World War I, 1914–1918

Explore ONLINE!

Legend

- Allied powers, 1916
- Central powers, 1916
- Neutral Countries
- Allied powers troop movements
- Central powers troop movements
- British naval blockade
- Farthest Russian advance (1914)
- Farthest Central powers advance
- Trench line, western front
- Armistice line, Nov. 11, 1918
- Allied victory
- Central powers victory
- Undecided battle
- German submarine activity

0 200 400 Miles
0 200 400 Kilometers

ATLANTIC OCEAN

NORWAY
SWEDEN
FINLAND
Petrograd

GREAT BRITAIN
North Sea
DENMARK
RUSSIA

Lusitania sunk May 1915
London
Sussex torpedoed March 1916

NETHERLANDS
Berlin
EASTERN FRONT DEC. 1917

English Channel

BELGIUM
GERMANY
Stebark Aug. 1914

Ypres Oct.–Nov. 1914 Apr.–May 1915
Somme July–Nov. 1916
LUXEMBOURG
Battle of the Marne Sept. 1914, July 1918
Château-Thierry June 1918
Paris
ALSACE-LORRAINE
Argonne Forest Sept.–Oct. 1918
Verdun Feb.–Dec. 1916
WESTERN FRONT
Vienna
AUSTRIA-HUNGARY
Budapest

Bay of Biscay

SWITZERLAND
FRANCE

Kobarid Oct.–Nov. 1917

PORTUGAL
SPAIN

ITALY
Rome
Adriatic Sea

BOSNIA and HERZEGOVINA
Sarajevo
SERBIA
ROMANIA
Black Sea
Bosporus

MONTENEGRO
BALKANS
BULGARIA
Constantinople

Mediterranean Sea
ALBANIA

GREECE (Joined Allied Powers 1917)

Dardanelles
Gallipoli April 1915–Jan. 1916

OTTOMAN EMPIRE

Interpret Maps

1. **Human-Environment Interaction** Why was the British naval blockade located where it was?

2. **Location** In which country were the most battles fought, according to this map?

The 369th Infantry spent 191 days in combat, longer than any other American force sent to Europe during World War I. The "Harlem Hellfighters" became famous throughout Europe and America for their valor.

Among the many heroes of these battles was a young man from Tennessee named Alvin York. In October 1918 York killed 25 German gunners and captured 132 prisoners. His heroism earned him fame and many awards, including the Congressional Medal of Honor. His life story even became the basis for a popular movie in 1941.

Also among the brave American troops were the African American soldiers of the 369th Infantry. Known as the "Harlem Hellfighters," the 369th spent more time in combat than any other American unit. Its members were the first to reach the Rhine River on the German border. They aided French forces at Château-Theirry and Belleau Wood. France awarded them the prized Croix de Guerre (Cross of War) medal for their bravery.

The Allies were also winning the war at sea. Allied war planners used a new **strategy** called the convoy system to protect their ships. This meant that destroyers capable of sinking U-boats escorted and protected groups of Allied merchant ships.

By November 1918 American soldiers were making rapid advances toward Germany. "For the first time the enemy lines were completely broken through," reported General Pershing.

Academic Vocabulary
strategy a plan for fighting a battle or war

Reading Check
Sequence Identify significant events leading to the turning of the tide in the war.

Armistice

At home and on the battlefield, Germans were tired of war. Food was so scarce in Germany that more than 800 German civilians were dying of starvation every day. In Germany and other nations of the Central powers, food riots and strikes occurred. Germany was also running out of soldiers. In addition to those killed or wounded in 1918, one-quarter of Germany's fighting men had been captured by the Allies.

Germany's allies were also eager to end the war. Bulgaria and the Ottoman Empire quit the war in the fall of 1918. Austria-Hungary reached a peace agreement with the Allies on November 3. Seeing that his country was beaten, the German leader, Kaiser Wilhelm II, gave up his throne and fled to the Netherlands.

The Germans then agreed to a cease-fire. The Allies demanded that Germany pull back from all its conquered territory. They insisted that Germany destroy its aircraft, tanks, and big guns and surrender its U-boats. The Germans had no choice but to accept these demands to disarm. The **armistice**, or truce, went into effect on the 11th hour of the 11th day of the 11th month of 1918. "At eleven o'clock everything got so quiet that the silence was nearly unbearable," remembered an American soldier. Then the silence was broken with shouts like "I've lived through the war!"

Summary and Preview America's entry into World War I helped the Allies achieve victory. In the next lesson you will learn about the effort to work out a permanent peace agreement.

Reading Check
Identify Which circumstances led Kaiser Wilhelm II to give up his throne?

Lesson 3 Assessment

Review Ideas, Terms, and People

1. a. Recall What was the American Expeditionary Force?

b. Analyze How did the Russian Revolution change the course of the war?

c. Evaluate Why did Russia leave the war?

2. a. Recall How was the Second Battle of the Marne a turning point in the war?

b. Analyze How did U.S. troops make a difference in the final battles of the war?

3. a. Describe What was Germany required to surrender in the armistice?

b. Explain Were the terms of the armistice fair? Explain your answer.

Critical Thinking

4. Categorize In this lesson you learned about the victories of the American Expeditionary Force. Create a graphic organizer similar to the one below and use it to list challenges the Allies faced from 1917 to 1918. List the Allies' achievements during the same time period.

Allied Challenges	
Allied Achievements	

★ Establishing Peace

The Big Idea

The United States and the victorious Allied powers clashed over postwar plans.

Main Ideas

- The costs of war included millions of human lives as well as financial burdens.
- President Woodrow Wilson and European leaders met to work out a peace agreement.
- The U.S. Senate rejected the Treaty of Versailles.

Key Terms and People

League of Nations
reparations
Treaty of Versailles
Henry Cabot Lodge

If YOU were there . . .

Your older brother was drafted in 1917 and sent to fight on the western front in Europe. He has written home about the terrible conditions in the trenches and the horror of seeing men killed in battle. Now the war is over. You read in the newspaper that a peace treaty is being negotiated in Paris, France.

What do you hope the peace treaty will say?

The Costs of War

While soldiers and civilians around the world celebrated the end of World War I in November 1918, the tragedy of war was never far from people's minds. When asked what the armistice meant, one British soldier simply said, "Time to bury the dead."

War Dead The number of soldiers killed in World War I was beyond anything the world had ever experienced. About 5 million Allied soldiers and 3.5 million soldiers from the Central powers died in combat. More than 20 million soldiers on both sides were wounded. The war devastated an entire generation of young men in many European nations. In France, for example, 90 percent of the healthy young men had served in World War I. More than seven out of ten of these men were killed or wounded. While the United States

Memorials to soldiers killed in World War I, like this one at Somme, France, are located throughout Europe.

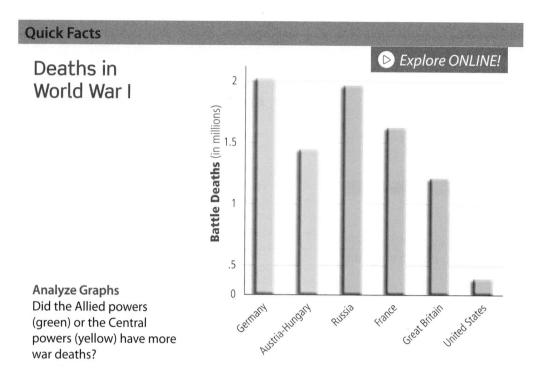

Deaths in World War I

Explore ONLINE!

Analyze Graphs
Did the Allied powers (green) or the Central powers (yellow) have more war deaths?

escaped this extreme level of devastation, American forces did suffer heavy losses. Some 116,000 U.S. troops died and about 200,000 were wounded.

Financial Losses Along with the shocking human losses, the war brought financial disaster to many parts of Europe. Factories and farms were left in ruins. "For mile after mile nothing was left," said one British visitor about the French countryside. "No building was habitable [livable] and no field fit for the plow." With farmers unable to raise crops, severe food shortages occurred.

The overall economic cost of the war was huge. Property worth $30 billion had been destroyed. The Allies had spent $145 billion on the war effort, and the Central powers had spent $63 billion. France and Britain had borrowed large amounts of money to fight the war, and now they were deeply in debt to American banks. Germany was also in debt, and its people faced starvation.

The Influenza Epidemic The world was in for another shock in 1918 when a worldwide epidemic of influenza, or flu, broke out. The virus was extremely contagious and deadly. Over the next two years, it spread around the world, killing approximately 30 million people—even more than the war itself.

The epidemic started in an army training camp in Kansas. Because the flu is transmitted through the air, it spread rapidly. American soldiers unknowingly spread the disease to other army camps, to American civilians, and eventually to soldiers and civilians in Europe. One American doctor said that seeing stacks of bodies at an army camp in Massachusetts "beats any sight they ever had in France after a battle." Half of the Americans who died during this period died from influenza.

The epidemic changed life everywhere in the United States. In Chicago, for example, the flu more than doubled the normal death rate in the fall of 1918. Many of those killed were young and strong. State and local governments took measures to prevent the spread of the disease. Kearney, Nebraska, imposed a quarantine, forbidding people who were ill from leaving their homes. Many cities banned public gatherings, including school classes. A man named Dan Tonkel remembered what life was like for children in his hometown of Goldsboro, North Carolina:

> "I felt like I was walking on eggshells. I was afraid to go out, to play with my playmates, my classmates, my neighbors . . . I remember I was actually afraid to breathe. People were afraid to talk to each other. It was like—don't breathe in my face, don't even look at me, because you might give me germs that will kill me."
>
> —Dan Tonkel, quoted in *Influenza 1918: The Worst Epidemic in American History*, by Lynette Lezzoni

Although there was no cure for the flu, people would try anything. One woman surrounded her daughter with raw onions. Another remembered, "We hung bags of . . . garlic about our necks. We smelled awful, but it was okay, because everyone smelled bad." By the time the influenza epidemic ended in 1919, it had killed 800,000 Americans at home and abroad. Today, vaccinations help prevent major outbreaks of the flu and other contagious diseases.

Reading Check
Find Main Ideas
What made the influenza epidemic of 1918 so deadly?

The Peace Agreement

Even before the United States entered World War I, President Woodrow Wilson began making plans for a peace agreement. This peace agreement was one example of the United States leadership role at the conclusion of the war. Wilson was determined to do everything possible to prevent another world war. On January 8, 1918, he outlined his vision for the postwar world in a plan known as the Fourteen Points.

Wilson's Fourteen Points Wilson's Fourteen Points was a list of specific proposals for postwar peace. Several of the points would settle national border disputes. Others called for military cutbacks, proposed lower tariffs, and banned secret agreements between nations. Another proposed settlements for colonial peoples who wished to be independent. This reflected Wilson's strong belief in self-determination—the right of people to choose their own political status. The final point called for the creation of an international assembly of nations called the **League of Nations**. The league's mission would be to work to settle international disputes and encourage democracy.

European leaders disagreed with Wilson's vision for the peace settlement. They wanted it to clearly punish Germany for

Quick Facts

Key Goals of the Fourteen Points

- End secret alliances
- Encourage free shipping
- Remove barriers to trade
- Reduce armies and navies
- Resolve colonial claims
- Support the right of people to choose their own government
- Settle border disputes
- Establish the League of Nations

its role in the war. European leaders wanted to prevent Germany from ever again becoming a world power.

The Treaty of Versailles President Wilson traveled to Europe to attend the Paris Peace Conference, which was held at the palace of Versailles (ver-SY), outside of Paris. Wilson felt it was his duty to "play my full part in making good what [our soldiers] offered their lives to obtain."

The leaders, called the Big Four, were President Wilson, British prime minister David Lloyd George, French premier Georges Clemenceau, and Italian prime minister Vittorio Orlando. They took control of the conference. No representatives from Russia or the Central powers attended.

Many Allied leaders defended their own country's interests and insisted on severe punishment for Germany. They wanted Germany to accept complete blame for the war and pay for the damage it had caused. These **reparations**, or payments for war damages, were set at $33 billion. France and the other Allies also wanted to take control of large parts of German territory.

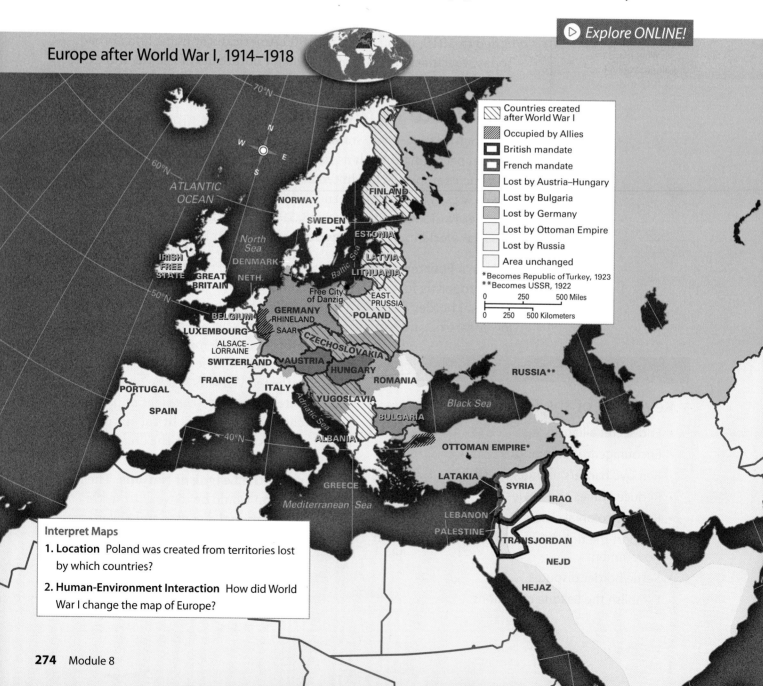

Europe after World War I, 1914–1918

▷ *Explore ONLINE!*

Legend:
- Countries created after World War I
- Occupied by Allies
- British mandate
- French mandate
- Lost by Austria–Hungary
- Lost by Bulgaria
- Lost by Germany
- Lost by Ottoman Empire
- Lost by Russia
- Area unchanged

*Becomes Republic of Turkey, 1923
**Becomes USSR, 1922

0   250   500 Miles
0   250   500 Kilometers

Interpret Maps

1. **Location** Poland was created from territories lost by which countries?

2. **Human-Environment Interaction** How did World War I change the map of Europe?

Woodrow Wilson
1856–1924

Woodrow Wilson was born in Virginia in 1856. The terrible destruction he saw as a child during the Civil War would later influence his response to World War I. As president, he backed reforms such as child-labor restrictions and an eight-hour workday for railroad workers. Although he eventually abandoned American neutrality during World War I, Wilson was committed to world peace after the war. For his role in helping found the League of Nations, Wilson won the Nobel Peace Prize in 1919.

Make Inferences
How did Wilson's childhood experiences affect his reaction to World War I?

Wilson reluctantly agreed to the **Treaty of Versailles**, the peace settlement of World War I. In it, the League of Nations was established. Estonia, Finland, Latvia, Lithuania, Czechoslovakia, and Yugoslavia became independent countries. Poland was restored as a nation. The Central powers turned over their colonies to the League of Nations. The league assigned their colonies to other European powers to rule. Though the Treaty of Versailles did not give Wilson everything he wanted, he hoped the League of Nations would solve remaining problems.

Reading Check
Analyze Information
Why did Allied leaders object to Wilson's plan?

Treaty of Versailles Rejected

The U.S. Constitution states that treaties must be ratified by at least two-thirds of the members of the Senate. Wilson knew he was going to have a hard time convincing some senators to vote to ratify the Versailles Treaty. Republican senator **Henry Cabot Lodge** declared: "No peace that satisfied Germany in any degree can ever satisfy us." Lodge wanted the winners to set the terms of the peace.

Republicans insisted on changes to the treaty before they would ratify it. Their main objection was the League of Nations' power to use military force. They were worried that as a member of the League, the United States could be forced to send troops to war based on decisions made by the League of Nations. This, they argued, conflicted with Congress's constitutional power to declare war.

Wilson refused to compromise. He insisted that the treaty be ratified exactly as it was written. He traveled around the country, trying to convince the public to pressure Republican senators to vote for the treaty. Before he completed his tour, however, Wilson was weakened by a stroke.

Lodge announced that he was prepared to accept most of the treaty. He still wanted to limit U.S. military commitment to the League of Nations. Wilson demanded that Democrats in the Senate refuse to change

Causes and Effects of World War I

Causes

- Nationalism
- Militarism
- Competition for territory
- Alliance system in Europe

Effects

- U.S. entry into the war in 1917
- Millions of deaths and widespread destruction in Europe
- Treaty of Versailles
- Creation of several new nations
- League of Nations

Reading Check
Support Points of View
Do you think Wilson should have compromised with Republicans in the Senate on the Treaty of Versailles? Why or why not?

the treaty. When the vote was taken on November 19, 1919, neither the Democrats nor the Republicans would compromise. The Treaty of Versailles was defeated in the Senate. Following extensive political debate, the United States refused to ratify the Treaty of Versailles.

It was a bitter disappointment for President Wilson. The United States signed separate peace treaties with Austria, Hungary, and Germany. They never joined the League of Nations.

Summary and Preview World War I changed the world map and affected the lives of millions. But efforts to build a lasting peace in the years that followed failed.

Lesson 4 Assessment

Review Ideas, Terms, and People

1. **a. Recall** Approximately how many soldiers were killed or wounded in World War I?

   b. Draw Conclusions How did the war affect the European economy?

   c. Summarize How did Americans try to fight the influenza epidemic of 1918?

2. **a. Recall** What was the League of Nations?

   b. Explain How did the Treaty of Versailles change the map of Europe?

   c. Elaborate Which countries did not attend the Paris Peace Conference? How do you think this affected the outcome?

   d. Evaluate What were Wilson's Fourteen Points?

3. **a. Identify** Who was Henry Cabot Lodge?

   b. Predict How might Wilson have ensured that the U.S. Senate would ratify the Treaty of Versailles?

   c. Evaluate What were reasons why the U.S. Senate refused to support the Treaty of Versailles?

Critical Thinking

4. **Identify Points of View** In this lesson you learned about the Treaty of Versailles. Create a graphic organizer similar to the one below and use it to compare the positions of Woodrow Wilson, Allied leaders, and Senate Republicans. Fill in the results of each person's or group's goals.

	Goals	Results
Woodrow Wilson		
Allied Leaders		
Senate Republicans		

Social Studies Skills

Use Visual Resources

Define the Skill

A major part of history is understanding the events and ideas of the past. Visual resources are good sources of information about the past. Visual resources include paintings, drawings, cartoons, posters, and photographs. The symbols and images in these resources tell us about the ideas and values of a time period. They often provide different information and points of view than do written documents.

Learn the Skill

Visual resources can have special purposes. For example, the poster above was produced by the U.S. government to inspire patriotism and encourage support for the war effort. It uses symbols and images to suggest that all Americans can contribute to the war effort.

You know from reading the module that conserving food to provide supplies for troops was an important part of the war effort. This poster encourages Americans to can fruits and vegetables. The pictures show canned tomatoes and peas in glass jars.

The poster also shows the German kaiser in a jar. He cannot reach his sword, which is outside the jar. He is helpless. This suggests that, by canning fruit and vegetables, Americans can help defeat the German leader.

Practice the Skill

Study the World War I poster below. Like the other poster, it was produced by the U.S. government to encourage support for the war effort. Write a paragraph describing the poster. Your paragraph should include the specific purpose of the poster, the symbols it uses, and whether it conveys its message effectively. You can use the text above as a model.

Module 8 Assessment

Review Vocabulary, Terms, and People

Identify the descriptions below with the correct term or person from the module.

1. International assembly of nations designed to settle international disputes and encourage democracy

2. Strategy of defending a position by fighting from the protection of deep ditches

3. American fighting force trained and led by General John J. Pershing

4. Law that required men between the ages of 21 and 30 to register to be drafted into the armed forces

5. Senate leader who opposed the Treaty of Versailles

6. Truce between warring nations

7. Telegram from the German foreign minister proposing an alliance between Germany and Mexico against the United States

Comprehension and Critical Thinking

Lesson 1

8. a. **Identify** What event sparked World War I?

    b. **Explain** How did tensions in Europe lead to war?

    c. **Draw Conclusions** Why did the war in Europe become a stalemate?

Lesson 2

9. a. **Recall** What happened to the *Lusitania*? How did the American public react?

    b. **Analyze** How did the country's mobilization for war affect American women?

    c. **Evaluate** Do you think U.S. efforts to prepare for war were successful? Why or why not?

Lesson 3

10. a. **Identify** How did the American Expeditionary Force prepare for war?

    b. **Contrast** How was the Second Battle of the Marne different from the First Battle of the Marne?

    c. **Draw Conclusions** Do you think the Allies would have won World War I without American help? Explain your answer.

Lesson 4

11. a. **Recall** Which nations' leaders dominated the Paris Peace Conference?

    b. **Summarize** What were the main ideas of Wilson's Fourteen Points?

    c. **Predict** How effective do you think the League of Nations was? Why?

Module 8 Assessment, continued

Review Themes

12. **Economics** How did World War I affect the economy of the United States?

13. **Politics** What lasting political changes were brought about by World War I?

Social Studies Skills

Use Visual Resources *Use the Social Studies Skills taught in this module to answer the question below.*

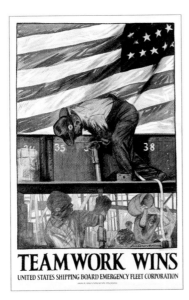

TEAMWORK WINS
UNITED STATES SHIPPING BOARD EMERGENCY FLEET CORPORATION

14. What parts of the U.S. war effort are shown in this poster?

Reading Skills

Recognize Fallacies in Reasoning *Use the Reading Skills taught in this module to answer the question about the reading selection below.*

The number of soldiers killed in World War I was beyond anything the world had ever experienced. About 5 million Allied soldiers and 3.5 million soldiers from the Central powers died in combat. More than 20 million soldiers on both sides were wounded.

15. Which of the following is an example of a false conclusion drawn from the selection above?
   a. More soldiers were killed in World War I than in any war up to that point.
   b. World War I devastated the European population.
   c. Europe would never recover from World War I.
   d. The number of soldiers wounded was more than two times the number of soldiers killed.

Focus on Speaking

16. **Present a Persuasive Speech** You have learned that before the United States entered World War I, Americans debated joining the fight. Think about the arguments on both sides of the debate. Then form an opinion on whether the United States should have entered the war and prepare a speech presenting your point of view. You will have about five minutes to present your speech. Use note cards to organize your ideas. Begin by writing a one-sentence introduction clearly stating your opinion. Then write several sentences with details and examples from the module that support your point of view. Conclude your speech with a sentence that summarizes your ideas. Practice your speech and then present it to the class.

Dear home: LETTERS FROM WWI

When U.S. troops arrived in Europe in 1917 to fight in World War I, the war had been dragging on for nearly three years. The American soldiers suddenly found themselves in the midst of chaos. Each day, they faced the threats of machine-gun fire, poison gas, and aerial attacks. Still, the arrival of American reinforcements had sparked a new zeal among the Allies, who believed the new forces could finally turn the tide in their favor. The letters soldiers wrote to their families back home reveal the many emotions they felt on the battlefield: confusion about their surroundings, fear for their own safety, concern for friends and loved ones, and hope that the war would soon be over.

Explore World War I online through the eyes of the soldiers who fought in it. You can find a wealth of information, video clips, primary sources, activities, and more through your online textbook.

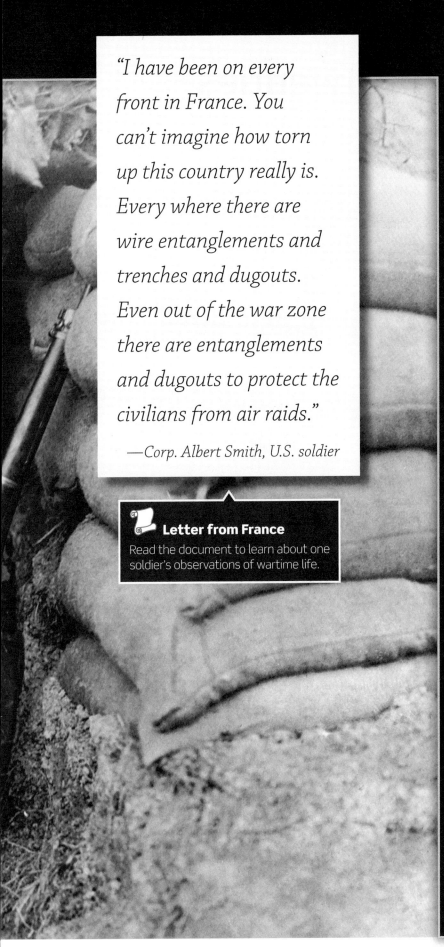

> "I have been on every front in France. You can't imagine how torn up this country really is. Every where there are wire entanglements and trenches and dugouts. Even out of the war zone there are entanglements and dugouts to protect the civilians from air raids."
>
> —Corp. Albert Smith, U.S. soldier

Letter from France
Read the document to learn about one soldier's observations of wartime life.

Over There
Watch the video to learn about the experiences of American soldiers on the way to Europe and upon their arrival.

War on the Western Front
Watch the video to hear one soldier's vivid account of battle and its aftermath.

Surrender!
Watch the video to experience soldiers' reactions to the news that the war was finally over.

Module 9
The Roaring Twenties

⭐

Essential Question
How did American society change during the Roaring Twenties?

About the Painting: People flocked to bustling city centers like New York City's Times Square.

In this module you will learn about how American life changed in the years after World War I. You will also read about important artists of the Jazz Age.

What You Will Learn . . .

▶ Explore ONLINE!

HISTORY.

VIDEOS, including...
- America Goes Dry with Prohibition
- Warren G. Harding
- Growth of Radio

☑ Document-Based Investigations

☑ Graphic Organizers

☑ Interactive Games

☑ Image Carousel: Model T Assembly Line

☑ Image Slider: The 1928 Presidential Election

☑ Image Carousel: American Heroes

Timeline of Events 1918–1930

▶ *Explore ONLINE!*

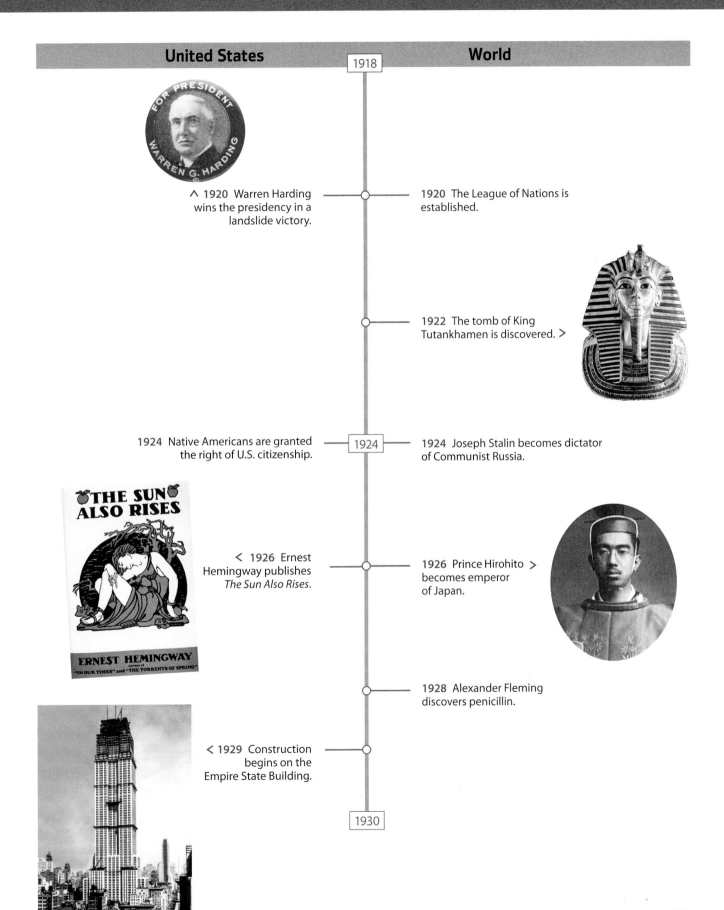

United States

1918

1930

∧ **1920** Warren Harding wins the presidency in a landslide victory.

1924 Native Americans are granted the right of U.S. citizenship.

< **1926** Ernest Hemingway publishes *The Sun Also Rises*.

< **1929** Construction begins on the Empire State Building.

World

1920 The League of Nations is established.

1922 The tomb of King Tutankhamen is discovered. >

1924

1924 Joseph Stalin becomes dictator of Communist Russia.

1926 Prince Hirohito > becomes emperor of Japan.

1928 Alexander Fleming discovers penicillin.

Reading Social Studies

Society and Culture, Science and Technology

In this module you will learn about the decade of the 1920s, a period called the Roaring Twenties. During this time, many in society thought that the Great War would be the last major war and that the future was bright. Also during this time, science and technology made leaps forward that would make life easier for millions of Americans.

READING FOCUS:

Synthesize Information

Learning about history means synthesizing, or combining, many different sources about the past. When you read these modules, you are reading a synthesis of other sources, accounts, and ideas about history.

Synthesize Once you have identified the subject you are studying, you should try to read as many different accounts of the story as you can. Be sure to investigate the author of a source to learn what his or her goals might be. Compare and contrast the different sources and evaluate which ones you believe. Finally, use all the various stories you have read to form your own interpretation of what happened in history.

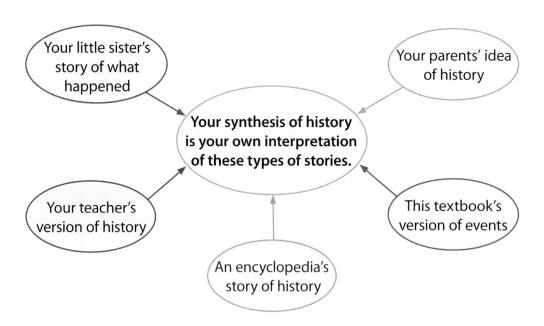

Your little sister's story of what happened

Your parents' idea of history

Your synthesis of history is your own interpretation of these types of stories.

Your teacher's version of history

This textbook's version of events

An encyclopedia's story of history

You Try It!

Read these two accounts of the assassination of Archduke Francis Ferdinand and his wife, Sophie. Then write your own version of the story.

> "As the car came abreast he stepped forward from the curb, drew his automatic pistol from his coat and fired two shots. The first struck the wife of the Archduke, the Archduchess Sofia, in the abdomen. . . . She died instantly. The second bullet struck the Archduke close to the heart. He uttered only one word, 'Sofia'—a call to his stricken wife. Then his head fell back and he collapsed. He died almost instantly."
>
> —conspirator Borijove Jevtic

> "As I was pulling out my handkerchief to wipe the blood away from his mouth, the duchess cried out to him, 'In Heaven's name, what has happened to you?' At that she slid off the seat and lay on the floor of the car. . . . I had no idea that she too was hit and thought she had simply fainted with fright. Then I heard His Imperial Highness say, "Sopherl, Sopherl, don't die. Stay alive for the children!"
>
> —guard Count Franz von Harrach, quoted in "Assassination of an Archduke," *Eyewitness to History*

1. What differences do you notice between the two accounts?
2. Why might these different authors have a different view of the assassination?
3. How can you tell what each author's viewpoint is?
4. Write your own version of what might have happened. Use details that you believe from the sources above.

As you read Module 9, notice any differing views from different sources.

★
Boom Times

The Big Idea

American industries boomed in the 1920s, changing many Americans' way of life.

Main Ideas

- President Harding promised a return to peace and prosperity.

- Calvin Coolidge supported a probusiness agenda.

- American business boomed in the 1920s.

- In 1928 Americans elected Herbert Hoover, hoping he would help good financial times continue.

Key Terms and People

Warren G. Harding
Calvin Coolidge
Teapot Dome scandal
Kellogg-Briand Pact
Model T
moving assembly line
Herbert Hoover

If YOU were there . . .

You have been working in a car factory for years, and now you have finally bought a car of your own—a shiny new 1920 Ford Model T. As you set out on your first drive, the car rattles and bounces over unpaved roads that were designed for horse-and-buggy travel. But you don't mind the rough ride. You now have the freedom to drive anywhere you want to go!

How will owning a car change your life?

Return to Peace and Prosperity

The end of World War I had an immediate impact on the economy. Because the government no longer needed war supplies, it canceled billions of dollars' worth of contracts with American factories. This meant that factories cut back on production at the very moment that millions of soldiers left the military and began looking for jobs. The result was a sharp rise in unemployment. Meanwhile, many people who did have jobs rushed to buy products they could not buy during the war. Prices soared. Wages could not keep up with the rising prices, and thus workers could no longer afford to buy the goods they needed and wanted. Many went on strike for higher wages— more than 4 million in 1919 alone.

As the 1920 presidential election approached, the economic difficulties were bad news for the party in power, Woodrow Wilson's Democratic Party. Many voters blamed the Democrats for the hard times. Sensing the public's anger, the Republicans looked for a candidate who would offer new hope for American voters. They chose **Warren G. Harding**, a senator from Ohio. Harding picked Governor **Calvin Coolidge** of Massachusetts as his running mate.

Harding based his campaign strategy on a promise to return the country to stability and prosperity, what he called "normalcy." His conservative policies contrasted with the reform-minded policies of the Progressive Era.

Academic
Vocabulary
incentive something
that encourages
people to behave a
certain way

Democrats believed there was still support for Wilson's ideas for reform. They ran Ohio governor James M. Cox for president, and New York's Franklin D. Roosevelt for vice president. But Harding's promise of a return to normalcy captured the public's mood in 1920. Harding won a landslide victory with about 60 percent of the popular vote.

Harding worked quickly to help strengthen the economy. He put together a cabinet of experts who believed in reducing money owed by the government and limiting government involvement in the economy. Secretary of the Treasury Andrew Mellon pushed for tax cuts for wealthy Americans. Mellon believed that this policy would give the wealthy an **incentive** to invest in new businesses and create new jobs for other Americans. Mellon's opponents called this idea the trickle-down theory, arguing that money would only "trickle down" in small drops to less-well-off Americans.

While Harding was president, businesses did in fact bounce back from the postwar recession. The economy created new, better-paying jobs, leading to an economic boom that lasted for most of the decade.

Harding faced problems in other areas, however. He had appointed many of his trusted friends to high positions. Some of these men used their positions to gain wealth through illegal means. "I have no trouble with my enemies," Harding once said. "But my . . . friends . . . keep me walking the floor nights."

What came to be known as the **Teapot Dome scandal** involved Secretary of the Interior Albert Fall, who accepted large sums of money and valuable gifts from private oil companies. In exchange, Fall allowed the companies to control government oil reserves in Elk Hills, California, and Teapot Dome, Wyoming. The U.S. Senate soon began investigating Fall, who was convicted of accepting bribes. He was the first cabinet member ever to be convicted of a crime for his actions while in office.

Reading Check
Summarize What
did Harding mean
when he promised a
return to normalcy?

Coolidge's Probusiness Administration

Just before details of the Teapot Dome scandal became public, President Harding died of a heart attack. In August 1923 Vice President Calvin Coolidge took charge. Coolidge had a strong reputation as an honest and trustworthy leader. These qualities helped him restore confidence in the government.

Coolidge acted quickly to fire all officials who had been involved in the bribery scandals of Harding's administration. This helped him win the presidential election in 1924. He received nearly twice as many votes as the Democratic candidate, John W. Davis.

Coolidge proved to be even more probusiness than Harding had been. He once declared that "the business of America is business." He expanded the policies started under Harding, such as tax cuts for wealthier citizens. He also supported raising tariffs on foreign goods to decrease competition with domestic products. Despite higher tariffs, trade with other countries actually increased under Coolidge. This was mainly because many nations depended on trade with the United States to rebuild their economies after

World War I. Not everyone profited from Coolidge's efforts, however. Coolidge vetoed congressional attempts to provide aid to farmers through the regulation of prices.

Like the United States, European nations wanted a return to prosperity. Europeans also wanted to avoid another devastating war. In 1928 the United States and 14 other nations signed the **Kellogg-Briand Pact**, an agreement that outlawed war. Eventually, 62 nations accepted the pact. There was no way to enforce the pact, however. One U.S. senator complained that the treaty would be "as effective to keep down war as a carpet would be to smother an earthquake." Still, it was a sign that most countries wanted to prevent another global conflict. Today, countries still try to prevent wars with international agreements. More than 180 nations have signed the Treaty on the Non-Proliferation of Nuclear Weapons, an agreement to prevent the spread of nuclear weapons.

Reading Check
Compare and Contrast How were Harding and Coolidge similar, and how were they different?

Business Booms

The 1920s were years of rapid economic growth in the United States. Between 1921 and 1929, U.S. manufacturing nearly doubled. As jobs and wages increased, so did people's ability to buy new products. Some of these products as well as developments in factory and labor productivity and transportation changed the way Americans lived. Their standard of living also changed.

Ford's Model T Today, we think of cars as a major part of American life. In the early 1900s, though, cars were seen as luxury items that only the wealthy could afford. Henry Ford, an inventor and business leader from Detroit, helped to change this. Ford dreamed of building a car that most Americans could afford:

> "I will build a motor car for the great multitude [most of the people]. It will be large enough for the family but small enough for the individual to run and care for. It . . . will be so low in price that no man making a good salary will be unable to own one."
>
> —Henry Ford, quoted in *My Life and Work*

Ford achieved his goal by building a sturdy and reliable car called the **Model T**, nicknamed the Tin Lizzie. In 1908 the Model T sold for $850. By 1925 it cost just $290. Ford was able to make his car affordable by cutting costs of production. For example, every car looked the same. The Model T came only in black for many years.

To decrease the time it took to make the cars, Ford also began using a **moving assembly line**. This system used conveyer belts to move parts and partly assembled cars from one group of workers to another. The workers stood in one place and specialized in one or two simple assembly tasks that they performed as parts moved past them. The moving assembly line greatly increased the efficiency of mass production.

In 1914 Ford raised the wages for his factory workers to $5 a day. This was good pay, compared with the $2 or $3 per day offered by many other factories. Ford believed the wage increase would keep his employees from

The Model T Assembly Line

These workers are building flywheel magnetos, a part of the ignition system of early engines. The workers perform the same action on each part as the part passes them. Ford's system reduced the time to build a flywheel from 20 minutes to 5 minutes.

The chassis, or frame, and the engine are assembled on separate lines. Workers on a third line then attach them.

The assembled chassis is then connected to the body of the car.

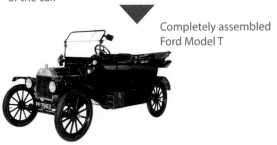

Completely assembled Ford Model T

Analyze Visuals
How does the moving assembly line reduce the time it takes to build a car?

quitting. He also lowered the workday to eight hours and employed people that other factories would not hire, such as African Americans and people with disabilities.

Even with the good wages, many workers had a hard time adjusting to the fast-paced and repetitive work on Ford's assembly line. One wife of an autoworker wrote to Ford saying, "My husband has come home and thrown himself down and won't eat his supper—so done out [tired]! . . . That $5 a day is a blessing—a bigger one than you know, but oh they earn it."

Ford wanted to help make his cars more affordable. He allowed customers to buy cars using an installment plan. Most people were used to saving up for years to buy items. Installment plans let people pay a small amount of the cost every month until the entire car was paid for. Ford's competitors also allowed customers to pay with installment plans. For a slightly higher price than the Model T, companies such as General Motors offered cars in a variety of colors and with more power.

The automobile changed, or impacted, the way Americans lived. With this advancement in transportation, they could now go on long drives or take jobs farther away from where they lived. Cars gave people a sense of freedom and adventure. As *Motor Car* magazine told drivers, "You are your master, the road is ahead . . . your freedom is complete."

Growing Industries The rise of the automobile affected the entire American economy. Millions of Americans found work. They made steel for car bodies, rubber for tires, or glass for windows. The government spent millions of dollars to improve road safety. The government hired workers to pave highways and build new bridges. People opened roadside businesses to serve travelers, such as gas stations, restaurants, and motels. The rising number of cars also created a demand for car repair shops and car insurance.

The Model T ▷ Explore ONLINE!

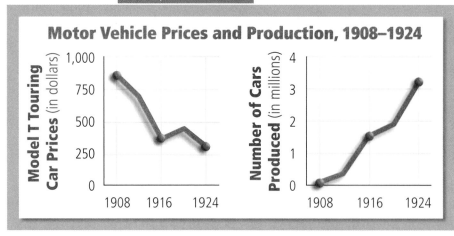

Analyze Graphs
Why did sales of the Model T increase?

Reading Check
Identify Cause and Effect How did the automobile change society?

Manufacturers of other types of products followed Ford's example. They began using assembly lines and allowing customers to pay on installment plans. Many companies also took advantage of the increasing number of homes with electricity. By 1929 about 85 percent of all Americans living in towns or cities had electricity. Companies responded by building new electrical appliances designed to make household chores easier. These companies made appliances such as washing machines, vacuum cleaners, and refrigerators.

As companies competed to sell these new goods, the advertising industry boomed. Companies advertised in magazines and on the radio to convince people that their lives would be improved if they owned a certain product. Many advertisers targeted women. They hoped to convince women that they needed the newest technological labor-saving products. For example, one advertisement for an electric dishwasher called its product "the greatest gift of electricity to the modern housewife."

Hoover Elected

With the economy booming, public support for the Republican Party remained strong. President Coolidge decided not to run for reelection in 1928. The Republican Party chose Coolidge's secretary of commerce, **Herbert Hoover**, as its nominee. The Democrats nominated New York governor Alfred E. Smith.

Hoover told voters that he was the right choice to maintain economic prosperity. Hoover boldly claimed that "we in America today are nearer to the final triumph over poverty than ever before in the history of any land."

Smith's campaign focused mainly on issues facing city dwellers. This concerned some rural voters. Smith's religious faith also became an issue. He was the first Catholic to run for president. His opponents stirred up fears that the pope and other church officials would control Smith. In the end, Hoover won easily, gaining 58 percent of the popular vote.

Reading Check
Draw Conclusions What helped Herbert Hoover win the presidency in 1928?

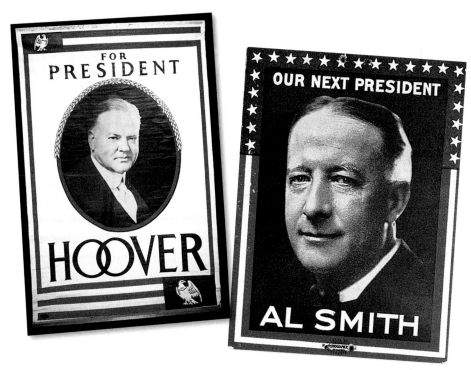

Republican Herbert Hoover defeated Democrat Alfred E. Smith in the 1928 presidential election.

Summary and Preview In this lesson you learned about politics and the economy in the 1920s. In the next lesson you will learn more about how society changed during the decade.

Lesson 1 Assessment

Review Ideas, Terms, and People

1. a. **Describe** What was the result of the 1920 presidential election, and why?

   b. **Summarize** What did the Teapot Dome scandal reveal about Warren G. Harding's administration?

2. a. **Identify** Who succeeded Harding as president, and what were his main policies?

   b. **Analyze** What was the main weakness of the Kellogg-Briand Pact?

3. a. **Recall** Why did American businesses grow during the 1920s?

   b. **Explain** Why were Model T prices low?

4. a. **Recall** Why was Herbert Hoover elected?

   b. **Elaborate** Whom would you have voted for in the 1928 election? Explain your answer.

Critical Thinking

5. **Summarize** In this lesson you learned about the U.S. presidents in the 1920s. Create a chart similar to the one below and expand on your notes by summarizing the main ideas or achievements of each president.

President	Ideas/Achievements

Life during the 1920s

The Big Idea

Americans faced new opportunities, challenges, and fears as major changes swept the country in the 1920s.

Main Ideas

- In the 1920s many young people found new independence in a changing society.

- Postwar tensions occasionally led to fear and violence.

- Competing ideals caused conflict between Americans with traditional beliefs and those with modern views.

- Following the war, minority groups organized to demand their civil rights.

Key Terms and People

flappers
Red Scare
Twenty-First Amendment
fundamentalism
Scopes trial
Great Migration
Marcus Garvey

If YOU were there . . .

The year is 1925. You have just finished school and you are visiting a big city for the first time. You and your friends go to a club and watch young people dancing energetically to popular music. The women have short hair and wear makeup, trying to copy the glamorous style of movie stars. Some of your friends start talking about finding an apartment and looking for jobs in the city.

Would you want to move to a big city in 1925? Why?

A Changing Society

The experience of living through World War I changed the way many young people saw the world around them and inspired social changes. Young men returning from Europe had visited far-off countries and learned about other cultures. Many of them came home with a desire to continue expanding their horizons. The title of one popular song in 1919 asked, "How 'Ya Gonna Keep' em Down on the Farm after They've Seen Paree [Paris]?"

Many young people moved away from farms and small towns to cities. By 1920, for the first time in American history, more than half of the country's population lived in urban areas. Young people took advantage of the economic opportunities of the 1920s to gain independence. In the past most young people had lived and worked at home until they got married. Now more young adults were experiencing a time of freedom before settling down. A new youth culture developed, which included going to parties and dance clubs, listening to popular music, and driving fast cars.

For many young Americans, access to education was an important part of this new independence. High school attendance doubled during the decade. The percentage of students going on to college was higher in the United States than in any other country. This included women, who were

Bryn Mawr and other colleges provided education to women in new fields.

Bessie Coleman became the first African American woman to obtain her international pilot's license. She traveled the United States, performing stunts under the name "Brave Bessie."

Flappers challenged many of society's ideas about womanhood. They established new rules of speech, dress, and behavior.

Analyze Visuals
How do these images reflect new roles for women during the 1920s?

Reading Check
Summarize How did women in the 1920s express their independence?

attending college in higher numbers than ever before.

The number of women in the workforce continued to grow as well. Women with college degrees worked as nurses, teachers, librarians, and social workers.

Women were also finding new opportunities in politics. In 1923 suffrage leader Alice Paul introduced the Equal Rights Amendment to Congress, calling for equality of rights regardless of a person's gender. The U.S. Senate passed the amendment 49 years later, but it was never ratified by the states. In 1925 Nellie Tayloe Ross (Wyoming) and Miriam "Ma" Ferguson (Texas) became the first women to serve as governors in the United States. Three years later, there were 145 women serving in state legislatures. Five women had won terms in the U.S. House of Representatives.

Still, women were discouraged from careers in medicine, law, and architecture. By the end of the 1920s, less than 5 percent of the country's doctors, lawyers, and architects were women. The percentage was small—but it was beginning to rise.

Some young women found other ways, including fashion, to express their freedom. Young women known as **flappers** cut their hair short and wore makeup and short dresses, openly challenging traditional ideas of how women were supposed to behave. Many older Americans considered this behavior scandalous. One 1920s writer expressed her admiration for flappers, by saying about her daughter:

"I want my girl to do what she pleases, be what she pleases. . . . I want her to be a flapper, because flappers are brave."

—Zelda Fitzgerald, quoted in *Zelda*, by Nancy Milford

Fashion magazines, Hollywood movies, and advertising helped promote these new images and ideas of youthful freedom.

Fear and Violence

Not all social changes during the 1920s were peaceful. You have read about the hard times that hit the U.S. economy after World War I—unemployment, inflation, and labor disputes that resulted in large strikes.

These troubles worried many Americans. In this atmosphere, suspicion of foreigners and radicals, or people who believe in an extreme change in government, sometimes led to violence.

The Red Scare After the Communists took power in Russia in 1917, many Americans began to fear Communist ideas. They worried that Communists would soon try to gain power in the United States. This fear increased when millions of American workers went on strike in 1919. Many Americans blamed Communists and radicals for the upheaval.

These attitudes led to a **Red Scare**, a time of fear of Communists, or Reds. The Red Scare began in April 1919, when U.S. postal workers found bombs hidden in several packages addressed to famous Americans. Officials never found out who sent the bombs, but they suspected members of the Communist Party.

In June a bomb exploded outside the home of Attorney General A. Mitchell Palmer. Palmer responded by organizing police raids to break up Communists and other groups. In what became known as the Palmer raids, government agents arrested thousands of suspected radicals, often without evidence. Palmer frightened the public by warning that radicals were planning a revolution.

Sacco and Vanzetti

Supporters of Sacco and Vanzetti held rallies and raised money for the immigrants' defense. The men were found guilty and were executed in 1927.

Why did the Sacco and Vanzetti case become so famous?

The Red Scare led to one of the best-known criminal cases in American history. In 1920 police arrested Italian-born anarchists Nicola Sacco and Bartolomeo Vanzetti for the robbery and murder of a factory paymaster and his guard. (Anarchists are people opposed to organized government.) Though both men declared themselves innocent of the crime, Sacco and Vanzetti were found guilty. The American Civil Liberties Union (ACLU), founded in 1920 to defend people's civil rights, tried unsuccessfully to get the verdict overturned. Sacco and Vanzetti were convicted. They were executed in 1927.

Restricting Immigration Some people thought that a general fear of foreigners from different ethnic groups influenced the Sacco and Vanzetti case. Many recent immigrants were poor and did not speak English. Some Americans saw them as a threat to their jobs and culture. Immigrants "fill places that belong to the loyal wage-earning citizens of America," said Alabama senator James Thomas Heflin.

The government responded to these concerns with new laws. Immigration legislation, such as the Emergency Quota Act of 1921, limited the total number of immigrants allowed into the country. It also favored immigrants from western Europe. The National Origins Act of 1924 banned immigration from East Asia entirely. It also further reduced the number of immigrants allowed to enter the country. These laws caused a dramatic drop in immigration to the United States.

Competing Ideals

Fear of radical ideas and foreigners was part of a larger clash over ideals and values in America. In these social conflicts, differences were growing between older, rural traditions and the beliefs and practices of modern urban society. Americans had very different ideas about what was best for the country's future.

Prohibition An issue that highlighted this conflict was prohibition. The Eighteenth Amendment went into effect in 1920. It outlawed the manufacture, sale, and transportation of alcoholic beverages. Support for prohibition was strongest in rural areas, while opposition was strongest in cities.

Government officials found it nearly impossible to enforce prohibition. Congress passed the Volstead Act. This act set fines and punishments for disobeying prohibition. Even respectable citizens, however, broke the law. Many people found ways to make alcohol at home using household products. Others bought alcohol at speakeasies, or illegal bars.

Organized criminals called bootleggers quickly seized control of the illegal alcohol business. They made their own alcohol or smuggled it in from Canada or Mexico. Gangsters bribed local police and politicians to avoid arrest. Competition between gangs often led to violent fighting. In Chicago, gangster Al "Scarface" Capone murdered his rivals to gain control of the alcohol trade. By 1927 Capone was earning more than $60 million a year from his illegal businesses.

Historical Source

Prohibition

Agents of federal and state governments tried to enforce the Eighteenth Amendment against great odds. They usually destroyed any liquor that they found. This photograph shows an illegal barrel of beer being broken with an ax. More illegal beer and liquor would soon turn up, however. Faced with a lack of public support and an impossible task of enforcing the ban on alcohol, prohibition was repealed with the Twenty-First Amendment in 1933.

Analyze Historical Sources
Why was enforcing prohibition such a hard task?

By the end of the decade, the nation was weary of the effects and impact of prohibition. The law had reduced alcohol consumption but had not stopped Americans from drinking. Prohibition had also created new ways for criminals to grow rich. Without government supervision of alcohol production, much of the alcohol consumed in speakeasies was more dangerous than what had been produced before prohibition. Many people came to believe that it would be better to have a legal alcohol trade that the government could monitor. In 1933 state and federal governments responded with the **Twenty-First Amendment**. This amendment ended prohibition. It made the manufacture and sale of alcohol legal again, but laws today still regulate drinking. The National Minimum Drinking Age Act of 1984 raised the minimum drinking age from 18 to 21 in every state.

Religious Ideals Youth culture of the 1920s and prohibition's failure concerned many religious leaders and religious groups. They saw these changes as movements away from **traditional** values. This led to a Protestant religious movement known as **fundamentalism**. Fundamentalism was characterized by the belief in a literal, or word-for-word, interpretation

Academic
Vocabulary
traditional
customary,
time-honored

Historical Sources

The Scopes Trial

The focus of the Scopes trial was whether or not John Scopes had broken the law. Prosecution witness **William Jennings Bryan**, however, saw the conflict as one between science and faith.

"*Science is a magnificent force, but it is not a teacher of morals. It can perfect machinery, but it adds no moral restraints to protect society from the misuse of the machine. . . . The [Scopes] case has assumed the proportions of a battle-royal [a struggle involving many people] between unbelief that attempts to speak through so-called science and the defenders of the Christian faith.*"

—William Jennings Bryan, from Bryan's Last Speech: *Undelivered Speech to the Jury in the Scopes Trial*

Analyze Historical Sources
Why did Darrow believe the Scopes trial was about free speech?

Clarence Darrow saw the conflict as a battle over free speech.

"*If today you can take a thing like evolution and make it a crime to teach it in the public school, tomorrow you can make it a crime to teach it in the private schools, and the next year you can make it a crime to teach it . . . in the church. At the next session you may ban books and the newspapers. Soon you may set Catholic against Protestant and Protestant against Protestant, and try to foist [force] your own religion upon the minds of men.*"

—Clarence Darrow, from the Scopes trial"

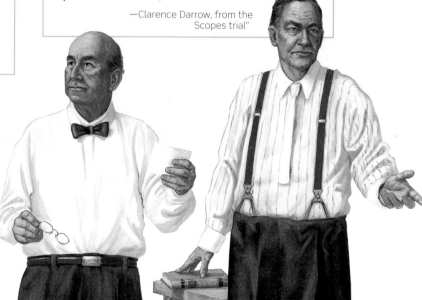

of the Bible. Popular preachers like Aimee Semple McPherson used the radio and modern marketing tools to draw followers. Fundamentalism was especially strong in rural areas and small towns. In these areas, people often blamed society's problems on the culture of urban areas.

Many fundamentalists believed that modern scientific theories conflicted with the teachings of the Bible. This included theories such as Charles Darwin's theory of evolution. Darwin's theory states that species evolve over time by adapting to their environment. To fundamentalists, this contradicted the biblical account of how the world was made. They opposed the teaching of evolution in public schools. Many cities and states passed laws to prevent the teaching of evolution.

In May 1925 a Dayton, Tennessee, high school science teacher named John T. Scopes was put on trial for teaching evolution. This became known as the **Scopes trial**. The fact that famous Americans represented each side heightened national interest in the event. Criminal attorney Clarence Darrow led the ACLU defense team. Three-time presidential candidate William Jennings Bryan assisted the prosecution.

Over live radio, Darrow and Bryan attacked each other's ideas. After more than a week on trial, Scopes was convicted and fined $100 for breaking the law. The state supreme court later overturned his conviction, but the debate over evolution continued.

Reading Check
Analyze Information
What cultural conflict did the Scopes trial represent?

Minority Rights

During World War I large numbers of African Americans began leaving the South to take jobs in northern factories. This movement, or migration, continued during the economic boom of the 1920s. It was called the **Great Migration**. While African Americans found jobs in the North, they did not escape racism. During the Great Migration, northern cities, such as New York City, grew.

Racial Tensions The economic recession that followed the war led to increased racial tensions. Many white laborers feared the competition for jobs. Several race riots broke out. In 1919, a race riot in Chicago left 38 dead. This riot was considered the worst of the approximately 25 riots that occurred during the Red Summer of 1919. In 1921 a group of whites attacked a community of African Americans in Tulsa, Oklahoma. This resulted in the businesses and homes of the Greenwood District being destroyed. At that time the Greenwood District was the wealthiest black community in the United States.

The Silent Parade, also called the Silent March or the Silent Protest Parade, happened on July 28, 1917, in New York City. The parade was partially a response to the East St. Louis riots in May and July 1917. White mobs killed between 40 and 250 blacks in these riots. In the Silent Parade between 8,000 and 10,000 African Americans marched. They protested lynching and anti-black violence. The National Association for the Advancement of Colored People, or NAACP, organized the parade. This was one of the first parades of this kind in New York City. It was also one of the first instances of blacks publicly demonstrating for civil rights.

The Great Migration

From 1940 to 1941, artist Jacob Lawrence created a series of paintings. They told the story of African Americans moving from the South to northern cities in search of jobs and equality. This is one of 60 paintings in the Migration Series. It shows African Americans about to begin their journey.

Draw Conclusions
Where are the people in the painting going?

Racial tensions and fear of foreigners helped give rise to a new form of the Ku Klux Klan. This racist group had terrorized African Americans during Reconstruction. The new Klan harassed Catholics, Jews, and immigrants, as well as African Americans. It also worked against urbanization, women's rights, and modern technology. By the mid-1920s the Klan had more than 5 million members. It had become an influential force in American politics. Its influence then began to decline as news of financial corruption became public.

Protecting Rights People who were the targets of the Klan's hatred found new ways to protect their rights. In 1922, for example, the NAACP began placing advertisements in newspapers. The ads presented the harsh facts about the large number of lynchings taking place across the South.

Another way minorities tried to protect their rights was to strengthen their culture. During the 1910s and 1920s, **Marcus Garvey** encouraged black people around the world to express pride in their culture. Garvey argued that black people should build their own businesses and communities to establish economic independence. These ideas were the basis of a movement known as black nationalism. The *New York Amsterdam News* praised Garvey's work, saying he "made black people proud of their race."

Hispanic Americans also organized to fight prejudice and promote civil rights. In 1929 Mexican American leaders met in Corpus Christi, Texas, to form the League of United Latin American Citizens (LULAC). This group worked to end unfair treatment such as segregation in schools and voting restrictions.

Most Native Americans lacked the legal protections of citizenship and the right to vote because they were not citizens of the United States. The

Marcus Garvey 1887–1940

Marcus Garvey grew up in Jamaica and moved to the United States in 1916. A talented speaker, he quickly became one of the country's most famous and controversial black leaders. His newspaper *Negro World* promoted the idea of building an independent black economy. To encourage worldwide trade among black people, he created the Black Star Steamship Line. Some black leaders, including W.E.B. Du Bois, considered Garvey's ideas dangerous and extremist. After a series of legal problems related to his steamship company, Garvey was arrested in 1922 and was later deported.

Make Inferences
How did Marcus Garvey try to help African Americans?

**Reading Check
Find Main Ideas**
How did minorities react to discrimination in the 1920s?

fact that thousands of Native Americans had performed military service in World War I helped bring about change. In 1924 Congress passed the Indian Citizenship Act. The act granted citizenship to all Native Americans. However, the federal government also attempted to buy or take back some of the reservation lands. Native Americans successfully organized to stop these attempts, which were part of a larger effort to encourage Indians to adopt the culture of white Americans.

Summary and Preview Americans saw many conflicts as their culture changed. In the next lesson you will learn about entertainment and the arts in the 1920s.

Lesson 2 Assessment

Review Ideas, Terms, and People

1. **a. Recall** How did flappers express their freedom?
   b. Elaborate How were young people of the 1920s more independent than their parents?

2. **a. Identify** What caused the Red Scare, and what was its result?
   b. Explain Describe the results of the immigration laws of the 1920s.

3. **a. Recall** What kinds of social conflicts developed during the 1920s?
   b. Describe What did the Twenty-First Amendment accomplish?
   c. Analyze How did fundamentalism influence the Scopes trial?

4. **a. Identify** How did minorities fight for their rights in the 1920s?

   b. Recall What was the Great Migration?
   c. Draw Conclusions Why did Marcus Garvey call for African Americans to build their own businesses?

Critical Thinking

5. **Identify Cause and Effect** In this lesson you learned about the social changes that took place in the 1920s. Create a chart similar to the one below and use it to identify the causes and effects of several changes in American society.

Cause		Effect
	→	
	→	
	→	

The Jazz Age

The Big Idea

Musicians, artists, actors, and writers contributed to American popular culture in the 1920s.

Main Ideas

- Radio and movies linked the country in a national culture.

- Jazz and blues music became popular nationwide.

- Writers and artists introduced new styles and artistic ideas.

Key Terms and People

talkie
Jazz Age
Harlem Renaissance
Langston Hughes
Lost Generation
expatriates
Georgia O'Keeffe

If YOU were there . . .

The year is 1924. The New York Giants are playing the Washington Senators in the World Series. You just bought your first radio, and you are listening to an announcer describe the tense action as the seventh and deciding game goes into extra innings. You used to have to wait to read about the games in the newspaper. Now you can follow your favorite team pitch by pitch!

What other forms of entertainment could the radio bring to you?

A National Culture

On November 2, 1920, KDKA, the first commercial radio station, announced that Warren Harding had won the presidential election held that day. Just one year later, stations broadcast the action from the 1921 World Series. One newspaper writer predicted, "It might not be too long before farmers at the four corners of the Union may sit in their own houses and hear the president of the United States." Such an event seemed amazing to Americans in the early 1900s. But it quickly became a reality. Soon, hundreds of radio stations began broadcasting all over the United States.

National radio networks, such as the National Broadcasting Company (NBC) and Columbia Broadcasting System (CBS), allowed people all over the country to listen to the same programs. People suddenly had access to music, news, weather reports, children's bedtime stories, sports broadcasts, and political speeches without leaving their homes. Business owners loved this technology. It allowed their advertisements to reach millions of listeners. Radio helped build a new national culture by allowing Americans everywhere to share common experiences.

Movies also became a major national passion in the 1920s. Early motion pictures had no sound. However, they opened a new world of exciting adventures for audiences. People packed theaters to see Westerns, romances, and stories about bootlegging gangsters. The 1927 movie *The Jazz Singer* thrilled movie fans. In the movie, actor Al Jolson shouted the line "You ain't heard nothin' yet!" This was the first **talkie**, or motion picture with sound.

The movies quickly became big business. By the end of the decade, Americans were buying 95 million movie tickets each week. This was an amazing figure, considering that the U.S. population was only 123 million.

Young movie fans copied hair and clothing styles of movie stars. Fans felt a personal connection to stars like Douglas Fairbanks, Charlie Chaplin, and Mary Pickford, who was known as "America's Sweetheart." Few fans at the time realized that Pickford was also a smart businesswoman. She was one of the highest paid actors in Hollywood and a founder of United Artists, one of the nation's most successful film companies.

Movie stars were not the only national heroes. Fans packed baseball stadiums to watch the great players of the 1920s, especially George Herman "Babe" Ruth. Ruth shattered home-run records, drawing thousands of new fans to the sport. Because baseball was segregated, African American players and business leaders started their own league. Negro League stars such as Satchel Paige and Josh Gibson are considered to be among the best baseball players in history.

Charles Lindbergh specially modified his plane, the *Spirit of St. Louis,* for his transatlantic flight.

Fans always loved to see athletes break records. In 1926 American swimmer Gertrude Ederle became the first woman to swim the English Channel between England and France. Ederle beat the men's world record by almost two hours.

Pilots also became national heroes in the 1920s. Charles Lindbergh dominated the national news in 1927. He completed the first nonstop solo flight across the Atlantic Ocean, traveling from New York to Paris. A few years later, Amelia Earhart became the first woman to fly solo across the Atlantic.

New ideas like psychoanalysis became more popular. Developed by physician Sigmund Freud, psychoanalysis is a method for examining human behavior to find out why people behave the way they do.

Reading Check
Summarize
How did American culture change during the 1920s?

Popular Music

With a booming economy and exciting forms of entertainment, the 1920s became known as the Roaring Twenties. An explosion in the popularity of jazz music gave the decade another nickname—the **Jazz Age**.

Jazz developed in New Orleans. African American musicians in this city blended spirituals with European harmonies and West African rhythms. When African Americans moved north during the Great Migration, they brought their music with them.

As with many new forms of popular culture, jazz sparked arguments between older and younger generations. "When my grandmother found out that I was playing jazz music . . . she told me that I had disgraced the family," remembered "Jelly Roll" Morton, an early jazz composer. But young Americans loved the music and the wild, fast-paced dances that went along with it. Dance crazes sweeping the nation included the Charleston, the Toddle, and the Shimmy. New magazines arose that taught dance steps to subscribers.

Timeline: Popular Culture of the 1920s

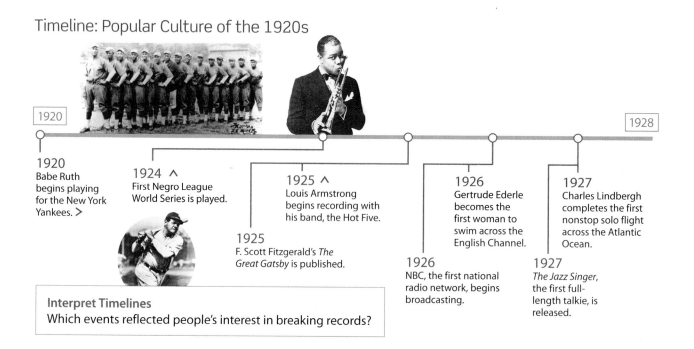

1920

1928

1920
Babe Ruth begins playing for the New York Yankees. >

1924 ∧
First Negro League World Series is played.

1925 ∧
Louis Armstrong begins recording with his band, the Hot Five.

1925
F. Scott Fitzgerald's *The Great Gatsby* is published.

1926
Gertrude Ederle becomes the first woman to swim across the English Channel.

1926
NBC, the first national radio network, begins broadcasting.

1927
Charles Lindbergh completes the first nonstop solo flight across the Atlantic Ocean.

1927
The Jazz Singer, the first full-length talkie, is released.

Interpret Timelines
Which events reflected people's interest in breaking records?

Academic Vocabulary
innovation a new idea or way of doing something

Jazz musicians such as Louis Armstrong experimented with various sounds and rhythms to create a new kind of music. Armstrong, who played the trumpet, was known for his solo numbers. His method of stepping out from the band to perform a solo was an **innovation** that is still copied by musicians today. Another major figure of the Jazz Age was conductor and composer Edward "Duke" Ellington. His "big band" sound blended many instruments together in songs such as "Take the A Train." Ellington described the exciting life of Jazz Age musicians in New York City:

"A lot of guys liked to play so much that in spite of being on a regular job, they'd still hire out to work matinees, or breakfast dances. . . . Nobody went to bed at nights and round three or four in the mornings you'd find everyone making the rounds bringing their horns with them."
—Duke Ellington, quoted in *Reminiscing in Tempo*, by Stuart Nicholson

Reading Check
Find Main Ideas Where did jazz originate, and what musical styles influenced it?

Blues music came from the rural South of the Mississippi delta. It also gained national popularity in the 1920s. Blues began as an expression of the suffering of African Americans during slavery. One of the leading blues singers of the 1920s was Bessie Smith, nicknamed the Empress of the Blues. "She had music in her soul," said Louis Armstrong.

Writers and Artists

As new forms of music were being created, writers and artists were also reshaping culture. Many works of the 1920s are still admired today.

The Harlem Renaissance Many of the African Americans who came north in the Great Migration built a thriving community in the Harlem neighborhood of New York City. This community became the center of the **Harlem Renaissance**, a period of African American artistic accomplishment. Artists of the Harlem Renaissance celebrated the cultural traditions and the life experiences of African Americans.

Harlem Renaissance writers included **Langston Hughes** and Claude McKay. Hughes produced poems, plays, and novels about African American life. His works often incorporated African American slang and jazz rhythms. McKay was a poet and activist. He spoke out against racial discrimination and called on African Americans to stand up against lynchings and other violence. Another important writer of the Harlem Renaissance was Zora Neale Hurston. Her novels, such as *Their Eyes Were Watching God*, reflected the experiences of African American women.

The Lost Generation Other Americans also wrote of their experiences living in the United States and in places around the world. Soon after he graduated from high school in Illinois, Ernest Hemingway volunteered as an ambulance driver in World War I. Hemingway called the war "the most colossal, murderous, mismanaged butchery that had ever taken place on earth." He began writing short stories and novels. Soon, he gained fame for his powerful and direct writing. Hemingway was among a group of young American writers who expressed disillusionment in the American society. They felt it denied them a voice in their own futures. Author Gertrude Stein called these writers "a lost generation." Writers who criticized American society in the 1920s thus became known as the **Lost Generation**.

Many members of the Lost Generation moved to Paris in the 1920s. They formed a community of **expatriates**—people who leave their home country to live elsewhere. Hemingway wrote about the expatriate community in his best-selling novel *The Sun Also Rises*. Another Lost Generation writer was F. Scott Fitzgerald, who wrote *The Great Gatsby*. His novel focused on what he saw as the loss of morality behind the seemingly fun and free-spirited times of the Jazz Age. Another writer of the time, Sinclair Lewis, became the first American to receive the Nobel Prize in literature.

Historical Sources

America

In one of his most celebrated poems, Claude McKay expressed his conflicted feelings about the United States. The poem describes how he feels resentment, love, and admiration for the country all at the same time.

Analyze Historical Sources
Who do you think McKay is referring to when he speaks of "her"?

"*Although she feeds me bread of bitterness,*
And sinks into my throat her tiger's tooth,
Stealing my breath of life, I will confess
I love this cultured hell that tests my youth!
Her vigor flows like tides into my blood,
Giving me strength erect against her hate.
Her bigness sweeps my being like a flood.
Yet as a rebel fronts a king in state,
I stand within her walls with not a shred
Of terror, malice, not a word of jeer.
Darkly I gaze into the days ahead,
And see her might and granite wonders there,
Beneath the touch of Time's unerring hand,
Like priceless treasures sinking in the sand."

Georgia O'Keeffe 1887–1986

Georgia O'Keeffe grew up in Wisconsin and studied art in Chicago and New York. While teaching art at a college in Canyon, Texas, she would sometimes hike in Palo Duro Canyon, where she sketched scenes of amazing colors and rock formations. This was the start of a lifelong fascination with the beauty of the desert landscape. O'Keeffe lived much of her life in rural New Mexico, where many of her paintings were created. Animal bones, rocks, and desert flowers fill her works. She would often paint these objects in close-up view, showing tiny details. O'Keeffe said, "Most people in the city rush around so, they have no time to look at a flower. I want them to see it whether they want to or not."

Find Main Ideas
How did Georgia O'Keeffe's life influence her painting?

Reading Check
Compare and Contrast How were the artists of the Harlem Renaissance and the Lost Generation similar and different?

New Directions in Art Painters were also experimenting with new artistic styles in the 1920s. Edward Hopper painted images of the loneliness of modern urban life. **Georgia O'Keeffe** was well known for her detailed paintings of flowers and of the Southwest.

Architects of the 1920s embraced a style they called art deco. Buildings constructed in this style had clean, sharp lines that resembled machines. Today, art deco skyscrapers still stand out in American skylines. New York City's Chrysler and Empire State Buildings are examples of art deco style.

In 1929, the Museum of Modern Art in New York City was founded. Photography was also being accepted as an art form during this time.

Summary and Preview Americans became interested in new forms of entertainment and art in the 1920s. In the next module you will learn about how life changed in the 1930s.

Lesson 3 Assessment

Review Ideas, Terms, and People

1. **a. Recall** What new forms of entertainment dominated American society during the 1920s?
   b. Identify What was the first talkie?
2. **a. Explain** Why were the 1920s called the Jazz Age?
   b. Make Inferences Why do you think jazz music became so popular?
3. **a. Recall** How did writers and artists express new ideas during the 1920s?
   b. Describe What did the Lost Generation writers express in their works?
   c. Predict How might the artists of the Harlem Renaissance influence African American artists of later generations?

Critical Thinking

4. **Categorize** In this lesson you learned about the popular culture in the 1920s. Create a chart similar to the one below and use it to categorize examples of popular culture in the 1920s.

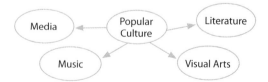

Social Studies Skills

Compare Graphs

Define the Skill

Graphs are often a very useful way to organize historical information. They can present a large amount of detailed information clearly. Graphs can be an especially good way of showing how something like population or average income changed over time.

When information is organized in a graph, it is often easy to see patterns. Looking at two related graphs, you can compare patterns and make conclusions. For example, you can ask yourself, "Do the numbers in the graphs go up or down for the same reasons? What are the causes behind the changes shown by these graphs?"

Learn the Skill

These guidelines will help you to compare information in two or more graphs.

1. Use your basic graph-interpreting skills. Identify each graph's subject, purpose, and type. Study its parts and categories.

2. Analyze the data in each graph. Then compare any increases, decreases, changes, or patterns you find.

3. Finally, draw conclusions about the relationship between the information in each graph. Think about what could cause such relationships. It will probably help you to review what you know about related events at the same time.

Practice the Skill

Compare the graphs below to answer the following questions.

1. What are the topics of these graphs?

2. What percentage of American households had electricity in 1922? What was the first year when more than half of American households had electricity?

3. Based on the information in the graphs, draw a conclusion about how electricity changed American households.

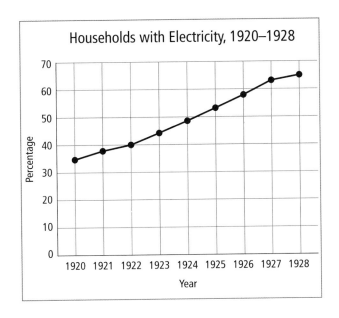

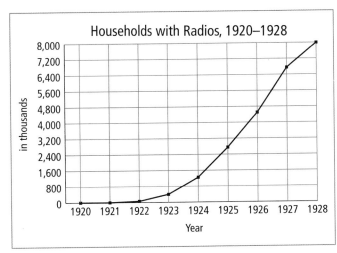

Source: Historical Atlas of the United States

Module 9 Assessment

Review Vocabulary, Terms, and People

Complete each sentence by filling in the blank with the correct term or person from the module.

1. Harlem Renaissance writer _____ wrote poems, plays, and novels about African American life.

2. The United States and other nations signed the _____, which outlawed war.

3. In the _____, Clarence Darrow defended a high school teacher tried for teaching evolution.

4. The _____ repealed prohibition.

5. Writers who criticized American culture during the 1920s were known as the _____.

6. African Americans moved north for jobs during the _____.

Comprehension and Critical Thinking

Lesson 1

7. **a. Describe** What was President Warren Harding's plan for strengthening the U.S. economy?

   b. Explain What methods did Henry Ford's competitors use to attract customers?

   c. Elaborate What do you think might have made the Kellogg-Briand Pact more effective?

Lesson 2

8. **a. Recall** What was the Red Scare?

   b. Analyze What are some reasons women had more opportunities in the 1920s?

   c. Evaluate Would you have become involved in the youth culture if you had lived during the 1920s? Why or why not?

Lesson 3

9. **a. Identify** What were talkies?

   b. Explain How did African Americans play an important role in Jazz Age culture?

   c. Predict How do you think new aspects of American culture affected life after the 1920s?

Review Themes

10. **Society and Culture** How did the prosperity of the 1920s change American culture?

11. **Science and Technology** What new forms of technology emerged in the 1920s?

Social Studies Skills

Compare Graphs *Use the Social Studies Skills taught in this module to answer the question below.*

12. Look back at the line graphs in the Social Studies Skills. Do you think a graph showing the number of radio stations in the United States during the 1920s would look similar to these graphs? Explain your answer.

Reading Skills

Synthesize Information *Use the Reading Skills taught in this module to answer the question below.*

> The number of women in the workforce continued to grow as well. Women with college degrees worked as nurses, teachers, librarians, and social workers. . . . Women were still discouraged from pursuing fields such as medicine, law, and architecture, however. By the end of the 1920s, less than 5 percent of the country's doctors, lawyers, and architects were women. The percentage was small—but it was beginning to rise.

13. Which of the following sources might have been used to synthesize the information above?
    a. a history of architecture
    b. an instructional manual for nurses
    c. a history of working women in the 1920s
    d. the list of graduates from a women's college in 1910

Focus on Writing

14. **Write a Radio Advertisement** Radio stations began to air regular broadcasts in the 1920s. Radios linked Americans from coast to coast, allowing them to hear the same programs and the same advertisements. In the 1920s Americans with means could afford to buy various products and could choose different entertainment, travel, fashion, and convenience. Choose one product that was popular in the 1920s that is mentioned in the module. Write a radio ad for that product. Think about these questions as you design your radio ad: Who is your audience? How will this product improve people's lives? What words or sounds will best describe your product? Write the dialogue for your ad, including directions for the actors. Also, include information about music or sound effects you want to use.

$100. WILL BUY THIS CAR. MUST HAVE CASH. LOST ALL ON THE STOCK MARKET

Module 10

The Great Depression

★

Essential Question
Was the Great Depression inevitable?

About the Photo: The Great Depression forced many people to sell everything they owned just to survive.

▷ *Explore ONLINE!*

HISTORY.

VIDEOS, including...
- The Great Depression
- Run on Banks
- FDR's Fireside Chat
- Tennessee Valley Authority
- FDR's New Deal

✓ Document-Based Investigations

✓ Graphic Organizers

✓ Interactive Games

✓ Image with Hotspots: Blame It on Hoover

✓ Image with Hotspots: Packing the Supreme Court

✓ Interactive Map: The Dust Bowl, 1933–1936

In this module you will learn about how Americans coped with the economic problems of the 1930s. You will also learn about the Dust Bowl and its effects.

What You Will Learn . . .

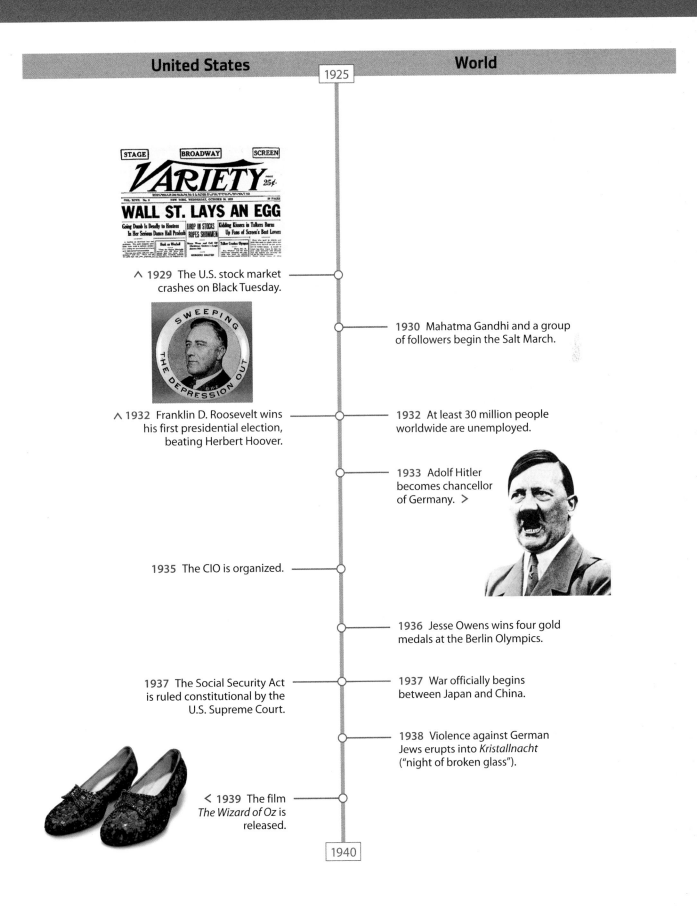

United States

World

1925

∧ **1929** The U.S. stock market crashes on Black Tuesday.

1930 Mahatma Gandhi and a group of followers begin the Salt March.

∧ **1932** Franklin D. Roosevelt wins his first presidential election, beating Herbert Hoover.

1932 At least 30 million people worldwide are unemployed.

1933 Adolf Hitler becomes chancellor of Germany. ›

1935 The CIO is organized.

1936 Jesse Owens wins four gold medals at the Berlin Olympics.

1937 The Social Security Act is ruled constitutional by the U.S. Supreme Court.

1937 War officially begins between Japan and China.

1938 Violence against German Jews erupts into *Kristallnacht* ("night of broken glass").

‹ **1939** The film *The Wizard of Oz* is released.

1940

Reading Social Studies

THEME FOCUS:

Economics, Politics

In this module you will learn about the Great Depression, one of the most serious economic crises in America's history. You will also learn about the politics that arose to try to deal with this crisis. Finally, you will read about how the Depression affected the global economy and how world leaders responded to it.

READING FOCUS:

Recognize Implied Main Ideas

When you read, you will notice that not every paragraph has a main idea sentence. Sometimes the main idea is implied.

Implied Main Ideas While main ideas give a basic structure to a paragraph, supporting details help convince the reader of the author's point. Main ideas can be presented in a sentence, or simply implied. Usually, a paragraph without a main idea sentence will still have an implied main idea that ties the sentences together.

Notice how one reader found the main idea of the following paragraph.

During the boom years of the 1920s, one General Motors executive boldly declared: "Anyone not only can be rich, but ought to be rich." For almost all of the Roaring Twenties, the stock market was a bull market, or one with rising stock values. It seemed easy to make money by investing in stocks. For example, you could have bought shares in the Radio Corporation of America for $85 each at the beginning of 1928. You could have sold them a year later for $549 each.

This quote is about making money and being rich. Maybe the main idea is about money or economics.

This sentence is about making money through the stock market. I guess the main idea has to do with investing.

Here is a great example of how easy it was to make money in the 1920s. I think the main idea is something like "The stock market provided an easy way for many to become rich in the 1920s."

You Try It!

Read the following paragraph and then answer the questions below.

The action began when Roosevelt called Congress into a special session. Known as the Hundred Days, the session started just after the inauguration and lasted until the middle of June. During the Hundred Days, Roosevelt and Congress worked together to create new programs to battle the Depression and aid economic recovery. These programs became known as the New Deal.

1. List two ideas that this paragraph discusses.
2. How are these two ideas related to each other?
3. Write an example of the main idea of this paragraph.
4. Which details support your main idea?

As you read Module 10, think of a main idea for any paragraph that does not have a main idea sentence.

The End of Prosperity

The Big Idea

The collapse of the stock market in 1929 helped lead to the start of the Great Depression.

Main Ideas

- The U.S. stock market crashed in 1929.
- The economy collapsed after the stock market crash.
- Many Americans were dissatisfied with Hoover's reaction to economic conditions.
- Roosevelt defeated Hoover in the election of 1932.

Key Terms and People

buying on margin
Black Tuesday
business cycle
Great Depression
Bonus Army
Franklin D. Roosevelt

If YOU were there . . .

For almost a year you've been working part-time at a neighborhood store. You earn money for your family and still have time to go to school. But when you arrive at work today, your boss says business has been so bad that he can't afford to pay you anymore. With your father out of work, your family had been counting on your income from this job.

How can you continue earning money to help your family?

The Stock Market Crashes

During the boom years of the 1920s, one General Motors executive boldly declared: "Anyone not only can be rich, but ought to be rich." Many people relied on the stock market to increase their wealth. The stock market is a market that people can use to buy or sell shares of ownership in a company. For almost all of the Roaring Twenties, the stock market was a bull market, or one with rising stock values. It seemed easy to make money by investing in stocks. For example, you could have bought shares in the Radio Corporation of America for $85 each at the beginning of 1928. You could have sold them a year later for $549 each.

The chance to make huge profits from small investments encouraged many people to buy stocks. Some people could not afford the stocks' full price. They began **buying on margin**—purchasing stocks on credit, or with borrowed money. These stockholders planned to sell the stocks at a higher price. Then they would pay back the loan and keep what remained as profit. But this plan was risky because it only worked if stock values went up. Few considered what would happen if the bull market turned into a bear market, or one with declining stock prices.

The Federal Reserve Board became concerned about the growing popularity of buying on margin. In the late 1920s the Board tried to make it more difficult and more costly for

Black Tuesday

More than 16 million shares were traded on Wall Street on Black Tuesday, a record that stood for 39 years. Just weeks later, roughly one-third of the value of the stock market had disappeared.

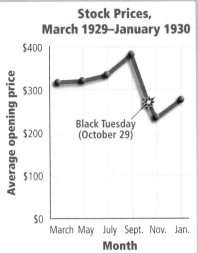

Stock Prices, March 1929–January 1930

Black Tuesday (October 29)

Average opening price

$400
$300
$200
$100
$0

March May July Sept. Nov. Jan.

Month

Analyze Graphs
How are the events of Black Tuesday shown on the graph?

brokers to offer margin loans to investors. These actions helped decrease the amount that brokers borrowed from banks. However, soon, brokers began borrowing from large corporations and the risky investing practice continued.

Stock prices peaked in the late summer of 1929. Then prices started to drop. Frightened investors who had bought stocks on margin rushed to sell their stocks in order to pay off their loans. On Thursday, October 24, panic hit the stock market. Within three hours the market had lost $11 billion in value. The following Monday, prices dropped again. On Tuesday, October 29—a day that became known as **Black Tuesday**—the stock market crashed. So many people wanted to sell their stocks, and so few wanted to buy, that stock prices collapsed. One journalist described the nightmare:

> "The wires to other cities were jammed with frantic orders to sell [stock]. So were the cables, radio, and telephones to Europe and the rest of the world. Buyers were few, sometimes wholly absent . . . This was real panic . . . When the closing bell rang, the great bull market was dead and buried."
>
> —Jonathan Norton Leonard, from *Three Years Down*

In September 1929 the total value of all stocks was $87 billion. Less than two months later, more than $30 billion in stock value had disappeared. Investors who had bought stocks on margin became stuck with large debts.

Reading Check
Analyze Information
Why was buying on margin risky?

The Economy Collapses

President Herbert Hoover tried to calm public fears by assuring Americans that the economy was still strong. "The fundamental business of the country . . . is on a sound and prosperous basis," he said. But this was just the beginning of more than ten years of economic hard times.

The Banking Crisis One immediate effect of the stock market crash was a banking crisis. Banks had invested heavily in the stock market, so they lost heavily when the market crashed. Banks had also lent their customers money to buy stocks on margin. Now those customers were unable to pay back their loans. Some banks went out of business. People who had deposited their life savings in those banks lost everything.

This created a panic all over the country, as customers rushed to their banks to withdraw their money. But since banks usually do not keep enough cash on hand to cover all deposits, the banks soon ran out of money. Many had to close their doors. In 1931 alone, more than 2,200 banks closed. The banking crisis contributed to a business crisis. Some businesses lost their savings in failed banks and had to close. Others were forced to cut back production, which meant they needed fewer workers. Nearly 3 million people lost their jobs. In the last three months of 1929, U.S. unemployment soared from under half a million workers to more than 4 million.

Unemployment during the Depression

Connect to Economics People are considered unemployed if they are trying to find work but do not have a job. High rates of unemployment hurt the economy because unemployed people cannot buy many goods and services. This causes businesses to lose money.

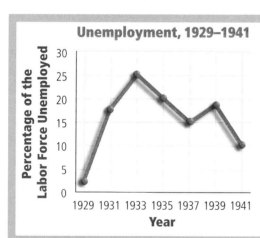

Unemployment, 1929–1941

Analyze Graphs
During what year was unemployment the highest?

The Causes Throughout the history of the United States, the economy has followed a pattern of ups and downs. When businesses produce more than they can sell, unsold goods pile up. Businesses then cut back on their production and lay off workers. People who have lost their jobs, and others who are afraid they might soon lose their jobs, buy fewer goods. This causes more businesses to fail. This economic event is called a recession. Deep and long-lasting recessions are known as depressions.

As time passes, an economy will tend to bounce back. Consumers buy surplus goods, and companies increase production to meet the demand. Soon, more workers are hired and unemployment drops. This up-and-down pattern, known as the **business cycle**, continues in today's economy.

The United States had experienced recessions and depressions before 1929. Each time, the economy followed the business cycle and recovered. But the economy did not recover quickly from the downturn that began in 1929. Because of its severity and length, it was called the **Great Depression**.

Historians and economists still debate the exact causes of the Great Depression. Some believe that the government's monetary policy was a cause. Others believe that limited market competition and protectionism, or restriction of trade, played a part. However, most agree that a major factor was the overproduction of goods at a time when the market for those goods was shrinking. Companies built millions of cars and appliances during the 1920s. By the late 1920s, however, most people who could afford these products already had bought them. That meant that American businesses were producing far more goods than people were consuming.

Uneven distribution of wealth made this problem worse. In 1929 the wealthiest 5 percent of Americans earned one-third of all income, while the bottom 40 percent earned only one-eighth of all income. Millions of Americans simply did not earn enough money to buy expensive new products. Many of them lost their jobs, their wealth, and their homes.

Declining world trade also hurt American manufacturers. Europeans were still recovering from World War I and could not afford many American goods. At the same time, high tariffs made it difficult for European nations to sell products to the United States. As a result, Europeans had even less money to buy American goods.

Hoover's Reaction

As unemployment skyrocketed, more and more Americans struggled just to feed themselves and their families. Hungry people searched city dumps for scraps of food. One woman remembered taking off her glasses when she cooked so she could not see the maggots in the meat her family was about to eat. Private charities, as well as state and local governments, set up soup kitchens and breadlines in New York and across the country. But the need far exceeded the available resources. Many people turned to President Herbert Hoover and the federal government to lead the relief effort.

Reading Check
Make Predictions
Do you think the Great Depression could have been avoided? How?

"Blame It on Hoover"

Presidents can affect the economy to some degree through their policies. During the Great Depression, President Hoover was blamed for the financial crisis. Political cartoons like this one gave voice to those Americans who thought Hoover could have prevented the crisis or could have brought it to an end quickly through government programs.

How does the cartoonist show Hoover reacting to the crisis?

What kind of people are blaming Hoover?

Analyze Historical Sources
Why is this cartoon useful for showing the feelings of the American public during the Great Depression?

A Most Vicious Circle
—Costello in the Albany "News."

Academic Vocabulary
implement put in place

Hoover knew that many Americans needed help. He did not believe, however, that it was the federal government's role to provide direct relief to Americans. Hoover felt it was up to private individuals and institutions, not the government, to offer relief. Despite this belief, Hoover did **implement** some new government programs. In 1932 he created the Reconstruction Finance Corporation (RFC). That year, the RFC loaned $1.2 billion to 5,000 different financial institutions, including banks and farm mortgage companies. Hoover continued to resist giving direct assistance to individuals.

This angered Americans who believed the president should do more to fix the economy. People bitterly referred to empty pockets turned inside out as Hoover flags. Groups of tin and cardboard shacks built by homeless families were nicknamed Hoovervilles. These camps were built in cities and towns across the United States from New York to Los Angeles.

In 1932 a new Hooverville was built in Washington, DC. Its more than 17,000 residents were World War I veterans, some with their families. Called the **Bonus Army**, they had come to the capital to demand early payment of a military bonus. After the government denied the payment, most of the veterans returned home. About 2,000, however, stayed in their shantytown.

President Hoover authorized General Douglas MacArthur to use U.S. troops to evict the Bonus Army. MacArthur used force, including tear gas and tanks, to scatter the veterans. Several veterans were killed. The public reacted with outrage to the government's treatment of war veterans. Americans would have a chance to express this frustration in the upcoming election.

Reading Check
Make Generalizations
How would you describe President Hoover's response to the Depression?

Election of 1932

The Republican Party nominated Herbert Hoover again for president in 1932, but few people believed he could win. Regarding his chances of re-election, even Hoover realized that "the prospects are dark." Still, he began campaigning hard for a second term.

He called the election "a contest between two philosophies of government." He warned that the government aid programs Democrats were promising would weaken Americans' spirit of self-reliance.

By 1932, however, much of the public had lost confidence in Hoover. His insistence on limited government action earned him the reputation as a "do-nothing" president. Many even blamed him for the Depression. In contrast, as governor of New York during the first years of the Depression, Democratic presidential candidate **Franklin D. Roosevelt** had taken active steps to provide aid. He directed the state government to provide relief for the state's citizens, especially farmers. He also helped establish the Temporary Emergency Relief Administration, which gave unemployment assistance to many out-of-work New Yorkers. Roosevelt's programs provided help for one in every ten New York families.

BIOGRAPHY

Franklin Delano Roosevelt
1882–1945

Roosevelt lived much of his life in New York State, where he served in the state senate and as governor. He also lived in Washington, DC, while he was serving as assistant secretary of the navy and later as president.

As president, he began the New Deal, a set of government programs designed to help the country survive and recover from the Great Depression. He gave many Americans hope for the future when he spoke to them in his fireside chats.

Roosevelt led the United States during two of the most serious crises that our country has ever faced: the Great Depression and World War II. He served as president for 12 years, longer than any other president.

"The only thing we have to fear is fear itself, nameless, unreasoning, unjustified terror."

—Franklin Roosevelt,
1933 inaugural address

Make Predictions
How do you think Franklin Roosevelt's experience as president during the Depression might have helped him lead the country during World War II?

Reading Check
Analyze Information
How did Franklin
D. Roosevelt win the
1932 presidential
election?

Roosevelt's confident and optimistic personality appealed to many voters. At the Democratic Party convention, Roosevelt declared to Americans: "I pledge you, I pledge myself, to a new deal for the American people." Voters responded overwhelmingly to this message of hope. Roosevelt won the 1932 election in a landslide. He received 57 percent of the popular vote and swept the electoral vote in all but six states. In addition, the Democrats won strong majorities in both houses of Congress.

Summary and Preview Overproduction of goods, buying stocks on margin, and other economic practices in the 1920s contributed to the start of the Great Depression. After the stock market crash and the start of the Great Depression, Franklin Roosevelt offered hope for the future. In the next lesson you will learn about his programs for relief.

Lesson 1 Assessment

Review Ideas, Terms, and People

1. **a. Recall** Why did the stock market crash in 1929?

   b. Compare How is buying on margin similar to buying on an installment plan?

2. **a. Recall** What happened to the economy as a result of the stock market crash?

   b. Explain Why did many banks close in the late 1920s and early 1930s?

   c. Compare What similarities does the economy in the 1920s and 1930s share with the economy today?

   d. Draw Conclusions What do you think was the goal of U.S. tariffs?

3. **a. Make Inferences** Why did many Americans blame President Hoover for the Depression?

   b. Describe What did the Bonus Army want?

   c. Elaborate Do you think Americans were justified in blaming Hoover for the hard times?

4. **a. Identify** Which party was more successful in the 1932 elections?

   b. Make Inferences Why do you think voters did not listen to Hoover's ideas about government?

   c. Elaborate How do you think Franklin D. Roosevelt's experiences as governor of New York helped him appeal to voters?

Critical Thinking

5. **Identify Cause and Effect** In this lesson you learned about the American economy in the 1920s and 1930s. Create a chart similar to the one below and use it to identify the economic causes of the Depression and their effects.

Economic Causes 1920s → The Depression 1930s

Roosevelt's New Deal

The Big Idea

Franklin Roosevelt's New Deal included government programs designed to relieve unemployment and help the economy recover.

Main Ideas

- Congress approved many new programs during the Hundred Days.

- Critics expressed concerns about the New Deal.

- New Deal programs continued through Roosevelt's first term in what became known as the Second New Deal.

- Roosevelt clashed with the Supreme Court over the New Deal.

Key Terms and People

New Deal
fireside chats
Tennessee Valley Authority
Frances Perkins
Eleanor Roosevelt
Social Security Act
Congress of Industrial
    Organizations
sit-down strike

If YOU were there . . .

It has been five months since you lost your job. One of your friends has found work in a new government program that is hiring young people to work in national parks and forests. The pay is low, and you would have to leave home, but you would have enough food, a place to live, and a little money to send back to your family every month.

Would you take a job with the Civilian Conservation Corps? Why or why not?

The Hundred Days

Immediately after taking the oath of office in March 1933, President Franklin Roosevelt spoke to the nation. In his first inaugural address, Roosevelt told nervous Americans that economic recovery was possible. "The only thing we have to fear is fear itself," he said, "nameless, unreasoning, unjustified terror." It was only fear of the future, he argued, that could keep America from moving forward. Roosevelt spoke openly of the severe problems facing the American people—unemployment, failing banks, and products with no markets. He promised that the government would help. "This nation asks for action," he said, "and action now."

The action began when Roosevelt called Congress into a special session. Known as the Hundred Days, the session started just after the inauguration and lasted until the middle of June. During the Hundred Days, Roosevelt and Congress worked together to create new programs to battle the Depression and aid economic recovery. These programs became known as the **New Deal**.

Restoring Confidence One of Roosevelt's first goals was to restore confidence in American banks. The day after his inauguration, Roosevelt announced a "bank holiday." He ordered all banks to close temporarily. Three days later,

Congress's special session began. Congress quickly passed the Emergency Banking Relief Act. President Roosevelt signed it into law.

That Sunday, President Roosevelt gave the first of his **fireside chats**—radio addresses in which he spoke directly to the American people. In this first fireside chat, he explained the new bank relief law. The government would inspect the finances of every bank and allow only healthy banks to reopen. The Federal Deposit Insurance Corporation (FDIC) was established to help maintain stability in the United States financial system. It provided government insurance for deposits made into eligible banks. People no longer needed to fear losing their savings in the event of another bank failure. The new bank law and Roosevelt's fireside chat helped Americans trust banks with their money again. As banks reopened, there were no rushes to withdraw money. Over the next month Americans deposited almost $1 billion in banks.

Under Roosevelt's leadership, Congress also established the Securities and Exchange Commission (SEC). The SEC was an organization that would regulate operations within the stock market. Created to restore the confidence of investors in the market, the Securities and Exchange Commission established rules to prevent misleading sales practices.

Relief and Recovery Roosevelt next turned his attention to other serious problems. In 1933 some 13 million Americans were unemployed.

Historical Sources

Fireside Chats

An American family sits around the radio listening to President Roosevelt answer his critics in his first fireside chat.

"There is an element in . . . our financial system more important than currency [money], more important than gold, and that is the confidence of the people. Confidence and courage are the essentials of success in carrying out our plan. You people must have faith; you must not be stampeded by rumors or guesses. Let us unite in banishing [driving away] fear. We have provided the machinery to restore our financial system; it is up to you to support and make it work. It is your problem no less than it is mine. Together we cannot fail."

Analyze Historical Sources
According to Roosevelt, how should the American people help the government deal with the banking crisis?

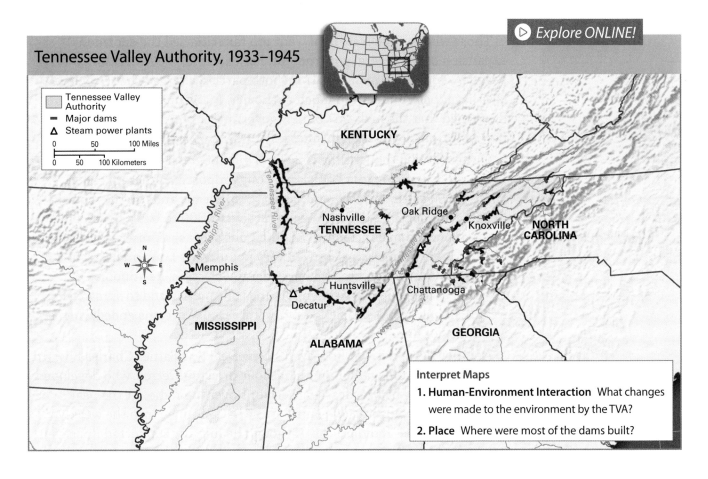

Tennessee Valley Authority, 1933–1945

Explore ONLINE!

Legend:
- Tennessee Valley Authority
- ■ Major dams
- △ Steam power plants

0   50   100 Miles
0   50   100 Kilometers

KENTUCKY

Nashville   Oak Ridge
TENNESSEE   Knoxville   NORTH CAROLINA

Memphis

Huntsville   Chattanooga
Decatur

MISSISSIPPI   ALABAMA   GEORGIA

Mississippi River
Tennessee River

Interpret Maps

1. **Human-Environment Interaction** What changes were made to the environment by the TVA?

2. **Place** Where were most of the dams built?

This represented about 25 percent of the nation's workforce. New Deal programs helped to get Americans back to work. The Civil Works Administration (CWA) employed more than 4 million Americans, building roads and airports. One grateful CWA worker expressed the feelings of many when he said, "I was working, and I could again hold my head up when I met people." The Civilian Conservation Corps (CCC) provided jobs for hundreds of thousands of people. They worked on projects such as planting trees and improving national parks.

Another federal project, the **Tennessee Valley Authority** (TVA), hired people to build dams and generators. This brought electricity and jobs to communities in the Tennessee River valley. The New Deal also included programs to help farmers. The Farm Credit Administration (FCA) helped farmers refinance their mortgages so they could keep their farms. The Agricultural Adjustment Act (AAA) helped stabilize agricultural prices.

The National Industrial Recovery Act (NIRA) addressed business concerns. It eliminated unfair competition among companies. This law was passed with support from Secretary of Labor **Frances Perkins**, the nation's first woman cabinet member.

Reading Check
Categorize Which New Deal programs employed people to build public projects?

New Deal Critics

While many Americans approved of the New Deal, others criticized President Roosevelt's programs. New Deal critics fell into two main groups—those who believed the New Deal went too far, and those who believed it did not go far enough.

Academic Vocabulary
authority power, right to rule

Those who felt the New Deal went too far criticized the enormous expansion of the federal government. For example, the American Liberty League, which drew members from both parties, charged that New Deal laws gave the president too much **authority**. Many business leaders were concerned that the high cost of new government programs would lead to new taxes, particularly on businesses.

One critic who thought the New Deal did not go far enough was Huey Long, a U.S. senator from Louisiana. Long proposed a program called Share Our Wealth, which would tax rich Americans and use the money to help the poor. Every family would receive $5,000 to buy a home, plus a guaranteed annual income of $2,500. Long's ideas, represented in the slogan "Every Man a King," proved very popular. As Long prepared to challenge Roosevelt in the 1936 presidential election, he announced his goal "to break up the swollen fortunes of America and to spread the wealth among all our people." Long's White House dreams ended when an assassin shot him in 1935.

Another fierce critic of Roosevelt's New Deal was Father Charles Edward Coughlin. Coughlin was a Roman Catholic priest in Detroit who developed a large following by broadcasting sermons over the radio. At the peak of Coughlin's popularity, one-third of the nation tuned into the weekly broadcasts of the "radio priest." Although he initially supported Roosevelt and his programs, Coughlin eventually decided that the New Deal helped only business interests. Coughlin wanted the government to nationalize, or take over, all of the country's wealth and natural resources.

Dr. Francis Townsend criticized the New Deal for not doing enough for older Americans. He proposed a plan providing for a monthly pension for people over the age of 60. Like Long and Coughlin, Townsend attracted many followers. Some of his ideas later would shape Roosevelt's thinking and policies.

Reading Check
Support a Point of View Do you agree with any of the New Deal critics? Why or why not?

The New Deal Continues

Despite criticism of the New Deal, Democrats increased their majorities in both houses of Congress in the 1934 election. With this show of support from the American people, Roosevelt continued to introduce additional New Deal legislation. These later laws were known as the Second New Deal.

The Second New Deal After the Civil Works Administration ended in 1934, Congress formed a new agency to provide jobs for unemployed Americans. Between 1935 and 1943, the Works Progress Administration (WPA) employed some 8.5 million people on tens of thousands of projects all over the country. WPA employees built more than 650,000 miles of roads; 75,000 bridges; 8,000 parks; and 800 airports. WPA workers built the Grand Coulee Dam in Washington and New York City's Lincoln Tunnel. They also built prisons, swimming pools, hospitals, and courthouses.

First Lady **Eleanor Roosevelt** was an active supporter of New Deal programs. She was concerned, however, that the WPA was not solving the problem of unemployment among young Americans in their teens and

Eleanor Roosevelt visits a WPA project to convert a city dump into a waterfront park.

National Youth Administration

A New Deal program called the National Youth Administration (NYA) helped thousands of young people continue their education while working to support their families. Eleanor Roosevelt was a strong supporter of the program, which aimed to teach young people the skills they would need to remain part of the workforce.

early twenties. "I live in real terror when I think we may be losing this generation," she said. "We have got to bring these young people into the active life of the community and make them feel that they are necessary." The First Lady helped convince the president to create the National Youth Administration (NYA). The NYA gave part-time jobs to many students. These jobs allowed young workers to stay in school and help their families. One NYA worker said, "I tell you, the first time I walked through the front door with my paycheck, I was somebody!"

President Roosevelt also wanted to help those who were "unable . . . to maintain themselves independently . . . through no fault of their own." The **Social Security Act**, passed in 1935, provided some financial security for the elderly, the disabled, children, and the unemployed. To help pay for these programs, the law placed a new tax on workers and employers. The passage of the Social Security Act marked the first time the federal government took direct responsibility for many citizens' economic well-being. In a national radio address, Secretary of Labor Perkins told Americans she believed Social Security was "a most significant step in our national development, a milestone in our progress toward the better-ordered society." Social Security is still an important financial safety net for many Americans. Nine out of ten individuals over the age of 65 receive benefits from the program.

New Deal Labor Programs The National Industrial Recovery Act of 1933 helped regulate business by requiring minimum wage and allowing collective bargaining. In 1935, however, the Supreme Court declared the NIRA unconstitutional.

Selected New Deal Programs

Program	Purpose
Emergency Banking Relief Act	Gave the executive branch the right to regulate banks
Farm Credit Act (FCA)	Refinanced loans to keep farmers from losing their land
Civilian Conservation Corps (CCC)	Created jobs for single, unemployed young men
Agricultural Adjustment Act (AAA)	Paid farmers to grow less (declared unconstitutional)
Tennessee Valley Authority (TVA)	Built dams and power plants in the Tennessee Valley
Federal Deposit Insurance Corporation (FDIC)	Guaranteed deposits in individual bank accounts
National Industrial Recovery Act (NIRA)	Established fair competition laws (declared unconstitutional)
Civil Works Administration (CWA)	Provided jobs for the unemployed
Works Progress Administration (WPA)	Created jobs in construction, research, and the arts
National Youth Administration (NYA)	Provided part-time jobs to students
National Labor Relations Act (Wagner Act)	Recognized unions' right to bargain collectively
Social Security Act	Provided government aid to the retired and unemployed

In response to this setback, Congress passed the National Labor Relations Act (NLRA). This law is sometimes called the Wagner Act, after its sponsor, Senator Robert F. Wagner of New York. This law allowed workers to join labor unions and work together for better working conditions or salaries with collective bargaining. It also established the National Labor Relations Board to oversee union activities. Union membership grew after the passage of the Wagner Act. Organized labor became a powerful political force.

At the start of the Depression, many skilled workers belonged to craft unions. Such unions were often associated with the American Federation of Labor, which had existed since the 1880s. Unskilled workers, however, such as those who worked on assembly lines, did not qualify to belong to AFL unions. In 1935 a new union called the **Congress of Industrial Organizations** (CIO) organized workers into unions based on industry, not skill level. For example, all workers in the automobile industry would belong to the same union. The CIO also welcomed African American and Hispanic members, as well as women and immigrants.

Unions led a number of major strikes during the Depression. On New Year's Eve 1936, the CIO went on strike against General Motors for 44 days. Instead of leaving the buildings as strikers usually did, workers stayed in the factories so they could not be replaced by new workers. This strategy became known as the **sit-down strike**. The success of the General Motors strike attracted more workers to CIO unions.

Reading Check
Compare and Contrast How were the WPA and the Social Security Act similar, and how were they different?

Clashes with the Court

Roosevelt won re-election by a huge margin in 1936, carrying every state but Maine and Vermont. Democrats expanded their dominant control of Congress. But Roosevelt and the Democrats in Congress could not control the Supreme Court.

In 1935 the Supreme Court issued a series of rulings declaring several New Deal programs, including the AAA, unconstitutional. Roosevelt and his advisers felt that the entire New Deal was in danger. "Mr. President, they mean to destroy us," said Attorney General Homer Cummings.

Roosevelt decided to propose a plan for reorganizing the federal judiciary that was soon to be labeled the "court-packing" bill. This bill would allow the president to appoint a new Supreme Court justice for every justice who was 70 years old or older. If the bill passed, Roosevelt would be able to appoint six new justices immediately.

Roosevelt's judiciary plan drew harsh criticism from Congress and the public. Critics charged that Roosevelt was trying to change the balance of power so carefully defined in the U.S. Constitution. After a heated debate, Congress rejected the bill. The Supreme Court, however, did not overturn any more New Deal legislation. Roosevelt eventually had the opportunity to nominate nine new Supreme Court justices to replace those who had retired or died.

Reading Check
Analyze Information
Why did Roosevelt try to alter the Supreme Court?

Summary and Preview Roosevelt's New Deal programs brought economic relief to many Americans; however, the reforms did not resolve all of the hardships that people faced. In the next lesson you will read about how the country continued to suffer the effects of the Depression.

Lesson 2 Assessment

Review Ideas, Terms, and People

1. a. **Recall** What were the Hundred Days?
   b. **Make Inferences** What was the purpose of the bank holiday Roosevelt declared?
   c. **Evaluate** Which of the New Deal programs that passed during the Hundred Days was most effective? Why?

2. a. **Describe** Who were some of the critics of the New Deal?
   b. **Contrast** How were the ideas of Huey Long and the American Liberty League different?
   c. **Elaborate** Why do you think people supported New Deal critics such as Huey Long and Father Coughlin?

3. a. **Identify** What programs were part of the Second New Deal?
   b. **Make Inferences** Why did the Wagner Act encourage people to join unions?

4. a. **Recall** What happened to some of the New Deal programs when they were challenged in court?
   b. **Make Inferences** What was the purpose of Roosevelt's judiciary reorganization bill?

Critical Thinking

5. **Problem Solving** In this lesson you learned about the challenges faced by the nation and the president during the Depression. Create a chart similar to the one below and use it to identify Depression problems and New Deal solutions.

Depression Problems	New Deal Solutions

Americans Face Hard Times

The Big Idea

All over the country, Americans struggled to survive the Great Depression.

Main Ideas

- Parts of the Great Plains came to be known as the Dust Bowl as severe drought destroyed farms there.

- Families all over the United States faced hard times.

- Depression-era culture helped lift people's spirits.

- The New Deal had lasting effects on American society.

Key Terms and People

Dust Bowl
Mary McLeod Bethune
John Steinbeck
Woody Guthrie

If YOU were there . . .

You own a wheat farm on the Great Plains, where you and your family live and work. Wheat prices have been low for years, and you have managed to get by only by borrowing thousands of dollars. Now the region is suffering through a terrible drought. Without water, you have been unable to grow any wheat at all. But if you do not start paying your debts, you will lose your farm.

Would you stay on your farm or leave and start a new life somewhere else?

The Dust Bowl

For American farmers, hard times began well before the start of the Great Depression. Despite the widespread prosperity of the 1920s, prices for farm products remained low. Many farmers went into debt or lost their farms. The Depression worsened this already bad situation. Conditions worsened again when a severe drought hit the Great Plains in the early 1930s and lasted most of the decade. From North Dakota to Texas, crops withered away. With no roots to hold it in place, topsoil began to blow away.

Massive dust storms swept the region, turning parts of the Great Plains into the **Dust Bowl**. "These storms were like rolling black smoke," recalled one Texas schoolboy. "We had to keep the lights on all day. We went to school with the headlights on, and with dust masks on." A woman from Kansas remembered dust storms "covering everything—including ourselves—in a thick, brownish gray blanket . . . Our faces were as dirty as if we had rolled in the dirt; our hair was gray and stiff and we ground dirt between our teeth."

Unable to raise crops, farmers in the Dust Bowl region could not pay their mortgages. Many lost their farms. Several New Deal programs tried to assist farmers by offering loans and by working to stabilize prices for farm products. Scientists also began thinking of ways to prevent dust storms during future droughts. Soil

The Dust Bowl

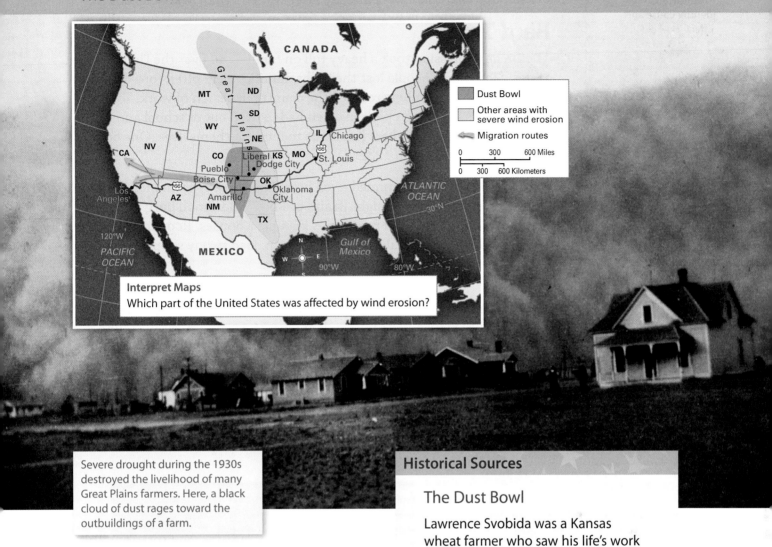

CANADA

Dust Bowl
Other areas with severe wind erosion
Migration routes

0 300 600 Miles
0 300 600 Kilometers

Interpret Maps
Which part of the United States was affected by wind erosion?

Severe drought during the 1930s destroyed the livelihood of many Great Plains farmers. Here, a black cloud of dust rages toward the outbuildings of a farm.

conservation experts encouraged farmers to adopt new farming methods to protect the soil. Grass was planted to hold soil in place, and rows of trees were planted to help break the wind. These changes have helped prevent another Dust Bowl in the years since the Great Depression.

For many farmers in the 1930s, however, the new programs came too late. After losing their crops and livestock to dust storms, about 2.5 million people left the area. Many packed up whatever they could fit in the family car or truck and drove to

Historical Sources

The Dust Bowl

Lawrence Svobida was a Kansas wheat farmer who saw his life's work destroyed in the 1930s.

"When I knew that my crop was irrevocably [forever] gone I experienced a deathly feeling which, I hope, can affect a man only once in a lifetime. My dreams and ambitions . . . and my shattered ideals seemed gone forever. The very desire to make a success of my life was gone, the spirit and urge to strive were dead within me. Fate had dealt me a cruel blow above which I felt utterly unable to rise."

Analyze Historical Sources
How did Svobida feel after his crop was destroyed?

California to look for any kind of work they could find. Once there, they often found that there were already more workers than available jobs.

Hard Times

The Great Depression took a heavy toll on families all over the United States. Since many people lost their jobs, families were often forced to split up, as individual members roamed the country in search of work. To help their families buy food, children often had to drop out of school and take very low-paying jobs. Others left home to fend for themselves. One boy wrote this diary entry in 1932:

> "Slept in paper box. Bummed swell breakfast three eggs and four pieces meat . . . Rode freight [train] to Roessville. Small burg [town], but got dinner. Walked Bronson . . . Couple a houses. Rode to Sidell . . . Hit homes for meals and turned down. Had to buy supper 20 cents. Raining."
> —Anonymous, quoted in *The Great Depression*, by Thomas Minehan

The Great Depression was especially hard on minority groups. As white families moved West in search of jobs, Mexican Americans found it harder to get work. In California local leaders and unions convinced the government to deport many Mexican-born workers. Some of the workers' children were American-born, which made them U.S. citizens, but they were deported anyway.

DOCUMENT-BASED INVESTIGATION   Historical Sources

Migrant Mother

Photographer Dorothea Lange gained fame in the 1930s for documenting the conditions of the poor during the Depression. Lange took this famous photograph of a widowed migrant worker and two of her seven children. The woman worked in the pea fields of Nipomo, California. Her family survived by eating frozen peas and birds the children caught. The woman had just sold her car's tires for money to buy food.

Analyze Historical Sources
How would you describe the expression on the face of the woman in the photograph?

African Americans also faced discrimination. Many lost jobs to unemployed white workers. By 1932 unemployment had reached 50 percent in the African American neighborhood of Harlem in New York City. One man recalled traveling around Michigan in search of work. He went into a factory that was hiring workers:

> "They didn't hire me because I didn't belong to the right kind of race. Another time I went into Saginaw, it was two white fellas and myself made three. The fella there hired the two men and didn't hire me. I was back out on the streets. That hurt me pretty bad, the race part."
> —Louis Banks, quoted in *Hard Times: An Oral History of the Great Depression*, by Studs Terkel

Marian Anderson singing at the Lincoln Memorial in Washington, DC, in 1939

In spite of this type of discrimination, hundreds of thousands of African Americans were able to find work through relief programs such as the CCC and WPA. President Roosevelt also consulted with African American leaders, including educator **Mary McLeod Bethune**. Bethune was one of several African Americans who Roosevelt appointed to his administration. Other members included Walter White, Robert C. Weaver, and William Henry Hastie. These advisers became known as the Black Cabinet. Their role was to advance the concerns of African Americans in the Roosevelt White House. They stood out as a powerful symbol of rising African American influence in government.

First Lady Eleanor Roosevelt was a strong supporter of equal rights. She encouraged the president to include African Americans in his recovery programs. In 1939 the Daughters of the American Revolution (DAR) refused to rent their auditorium to the African American opera singer Marian Anderson. In protest, Eleanor Roosevelt resigned her membership in the DAR. She then helped Anderson arrange a concert at the base of the Lincoln Memorial. Some 75,000 people attended. Millions more heard the national radio broadcast of the concert. Anderson later gave a private performance at the White House.

Reading Check
Draw Inferences
What weakened families during the Depression?

Depression-Era Culture

Starting in 1935, new Works Progress Administration projects began to put the country's painters, sculptors, writers, and actors to work. When he was criticized for hiring artists, WPA director Henry Hopkins said, "They've got to eat just like other people."

Some of the work done by WPA artists has become an important part of American culture. For example, WPA musicians went into the nation's rural areas to record cowboy ballads, folk songs, and African American spirituals. This music might have been lost without these recordings. Artists employed by the WPA made more than 2,500 murals and 17,000 pieces of sculpture for public spaces. WPA writers created a permanent record of American life by interviewing Americans of many different backgrounds about their lives and memories. Today many of the thousands of interviews conducted by WPA writers are available on the Internet. You can read the stories of former slaves, pioneers, Native American leaders, and others in their own words.

Escape to the Movies

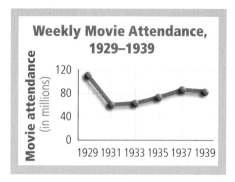

Weekly Movie Attendance, 1929–1939

Movie attendance (in millions)

120
80
40
0

1929 1931 1933 1935 1937 1939

Analyze Information
How many Americans attended movies in 1931?

The movies of child-star Shirley Temple, "America's Little Darling," were among Hollywood's top moneymakers in the late 1930s.

Like many people at the time, author **John Steinbeck** was deeply affected by the Great Depression. Depression life became a main theme of Steinbeck's most famous novel, *The Grapes of Wrath*. The novel tells the story of the Joads, a family of farmers who are forced to move to California for work.

Some of the music of the day expressed themes similar to Steinbeck's. Oklahoma-born folk singer **Woody Guthrie** crisscrossed the country singing his songs of loss and struggle. One contained the line, "All along your green valley I'll work till I die"—a grim reality for some Americans.

Swing music, meanwhile, became popular for a different reason. Instead of focusing on the sadness of the Depression, swing helped people forget their troubles. Big-band leaders such as Duke Ellington, Benny Goodman, and Count Basie helped make swing wildly popular in the 1930s. People tuned into swing-music shows on inexpensive radios and danced to the fast-paced rhythms. Radios provided people with other forms of entertainment as well. Every week millions of Americans put aside their worries to listen to radio shows such as *Little Orphan Annie* and *The Lone Ranger*.

Movies offered Americans another welcome escape from reality. One boy remembered how he and his friends would save their pennies for movie tickets. "[It] was two for a nickel," he said. "You'd come to the movie in the summer like 8:30 in the mornin' and you'd see about 200 kids." For 25 cents or less, adults, too, could forget their troubles as they watched historical dramas, gangster films, comedies, and musicals.

Reading Check
Evaluate How was the work of writers and musicians affected by the Great Depression?

Causes and Effects of the New Deal

Causes
- Stock market crash
- Banking crisis
- Soaring unemployment
- Farmers' troubles
- Widespread poverty

Effects
- Expanded role of federal government
- Created major programs such as Social Security and the FDIC
- Provided hope and relief to many Americans but did not end the Great Depression

Effects of the New Deal

People are still debating the effects of the New Deal today. New Deal critics point out that Roosevelt's programs did not end the Great Depression. Full recovery occurred in the early 1940s, after the United States entered World War II. Roosevelt's supporters, however, believe that the New Deal gave Americans help and hope in a time of severe economic crisis.

People today do agree that the New Deal greatly expanded the role of the federal government. Some of the programs and agencies created as part of the New Deal, such as Social Security and the Federal Deposit Insurance Corporation (FDIC), remain part of our lives. Social Security still provides economic relief to the elderly, children, and those with disabilities. The FDIC protects the savings of bank customers.

Summary and Preview The New Deal helped Americans but did not end the Great Depression. The Depression finally ended after the United States entered World War II, which you will learn about in the next module.

Reading Check
Find the Main Idea
What are some current government programs that began during the New Deal?

Lesson 3 Assessment

Review Ideas, Terms, and People

1. **a. Identify** What was the Dust Bowl?

   b. Explain What factors contributed to farmers' difficulties in the 1920s and 1930s?

2. **a. Recall** What were some of the problems people faced during the Depression?

   b. Compare How was the experience of African Americans and Mexican Americans in the Depression similar?

   c. Evaluate Do you think President Roosevelt did enough to help African Americans? Explain your answer.

3. **a. Draw Conclusions** Why do you think swing music, radio shows, and movies were popular during the Great Depression?

   b. Identify How did the WPA help the arts?

4. **a. Recall** What are the different viewpoints on the success of the New Deal?

   b. Identify How did the New Deal change the involvement of the federal government in the economy?

   c. Elaborate How are Social Security and the FDIC still important today?

Critical Thinking

5. **Categorize** In this lesson you learned about life during the Great Depression. Create a chart similar to the one below and use it to identify challenges people faced during the Depression and the ways they coped.

Challenges people faced	Ways people coped with challenges

Literature in History

Depression-Era Literature

Word Help

migrant a person who moves regularly

Divide The Continental Divide separates rivers that flow east from those that flow west.

tributary a stream that feeds into a larger river or lake (Steinbeck applies the word to the road system.)

❶ *From what are people on Highway 66 fleeing?*

❷ *How does Steinbeck describe what people are running from?*

About the Reading Published in 1939, *The Grapes of Wrath* described the impact of the Great Depression on the nation. In this passage, John Steinbeck describes a journey of Dust Bowl families to California.

As You Read Look for details that appeal to the five senses.

From *The Grapes of Wrath*
by John Steinbeck (1902–1968)

Highway 66 is the main migrant road. 66—the long, concrete path across the country, waving gently up and down the map, from the Mississippi [River] to Bakersfield [California]—over the red lands and the gray lands, twisting up into the mountains, crossing the Divide and down into the bright and terrible desert to the mountains again, and into the rich California valleys.

66 is the path of people in flight, ❶ refugees from dust and shrinking land, from the thunder of tractors and shrinking ownership, from the desert's slow northward invasion, from the twisting winds that howl up out of Texas, from the floods that bring no richness to the land and steal what little richness is there. ❷ From all of these the people are in flight, and they come into 66 from the tributary side roads, from the wagon tracks and the rutted country roads. 66 is the mother road, the road of flight.

Connect Literature to History

1. **Analyze** According to this passage, why might driving between towns be a terror? What does this tell you about the migrants?

2. **Draw Conclusions** Based on Steinbeck's description and on what you already know, how might people traveling on Route 66 have felt? Why?

Social Studies Skills

Conduct a Debate

Define the Skill

The First Amendment to the U.S. Constitution guarantees freedom of speech, assembly, and the press. These freedoms have become a key part of American democracy. They guarantee that both government officials and citizens can express their opinions. People also have the right to express disagreement with leaders or the government.

The ability to discuss opposing points of view is key to a democratic society. In the United States, citizens vote for their leaders. Having access to different points of view helps people decide which candidates to support in elections.

One way to express opposing points of view is to have a debate. Debates are organized to present two sides of an issue. Debate rules make sure that both sides are treated fairly. By learning about the strengths and weaknesses of two positions on an issue, people can decide which position is more convincing.

Learn the Skill

Think about the opposition President Franklin D. Roosevelt faced when he tried to begin new programs during the Great Depression. He had to convince people to support his ideas. Roosevelt and members of his administration used radio programs and newspaper articles to promote their point of view and answer questions from their critics.

In a debate, it is important to make your point of view clear. Explain why you support a certain position or give specific reasons why you oppose it. The more detailed the argument, the more persuasive it will be. When you are in a debate, make sure to prepare plenty of evidence and examples to support your case.

Debaters have the chance not only to present a case but also to argue against the opposite point of view. One way to get ready for this is to think of possible arguments against your position. Prepare responses to each of these arguments in advance. Having good answers to criticism makes your position stronger.

In a debate, it is important to follow any rules that have been set up. Not all debates have the same rules. They do share some basic guidelines, however. Only one person is allowed to speak at once, and speaking time is limited. The two sides take turns presenting their arguments. Debates may have additional rules as well.

Practice the Skill

Suppose that your class is the Senate in 1933. President Roosevelt has already begun several new government programs. Now he is asking you to pass more new laws, which he believes will help the economy. Follow the guidelines above to have a debate about the New Deal. One group should support expanding the New Deal, and one group should oppose it. When the debate is over, answer the following questions.

1. Did your group make its point of view clear? Did it explain the reasons for taking that position? What do you think was your group's most persuasive supporting detail or example?

2. Did your group prepare arguments against the other side in advance? Were any of these arguments particularly effective?

Module 10 Assessment

Review Vocabulary, Terms, and People

Read each question and write the letter of the best response.

1. Which of the following refers to a severe economic downturn that lasted for more than ten years?
   a. the Bonus Army
   b. the Great Depression
   c. the bull market
   d. the business cycle

2. Who was Franklin Roosevelt's secretary of labor and the first woman cabinet member?
   a. Frances Perkins
   b. Mary McLeod Bethune
   c. Eleanor Roosevelt
   d. Dorothea Lange

3. Parts of the Great Plains where a severe drought struck were known as the
   a. Tennessee Valley.
   b. New Deal.
   c. Dust Bowl.
   d. Hoovervilles.

4. Which of the following means purchasing stocks on credit with a loan?
   a. the installment plan
   b. buying on margin
   c. the banking crisis
   d. bear market

Comprehension and Critical Thinking

Lesson 1

5. a. **Describe** What happened on Black Tuesday—October 29, 1929?
   b. **Summarize** How did President Hoover respond to the Depression?
   c. **Elaborate** Why do you think Americans were so unprepared for difficult times?

Lesson 2

6. a. **Recall** What New Deal programs did lawmakers create during the Hundred Days?
   b. **Explain** How did the Works Progress Administration help Americans?
   c. **Evaluate** Do you think the New Deal was successful? Explain your answer.

Lesson 3

7. a. **Recall** How did the Great Depression affect Mexican Americans?
   b. **Contrast** How did Depression-era culture show both hope and the difficulties of everyday life?
   c. **Draw Conclusions** Why do you think many African Americans supported President Roosevelt, even though they continued to face discrimination and segregation?

Module 10 Assessment, continued

Review Themes

8. **Economics** How did the economy of the country change during the Great Depression?

9. **Politics** What role did politics play in easing the Great Depression?

Reading Skills

Recognize Implied Main Ideas *Use the Reading Skills taught in this module to complete the activity about the reading selection below.*

> Banks had invested heavily in the stock market, so they lost heavily when the market crashed. Banks had also lent their customers money to buy stocks on margin. Now those customers were unable to pay back their loans. Some banks went out of business. People who had deposited their life savings in those banks lost everything.

10. Write a main idea for the paragraph above.

Social Studies Skills

Conduct a Debate *Use the Social Studies Skills taught in this module to complete the activity below.*

11. Suppose you have been invited to participate in a debate on Franklin Roosevelt's plan to "pack" the Supreme Court by adding extra justices. First decide on your position. Then prepare several supporting arguments. Summarize the main points of your arguments in a paragraph.

Focus on Writing

12. **Write a Journal Entry** Think about what it was like to live during the Great Depression and how it affected the everyday lives, feelings, and thoughts of people. Then create a fictional character who lived during the Depression. Decide on the age of your character and a set of circumstances for your character. Choose one event from the Great Depression for your character to write about in a one-page journal entry. Include in your entry what your character's feelings and thoughts are about that event and about living during the Great Depression. Also include what your character's hopes and fears are for the future. Begin by placing a date from the 1930s at the top of the page.

Module 11

World War II

★

Essential Question

How did World War II impact the lives of Americans and the nation's role in the world?

About the Photo: The D-Day invasion at Normandy, France, was one of the most successful Allied invasions of the war.

In this module you will read about U.S. involvement in World War II. You will also learn about how this involvement changed the society and economy of the United States.

▶ *Explore ONLINE!*

HISTORY.

VIDEOS, including...
- D-Day Invasion of Europe
- Winston Churchill
- U.S. Victory at the Battle of Midway

✓ Document-Based Investigations

✓ Graphic Organizers

✓ Interactive Games

✓ Interactive Map: World War II in Europe, 1942–1945

✓ Interactive Map: War in the Pacific, 1942–1945

✓ Image with Hotspots: Navaho Code Talkers

What You Will Learn . . .

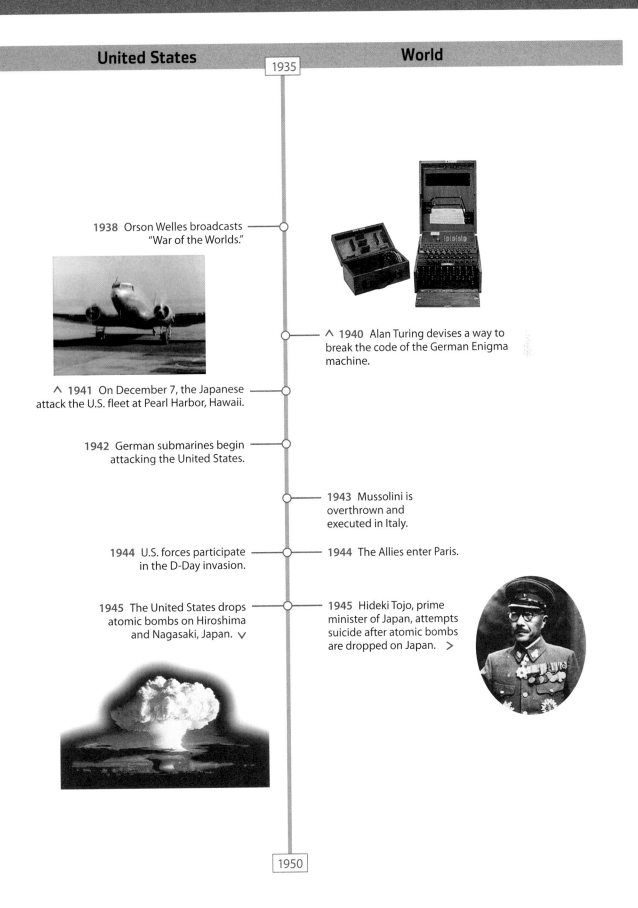

United States		World
	1935	

1938 Orson Welles broadcasts "War of the Worlds."

∧ **1940** Alan Turing devises a way to break the code of the German Enigma machine.

∧ **1941** On December 7, the Japanese attack the U.S. fleet at Pearl Harbor, Hawaii.

1942 German submarines begin attacking the United States.

1943 Mussolini is overthrown and executed in Italy.

1944 U.S. forces participate in the D-Day invasion.

1944 The Allies enter Paris.

1945 The United States drops atomic bombs on Hiroshima and Nagasaki, Japan. ∨

1945 Hideki Tojo, prime minister of Japan, attempts suicide after atomic bombs are dropped on Japan. >

1950

Reading Social Studies

THEME FOCUS:

Geography, Society and Culture

In this module you will read about the causes and consequences of World War II. You will learn about how geography played an important role in the fighting of the war. You will also read about how society and culture reacted to the Second World War.

READING FOCUS:

Categorize

Have you ever read a schoolbook and been overwhelmed by the amount of information it contained? Categorizing events, people, and ideas can help you make sense of the facts you learn in this book.

Understand Categorizing Ideas, people, events, and things can all be categorized in many different ways. For the study of history, some of the most useful ways are by time period and by similarity between events. Categorizing events by the people involved can also be helpful. Within a category, you can make subcategories to further organize the information.

People Involved in WWII	Events of WWII
• Winston Churchill • Franklin D. Roosevelt • Adolf Hitler • Benito Mussolini • Hideki Tojo • Soldiers • Civilians	• Key battles • Treaties • Invasions ↓ **Invasions** • China • Rhineland • Czechoslovakia • Poland • Dunkirk • French Indochina • D-Day

You Try It!

The following passage is from the module you are getting ready to read. As you read the passage, look for ways to organize the information.

> **Japan Advances** American and Filipino forces under the command of American general Douglas MacArthur could not stop Japan's advance in the Philippines. MacArthur left the islands in March 1942, vowing to return. More than 70,000 American and Filipino soldiers surrendered to the Japanese. The atrocities that followed were clear violations of human rights. The exhausted soldiers were forced to march 63 miles up the Bataan Peninsula to prison camps. Many prisoners were starved and beaten by Japanese soldiers. More than 600 Americans and about 10,000 Filipinos died in the Bataan Death March.

After you read the passage, answer the following questions.

1. What are two categories you could use to organize the information in this passage?
2. How many different kinds of people are mentioned in this passage?
3. What different places are mentioned in this passage?
4. Complete the chart below using the information from the passage above.

People involved	Countries involved	Places mentioned

As you read Module 11, remember to look for categories that can help you organize the information you read.

Key Terms and People

Lesson 1
totalitarianism
Benito Mussolini
fascism
Adolf Hitler
Nazis
Joseph Stalin
Axis Powers
appeasement
Winston Churchill
Allied Powers
Lend-Lease Act
Pearl Harbor

Lesson 2
War Production Board
A. Philip Randolph
Tuskegee Airmen
Benjamin O. Davis Jr.
zoot-suit riots
internment

Lesson 3
Battle of El Alamein
Dwight D. Eisenhower
Battle of Stalingrad
D-Day

Lesson 4
Douglas MacArthur
Bataan Death March
Chester Nimitz
Battle of the Coral Sea
Battle of Midway
island hopping
Battle of Leyte Gulf
kamikaze

Lesson 5
Battle of the Bulge
Harry S. Truman
Holocaust
genocide
Manhattan Project
atomic bomb

The War Begins

If YOU were there . . .

The year is 1933, and your family is struggling through the Great Depression along with millions of others. Sometimes your parents wonder if they should have left Italy to come to the United States. But conditions in Italy are far from ideal. A dictator rules the country, and the people have little personal freedom.

What would you say to your parents?

The Rise of Totalitarianism

Desperate to end the hard times, many people were willing to give up their individual rights to leaders who promised to deliver prosperity and national glory. As a result, in the 1920s and 1930s, several European countries moved toward **totalitarianism**, a political system in which the government controls every aspect of citizens' lives. These governments were inspired by militant nationalism to expand their territory and power.

Italy In the years after World War I, the people of Italy suffered through economic depression, unemployment, strikes, and riots. Many Italians looked for a strong leader who could bring stability to the country. They found such a leader in **Benito Mussolini**, who gained complete control of Italy in 1922. Mussolini's rule was based on **fascism**, a political system in which the "state"—or government—is seen as more important than individuals. Fascist systems are typically militaristic and headed by a strong leader.

Mussolini restored order to Italy and improved the economy through public works projects. But the fascist government violently crushed all opposition, destroying basic individual rights such as freedom of speech. In 1935 Mussolini tried to expand Italy's territory by attacking the nation of Ethiopia, making it a colony. Haile Selassie, Ethiopia's overthrown emperor, warned the world, "It is us today. It will be you tomorrow."

Germany Germany was also suffering the effects of the global depression. In addition, many Germans were furious about the Treaty of Versailles, which forced Germany to make crippling reparation payments for its role in World War I. Politician, World War I veteran, and militant nationalist **Adolf Hitler** took advantage of public anger to gain power. A fiery speaker, he inspired huge audiences by vowing to restore Germany to prosperity and a position of international power.

Hitler also offered Germans a scapegoat, or someone to blame for their problems. He accused intellectuals, Communists, and especially Jews of causing Germany's defeat in World War I and its economic problems after the war. Only by ridding itself of Jews, Hitler declared, would Germany again rise to greatness. Hitler's National Socialist Party, or **Nazis**, gained a large following. Hitler became chancellor in 1933 and quickly seized all government power.

The Soviet Union Hitler spoke with fury of his hatred of communism. But he had something in common with the Communist ruler of the Soviet Union—both ruled as ruthless dictators. By 1928 **Joseph Stalin** had become dictator of the Soviet Union. In the 1930s Stalin terrorized those he saw as political enemies, killing or imprisoning millions of Soviet citizens. As one Soviet artist put it, "There isn't a single thinking adult in this country who hasn't thought that he might get shot."

The Third Reich

Hitler gained much of his power through the use of propaganda. Films and photographs like the one shown here showed Hitler and the Nazi Party as the best leaders for Germany. The propaganda often ignored or lied about aspects Hitler wanted hidden from the public.

How did propaganda help Hitler rise to power?

Japan Though Japan never had one single dictator, a group of nationalist military leaders slowly gained complete control over the government during the early 1900s. By the early 1930s this group had more influence than the Japanese emperor. The military leaders wanted to build a large Japanese empire in East Asia. In 1931 Japan invaded and conquered a region in northern China and called it Manchukuo. China's capital, Nanjing, was the site of massacres that claimed up to 300,000 Chinese victims. (Between 1937 and 1945 Japan's invasion of China would cost some 20 million lives.) The United States protested the invasion. Fearful of another world war, however, most Americans opposed using force to help China. The League of Nations also condemned Japan for the attack but was unable to take forceful action.

Germany Expands

Hitler dreamed of avenging Germany's defeat in World War I. "The lost land will never be won back by solemn appeals to God," he told Germans, "nor by hopes in any League of Nations, but only by force of arms." Hitler wanted to build an empire, uniting all German-speaking people in Europe. He also wanted "living space" for the growing German population.

In violation of the Treaty of Versailles, Hitler began to rebuild the German military. In 1936 Nazi troops invaded the Rhineland, a former German territory lost during World War I. That year he also signed an alliance with Mussolini, forming the **Axis Powers**. Japan later joined this pact. In 1938 Hitler forced Austria to unite with Germany. Then he demanded control of the Sudetenland, a region in Czechoslovakia where many Germans lived. When the Czechs refused, Hitler threatened war.

Appeasement Fails Czech leaders looked to their allies in France and Great Britain for help. But neither country wanted to be pulled into an armed conflict. British prime minister Neville Chamberlain organized a meeting with Hitler to work out a peaceful solution. At the 1938 Munich Conference, Germany was given control over the Sudetenland in return for a promise not to demand more land. This approach was known as **appeasement**—a policy of avoiding war with an aggressive nation by giving in to its demands. British admiral **Winston Churchill** was convinced that this strategy would not stop Hitler. "The government had to choose between shame and war," Churchill warned. "They have chosen shame. They will get war."

Churchill was right. In March 1939 German troops seized the rest of Czechoslovakia and began demanding territory from Poland. Great Britain and France pledged to defend Poland if Hitler attacked. To keep the Soviets out of the conflict, Hitler signed a nonaggression pact with Joseph Stalin in August 1939. In addition to promising not to attack each other, the two countries secretly agreed to divide Poland between them.

On September 1, 1939, Hitler's troops and tanks rushed into Poland. This was the start of World War II. Two days later, Britain and France, known as the **Allied Powers**, declared war on Germany. Neville

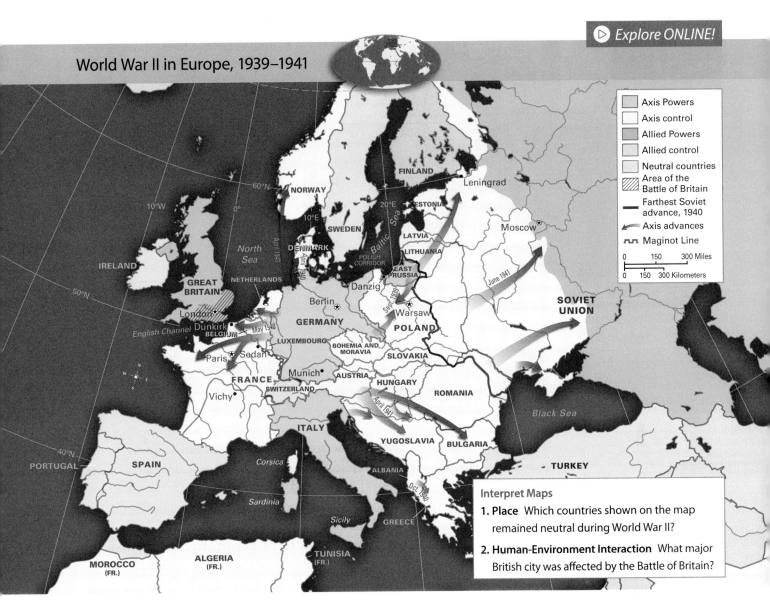

World War II in Europe, 1939–1941

Axis Powers
Axis control
Allied Powers
Allied control
Neutral countries
Area of the Battle of Britain
Farthest Soviet advance, 1940
Axis advances
Maginot Line

0   150   300 Miles
0   150   300 Kilometers

FINLAND
NORWAY
SWEDEN
DENMARK
Baltic Sea
North Sea
IRELAND
GREAT BRITAIN
London
English Channel
Dunkirk
BELGIUM
Paris
Sedan
FRANCE
Vichy
SWITZERLAND
LUXEMBOURG
GERMANY
Berlin
Munich
AUSTRIA
HUNGARY
POLISH CORRIDOR
EAST PRUSSIA
Danzig
Warsaw
POLAND
BOHEMIA AND MORAVIA
SLOVAKIA
ESTONIA
LATVIA
LITHUANIA
Leningrad
Moscow
SOVIET UNION
ROMANIA
Black Sea
ITALY
YUGOSLAVIA
BULGARIA
ALBANIA
GREECE
TURKEY
Corsica
Sardinia
Sicily
PORTUGAL
SPAIN
MOROCCO (FR.)
ALGERIA (FR.)
TUNISIA (FR.)

April 1940
May 1940
Sept. 1939
June 1941
April 1941
Oct. 1940

Interpret Maps

1. **Place** Which countries shown on the map remained neutral during World War II?

2. **Human-Environment Interaction** What major British city was affected by the Battle of Britain?

Chamberlain spoke bitterly of the failure of appeasement, saying, "Everything that I believed in during my public life has crashed into ruins."

Hitler Moves West The Allied Powers had little time to organize their forces to protect Poland. Using a strategy called *blitzkrieg*, or "lightning war," German tanks and airplanes broke through Polish defenses. As German forces drove into Poland from the west, the Soviets attacked from the east. Within a month, the two powers had taken control of Poland.

With Poland secure, Hitler turned toward western Europe. In the spring of 1940, Germany quickly conquered the countries of Denmark, Norway, Belgium, Luxembourg, and the Netherlands. German troops then invaded France, trapping hundreds of thousands of Belgian, British, and French soldiers in the French port city of Dunkirk. British ships and boats of all kinds raced to Dunkirk and carried the soldiers across the English Channel to safety in Britain.

German forces, meanwhile, continued their march through France. As the Germans approached the French capital of Paris, Italy declared war on the Allied Powers. France surrendered to Germany on June 22, 1940.

Nazi planes bombed London from September 1940 to May 1941. During that time, residents of London sought shelter wherever they could, including subway stations. Here, a merchant is open for business after a bombing raid.

Many of the French soldiers who had escaped at Dunkirk, however, continued to resist Germany's occupation of France. In London, French general Charles de Gaulle organized a "Free French" army to fight alongside the Allies. "France has lost a battle," de Gaulle declared, "but France has not lost the war!"

The Battle of Britain Britain now stood alone against Hitler's war machine. "The final German victory over England is now only a question of time," said German general Alfred Jodl. Hitler prepared to invade Britain. To move troops and equipment across the English Channel, Germany first had to defeat the British Royal Air Force (RAF). In July 1940 the Luftwaffe, or German air force, began attacking British planes and airfields in what became known as the Battle of Britain.

In August Hitler ordered the Luftwaffe to begin bombing British cities in the hope of crushing British morale. But Winston Churchill, the new prime minister, refused to give in. "We shall fight on the beaches," he vowed. "We shall fight in the fields and in the streets, we shall never surrender." Using the new technology of radar, the RAF was able to detect and destroy some 2,300 of the Luftwaffe's aircraft. Hitler canceled the invasion of Britain.

The United States Joins the War

Most Americans opposed Hitler's actions, but they did not want to join the war. When President Franklin Roosevelt ran for re-election in 1940, he told voters that "your boys are not going to be sent into any foreign wars." Privately, however, Roosevelt was convinced that the United States would soon be at war.

Helping the Allies In 1941 Roosevelt proposed new programs to assist the Allies. "We must be the great arsenal [arms supply] of democracy," he told Congress. In March 1941 Congress passed the **Lend-Lease Act**, allowing the president to aid any nation believed vital to U.S. defense. Under Lend-Lease, the United States sent billions of dollars' worth of aid in the form of weapons, tanks, airplanes, and food to Britain, the Nationalists in

Reading Check
Sequence What event sparked World War II?

China, and other Allied countries. In June 1941 Hitler violated his nonaggression pact with Stalin and invaded the Soviet Union. The Soviets then joined the Allies in the fight against Germany. In November the United States extended the Lend-Lease program to the Soviet Union, though many Americans worried about giving aid to a Communist country.

Japan Attacks Pearl Harbor Like Germany and Italy, Japan was quickly building an empire. After conquering much of China in the 1930s, Japanese forces moved into Southeast Asia. Japan's leaders wanted control of oil and other resources there.

When Japanese forces captured French Indochina in July 1941, Roosevelt protested. He demanded that Japan withdraw. Then the United States froze Japanese funds in its banks and cut off exports to Japan.

Japanese military leaders had already begun planning a large-scale attack to destroy the U.S. naval fleet stationed at **Pearl Harbor**, in Hawaii. This would give Japan time to secure control of East Asia before the U.S. military could respond.

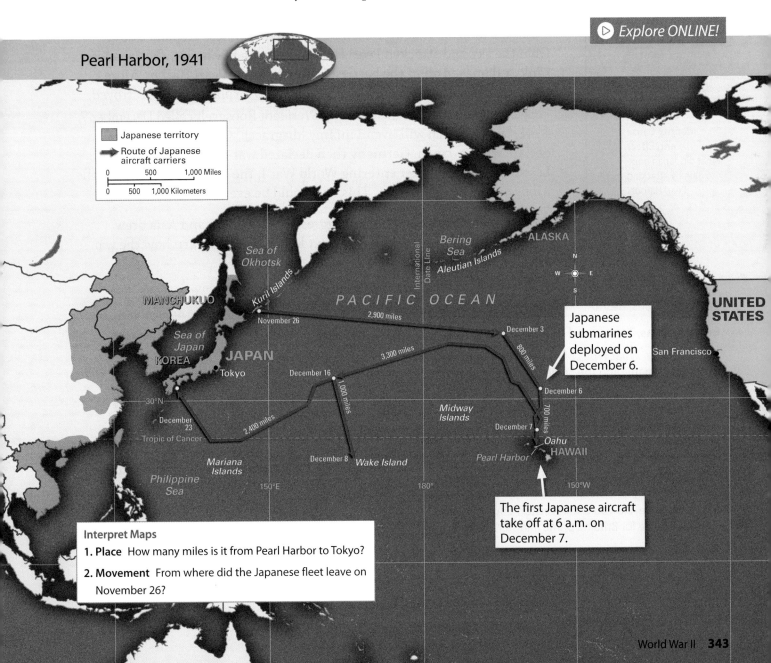

▷ *Explore ONLINE!*

Pearl Harbor, 1941

Japanese territory

Route of Japanese aircraft carriers

0   500   1,000 Miles

0   500   1,000 Kilometers

Sea of Okhotsk

Kuril Islands

MANCHUKUO

November 26

Bering Sea

Aleutian Islands

International Date Line

ALASKA

PACIFIC OCEAN

2,900 miles

December 3

UNITED STATES

Sea of Japan

KOREA

JAPAN

Tokyo

December 16

3,300 miles

1,000 miles

800 miles

Japanese submarines deployed on December 6.

San Francisco

December 6

30°N

December 23

2,400 miles

Tropic of Cancer

Midway Islands

December 7

700 miles

December 8

Wake Island

Oahu

Pearl Harbor

HAWAII

Mariana Islands

150°E

180°

150°W

Philippine Sea

The first Japanese aircraft take off at 6 a.m. on December 7.

Interpret Maps

1. **Place** How many miles is it from Pearl Harbor to Tokyo?

2. **Movement** From where did the Japanese fleet leave on November 26?

Japanese forces bombarded the American naval fleet for several hours in the attack on Pearl Harbor. Eighteen ships were hit, and more than 2,400 Americans were killed.

At 7:55 a.m. on Sunday, December 7, 1941, Japanese airplanes dove from the sky and attacked Pearl Harbor. In just a few hours, the Japanese sank or damaged all of the battleships anchored at Pearl Harbor. More than 2,400 Americans were killed. Almost 200 airplanes were destroyed.

Speaking to Congress the next day, President Roosevelt called December 7, 1941, "a date which will live in infamy [disgrace]." Congress voted to declare war on Japan. Germany then declared war on the United States. Less than 25 years after entering World War I, the United States joined the Allies in another global war. This one would be even more devastating.

Reading Check
Identify Cause and Effect
What did Japan hope to gain by attacking Pearl Harbor?

Summary and Preview Military aggression in Europe and Asia drew the United States into war. In the next lesson you will learn how the war affected the home front.

Lesson 1 Assessment

Review Ideas, Terms, and People

1. a. Identify What types of leaders came to power in Italy, Germany, and the Soviet Union before World War II?

b. Explain Why did some Europeans have faith in these leaders?

2. a. Recall Which countries formed the Axis Powers and the Allied Powers?

b. Summarize What did Adolf Hitler promise the German people, and how did he act on this promise?

c. Elaborate Do you think Winston Churchill was a good choice for Britain's prime minister? Explain your answer.

3. a. Describe How did the Lend-Lease Act help the Allies?

b. Explain What event brought the United States into World War II?

Critical Thinking

4. Identify Cause and Effect In this lesson you learned about totalitarian countries and their leaders prior to World War II. Create a graphic organizer similar to the one below and use it to give details on the causes of World War II.

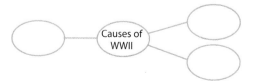

Causes of WWII

The Home Front

The Big Idea

American involvement in World War II helped the U.S. economy and changed the lives of many Americans.

Main Ideas

- Businesses, soldiers, and citizens worked to prepare the United States for war.

- The war brought new opportunities for many women and minorities.

- Japanese Americans faced internment during the war.

Key Terms and People

War Production Board
A. Philip Randolph
Tuskegee Airmen
Benjamin O. Davis Jr.
zoot-suit riots
internment

If YOU were there . . .

Shopping for food has become a whole new experience since the United States entered World War II. When your mother sends you to the grocery store these days, she gives you government-issued ration stamps. These stamps limit the amount of sugar, butter, and meat each family can buy. The sacrifice is difficult, but you know it will help the soldiers fighting overseas.

In what other ways can you help the war effort?

Preparing for War

The United States was still experiencing the effects of the Great Depression when the Japanese attacked Pearl Harbor in December 1941. The enormous effort of mobilizing for war finally brought the Depression to an end. The economy was converted to war production. Factories ran 24 hours a day, producing ships, tanks, jeeps, guns, and ammunition. Americans turned their knowledge of mass production toward the production of war supplies. One remarkable example was the building of Liberty ships—transport vessels for troops and supplies. Workers could build an entire 441-foot-long Liberty ship in as little as four days.

American workers were soon doubling the war production of Germany, Japan, and all other Axis Power countries combined. Unemployment fell to 1 percent in 1944. Agricultural production increased as well, as farmers sent food overseas to feed Allied soldiers. On the home front, one could buy only limited amounts of many foods, from coffee to canned goods. To organize the war effort, the government created the **War Production Board** (WPB) to oversee the conversion of factories to war production. In 1942, for example, the WPB banned the production of cars so that auto plants could produce military equipment. Essential resources, such as rubber for tires and gasoline, were rationed to ensure adequate supplies for military use.

In addition to metal, Americans collected old tires and recycled the rubber to make gas masks, lifeboats, and wheels for military vehicles.

Reading Check
Identify Cause and Effect How did the war affect the U.S. economy?

The United States also needed millions of soldiers. Congress had begun to prepare for war by passing the Selective Training and Service Act in 1940. This was the first peacetime draft in the country's history. Men from the ages of 21 to 35 (later 18 to 38) were required to register for the draft. More than 16 million Americans served during the war.

To finance the war effort, the government increased taxes and sold war bonds. War bonds were essentially loans that people made to the government. People who bought war bonds in 1942, for example, would get their money back ten years later, with interest.

Americans also contributed to the war effort by collecting scrap metal that could be used in weapons factories. People learned to adjust to government rations limiting the supply of gasoline, rubber, shoes, and some foods. Posters urged Americans to "Use it up, wear it out, make it do, or do without."

Wartime Opportunities

You read that wartime production during World War I created new opportunities for many women and minorities. The same thing happened on an even larger scale during World War II.

New Roles for Women With so many men leaving home to fight in World War II, factories badly needed new workers. The government urged women to fill these positions. Women found themselves doing work that had traditionally been considered "unladylike." One female riveter (a person who fastens parts on a machine) recalled her experiences building airplanes:

> "[I] learned to use an electric drill . . . and I soon became an outstanding riveter. . . . The war really created opportunities for women. It was the first time we got a chance to show that we could do a lot of things that only men had done before."
>
> —Winona Espinosa, quoted in "Rosie the Riveter Remembers"
> *American Heritage*, February/March 1984

Women also filled new roles in military service. About 300,000 women served in the armed forces through special divisions such as the Women's Auxiliary Army Corps (WAAC) and Women's Airforce Service Pilots (WASP). WASP pilots flew test flights and ferried planes between factories and air bases. Army and navy nurses served in combat areas.

African Americans The Great Migration continued as African Americans moved to northern cities to find factory jobs. In most cases, however, black workers received lower pay than did white workers. They also were restricted in what kinds of jobs they were hired to perform.

To protest this unfair treatment, African American labor leader **A. Philip Randolph** began to organize a march to Washington, DC, in 1941. "If freedom and equality are not [granted for] the peoples of color, the war for democracy will not be won," he argued. Randolph canceled the march, however, after President Roosevelt issued an order prohibiting racial discrimination in the government and in companies producing war goods.

Supporting the War

Posters like these encouraged Americans to support their troops in a variety of ways. Building weaponry, growing food, saving scrap metal, and rationing all helped the war effort and allowed soldiers to have necessary supplies.

"Rosie the Riveter" became a symbol of women's work to support the war.

Victory gardens planted at home allowed more commercially produced food to be sent from farms to troops overseas.

Analyze Historical Sources
How did posters like these aim to help troops overseas?

About 1 million African Americans served in the armed forces during the war, mostly in segregated units. In the Navy, African Americans were assigned only to support positions and denied the right to participate in combat. Despite this, many black soldiers became national heroes during the war. One was Doris "Dorie" Miller, who displayed great courage during the attack on Pearl Harbor. Leaving his post as ship's cook, Miller manned a machine gun on the deck of the USS *West Virginia* until he was ordered to abandon the ship because it was sinking.

The **Tuskegee Airmen** were African American pilots who trained at the Tuskegee Army Air Field in Alabama. **Benjamin O. Davis Jr.**, who later became the first African American general in the U.S. Air Force, led the group. Davis and his pilots had to overcome prejudice in the military as well as the hazards of war. He later described the pilots as "outstanding Americans who served their country unselfishly. Despite treatment that would have demoralized men of lesser strength and character, they persisted through humiliations and dangers to earn the respect of their fellows." The Tuskegee Airmen flew thousands of successful combat missions in North Africa and Italy.

Mexican Americans About 300,000 Mexican Americans served in the military during the war. Many Mexican Americans also found wartime jobs on the West Coast and in the Midwest. Because of a shortage of farm workers, the federal government asked Mexico to provide agricultural workers. The workers, called *braceros*, were guaranteed a minimum wage, food, shelter, and clean living conditions. About 200,000 Mexicans worked in the *bracero* program.

Tuskegee Airmen

Benjamin O. Davis Jr. was a graduate of West Point who became the first African American Air Force officer to achieve the rank of general. During World War II he led the first African American flying unit, the 99th Fighter Squadron. These men had been trained at the Tuskegee Institute in Alabama.

Analyze Historical Sources
What advantages did the Tuskegee Airmen bring to battle?

"While no AAF [American Air Force] unit had gone into combat better trained or better equipped than the 99th Fighter Squadron, we lacked actual combat experience. So as we approached our first missions, my own inexperience and that of my flight commanders was a major source of concern. On the other hand, we had averaged about 250 hours per man in a P-40 (quite a lot for pilots who had not yet flown their first missions), and we possessed an unusually strong sense of purpose and solidarity."

—Benjamin O. Davis, *Benjamin O. Davis, American: An Autobiography*

Reading Check
Analyze Information
How did the war create both opportunities and challenges for minorities?

Young Mexican Americans of the time created their own culture by blending different music styles and clothing styles. Some men wore zoot suits—fancy, loose-fitting outfits with oversized hats. Despite their aiding of the war effort, many faced discrimination. In Los Angeles in June 1943, groups of sailors attacked Mexican Americans wearing zoot suits, beginning the **zoot-suit riots**. During the ten-day period, white mobs attacked many Mexican Americans.

Struggles at Home

Although members of every race participated in the war as American soldiers, life for minorities at home changed very little. African Americans were still subject to segregation, and Mexican Americans continued to have very little economic opportunity.

Japanese American Internment

Japanese Americans faced a different form of prejudice during World War II. After the Japanese attack on Pearl Harbor, some Americans began to look at Americans of Japanese descent with fear and suspicion. Most Japanese Americans lived on the West Coast at this time. It was feared that they would serve as secret agents for Japan and help Japan prepare an invasion of the West Coast or try to sabotage U.S. war efforts.

The U.S. government had no evidence to support these fears. In spite of this fact, President Roosevelt issued Executive Order 9066. This order allowed the government to begin the process of **internment**, or forced relocation and imprisonment, of Japanese Americans. About 115,000 Japanese Americans were evacuated from their homes and held in isolated internment camps. Half of those held in the camps were children. A smaller number of Americans of German and Italian ancestry were also held in internment camps during the war.

Fred Korematsu, a Japanese American citizen, refused to go to the camps and was arrested as a result. Saying that the internment order was unlawful and racist, Korematsu took his case all the way to the Supreme Court. In *Korematsu* v. *United States* (1944), the Supreme Court ruled against him, arguing that the unusual demands of wartime security justified the order.

At this time, some Japanese Americans were *Issei*, or immigrants born in Japan. But most were *Nisei*, American citizens born in the United States to Japanese immigrant parents. Whether they were U.S. citizens or not, Japanese Americans lost their jobs, homes, and belongings when they were

Japanese Americans

After the attack on Pearl Harbor, Japanese Americans were removed from their communities and ordered into internment camps far away from the West Coast.

Japanese American Internment

Not interned — 6%

Japanese citizens living in America interned — 37%

American citizens of Japanese descent interned — 57%

forced to move to internment camps. A farm owner named Yuri Tateishi spoke of feeling betrayed by his government. "You hurt," he said. "You give up everything that you worked for that far, and I think everybody was at the point of just having gotten out of the Depression and was just getting on his feet. And then all that happens! You have to throw everything away." After the Pearl Harbor attack, the government banned young Japanese American men from serving in the military. But Roosevelt reversed this policy in 1943. Daniel Inouye remembered the excitement he and his fellow Japanese Americans in Hawaii felt when they heard that the government was going to form an all-Nisei combat team. An army recruiter had prepared a pep talk for the young Japanese Americans, but this proved to be unnecessary:

> "As soon as he said that we were now eligible to volunteer, that room exploded into a fury of yells and motion. We went bursting out of there and ran—ran!—the three miles to the draft board . . . jostling for position, like a bunch of marathoners gone berserk."
>
> —Daniel Inouye, from *Journey to Washington*
> by Daniel Inouye and Lawrence Elliott

Inouye was one of about 33,000 Nisei who served in World War II. The Japanese American 100th/442nd Regimental Combat Team received more than 18,000 decorations for bravery—more than any other unit of its size in U.S. military history. Many of the soldiers of the 100th/442nd served while their families were held in internment camps back home.

Summary and Preview The war effort changed life on the home front. In the next lesson you will learn about the fighting in Europe and North Africa.

Reading Check
Analyze
Information
Why were Japanese Americans interned?

Lesson 2 Assessment

Review Ideas, Terms, and People

1. a. **Describe** How did people on the home front support the war effort?

   b. **Identify** What government agency oversaw factory production during the war?

2. a. **Recall** What were the WAAC and the WASP?

   b. **Explain** Why did A. Philip Randolph organize a march on Washington and then cancel it?

   c. **Elaborate** How did the *bracero* program benefit both Mexicans and Americans?

3. a. **Define** What was the internment program?

   b. **Contrast** How did the U.S. government change its policy toward Japanese Americans serving in the military? How did many respond?

Critical Thinking

4. **Categorize** In this lesson you learned about the challenges and opportunities for different groups of people in America during World War II. Create a graphic organizer similar to the one below and use it to list opportunities that women, African Americans, and Mexican Americans found during the war.

Wartime Opportunities

Women	African Americans	Mexican Americans

War in Europe and North Africa

The Big Idea

After fierce fighting in North Africa and Europe, the Allies stopped the German advance and slowly began driving back German forces.

Main Ideas

- The Allies fought back against the Axis Powers in North Africa and Europe.
- Key Allied victories halted the German advance.
- In the D-Day invasion, Allied forces attacked German-controlled France.

Key Terms and People

Battle of El Alamein
Dwight D. Eisenhower
Battle of Stalingrad
D-Day

If YOU were there . . .

The year is 1943, and you are a senior in high school. You know that you will be drafted into the armed forces as soon as you graduate. Every day after school you listen to radio reports about the battles being fought around the world. Your future, and the future of the whole world, seem so uncertain.

How do you feel about fighting in this war?

The Allies Fight Back

In December 1941, soon after the United States entered the war, President Roosevelt met with British prime minister Winston Churchill to work out a plan to defeat the Axis Powers. Roosevelt agreed that the United States would place "Europe first" in its plans to defeat the Axis, while still aiding China in the fight against Japan in the Pacific. In addition, Roosevelt and Churchill agreed on two initial strategies: a buildup of troops in Britain to be used to invade France, and an assault on German forces in North Africa.

Meanwhile, the Soviets had been demanding Allied help on the eastern front, where they had borne the brunt of the European war for months after Hitler's invasion. Stalin wanted the Allies to attack in Europe immediately, to take some of the pressure off of the Soviet forces in the east. In July 1942, however, the Allies decided to put a European invasion on hold and launch an initial offensive in North Africa. Stalin was angry. The Soviets would have to continue to fight the war on the eastern front without a western European assault to distract the Germans.

As they prepared their battle plans, the Allies faced many obstacles. One major threat the Allies had to combat was U-boat attacks. In 1942 alone German U-boats sank more than 6 million tons of Allied materials. To prevent further damage, the Allies used the convoy system of multiple ships traveling at once, along with new sonar technology. Sonar,

The Allies began using sonar to destroy German U-boats, shown here in a German harbor.

Reading Check
Sequence What battle plan did the Allies agree to pursue after U.S. entry into the war?

which uses sound waves to detect objects underwater, helped Allied ships find and destroy German U-boats. In addition, new long-range Allied planes protected the convoys from the air. Long-range planes could also fly into German territory to drop bombs on factories, railroads, and cities, inflicting tremendous damage on German targets.

Halting the German Advance

Churchill predicted that the road to victory would be long and difficult. By winning several key battles, however, Allied forces finally stopped the German advance.

North Africa and Italy As you have read, a main focus for the Allies when the United States entered the war was North Africa. The Germans and British were battling for control there because Axis leaders wanted to grab control of the Suez Canal, a crucial supply route in Egypt. Germany's Afrika Korps was led by General Erwin Rommel, nicknamed the Desert Fox for his bold, surprise attacks.

In the summer of 1942, Rommel began an offensive to take Egypt. General Bernard Montgomery led the British forces to stop the Germans. The British stopped the Afrika Korps in July at the **Battle of El Alamein**. At the same time, U.S. and British troops, led by American general **Dwight D. Eisenhower**, came ashore in Morocco and Algeria, west of Egypt. Caught between two Allied forces, the Afrika Korps surrendered in May 1943.

With North Africa under their control, the Allies prepared to attack the Axis Powers in Europe. Churchill identified Italy as the "soft underbelly" of the Axis. Allied forces invaded the island of Sicily in July 1943 and moved from there to the Italian mainland. Italian leaders overthrew Mussolini and surrendered to the Allies. But Hitler refused to recognize the Axis defeat. He sent German troops to Italy to block the Allied advance.

Major Allied Leaders in Europe

Winston Churchill Prime Minister of Great Britain

Franklin Roosevelt President of the United States

Joseph Stalin Premier of the Soviet Union

Major Axis Leaders in Europe

Adolf Hitler Chancellor of Germany

Benito Mussolini Prime Minister of Italy

In January 1944, Allied forces tried to get behind the Germans with a surprise attack at Anzio, on the western coast of Italy. American and British troops landed at Anzio but were pinned down on the beach for several months. The "soft underbelly" proved to be much tougher than expected. Finally, the Allied forces in southern Italy battled north to Anzio. The combined forces captured Rome, the capital of Italy, in June 1944. Early in 1945, German forces were driven out of Italy. Italian freedom fighters executed Mussolini.

The Battle of Stalingrad Meanwhile, massive German and Soviet armies were battling on the eastern front. By the middle of 1942, Axis armies had driven deep into Soviet territory. Millions of Soviet soldiers had been killed or captured.

German forces then advanced to the key industrial city of Stalingrad, now called Volgograd. German firebombs set much of the city on fire. But Soviet leader Joseph Stalin was determined to hold on to Stalingrad at all costs. At one point in the fighting, the Soviet forces occupied only a small strip of land along the Volga River. Savage street fighting dragged on for months. The city's remaining buildings were destroyed. Soviet snipers used the ruined buildings to their advantage, firing at German soldiers from behind piles of stone and brick.

German supplies began to run desperately low as the harsh Russian winter began. Hitler remained obsessed with capturing Stalingrad,

Tanks thundered across Europe, destroying much of what lay in their paths.

Airplanes dropped millions of bombs on opposing forces. They were also used for moving troops and for spying on the enemy.

however. He ordered his troops to keep fighting, though he did not send enough new supplies or soldiers. Thousands of Germans froze or starved to death. In late January 1943 the German commander at Stalingrad defied Hitler and surrendered to save his remaining troops. The **Battle of Stalingrad** thus became a key turning point of the war.

The Soviet victory came at an enormous cost—more than 1 million Soviet soldiers died at Stalingrad. About 800,000 Axis soldiers were killed. After Stalingrad, the Soviets won another victory in the city of Kursk, in the biggest tank battle ever fought. The Axis Powers now began to retreat from the Soviet Union. The tide of the war in the east had turned.

Reading Check Sequence What events led to the Allied victories in Italy and the Soviet Union?

The D-Day Invasion

After hard-fought victories in North Africa and Italy, the Allies were ready for an even tougher task—the invasion of German-occupied France. This was the first step toward the goal of liberating Europe and forcing Hitler to surrender.

Dwight Eisenhower was in charge of planning what would be the largest sea-to-land invasion ever attempted. Eisenhower knew that German forces were expecting an invasion of France. The Germans had planted mines and stretched barbed wire along the French coastline. Heavily armed German soldiers waited on the beaches in bombproof bunkers. Eisenhower warned his troops of the danger but expressed confidence in their ability to succeed. "The hopes and prayers of liberty-loving people everywhere march with you," he told them.

American, British, and Canadian troops invaded France on June 6, 1944—known as **D-Day**, or "designated day." They crossed the choppy waters of the English Channel and landed on five beaches in Normandy. More than 6,000 ships, 11,000 planes, and 156,000 men were part of the invasion. Soldiers jumped from boats and waded ashore, often under heavy fire.

World War II in Europe, 1942–1945

Legend:
- Axis controlled, June 1944
- Allied controlled, June 1944
- Neutral country
- Farthest Axis advance, 1942
- → Allied advance
- ✦ Major battle
- ✦ Allied air attack

0   150   300 Miles
0   150   300 Kilometers

Map labels:

NORWAY
SWEDEN
FINLAND
Leningrad
DENMARK
North Sea
Baltic Sea
IRELAND
GREAT BRITAIN
London
NETHERLANDS
Antwerp
BELGIUM
Elbe River
Berlin Apr.–May 1945
Oder River
Vistula River
SOVIET UNION
Stalingrad Nov. 1942–Feb. 1943
English Channel
Battle of the Bulge Dec. 1944
D-Day June 1944
Paris
GERMANY
Rhine River
Danube River
SLOVAKIA
HUNGARY
FRANCE
ATLANTIC OCEAN
SWITZERLAND
AUSTRIA
CROATIA
SERBIA
ROMANIA
Black Sea
VICHY FRANCE
AUG. 1944
ITALY
Adriatic Sea
MONTENEGRO
BULGARIA
ALBANIA
PORTUGAL
SPAIN
Corsica
Rome
Anzio Jan. 1944
Sardinia
GREECE
Aegean Sea
TURKEY
GIBRALTAR (BR)
NOV. 1942
SEPT. 1943
Sicily
Malta
JULY 1943
Crete
Mediterranean Sea
SPANISH MOROCCO
MOROCCO
ALGERIA
TUNISIA
El Alamein Oct.–Nov. 1942
EGYPT

Interpret Maps

Location In which country shown on the map did most of the major battles take place?

American soldiers landed on the beaches of Normandy during the D-Day invasion.

Timeline: World War II in Europe, 1942–1945

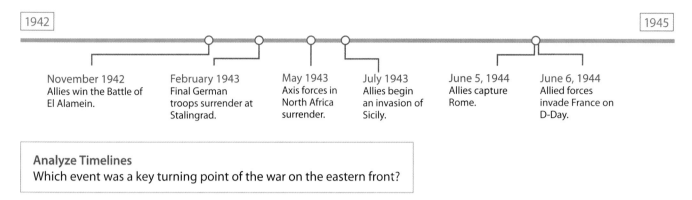

1942

November 1942	February 1943	May 1943	July 1943	June 5, 1944	June 6, 1944
Allies win the Battle of El Alamein.	Final German troops surrender at Stalingrad.	Axis forces in North Africa surrender.	Allies begin an invasion of Sicily.	Allies capture Rome.	Allied forces invade France on D-Day.

1945

Analyze Timelines
Which event was a key turning point of the war on the eastern front?

Reading Check
Summarize
What was the goal of the D-Day invasion?

The Americans landed on two beaches, codenamed Utah and Omaha. Fighting was especially fierce on Omaha Beach, where almost 3,000 men were killed or wounded. "The entire beach was strewn with mines," wrote one U.S. soldier to his wife. "With a stream of lead coming towards us, we were at the mercy of the Germans."

By the end of D-Day, all five beaches were secured. The Allies then began driving east through French villages and countryside toward Germany.

Summary and Preview Allied victories led to the D-Day invasion. In the next lesson you will read about the Pacific war.

Lesson 3 Assessment

Review Ideas, Terms, and People

1. **a. Describe** What new strategies did the Allies use in the fight in Europe and North Africa?

   b. Draw Conclusions Why was it important for no individual Allied Power to make peace with the Axis countries?

2. **a. Recall** What role did Dwight D. Eisenhower play in the North Africa campaign?

   b. Analyze Why did the Allies decide to invade North Africa and Italy?

   c. Evaluate Why is the Battle of Stalingrad often called a turning point in the war?

3. **a. Identify** What was D-Day?

   b. Elaborate What did Eisenhower mean when he said, "The hopes and prayers of liberty-loving people everywhere march with you"?

Critical Thinking

4. **Categorize** In this lesson you learned about the major World War II battles and campaigns in different areas of the world. Create a graphic organizer similar to the one below and use it to explain the significance of each event shown.

Event	Significance
Battle of El Alamein	
Capture of Rome	
Battle of Stalingrad	
D-Day invasion	

War in the Pacific

The Big Idea

Allied forces reversed Japan's expansion in the Pacific and battled toward the main Japanese islands.

Main Ideas

- The Japanese continued advancing across the Pacific in 1942.

- The Allies stopped Japan's advance with key victories over the Japanese navy.

- The Allies began battling toward Japan.

Key Terms and People

Douglas MacArthur
Bataan Death March
Chester Nimitz
Battle of the Coral Sea
Battle of Midway
island hopping
Battle of Leyte Gulf
kamikaze

Reading Check
Identify Cause and Effect Why could the U.S. Pacific Fleet not immediately stop the Japanese advance?

If YOU were there . . .

It is spring of 1945, and your older brother is fighting the Japanese in the Pacific. You've been following the news reports closely, and you know that fighting in the Pacific is terribly fierce. You hear that the Japanese soldiers often refuse to surrender, fighting to the death instead. Your brother reveals in his letters that he is lonely and suffering many hardships. Now you are writing to him.

What would you say to encourage him?

Japan Advances

Japan's attack on Pearl Harbor left the U.S. Pacific Fleet so weakened that it could not immediately respond to the Japanese advance. In addition, President Roosevelt had agreed to concentrate U.S. resources in Europe first. So, while the United States recovered from Pearl Harbor, Japan conquered Thailand, Burma, the British colonies of Hong Kong and Singapore, and the U.S. territories of Guam and Wake Island. The same day as the attack on Pearl Harbor, Japan invaded Hong Kong. British, Canadian, and Indian forces attempting to stop the invasion were outnumbered. Japan attacked the American-controlled Philippines the same day.

American and Filipino forces under the command of American general **Douglas MacArthur** could not stop Japan's advance in the Philippines. MacArthur left the islands in March 1942, vowing to return. More than 70,000 American and Filipino soldiers surrendered to the Japanese. The atrocities that followed were clear violations of human rights. The exhausted soldiers were forced to march 63 miles up the Bataan Peninsula to prison camps. Many prisoners were starved and beaten by Japanese soldiers. More than 600 Americans and about 10,000 Filipinos died in the **Bataan Death March**.

Key Allied Victories

The Allies feared the Japanese might next attack India, Australia, or even the United States mainland. Admiral **Chester Nimitz** led the U.S. Pacific Fleet. Nimitz was determined to stop the Japanese advance, and he had an important advantage—the ability to crack secret Japanese codes.

American code breakers helped the Allies in two key naval battles in the Pacific. Nimitz learned that the Japanese were planning an attack on Port Moresby, New Guinea, an island just north of Australia. If the Japanese took New Guinea, they would have a base from which to invade Australia. In May 1942 Nimitz sent Allied forces to stop the Japanese fleet. American and Japanese aircraft carriers and fighter planes clashed in the **Battle of the Coral Sea**. In this battle both sides used a new kind of strategy. The opposing ships did not fire a single shot. In fact, they often were not in view of each other. Instead, airplanes taking off from the huge aircraft carriers attacked the ships. Although each side suffered heavy losses, neither won a clear victory. Still, the Japanese assault on Port Moresby was stopped.

Allied leaders then learned that the Japanese planned a surprise attack on the Midway Islands. Nimitz was prepared. The **Battle of Midway** began

Code Talkers

More than 40,000 Native Americans served in the U.S. armed forces during the war. About 400 Navajo Native Americans served as "code talkers," relaying coded messages based on the complex Navajo language. Japan's expert code breakers were never able to crack the Navajo code.

Why might the Japanese have been unable to break the Navajo code?

on June 4, 1942, when Japan started bombing the islands. American aircraft carriers launched their planes, catching the Japanese aircraft carriers while many of their planes were refueling on deck. American dive bombers destroyed four of Japan's aircraft carriers, severely weakening Japanese naval power. "Pearl Harbor has now been partially avenged," said Nimitz.

The Allies then began the enormous and difficult task of recapturing territory from Japan. In August 1942 American marines invaded Guadalcanal, one of the Solomon Islands northeast of Australia. Intense fighting raged for nearly six months. Marine Louis Ortega remembered that enemy bombs and bullets were only part of the danger in the hot, rainy jungles of Guadalcanal. Soldiers also suffered from diseases, such as malaria, and from hunger due to lack of supplies. "I had gone to Guadalcanal weighing about 150," Ortega said. "I left weighing about 110." American forces finally took control of the island in February 1943.

Reading Check
Draw Conclusions
How did the Allied victory at Midway change the course of the war in the Pacific?

Battling toward Japan

Allied victories at Midway and Guadalcanal helped change the course of the war in the Pacific. The Allies now saw their chance to go on the offensive, with the goal of reaching Japan itself.

Island Hopping To fight their way toward Japan, Allied war planners developed a strategy called **island hopping**, where Allied forces took only the most strategically important islands, instead of each Japanese-held island. They could use each captured island as a base for the next attack, while isolating the Japanese forces on the bypassed islands.

Academic Vocabulary
execute perform, carry out

Island hopping proved to be a successful strategy, though very costly to **execute**. Japanese forces fortified key islands and fought fiercely to hold on to them. In November 1943, U.S. Marines leapt off their boats and waded toward Tarawa, one of the Gilbert Islands. They advanced into ferocious fire from Japanese machine guns. "The water seemed never clear of . . . men," one marine said. "They kept falling, falling, falling." Both sides sustained heavy casualties at Tarawa, but the marines captured the island. The Allies won similar victories in the Marshall, Mariana, Volcano, and Bonin islands.

In October 1944 General MacArthur led a mission to retake the Philippines. The Japanese navy confronted the Allies at the **Battle of Leyte Gulf**, the largest naval battle in history. The Allies crushed the Japanese fleet, crippling Japan's naval power for the remainder of the war. It also gave the Allies a base from which to attack the main shipping routes that supplied Japan. After splashing ashore on Leyte, MacArthur proudly declared: "People of the Philippines: I have returned." Securing the Philippines took many more months of fighting. Allied forces and Filipino guerrillas finally drove out or captured all of the Japanese defenders by the summer of 1945.

Final Battles With key islands close to Japan secured, Allied planes began bombing targets in Japan in November 1944. A recently developed airplane, the B-29, played a major role in the effort. These planes, which

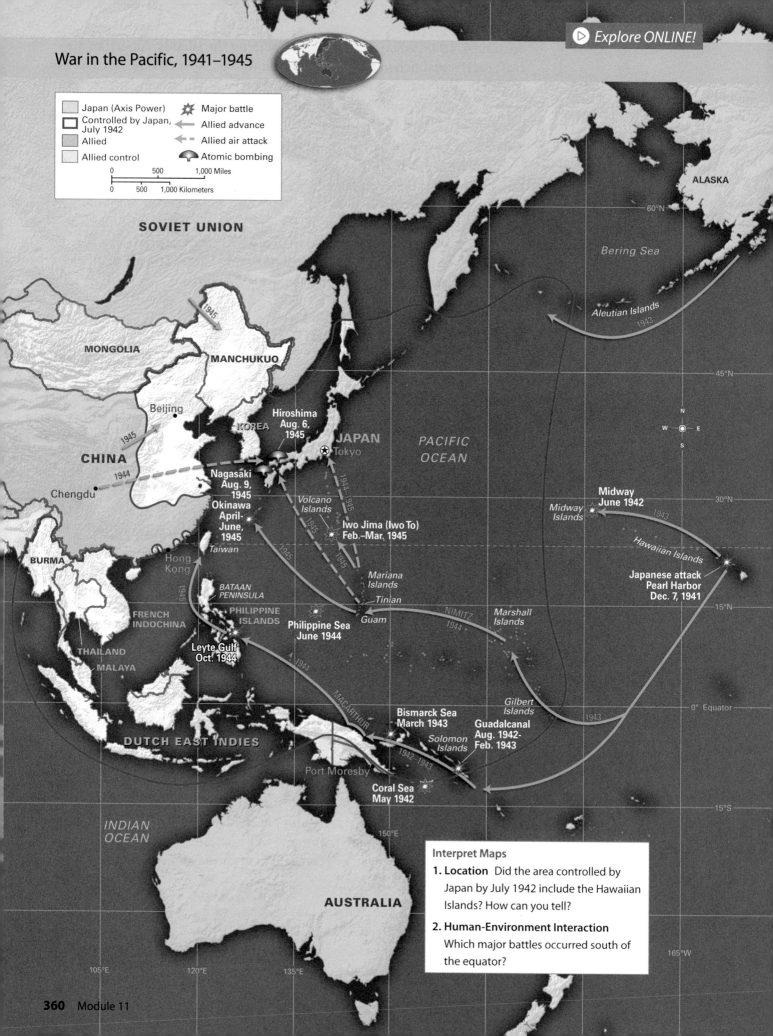

War in the Pacific, 1941–1945

▶ Explore ONLINE!

Legend:
- Japan (Axis Power)
- Controlled by Japan, July 1942
- Allied
- Allied control
- ✦ Major battle
- ← Allied advance
- ← - Allied air attack
- ⛑ Atomic bombing

0   500   1,000 Miles
0   500   1,000 Kilometers

SOVIET UNION

MONGOLIA

MANCHUKUO

Beijing

KOREA

CHINA

1945

1944

Chengdu

BURMA

Hong Kong

Taiwan

FRENCH INDOCHINA

THAILAND

MALAYA

BATAAN PENINSULA

PHILIPPINE ISLANDS

DUTCH EAST INDIES

Hiroshima Aug. 6, 1945

Nagasaki Aug. 9, 1945

Okinawa April–June, 1945

Volcano Islands

Iwo Jima (Iwo To) Feb.–Mar. 1945

JAPAN
Tokyo

PACIFIC OCEAN

N
W ⊙ E
S

ALASKA

Bering Sea

Aleutian Islands
1943

60°N

45°N

Midway June 1942

Midway Islands

1943

Hawaiian Islands

Japanese attack Pearl Harbor Dec. 7, 1941

30°N

15°N

Mariana Islands

Tinian

Guam

Leyte Gulf Oct. 1944

Philippine Sea June 1944

NIMITZ 1944

Marshall Islands

Gilbert Islands

Bismarck Sea March 1943

Guadalcanal Aug. 1942– Feb. 1943

Solomon Islands

MACARTHUR

1942–1943

Port Moresby

Coral Sea May 1942

1943

0° Equator

15°S

INDIAN OCEAN

AUSTRALIA

105°E   120°E   135°E   150°E   165°W

Interpret Maps

1. **Location** Did the area controlled by Japan by July 1942 include the Hawaiian Islands? How can you tell?

2. **Human-Environment Interaction** Which major battles occurred south of the equator?

Raising the Flag on Iwo Jima

Six marines are shown raising the American flag atop Mount Suribachi on the island of Iwo Jima after an important battle there. They were instructed to raise the flag on the highest point of the island so that all the men still fighting could see it.

could carry 20,000 pounds of explosives each, led bombing raids on more than 60 major Japanese cities. A March 1945 raid set Japan's capital city of Tokyo on fire, leaving 1 million people homeless. Japanese factories were destroyed, and food became so scarce that many people neared starvation. Even with the widespread loss of life and damage to the environment, Japan refused to surrender.

Two of the war's fiercest battles occurred on Japan's outer islands early in 1945. In February U.S. Marines stormed the beaches of Iwo Jima, now known as Iwo To. Japanese defenders were dug into caves, with orders to fight to the death. "On Iwo, we hardly ever saw the enemy," recalled one marine. After the marines raised the American flag on Iwo Jima, a month of bloody fighting followed. Of more than 20,000 Japanese defenders on Iwo Jima, about a thousand were taken prisoner—the rest were killed or wounded in battle. About 6,800 Americans had died.

Beginning in April an even deadlier battle was fought for the island of Okinawa. There were an estimated 100,000 Japanese soldiers on the island when U.S. forces began their attack. One U.S. Marine officer described the hard fighting at the Battle of Okinawa:

"We poured a tremendous amount of metal in on those positions. . . . It seemed nothing could possibly be living in that churning mass where the shells were falling and roaring but when we next advanced, [Japanese troops] would still be there and madder than ever."

—Colonel Wilburt S. Brown, quoted in *The Final Campaign: Marines in the Victory on Okinawa* by Colonel Joseph H. Alexander

Kamikaze pilots, some as young as 17, flew their airplanes directly into enemy targets, committing suicide to fulfill their duty.

In the waters near the island, Japanese planes struck U.S. ships with the tactic of **kamikaze**—purposely crashing piloted planes into enemy ships. In wave after wave, kamikaze pilots flew planes loaded with explosives straight down onto the decks of Allied ships. An American sailor who was on the deck of an aircraft carrier when a kamikaze attacked the ship described the scene. The plane "cartwheeled the length of the carrier and plowed into the planes we had on the [flight deck]. We were burning bow to stern . . . All the guys manning the guns were dead. Standing up. Pointing their guns. They never left their posts."

More than 2,500 kamikaze missions were flown, killing more than 4,000 Allied sailors. The fighting on Okinawa lasted nearly three months and led to terrible casualties. By the time the island was secure, some 12,000 Allied troops were dead and 36,000 wounded. The Japanese losses were staggering—some 110,000 troops and 80,000 civilians had been killed.

After their victories at Iwo Jima and Okinawa, the Allies were one step closer to final victory. Allied leaders began to plan for an all-out assault on the main Japanese islands.

Reading Check
Analyze
Information How did the Allied strategy in the Pacific change starting in 1943?

Summary and Preview The Allies made major gains in the Pacific war, moving closer to Japan. In the next lesson you will learn how the Allies achieved full victory.

Lesson 4 Assessment

Review Ideas, Terms, and People

1. a. **Identify** Why were the Japanese able to advance in the Pacific in 1942?

   b. **Explain** Why did so many prisoners die on the Bataan Death March?

2. a. **Recall** What Allied victories halted Japan's advance?

   b. **Analyze** Why was the Battle of the Coral Sea important?

   c. **Elaborate** How do you think the war might have been different if the Allies had lost the Battle of Midway?

3. a. **Identify** What was island hopping?

   b. **Explain** What event led to the retaking of the Philippines?

   c. **Evaluate** Why do you think someone would serve as a kamikaze pilot?

Critical Thinking

4. **Sequence** In this lesson you learned about the main events of the Pacific war. Create a graphic organizer similar to the one below and use it to put the main events of the Pacific war in the correct sequence.

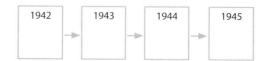

| 1942 | 1943 | 1944 | 1945 |

Victory and Consequences

The Big Idea

The Allies won World War II, the most devastating war in world history.

Main Ideas

- The Allies gained victory in Europe with Germany's surrender.

- Nazis murdered millions of Jews and other people in the Holocaust.

- Victory in the Pacific came after the United States dropped atomic bombs on Japan.

Key Terms and People

Battle of the Bulge
Harry S. Truman
Holocaust
genocide
Manhattan Project
atomic bomb

If YOU were there . . .

It is August 1944. You are an American soldier in France. You have seen the horrors of battle up close, but today is a day to rejoice. You and other Allied soldiers are marching through the streets of Paris, celebrating its liberation from Nazi control. It seems as if the whole city has come out to greet the Americans. People rush up to shake your hand. Children cheer and hand you flowers.

How does it feel to be part of this moment in history?

Germany Surrenders

In the weeks after the successful D-Day invasion, hundreds of thousands of Allied troops landed in France. Led by American general Omar Bradley, Allied forces began fighting their way across France toward Germany. At the same time, the Soviets were closing in on Germany from the east. Although Germany's defeat seemed certain to the Allies, Hitler refused to surrender.

In July 1944 Allied tank forces led by American general George Patton broke through German lines on the western front. While Patton drove forward, more Allied forces invaded southern France. Both groups of Allied forces fought their way toward Paris. Encouraged by the Allies' success, the citizens of Paris rebelled against the German-occupying forces. By the end of August, General Bradley was leading Allied troops through the streets of the freed city. "All Paris surged out to meet the Allied columns and welcome their liberators," remembered one witness. After securing Paris, the Allies continued driving through Belgium and Luxembourg, making their way toward Germany. Hitler drafted every able-bodied German man from the age of 16 to 60 and planned one last desperate attack.

Hitler's goal was for German forces to drive through a weak spot in the Allied lines and capture the city of Antwerp,

In the Battle of the Bulge, American soldiers faced a strong German attack in snowy forests during the coldest winter northern Europe had in 40 years.

Belgium. On December 16 the Germans seized a moment when Allied planes were grounded due to bad weather. In heavy snow some 25 German divisions attacked the Ardennes (ahr-DEN), a densely forested region defended by just a few American divisions. The Germans quickly pushed the Allied forces back about 65 miles, creating a huge bulge in the Allied lines. This gave the battle its name—the **Battle of the Bulge**.

Allied forces recovered rapidly and stopped the German advance. When the skies cleared in late December, Allied planes began pounding German troops. In early January 1945 the Germans began to retreat. American losses were heavy—between 70,000 and 81,000 casualties. Germany's losses were even greater, and Hitler's ability to wage offensive war was now completely crushed.

In the final months of the war, Allied bombing raids devastated major German cities such as Berlin and Hamburg. Both sides in World War II had used these kinds of bombing raids against the enemy's cities. German raids, for example, killed about 30,000 civilians in the British capital of London. In February 1945 Allied bombers attacked the German city of Dresden, igniting a firestorm that destroyed the city and killed more than 35,000 civilians. "Dresden was an inferno," recalled one U.S. soldier. "I have nightmares, even today."

As Allied forces surrounded Berlin, Hitler retreated to an underground bunker in the heart of the ruined city. On April 30, as Soviet troops entered Berlin, Hitler committed suicide. A week later, the Germans surrendered. The war in Europe had finally come to an end. The Allies celebrated May 8, 1945, as V-E (Victory in Europe) Day.

President Franklin Roosevelt, who had led the United States throughout World War II, did not live to see V-E Day. He died of a stroke on April 12. **Harry S. Truman** became president and immediately faced the challenge of winning the war in the Pacific.

Reading Check
Sequence What events led to Germany's surrender?

Horrors of the Holocaust

When Allied forces liberated Europe, they uncovered evidence of horrifying Nazi crimes against humanity. In a program of mass murder that became known as the **Holocaust**, Hitler and the Nazis had attempted to exterminate the entire Jewish population of Europe in the name of Aryan supremacy.

The Final Solution Soon after gaining power in Germany, Hitler began his campaign of terror against the Jews. The Nazis stripped German Jews of their citizenship and seized their property. On the "night of broken glass," or *Kristallnacht*, many Jewish homes and businesses were destroyed. Many Jews who did not escape the country were imprisoned in concentration camps such as Dachau (DAH-kow), near Munich.

When Germany conquered huge sections of Europe and the Soviet Union early in World War II, nearly 10 million Jews came under Hitler's control. The Nazis forced many Jews into urban centers called ghettos. Others were sent to concentration camps and used as slave labor. Many died from hunger or disease. The Nazis also formed special killing squads that rounded up groups of Jews, shot them, and buried them in mass graves. When the Germans invaded the Soviet Union, these squads murdered more than 33,000 Soviet Jews near Kiev in three days. By the end of 1941 the death squads had executed nearly 1 million people.

The Death Camps In January 1942 senior Nazi officials met to plan what they called "a final solution to the Jewish question." Hitler's "final solution" was **genocide**, or the extermination of an entire group of people. The Nazi plan was to kill the Jews in specially built death camps, mainly in German-occupied Poland. The camps were equipped with gas chambers designed to kill large numbers of people, and furnaces were used to cremate the bodies of victims.

By mid-1942 the Nazis had begun to ship Jews from throughout German-occupied Europe to the camps. Several hundred thousand Jews, for example, were transported by train from the ghetto in the Polish capital of Warsaw to a death camp called Treblinka. In April 1943 Jews in the Warsaw ghetto staged a violent uprising, attacking the Germans with guns and homemade bombs. It took German troops nearly a month to crush the revolt. Survivors were sent to Treblinka.

At the death camps most children, the elderly, and the sick were immediately executed. Those strong enough to work were used as laborers. When they became too weak to work, they too were sent to the gas chambers. Moritz Vegh was 13 when his family was sent from Czechoslovakia to Auschwitz, one of the most notorious of the death camps. He later described what happened to his mother and sister.

Buchenwald

Jews, Roma (also known as Gypsies), and other victims of Hitler and the Nazis were sent to concentration camps. Many were killed immediately upon arrival at the camps, while others were executed later. Families were forced apart, and prisoners were poorly fed and clothed. Some were used as subjects for medical experiments. This photo shows survivors of the Buchenwald concentration camp after their liberation.

How did Hitler use the concentration camps to fulfill part of his goals for Germany?

"When we got off the cattle truck, they ordered, 'Men, right; women, left.' . . . I went with my father. My little sister, Esther, she went with my mother. Esther was only eleven. She was holding my mother's hand. When they made a selection of the women, Esther clung to my mother. My mother wouldn't give her up. . . . They went straight to the gas chamber."

—Moritz Vegh, quoted in *The Boys: The Untold Story of 732 Young Concentration Camp Survivors*

Reading Check
Summarize What was the purpose of the Nazis' Final Solution?

Moritz survived the war, working as a laborer at Auschwitz.

The Allied soldiers who liberated the death camps were horrified by what they found. About 6 million Jews—some two-thirds of Europe's pre-war Jewish population—had been killed in the Holocaust. The Nazis had also murdered millions of others, including Roma (often known as Gypsies), Slavs, political opponents, and people with physical or mental disabilities.

Victory in the Pacific

In the Pacific, Allied planners prepared to invade Japan. They estimated that the invasion could result in more than 1 million Allied casualties.

The Allies had another option. Since 1942 Allied scientists had been working on a secret program known as the **Manhattan Project**. The goal was to develop an **atomic bomb**, a weapon that produces tremendous power by splitting atoms. (Germany had started trying to develop atomic weapons since before the war began. The Allies were determined to achieve that goal before the Nazis.) On July 16, 1945, the Allies successfully tested the first atomic bomb in the New Mexico desert. The massive explosion melted the desert sand into glass for 800 yards in all directions.

When Japanese leaders refused the Allies' demand for an unconditional surrender, President Truman gave the order to use the atomic bomb. On August 6, 1945, the B-29 bomber *Enola Gay* dropped an atomic bomb above the city of Hiroshima. "When I saw a very strong light, a flash, I put my arms over my face unconsciously," said one Japanese survivor. "Almost instantly I felt my face was inflating . . . I saw people looking for water and they died soon after they drank it . . . The whole city was destroyed and burning. There was no place to go." The explosion killed almost 80,000 people instantly. Thousands more died later from burns and radiation poisoning.

The atomic blast over Hiroshima destroyed the city. Almost 80,000 people were killed instantly, and thousands more died later from the effects of radiation.

Japanese leaders still refused to surrender. On August 9 U.S. forces dropped a second atomic bomb on the city of Nagasaki. About one-third of the city was destroyed, and approximately 22,000 people died immediately. The Japanese announced their surrender on August 15, 1945.

After the War

After six years, World War II was finally over. More than 50 million people had been killed—more than half of them civilians. National economies in Europe and Asia were devastated, and millions of people were left without food, water, or shelter. Since the war had been fought far from American soil, the United States escaped this level of destruction. As the strongest power left in the world, much of the responsibility for postwar rebuilding fell to the United States, which sent billions of dollars to its European allies and even its defeated enemies.

Reading Check
Summarize How
did Japan go from
being an enemy to
being an ally?

Japan was in ruins. Bombing raids had almost destroyed Tokyo, and the atomic bombs had flattened Hiroshima and Nagasaki. Japan had lost its empire. A legitimate government had to be established. General Douglas MacArthur took charge of rebuilding Japan. He disbanded the military and brought war criminals to trial. MacArthur and his team drew up a new constitution built on democratic principles, and it was quickly adopted. Although reviving the country's economy was not really part of his job, MacArthur also pushed through a plan for land reform. Other reforms gave workers the right to create labor unions. By the early 1950s Japan was well on the road to recovery. Once bitter enemies, the United States and Japan became allies.

Summary and Preview In this lesson you learned how World War II ended. In the next module you will learn how the world recovered from the war and worked to prevent such wars in the future.

Lesson 5 Assessment

Review Ideas, Terms, and People

1. **a. Identify** What was the last major battle of the war in Europe?

   b. Evaluate What was the biggest task facing Harry S. Truman when he became president?

2. **a. Identify** What was the Holocaust?

   b. Elaborate How did the oppression of Jews increase during the war?

3. **a. Recall** What was the purpose of the Manhattan Project, and how did it result in the end of the war against Japan?

   b. Explain What was the status of the United States after the war?

   c. Predict How do you think the invention of the atomic bomb changed people's views of war?

Critical Thinking

4. **Identify Causes** In this lesson you learned about the final days of the war in both Europe and the Pacific. Create a graphic organizer similar to the one below and use it to show the short-term causes of Germany's and Japan's surrenders.

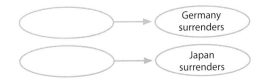

Literature in History

Literature of the Holocaust

Word Help

molten melted

phylacteries wooden prayer boxes strapped to the forehead and arm

ghetto neighborhood set aside for Jews

indiscriminately without care

surreptitiously secretly

convoy military escort

❶ The Hungarian police used physical force to gather people together.

About the Reading Elie Wiesel was taken to Auschwitz when he was age 15. Though he survived the camp, not all of his family did. Years after the war, Wiesel wrote about his time spent imprisoned at Auschwitz.

As You Read Look for ways that Wiesel describes the trauma of being taken away.

From *Night*
by Elie Wiesel (1928–2016), translated by Marion Wiesel

By eight o'clock in the morning, weariness had settled into our veins, our limbs, our brains, like molten lead. I was in the midst of prayer when suddenly there was shouting in the streets. I quickly unwound my phylacteries and ran to the window. Hungarian police had entered the ghetto and were yelling in the street nearby:

"All Jews, outside! Hurry!"

They were followed by Jewish police, who, their voices breaking, told us:

"The time has come . . . you must leave all this . . ."

The Hungarian police used their rifle butts, their clubs to indiscriminately strike old men and women, children and cripples. ❶

One by one, the houses emptied and the street filled with people carrying bundles. By ten o'clock, everyone was outside. The police were taking roll calls, once, twice, twenty times. The heat was oppressive. Sweat streamed from people's faces and bodies.

Children were crying for water.

Water! There was water close by in the houses, the backyards, but it was forbidden to break rank.

"Water, Mother, I am thirsty!"

Some of the Jewish police surreptitiously went to fill a few jugs. My sisters and I were still allowed to move about, as we were destined for the last convoy, and so we helped as best we could.

Connect Literature to History

1. **Analyze** During the early years of World War II, European Jews faced oppression. In time oppression changed to removal. How does Wiesel describe the removal of the Jews from his hometown?

2. **Describe** Jews were treated with physical violence by Nazi supporters. Give an example of violence against Jews found in this passage.

Social Studies Skills

Construct Timelines

Define the Skill

Timelines are a good way to organize historical information. Timelines clearly show a sequence of historical events over a certain period of time. Many timelines focus on a specific theme within a time period.

When you construct a timeline, it often makes the sequence of events easier to follow. Timelines show events in the order they happened and the amount of time between events. Constructing a timeline can therefore help you better understand events' context. For example, organizing events on a timeline can help you determine their causes and effects.

Learn the Skill

When you construct a timeline, you need to make some basic decisions. First, the timeline needs a topic. This topic can be general or specific. One example of a general topic is the 1940s. A more specific topic might be major battles of World War II. The timeline should cover a time period that includes the main events related to the topic. For example, it would make sense for a timeline on American battles in World War II to cover the period 1941 to 1945.

The next step in constructing a timeline is gathering information. This includes taking notes on events from the chosen time period related to the topic. It is important to write down the date when each event happened. Putting the events in order before making the timeline is often helpful. If there are too many events, it is a good idea to include only the most important ones.

The first step in actually constructing the timeline is to draw a straight line using a ruler. The next step is to mark even intervals on the timeline. Intervals are dates that divide the timeline into smaller, equal time periods. For example, a timeline of the 1940s might include two-year intervals: 1940, 1942, 1944, and so on. Then add events in the correct places on the timeline. The beginning and end of the timeline, each interval, and each event should be labeled with dates. The finished timeline should include at least six events. As a final touch, the timeline needs a title. The title tells what the entries in the timeline are about and may include the dates the timeline covers.

Practice the Skill

Follow these instructions to construct a timeline.

1. Using your textbook, choose a topic related to World War II for your timeline. Decide on the dates your timeline will need to cover.

2. Use your textbook to take notes on events to include in your timeline and their dates. Put the events in order.

3. Following the steps described above, construct your timeline. The finished timeline should include clearly labeled dates, at least six events, and a title.

Module 11 Assessment

Review Vocabulary, Terms, and People

Identify the term or person from the module that best fits each of the following descriptions.

1. The first African American flying unit in the U.S. military
2. American general who retreated from and then retook the Philippines
3. The dictator of the Soviet Union
4. A weapon that produces a massive explosion by splitting atoms
5. Battle at which British troops stopped the German Afrika Korps
6. Policy of avoiding war with an aggressive nation by giving in to its demands
7. Extermination of an entire group of people

Comprehension and Critical Thinking

Lesson 1

8. a. **Identify** What is fascism?
   b. **Make Inferences** Before Pearl Harbor, what U.S. policies suggested that the United States would join the Allies?
   c. **Evaluate** How well did the policy of appeasement work? Explain your answer.

Lesson 2

9. a. **Recall** What happened during the zoot-suit riots?
   b. **Analyze** Why was the War Production Board important to the war effort?
   c. **Elaborate** How do you think Japanese Americans felt about internment?

Lesson 3

10. a. **Identify** What led the Axis Powers to retreat from the Soviet Union?
    b. **Summarize** In which regions and countries did the Allies win major victories against Germany?
    c. **Draw Conclusions** Why do you think D-Day succeeded?

Lesson 4

11. a. **Describe** What did kamikaze pilots do?
    b. **Explain** How did cracking Japanese codes help the Allies in the Pacific?
    c. **Draw Conclusions** Why do you think Japan was determined to continue fighting?

Lesson 5

12. a. **Recall** What were the effects of the atomic bombs on Hiroshima and Nagasaki?
    b. **Contrast** How was the Holocaust different from other wartime tragedies?
    c. **Evaluate** Do you think the strategy of bombing civilian centers was fair? Why or why not?

Module 11 Assessment, continued

Review Themes

13. Geography How did geography affect the course of World War II?

14. Society and Culture What changes in society did World War II bring about?

Reading Skills

Categorize *Use the Reading Skills taught in this module to answer the question from the reading selection below.*

> American, British, and Canadian troops invaded France on June 6, 1944—known as D-Day, or "designated day." They crossed the choppy waters of the English Channel and landed on five beaches in Normandy. More than 6,000 ships, 11,000 planes, and 156,000 men were part of the invasion. Soldiers jumped from boats and waded ashore, often under heavy fire.

15. Which of the following general categories could help you organize this information?
  a. generals of the American forces
  b. types of ammunition used
  c. resources of invading forces
  d. leaders of Allied nations

Social Studies Skills

Construct Timelines *Use the Social Studies Skills taught in this module to answer the question below.*

16. Make a timeline about the end of World War II, covering the events of 1945.

Focus on Writing

17. Write Your Radio News Broadcast During World War II, millions of Americans had relatives fighting overseas. They relied on radio broadcasts for up-to-date news from the battlefronts around the world. Choose one event or story from World War II as the focus of your radio broadcast. You can include quotes from soldiers or national leaders. Remember that people cannot see your broadcast, so use descriptive language. Be sure to answer the following questions: Who? What? Where? When? Why? and How?

Memories of
WORLD WAR II

A global conflict, World War II shaped the history of both the United States and the world. Americans contributed to the war effort in numerous ways. Many enlisted in the military and served in Africa, Europe, and the Pacific. Others contributed by working in factories to produce the massive amounts of ships, planes, guns, and other supplies necessary to win the war. In the process, these Americans left behind firsthand accounts of their experiences during the war, both at home and abroad. Explore some of the personal stories and recollections of World War II online. You can find a wealth of information, video clips, primary sources, activities, and more through your online textbook.

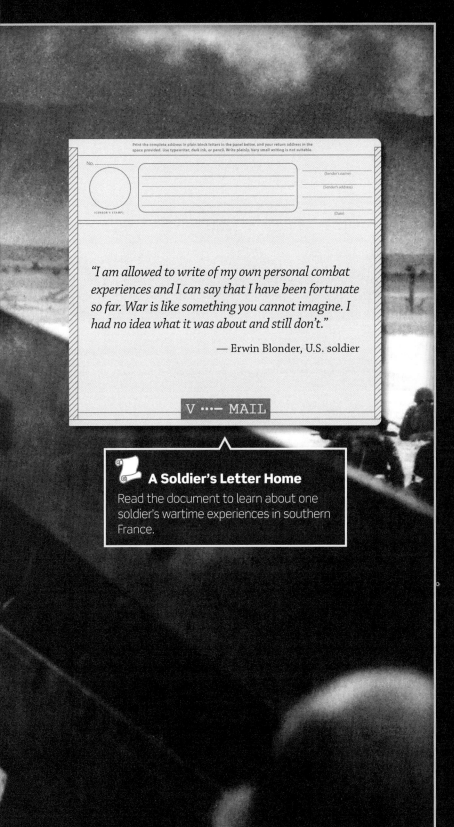

> "I am allowed to write of my own personal combat experiences and I can say that I have been fortunate so far. War is like something you cannot imagine. I had no idea what it was about and still don't."
>
> — Erwin Blonder, U.S. soldier

V ···— MAIL

A Soldier's Letter Home

Read the document to learn about one soldier's wartime experiences in southern France.

America Mobilizes for War

Watch the video to see how the United States mobilized its citizens for war and how society changed as a result.

Air War Over Germany

Watch the video to see how the P-51 Mustang helped the Allies win the air war over Germany.

The Pacific Islands

Watch the video to hear veterans describe their experiences fighting in the Pacific theater.

The Cold War

★

Essential Question

How might the Cold War have been prevented?

About the Photo: After World War II, the United States and the Soviet Union engaged in a nuclear arms race. Here, American students practice a "duck-and-cover" drill, designed to protect them from a nuclear bomb blast.

▶ Explore ONLINE!

HISTORY.

VIDEOS, including...
- The Arms Race
- The Berlin Airlift
- Korean War Begins
- Suburbia and the Baby Boom

☑ Document-Based Investigations

☑ Graphic Organizers

☑ Interactive Games

☑ Interactive Map: Postwar Germany

☑ Image with Hotspots: Fear of Communism

☑ The Korean War Begins

☑ Image Carousel: Major Spy Cases

☑ Interactive Graphs: Postwar Boom, 1945–1960

In this module you will learn how American life changed as a result of the Cold War.

What You Will Learn . . .

Timeline of Events 1945–1960

▶ Explore ONLINE!

United States	World

1945

1945 After Roosevelt's death, Harry S. Truman becomes president.

1946 Winston Churchill declares an "iron curtain" between Western powers and the Soviet Union.

⋁ **1948** The nation of Israel is established.

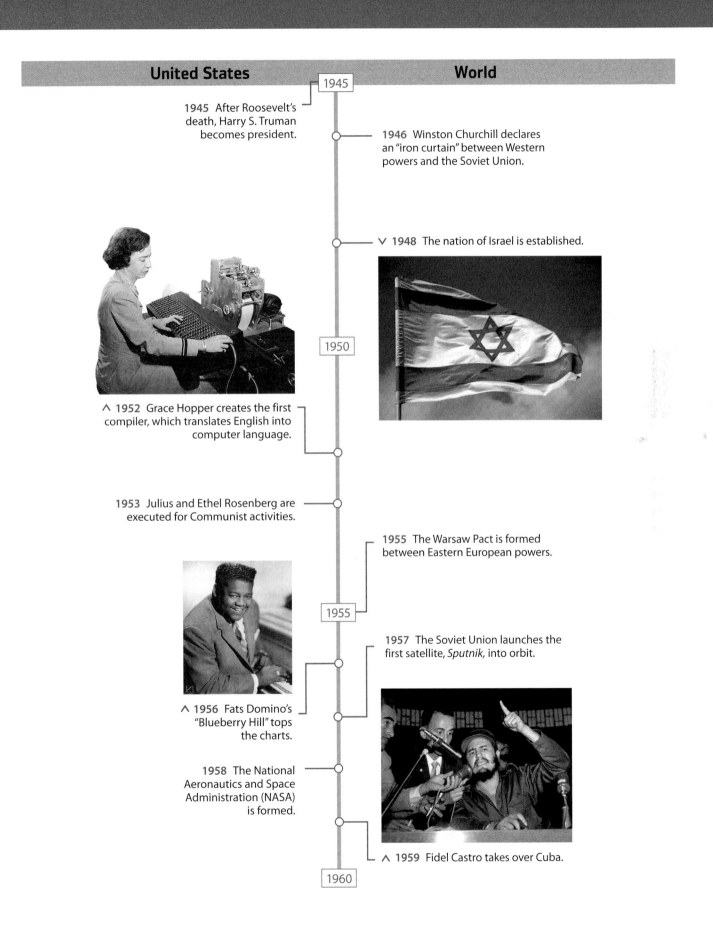

1950

∧ **1952** Grace Hopper creates the first compiler, which translates English into computer language.

1953 Julius and Ethel Rosenberg are executed for Communist activities.

1955 The Warsaw Pact is formed between Eastern European powers.

1955

1957 The Soviet Union launches the first satellite, *Sputnik,* into orbit.

∧ **1956** Fats Domino's "Blueberry Hill" tops the charts.

1958 The National Aeronautics and Space Administration (NASA) is formed.

∧ **1959** Fidel Castro takes over Cuba.

1960

Reading Social Studies

Politics, Science and Technology

In this module you will learn about the Cold War between the United States and the Soviet Union. This war was unlike other wars in that it was often fought between politicians instead of soldiers. Each country used developments in science and technology to declare itself superior. You will also read about U.S. society and its reaction to the Cold War.

READING FOCUS:

Understand through Visualizing

Visualizing how your life might have been different if you had been alive during a period in history can help you understand life at that time.

Visualizing Using clues about everyday life that you find in a history module like this one can help you imagine what life was like in the past. You can imagine yourself and your life, and how life would have been different if you had lived in the past. Or, you can try to imagine what life was like for the people then.

Notice the clues in this passage that give you an idea of the thinking of people living during the Cold War.

All the time, in the homely [plain], cluttered rooms of our private lives the television displayed the continuing spectacle of public life—all of it still going on in the windless places on the other side of the screen. Presidents and First Secretaries trod [climbed] down the metal staircases from the bellies of great aircraft to shake hands on the tarmac [runway] and climb into big black cars. Tanks wheeled down blind streets and across muddy fields. Rolls of heavy wire netting were unwound and veered [turned] upwards against a dawn sky.

—From *The Cruel Peace*, by Fred Inglis

> The author is using description to inform the reader about the feeling of watching the Cold War unfold on television.

> Here the author uses frightening images to help the reader understand the fear of the Cold War.

You Try It!

The following passage is from the module you are getting ready to read. As you read the passage, look for details that help you visualize the past.

In 1946 Winston Churchill described how Soviet control cut these countries off from the Western world. "An iron curtain has descended [fallen] across the [European] Continent," he said. The term *iron curtain* thus came to be used to describe this division. Presidential adviser Bernard Baruch warned of the seriousness of the Soviet threat, saying, "Let us not be deceived—we are today in the midst of a cold war." The phrase *Cold War* came to be used to describe the struggle for global power between the United States and the Soviet Union.

After you read the passage, answer the following questions.

1. Which visual description helps you understand the attitude existing between the United States and the Soviet Union?

2. How does the quote by Winston Churchill help you visualize the political atmosphere of the time?

3. How does the phrase *Cold War* help you visualize the political atmosphere of the time?

As you read Module 12, look for details that help you visualize the past.

Key Terms and People

Lesson 1
Yalta Conference
Nuremberg trials
United Nations
superpowers
Cold War
containment
Truman Doctrine
Marshall Plan
North Atlantic Treaty Organization
GI Bill of Rights
Fair Deal

Lesson 2
Mao Zedong
38th parallel
Joseph McCarthy
hydrogen bomb
arms race
Sputnik
brinkmanship

Lesson 3
baby boom
Sun Belt
urban renewal
beats

Adjusting to Peace

The Big Idea

After World War II, Americans adjusted to new challenges both at home and around the world.

Main Ideas

- As World War II ended, leaders began planning the future of the postwar world.

- The United States and the Soviet Union went from being allies to enemies after World War II.

- Americans adjusted to postwar life.

Key Terms and People

Yalta Conference
Nuremberg trials
United Nations
superpowers
Cold War
containment
Truman Doctrine
Marshall Plan
North Atlantic Treaty
    Organization
GI Bill of Rights
Fair Deal

If YOU were there . . .

You are an adviser to President Harry S. Truman in July 1945. You have traveled with him to Potsdam, outside the ruined city of Berlin, where Allied leaders are discussing postwar plans. Everyone agrees that steps must be taken to prevent another world war. But you are worried that Soviet leader Joseph Stalin cannot be trusted.

What advice would you give to President Truman?

The Future of the Postwar World

As 1945 began, it was becoming clear that the Allies were going to win World War II. In February Allied leaders known as the Big Three—Franklin D. Roosevelt of the United States, Winston Churchill of Great Britain, and Joseph Stalin of the Soviet Union—met in the Soviet city of Yalta to discuss plans for peace.

In February, at the **Yalta Conference**, the three leaders made important decisions about the future of European governments. They expressed support for the creation of an international peacekeeping organization. They also agreed that nations freed from Germany should have the right "to create democratic institutions of their own choice." Stalin promised to allow free elections in the Soviet-occupied countries in Eastern Europe. However, after driving German troops out of Poland, Soviet forces set up a pro-Soviet Communist government.

In July 1945 President Truman met with the new British prime minister Clement Atlee and Soviet leader Joseph Stalin near Berlin, Germany, at the Potsdam Conference. The Allied leaders divided conquered Germany into four zones. Britain, France, the United States, and the Soviet Union would each occupy one zone. The capital city of Berlin—located deep inside the Soviet zone—was also divided into four zones.

Winston Churchill, Franklin Roosevelt, and Joseph Stalin (seated left to right) met at Yalta in 1945.

Clement Atlee, Harry Truman, and Joseph Stalin (seated left to right) met at Potsdam in 1945.

War Crimes Trials After World War II, Allied leaders formed a special court, called the International Military Tribunal, to try Axis leaders accused of war crimes. In November 1945 the tribunal put high-ranking Nazis on trial in the German city of Nuremberg in what became known as the **Nuremberg trials**. U.S. Supreme Court justice Robert H. Jackson served as the chief American attorney. In his opening statement, Jackson explained the importance of the trials:

> "The wrongs which we seek to condemn and punish have been so calculated [well planned], so malignant [evil] and devastating, that civilization cannot tolerate their being ignored because it cannot survive their being repeated."
>
> —Robert H. Jackson, quoted in *The Nuremberg Trial*, edited by Mitchell Bard

The court charged Nazi officials with "crimes against humanity." One defendant was Hermann Goering, a key planner of Hitler's "final solution." Another was Hans Frank, Poland's wartime governor, who had organized the killing of hundreds of thousands of Poles and Polish Jews. The tribunal found 19 Nazi leaders guilty. Of these, 12 leaders, including Goering and Frank, were sentenced to death.

The International Military Tribunal for the Far East held trials in Japan. Japan's wartime leader Hideki Tojo was convicted and executed. Seven other Japanese leaders were also sentenced to death. The trials in Germany and Japan helped establish the principle that individuals must be held responsible for committing war crimes, even when acting on behalf of a government.

The United Nations During the war, President Roosevelt had spoken of the need for a new international organization to promote world peace. Roosevelt did not believe the United States alone could bring peace to the whole world. "The structure of world peace," he said, "must be a peace which rests on the cooperative effort of the whole world."

In 1944 American, British, Soviet, and Chinese representatives met to draft a plan for the **United Nations** (UN)—an organization dedicated to

Today, the United Nations has more than 190 members and works to prevent war, provide disaster relief, prevent hunger and disease, and combat international terrorism.

resolving international conflicts. In 1945 representatives from 50 countries met to write the United Nations Charter. The UN Charter declared the organization's commitment "to unite our strength to maintain international peace and security." President Truman appointed Eleanor Roosevelt as one of the first U.S. delegates to the UN.

At the UN, Eleanor Roosevelt helped write and advocate for the Universal Declaration of Human Rights, which the UN adopted in 1948. During Franklin Roosevelt's presidency, she had changed the role of First Lady by holding her own press conferences, making speeches, and writing newspaper columns that actively promoted human rights, children's welfare, and equal rights for women and minorities.

One of the UN's first actions concerned Palestine, occupied by the British after World War I. The UN General Assembly voted to divide the area into separate Arab and Jewish states. Jews had begun moving to Palestine, an area important to the Jewish, Christian, and Islamic religions, after World War I. Many more moved there before and during World War II. On May 14, 1948, Jewish leaders announced the creation of the nation of Israel.

The United States quickly recognized the new Jewish state. Arab leaders refused to do so and claimed the land as their own. Armies from five Arab states attacked Israel. Israeli forces drove them back, and the two sides reached a truce in 1949. Israel then joined the UN. But tensions remained high.

Reading Check
Find Main Ideas
What steps did world leaders take to establish peace?

From Allies to Enemies

After World War II, the United States and the Soviet Union emerged as **superpowers**, or powerful countries who influenced events in their regions of the world. During World War II, the two countries had cooperated to win the war. Afterward, the differences between the two nations led to new hostility. The Soviet Union hoped to spread communism around the world. Americans remained committed to capitalism and democracy.

The Iron Curtain After Stalin created a Communist government in Poland, the Soviet Union expanded its control over Eastern Europe by creating "satellite states"—countries under complete Soviet control. In 1946 Winston Churchill described how Soviet control cut these countries off from the Western world. "An iron curtain has descended [fallen] across the [European] Continent," he said. The term *iron curtain* thus came to be used to describe this division. Presidential adviser Bernard Baruch warned of the seriousness of the Soviet threat, saying, "Let us not be deceived—we are today in the midst of a cold war." The phrase **Cold War** came to be used to describe the struggle for global power between the United States and the Soviet Union.

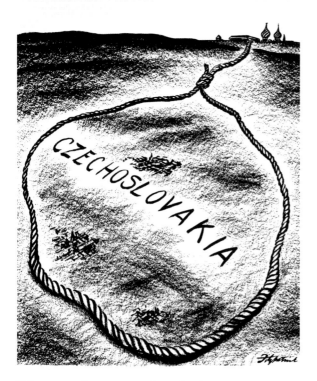

This cartoon shows a noose from the distant Soviet Union encircling the nation of Czechoslovakia.

Cold War Policies The United States quickly developed a new foreign policy to deal with the Cold War. It was based on the goal of **containment**, or preventing the Soviet Union from expanding its influence around the world.

In 1945 the Soviet Union began demanding control over areas in the Mediterranean Sea that were under Turkish authority. In 1946 Communist rebels in Greece threatened to topple the Greek monarchy. At Truman's request, Congress passed an aid package worth millions of dollars for Greece and Turkey. The money, the president said, would "support free peoples who are resisting attempted subjugation [conquest] by armed minorities or outside pressures." U.S. aid helped the Greek army defeat the Communist rebels and protected Turkey from Soviet expansion. This policy of providing aid to help foreign countries fight communism became known as the **Truman Doctrine**.

The nations of Europe, meanwhile, were still devastated from World War II. American secretary of state George C. Marshall saw this as a threat both to stability in Europe and to the U.S. economy, which depended on trade with Europe. Marshall called on European leaders to develop plans for economic recovery, which the United States would help fund. Under the **Marshall Plan**, Western Europe received more than $13 billion in U.S. loans and grants for European economic recovery between 1948 and 1952. Soviet leaders rejected Marshall Plan aid. They also kept Eastern European nations from participating.

Japan was also left devastated by World War II. With the end of the war, U.S. forces under General Douglas MacArthur occupied Japan and began a series of reforms to help rebuild the country and to keep communism from taking hold. As part of the reform, Japan's emperor lost most of his authority. Power was given instead to an elected parliament. The Americans also helped strengthen and modernize the Japanese economy.

Cold War tensions rose further in 1948 when France, Britain, and the United States decided to join their occupation zones of Germany into one unit. The Soviet Union had good reason to fear the creation of a strong West German state. On June 24, the Soviet Union suddenly blocked all rail, highway, and water traffic between western Germany and the city of Berlin. West Berlin's 2 million residents were trapped behind the iron curtain.

To respond to this crisis without using military force, U.S. and British planes began airlifting supplies into West Berlin. For more than a year, planes delivered lifesaving food, fuel, and machinery to West Berliners. The Soviet Union made no determined effort to stop the airlift, fearing a war. It then lifted the blockade in May 1949.

That same year, the United States joined nine Western European countries, along with Iceland and Canada, to form the **North Atlantic Treaty Organization** (NATO). NATO members promised to defend each other if attacked. In 1955 the Soviet Union created the Warsaw Pact, which provided a unified system of military command between the Soviet Union and its Eastern European satellite countries for their mutual defense. When the Cold War ended, many former Warsaw Pact nations joined NATO. Today, NATO has 28 member nations.

Reading Check
Compare
How were NATO
and the Warsaw
Pact similar?

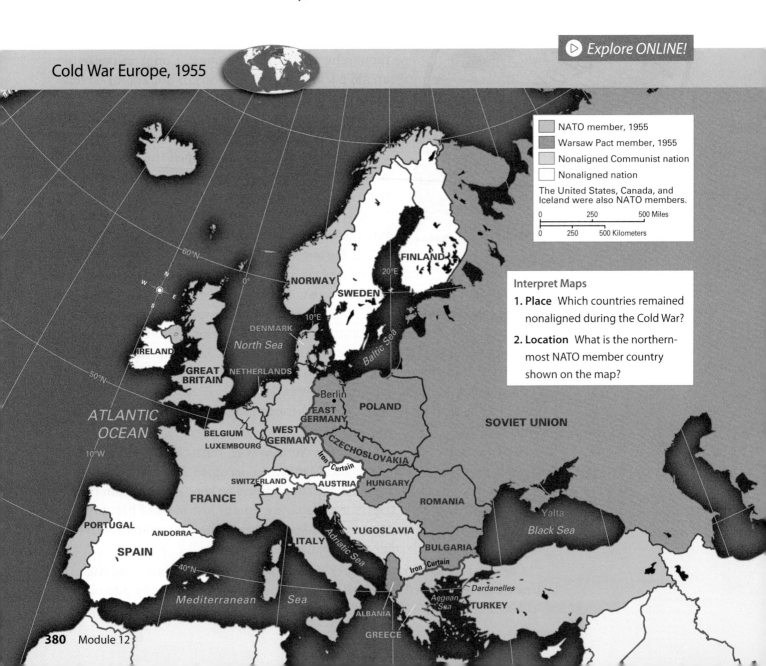

▷ Explore ONLINE!

Cold War Europe, 1955

NATO member, 1955
Warsaw Pact member, 1955
Nonaligned Communist nation
Nonaligned nation
The United States, Canada, and Iceland were also NATO members.

0   250   500 Miles
0 250 500 Kilometers

Interpret Maps
1. **Place** Which countries remained nonaligned during the Cold War?
2. **Location** What is the northernmost NATO member country shown on the map?

In the aftermath of World War II, President Truman was charged with transitioning the nation's economy and people to peacetime.

Postwar America

You have read about the economic depression that followed the end of World War I. As World War II ended, President Truman was worried about a similar downturn. More than 16 million Americans had served in the armed forces during the war. Now they were coming home, and most would be looking for work.

President Truman, who was sworn in as president when Roosevelt died in 1945, led the country through the end of World War II and the start of the Cold War. He had been an artillery officer in France during World War I, and he was familiar with the issues veterans faced returning from war.

The Postwar Economy To provide jobs for returning veterans, the government urged the millions of women who had gone to work during the war to give up their jobs. New laws also eased the transition for returning soldiers. The Servicemen's Readjustment Act, or **GI Bill of Rights**, offered veterans money for school as well as loans for houses, farms, and businesses. The GI Bill's home loans enabled veterans to buy about 20 percent of the new houses built right after the war. Some 8 million veterans used the GI Bill's educational benefits to attend colleges and technical schools to receive training for jobs. Thousands more took out loans to open their own businesses. Bob Dole, former U.S. senator from Kansas, described how the GI Bill changed his life:

> "In my case, I went from a couple of nondescript [ordinary] years in college before the war, and came back and made excellent grades. I went on to law school and got involved in politics. None of that would have happened without the GI Bill."
>
> —Bob Dole, quoted in *GI Bill: The Law That Changed America*, by Milton Greenberg

Another major postwar change was Truman's decision to end the rationing of scarce products. Prices skyrocketed as people rushed to buy gasoline and other products that had been limited during the war. The inflation rate in 1946 rose above 18 percent. The U.S. economy remained strong, however.

Labor Unrest More than 35 percent of all nonfarm workers were members of unions in 1946, more than ever before. With prices rising quickly, workers went on strike to demand higher wages. In 1946 alone, 4.5 million workers participated in nearly 5,000 strikes.

The strikes became a major political problem for President Truman. Many people began to wonder if he could handle the presidency. In April 1946 the 400,000-member United Mine Workers of America union went on strike. When Truman was unable to negotiate a settlement, he placed the mines under government control. In May Truman ended a railroad strike by threatening to draft all the striking workers into the army.

To reduce the power of labor unions, Congress passed the Taft-Hartley Act in 1947. This act outlawed closed shops—businesses that could hire only union members. It also allowed the president to order an 80-day "cooling-off" period before a strike began. In addition, union leaders had to swear they were not Communists. In spite of his clashes with unions, Truman thought this bill went too far to weaken unions. He vetoed the bill, but Congress overrode his veto.

Civil Rights After serving their country in World War II, many African Americans faced prejudice and segregation at home. "Black servicemen were overseas dying for this country," said civil rights lawyer Constance Baker Motley. "And . . . they would be coming home to a situation that said, in effect, You're a second-class citizen." African American veterans helped lead a major effort to gain equal rights.

Truman responded in 1946 by appointing the Committee on Civil Rights to investigate discrimination and suggest solutions. As a result of the committee's report, Truman recommended that Congress pass anti-lynching laws, outlaw segregation, and protect civil rights. Congress failed to act on Truman's ideas. But in 1948, under pressure from African American groups, Truman issued an executive order ending segregation in the armed forces. He also banned discrimination in the hiring of federal employees.

The Election of 1948 As the election of 1948 drew near, President Truman's chances of re-election looked bleak. The Republicans had gained control of Congress in 1946. They felt confident that their presidential candidate, New York governor Thomas Dewey, could beat Truman.

Truman faced challenges from within the Democratic Party as well. Some southern Democrats protested Truman's support for civil rights laws by walking out of the 1948 Democratic National Convention. Many joined the States' Rights Party, or Dixiecrats, which favored racial segregation. The Dixiecrats nominated their own presidential candidate—South Carolina governor Strom Thurmond.

Truman took his case for re-election directly to the American people. He traveled more than 30,000 miles by train and delivered hundreds of speeches. He attacked what he called the "do-nothing, good-for-nothing" Congress for refusing to pass his legislation.

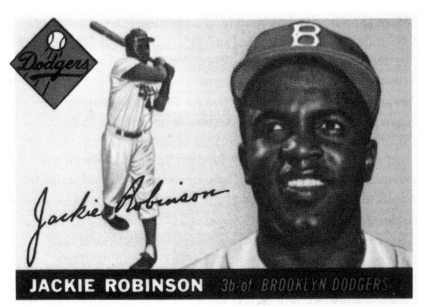

Jackie Robinson

On April 15, 1947, Jackie Robinson played his first game for the Brooklyn Dodgers. Robinson became a hero to millions by ending segregation in major league baseball. He went on to be a Hall of Fame player—and an outspoken supporter of equal rights. "The right of every American to first-class citizenship is the most important issue of our time," Robinson said.

How did Robinson show his support for equal rights for all Americans?

"I spoke I believe altogether to between fifteen and twenty million people," he later said. "I met them face to face, and I convinced them, and they voted for me." Truman won a surprise victory. The Democratic Party also regained control of both houses of Congress.

In his 1949 State of the Union Address, Truman urged Congress to support his plans for the nation. Truman's domestic program, called the **Fair Deal**, included a higher minimum wage, the creation of a national health insurance plan for all Americans, and expanded Social Security benefits for the elderly. It also asked for federal protection of civil rights and an end to racial discrimination in hiring.

Congress approved some parts of the Fair Deal, such as a higher minimum wage and expanded Social Security benefits. Congress rejected other Fair Deal proposals. These included civil rights legislation that would have created a permanent Fair Employment Practices Committee.

Reading Check
Analyze Information
How did the GI Bill help returning soldiers?

Summary and Preview The United States faced a series of new challenges after World War II. In the next lesson you will learn how the fear of communism grew in the 1950s.

Lesson 1 Assessment

Review Ideas, Terms, and People

1. a. **Describe** How did the Allies divide Germany at the Potsdam Conference?

   b. **Explain** Why were the Nuremberg trials important?

   c. **Predict** Based on its founding and early years, do you think the United Nations would be an effective organization?

2. a. **Identify** What was the Truman Doctrine?

   b. **Analyze** How did the Marshall Plan help stabilize Western Europe?

   c. **Elaborate** Why do you think the United States and Western European countries were concerned about Soviet expansion?

3. a. **Recall** What kinds of programs were included in President Truman's Fair Deal?

   b. **Explain** What was the purpose of the Taft-Hartley Act?

   c. **Evaluate** Do you think President Truman did enough to promote civil rights? Why or why not?

Critical Thinking

4. **Categorize** In this lesson you learned about changes that happened as a result of World War II. Create a chart and use it to identify the effects of the war's end on the United States and the world.

Results of World War II	
In the United States	In the World

War in Korea and a New Red Scare

The Big Idea

During the Cold War, the U.S. government confronted communism globally and within the United States.

Main Ideas

- The United States fought Communist North Korea in the Korean War.

- Fear of Communists led to a new Red Scare at home.

- President Eisenhower faced Cold War crises around the world.

Key Terms and People

Mao Zedong
38th parallel
Joseph McCarthy
hydrogen bomb
arms race
Sputnik
brinkmanship

If YOU were there . . .

A radio broadcast on June 26, 1950, delivers a shocking announcement. Communist forces from North Korea have just invaded South Korea. President Truman has demanded that the North Koreans halt their invasion, but they seem to be ignoring this demand. Now Truman has to decide whether to use American military force to stop the North Koreans.

Do you think the United States should send troops to Korea? Why or why not?

The Korean War

The Cold War began in Europe but quickly spread to the Asian nations of China and Korea. In China the Communist Party and the Nationalist Party had been struggling for control of the country since the early 1900s. The two rivals joined forces against Japan during World War II but then resumed their civil war after Japan's defeat. The United States, as part of its commitment to stop the spread of communism, backed the Nationalists. The Nationalists were defeated, however, and were forced to flee to the island of Taiwan. Led by **Mao Zedong**, the Communists officially established the People's Republic of China on October 1, 1949. Many Americans saw this as a disastrous failure of U.S. foreign policy. They feared that all of Asia might soon fall to communism.

These fears were heightened by a crisis in Korea. Japan had controlled Korea from 1910 to the end of World War II. After the war, the Allies divided Korea at the **38th parallel**. The Soviet Union controlled the northern part of Korea, and the United States occupied the south. Both sides set up governments, neither of which recognized the other as legitimate.

Fighting in Korea On June 25, 1950, North Korea's Soviet-trained and -equipped army stormed across the 38th parallel and invaded South Korea. The United Nations called for a cease-fire. But the North Koreans continued their attack.

The Korean War

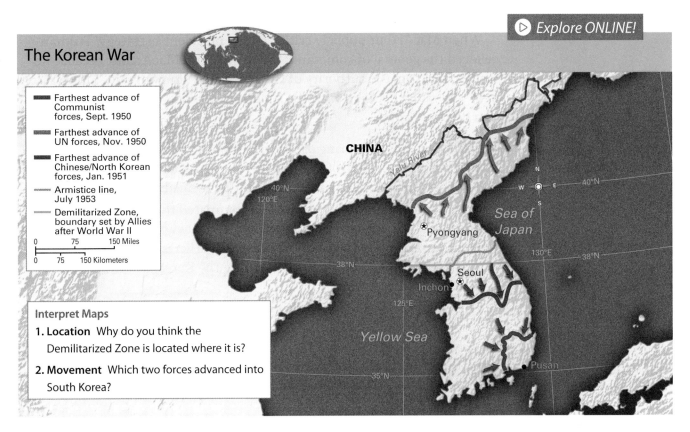

Farthest advance of Communist forces, Sept. 1950

Farthest advance of UN forces, Nov. 1950

Farthest advance of Chinese/North Korean forces, Jan. 1951

Armistice line, July 1953

Demilitarized Zone, boundary set by Allies after World War II

0   75   150 Miles

0   75   150 Kilometers

CHINA

Yalu River

Sea of Japan

Pyongyang

Seoul

Inchon

Yellow Sea

Pusan

Interpret Maps

1. Location Why do you think the Demilitarized Zone is located where it is?

2. Movement Which two forces advanced into South Korea?

President Truman had to make an immediate decision: Should the United States use force to try to stop the North Korean invasion? On June 27 Truman announced: "I have ordered United States air and sea forces to give the [South] Korean government troops cover and support." That same day, the UN decided to help South Korea "to repel the armed attack." American general Douglas MacArthur was put in command of the UN forces, which included troops from the United States and 15 other countries. The majority of the troops were from the United States and South Korea.

Douglas MacArthur graduated first in his class at West Point, and then began an army career that would last more than 50 years. He reached the rank of general in 1918 and commanded troops in World War I, World War II, and the Korean War.

In the early battles in the Korean War, MacArthur's forces were driven back to the southeastern tip of the Korean Peninsula, near the city of Pusan. Fierce fighting raged for six weeks before the UN troops turned the tide of the war with a surprise attack. Landing at the port city of Inchon on September 15, UN forces attacked the North Koreans from behind. About a month later, MacArthur's troops captured Pyongyang, North Korea's capital. They then advanced north to the Yalu River, the border between North Korea and China. MacArthur told Truman he would "have the boys home by Christmas."

Then China suddenly sent hundreds of thousands of soldiers across the border to join the North Koreans. They drove UN forces south again, back below the 38th parallel. MacArthur suggested air strikes on Chinese cities and an attack on mainland China. Truman refused permission. He was determined to contain the war in Korea.

When MacArthur publicly criticized the president's strategy, Truman relieved the general of command. "I fired General MacArthur because he wouldn't respect the authority of the president," Truman said. This was a very unpopular decision with the American public. MacArthur came home to a hero's welcome.

The War Ends By the spring of 1951 the fighting in Korea settled into a violent stalemate. The UN forces had driven the North Koreans and Chinese back across the 38th parallel. But neither side seemed able to win the war.

Americans' frustration with the war dominated the 1952 presidential election. The Republicans nominated war hero Dwight D. Eisenhower. He promised to end the increasingly unpopular conflict, saying, "The first task of a new administration will be to . . . bring the Korean War to an early and honorable end."

This promise helped Eisenhower win the election. Eisenhower visited Korea, but the conflict dragged on. A cease-fire finally ended the fighting on July 27, 1953. After three years of fighting, North and South Korea were again divided near the 38th parallel. More than 130,000 Americans had been killed or wounded. Korean and Chinese casualties topped 2 million.

Reading Check
Summarize
What were the effects of the Korean War?

A New Red Scare

The first Red Scare swept America after the Russian Revolution in 1917. Cold War fears led to another Red Scare in the late 1940s and 1950s. Attorney General J. Howard McGrath summed up these fears when he said, "There are today many Communists in America. They are everywhere—in factories, offices, butcher shops, on street corners."

Fear of Communists A congressional committee called the House Un-American Activities Committee (HUAC) investigated Communist influence in America. In 1947 HUAC launched a series of hearings to expose what it believed was Communist influence in the Hollywood movie industry. The committee branded as "red," or Communist, actors and writers who would not answer questions or who refused to reveal the names of suspected Communists. People suspected of Communist sympathies were often blacklisted, or denied work. Some of these people never worked in movies again.

Explosive spy cases also fed the fears that Communists were at work in the United States. In 1950 a German-born physicist was convicted of providing the Soviets information about the atomic bomb project at Los Alamos, New Mexico, that allowed them to develop an atomic bomb at least one year earlier than they would have. In 1951 Julius and Ethel Rosenberg also were tried for providing Soviet spies with secret details about atomic bomb design. The Rosenbergs denied the charges but were found guilty and executed in 1953.

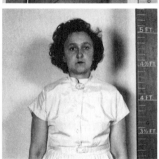

Ethel and Julius Rosenberg passed military secrets related to the atomic bomb to the Soviets in the late 1940s. They were accused and convicted in 1951.

The Rise of McCarthy Wisconsin senator **Joseph McCarthy** contributed to fears in the early 1950s by charging that Communists were working inside the State Department. He claimed to have the names of 57 people

Fear of Communism

In the 1950s the fear of communism caused some government leaders to ignore the civil liberties of suspected Communists. Some critics, like this cartoonist, believed these tactics threatened the freedom of all Americans. Here, a frightened man climbs the arm of the Statue of Liberty to put out her torch.

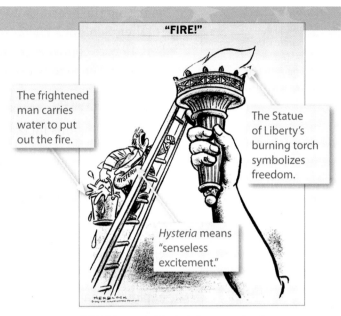

"FIRE!"

The frightened man carries water to put out the fire.

The Statue of Liberty's burning torch symbolizes freedom.

Hysteria means "senseless excitement."

"FIRE!" from *Herblock: A Cartoonist's Life* (Times Books 1998)

Analyze Historical Sources
Why is the man shown to be putting out Liberty's torch?

Academic Vocabulary
concrete specific, real

who were "either card-carrying members or certainly loyal to the Communist Party."

McCarthy produced no **concrete** proof of crimes. Many people spoke out about McCarthy's accusations. When challenged, he made up new charges, labeling those who questioned him as "soft on communism." This method of making aggressive accusations without proof became known as McCarthyism.

Edward R. Murrow, a prominent journalist of the time, frequently criticized Senator McCarthy's tactics.

"If none of us ever read a book that was 'dangerous,' nor had a friend who was 'different,' or never joined an organization that advocated 'change,' we would all be just the kind of people Joe McCarthy wants. Whose fault is that? Not really [McCarthy's]. He didn't create this situation of fear. He merely exploited [took advantage of] it, and rather successfully."

"Murrow is a symbol—the leader and the cleverest of the jackal [wild dog] pack which is always found at the throat of anyone who dares to expose individual Communists and traitors. I am compelled by the facts to say to you that Mr. Edward R. Murrow, as far back as twenty years ago, was engaged in propaganda for Communist causes."

McCarthy finally went too far in 1954. In televised Senate hearings he charged that there were Communists in the U.S. Army. For five weeks Americans watched McCarthy's bullying tactics. At one point McCarthy tried to discredit Joseph Welch, the army's attorney, by attacking a young assistant in Welch's law firm. This shocked Welch—and the nation

Reading Check
Compare How were HUAC's and McCarthy's actions similar?

watching the hearings on television. "Let us not assassinate this lad further, Senator," Welch said. "Have you left no sense of decency?" A later Senate vote condemned McCarthy's actions, but it came too late for those whose careers had been ruined by his attacks.

Eisenhower and the Cold War

Cold War tensions increased around the world during the presidency of Dwight Eisenhower. In this hostile atmosphere, Americans adjusted to the reality of living with the constant threat of nuclear war.

The Arms Race In 1950 President Truman approved work on the **hydrogen bomb**, a weapon far more powerful than the atomic bombs used in World War II. American scientists tested the first hydrogen bomb in the South Pacific in 1952. "The fireball expanded to three miles in diameter," said a test observer. He soon saw that the entire island on which the bomb exploded "had vanished, vaporized."

The Soviet Union tested its first atomic bomb in 1949 and its first hydrogen bomb in 1953. With these tests, the Soviet Union became the world's second nuclear superpower, or powerful country in possession of nuclear weapons. In what became a nuclear **arms race**, both the United States and the Soviet Union rushed to build more and more weapons. American school children practiced "duck-and-cover" drills, in which they were taught to crouch under their desks in case of nuclear attack. Some families built underground bomb shelters in their backyards for use in a nuclear emergency. The shelters were stocked with essentials.

In October 1957 the Soviets launched *Sputnik*, the world's first artificial satellite. Americans feared that if the Soviet Union could launch a satellite, it could launch missiles to attack the United States. In January 1958 the

Families kept essentials in their bomb shelters such as food, water, first aid supplies, and clothing.

United States responded by launching its own satellite. Later that year, the U.S. government established the National Aeronautics and Space Administration (NASA) to conduct space research.

Cold War Crises President Eisenhower modified Truman's policy of containment. He and Secretary of State John Foster Dulles supported **brinkmanship**—a willingness to go to the brink of war to oppose communism. "The ability to get to the verge [edge] without getting into war is the necessary art," Dulles explained. The president and Dulles also threatened the Soviet Union with "massive retaliation" against Soviet advances.

As part of his effort, Eisenhower used covert, or secret, operations around the world. In 1953, for example, the Central Intelligence Agency (CIA) helped overthrow the premier of Iran. American officials had feared he was a Communist. In 1954 the CIA helped organize the removal of the Guatemalan president for similar reasons.

In 1956 a crisis in Egypt seemed to push the world to the brink of a third world war. Egyptian leader Gamal Abdel Nasser nationalized the Suez Canal, a vital waterway connecting the Mediterranean and Red seas, in an attempt to collect tolls from the canal to finance a major dam project. Britain and France, which relied on the canal for trade, allied with Israel, a longtime enemy of Egypt, and invaded the area around the canal. The Soviet Union, an ally of Egypt, threatened to crush the invaders. This would force the United States to defend its allies. Finally, the Americans and the Soviet Union agreed to condemn the invasion, and the Suez crisis ended. After the brief moment of cooperation, the Cold War continued.

Summary and Preview After World War II, Americans responded to Communist threats at home and abroad. In the next lesson you will read about how America prospered during these challenging times.

Reading Check
Analyze Information
How was the arms race a display of brinkmanship?

Lesson 2 Assessment

Review Ideas, Terms, and People

1. a. **Identify** What is the 38th parallel, and why was it important in the Korean War?

   b. **Analyze** How did the outcome of China's civil war affect the U.S. response to North Korea's attack?

   c. **Evaluate** Do you think President Truman should have fired MacArthur? Explain your answer.

2. a. **Describe** Why did a second Red Scare occur in the late 1940s and 1950s?

   b. **Explain** How did television affect Joseph McCarthy's power?

   c. **Elaborate** Why do you think the Red Scare lasted so long?

3. a. **Recall** How did Eisenhower deal with Cold War crises during his administration?

b. **Make Inferences** How can you tell that the U.S. government took the launch of *Sputnik* seriously?

c. **Elaborate** Why do you think the United States and the Soviet Union were able to cooperate during the Suez crisis?

Critical Thinking

4. **Categorize** In this lesson you learned about Cold War conflicts and crises. Create four boxes similar to the ones below and use each box to list each event under its appropriate location.

Asia | Soviet Union | United States | Others

The Nation Prospers

The Big Idea

An expanding economy led to new ways of life for many Americans in the 1950s.

Main Ideas

- America's economy boomed in the 1950s.
- Americans enjoyed new forms of popular culture.
- Social critics found fault with 1950s society.

Key Terms and People

baby boom
Sun Belt
urban renewal
beats

If YOU were there . . .

You live with your parents in an apartment building in 1954. You have grown up in the city, and you are used to walking or taking the subway everywhere you need to go. But your parents are talking about moving out to the suburbs. They like the idea of having a house of their own, with a driveway and a backyard. They ask what you think about moving to the suburbs.

How would you respond?

America's Economy in the 1950s

The American economy boomed during the 1950s. Millions of Americans earned more money than ever before and, therefore, had more money to spend on homes, cars, vacations, and large appliances. Feeling better off than they had during the Depression and World War II, many young Americans were getting married and starting families. This led to a **baby boom**, or a significant increase in the number of babies born.

A Nation on the Move Americans were also on the move in the 1950s, as people relocated to new parts of the country to take jobs and improve the quality of their lives. Many businesses and workers moved to the **Sun Belt**—southern and western states that offered a warm climate year-round and low tax rates. As a result, the region's population doubled in the 30 years after World War II.

The 1956 Highway Act also encouraged travel. This new law provided billions of dollars for the construction of a 41,000-mile interstate highway system. New highways helped to greatly increase both business and personal travel between cities throughout the country. The roads also made it easier for people to move to suburbs and commute to jobs in cities.

Suburbs and Cities The rising demand for homes in the suburbs encouraged developers to build new suburban neighborhoods. On Long Island, New York, William Levitt

Postwar Boom, 1945-1960

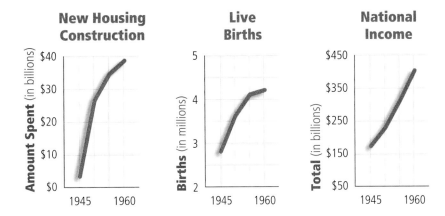

New Housing Construction

Live Births

National Income

Analyze Visuals
How did rising wealth affect families in the 1950s?

created Levittown, one of the nation's first preplanned suburbs. Between 1946 and 1951, Levitt built more than 17,000 low-priced, mass-produced houses. Like Henry Ford's Model T, Levitt's homes were designed to be simple and affordable. By the mid-1950s, builders were constructing similar suburban homes all over the country. By 1970 more Americans lived in suburbs than in cities.

Many families welcomed the comfort and convenience of suburban living. Suburban homes usually had driveways, large lawns, and labor-saving appliances. New schools were built in suburbs across the country to accommodate the increased number of students. Suburban children could participate in a wide variety of sports and other activities. Many mothers spent so much time driving their children from one activity to another that one commentator referred to the task as "motherhood on wheels."

Some critics of suburbs complained that suburban life was too heavily based on consumer culture. They also criticized the suburbs for encouraging conformity, or sameness. Most of the people living in the suburbs were white and middle class. In fact, some communities— including Levittown— refused to sell homes to black families.

Many American families used their newfound wealth to buy consumer products like houses, automobiles, and appliances. Advertisements like this one used an idealized version of an American family to sell products.

Some critics also complained that Levitt and other developers turned productive farmland into less productive residential areas. As more suburbs were built surrounding major cities—a process known as urban sprawl—less land was available to farmers. In the late 1970s and 1980s, many states, fearing that the country's most productive farmland would all be lost, passed laws to protect and preserve local farms.

As middle-class families moved to the suburbs, cities collected fewer tax dollars. This led to a decline in city services. Those who were unable to afford a move to the suburbs lived in increasingly decaying urban areas. As conditions worsened, the federal government began an **urban renewal** program—a plan to improve life in cities. Urban renewal projects focused on improving city services and urban housing. In reality, however, the programs sometimes led to more problems for urban residents.

Reading Check
Contrast
How was life different in suburbs and cities?

American Pop Culture

American life was changing quickly in the 1950s as new technology developed. More money was available to buy a wider variety of products, and technological advances made life safer and easier for many.

Life in the 1950s

Life for the average citizen in the United States changed dramatically in the prosperous years after World War II. More money was available to buy a wider variety of products, and technological advances made life safer and easier for many.

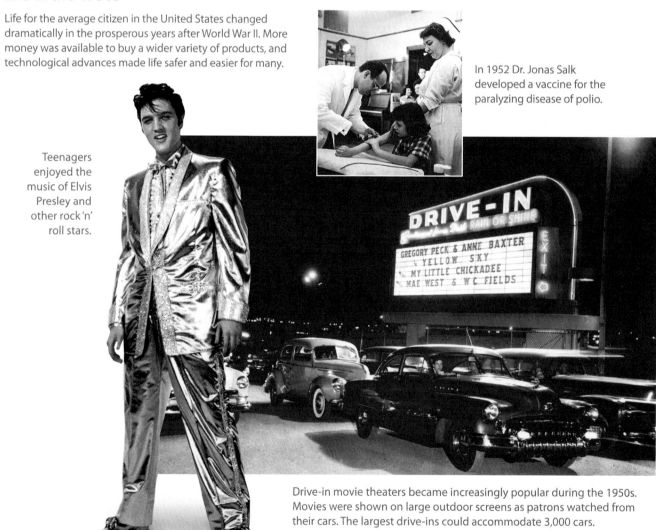

In 1952 Dr. Jonas Salk developed a vaccine for the paralyzing disease of polio.

Teenagers enjoyed the music of Elvis Presley and other rock 'n' roll stars.

DRIVE-IN RAIN OR SHINE

GREGORY PECK & ANNE BAXTER
YELLOW SKY
MY LITTLE CHICKADEE
MAE WEST & W C FIELDS

EXIT

Drive-in movie theaters became increasingly popular during the 1950s. Movies were shown on large outdoor screens as patrons watched from their cars. The largest drive-ins could accommodate 3,000 cars.

Many people began shopping in malls and eating at new fast-food restaurants. By the end of the decade, nearly 90 percent of all American families owned at least one television set. On average, American families watched about six hours of television a day.

Americans all over the country shared the experience of watching the same news, comedies, and sports programs. Many shows, such as *The Lone Ranger,* were versions of shows that began on the radio. Early hits included Milton Berle's variety show *Texaco Star Theater* and the Western drama *Gunsmoke.* But the most popular show was *I Love Lucy,* a situation comedy (or sitcom) starring Lucille Ball and her real-life husband, Cuban American bandleader Desi Arnaz. About 44 million Americans tuned in to one episode of *I Love Lucy* in 1953 to see the birth of their son—twice the number that watched President Eisenhower's inauguration the next day.

New styles of music also helped reshape American culture in the 1950s. African American jazz greats Charlie Parker and Dizzy Gillespie became known as the Fathers of Bebop, a complex jazz style often played at a rapid pace. Meanwhile, musicians like Elvis Presley, Buddy Holly, Chuck Berry, and Little Richard helped rock 'n' roll sweep the nation. Teenage music fans powered the rock 'n' roll revolution, buying more than 70 percent of all records sold in the late 1950s. Just like jazz in the 1920s, rock music drew criticism from some adults. One journalist even labeled rock 'n' roll "a menace to morals." An Arizona teenager responded to this type of criticism by saying, "Man, I believe the older generation just doesn't want the younger generation to have any fun."

Reading Check
Find Main Ideas
What changes took place in American pop culture during the 1950s?

Social Critics

Though the postwar years were happy and productive for many Americans, not everyone was happy with American society in the 1950s. Some women, for instance, were frustrated that they could only find work in a limited number of fields such as teaching, nursing, or office work. Others were discouraged by the expectation that they would give up their jobs when they got married. One woman recalled,

"There was always the assumption, even when I was getting my graduate degree in education, that any work I did was temporary, something to do until I assumed [began] my principal role in life which was to be the perfect wife and mother, supported by my husband."
—Sally Ann Carter, quoted in *The Fifties: A Women's Oral History,* by Brett Harvey

Many writers commented on 1950s society in their work. In 1951 J. D. Salinger published *The Catcher in the Rye.* The novel's teenage

Ralph Ellison began his writing career with the Federal Writers' Project during the Great Depression. He eventually became famous for writing about discrimination against African Americans.

narrator, Holden Caulfield, criticizes the "phoniness" of the adults around him, who he believed loved only money and wanted everyone to be the same. In his 1952 novel *Invisible Man,* Ralph Ellison wrote about how African Americans felt left out by American society. "I am an invisible man," Ellison wrote. "I am invisible, understand, simply because people refuse to see me."

Young people known as beatniks, or **beats**, criticized society with unusual writing styles and rebellious behavior. The works of beat poet Allen Ginsberg and novelist Jack Kerouac inspired many young people to question the rules of mainstream American society. Many young people also identified with rebellious characters in popular movies of the 1950s. In the 1953 film *The Wild One,* actor Marlon Brando plays Johnny, a wild biker who challenges the rules of society. When asked, "Hey Johnny, what are you rebelling against?" Johnny replies, "Whadda ya got?"

Summary and Preview In the 1950s, suburban life, television, and pop culture changed American society. In the next module you will learn how the civil rights movement affected the United States.

Reading Check
Find Main Ideas
Why did people criticize 1950s society?

Lesson 3 Assessment

Review Ideas, Terms, and People

1. **a. Recall** How did a booming economy affect life in the United States in the 1950s?

   b. Explain How did the growth of suburbs affect cities?

   c. Elaborate How do you think the baby boom affected 1950s society?

2. **a. Identify** How did American pop culture change in the 1950s?

   b. Make Inferences Based on what you have read, how was teenage culture in the 1950s different from adult culture?

3. **a. Describe** What was the novel *Invisible Man* about?

   b. Compare What did J. D. Salinger and Jack Kerouac have in common?

   c. Predict How do you think some women in the 1950s might have wanted to change their lives?

Critical Thinking

4. **Analyze Information** In this lesson you learned about 1950s suburban life and culture. Create a chart similar to the one below and use it to list the benefits and challenges of suburban life and culture.

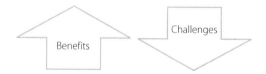

Social Studies Skills

Interpret Battle Maps

Define the Skill

Battle maps show events during a battle or war. They may show army movements or locations of battles. A single battle map often shows events that occurred at different times. Reading the map key is very important when you interpret battle maps. Battle maps usually include many different symbols. The map key explains the symbols used on the map.

Learn the Skill

Follow these steps to interpret battle maps.

1. Read the title to determine what the map is about.

2. Study the map key to understand what the symbols on the map mean. Locate the symbols from the key on the map.

3. Look for labels and other information on the map. Use what you already know about the time period to determine the importance of these features.

4. Use the map to make a generalization about a battle or war, such as which side won.

Practice the Skill

1. What is this map about?

2. What does the solid blue line on this map represent? What does the solid red line represent?

3. What does the green line on the 38th parallel show? Why is this important? Based on this map, make a generalization about the Korean War.

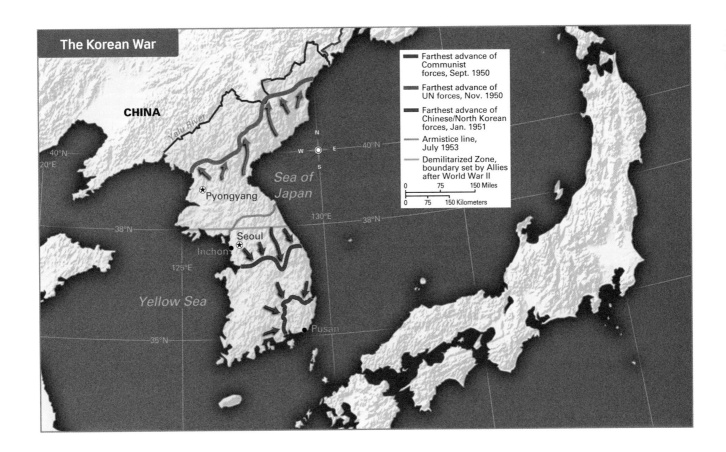

The Korean War

Map key:
- Farthest advance of Communist forces, Sept. 1950
- Farthest advance of UN forces, Nov. 1950
- Farthest advance of Chinese/North Korean forces, Jan. 1951
- Armistice line, July 1953
- Demilitarized Zone, boundary set by Allies after World War II

0   75   150 Miles
0   75   150 Kilometers

CHINA · Yalu River · Sea of Japan · Pyongyang · Seoul · Inchon · Yellow Sea · Pusan · 40°N · 20°E · 38°N · 35°N · 130°E · 125°E

Module 12 Assessment

Review Vocabulary, Terms, and People

Match the numbered person or term with the correct lettered definition.

1. GI Bill of Rights
2. Yalta Conference
3. Truman Doctrine
4. Joseph McCarthy
5. Fair Deal

a. U.S. senator who unfairly accused many citizens of being Communists
b. meeting at which Franklin Roosevelt, Winston Churchill, and Joseph Stalin discussed strategy for postwar peace
c. package of domestic reforms proposed by President Truman
d. U.S. policy of containing communism through economic aid
e. program that offered veterans money for school after World War II

Comprehension and Critical Thinking

Lesson 1

6. a. **Recall** What is the United Nations?
    b. **Explain** Why did Franklin Roosevelt support the formation of the UN?
    c. **Elaborate** Would you have supported the policy of containment? Why or why not?

Lesson 2

7. a. **Identify** How did the United States battle communism in Asia in the 1950s?
    b. **Explain** What effect did the launch of *Sputnik* have on the United States?
    c. **Evaluate** What were some risks and advantages of the strategy of brinkmanship?

Lesson 3

8. a. **Describe** How did life in the United States change in the 1950s?
    b. **Summarize** Why were some women frustrated with 1950s society?
    c. **Elaborate** How has American popular culture changed since the 1950s? How has it stayed the same?

Module 12 Assessment, continued

Review Themes

9. **Politics** How did the Cold War affect political relations between the United States and the Soviet Union?

10. **Economics** What steps did the United States take to help rebuild Europe and Japan after World War II?

11. **Science and Technology** How did science and technology advance during the 1950s?

Reading Skills

Understand through Visualizing *Use the Reading Skills taught in this module to answer the question below.*

Wisconsin senator Joseph McCarthy contributed to fears in the early 1950s by charging that Communists were working inside the State Department. He claimed to have the names of 57 people who were "either card-carrying members or certainly loyal to the Communist Party."

12. What elements of the selection above help you visualize the feelings created by the Red Scare?

Social Studies Skills

Interpret Battle Maps *Use the Social Studies Skills taught in this module to answer the question below.*

13. Look back at the battle map in Lesson 2. In what year did North Korean forces make their farthest advance?

Focus on Writing

14. **Write Song Lyrics** To begin to write a song about the 1950s, first decide on a theme for your song. That theme can focus either on one event or idea or on several events. The lyrics should address something specific about what it was like to live in the United States in the 1950s. You may even want to write the song from the point of view of a young person living in the 1950s. What would that person think about? What would be his or her hopes and fears?

The Vietnam War Years

★

Essential Question
Why did some Americans oppose the Vietnam War?

About the Photo: Soldiers from the U.S. 173rd Airborne Brigade take part in the Iron Triangle assault.

In this module you will learn how the U.S. commitment to stop the spread of communism worldwide led the United States into a long and costly war in Vietnam.

What You Will Learn . . .

▷ *Explore ONLINE!*

HISTORY

VIDEOS, including...
- Causes of the Vietnam War
- Reaction to the Crisis
- Gulf of Tonkin Incident
- Kent State

☑ Document-Based Investigations

☑ Graphic Organizers

☑ Interactive Games

☑ Interactive Map: Crises in Cuba

☑ Image with Hotspots: The Apollo Space Program

☑ Interactive Map: The Vietnam War, 1968

☑ Image Slider: A Society Divided

Timeline of Events 1960–1975

▶ Explore ONLINE!

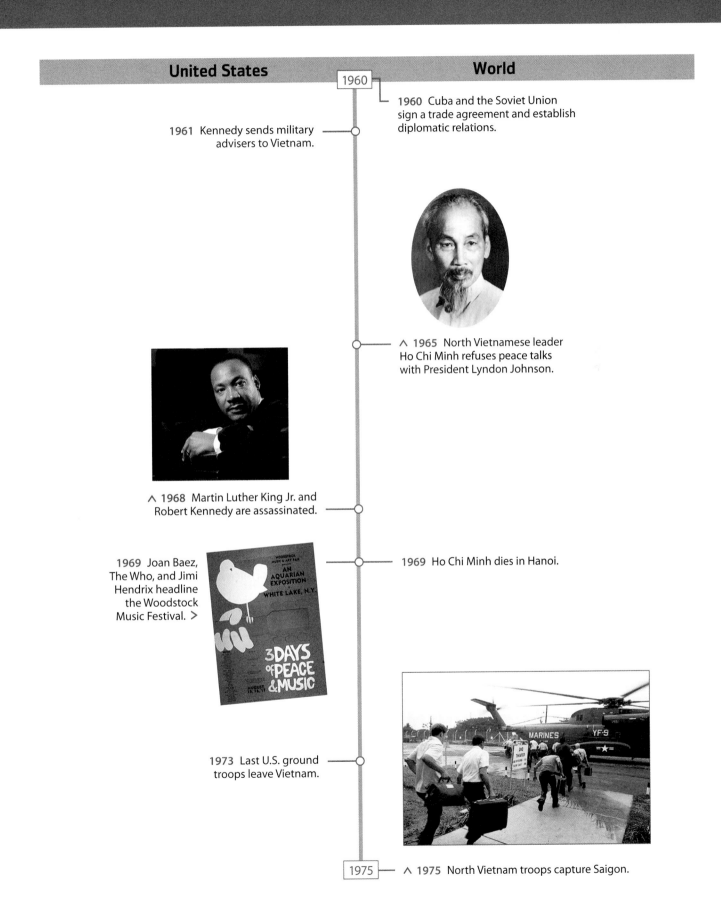

United States

World

1960

1961 Kennedy sends military advisers to Vietnam.

1960 Cuba and the Soviet Union sign a trade agreement and establish diplomatic relations.

∧ **1965** North Vietnamese leader Ho Chi Minh refuses peace talks with President Lyndon Johnson.

∧ **1968** Martin Luther King Jr. and Robert Kennedy are assassinated.

1969 Joan Baez, The Who, and Jimi Hendrix headline the Woodstock Music Festival. >

1969 Ho Chi Minh dies in Hanoi.

1973 Last U.S. ground troops leave Vietnam.

1975 — ∧ **1975** North Vietnam troops capture Saigon.

Reading Social Studies

Geography

In this module you will learn about the Vietnam War years. American soldiers faced many obstacles in Vietnam, including the country's geography. Jungles and mountains prevented Americans from gaining an easy victory. You will read about how the long, drawn-out conflict caused divisions between the nation's leaders and many Americans.

READING FOCUS:
Set a Purpose

Setting a purpose for your reading can help you to understand the things that you read. Understanding the author's goal is often an important part of this task.

Set a Purpose When you open this book to a page you have been assigned to read, there will be clues about what you will be learning. The information in this book is organized under headings that help explain the text. When you read a section like the one below, try to determine how the text explains the heading.

Notice how one reader used the headings to determine his purpose for reading the passage below.

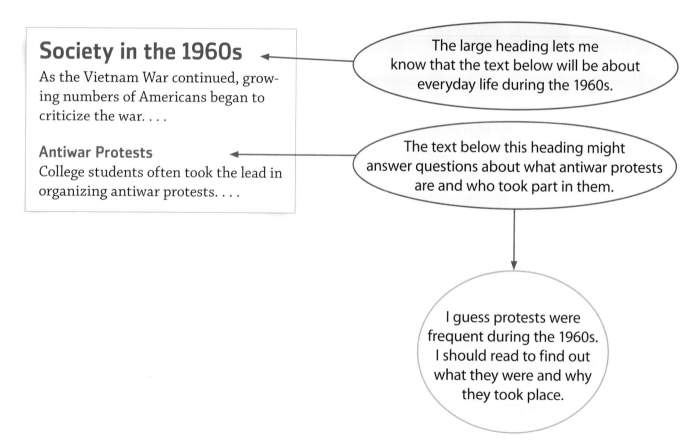

Society in the 1960s

As the Vietnam War continued, growing numbers of Americans began to criticize the war. . . .

Antiwar Protests
College students often took the lead in organizing antiwar protests. . . .

The large heading lets me know that the text below will be about everyday life during the 1960s.

The text below this heading might answer questions about what antiwar protests are and who took part in them.

I guess protests were frequent during the 1960s. I should read to find out what they were and why they took place.

You Try It!

The following passage is from the module you are getting ready to read. As you read the passage, look for information in the headings that tell you what to look for.

The Vietnam War Ends

While Nixon was running for re-election in 1972, Henry Kissinger continued peace negotiations with the North Vietnamese. . . .

The Impact in Southeast Asia

The war ended when North Vietnamese forces captured Saigon in April 1975. . . .

The Impact at Home

The Vietnam War carried heavy costs for the United States as well. . . .

After you read the passage, answer the following questions.

1. After reading the headings, what do you think this section is going to be about?
2. What are some questions you might ask before reading this section?
3. What information do you think you will learn from the section?

As you read Module 13, set a purpose before you read each section.

Key Terms and People

Lesson 1
Peace Corps
Fidel Castro
Berlin Wall
Cuban missile crisis
Neil Armstrong
Edwin "Buzz" Aldrin
Ho Chi Minh
domino theory
Vietcong

Lesson 2
Tonkin Gulf Resolution
Ho Chi Minh Trail
escalation
William Westmoreland
search-and-destroy missions
Tet Offensive
doves
hawks

Lesson 3
Students for a Democratic
Society
hippies
Richard M. Nixon
Henry Kissinger
Vietnamization
Twenty-Sixth Amendment
War Powers Act
Vietnam Veterans Memorial

Kennedy and Foreign Policy

The Big Idea

The United States confronted Communist nations in Cold War conflicts around the world.

Main Ideas

- President Kennedy confronted Communist threats around the world.

- The United States and the Soviet Union raced to send a person to the moon.

- The Cold War conflict in Vietnam led the United States into war.

Key Terms and People

Peace Corps
Fidel Castro
Berlin Wall
Cuban missile crisis
Neil Armstrong
Edwin "Buzz" Aldrin
Ho Chi Minh
domino theory
Vietcong

If YOU were there . . .

You are a student in 1960. Whenever you discuss current events in class, students talk nervously about the ongoing nuclear arms race between the United States and the Soviet Union. If Cold War tensions ever spark an all-out nuclear war, entire cities and populations could be destroyed in just a matter of minutes.

Do you think Cold War tensions will lead to a nuclear war?

Kennedy Confronts Communism

As president, John F. Kennedy was committed to the Cold War policy of stopping the spread of communism worldwide. He maintained strong military forces and expanded the nation's supply of nuclear weapons. He also sought nonmilitary ways to defeat communism. For example, in a program called the Alliance for Progress, the United States pledged $20 billion in aid to countries in Latin America. This assistance did little to improve conditions in Latin America or U.S.–Latin American relations, however. Another nonmilitary program was more successful. Beginning in 1961, the **Peace Corps** sent volunteers to developing countries to help with projects such as digging wells and building schools.

Bay of Pigs In his early days as president, much of Kennedy's attention involved confronting communism with U.S. military forces. The first Cold War crisis during his administration took place in Cuba. In the late 1950s Cuban rebel **Fidel Castro** had led a revolution against an unpopular dictator. In 1959 he overthrew the dictator. Castro soon established a Communist government allied to the Soviet Union. Many Cubans who had opposed Castro fled to the United States.

Castro's close ties with the Soviet Union worried Kennedy, especially since Cuba is only about 90 miles from Florida. Soviet leaders could use Cuba as a base from which to attack the United States.

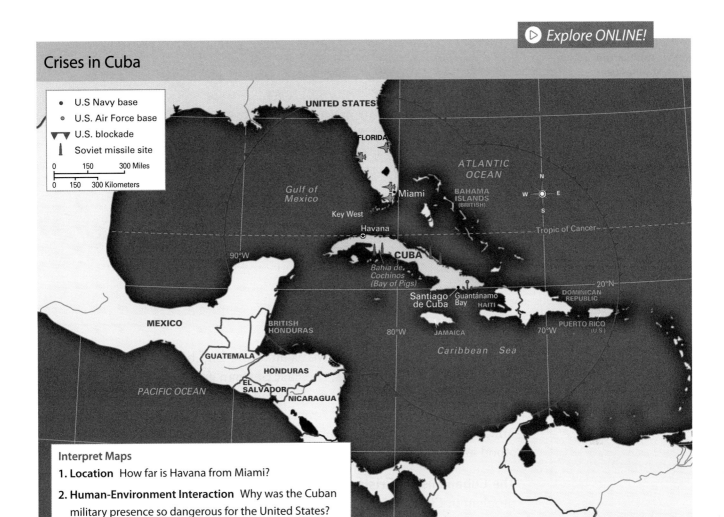

Crises in Cuba

- • U.S Navy base
- • U.S. Air Force base
- ▼ U.S. blockade
- | Soviet missile site

0   150   300 Miles

0   150   300 Kilometers

Interpret Maps

1. **Location** How far is Havana from Miami?

2. **Human-Environment Interaction** Why was the Cuban military presence so dangerous for the United States?

While president, Dwight Eisenhower had developed a plan to remove Castro from power. The Central Intelligence Agency began training Cuban exiles to invade the island and overthrow Castro. Kennedy learned of the plan when he became president. He approved the operation.

On April 17, 1961, about 1,500 Cuban exiles landed by boat at Cuba's Bay of Pigs. Castro's forces quickly responded, killing about 300 of the invaders and capturing the rest. Many Americans criticized Kennedy for the disastrous invasion attempt. His administration was off to a shaky start.

The Berlin Wall Located behind the Iron Curtain in East Germany, the city of Berlin was the site of Kennedy's second crisis. East Berlin was part of Communist East Germany. West Berlin remained a part of democratic West Germany. It stood as a model of prosperity and freedom. About 2.5 million East Germans fled to West Berlin between 1949 and 1961. They were desperate for freedom and better economic opportunities. The steady loss of skilled workers alarmed Communist officials. Calling the open border between East and West Berlin a "handy escape route," Soviet premier Nikita Khrushchev demanded that the border be closed.

Khrushchev threatened to take over West Berlin. President Kennedy responded by vowing to defend the free city. "We cannot and will not

This map of Cuba was marked by President Kennedy during a cabinet briefing on the Cuban missile crisis.

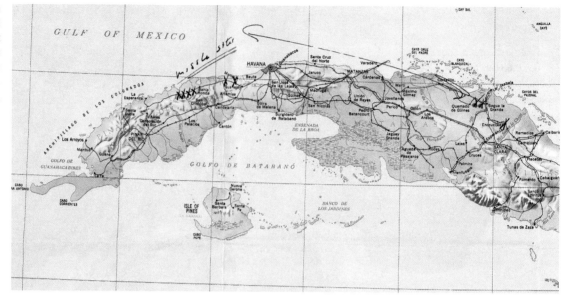

permit the Communists to drive us out of Berlin," he warned. Then, on the night of August 12–13, 1961, the East German government began building the **Berlin Wall**, a barrier of concrete and barbed wire between East and West Berlin. Kennedy rushed American troops to West Berlin. But he was unwilling to go to war with the Soviet Union over the Berlin Wall. The wall stood as a symbol of the Cold War for nearly three decades.

The Cuban Missile Crisis In October 1962 Kennedy faced yet another problem in Cuba. American U-2 spy planes discovered that the Soviets were installing nuclear missiles in Cuba. If launched, the missiles could reach, and possibly destroy, American cities within minutes.

At a press conference on October 22, Kennedy demanded that the Soviet Union remove the missiles. During the **Cuban missile crisis**, the U.S. Navy formed a blockade around Cuba. The blockade was designed to prevent Soviet ships from bringing in more weapons. As Soviet ships approached the blockade, terrified Americans waited tensely for news updates. Then came some welcome news—the Soviet ships had turned back.

After the crisis ended, Khrushchev agreed to remove the nuclear missiles from Cuba. In return, Kennedy promised not to invade Cuba. He also agreed to remove some missiles in Italy and Turkey. To improve future communication, Kennedy and Khrushchev set up a telephone "hotline" so the leaders could talk directly to each other at a moment's notice. They also signed the Limited Nuclear Test Ban Treaty, which banned the testing of new nuclear weapons aboveground.

Reading Check
Sequence When did Kennedy's three Cold War crises occur?

Race to the Moon

Although Kennedy and Khrushchev had taken some steps to prevent conflicts, the Cold War continued. One **aspect** of the Cold War that heated up in the 1960s was the space race—the competition between the United States and the Soviet Union to explore space. The Soviet Union pulled ahead in April 1961 when Soviet cosmonaut Yuri Gagarin became the first person to travel into space, orbiting Earth once.

Academic Vocabulary
aspect part

The United States was determined to catch up to and surpass the Soviet Union in the space race. Kennedy outlined a bold plan in a 1961 speech to Congress:

> "I believe that this nation should commit itself to achieving the goal, before this decade is out, of landing a man on the moon and returning him safely to the earth."
>
> —John F. Kennedy, speech to Congress, May 25, 1961

It is difficult for us to imagine what it was like for Kennedy's audience to hear these words. Space travel seems normal to us today. But to people in the early 1960s, the idea of humans landing on the moon seemed like something out of a science fiction novel. Still, Americans supported the project. Congress provided NASA with billions of dollars to fund the development of new space-travel technology.

In May 1961 astronaut Alan Shepard Jr. became the first U.S. astronaut in space. The next year, John Glenn became the first American to orbit Earth. Then NASA pushed ahead with Project Apollo, with the goal of landing an astronaut on the moon. Even with careful planning, Apollo astronauts faced great danger. Three astronauts died in a fire during a prelaunch test in 1967.

On July 20, 1969, while millions of people around the world watched on television, the lunar module *Eagle* landed on the surface of the moon. American astronauts **Neil Armstrong** and **Edwin "Buzz" Aldrin** climbed out and became the first people to walk on the moon. "That's one small step for [a] man, one giant leap for mankind," said Armstrong as he touched the lunar surface. Armstrong and Aldrin planted the American flag on the moon's surface and collected samples of moon rocks. The Apollo program continued, achieving five more successful moon landings by 1972.

A vehicle known as the moon lander took two astronauts to the moon and returned them to the orbiting spacecraft.

The astronauts guided the spacecraft from a capsule perched on the nose of the rocket. This capsule was the only part that returned to Earth.

The power from this rocket was needed to escape the pull of Earth's gravity at liftoff.

Connect to Science and Technology

The Apollo space program led to the creation of new technology to land people on the moon and bring them safely back to Earth. The design of the *Apollo 11* spacecraft involved separate pieces that played a role in different stages of the voyage. These included a rocket that could escape Earth's gravity, a spacecraft that orbited the moon, and a craft that could land on the moon and return to the orbiting spacecraft.

Analyze Visuals
What were some of the challenges of landing humans on the moon?

Reading Check
Analyze How did the events of July 20, 1969, fulfill the hope Kennedy had expressed in 1961?

The technology NASA developed enabled people to land on the moon and return safely back to Earth. The design of the *Apollo 11* spacecraft that first took astronauts to the moon involved separate pieces that played a role in different stages of the voyage. These included a rocket that could escape Earth's gravity, a spacecraft that orbited the moon, and a craft that could land on the moon and return to the orbiting spacecraft.

Conflict in Vietnam

The most serious and deadly event of the Cold War took place in Vietnam, a country in Southeast Asia. The Vietnamese struggled against the domination of China for centuries. By the early 1880s all of Vietnam was conquered by France. The French combined Vietnam with neighboring Laos and Cambodia to create a colony called French Indochina. French leaders imposed harsh taxes and put limits on political freedoms. Vietnamese nationalists began a struggle for independence in the early 1900s.

France and Vietnam One of the leading Vietnamese nationalists was **Ho Chi Minh**. Ho believed that only a Communist revolution could free the Vietnamese people.

During World War II, Japan drove the French out of Indochina. Ho Chi Minh did not want Vietnam to be controlled by yet another foreign power.

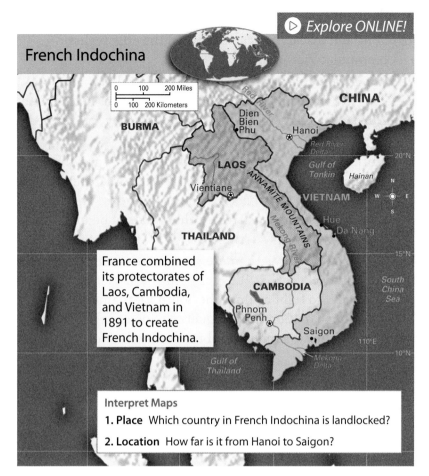

French Indochina

Explore ONLINE!

0 100 200 Miles
0 100 200 Kilometers

CHINA

BURMA

Dien Bien Phu

Hanoi

Red River Delta

Gulf of Tonkin

Hainan

20°N

LAOS

Vientiane

ANNAMITE MOUNTAINS

VIETNAM

N

W E

S

Hue

Da Nang

15°N

THAILAND

France combined its protectorates of Laos, Cambodia, and Vietnam in 1891 to create French Indochina.

South China Sea

CAMBODIA

Phnom Penh

Saigon

110°E

10°N

Mekong Delta

Gulf of Thailand

Mekong River

Red River

Interpret Maps

1. **Place** Which country in French Indochina is landlocked?

2. **Location** How far is it from Hanoi to Saigon?

He organized a group called the Vietminh to resist Japanese occupation. When Japan was defeated by the Allies in 1945, Ho declared Vietnamese independence. Using words echoing those of the American Declaration of Independence, he said, "All men are born equal: the Creator has given us inviolable rights, life, liberty, and happiness." In reality, Ho did not believe in the democratic principles outlined in the American document.

Vietnam was still not free of foreign rule. France insisted that Vietnam was a French colony. French forces moved to regain control of Vietnam, leading to new fighting between the two sides.

Presidents Truman and Eisenhower both supported France with military aid. Military aid is often used by countries as a tool of foreign policy. In this case, American leaders were concerned that a Vietminh victory would lead to the spread of communism in Asia. They feared that if one country became Communist, nearby countries would also fall to communism. This was called the **domino theory**. Americans had already watched Communist victories in China and North Korea. They did not want Vietnam to be next.

The Vietminh had fewer weapons and supplies than the French, but they used hit-and-run guerrilla tactics to gradually weaken French forces. In May 1954 the Vietminh trapped a French army at Dien Bien Phu, where the French surrendered. In July French and Vietnamese leaders worked out an agreement called the Geneva Accords. This compromise temporarily divided Vietnam into North and South. It also called for democratic elections in July 1956 that would unite the two countries under one government.

North and South Vietnam North Vietnam became a Communist dictatorship led by Ho Chi Minh. South Vietnam had a Western-style government led by Ngo Dinh Diem (en-GOH DIN de-EM) and supported by the United States. U.S. officials hoped Diem would win control of the country in the 1956 elections.

Diem, however, quickly proved to be a disappointing leader. He put his own family members in top government positions and used his security forces to imprison and torture his political enemies. President Eisenhower was concerned, but he and his advisers saw Diem as the only realistic alternative to a Communist Vietnam.

In North Vietnam, meanwhile, Ho Chi Minh introduced land redistribution plans. Like Diem, Ho and the Vietminh violently persecuted their opponents. During the land redistribution process, they imprisoned and killed thousands of landowners.

As the 1956 reunification elections approached, however, a growing number of South Vietnamese supported Ho and the Vietminh. Diem refused to allow South Vietnam to participate in the elections. The United States backed this decision. Diem also arrested thousands of people who supported Ho.

In 1960 members of the North Vietnamese government formed the National Liberation Front (NLF). The NLF recruited South Vietnamese who were opposed to Diem to fight against the South Vietnamese government. The NLF relied on Communist guerrilla forces called the **Vietcong** as its army, which was supplied and funded by the North Vietnamese.

American Involvement The United States government felt it had a national interest in stopping the spread of communism. President Eisenhower sent aid, weapons, and military advisers to South Vietnam to aid Diem. Soon after taking office in 1961, President Kennedy sent more advisers and special forces. Although they were not official combat troops, the U.S. military advisers often accompanied the South Vietnamese army on combat missions. Some were killed in action. By late 1963 about 16,000 U.S. military personnel were serving in Vietnam.

South Vietnamese soldiers plot a firing pattern under the guidance of American military personnel.

The Beginning of the Vietnam War

Causes
- French lose control of Vietnam
- Cold War tensions
- Civil war in Vietnam
- Assassination of President Diem

Effects
- Eisenhower and Kennedy send military advisers
- Gulf of Tonkin Resolution

The increased U.S. support did not help Diem, who was becoming less and less popular in South Vietnam. Several attempts were made to overthrow his government, all of which failed. Diem would not hold elections, and his opponents began to consider violence as their only option. He lost more support when he ordered his troops to fire on Buddhist demonstrators.

Some Buddhist monks protested by setting themselves on fire. Horrifying images of these protests helped turn U.S. public opinion against Diem.

In November 1963 a group of South Vietnamese army officers seized power and killed Diem and his brother. Only weeks later, Kennedy was assassinated, and Vice President Lyndon Johnson became president. Johnson immediately faced tough decisions about how to handle an increasingly unstable South Vietnam.

Reading Check
Evaluate Why did the United States see the Vietnam conflict as a Cold War struggle?

Summary and Preview In the 1950s and early 1960s, Cold War tensions caused conflicts around the world. In the next lesson you will read about increased U.S. involvement in Vietnam.

Lesson 1 Assessment

Review Ideas, Terms, and People

1. a. **Describe** What nonmilitary tactics did President Kennedy use to confront communism?

   b. **Explain** How was the Cuban missile crisis resolved?

   c. **Evaluate** In which Cold War crisis do you think President Kennedy showed the strongest leadership? Explain your answer.

2. a. **Recall** How did the Soviet Union take the lead in the space race in 1961?

   b. **Predict** How do you think the Soviet Union responded to the successful U.S. landing of a man on the moon?

3. a. **Identify** Who was Ho Chi Minh?

   b. **Describe** According to the domino theory, what did U.S. leaders think might happen if Vietnam became a Communist country?

c. **Analyze** Do you think the United States was justified in supporting Ngo Dinh Diem? Why or why not?

Critical Thinking

4. **Identify Cause and Effect** In this lesson you learned about the Cold War crises during the Kennedy administration. Create a chart similar to the one below and use it to list the causes and effects of each crisis.

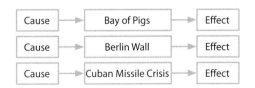

Cause	→	Bay of Pigs	→	Effect
Cause	→	Berlin Wall	→	Effect
Cause	→	Cuban Missile Crisis	→	Effect

Escalation in Vietnam

The Big Idea

Johnson quickly expanded U.S. involvement in Vietnam, but American soldiers faced a determined enemy.

Main Ideas

- President Johnson committed the United States to victory in Vietnam by expanding U.S. involvement.

- American soldiers faced new challenges fighting the Vietnam War.

- The Tet Offensive was an important turning point in the war.

Key Terms and People

Tonkin Gulf Resolution
Ho Chi Minh Trail
escalation
William Westmoreland
search-and-destroy missions
Tet Offensive
doves
hawks

If YOU were there . . .

It is 1965, and you have just been elected to Congress. You know voters are concerned about events in Vietnam, and you are carefully following the progress of the war. No one knows what will happen if the United States gets more deeply involved in the conflict. It might turn back the tide of communism. On the other hand, thousands of young soldiers might die.

Would you support sending U.S. troops to Vietnam? Why or why not?

Johnson Commits to Victory

Lyndon Johnson was determined to prevent Communists from taking over in South Vietnam. "We have the resources and the will to follow this course as long as it may take," Johnson said. He waited for a spark that might allow him to take action.

The Tonkin Gulf Resolution In the summer of 1964, a naval skirmish led to a rapid expansion of U.S. involvement in Vietnam. On August 2, 1964, the USS *Maddox* reportedly exchanged gunfire with North Vietnamese torpedo boats in the Gulf of Tonkin, off the North Vietnamese coast. Two days later, during a night of thunderstorms, U.S. ships reported a second attack. The captain of the *Maddox* was not sure his ship had actually been attacked, but the USS *Turner Joy* claimed to have picked up high-speed vessels on its radar. Despite the conflicting stories, President Johnson declared the incident an act of war.

Johnson asked Congress to give him the authority to take military action. Congress passed the **Tonkin Gulf Resolution**. The resolution gave the president the authority "to take all necessary measures to repel any armed attack against the forces of the United States." Johnson used the Tonkin Gulf Resolution to greatly expand the U.S. role in Vietnam.

Air Strikes Begin Johnson sent the first U.S. combat troops to South Vietnam in March 1965. At the same time, he ordered Operation Rolling Thunder, a series of air strikes on war industries in North Vietnam. The air strikes were also designed to disrupt the **Ho Chi Minh Trail**, a supply route the North Vietnamese used. The trail was a network of paths and tunnels that led from North Vietnam, through Laos and Cambodia, and into South Vietnam.

Because some of the Ho Chi Minh Trail was located in neutral countries, U.S. soldiers could not surround it on the ground. Instead, U.S. airplanes bombed the route. Sometimes planes bombed with napalm, or jellied gasoline, to kill troops and destroy supplies. Planes also released chemicals such as Agent Orange to kill the dense forests on the trail and to increase visibility from the air. American veterans and Vietnamese civilians later suffered serious health problems from exposure to these chemicals.

By late 1968 more than a million tons of explosives had been dropped on North and South Vietnam. Many Vietnamese soldiers and civilians were killed. The Communists' ability to wage war, however, was not destroyed.

Reading Check
Summarize
What authority did the Tonkin Gulf Resolution give to President Johnson?

U.S. Soldiers in Vietnam

From 1965 to 1968, President Johnson pursued a policy of **escalation**, or increased involvement, in the war. By 1968 more than 500,000 U.S. troops were serving in Vietnam. Backed by superior military technology, U.S. generals expected to win a quick victory. But the Vietnam War proved to be different from previous wars.

--- BIOGRAPHY ---

John McCain 1936–

John McCain's father and grandfather were both U.S. Navy admirals. The younger McCain also attended the Naval Academy and served in Vietnam as a combat pilot. On a bombing mission over Hanoi in 1967, his plane was shot down. McCain was held as a prisoner of war (POW) for more than five years. He was often tortured and kept in solitary confinement. McCain entered politics after the war. In 2010 he was elected to his fifth term as U.S. senator from Arizona. One of his priorities as a senator has been to help repair and strengthen U.S. relations with Vietnam. McCain was the Republican nominee for president in 2008.

As a lieutenant, John McCain served as a flight instructor.

Draw Inferences
If you were John McCain, would you want to establish good relations with Vietnam? Why or why not?

Strategies and Tactics In Vietnam there was rarely a front line where armies met face to face. Much of the war was fought in the jungles and villages of South Vietnam. General **William Westmoreland** commanded the U.S. ground forces involved in Vietnam. He developed a strategy based on **search-and-destroy missions**. During these missions U.S. patrols searched for hidden enemy camps, then destroyed them with massive firepower and air raids.

To make up for their disadvantage in firepower, Vietcong and North Vietnamese Army (NVA) troops used guerrilla warfare tactics. Moving quickly, they set deadly traps and land mines. They also knew the local geography. This allowed them to make quick surprise assaults on small groups of U.S. soldiers. Though the Vietcong and NVA suffered high casualty rates, they were able to match U.S. escalation by continuing to send new troops into combat. They also received supplies and weapons from Communist China and the Soviet Union.

The civilians of South Vietnam were often caught in the middle of the fighting. Vietcong forces entered villages at night. The forces killed people they believed were cooperating with the South Vietnamese government. South Vietnamese and American troops attacked villages they suspected of assisting the Vietcong. About 4 million South Vietnamese were driven from their homes. This undermined the crucial U.S. goal of winning the support and loyalty of South Vietnamese civilians.

Soldiers' Stories More than 2 million American soldiers served in the Vietnam War. Their average age was 18–21, several years younger than in previous American wars. About one-quarter of the soldiers were drafted, many from minority groups and poor families. College students—most

---

Historical Sources

Vietnam War

Charley Trujillo was a soldier in the Vietnam War. He later became a writer and filmmaker, focusing on the experiences of Latinos and Chicanos in the Vietnam War. Here he describes a day in Vietnam.

"Throughout the day we received mortar and sniper fire. By that evening we had suffered more casualties. The one I remember most was a guy we called the yippie. He was totally against the war and usually tried to avoid any violence. He was even thinking, for a while, of not carrying a rifle. It didn't help him much because the dude lost his leg that afternoon."

—Charley Trujillo, quoted in *Soldados: Chicanos In Việt Nam*

Analyze Historical Sources
Why might Trujillo have remembered this casualty the most?

of whom were white and from wealthier families—were able to get draft releases called deferments.

American troops patrolled jungles and rice paddies, carrying 75–90 pounds of equipment through 100-degree heat and rainstorms that could last for days. They never knew when they might run into enemy fire. Soldiers also faced the constant danger of land mines and booby traps. "We required this kind of instant hair-trigger alertness," said marine officer Philip Caputo. "You simply trusted absolutely no one. I mean, from a 5-year-old kid to a 75-year-old woman."

While American troops were often able to win individual battles, they were rarely able to control the territory they had won for long. "You were just constantly walking out over the same ground," Caputo explained. "The enemy you were supposed to be defeating statistically kept coming back for more."

Reading Check
Compare and Contrast
How was Vietnam different from previous wars for U.S. soldiers?

Turning Points in Vietnam

By the end of 1967, U.S. military leaders argued that they were nearing victory in Vietnam. General Westmoreland said that he saw "a light at the end of the tunnel." But events in 1968 weakened the American public's confidence in this claim.

The Tet Offensive On January 30, 1968, the Vietnamese celebrated their New Year, called Tet. In previous years, a cease-fire had halted fighting on this holiday. In 1968, however, Vietcong and North Vietnamese forces launched the **Tet Offensive**—surprise attacks all over South Vietnam, including an attack on the U.S. Embassy in Saigon, South Vietnam's capital.

This Vietcong propaganda poster reads, "Vietnam will surely be victorious and America will surely be defeated."

South Vietnamese and U.S. forces successfully fought off the enemy strikes. Still, the massive size of the Tet Offensive shocked Americans. They had been told that the war would soon be over. Now they saw that the enemy was still strong and determined. Many began to wonder if government officials were being honest about the war. One poll taken after the Tet Offensive showed that only 33 percent of Americans believed that the United States was winning the war in Vietnam. About 49 percent said that the United States should never have become involved in the war.

In February 1968 Westmoreland asked for some 200,000 more troops. Many Americans questioned the wisdom of further escalation in Vietnam. President Johnson denied the general's request.

Hawks and Doves Television reports had an important impact on public opinion about the war. Americans could watch action from the battlefield and see real images of the war's brutality on nightly news broadcasts. Many were dismayed by what they saw.

Gradually, some Americans who had been supporters of the Vietnam War began to call for an end to U.S. involvement. Opponents of the war were called **doves**—named after the birds that symbolize peace. Many doves believed that the war was draining money that should be spent on

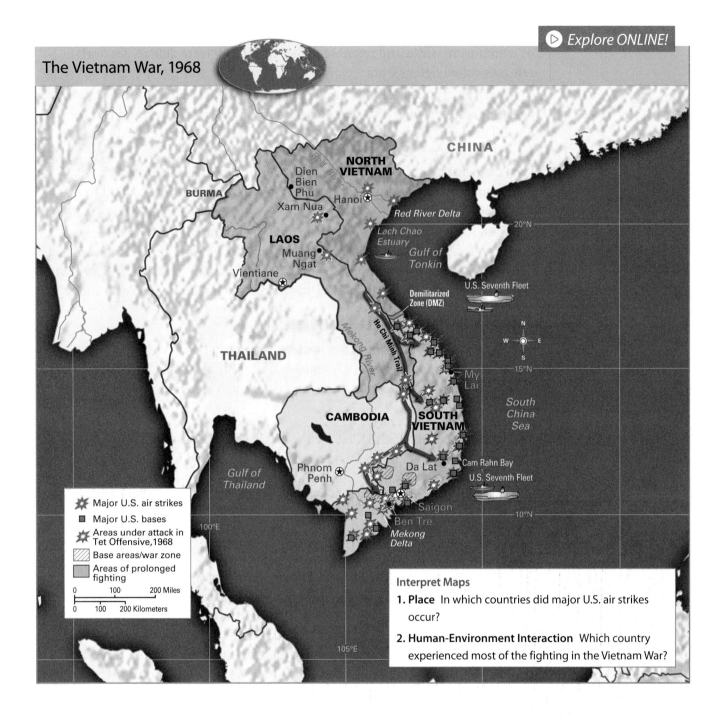

The Vietnam War, 1968

CHINA

NORTH VIETNAM

Dien Bien Phu

BURMA

Xam Nua

Hanoi ✪

Red River Delta

20°N

Lach Chao Estuary

Gulf of Tonkin

LAOS

Muang Ngat

U.S. Seventh Fleet

Vientiane ✪

Demilitarized Zone (DMZ)

THAILAND

Ho Chi Minh Trail

Mekong River

N
W — E
S

15°N

My Lai

South China Sea

CAMBODIA

SOUTH VIETNAM

Da Lat

Cam Rahn Bay

U.S. Seventh Fleet

Gulf of Thailand

Phnom Penh ✪

Saigon ✪

10°N

Ben Tre

Mekong Delta

✸ Major U.S. air strikes
■ Major U.S. bases
✸ Areas under attack in Tet Offensive,1968
▨ Base areas/war zone
▨ Areas of prolonged fighting

0   100   200 Miles
0   100   200 Kilometers

100°E

105°E

Interpret Maps

1. **Place** In which countries did major U.S. air strikes occur?

2. **Human-Environment Interaction** Which country experienced most of the fighting in the Vietnam War?

social programs at home. Supporters of the war were called **hawks**. Hawks called for increased military spending, based on the belief that winning the Cold War took priority over domestic programs.

The bitter divisions between hawks and doves deepened as the Vietnam War continued. On March 16, 1968, a company of U.S. soldiers under the command of Lieutenant William Calley entered the South Vietnamese village of My Lai. Calley and his men expected to find Vietcong forces in My Lai. Their search-and-destroy mission turned into a massacre when American soldiers opened fire, killing about 500 unarmed villagers, including women and children.

Millions of Americans watched correspondent Walter Cronkite report the Vietnam War from the field. When Cronkite called the war a stalemate, or tie, President Johnson said, "I've lost middle America."

Reading Check
Summarize
What events made some Americans oppose the war?

At first, U.S. military officials tried to cover up news of the massacre. But former soldiers eventually made details of the events public. Lieutenant Calley was tried by the military and convicted of murder. As with the Tet Offensive, the My Lai massacre caused many Americans to question U.S. involvement in Vietnam.

Summary and Preview The Vietnam War escalated steadily under President Johnson. In the next lesson you will learn about the final years of the war.

Lesson 2 Assessment

Review Ideas, Terms, and People

1. **a. Recall** What events led Johnson to ask Congress for authority to take military action in Vietnam?

   b. Explain Why was the Ho Chi Minh Trail the target of U.S. air strikes?

   c. Predict What problems might arise from giving a president powers such as those defined in the Tonkin Gulf Resolution?

2. **a. Define** What was escalation?

   b. Contrast How did strategies and tactics of U.S. troops differ from those of the NVA and Vietcong?

3. **a. Describe** What were the goals of the doves and the hawks during the Vietnam War?

   b. Analyze How did television influence public opinion during the Vietnam War?

   c. Elaborate Why was the Tet Offensive such a surprise to U.S. forces?

Critical Thinking

4. **Sequence** In this lesson you have learned about the events that led to increased U.S. involvement in the Vietnam War. Create a chart similar to the one below and use it to put the events in the correct order.

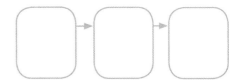

The Vietcong Tunnels

Besides knowing the geography and terrain much better than U.S. forces, the Vietcong had the advantage of an underground system of tunnels. One large system of tunnels was installed some 47 miles north of Saigon in the Cu Chi district of South Vietnam. The picture on these pages is a re-created representation of these tunnels. The tunnels provided a place from which to fight that the Americans could not attack. A tunnel complex included special rooms in which to sleep, eat, plan, store weapons and supplies, and tend wounded soldiers.

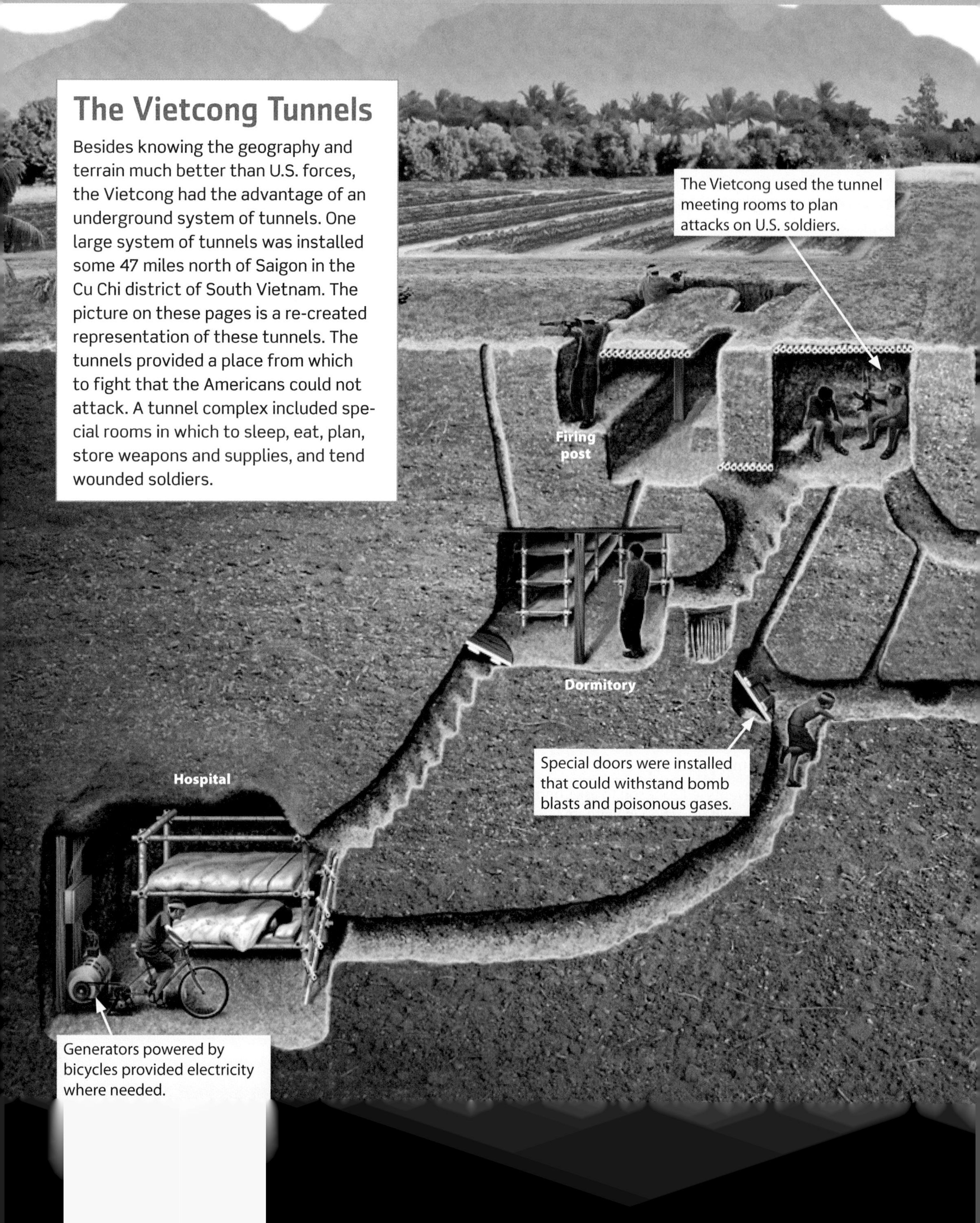

The Vietcong used the tunnel meeting rooms to plan attacks on U.S. soldiers.

Firing post

Dormitory

Special doors were installed that could withstand bomb blasts and poisonous gases.

Hospital

Generators powered by bicycles provided electricity where needed.

American soldiers had trouble finding the hidden tunnel entrances, like the one in this photograph.

Air vents

Kitchen

Bomb shelter

Some tunnels contained traps that would harm invaders.

Some tunnel complexes like this one were connected to others through longer tunnels.

Weapons storage

The Vietcong dug wells so that they could have freshwater without leaving the tunnel system.

Analyze Visuals
How did the Vietcong's tunnel system help their soldiers fight U.S. forces?

The End of the War

If YOU were there . . .

You are a high school student in 1969. You follow events in Vietnam very closely and often talk about the war with your friends. Some of your friends are active in the antiwar movement, but you also have friends who support the war. You think each group makes good points, but you are having a hard time deciding which position you support.

Would you join the antiwar protests?
Why or why not?

Society in the 1960s

As the Vietnam War continued, growing numbers of Americans began to criticize the war. "The peaceniks [war protesters] these days are legion [many]," said Charlotte Keyes, who helped organize a group called Women Strike for Peace. "They are ninety-years-old and fifteen, heads of families and housewives with babies, students, [and] young people."

Antiwar Protests College students often took the lead in organizing antiwar protests. One of the most active protest groups was **Students for a Democratic Society** (SDS). Members of SDS protested the draft as well as companies that made weapons used in Vietnam.

By the end of 1968, students had held antiwar demonstrations on nearly 75 percent of college campuses. Some young men protested by publicly burning their draft cards. Others avoided military service by moving to Canada. Many Americans, however, criticized the antiwar movement as anti-American. In 1970, for example, thousands of construction workers marched in New York City, shouting, "All the way with the U.S.A."

For some Americans, the antiwar movement was part of a rejection of traditional **values** and government authority. Some young people chose to "drop out" of mainstream

A Society Divided

Some young Americans supported the war in Vietnam. Many saw it as the only way to stop the spread of communism. Other young Americans protested the war. They believed the United States should not be involved in a violent conflict in Southeast Asia.

society and built a counterculture—a culture with its own values and ways of behaving. Members of this counterculture, called **hippies**, emphasized individual freedom, nonviolence, and communal sharing. Hippies expressed their rejection of traditional society by growing their hair long and wearing unusual clothes. They promoted openness and were sometimes called "flower children."

The views of hippies and war protesters upset many Americans. Commentators described a "generation gap," or division between older and younger Americans. "I know of no time in our history when the gap between the generations has been wider," said one university professor.

The Election of 1968 News of the Tet Offensive led to a sharp drop in the popularity of President Johnson. In early 1968 the percentage of Americans who approved of Johnson's performance as president fell from 48 to 36. The number of Americans who approved of the way Johnson was handling the war was even lower. As the 1968 presidential election approached, Johnson was even losing support within his own Democratic Party. On March 31 he went on live television and told Americans: "I shall not seek, and I will not accept, the nomination of my party for another term as president."

Several other candidates campaigned for the Democratic nomination. Johnson backed his vice president, Hubert Humphrey. Eugene McCarthy, a senator from Minnesota, ran as an outspoken antiwar candidate. Senator Robert F. Kennedy of New York argued that the United States should do everything possible to negotiate a quick and peaceful end to the war.

Kennedy won the California primary on June 5, 1968—an important step before the upcoming Democratic National Convention in Chicago. After giving his victory speech that night, he was assassinated by a man named Sirhan Sirhan.

National Guardsmen and antiwar protestors face off at the 1968 Democratic National Convention in Chicago.

Reading Check
Compare Who were the candidates in the 1968 election? What was the outcome of the election?

The Democrats were badly divided going into their party's convention in Chicago. Vice President Humphrey seemed certain to win the nomination. But many delegates disliked his close ties with President Johnson and the Vietnam War. Angry debates inside the convention hall were matched by antiwar protests on the streets. When police officers moved in to stop the demonstrations, a riot broke out. Television cameras broadcast live images of the violent chaos in Chicago. More than 100 police officers and 100 demonstrators were injured.

Humphrey won the Democratic nomination for president, but the events in Chicago damaged his chances of victory. Republican nominee **Richard M. Nixon** promised to restore order to American society and bring "peace with honor" to Vietnam. Nixon won the election, receiving 301 electoral votes to Humphrey's 191. Southern voters gave 46 electoral votes to George Wallace, a segregationist candidate of the American Independent Party.

The War under Nixon

President Nixon wanted to get U.S. troops out of Vietnam without creating the appearance of an American defeat. "I will not be the first president of the United States to lose a war," he told his fellow Republicans. With his national security adviser, **Henry Kissinger**, Nixon created a plan to pull U.S. troops from Vietnam and have the South Vietnamese Army take over all the fighting. This strategy was called **Vietnamization**.

Nixon began slowly withdrawing American troops from Vietnam. Without the knowledge of Congress or the American public, however, he approved bombing raids on Cambodia and Laos. The goal of these raids was to disrupt Vietcong supply lines. On April 30, 1970, Nixon announced that he had sent U.S. troops into Cambodia to attack Communist bases. "If, when the chips are down," he said, "the United States of America acts like a pitiful helpless giant, the forces of totalitarian anarchy will threaten free nations." Many Americans were furious. Rather than seeking peace, Nixon seemed to be expanding the war.

Student protests erupted on hundreds of college campuses. On May 4, at Kent State University in Ohio, the National Guard was called in to break up a demonstration. When the students refused to leave, guard troops used tear gas. Some students began throwing rocks at the National Guard. Several guard troops then opened fire into the crowd. Four students were killed. Horrified by the killings, antiwar activists expanded their protests all over the nation.

Antiwar feelings grew in June 1971, when the *New York Times* published secret government documents known as the Pentagon Papers. These documents revealed that U.S. officials had been lying to the American public about the progress of the war for years.

Public opinion was hardening against the war as the 1972 presidential race began. Democratic candidate George McGovern was an outspoken opponent of the war who promised voters an immediate U.S. troop withdrawal from Vietnam. "The doors of government will be opened, and that brutal war will be closed," he said.

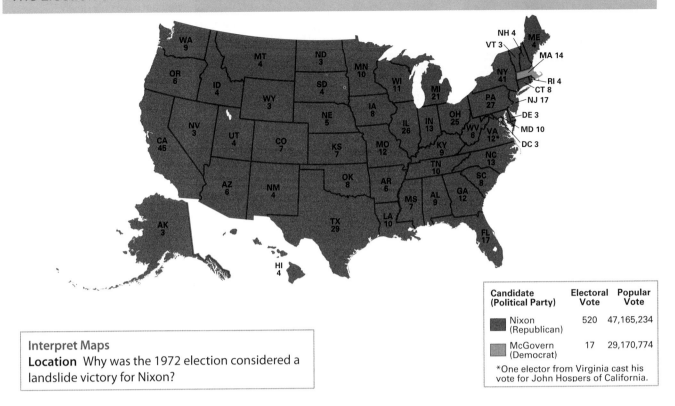

Candidate (Political Party)	Electoral Vote	Popular Vote
■ Nixon (Republican)	520	47,165,234
■ McGovern (Democrat)	17	29,170,774

*One elector from Virginia cast his vote for John Hospers of California.

Interpret Maps
Location Why was the 1972 election considered a landslide victory for Nixon?

Reading Check
Draw Conclusions
Why did McGovern lose in a landslide?

McGovern hoped to appeal to young voters, many of whom would be voting for the first time. The **Twenty-Sixth Amendment**, which was ratified in 1971, lowered the federal voting age from 21 to 18. McGovern did win a majority of these younger voters in 1972, but a majority of voters over 21 from both parties supported Nixon. Many of these voters feared that a McGovern victory would lead to greater disorder and protests. Nixon won by a landslide, receiving 520 electoral votes to McGovern's 17.

The Vietnam War Ends

While Nixon was running for re-election in 1972, Henry Kissinger continued peace negotiations with the North Vietnamese. On January 27, 1973, the United States signed a cease-fire called the Paris Peace Accords with representatives of North Vietnam, South Vietnam, and the Vietcong. The United States agreed to withdraw all its troops from Vietnam. North Vietnam agreed to return all American prisoners of war. Despite the peace agreement, fighting broke out between North and South Vietnam in 1974. The United States refused to send troops back to South Vietnam.

In 1975 North Vietnam invaded the South. Thousands of panic-stricken American Embassy workers and South Vietnamese scrambled to evacuate Saigon. "The city was in flames," remembered one American worker. "And the Communists had the city surrounded with missiles. . . . We realized that we were down to hours if not minutes." Helicopters lifted many people to ships waiting off the coast.

Today, relations between the United States and the united Vietnam have only slowly improved. In 1994 the United States lifted its long-standing trade embargo against Vietnam. In 1995 the former enemies officially established diplomatic relations. Many American veterans and tourists now visit Vietnam.

The Impact in Southeast Asia The war ended when North Vietnamese forces captured Saigon in April 1975. Communist leaders created the Socialist Republic of Vietnam, uniting the former countries of North and South Vietnam. Hanoi became the capital, and Saigon was renamed Ho Chi Minh City.

Life remained extremely difficult in Vietnam after the war. Cities, villages, forests, and farms had been destroyed during the war. Some 250,000 South Vietnamese soldiers died in the war. About 1 million North Vietnamese and Vietcong soldiers were killed. The number of civilians killed is estimated at 2 million. Hundreds of thousands of former soldiers, officials, and other professionals were forced to live in "re-education camps." Another 1.5 million Vietnamese fled the country. About half of them settled in the United States. Thousands of other refugees from Southeast Asia joined them, such as the Hmong of Laos. The Hmong fought bravely alongside the U.S. military against the Communists during the war. Communist dictators took over Laos and Cambodia in 1975. The Cambodian Communist army, the Khmer Rouge, killed about 1.5 million people in a massive campaign to destroy supposed enemies of communism.

According to a 2007 U.S. Census survey, more than a million Vietnamese immigrants now live in the United States. Vietnamese, Laotian, and Cambodian immigrants to the United States have made significant contributions to the communities they join. Many of these communities are along the West and Gulf coasts.

The Impact at Home The Vietnam War carried heavy costs for the United States as well. Some 58,000 Americans were killed, and more than 300,000 were wounded.

Returning American soldiers were not always welcomed home as heroes as other war veterans had been. Some were insulted by antiwar protesters. As veterans struggled to readjust to civilian life, many suffered from post-traumatic stress disorder. This condition includes symptoms such as nightmares and flashbacks to traumatic experiences. Today, the U.S. government is more prepared to meet the needs of veterans with post-traumatic stress disorder. It offers counseling and information to vets and their families on how to deal with symptoms of trauma.

Another effect of the Vietnam War was that Americans had less trust in government officials, including the president. This led to the passage in 1973 of the **War Powers Act**. The act requires the president to get congressional approval before committing U.S. troops to an armed struggle.

The war also left a dismal economic legacy, affecting the development of the United States. Some estimates place the cost to American taxpayers at more than $150 billion. This cost added to the national debt and fueled inflation. The money spent on the war used funds that might have gone to domestic programs, such as those that help the poor.

Americans took a step toward healing the wounds of the war with the 1982 dedication of the **Vietnam Veterans Memorial**. Maya Ying Lin designed the black granite memorial. It lists the names of dead or missing American soldiers. Lin insisted that the names be listed in chronological order rather than in alphabetical order or by rank.

—————— BIOGRAPHY ——————

Maya Ying Lin
1959–

Ohio-born Maya Lin was a 21-year-old architecture student when she designed the Vietnam Veterans Memorial. Her design was chosen from more than 1,400 proposed memorial designs. The memorial is a V-shaped black granite wall that lists the names of more than 58,000 dead and missing Americans. Explaining the design, Lin said, "It was important to me to be extremely honest; not be concerned with the politics of war, but the results. I wanted to bring the visitor a concrete realization of the great loss."

The memorial is now one of the most-visited spots in Washington, DC. Many visitors leave letters, flowers, or other objects at the memorial to honor loved ones.

Draw Conclusions
How does Lin's design achieve the goal she describes?

The smooth, black-granite wall of the Vietnam Veterans Memorial, nearly 500 feet long, lists the 58,249 names of military men and women who died or were listed as missing in action.

Reading Check
Summarize What were the longterm effects of the Vietnam War?

The memorial has become a symbol of healing after a long and divisive war. Hundreds of people visit it daily. Some visitors leave flowers, personal mementos, or written messages. Others simply ponder the meaning of the memorial.

Summary and Preview The Vietnam War deeply divided American society. In the next module you will read about how American life changed in the 1970s and 1980s.

Lesson 3 Assessment

Review Ideas, Terms, and People

1. **a. Identify** What was Students for a Democratic Society?

   b. Elaborate How did hippies express their disapproval of traditional culture?

   c. Evaluate How did the Republicans win the presidential election of 1968?

2. **a. Explain** What was Vietnamization?

   b. Summarize Why did the Pentagon Papers fuel antiwar feelings?

   c. Elaborate How did the Twenty-Sixth Amendment affect the 1972 presidential election?

3. **a. Recall** How did the Vietnam War end?

   b. Describe What was the experience of veterans returning home from Vietnam?

   c. Analyze Do you think U.S. leaders made the right decision in signing the Paris Peace Accords? Why or why not?

Critical Thinking

4. **Identify Effects** In this lesson you learned about the causes of the end of the Vietnam War. Create a chart similar to the one below and use it to list the effects of the end of the war.

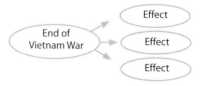

Social Studies Skills

Use Primary Sources: Oral Histories

Define the Skill

An important part of history is understanding the lives and experiences of people in the past. Oral histories and personal memoirs are primary sources that help historians understand how people in the past acted and felt.

Oral histories are interviews in which people talk about events they participated in or witnessed. In personal memoirs, people write about their memories of such events. Both oral histories and personal memoirs are different from other kinds of primary sources because they can be written long after an event takes place. However, they both include descriptions of firsthand experiences.

Learn the Skill

Follow these guidelines to analyze oral histories and personal memoirs.

1. Identify the situation that the oral history or memoir describes.

2. Find the emotions or events that stand out in the description.

3. Make a generalization about how the individual's experience helps us understand the time period or event. Do you think other people might have had similar experiences?

In the following quotation, Diana Dwan Poole describes her experience serving in the Army Nurse Corps in Vietnam.

"One of my rules was that nurses were not allowed to cry. The wounded and dying men in our care need our strength, I told them. We couldn't indulge in the luxury of our own feelings. . . . I was always straight with the soldiers. I would never say, 'Oh, you're going to be just fine,' if they were on their way out. I didn't lie."

Poole was a nurse in Vietnam. In this quotation, she describes working with wounded and dying patients. Her strength in the face of sadness and her honesty stand out.

Other nurses might have had experiences similar to Poole's. The nurses' situation—treating the wounded and the dying—also suggests the dangers soldiers faced.

Practice the Skill

Todd B. Walton was a sergeant in Iraq who found adjusting back to life at home challenging. Read the primary source quotation from Walton below.

"I would scan the overpasses for IEDs or something down on the bottom. Is there anybody on the top that is going to be trying to throw stuff in, obliviously I'm in truck mentality, you know, are they going to try to drop something into your truck. . . . Is there somebody manning a . . . weapon."

1. What situation does Walton describe?

2. Based on this description, how do you think Walton felt at the time?

3. How can Walton's experience help us better understand soldiers serving in Iraq?

Module 13 Assessment

Review Vocabulary, Terms, and People

Identify the descriptions below with the correct term or person from the module.

1. The Cuban rebel who overthrew an unpopular dictator and established a Communist government

2. A barrier made of concrete and barbed wire that separated East Berlin and West Berlin

3. The commander of U.S. ground forces in Vietnam who developed the strategy of search-and-destroy missions

4. Supporters of the Vietnam War who believed winning the Cold War took priority over domestic reform

5. The Republican nominee who won the 1968 election for president of the United States

6. The amendment that lowered the voting age from 21 to 18

Comprehension and Critical Thinking

Lesson 1

7. **a. Recall** What is the Peace Corps?

   b. Sequence Describe the sequence of events that led to American astronauts landing on the moon in 1969.

   c. Evaluate How do you think the Cuban missile crisis would have ended had the United States pursued air strikes or an invasion of Cuba?

Lesson 2

8. **a. Define** What is guerrilla warfare?

   b. Describe How did the American military try to disrupt the Ho Chi Minh Trail?

   c. Predict Do you think Americans' opinions about the war would have been different had there been no television reporting? Explain your answer.

Lesson 3

9. **a. Identify** What was the War Powers Act?

   b. Explain What was Henry Kissinger's role in the Vietnam War?

   c. Summarize What long-term effects did the Vietnam War have on the United States?

Module 13 Assessment, continued

Review Themes

10. **Geography** How did the geography of Vietnam help the Vietcong?

11. **Geography** How did the geography of Vietnam affect American forces?

Reading Skills

Set a Purpose *Use the Reading Skills taught in this module to answer the question about the reading selection below.*

> ### Johnson Commits to Victory
>
> Lyndon Johnson was determined to prevent Communists from taking over in South Vietnam. "We have the resources and the will to follow this course as long as it may take," Johnson said. . . .
>
> **The Tonkin Gulf Resolution**
> In the summer of 1964, a naval skirmish led to a rapid expansion of U.S. involvement in Vietnam. On August 2, 1964, the USS *Maddox* reportedly exchanged gunfire with North Vietnamese torpedo boats in the Gulf of Tonkin, off the North Vietnamese coast. . . .

12. Which of the following is an example of a purpose you could set for the passage above?
    a. Find out why the Vietnam War was fought.
    b. Find out Johnson's view of the Vietnam War.
    c. Find out when the Vietnam War ended.
    d. Find out what the Vietnam Veterans Memorial is.

Social Studies Skills

Use Primary Sources: Oral Histories *Read this passage from marine officer Philip Caputo. Then use the Social Studies Skills taught in this module to answer the question below.*

> "You simply trusted absolutely no one. I mean, from a 5-year-old kid to a 75-year-old woman."

13. How do you think Caputo felt about not being able to trust anyone? Do you think he felt safe? Why or why not?

Focus on Writing

14. **Present a Newscast** Newscasts during the Cold War were a big source of information that reported world and war events to the American people. You will present a five-minute newscast to your class about events in the Cold War. Make notes and include several segments on different topics from the module. One could be an interview with a friend in the role of a soldier back from Vietnam, a government official, or an antiwar protester. You can also use pictures to illustrate the events you are reporting. Write your script and practice reading it before your presentation.

OCTOBER FURY:
THE CUBAN MISSILE CRISIS

The Cuban missile crisis was perhaps the most dangerous event of the Cold War period. For several days in October 1962, the United States and the Soviet Union stood on the brink of nuclear war. The crisis began when the Soviet Union sent weapons, including nuclear missiles, to Cuba. It deepened when the United States blockaded Cuba to prevent the Soviets from delivering more missiles. With Soviet ships sailing toward the blockade, a confrontation seemed inevitable. However, at the last moment, the Soviet ships turned back and war was averted.

Explore the development and resolution of the Cuban missile crisis online. You can find a wealth of information, video clips, primary sources, activities, and more through your online textbook.

Prelude to Crisis

Watch the video to learn about the buildup
to the Cuban missile crisis.

UNITED KINGDOM

UNITED STATES

Getting Ready for War

Watch the video to see how the missiles in Cuba
created tension between the United States and
the Soviet Union.

FALLOUT SHELTER
IN BASEMENT

Crisis Averted?

Watch the video to see how the Cuban missile crisis
brought the United States and the Soviet Union to
the brink of nuclear war.

Lessons Learned

Watch the video to learn about the impact of the
Cuban missile crisis.

The Civil Rights Movement

Essential Question

How successful was the civil rights movement?

About the Photo: African Americans launched a major civil rights movement in the years following World War II. Members of the movement organized demonstrations to protest unfair treatment, like the March on Washington shown here.

In this module you will learn about the efforts of African Americans and others to gain civil rights protections in the 1950s, 1960s, and 1970s.

What You Will Learn . . .

▶ *Explore ONLINE!*

HISTORY

VIDEOS, including...
- Civil Rights Act of 1964
- Little Rock Nine
- March on Washington

☑ Document-Based Investigations

☑ Graphic Organizers

☑ Interactive Games

☑ Image Carousel: The Montgomery Bus Boycott

☑ Interactive map: Freedom Rides, 1961

☑ Image Carousel: Women and Equal Rights

Timeline of Events 1950–1975

▶ *Explore ONLINE!*

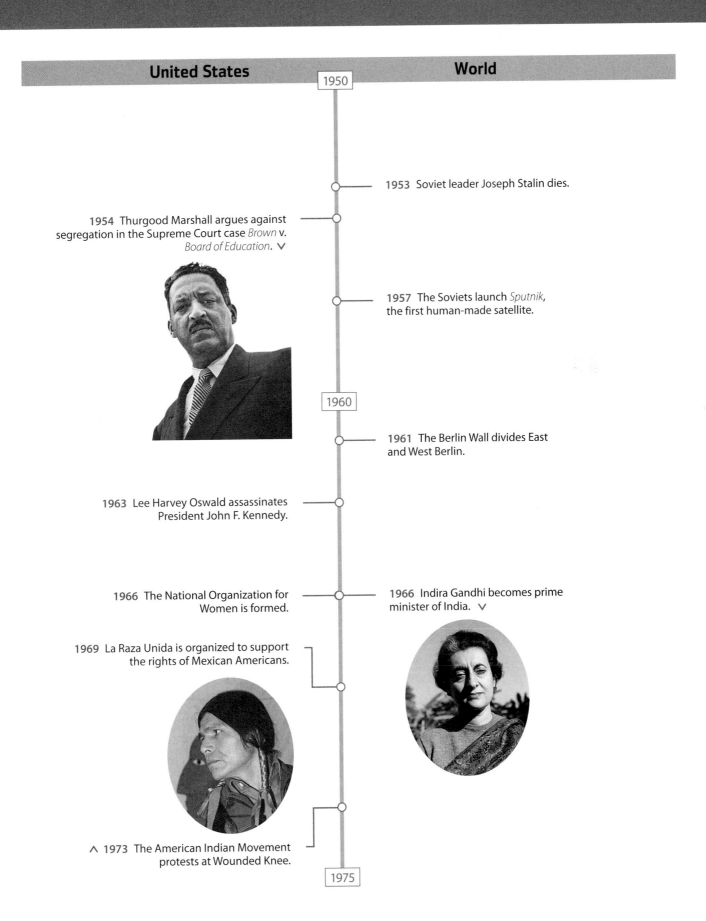

United States	World
	1950
	1953 Soviet leader Joseph Stalin dies.
1954 Thurgood Marshall argues against segregation in the Supreme Court case *Brown* v. *Board of Education*. ∨	
	1957 The Soviets launch *Sputnik*, the first human-made satellite.
	1960
	1961 The Berlin Wall divides East and West Berlin.
1963 Lee Harvey Oswald assassinates President John F. Kennedy.	
1966 The National Organization for Women is formed.	**1966** Indira Gandhi becomes prime minister of India. ∨
1969 La Raza Unida is organized to support the rights of Mexican Americans.	
∧ **1973** The American Indian Movement protests at Wounded Knee.	
	1975

Reading Social Studies

Politics, Society and Culture

In this module you will read about the important changes in American society during the period called the civil rights era. You will learn about how many people came to see politics as a way to correct social inequalities that existed for certain groups in the United States, such as African Americans, women, Mexican Americans, Native Americans, and people with disabilities. You will also read about life in the 1960s.

READING FOCUS:

Use Context Clues: Synonyms

Some words mean almost the same thing. Understanding the similarities can help you understand words whose meaning you may not know.

Understand Synonyms Words that have similar meanings are called synonyms. Often, a synonym is given as a definition. The synonym will probably be a word you already understand. This will help you learn the new word through context clues.

Notice how one reader uses synonyms to understand words she does not understand.

An AIM leader described the groups' goals, saying, "We don't want civil rights in the white man's society—we want our own sovereign [self-governing] rights."

This is a word I don't know the meaning of.

These brackets mean that the word inside is a synonym of the word or phrase that comes before. The word inside is a synonym of *sovereign*.

The word *sovereign* must mean to govern on one's own.

You Try It!

The following passage is from the module you are getting ready to read. As you read the passage, look for synonyms in the definitions of unfamiliar words.

On February 1, 1960, the students went into Woolworth and staged a sit-in—a demonstration in which protesters sit down and refuse to leave. They sat in the "whites-only" section of the lunch counter and ordered coffee. They were not served, but they stayed until the store closed. The next day, they returned with dozens more students to continue the sit-in. Soon, another sit-in began at the lunch counter of a nearby store.

After you read the passage, answer the following questions.

1. What word is a synonym of *sit-in* that is given in that word's definition?
2. What clue is given that helps you find the synonym in the above passage?
3. Can you think of another synonym for *sit-in* that might have been used?

As you read Module 14, look for synonyms that can help you define words you don't know.

The Civil Rights Movement Takes Shape

The Big Idea

Civil rights activists used legal challenges and public protests to confront segregation.

Main Ideas

- Civil rights leaders battled school segregation in court.
- The Montgomery bus boycott helped end segregation on buses.
- Students organized sit-ins to protest segregation.

Key Terms and People

Thurgood Marshall
Brown v. Board of Education
Little Rock Nine
Emmett Till
Rosa Parks
Montgomery bus boycott
Martin Luther King Jr.
sit-in
Student Nonviolent
  Coordinating Committee

If YOU were there . . .

You are an African American student in the 1950s. You get up early every day and take a long bus ride across the city to an African American public school. There is another school just three blocks from your home, but only white students are welcome there. You have heard, however, that this school will soon be opening its doors to black students as well.

Would you want to be one of the first African Americans to attend this school? Why or why not?

Battling Segregation

The push for black civil rights in the United States gained new momentum after World War II. As black veterans came home, many of them were no longer willing to put up with discrimination. They and other African Americans began to call for an end to racial inequality and campaigned for change. As a result, African Americans made a number of key gains. In 1948 President Harry S. Truman desegregated the armed forces. That same year, Truman also banned discrimination in the hiring of federal employees. President Dwight D. Eisenhower, elected in 1952, took further steps to reduce racial discrimination in hiring practices. Meanwhile, at the state level, several northern and western states passed laws banning racial discrimination in public housing.

Despite these gains, many opportunities remained closed to African Americans in the 1950s. Although this period was a time of economic prosperity for many white Americans, few black Americans shared in this new wealth. Furthermore, white resistance to black equality remained strong. Such opposition was particularly evident in the South. White citizens continued to use unfair laws, fear, and violence to keep black citizens from voting or standing up for their rights.

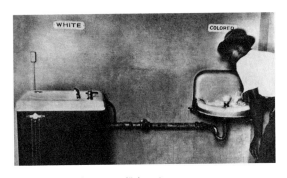

The "separate-but-equal" doctrine legalized the racial segregation of public facilities, so long as the facilities were equal. However, separate facilities, such as these water fountains, were rarely equal.

One major barrier to equality for blacks was segregation. The 1896 Supreme Court case *Plessy* v. *Ferguson* established the "separate-but-equal" doctrine. This doctrine stated that federal, state, and local governments could allow segregation as long as separate facilities were equal. One result of this ruling was that states in both the North and South maintained separate schools for white and black students. Government officials often insisted that though these schools were separate, they were equal in quality.

In fact, however, schools for black children typically received far less funding. Early civil rights leaders focused on ending segregation in America's public schools. Leaders of the movement were members of the National Association for the Advancement of Colored People (NAACP).

Brown v. Board of Education The NAACP's strategy was to show that separate schools were unequal. The NAACP attorneys **Thurgood Marshall**, who went on to become Supreme Court justice, and Jack Greenberg led the courtroom battles against segregation. In the early 1950s, five school segregation cases from Delaware, Kansas, South Carolina, Virginia, and Washington, DC, came together under the title of *Brown v. Board of Education*. The "Brown" in the case title was a seven-year-old African American girl from Topeka, Kansas, named Linda Brown. Though she lived near a school for white children, Linda Brown had to travel across town to a school for black children. Linda's father and the NAACP sued to allow Linda to attend the school closer to her home.

On May 17, 1954, the Supreme Court issued a unanimous ruling on *Brown* v. *Board of Education*. Segregation in schools and other public facilities was illegal.

The next year, the Court ordered public schools to desegregate, or integrate, "with all deliberate speed." These rulings would prove difficult to enforce.

Little Rock Nine In the entire South, only three school districts began desegregating in 1954. Most others **implemented** gradual integration plans. In Little Rock, Arkansas, the school board started by integrating one high school. It allowed nine outstanding black students to attend Central High School. These students became known as the **Little Rock Nine**. Arkansas governor Orval Faubus worked to prevent desegregation at Central High School, however. He used National Guard troops to block the Little Rock Nine from entering the school.

On the morning of September 4, 1957, eight of the nine students arrived at the school together and were turned away by the National Guard. Then the ninth student, 15-year-old Elizabeth Eckford, arrived at the school by herself. She found the entrance blocked by the National Guard. Turning around, she faced a screaming mob. Someone began yelling, "*Lynch her! Lynch her!*" Finally, a white man and woman guided Eckford to safety.

Elizabeth Eckford and the rest of the Little Rock Nine went home. For weeks, Governor Faubus refused to allow them to attend the school. The

Academic Vocabulary
implemented put in place

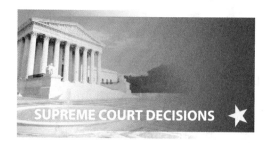

Brown v. Board of Education (1954)

Background of the Case

In 1896 the Supreme Court had ruled in *Plessy v. Ferguson* that "separate-but-equal" facilities were constitutional. In 1951 the NAACP sued the Board of Education of Topeka, Kansas. It argued that segregated schools did not give equal opportunities to black and white children. After hearing many arguments, the Court made its ruling in 1954.

The Court's Ruling

The Supreme Court overturned the *Plessy* doctrine of "separate-but-equal." It ruled that racially segregated schools were not equal and were therefore unconstitutional. All of the justices agreed to the ruling, making it unanimous.

The Court's Reasoning

The Supreme Court decided that segregation violated the Fourteenth Amendment's guarantee of "equal protection of the laws." Its opinion stated, "We conclude that, in the field of public education, the doctrine of 'separate-but-equal' has no place. Separate educational facilities are inherently [naturally] unequal."

Why It Matters

The ruling in *Brown v. Board of Education* led to integrated public schools. It also opened the door to other successful challenges to segregation in public places.

Linda Brown, age 9

Analyze Information

1. How did the ruling in *Brown v. Board of Education* overturn the 1896 Supreme Court ruling in *Plessy v. Ferguson*?

2. How might parents of both black and white children at the time have reacted to the ruling in *Brown v. Board of Education*?

---

tense situation lasted until President Eisenhower sent federal troops to escort the students into the school.

The Little Rock Nine began attending classes, but resistance to integration continued. Some white students insulted, harassed, and attacked the black students. In spite of these obstacles, eight of the nine remained at the school. In May 1958 Ernest Green became the first African American student to graduate from Central High. When Green's name was called at the graduation ceremony, no one clapped. "But I figured they didn't have to," he later said. "After I got that diploma, that was it. I had accomplished what I had come there for."

The Murder of Emmett Till Despite early victories against segregation, blacks remained second-class citizens to many white Americans, particularly in the South. This situation gained nationwide attention in 1955 with the murder of **Emmett Till**, a 14-year-old boy from Chicago, Illinois. Till had gone to the town of Money, Mississippi, to visit relatives. Having

This famous photograph shows Elizabeth Eckford walking to Little Rock's Central High School on September 4, 1957. The young woman shouting at Eckford is Hazel Bryan Massery. In 1963 Massery apologized to Eckford. Massery had decided she did not want to be, she said, the "poster child of the hate generation." The two women later became friends.

grown up in the North, the black teenager did not understand the South's strict racial etiquette. Shortly after arriving in Money, Till visited a local grocery store where he said something to the owner, a young white woman named Carolyn Bryant. She later claimed he asked her for a date and whistled at her, but there is some doubt that this was the case. Whatever Till said, she took offense. Her husband, Roy, soon found out about the incident.

Four days later, Roy Bryant and his half brother J. W. Milam kidnapped Till in the middle of the night. They brutally beat him, shot him, and tossed his body in the Tallahatchie River. National reports of Till's murder deeply moved many Americans.

Bryant and Milam stood trial for the crime, but a jury of 12 white men found them not guilty. Months later, the two men confessed to the killing to a reporter for *Look* magazine. Till's senseless murder—and his killers' acquittal—awakened more Americans to the racism that southern blacks faced and to the need for action.

Montgomery Bus Boycott

The victory in *Brown* v. *Board of Education* had a major impact on American society. However, segregation continued to be enforced in many other public places and facilities in the South. One major area that remained segregated was public transportation.

The NAACP decided to continue the battle against segregation in Montgomery, Alabama. Black passengers there were required to sit in the back of city buses. If the whites-only front section filled up, black passengers had to give up their seats.

On December 1, 1955, a seamstress and NAACP worker named **Rosa Parks** boarded a bus and sat in the front row of the section reserved for black passengers. When the bus became full, the driver told Parks and

Reading Check
Summarize
What obstacles faced supporters of desegregation?

Rosa Parks 1913–2005

Rosa Parks was born in Tuskegee, Alabama, and spent most of her childhood in Montgomery. While working as a seamstress, Parks became an active member of the NAACP.

She was fired from her seamstress job for her leading role in the Montgomery bus boycott. After the boycott succeeded, she and her husband moved to Detroit, Michigan. She continued working for fair treatment for all Americans and started a program to teach children about the Underground Railroad and the civil rights movement.

Find the Main Idea
How did Rosa Parks work for equal rights?

three others to give their seats to white passengers. Parks refused. The bus driver called the police, and Parks was taken to jail.

To protest Parks's arrest, African American professor Jo Ann Robinson organized a boycott of Montgomery buses. Local leaders formed the Montgomery Improvement Association (MIA) to help strengthen the boycott. In the **Montgomery bus boycott**, thousands of African Americans stopped riding the buses. Some white residents supported the boycott as well. Bus ridership fell by 70 percent.

To lead the MIA, African American leaders turned to **Martin Luther King Jr.**, a young Baptist minister. The 26-year-old King already had a reputation as a powerful speaker whose words could motivate and inspire listeners.

As the boycott continued, bus drivers guided nearly empty buses down the city streets. Leaders planned a carpool system that helped people find rides at more than 40 locations throughout Montgomery. For 381 days, boycotters carpooled, took taxis, rode bicycles, and walked. Still, Montgomery's leaders refused to integrate the bus system.

As in Little Rock during the school segregation fight, many white residents were angry about the attempt to end segregation. Some people resorted to violence. King's home was bombed, and he received hate mail and phone calls threatening him and his family. The police also harassed and arrested carpool drivers. In spite of this intimidation, the boycott gained national attention, sparking similar protests in other cities.

Finally, in November 1956 the Supreme Court ruled that segregation on public transportation was illegal. The next month, King joined other black and white ministers to ride the first integrated bus in Montgomery. "It . . . makes you feel that America is a great country and we're going to do more to make it greater," remembered Jo Ann Robinson.

The Montgomery bus boycott helped make Martin Luther King Jr. a nationally known civil rights leader. He formed the Southern Christian Leadership Conference (SCLC), which led campaigns for civil rights throughout the South.

Reading Check
Identify Cause and Effect
What event sparked the Montgomery bus boycott?

Sit-ins and the SNCC

Like public schools and buses, many private businesses in the South were segregated. In Greensboro, North Carolina, four students decided to challenge this form of segregation. They targeted a lunch counter at Woolworth, a popular department store. Black customers were supposed to eat standing up at one end of the counter. White customers sat down to eat at the other end.

On February 1, 1960, the students went into Woolworth and staged a **sit-in**—a demonstration in which protesters sit down and refuse to leave. They sat in the whites-only section of the lunch counter and ordered coffee. They were not served, but they stayed until the store closed. The next day, they returned with dozens more students to continue the sit-in. Soon, another sit-in began at the lunch counter of a nearby store.

People across the country read newspaper stories about the Greensboro sit-ins. Picket lines supporting the sit-ins began to appear outside of Woolworth stores in northern cities. Other black students in North Carolina and across the South began to hold similar protests at segregated facilities such as libraries, restaurants, and churches. The student protesters practiced the strategy of nonviolent resistance. No matter how much they were insulted or threatened, they refused to respond with violence. They were inspired by Martin Luther King Jr., who was a strong supporter of nonviolent action.

———— BIOGRAPHY ————

Martin Luther King Jr. 1929–1968

King grew up in Atlanta, Georgia, where his father was a pastor. He studied to become a minister in Pennsylvania. He received his doctorate in Massachusetts, then became pastor of a church in Alabama. He traveled throughout the country as a civil rights leader.

As a powerful and moving speaker, King became one of the leading voices of the civil rights movement. He was committed to achieving equality through nonviolent protest. He led a series of successful marches and protests, including the 1955 Montgomery bus boycott and the 1963 March on Washington.

His leadership helped make the civil rights movement a success. His belief in and passion for nonviolence led to the boycotts, sit-ins, and marches that helped African Americans gain equal treatment. King's work helped bring an end to legal segregation and led to new laws guaranteeing equal rights for all Americans.

Evaluate
Which of Martin Luther King Jr.'s contributions to the civil rights movement was most important? Why?

During this sit-in at a segregated lunch counter, young African Americans sat with their white friends and asked to be served. The activists reacted calmly as onlookers harassed them.

Reading Check
Compare
How were sit-ins similar to other civil rights protests?

These social conflicts led to change in North Carolina and the rest of the United States. Over time, some restaurants and businesses, including Woolworth, began the process of integration. To continue the struggle for civil rights, the leaders of the student protests formed the **Student Nonviolent Coordinating Committee** (SNCC) in the spring of 1960. The SNCC activists trained protesters and organized civil rights demonstrations. Bob Moses, a leader of the SNCC, helped organize sit-ins and voter registration drives.

Summary and Preview In the 1950s, court rulings and protests challenged segregation. In the next lesson you will learn how the civil rights movement continued the fight against inequality.

Lesson 1 Assessment

Review Ideas, Terms, and People

1. **a. Analyze** In what areas did early laws ban racial discrimination?

   b. Summarize How did the Supreme Court impact the desegregation of public schools?

   c. Identify Who were the Little Rock Nine?

2. **a. Recall** What was the purpose of the Montgomery bus boycott?

   b. Analyze Why was the arrest of Rosa Parks a turning point in the civil rights movement?

   c. Elaborate Why do you think the bus boycott lasted so long?

3. **a. Identify** What means did the Student Nonviolent Coordinating Committee use to protest segregation?

   b. Make Inferences What might have inspired the Greensboro students to stage a sit-in?

   c. Evaluate Do you think picketing and boycotts are an effective form of protest? Why or why not?

Critical Thinking

4. **Sequence** In this lesson you learned about events that challenged segregation. Create a graphic organizer similar to the one below and use it to show the sequence of major events in the civil rights movement described in this lesson.

Kennedy, Johnson, and Civil Rights

The Big Idea

The civil rights movement made major advances during the presidencies of John F. Kennedy and Lyndon B. Johnson.

Main Ideas

- John F. Kennedy was elected president in 1960.

- Civil rights leaders continued to fight for equality.

- Lyndon B. Johnson became president when Kennedy was assassinated.

- Changes occurred in the civil rights movement in the late 1960s.

Key Terms and People

John F. Kennedy
Freedom Rides
Medgar Evers
March on Washington
Lyndon B. Johnson
Civil Rights Act of 1964
Voting Rights Act of 1965
Great Society
Black Power
Malcolm X

If YOU were there . . .

You are a civil rights activist living and working in the South. It is 1960, a presidential election year. The battle for fair treatment has been difficult, and you hope that the next president will support civil rights. Both major presidential candidates will be visiting your area soon. You might have a chance to meet them and ask some questions.

What questions would you ask the candidates?

Kennedy Elected

When **John F. Kennedy** won the election of 1960, he became the youngest person ever elected president of the United States. For many Americans, Kennedy and his wife, Jacqueline, brought a sense of style and excitement to the White House. Kennedy was also the first Roman Catholic to become president.

In his inaugural address, Kennedy spoke of the opportunities and dangers facing Americans. "Man holds in his mortal hands the power to abolish all forms of human poverty and all forms of human life," he said. He encouraged all Americans to support freedom throughout the world. He said, "And so, my fellow Americans, ask not what your country can do for you—ask what you can do for your country."

As president, Kennedy pursued a set of proposals he called the New Frontier. His plan included a higher minimum wage and tax cuts to help stimulate economic growth. It called for new spending on the military and on the space program, and new programs to help poor and unemployed Americans. Kennedy also proposed providing greater financial help to public schools. However, political conflicts slowed the development of these programs. Fearing a budget imbalance, Republicans and conservative southern Democrats blocked much of the legislation Kennedy introduced.

John F. Kennedy 1917–1963

John F. Kennedy was born to a politically powerful and wealthy family in Massachusetts. He graduated from Harvard University, then joined the U.S. Navy. He commanded a patrol boat in the South Pacific during World War II and was wounded in a sea battle. Kennedy was elected to the House of Representatives at the age of 29 and to the Senate six years later. He was elected president in 1960, bringing a youthful energy to the White House. He had served for fewer than three years when he was assassinated.

Identify
What experiences helped prepare Kennedy to lead the nation?

Reading Check
Draw Inferences
What do you think African American voters hoped for from the new president?

Kennedy also spoke of his support for the goals of the civil rights movement. This had helped convince many African Americans to vote for him in the election of 1960. As president, however, Kennedy moved slowly on civil rights legislation. He was reluctant to anger Republicans and conservative southern Democrats in Congress. He needed their support to pass other items on his agenda. Kennedy was also busy dealing with foreign policy crises.

The Fight for Rights Continues

Public schools and some businesses had begun to desegregate. But other facilities remained strictly segregated.

Freedom Rides In 1947 a civil rights group called the Congress of Racial Equality (CORE) began protests in which African Americans rode in the whites-only section of interstate buses. In 1960 the Court ruled that segregation of bus stations was illegal. CORE decided to put pressure on President Kennedy to enforce this ruling.

To accomplish this, CORE organized a series of protests called the **Freedom Rides**. On these rides black and white bus riders traveled together to segregated bus stations in the South. White riders planned to use facilities set aside for African Americans in bus stations. Black riders would use whites-only facilities.

The Freedom Rides began in May 1961, when 13 riders boarded a bus traveling from Washington, DC, to New Orleans, Louisiana. In one Alabama town, the riders were viciously attacked by a white mob. After more attacks, CORE leaders decided to stop the protest to protect the riders' lives.

The leaders of the SNCC decided to continue the Freedom Rides. The SNCC activists faced the same violence as the CORE riders. Arriving in Montgomery, Alabama, in late May, they were attacked by a furious mob.

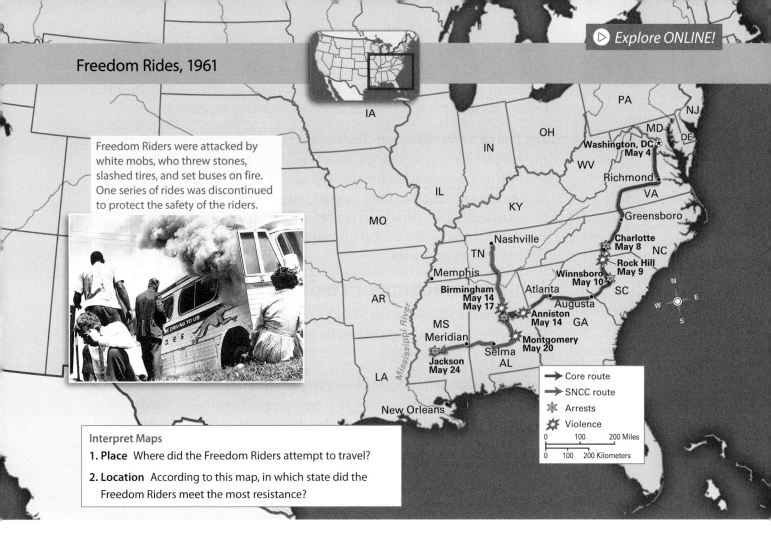

Freedom Rides, 1961

▶ Explore ONLINE!

Freedom Riders were attacked by white mobs, who threw stones, slashed tires, and set buses on fire. One series of rides was discontinued to protect the safety of the riders.

Washington, DC ★ May 4
Richmond
Greensboro
Charlotte May 8
Rock Hill May 9
Winnsboro May 10
Nashville
Memphis
Birmingham May 14 May 17
Atlanta
Augusta
Anniston May 14
MS Meridian
Montgomery May 20
Selma
Jackson May 24
New Orleans

Core route
SNCC route
Arrests
Violence

0   100   200 Miles
0 100   200 Kilometers

Interpret Maps

1. **Place** Where did the Freedom Riders attempt to travel?

2. **Location** According to this map, in which state did the Freedom Riders meet the most resistance?

Many Freedom Riders were jailed in Jackson, Mississippi. That same month, President Kennedy ordered the Interstate Commerce Commission to enforce strict bans on segregation in interstate bus terminals.

King in Birmingham In 1963 Martin Luther King Jr. organized marches in Birmingham, Alabama. King was arrested and jailed for marching without a permit. While jailed, he wrote a "Letter from Birmingham Jail," explaining his commitment to nonviolence. "We will reach the goal of freedom in Birmingham and all over the nation, because the goal of America is freedom."

King was released from jail and led a new round of marches. In May 1963 some 2,500 demonstrators marched through downtown Birmingham. Police commissioner Eugene "Bull" Connor ordered his officers to unleash their attack dogs and blast the marchers with high-pressure water hoses. Televised images of their tactics shocked Americans.

The Assassination of Medgar Evers Pressure for civil rights legislation continued to grow. President Kennedy called racial discrimination "a moral crisis." In June 1963 he announced support for a sweeping civil rights bill to end racial discrimination completely. Just hours later, the head of the NAACP in Mississippi, **Medgar Evers**, was murdered in front of his home in Jackson, Mississippi. Evers was one of the movement's most effective leaders. His slaying shocked many Americans.

Police quickly arrested a Ku Klux Klan member named Byron De La Beckwith. All-white juries failed to reach a verdict in two trials, and De La Beckwith went free. In 1994 he was tried again based on some comments he had made. He was convicted and died in prison in 2001.

The March on Washington To demonstrate support for the civil rights movement, African American leaders held the **March on Washington**— a massive demonstration for civil rights. On August 28, 1963, Martin Luther King Jr. stood at the Lincoln Memorial before a diverse crowd of more than 200,000 people. In his famous "I Have a Dream" speech, King expressed his hope for a future in which all Americans would enjoy equal rights and opportunities.

Reading Check
Summarize How did the Birmingham marches affect public opinion?

Johnson Becomes President

In the months following the March on Washington, Congress debated Kennedy's civil rights legislation. In November 1963 Kennedy began a quick tour of Texas cities.

Kennedy Assassinated On November 22, 1963, Kennedy rode through Dallas in a convertible, waving to supporters in the streets. Suddenly, gunshots rang out. Kennedy had been shot twice, and he died soon afterward in a Dallas hospital. Vice President **Lyndon B. Johnson** was quickly sworn in as president. Dallas police arrested an alleged assassin, Lee Harvey Oswald.

The assassination stunned Americans, who grieved the young president's death. Many of Kennedy's goals were left unfinished. Vowing to continue Kennedy's work, President Johnson urged Congress to pass a civil rights bill.

Civil Rights Laws On July 2, 1964, President Johnson signed the **Civil Rights Act of 1964**. The act banned segregation in public places. It also outlawed discrimination in the workplace on the basis of color, gender, religion, or national origin.

—— BIOGRAPHY ——

Lyndon B. Johnson 1908–1973

Lyndon B. Johnson grew up in rural Texas. After working his way through college, Johnson taught school for a year. In 1937, at the age of 29, he was elected to the House of Representatives. He was elected to the Senate in 1948. Johnson was known for his ability to guide bills through Congress by convincing members from both political parties to support them. As one fellow member of Congress said, "Lyndon got me by the lapels [jacket collar] and put his face on top of mine and he talked and talked." Johnson was elected vice president in 1960 and became president in 1963.

Compare and Contrast
How was Johnson's career similar to Kennedy's, and how was it different?

Johnson and Civil Rights

After he became president, Lyndon Johnson promised to continue Kennedy's plans for civil rights legislation. Johnson worked with Congress and African American leaders to create and pass laws that would help ensure equality for all Americans. Here, Johnson is shown signing the Civil Rights Act of 1964 as Martin Luther King Jr. and other leaders look on.

That summer, activists began to push for equal voting rights for African Americans in the South. Legally, of course, African Americans had the right to vote. But in much of the South, threats and unfair election rules often kept them from the polls. During the "Freedom Summer" of 1964, hundreds of volunteers, including many white college students, came to Mississippi. Their goal was to help African Americans register to vote.

Volunteers were threatened and attacked. On June 21 three civil rights workers—James Chaney, a young black Mississippian plasterer's apprentice; Andrew Goodman, a Jewish Queens College student; and Michael Schwerner, a Jewish social worker from New York City—were murdered by members of the Ku Klux Klan. Martin Luther King Jr. organized a voting rights march from Selma, Alabama, to Montgomery, during which many marchers were beaten and jailed. Violence against civil rights workers convinced many people to support voter registration efforts.

Congress approved the **Voting Rights Act of 1965**, which Johnson signed into law in August. This law gave the federal government new powers to protect African Americans' voting rights. Within three years, more than half of all qualified African Americans in the South registered to vote.

Quick Facts

The Great Society

Great Society Legislation:

- Civil Rights Act of 1964
- Voting Rights Act of 1965
- Elementary and Secondary Education Act of 1965
- Medicare and Medicaid Bill, 1965
- Department of Housing and Urban Development Act of 1965

The Great Society President Johnson won the election of 1964 by a huge margin. He saw this as a vote of approval for his program of domestic reforms that he called the **Great Society**. "The Great Society rests on abundance and liberty for all," Johnson said.

Congress quickly passed most of Johnson's Great Society legislation. Great Society programs included Medicare, which helps senior citizens afford health care, and Medicaid, which gives health care aid to low-income citizens. Another act gave local schools more than $1 billion to help students

Timeline: Civil Rights Movement, Key Events

1950 —— 1965

1955
Rosa Parks refuses to give up her seat on a Montgomery, Alabama, bus, sparking a citywide bus boycott. >

1960
The first sit-in at a segregated lunch counter occurs in Greensboro, North Carolina.

1963
Four young girls die in a bombing of a Birmingham, Alabama, church. The deaths lead to riots and civil unrest during which police attack African Americans. ∨

1964 ∧
Civil rights leader Martin Luther King Jr. receives the Nobel Peace Prize for his work in nonviolent demonstrations against segregation.

Interpret Timelines
Which events in the timeline are examples of nonviolent protest?

Reading Check
Summarize How did President Johnson support civil rights?

with special needs. The Department of Housing and Urban Development (HUD) was created to help low-income families get better housing. Robert Weaver served as HUD's secretary, becoming the first African American appointed to a presidential cabinet.

Changes in the Civil Rights Movement

Many young civil rights reformers found the pace of change too slow. Others entirely rejected the goal of racial integration.

New Directions One such activist was Stokely Carmichael, who had participated in the Freedom Rides and many marches. But in the mid-1960s, he broke with the goal of nonviolence. Carmichael was a founder of the **Black Power** movement, which called for African American independence. Black Power activists believed that blacks should reject integration, focusing instead on controlling their own communities.

Malcolm X helped inspire the Black Power movement. He was a leader of the Nation of Islam, an organization that combined ideas about African American independence with the teachings of Islam. Malcolm X argued that African Americans should work for social and political independence. He believed that African Americans had the right to defend themselves, using violence if necessary.

In 1964 Malcolm X traveled to the Muslim holy city of Mecca, where he met Muslims of many races. He began to hope that different races could coexist in peace, although he still supported freedom "by any means necessary." But in 1965 Malcolm X broke with the Nation of Islam and was killed by three of its members.

Reading Check

Contrast How did Malcolm X's goals differ from Martin Luther King Jr.'s?

Violence in the Streets Slow progress in the civil rights movement frustrated many members of the black community. In some U.S. cities, tensions exploded into violent, sometimes deadly, riots. One such riot occurred in August 1965 in the Watts section of Los Angeles. Twenty-four people were killed, and much of Watts was destroyed.

In April 1968 Martin Luther King Jr. was shot and killed in Memphis, Tennessee. As televised reports spread the news of King's assassination, furious rioters took to the streets in more than 100 American cities. The movement had lost its most visible leader.

Summary and Preview Under Kennedy and Johnson, major civil rights legislation was passed. In the next lesson you will learn how more groups began to push for equal rights.

Lesson 2 Assessment

Review Ideas, Terms, and People

1. **a. Describe** How was John F. Kennedy different from previous presidents?

   b. Analyze Why did many African Americans vote for Kennedy? Did his election to office bring the results they might have expected?

2. **a. Identify** What were the Freedom Rides?

   b. Explain How did television influence public opinion about the civil rights movement?

3. **a. Recall** What happened in Dallas, Texas, on November 22, 1963?

   b. Draw Conclusions Based on Johnson's plans for the Great Society, what do you think he believed was the purpose of government?

4. **a. Recall** What challenges did the civil rights movement face in the late 1960s?

   b. Elaborate Why did Malcolm X reject the goal of racial integration?

Critical Thinking

5. **Evaluate** In this lesson you learned about the goals and achievements of leaders who supported civil rights. Create a graphic organizer similar to the one below and use it to evaluate the leaders discussed in the section. Tell whether or not you think the leaders' actions were effective.

Leader	Evaluation

Rights for Other Americans

The Big Idea

Encouraged by the success of the civil rights movement, many groups worked for equal rights in the 1960s.

Main Ideas

- Hispanic Americans organized for civil rights and economic opportunities.

- The women's movement worked for equal rights.

- Other Americans also fought for change.

Key Terms and People

Cesar Chavez
Dolores Huerta
United Farm Workers
Betty Friedan
National Organization for Women
Shirley Chisholm
Equal Rights Amendment
Phyllis Schlafly
American Indian Movement
Earl Warren
Warren Court
Disabled in Action

If YOU were there . . .

Your parents came to the United States from Mexico, and you were born in California in the 1950s. You and your family work year-round picking crops—the work is hard, and the pay is low. You're trying to put aside some money for school, but your family barely makes enough to get by. Some farmworkers are talking about going on strike for better wages.

**Would you join the strike?
Why or why not?**

Hispanic Americans Organize for Change

The Hispanic population of the United States grew to 4 million by 1960 and to more than 10 million by 1970. Though people of Mexican descent made up the majority of this population, Hispanic Americans were a diverse group. Many people from Puerto Rico, Cuba, and other Latin American countries also lived in the United States.

The success of African Americans in battling segregation encouraged Hispanic Americans to fight for their own rights. **Cesar Chavez** was one of many Hispanic Americans who worked to improve conditions. In 1962, with help from **Dolores Huerta** and Gil Padilla, Chavez formed a union. It would later become the **United Farm Workers** (UFW). This union was committed to the goal of better pay and working conditions for migrant farmworkers—those who move seasonally from farm to farm for work. Chavez led the UFW in a five-year strike and boycott against California grape growers. Huerta worked by his side as the union's chief negotiator for contracts. They negotiated to guarantee farmworkers fair wages, benefits, and humane working conditions. The workers finally won better wages and benefits in 1970. The UFW became a national organization in 1976.

Chavez shared Martin Luther King Jr.'s commitment to nonviolent protest. To those who complained about the slow

Cesar Chavez 1927–1993

Cesar Chavez was born on a small family ranch in Arizona. After losing their land during the Great Depression, Chavez and his family began working as migrant farmworkers. Moving from town to town in search of work, Chavez went to more than 30 different schools. He served in the U.S. Navy during World War II, then returned to the fields to help migrant workers fight for better pay and working conditions. The soft-spoken Chavez seemed to many an unlikely leader of a protest movement. But Chavez quickly became an influential leader, continuing to lead the struggle for farmworkers' rights into the 1990s. Before his death, Chavez insisted, "It's not me who counts, it's the Movement."

Make Inferences
Why do you think Chavez began the farmworkers' movement?

Academic Vocabulary
consequences the effects of a particular event or events

Reading Check
Sequence What group helped inspire the Chicano movement?

pace of change, he pointed out that nonviolence takes time, and he urged them to be patient.

Chavez helped inspire young leaders in what became known as the Chicano movement. To fight discrimination and gain greater political influence, Chicano activists formed a political party called *La Raza Unida*, or the United Race. The Hispanic civil rights movement had important **consequences**. A 1968 amendment to the Elementary and Secondary Education Act required schools to teach students whose first language was not English in both languages until they learned English. The Voting Rights Act of 1975 required communities with large immigrant populations to print ballots in the voters' preferred language.

The Women's Movement

Activists also brought public attention to women's position in society. In 1963 a government commission reported that women had fewer job opportunities than men and were often paid less for the same work. President Kennedy responded by ordering an end to discrimination based on gender in civil service jobs. That same year Congress passed the Equal Pay Act. This act required many employers to pay men and women equal salaries for the same work. The Civil Rights Act of 1964 banned discrimination based on both gender and race.

Some women also began to question their traditional roles in society. In her 1963 book *The Feminine Mystique*, **Betty Friedan** described the dissatisfaction some women felt with their traditional roles of wife, mother, and homemaker.

Friedan became a leader of the modern women's rights movement. In 1966 she helped found the **National Organization for Women** (NOW)

In the 1960s women began to organize to demand equal rights. The movement became known as women's liberation. Many activists supported a woman's right to equal pay and equal protection under the law.

Shirley Chisholm became the first African American woman elected to Congress in 1968.

Betty Friedan authored *The Feminine Mystique*, a book declaring that many women wanted achievements beyond those of becoming a wife and mother.

to fight for equal educational and career opportunities for women. Other women worked for change by running for and holding public office. In 1968 **Shirley Chisholm** was elected to represent a New York City district in the House of Representatives. She was the first African American woman elected to the U.S. Congress.

In the early 1970s NOW and other women's rights activists supported and lobbied for an amendment to the Constitution. The **Equal Rights Amendment** (ERA) would outlaw all discrimination based on sex. The ERA was approved by Congress in 1972.

For an amendment to go into effect, it must be ratified by three-fourths of the states—or 38 out of 50 states. The ERA was ratified by 30 state legislatures by the end of 1973. But many opponents came forward to block the ERA. **Phyllis Schlafly**, a conservative activist, founded the group STOP ERA to prevent its ratification. Schlafly and her supporters argued that the ERA would hurt families by encouraging women to focus on careers rather than on motherhood. Such opposition weakened support for the ERA. In June 1982 the amendment fell three states short of ratification.

Despite this failure, the women's movement achieved many of its goals. Women found new opportunities in education and the workplace. For example, women began attending many formerly all-male universities. Increasing numbers of women pursued careers in traditionally all-male fields such as law and medicine. Many women also won political office at all levels of government.

Reading Check
Find Main Ideas
What were some achievements of the women's movement of the 1960s?

Other Voices for Change

Other Americans also began to demand change in laws and other discriminating practices during the 1960s and 1970s. In 1974 the Asian American Legal Defense and Education Fund was founded. Its purpose was to build an "informed and active Asian America." The National Italian American Foundation (1975) advocated for Italian Americans. League of United Latin American Citizens was founded much earlier. It played an important

Some activists worked to maintain what they saw as women's protected status under the law. Phyllis Schlafly argued against the Equal Rights Amendment, saying it would reduce the legal rights of wives and mothers.

activist role for Hispanic Americans during this period as well and continues to do so today. Native Americans and people with disabilities were also inspired by the civil rights movement.

Native Americans One major issue for Native Americans was their lack of control over tribal lands. Many worked through the National Congress of American Indians (NCAI) to gain more control over reservation lands from the federal government. They helped win passage of the Indian Civil Rights Act of 1968.

Other activists thought that groups like the NCAI worked too slowly. In November 1969 a group of young Native Americans occupied Alcatraz Island in San Francisco Bay. They did this to protest the government's takeover of Native American lands.

One of the groups that participated in the Alcatraz protest was the **American Indian Movement** (AIM). It was founded in 1968 to fight for Native Americans' rights. In February 1973 AIM activists seized a trading post and church at Wounded Knee, South Dakota. Wounded Knee is the site of the U.S. Army's massacre of Sioux Indians in 1890. Federal marshals surrounded Wounded Knee. The standoff ended with a gun battle killing two protesters and wounding one federal agent.

Such protests brought attention to issues facing Native Americans. In the early 1970s Congress began passing laws granting Native Americans greater self-government on tribal lands.

Rights for Individuals During the 1960s Supreme Court decisions brought major changes to American society. Under the leadership of Chief Justice **Earl Warren**, Court rulings greatly extended individual rights and freedoms. In *Escobedo* v. *Illinois* (1964), the justices decided that a person has the right to a lawyer during police questioning. In 1966 the Court extended these rights again in the case of *Miranda* v. *Arizona*. The Court ruled that accused persons must be informed of their rights at the time of their arrest. Today police in the United States carry cards with the Miranda warnings printed on them. They routinely "Mirandize" suspects by "reading them their rights."

The **Warren Court** issued many landmark decisions that further defined individual rights. One of these decisions was made in *Tinker* v. *Des Moines Independent Community School District* (1969). The Court established the right of public school students to express political opinions at school. The ruling stated that speech protected by the First Amendment includes not only spoken words but also "symbolic speech," or acts that express an opinion.

In this time of activism, some advocates felt that bringing cases before the Supreme Court might be a way to gain more rights for the LGBT (lesbian, gay, bisexual, and transgender) community. Their attempts, however, were not successful. During the 1970s and 1980s, members of the LGBT community began to fight openly for civil rights. Direct action groups sprang up throughout the country. They called for an end to antigay discrimination. Some people condemned this activism but were unable to slow the pace of change. By the early 1990s, several states and more than 100 local communities had outlawed such discrimination.

The Disability Rights Movement In 1970 Judy Heumann and other activists created **Disabled in Action** (DIA) to make people aware of challenges facing people with disabilities. People with disabilities often lacked access to both job opportunities and to public places. The DIA's work led to the passage of new laws. The Rehabilitation Act of 1973 banned federal agencies from discriminating against people with disabilities. The Education of Handicapped Children Act of 1975 required public schools to provide a quality education to children with disabilities. In 1990 the Americans with Disabilities Act (ADA) outlawed all discrimination against people with disabilities.

Judy Heumann and other activists formed Disabled in Action in 1970. The group promotes legislation and access to independent living for people with disabilities.

Reading Check
Contrast How were the tactics of AIM and DIA different?

Summary and Preview The fight for equal rights had far-reaching effects on American society. In the next module you will learn about world conflicts that also affected Americans.

Lesson 3 Assessment

Review Ideas, Terms, and People

1. a. **Evaluate** How did Hispanic Americans fight for civil rights?

   b. **Describe** Who benefited from laws like the Elementary and Secondary Education Act of 1968 and the Voting Rights Act of 1975?

2. a. **Analyze** What democratic rights and freedoms did women have to fight to obtain?

   b. **Explain** What happened during the ratification process of the Equal Rights Amendment?

   c. **Evaluate** Do you think holding elected office and lobbying are effective methods to cause change? Explain your answer.

3. a. **Analyze** In what way was the American Indian Movement similar to the Black Power movement?

   b. **Identify** What laws banned discrimination against people with disabilities?

Critical Thinking

4. **Categorize** In this lesson you learned about the achievements of groups that worked for equal rights. Create a graphic organizer similar to the one below and use it to identify the achievements of each group.

Hispanic Americans	Women	Native Americans	People with Disabilities

Social Studies Skills

Make Speeches

Define the Skill

In a democracy, activists, government leaders, and candidates for public office often need to address people directly. Speeches allow public figures to deliver a message to many people at once. People can use speeches to make their views known. They can use speeches to try to persuade people to support their ideas or programs.

Learn the Skill

Think about the role of speeches in the civil rights movement. Politicians and civil rights leaders used speeches to increase awareness of and support for the movement's goals. President John F. Kennedy is remembered as a powerful and effective speaker. On June 11, 1963, he gave a speech on civil rights that moved and inspired many listeners. Here is a brief excerpt from that speech, which he broadcast from the White House:

"The heart of the question is whether all Americans are to be afforded equal rights and equal opportunities, whether we are going to treat our fellow Americans as we want to be treated. If an American, because his skin is dark, cannot eat lunch in a restaurant open to the public, if he cannot send his children to the best public school available, if he cannot vote for the public officials who will represent him, if, in short, he cannot enjoy the full and free life which all of us want, then who among us would be content to have the color of his skin changed and stand in his place? Who among us would then be content with the counsels of patience and delay?"

Kennedy used repetition to express his message about the need for a civil rights bill. For example, notice that he included a series of phrases beginning with the word *if* to emphasize the injustices faced by African Americans. Not only do these phrases begin with the same word, but they also repeat the same grammatical pattern. Through this technique, Kennedy created a powerful rhythm that helped persuade his listeners.

The words of Kennedy's civil rights speech are powerful, but Kennedy's delivery made the speech even stronger. Kennedy spoke with confidence in a loud, clear voice. He also used direct eye contact and appropriate facial expressions to connect with his television audience.

Following these steps can help you make a persuasive speech.

1. Write the speech. Make sure it includes a clear main idea, good examples, and convincing language.

2. Practice. Practice reading your speech out loud to a friend. You can also practice at home in front of a mirror.

3. Give the speech. Remember to speak loudly and clearly and to look at your audience.

Practice the Skill

Suppose that you are a politician or civil rights leader in the 1960s. Following the steps above, write a short speech in favor of equal rights for African Americans, Hispanic Americans, women, Native Americans, or Americans with disabilities. After you have written and practiced your speech, give the speech to the class.

Module 14 Assessment

Review Vocabulary, Terms, and People

Complete each sentence by filling in the blank with the correct term or person from the module.

1. _____ was an African American civil rights leader and minister who believed in nonviolent, direct action.

2. In 1960 black students staged a(n) _____ at a Woolworth lunch counter in Greensboro, North Carolina.

3. The Congress of Racial Equality organized the _____ to protest segregation in bus stations throughout the South.

4. The _____ protected the voting rights of African Americans.

5. The _____ worked to get better pay and working conditions for migrant farmworkers.

6. _____ was the first African American woman elected to the U.S. Congress.

Comprehension and Critical Thinking

Lesson 1

7. **a. Describe** What was the Court's ruling in the *Brown* v. *Board of Education* case?

   b. Explain What did the Student Nonviolent Coordinating Committee do to fight segregation?

   c. Draw Conclusions Why do you think Martin Luther King Jr. was chosen to lead the MIA?

Lesson 2

8. **a. Recall** What was the New Frontier?

   b. Contrast What roles did leaders from CORE and SNCC play in the Freedom Rides?

   c. Compare and Contrast How were Malcolm X's ideas and strategies similar to those of Martin Luther King Jr.? How did they differ?

Lesson 3

9. **a. Identify** What is the National Organization for Women?

   b. Summarize How did Cesar Chavez help migrant farmworkers?

   c. Elaborate How did the Americans with Disabilities Act help disabled Americans?

Module 14 Assessment, continued

Review Themes

10. **Politics** How did political changes help minorities achieve their goals?

11. **Society and Culture** How did society change during the civil rights era?

Reading Skills

Use Context Clues: Synonyms *Use the Reading Skills taught in this module to answer the question below.*

> The Little Rock Nine began attending classes, but resistance to integration continued. Some white students insulted, harassed, and attacked the black students. In spite of these obstacles, eight of the nine remained at the school.

12. Which of the following would be a good synonym for the word *harassed*?
    - **a.** comforted
    - **b.** assisted
    - **c.** helped
    - **d.** insulted

Social Studies Skills

Make Speeches *Use the Social Studies Skills taught in this module to answer the question below.*

13. What steps should you follow to make a persuasive speech?

Focus on Writing

14. **Write a Bill** In this module you learned about the civil rights movement and the passage of new civil rights laws. Imagine that you are a member of Congress during the 1950s and 1960s. You want to write a new civil rights bill to help people gain fair treatment under the law. What is its goal? How will it expand civil rights? Is it designed to help a certain group of people? Discuss the reasons you believe it is important to expand civil rights in this way. You may refer to problems or events the bill responds to as well as to earlier civil rights laws and legal decisions.

Module 15

Searching for Order

Essential Question
Did the United States mainly experience progress or decline in the late 20th century?

About the Photo: The nation's 200th birthday was celebrated on July 4, 1976.

In this module you will read about the economic and foreign policies of presidents in the late twentieth century. You will also learn about social issues in this period and about the Watergate scandal that led to President Nixon's resignation.

Explore ONLINE!

VIDEOS, including...
- Watergate
- Impeachment
- Carter Promotes Human Rights
- Reagan's Foreign Policy

☑ Document-Based Investigations

☑ Graphic Organizers

☑ Interactive Games

☑ Interactive Graph: Affirmative Action and Education

☑ Interactive Chart: Supply-Side Economics

☑ Interactive Map: Central American Conflicts in the 1980s

What You Will Learn . . .

Timeline of Events 1968–2000

▶ Explore ONLINE!

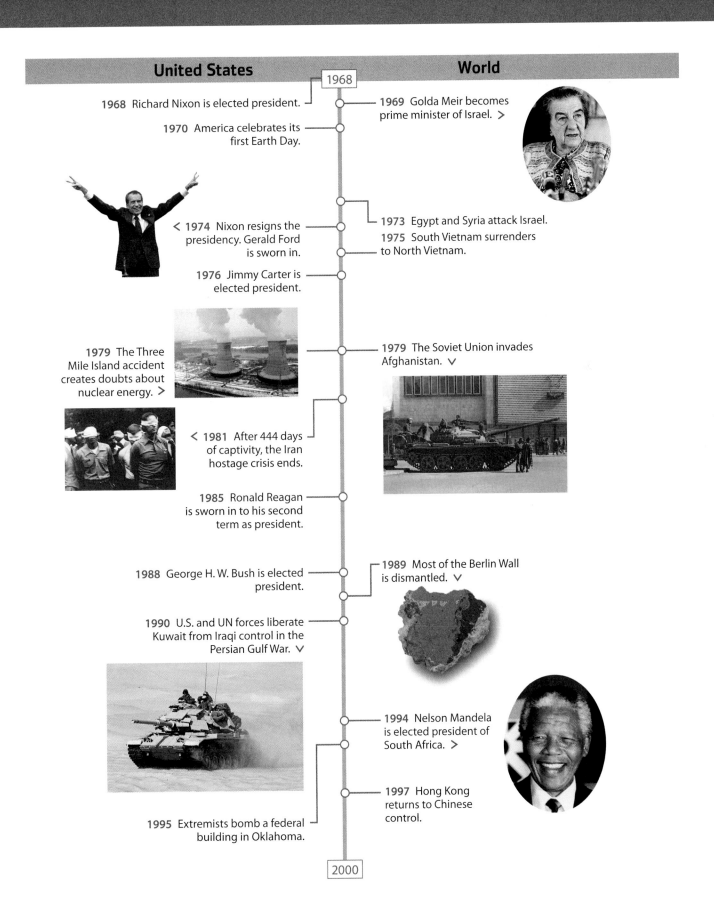

United States

1968

World

1968 Richard Nixon is elected president.

1969 Golda Meir becomes prime minister of Israel. >

1970 America celebrates its first Earth Day.

< **1974** Nixon resigns the presidency. Gerald Ford is sworn in.

1973 Egypt and Syria attack Israel.

1975 South Vietnam surrenders to North Vietnam.

1976 Jimmy Carter is elected president.

1979 The Three Mile Island accident creates doubts about nuclear energy. >

1979 The Soviet Union invades Afghanistan. ∨

< **1981** After 444 days of captivity, the Iran hostage crisis ends.

1985 Ronald Reagan is sworn in to his second term as president.

1988 George H. W. Bush is elected president.

1989 Most of the Berlin Wall is dismantled. ∨

1990 U.S. and UN forces liberate Kuwait from Iraqi control in the Persian Gulf War. ∨

1994 Nelson Mandela is elected president of South Africa. >

1997 Hong Kong returns to Chinese control.

1995 Extremists bomb a federal building in Oklahoma.

2000

Reading Social Studies

Economics, Politics

In this module you will learn about issues faced by several modern presidents. You will also read about crises in the economy and in politics that changed the way Americans viewed their role as a nation. Finally, you will learn about American society in the 1970s.

READING FOCUS:

Summarize

After reading a large amount of information, you can summarize it into a shorter amount that is easier for you to understand.

Understand Summarizing Using the ideas and information presented in a book can be easier if you summarize what the author is saying. When you summarize, you can use some of the key ideas and words to write your own sentences that explain the information. When you write a summary, some details can be left out.

Read the following passage and its summary. Notice which details the author chose to include and which to leave out.

The American population was changing in the 1970s. Throughout American history, most immigrants to the United States had come from Europe. Beginning in the 1970s, however, a majority of new immigrants came from the Americas and Asia. This pattern continues today.

Summary The population immigrating to the United States began changing during the 1970s. Now the majority of immigrants come from Latin America and Asia.

This passage contains most of the same information but is shorter. Not all of the information is included.

You Try It!

The following passage is from the module you are getting ready to read. As you read the passage, look for information that is important enough to go in a summary.

"Are you better off than you were four years ago?" That was the question Republican candidate Ronald Reagan asked voters during the 1980 presidential campaign. Millions of voters answered "No," giving Reagan an easy victory over President Carter. Reagan won 489 electoral votes to Carter's 49. On January 20, 1981—the day of Reagan's inauguration—Iran finally released the American hostages after 444 days in captivity.

After you read the passage, answer the following questions.

1. Do you think the campaign slogan from the passage above is essential information for a summary of the election?

2. Do you think the number of electoral votes should be included in your summary?

3. Write a two-sentence summary of the passage above.

As you read Module 15, practice summarizing the information from several paragraphs.

Key Terms and People

Lesson 1
stagflation
Organization of Petroleum Exporting Countries
realpolitik
Strategic Arms Limitation Talks
détente
Watergate
Gerald Ford
pardon

Lesson 2
affirmative action
Rachel Carson
Jimmy Carter
human rights
apartheid
sanctions
Camp David Accords
Iran hostage crisis

Lesson 3
Ronald Reagan
supply-side economics
deficit
Iran-Contra affair
Mikhail Gorbachev

Lesson 4
George H. W. Bush
Saddam Hussein
Operation Desert Storm
Colin Powell
Bill Clinton
North American Free Trade Agreement
Madeleine Albright
terrorism

Nixon's Presidency and Watergate

The Big Idea

Richard Nixon's policies helped ease Cold War tensions before the Watergate scandal brought down his presidency.

Main Ideas

- Americans faced domestic challenges, including an energy and economic crisis.

- Nixon's foreign policy led to improved relations with Communist powers.

- The Watergate scandal forced Nixon to resign.

- Gerald Ford became president upon Nixon's resignation and faced many challenges.

Key Terms and People

stagflation
Organization of Petroleum
    Exporting Countries
realpolitik
Strategic Arms Limitation Talks
détente
Watergate
Gerald Ford
pardon

If YOU were there . . .

You experienced a decade of conflict and change in the 1960s. You were a witness to major events in the civil rights movement, and you lived through frightening Cold War crises. You saw leaders assassinated and astronauts walk on the moon. You have some friends who fought in Vietnam and others who led antiwar protests.

Do you think the United States is now headed in the right direction? Why or why not?

Domestic Challenges

As president, Richard Nixon promised to work on behalf of Americans who opposed protests and supported his plan for ending the war. Nixon called these Americans the Silent Majority. He criticized student protesters and called on them to stop their activities. He did not believe Americans should leave Vietnam quickly.

New Federalism Nixon also had a new plan for government. Nixon knew that his supporters blamed the federal government for setting high taxes and interfering in citizens' lives. He proposed a plan called the New Federalism. The plan would limit the power of the federal government. His policies represented a major shift in direction from Lyndon Johnson's Great Society ideas. Under Nixon's plan, grants of money from the federal government went directly to state and local governments, who decided how to spend the money. This plan reflected Nixon's conservatism, or a belief in limiting the involvement of government in citizens' lives.

President Nixon promised to reduce welfare spending and to restore law and order. He supported policies that gave more power to police and to the courts.

His political philosophy affected the Supreme Court as well. As president, he appointed four new justices. Many Court decisions soon began to reflect a more conservative point of view.

Nixon did not push for new civil rights legislation. He believed that the government had done enough in the 1960s, saying, "The laws have caught up with our consciences."

Economic Troubles Nixon faced the difficult economic challenge of so-called **stagflation**—the economic condition of combined stagnant economic growth and high inflation. From 1967 to 1974, rising prices reduced the purchasing power of the U.S. dollar by more than 30 percent.

One cause of inflation was the rising cost of oil. By the early 1970s the United States was importing about one-third of its oil. Much of this oil was purchased from Middle Eastern nations that were members of the **Organization of Petroleum Exporting Countries**, or OPEC. This group worked to control the production and sale of oil to keep prices high.

Most OPEC countries were Arab countries that had been opposed to the creation of the Jewish state of Israel. On October 6, 1973, the Jewish holy day of Yom Kippur, Egypt and Syria attacked Israel. The attack started what would become known as the Yom Kippur War. The United States sent military supplies to help Israel.

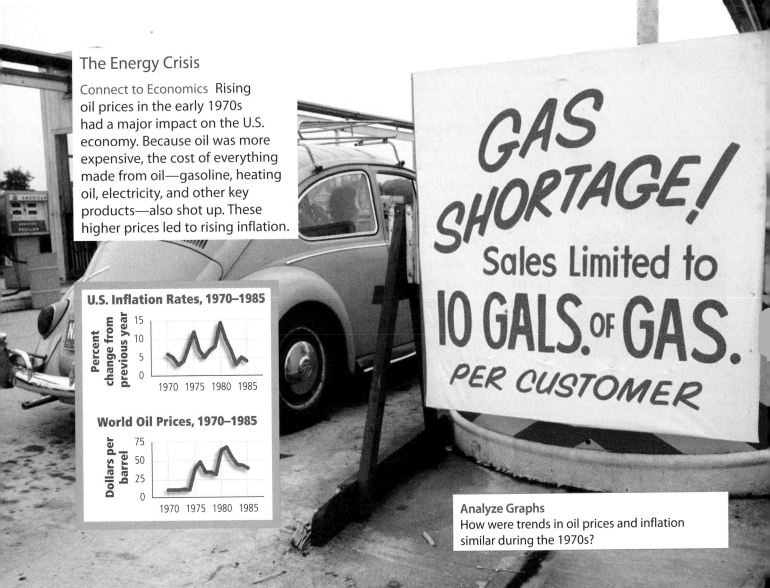

The Energy Crisis

Connect to Economics Rising oil prices in the early 1970s had a major impact on the U.S. economy. Because oil was more expensive, the cost of everything made from oil—gasoline, heating oil, electricity, and other key products—also shot up. These higher prices led to rising inflation.

U.S. Inflation Rates, 1970–1985

Percent change from previous year

15
10
5
0

1970 1975 1980 1985

World Oil Prices, 1970–1985

Dollars per barrel

75
50
25
0

1970 1975 1980 1985

GAS SHORTAGE! Sales Limited to 10 GALS. OF GAS. PER CUSTOMER

Analyze Graphs
How were trends in oil prices and inflation similar during the 1970s?

Reading Check
Identify Cause and Effect What was one cause of inflation?

Arab members of OPEC responded angrily to support for Israel. They declared an embargo, or ban, on oil sales to the United States. The oil embargo and soaring oil prices caused an energy crisis. This worsened an already weak U.S. economy.

Nixon's Foreign Policy

As the energy crisis demonstrated, international events could have a serious impact on life in the United States. Henry Kissinger, a German American professor who became Nixon's senior foreign policy adviser, helped Nixon develop a new approach to foreign policy. Nixon's foreign policy decisions would be based on practical American interests, not on moral or political ideals. This approach was known as **realpolitik**, the German term meaning "actual politics."

Nixon credited his realpolitik strategies with bringing an end to the Vietnam War. These strategies used political pressure from the Soviet Union and China to convince the North Vietnamese to negotiate. Realpolitik was controversial, however. In several Latin American countries, for example, the United States backed harsh military governments because they were friendly to U.S. interests.

In the ongoing Cold War rivalries with China and the Soviet Union, the realpolitik approach led to important changes. American officials had long feared China and the Soviet Union would work together to spread communism. But by 1970 it was clear that these two Communist powers had become bitter rivals. One cause of this rivalry was the Cultural Revolution. Chinese leader Mao Zedong launched this campaign in 1966 to regain control of his country's government. Mao and his allies attempted to rid China of capitalist and traditional influences. Millions of Chinese people were persecuted during the Cultural Revolution. In addition to attacking his internal enemies, Mao accused Soviet leaders of betraying the ideals of communism by being too "soft" in their policies dealing with capitalist countries.

On his visit to China in 1972, Nixon visited many sites, including the Great Wall.

Nixon believed it was in America's interest to widen this split and to improve U.S. relations with both Communist powers. He first turned his attention to China. Nixon lifted restrictions on trade and travel and opened negotiations. In 1972 Nixon became the first U.S. president to make an official visit to China. His visit received wide acclaim in the media. Newscasts showed Nixon and Mao shaking hands and trading jokes during their meeting.

Nixon's trip led to improved U.S.-China relations. It also caught the attention of Soviet leaders. They became more open to talks with the United States. In May 1972 Nixon flew to Moscow, where he and Soviet leader Leonid Brezhnev participated in the **Strategic Arms Limitation Talks** (SALT). These talks led to a treaty limiting each country's nuclear weapons. The SALT agreement opened a period of **détente** (day-TAHNT), or less hostile relations, between the United States and the Soviet Union. Détente brought economic benefits, as the Soviets began buying millions of tons of grain from American farmers.

Reading Check
Draw Conclusions Do you think realpolitik was a good strategy? Why or why not?

The Watergate Scandal

On June 17, 1972, five men were arrested while breaking into the Democratic National Committee's offices at the Watergate Hotel in Washington, DC. The burglars were carrying camera equipment and secret recording devices. Police soon discovered that some of them had ties to the Nixon administration. One had worked for the Committee to Reelect the President (CRP).

Nixon denied that anyone in his administration was involved in the Watergate break-in, and the White House public relations campaign was successful in keeping the trust of the American people. Nixon went on to win the 1972 election in a landslide. But early in Nixon's second term, the seemingly minor break-in exploded into a massive political scandal that became known as **Watergate**.

Investigating the Break-in

Did Nixon administration officials have anything to do with the Watergate break-in? Reporters Bob Woodward and Carl Bernstein investigated that question in a series of articles in the *Washington Post*. Key figures in the Nixon administration refused to talk to the reporters. Then a government official contacted Woodward. The official had inside information on the Watergate investigation. The informant was not revealed until 2005, more than 30 years later. W. Mark Felt, second-in-command at the FBI during Watergate, was the inside source. However, at the time, Woodward called Felt by a secret codename to protect his identity. With Felt's information, Woodward and Bernstein began publishing stories about Nixon administration officials and their illegal activities. The stories revealed that the CRP had hidden illegal campaign contributions and spread false rumors about Democratic candidates. They also presented evidence that officials in the Nixon White House were trying to cover up the facts of the Watergate break-in.

Senator Sam Ervin led a Senate committee that launched its own investigation of Watergate. When the committee began televised hearings in May 1973, millions of Americans tuned in. The most damaging witness was

Watergate Scandal

On May 28, 1972, five men burglarized the Democratic National Committee headquarters in the Watergate Hotel, shown here. They bugged telephones and took pictures of files. The burglars returned for more information on June 17 and were arrested.

Washington Post reporters soon linked the break-in to the presidential re-election campaign. A White House cover-up began.

The Senate formed a committee to investigate the break-in and possible cover-up. Its hearings (shown right) were televised.

Faced with impeachment for an illegal cover-up of the break-in, Nixon resigned. President Gerald Ford later pardoned Nixon.

Analyze Information
Why was Nixon threatened with impeachment by the House?

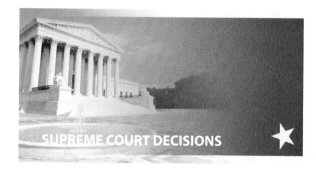

United States v. *Nixon* (1974)

Background of the Case

During the Watergate investigation, a special prosecutor asked for the tapes of President Nixon's Oval Office conversations. Nixon claimed that he did not have to obey court orders to turn over the tapes because of executive privilege. On July 8, 1974, the case went before the Supreme Court.

The Court's Ruling

The Supreme Court announced its unanimous decision on July 24. It stated, "the legitimate [lawful] needs of the judicial process may outweigh presidential privilege." Nixon could not use executive privilege to avoid the subpoenas.

The Court's Reasoning

The Court decided to hear the case more quickly than most cases because of its importance to the functioning of government and the interest of the American public. The Supreme Court ruled that to claim executive privilege, a president would have to show a convincing national security reason. Nixon had no such reason for refusing to hand over the tapes.

Why It Matters

The Supreme Court ruling showed that, despite their unique and important position, presidents do have to obey the law. It also showed that the government could use the powers defined in the Constitution to prevent one branch from becoming too powerful. Less than a week later, the House Judiciary Committee voted to impeach Nixon.

Analyze Information

1. How is this case an example of the checks and balances system?
2. What do you think was the most important impact of this Supreme Court decision?

---

former White House attorney John Dean. He testified that Nixon was personally involved in the Watergate cover-up. Dean could not prove this, however. Then another witness, former White House staffer Alexander Butterfield, revealed that Nixon had tape-recorded almost all of his Oval Office conversations.

Committee members asked Nixon to allow them to listen to the tapes. Nixon refused to hand the tapes over to a special prosecutor. He claimed executive privilege—a president's right to keep information secret for reasons of national security. In July 1974 the Supreme Court ordered Nixon to turn over the tapes. The recordings proved that Nixon had directed the Watergate cover-up and lied about it to Congress and the public.

While this investigation was unfolding, Vice President Spiro Agnew resigned. He faced charges that he had taken bribes and failed to pay taxes. Nixon appointed Michigan congressman **Gerald Ford** as vice president.

Nixon Resigns After studying the case, the House Judiciary Committee recommended impeachment. Judiciary Committee member Barbara Jordan of Texas explained why she thought Nixon should be impeached:

"My faith in the Constitution is whole, it is complete, it is total. And I am not going to sit here and be an idle spectator to the . . . destruction of the Constitution."

—Barbara Jordan, in a speech before Congress, 1974

On July 27, 1974, the committee approved its first article of impeachment. This article charged Nixon with obstruction of justice. Within the next week, the committee approved two more articles. One article was for the abuse of power and one for contempt of Congress.

On August 8, 1974, Nixon appeared on national television. He announced, "I shall resign the presidency effective at noon tomorrow." Nixon became the first president in American history to resign from office. Gerald Ford was sworn in as president on August 9.

One of the **consequences** of Watergate was that many Americans lost faith in government officials. In a poll taken in 1974, just 36 percent of Americans said they trusted the government. Others, however, saw a more positive side of Watergate. Senator Sam Ervin viewed the hearings and Nixon's resignation as evidence that the government was able to rid itself of corruption. "Watergate . . . proved our Constitution works," he said.

Academic Vocabulary
consequences the effects of a particular event or events

Reading Check
Sequence
What events led to Nixon's resignation?

Ford as President

Vice President Gerald Ford became the first modern president to hold the office without being elected to it. Ford lost some public support when he granted Richard Nixon a **pardon**, or freedom from punishment. He declared it was best for the nation that Nixon not be tried for his crime. Ford stated that Nixon would be "cruelly and excessively penalized" and "ugly passions would again be aroused [stirred]."

A U.S. Marine changes the official presidential photograph from one of Nixon to one of Ford.

Other issues added to Ford's difficulties. Oil prices and unemployment remained high, and stagflation continued. The United States also had an increasing trade deficit, an imbalance in which a country imports more than it exports.

Ford argued that inflation was the main cause of the economic troubles. He began a campaign called Whip Inflation Now (WIN). WIN encouraged people to save money and businesses to hold down wages and prices. Ford's plan met with resistance from many members of Congress, who wanted to increase spending to help the poor and unemployed. In 1975 Ford and Congress began to compromise. Still, inflation and unemployment remained high.

Summary and Preview Gerald Ford became president after the Watergate scandal ended Nixon's presidency. In the next lesson you will learn about life in the 1970s.

Reading Check
Analyze Information
Do you think President Ford was right to pardon Nixon?

Lesson 1 Assessment

Review Ideas, Terms, and People

1. **a. Describe** What challenges did the United States face during President Nixon's terms of office?

   b. Summarize Why do rising oil prices have such a widespread effect on the economy?

   c. Make Inferences Why do you think the Organization of Petroleum Exporting Countries objected to U.S. support for Israel?

2. **a. Identify** Who was Henry Kissinger?

   b. Contrast How was realpolitik different from other foreign policy approaches?

   c. Draw Conclusions Why do you think improved U.S.-China relations made the Soviets more open to talks with the United States?

3. **a. Recall** What was the Watergate scandal?

   b. Explain Why were President Nixon's tapes important?

   c. Elaborate Why do you think President Nixon decided to resign?

4. **a. Describe** How did Gerald Ford become president of the United States?

   b. Predict Do you think WIN was effective in helping the economy?

Critical Thinking

5. **Sequence** In this lesson you learned about Nixon's domestic policy, foreign policy, and the Watergate scandal. Create a table similar to the one below and use it to list, in order, the key events that took place during Nixon's presidency.

Event	Date

America in the 1970s

Main Ideas

- American society debated key social issues during the 1970s.
- Jimmy Carter was elected president in 1976.
- Carter had successes as well as failures in foreign policy during his administration.

Key Terms and People

affirmative action
Rachel Carson
Jimmy Carter
human rights
apartheid
sanctions
Camp David Accords
Iran hostage crisis

If YOU were there . . .

It is July 4, 1976. Today, the entire nation is celebrating the 200th anniversary of the signing of the Declaration of Independence. As you sit with your family watching a spectacular fireworks show, you think about the challenges this country has faced throughout its history. You think about the economic and foreign policy challenges facing Americans right now.

What are your hopes for the nation's future?

Social Issues of the 1970s

The American population was changing in the 1970s. Throughout American history, most immigrants to the United States had come from Europe. Beginning in the 1970s, however, a majority of new immigrants came from the Americas and Asia. This pattern continues today. Another change was that the birthrate, or number of births per 1,000 people, was declining. By 1970 Americans 65 and older became one of the fastest-growing population groups.

Debating Rights As the population grew and changed, American society faced challenges in trying to balance the views of all Americans. Some of these challenges involved women's issues. The Equal Rights Amendment caused nationwide debate in the 1970s. Although the ERA was not ratified, the women's movement did make important gains. A 1972 federal law known as Title IX banned discrimination on the basis of sex in educational programs that receive federal funds. The number of women admitted to medical and law schools climbed quickly. Title IX also opened the door for many more women to participate in college sports and earn athletic scholarships. In 1973 the Supreme Court legalized abortion in the case *Roe* v. *Wade*. Opponents of abortion began to form groups seeking to overturn the decision. Today, the issue of abortion remains highly controversial.

Issues of the 1970s

Environmental protection, women's rights, and affirmative action were among the major issues of the 1970s.

The environment became an important issue of national debate. Activists pushed for legislation and individual action to help protect the Earth.

Supporters of the Equal Rights Amendment urged states to ratify the amendment. They believed it would guarantee equal protection to women under the Constitution.

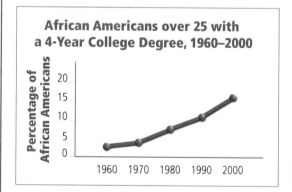

Affirmative action helped African Americans and other minorities gain access to universities and certain jobs. The issue also created much debate.

In the 1970s Americans also debated **affirmative action**, the practice of giving special consideration to nonwhites or women to make up for past discrimination. Supporters argued that minorities and women needed affirmative action to improve their educational and job opportunities. Opponents insisted that any preferences based on race or gender were unfair.

Many African Americans benefited from new opportunities in the 1970s. For example, the number of African Americans attending college increased. In 1976 the number was four times higher than it had been a decade earlier. Many people credited affirmative action programs with this increase.

Environmental Battles The environment also became a major issue in the 1970s. In her book *Silent Spring*, biologist **Rachel Carson** brought attention to the dangers of pollution. She explained how chemicals used to kill insects travel through the food chain and affect people's health.

"Man, however much he may like to pretend the contrary [opposite], is part of nature. Can he escape a pollution that is now so thoroughly distributed throughout our world?"

—Rachel Carson, *Silent Spring*

Silent Spring was first published in 1962. It helped inspire a nationwide movement to improve the environment. Environmentalists in the United States celebrated the first Earth Day on April 22, 1970. "Earth Day is to remind each person of his [or her] . . . equal responsibility . . . to preserve and improve the Earth," explained activists.

Environmentalists brought attention to other issues in addition to pollution. These issues included the risks of nuclear power, the overuse of natural resources, and the loss of natural habitats due to human development. Many environmentalists linked these problems to population growth. From 1900 to 1975, there were major changes in population. The population of the United States nearly tripled. The world's population grew from roughly 1.6 billion to 4 billion.

Congress passed new laws to limit the release of pollutants. The Environmental Protection Agency (EPA) was established in 1970 to carry out these laws. The mission of the EPA is to protect human health and the environment. It conducts research and writes and enforces rules to provide this protection.

One of the EPA's major efforts has been to reduce acid rain. It can form when air pollution mixes with water in the atmosphere. Acid rain can fall hundreds of miles from the source of pollution, harming plants and wildlife. In 1976 a scientist found that many of the lakes in Adirondack Park in New York State no longer had any fish because the water had become too acidic. In 1990 the EPA created a program to reduce pollution that causes acid rain.

The government also took action to repair damage caused by pollution. In 1980 Congress passed a law to promote the cleanup of heavily contaminated sites. The Love Canal disaster in the town of Niagara Falls, New York, inspired the creation of the law. Chemical companies had dumped large quantities of toxic waste into the canal before it was closed and covered with earth. A school and rows of homes were built nearby. Residents began to report high rates of serious health problems. Eventually, more than 900 families were moved from the site.

The environmental movement has claimed many victories since the 1970s. Americans are increasingly aware of how their actions affect the environment. As protections increased, however, debates have grown about how to balance business interests with environmental concerns.

Urban Decay In the 1970s many American cities fell into crisis, especially in the Midwest and the Northeast. As middle-class families moved to new suburbs following World War II, businesses followed them. Cities were harmed by the loss of jobs and taxpayers as well as by social problems such as crime and drug abuse. These conditions, known as urban decay, drove even more families to leave.

At times the downward spiral of urban decay seemed hopeless to reverse. For example, in 1975 New York City was on the verge of bankruptcy. After President Ford gave a speech in which he refused to provide the city with federal assistance, the *Daily News* published a front-page headline that read: "FORD TO CITY: DROP DEAD." New York began to stabilize in the 1980s, but other cities such as Detroit and Cleveland have continued to struggle.

Carter Elected

To oppose Republican Gerald Ford in the 1976 presidential election, Democrats nominated **Jimmy Carter**, a little-known former governor of Georgia. The Democrats purposely chose a candidate who was untouched by recent government scandals. Carter knew that the Vietnam War and Watergate had badly shaken American voters' trust in government. "I will never lie to you," he told voters.

Reading Check
Compare and Contrast
How are Title IX and affirmative action similar and different?

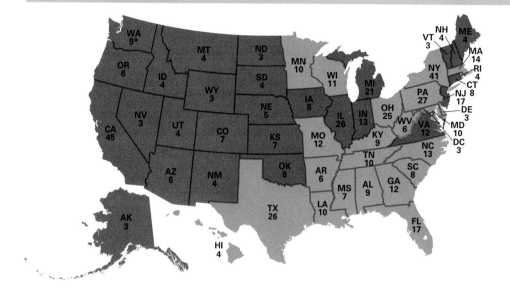

Jimmy Carter

Gerald Ford

Candidate	Party	Electoral Vote	Popular Vote	% Popular Vote
Carter	Democrat	297	40,828,929	50.1
Ford	Republican	240	39,148,940	48.0

*One electoral vote was cast for Ronald Reagan.
Source: World Almanac and Book of Facts, 2004

Interpret Maps
Place Which areas of the country did Carter win in 1976?

Carter defeated Ford in a close election. As president, Carter wanted to show a new spirit of informality and openness at the White House. On inauguration day, he and his family broke with tradition by walking to the inauguration rather than riding in a limousine.

Americans seemed to respond positively to his straightforward style. However, Carter faced serious challenges. High unemployment and inflation continued. The ongoing energy crisis also kept oil prices high. Many Americans became frustrated with the president's inability to solve these problems.

Although Democrats controlled Congress, Carter had a hard time convincing members to support his proposals. For example, Carter proposed a national energy plan. It called for conservation and the use of alternative energy sources such as solar energy. Congress demanded changes to the complex plan. The plan was never fully passed.

Carter also wanted to expand the use of nuclear power. This was one way he hoped to decrease the country's dependence on imported oil. But an accident at the Three Mile Island nuclear power plant in Pennsylvania caused new worries about the safety of nuclear energy. On March 28, 1979, a reactor core at Three Mile Island overheated. As a result, the plant released a small amount of radioactive gas into the air. This frightening incident damaged the nuclear power industry, and the federal government put in place a ban on building new reactors.

Reading Check
Draw Conclusions
How did the Three Mile Island incident affect Carter's energy plan?

Carter and Foreign Policy

President Carter rejected Nixon's realpolitik approach to foreign policy. He argued that "fairness, not force, should lie at the heart of our dealings with the nations of the world."

Changing Policies Carter favored policies that promoted **human rights**—the basic rights and freedoms of all people. He reduced U.S. aid to several former allies that committed human rights violations. In South Africa, Carter hoped to pressure the government into ending **apartheid**, a system of laws requiring racial segregation. He called for **sanctions**, or economic penalties, to encourage reform.

Carter's approach to foreign policy had effects in Latin America as well. Many Latin Americans resented previous U.S. interference in their countries. American control of the Panama Canal stood as a symbol of power in the region. In 1977 Carter signed treaties that would transfer control of the canal to Panama by the year 2000.

Carter had less success improving relations with the Soviet Union. Détente broke down when he criticized the Soviet Union for committing human rights abuses. Then in 1979 the Soviet Union invaded

Historical Sources

The Camp David Accords

In 1978 President Carter invited Israel's prime minister Menachem Begin and Egypt's president Anwar el-Sadat to meet at Camp David. The goal was to end conflict between their two nations, but the negotiations were very difficult. Carter later wrote about one moment when the talks nearly broke down.

"*Within a few minutes Sadat announced angrily that a stalemate [standstill] had been reached. He saw no reason for the discussions to continue. As far as he was concerned, they were over . . . They [Sadat and Begin] were moving toward the door, but I got in front of them to partially block the way. I urged them not to break off their talks, to give me another chance to use my influence and analysis, to have confidence in me. Begin agreed readily. I looked straight at Sadat; finally, he nodded his head. They left without speaking to each other.*"

Leaders Anwar el-Sadat (left), Jimmy Carter, and Menachem Begin (right) reached a peace agreement for the Middle East in the Camp David Accords.

Analyze Historical Sources
Why do you think Begin and el-Sadat agreed to continue their negotiations?

Afghanistan. Carter responded by breaking off arms-control talks and refusing to allow U.S. athletes to participate in the 1980 Summer Olympics in Moscow.

The Middle East While Cold War tensions increased, Carter worked to ease tensions in the Middle East. Egypt and Israel had been in conflict for 30 years. In 1978 Carter invited Egyptian president Anwar el-Sadat and Israeli prime minister Menachem Begin (men-AHK-uhm BAY-guhn) to the presidential retreat at Camp David, Maryland. After 13 days of meetings, the two leaders reached a peace agreement called the **Camp David Accords**. Many consider the agreement to be Carter's greatest achievement.

Carter also experienced disaster in the Middle East. The United States had supported the pro-American shah, or king, of Iran since the 1950s. Many Iranians resented the shah's reform efforts. They also disliked the country's shift from a traditional and agricultural society to a more urban and industrial one. The government severely punished its opponents and controlled all political participation. Many members of the opposition supported the views of Islamic spiritual leader Ruhollah Khomeini. Khomeini had been forced to leave the country because of his criticisms of the shah's policies.

In 1979 Khomeini's supporters drove the shah out of Iran. A month later, Khomeini took control of the government. On November 4, a group

Hostages Released

Approximately 52 Americans were held hostage by Iranian militants during the Iran hostage crisis. The men and women were kept blindfolded by their captors. After 444 days in captivity, the Americans were released.

of Iranian students attacked the U.S. embassy in Tehran, the capital of Iran, seizing about 90 American hostages. The **Iran hostage crisis** lasted for more than a year.

In the early days of the crisis, some hostages were released. The Iranian captors often blindfolded and beat the remaining hostages. Carter ended Iranian oil imports and froze Iranian assets in American banks. After a failed rescue attempt in April 1980, many Americans lost confidence in Carter's leadership.

Summary and Preview President Carter's policies included both successes and failures. In the next lesson you will learn about the policies of Ronald Reagan.

Reading Check
Make Inferences
Overall, do you think President Carter's foreign policy was effective? Why or why not?

Lesson 2 Assessment

Review Ideas, Terms, and People

1. **a. Recall** What social issues did Americans debate during the 1970s?

   b. Contrast How had immigration patterns changed by the 1970s?

   c. Draw Conclusions Why do you think *Silent Spring* remained important in the 1970s?

   d. Elaborate How is the EPA's mission reflected in its response to Love Canal and acid rain?

2. **a. Describe** How did Jimmy Carter break with tradition at his inauguration?

   b. Analyze Why did Carter's promise of honesty appeal to voters?

   c. Elaborate How did the Three Mile Island accident affect the energy crisis?

3. **a. Recall** What idea guided President Carter's approach to foreign policy?

   b. Explain What agreement was made in the treaties that Carter signed with Panama?

   c. Analyze Why did Carter lose political support during the Iran hostage crisis?

   d. Draw Conclusions Why do you think many people consider the Camp David Accords Carter's greatest achievement?

Critical Thinking

4. **Evaluate** In this lesson you learned about the new government policies in the 1970s. Create a graphic organizer similar to the one below to show President Carter's successes and failures.

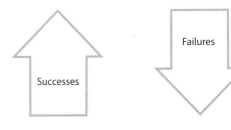

Successes   Failures

The Reagan Presidency

The Big Idea

President Reagan enacted conservative policies at home and took a strong anti-Communist stance in the Cold War.

Main Ideas

- President Reagan based his policies on conservative ideas.
- Reagan took a tough stand against communism in his foreign policy.

Key Terms and People

Ronald Reagan
supply-side economics
deficit
Iran-Contra affair
Mikhail Gorbachev

In July 1981, Reagan explained his plan to reduce taxes during a televised address to the nation from the Oval Office.

If YOU were there . . .

It is 1980, and you are a top adviser to the newly elected president, Ronald Reagan. You think about the challenges Reagan will face. High inflation and unemployment are plaguing the economy. Relations with the Soviet Union are falling apart. Also, 52 Americans are still being held hostage in Iran.

What would be your first recommendation to the president?

Reagan and Conservative Ideas

"Are you better off than you were four years ago?" That was the question Republican candidate **Ronald Reagan** asked voters during the 1980 presidential campaign. Millions of voters answered "No," giving Reagan an easy victory over President Carter. Reagan won 489 electoral votes to Carter's 49. On January 20, 1981—the day of Reagan's inauguration—Iran finally released the American hostages after 444 days in captivity.

Reagan's approach to government was based on conservative ideas. He wanted to cut taxes and reduce regulations on businesses. He promised to scale back the size of government, arguing that government involvement in business and society harmed individual ambition. "Government is not the solution to our problem; government is the problem," Reagan declared in his inaugural address.

Just two months into his presidency, Reagan was shot and severely wounded in an assassination attempt by John Hinckley Jr. Reagan was released from the hospital within two weeks and returned to work.

Reaganomics Reagan's economic policies, which some called Reaganomics, were based on a theory called **supply-side economics**. This theory calls for sharp tax cuts with the goal of increasing the amount of money people and businesses have to invest. This investment would lead to economic growth and the creation of new jobs. Over time, the expanding economic activity would produce increased tax revenues for the government.

Though many Democrats opposed this theory, Congress approved most of Reagan's plan for large cuts in business and personal taxes. To help balance the budget, Reagan called for spending cuts as well. Congress agreed to cut the rate of the growth of spending on social programs such as school lunches, low-income housing, and food stamps.

The economy experienced a brief recession early in Reagan's presidency. Then in 1983 the economy rebounded and began a long period of expansion. Business profits and tax revenues increased.

At the same time, spending on defense was increased dramatically, from $180 billion in 1981 to nearly $280 billion in 1985. The new spending outpaced the new tax revenues. The result was a rapidly rising **deficit**—the amount by which a government's spending exceeds its revenues.

Conservative Goals One of Reagan's conservative goals was to reduce government regulation of key industries. Reagan hoped fewer rules would encourage expansion in those industries, thereby improving the U.S. economy. Congress responded by reducing regulations on industries such as television, airlines, and banking.

Reagan was also able to move the Supreme Court in a more conservative direction by appointing politically conservative judges. In 1981 he appointed Sandra Day O'Connor to the Court. She became the first woman to serve as a Supreme Court justice. Reagan later appointed two more conservative justices: Antonin Scalia and Anthony M. Kennedy.

Election of 1984 President Reagan ran for re-election in 1984 against Democratic candidate Walter Mondale, who had served as Jimmy Carter's

Sandra Day O'Connor 1930–

Sandra Day O'Connor grew up on a ranch in Arizona and entered Stanford University at age 16. She graduated third in her class from Stanford Law School in 1952. When she applied for jobs as a lawyer, however, she found that law firms were not willing to hire women. She turned instead to public service in Arizona, holding jobs including assistant attorney general, state senator, and judge. She was serving on the Arizona Court of Appeals when she was nominated to the Supreme Court by Ronald Reagan. The Senate confirmed O'Connor's appointment by a vote of 99–0. O'Connor retired from the bench in 2005.

Analyze Information
Why did Sandra Day O'Connor begin working in public service?

vice president. Mondale chose Geraldine Ferraro as his running mate. Ferraro was the first woman to run for vice president on a major-party ticket. She spoke of the <u>implications</u> of her nomination:

> "By choosing an American woman to run for our nation's second-highest office, you send a powerful signal to all Americans. . . . We will place no limits on achievement. If we can do this, we can do anything."
>
> —Geraldine Ferraro, *Ferraro: My Story*

Reading Check
Summarize
What theories did
Reaganomics include?

The economy was booming as the election approached. Mondale argued that Reagan's economic policies unfairly favored the wealthy. Voters, however, gave Reagan a landslide victory. Reagan received 59 percent of the popular vote and captured 525 of the 538 electoral votes.

Reagan and Foreign Policy

President Reagan was an outspoken critic of communism and the Soviet Union, which he called an "evil empire." He saw the Cold War as a fight of "good versus evil, right versus wrong."

--- BIOGRAPHY ---

Ronald Reagan 1911–2004

Ronald Reagan grew up in Illinois. In 1937 he moved to California, where he became a well-known movie actor. He later entered politics and was elected governor of California. Then he served eight years as president.

Reagan worked to reshape the American government and economy based on conservative values. In foreign policy, he took an aggressive stand toward communism and the Soviet Union. Reagan challenged the Soviet leader to allow freedom in Eastern Europe. In a famous speech at the Berlin Wall, he said, "Mr. Gorbachev, tear down this wall!" Reagan and Gorbachev later signed the Intermediate-Range Nuclear Forces (INF) Treaty. It was the first treaty that reduced the number of nuclear weapons held by both countries.

Reagan was nicknamed the Great Communicator. He inspired many Americans with his sense of humor and his optimistic view of America's future. Many voters credited him with restoring their confidence after the difficulties of the 1970s. Many believe that Reagan's buildup of the U.S. military contributed to major changes in the Cold War and the eventual fall of Communist governments in the Soviet Union and Eastern Europe.

Find Main Ideas
What was Reagan's biggest foreign policy achievement? Use evidence from the reading to support your answer.

Central American Conflicts in the 1980s

▶ Explore ONLINE!

Legend:
- ✴ Guerrilla activity or civil war
- ◼ U.S. base in continuous operation since 1903
- ▲ U.S. military presence or intervention

0   200   400 Miles
0   200   400 Kilometers

UNITED STATES

ATLANTIC OCEAN

Gulf of Mexico

Miami

THE BAHAMAS

MEXICO

Havana

Mexico City

CUBA

CAYMAN IS. (U.K.) Guantánamo Bay

DOMINICAN REPUBLIC

PUERTO RICO (U.S.)

GUATEMALA   Belmopan
BELIZE HONDURAS
          1983, 1988

JAMAICA
Kingston

HAITI
Port-au-Prince

Santo Domingo

Guatemala City
EL SALVADOR
1981   San
             Salvador

Tegucigalpa

Caribbean Sea

NICARAGUA
Managua Panama Canal

PACIFIC OCEAN

COSTA RICA
San José

Panama City

GRENADA
1983

Caracas

1989
PANAMA

COLOMBIA

VENEZUELA
Georgetown
GUYANA

Interpret Maps

1. **Location** In which two countries did the United States intervene in 1983?

2. **Human-Environment Interaction** Why might the United States have intervened in the countries where it did?

Conflicts in Central America Civil wars raged in several Central American countries in the 1980s as communism spread in the area. Reagan supported anti-Communist governments in El Salvador and Guatemala with financial aid. Critics of this policy charged that the aid went to military governments that committed major human rights violations.

In Nicaragua, a revolutionary group called the Sandinistas overthrew the country's pro-American dictator in 1979. U.S. leaders became concerned when the Sandinistas formed closer ties with Communist Cuba. Reagan cut all U.S. aid to Nicaragua and began supporting anti-Sandinista rebels known as the Contras. This led to fears that the United States could be drawn into war. In 1984 Congress passed a ban on more U.S. military aid to the Contras.

A group of Reagan administration officials secretly found a way to continue funding the Contras. One member of the group was Oliver North, a marine officer serving as a national security aide. North helped arrange the sale of U.S. missiles to Iran. In exchange, Iran released U.S. hostages who had been taken by terrorists loyal to Iran. Profits from this secret deal were sent to the Contras. These profits were in violation of the congressional ban. The so-called **Iran-Contra affair** became a national controversy when it was exposed in 1986. Congressional hearings concluded that President Reagan was not guilty of illegal activity. Several White House officials, however, were convicted of crimes related to the affair.

Reagan and Gorbachev During his first term, President Reagan took a tough stand against the Soviet Union. He stopped arms negotiations and quickly expanded the U.S. military.

The Soviet Union tried to keep up with American spending in the arms race. This contributed to desperate economic times in the Soviet Union during the 1980s. In 1985 **Mikhail Gorbachev** became the new Soviet leader. To deal with his country's economic problems, he began a process of political and economic reforms called *perestroika*. He also adopted a new policy of political openness called *glasnost*. The newfound freedoms introduced by Gorbachev's policies threatened other leaders of the Soviet Union. But most of its citizens and leaders in the West supported these freedoms.

Reagan became convinced of Gorbachev's desire for change. In 1987 the two leaders signed the Intermediate-Range Nuclear Forces Treaty. The treaty eliminated all medium-range nuclear weapons in Europe. Cold War tensions were decreasing for the first time since the early 1970s.

Summary and Preview Conservative ideas influenced many of Ronald Reagan's policies. In the next lesson you will learn about the policies of presidents in the 1990s.

Reading Check
Identify Cause and Effect Why did President Reagan change his tough stand toward the Soviet Union?

Lesson 3 Assessment

Review Ideas, Terms, and People

1. **a. Recall** What was Ronald Reagan's view of government?

   b. Analyze Why did the federal budget deficit rise during Reagan's presidency?

   c. Draw Conclusions Why do you think so many Americans voted for Reagan in the 1984 election?

2. **a. Recall** What changes did Mikhail Gorbachev make in the Soviet Union?

   b. Explain How did Reagan administration officials violate the law in the Iran-Contra affair?

   c. Predict Do you think Reagan's policies were effective in fighting communism?

Critical Thinking

3. **Summarize** In this lesson you learned about the domestic and foreign policies of President Reagan. Create a table similar to the one below to list each policy with its correct geographic focus.

United States	Central America	Soviet Union

The End of the Twentieth Century

The Big Idea

The United States and the world faced many new challenges at the end of the twentieth century.

Main Ideas

- Major global changes took place during the presidency of George H. W. Bush.

- During Bill Clinton's presidency, the nation experienced scandal, economic growth, and the rise of terrorist threats.

Key Terms and People

George H. W. Bush
Saddam Hussein
Operation Desert Storm
Colin Powell
Bill Clinton
North American Free Trade
    Agreement
Madeleine Albright
terrorism

If YOU were there . . .

You are visiting the city of West Berlin in 1989. Just after midnight on November 9, you see huge crowds of people pouring into the streets to celebrate. You rush outside to find out what's going on. "The wall is falling!" people shout. You run toward the Berlin Wall, and there you see East and West Germans working together to rip down the hated wall.

What might the fall of the Berlin Wall mean for the future?

George H. W. Bush

Ronald Reagan was popular with a majority of voters as his second term as president came to an end. Republicans hoped this would help Reagan's vice president, **George H. W. Bush**, win the election of 1988. Bush's Democratic opponent was Massachusetts governor Michael Dukakis. After a hard-fought campaign, Bush won the election with 426 electoral votes to Dukakis's 111.

The Cold War Ends As Bush began his presidency, Mikhail Gorbachev continued his reform programs in the Soviet Union. In the Soviet-controlled states of Eastern Europe, people demanded even faster change and more freedom. Pro-democracy movements in Hungary, Poland, and other nations put increasing pressure on Communist governments. This pressure produced world-changing results in 1989, as pro-Soviet governments across Eastern Europe began to fall.

In October 1989 massive protests in East Germany led to the resignation of Communist leader Erich Honecker. The new government agreed to open the borders of East Germany. This included the border guarded by the Berlin Wall. At midnight on November 9, a wild celebration broke out as East and West Berliners jumped onto the Berlin Wall, shouting and dancing. Some smashed through parts of the wall with hammers and chisels. The wall began crumbling to

A man chisels a section of the Berlin Wall after the fall of communism in Germany.

the ground. It had stood as a symbol of the Cold War since 1961. Within a year, the two Germanys reunited as one democratic country.

Several Soviet republics soon declared independence from the Soviet regime. Hard-line Communists were desperate to hold on to power. They took Gorbachev hostage in August 1991 and tried to seize the government. Thousands of Soviets took to the streets in protest. Ignoring orders to stop the protesters, many soldiers joined the crowds. Pro-democracy leader Boris Yeltsin encouraged the protesters to stand strong. Within a few months, Gorbachev resigned and the Soviet Union broke apart.

After Gorbachev's resignation, Bush worked with Russian president Yeltsin to improve relations between the United States and Russia. In February 1992 they issued a formal statement declaring an end to the Cold War. In January 1993 Yeltsin and Bush signed the START II pact. This treaty was supposed to reduce the number of nuclear weapons held by both nations, but it was never put into effect.

The Persian Gulf War President Bush called for all countries to work together, especially during times of crisis. A major crisis soon developed in the Middle East. In August 1990 Iraq's dictator, **Saddam Hussein**, invaded neighboring oil-rich Kuwait.

Members of the United Nations called for the immediate withdrawal of Iraqi troops. President Bush, with strong public support, began assembling a coalition, or alliance, of nations to drive Iraq from Kuwait by force.

Saddam refused to withdraw from Kuwait. In response, a U.S.-led multi-national coalition launched **Operation Desert Storm**. This air offensive was led by U.S. generals Norman Schwarzkopf and **Colin Powell**. Powell was the chair of the joint chiefs of staff and the highest-ranking African American ever to serve in the U.S. military. After a six-week bombing campaign, ground forces entered Kuwait. Within days, Iraq agreed to a cease-fire.

About 22,300 Iraqi soldiers and civilians were killed in the Persian Gulf War. The coalition forces lost around 223 soldiers, 148 of whom were American. More than 35,000 American women served in the war, though federal laws prevented them from serving in combat.

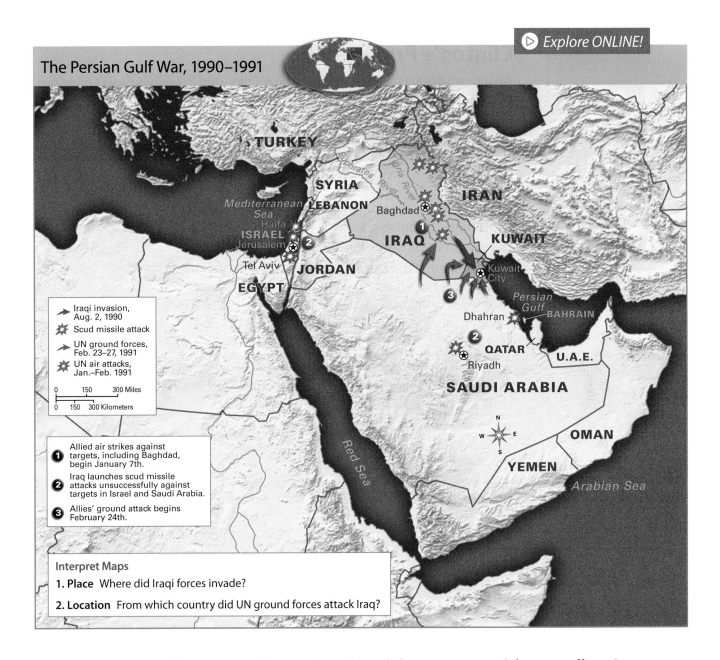

The Persian Gulf War, 1990–1991

▶ Explore ONLINE!

→ Iraqi invasion,
Aug. 2, 1990

✺ Scud missile attack

→ UN ground forces,
Feb. 23–27, 1991

✸ UN air attacks,
Jan.–Feb. 1991

0   150   300 Miles

0   150   300 Kilometers

1 Allied air strikes against targets, including Baghdad, begin January 7th.

2 Iraq launches scud missile attacks unsuccessfully against targets in Israel and Saudi Arabia.

3 Allies' ground attack begins February 24th.

Interpret Maps

1. Place Where did Iraqi forces invade?

2. Location From which country did UN ground forces attack Iraq?

President Bush explained the importance of the war, telling Congress:

"Now, we can see a new world coming into view. A world in which there is the very real prospect of a new world order . . . A world in which freedom and respect for human rights find a home among all nations."

—George H. W. Bush, March 6, 1991

Economic Policy Bush had campaigned on a firm pledge not to raise taxes. Once he was in office, however, he faced pressure due to the high federal deficit and a weakening economy. Bush proposed a plan to lower the deficit with spending cuts. The Democrats in Congress rejected his plan. In 1990 he compromised by agreeing to tax increases, which angered many conservatives. This step did not prevent the economy from entering a recession. In the spring of 1992, the unemployment rate climbed above 7 percent—a six-year high. Americans began to think that Bush was good at foreign policy but ineffective at home.

Reading Check
Summarize How did the world change between 1989 and 1991?

Clinton's Presidency

An overwhelming majority of Americans supported President Bush's handling of the Gulf War. By the time of the 1992 election, however, the struggling U.S. economy had become a more important issue for most voters. Arkansas governor **Bill Clinton** was the Democratic nominee for president. He told voters he would focus on improving the economy. Clinton won a three-way race against Bush and H. Ross Perot, who ran as an independent candidate.

Clinton and Congress Under President Clinton's leadership, Congress passed a budget. It was designed to reduce the deficit by cutting spending and raising taxes. He also convinced Congress to support the **North American Free Trade Agreement** (NAFTA). This treaty eliminated trade barriers between the United States, Canada, and Mexico. The treaty was controversial. Supporters claimed that it would strengthen the economies of all three nations. Critics argued that the United States would lose jobs to Mexico, where wages were lower.

In the 1994 congressional elections, House minority leader Newt Gingrich of Georgia helped lead Republicans to an important victory. Gingrich and other Republicans promoted a set of policies called the Contract with

Historical Sources

NAFTA

Just before Congress voted on NAFTA in 1993, Vice President Al Gore and former presidential candidate H. Ross Perot debated the controversial issue on national television.

"Everything that he [Perot] is worried about will get worse if NAFTA is defeated. We want jobs for America's working men and women. We want to get rid of the barriers that have prevented us from selling what we make in other countries. This is an historic opportunity to do that."

—Al Gore

"If we keep shifting our manufacturing jobs across the border [to Mexico] and around the world and deindustrializing our country, we will not be able to defend this great country, and that is a risk we will never take."

—H. Ross Perot

Analyze Historical Sources
According to Perot, how would NAFTA affect the United States? Why does Gore disagree?

Bill Clinton 1946–

Bill Clinton was born in Hope, Arkansas. As a teenager he met and shook hands with President John Kennedy. This experience heightened his interest in becoming a politician. He became a Rhodes scholar at Oxford after graduating from college. After graduating from Yale Law School, Clinton returned to Arkansas. He was elected governor in 1978. He lost his bid for re-election in 1980. Clinton ran again in 1982 and won, serving ten more years as governor. Clinton was elected president in 1992 and re-elected in 1996. The country experienced the longest period of continued economic growth during his presidency. In 1998, however, Clinton became only the second president in U.S. history to be impeached.

Draw Conclusions
Why might meeting President Kennedy have influenced Clinton?

America. These policies promised lower taxes and smaller government. Republicans gained control of both houses of Congress for the first time since 1952.

A growing economy helped Clinton win a second term in 1996 over Senator Bob Dole of Kansas. By 1998 the U.S. government was taking in more money than it was spending. However, questions about Clinton's personal and official conduct dominated his second term. Government investigators charged that the president had conducted an improper relationship with a White House intern and then lied about it under oath. In 1998 the House of Representatives voted to impeach Clinton for obstruction of justice. The Senate acquitted him of the charges in 1999. The scandal damaged Clinton's public image, though his approval ratings remained high, due in part to the booming economy.

A Dangerous World The collapse of the Soviet Union left the United States as the world's only superpower. In 1997 President Clinton appointed **Madeleine Albright** as the first woman to be secretary of state. Albright had been born in Prague. Her family then moved to the United States, fleeing the Holocaust. She helped adapt U.S. foreign policy to this complex new world.

The United States worked to promote global peace and democracy. In the Balkan region of Europe, for example, civil war erupted in Yugoslavia. Several of its republics declared independence. In Bosnia, one of the former republics, fighting broke out in 1992 among three groups: Bosniaks

(Bosnian Muslims), Croats, and Serbs. Many Bosniak civilians were killed or forced out of Serb-controlled territory. These actions were known as "ethnic cleansing." After more than three years of bloody fighting, the United States helped negotiate a peace agreement. President Clinton then sent 20,000 U.S. troops to Bosnia to help maintain peace.

Clinton also took an active role in the Oslo peace process. The process started in 1993, when Israel and the Palestinian Authority agreed to take steps toward a negotiated settlement of their conflict. The process broke down in 2000, after the failure of talks aimed at a final agreement.

In the 1990s, **terrorism**—the use of violence by individuals or small groups to advance political goals—became a major issue. In April 1995 American terrorists bombed a federal government office building in Oklahoma City. The attack killed 168 people and injured hundreds of others. Timothy McVeigh led the terrorists. McVeigh was an ex-Army soldier who held extreme views against the government. The United States also faced increasingly deadly attacks by extremist Islamic groups. Hundreds were killed in bomb attacks on U.S. embassies in Africa in 1998.

Reading Check
Identify Cause and Effect How did the end of the Cold War change the U.S. role in the world?

Summary and Preview The Cold War ended in 1990. In the next module you will learn about the challenges the nation and the world are facing in the twenty-first century.

Lesson 4 Assessment

Review Ideas, Terms, and People

1. a. **Recall** What domestic challenges did George H. W. Bush face during his presidency?
   b. **Summarize** What were some of the major world events during Bush's presidency?
   c. **Identify** What was the purpose of Operation Desert Storm?
   d. **Evaluate** How did the Persian Gulf War test President Bush's vision of a new world order?

2. a. **Recall** What were some of the high points and low points of Bill Clinton's presidency?
   b. **Contrast** How is terrorism different from standard warfare?
   c. **Elaborate** Do you think Congress was right to pass the North American Free Trade Agreement? Explain your answer.

Critical Thinking

3. **Sequence** In this lesson you learned about key events that occurred during the presidencies of George H. W. Bush and Bill Clinton. Create a table similar to the one below to identify the major events described in the lesson and the year they occurred.

Year	Event

Social Studies Skills

Determine the Strength of an Argument

Define the Skill

Studying history often involves learning about different opinions. In order to understand these opinions, it is important to recognize strong arguments. Strong arguments are based on convincing supporting evidence. Examples and points should be true and should make sense in the context of the argument. For example, supporting points should relate to the main idea of the argument. It is also important to consider any evidence against the argument.

Many people in the past have made decisions based on the strength of an argument. Determining the strength of an argument is important for the present as well. Your judgments can help you decide whether or not to support a policy, idea, or candidate.

During the 1970s Americans had to determine the strength of arguments during the Watergate scandal. If Nixon had not resigned, for example, members of the House of Representatives would have had to decide whether or not to vote to impeach the president. They would have had to weigh the evidence and determine the strength of arguments for and against him.

Learn the Skill

In *Silent Spring*, Rachel Carson argued that environmental pollution was harmful and had to be stopped. Here is part of her argument:

"Man, however much he may like to pretend the contrary, is part of nature. Can he escape a pollution that is now so thoroughly distributed throughout our world?"

How strong is Carson's argument? In *Silent Spring*, she gives many examples of the harmful effects of pollutants and insect poisons. This makes her argument stronger. In the quotation, Carson points out that humans rely upon nature. As nature becomes polluted, she argues, humans will not be able to avoid the harmful health effects of that pollution.

Carson's argument was strong enough to convince the American people and Congress to take action. The environmental movement grew, and new laws were passed to protect the nation's air and water.

Practice the Skill

Suppose that you are a member of Congress during the Watergate scandal. You have to decide whether or not to impeach President Nixon. Your decision will depend on the strength of the arguments in favor of impeachment. Review the module and answer the following questions to help determine the strength of those arguments.

1. What is the evidence against President Nixon? How does this evidence strengthen or weaken the case against him?

2. Is there any evidence that President Nixon is innocent? How strong is this evidence?

3. Would you vote to impeach the president? Explain your answer.

Module 15 Assessment

Review Vocabulary, Terms, and People

Read each question and write the letter of the best response.

1. Which of the following refers to a period of less hostile U.S.-Soviet relations in the 1970s?
   a. détente
   b. stagflation
   c. realpolitik
   d. *perestroika*

2. Which of the following was a theory that influenced President Reagan's policies?
   a. Whip Inflation Now
   b. supply-side economics
   c. SALT
   d. *glasnost*

3. One of President Clinton's major achievements was getting Congress to pass
   a. the ERA.
   b. the Camp David Accords.
   c. NAFTA.
   d. Operation Desert Storm.

Comprehension and Critical Thinking

Lesson 1

4. a. **Identify** Who were the reporters who uncovered the Watergate scandal?
   b. **Analyze** What were some results of Nixon's visit to China?
   c. **Elaborate** Why do you think Nixon called his supporters the Silent Majority?

Lesson 2

5. a. **Recall** What happened at Three Mile Island?
   b. **Analyze** How were new rules and laws in the 1970s used to protect individuals and the public in general?
   c. **Contrast** How were the foreign policies of Nixon and Carter different?
   d. **Draw Conclusions** Why do you think many Americans responded to *Silent Spring*?

Lesson 3

6 a. **Describe** What happened in the election of 1980?
   b. **Summarize** What were some results of Reagan's conservative policies?

c. **Evaluate** Do you think Congress was right to ban aid to the Contras in Nicaragua?

Lesson 4

7. a. **Recall** What events led to the breakup of the Soviet Union?
   b. **Explain** How did the Clinton administration attempt to end foreign conflicts?
   c. **Evaluate** Do you think NAFTA helped the U.S. economy? Explain.

Review Themes

8. **Economics** How did the energy crisis affect the economy of the United States?

9. **Politics** How did the politics of the presidents discussed in this module affect the foreign policy of the United States?

Module 15 Assessment, continued

Reading Skills

Summarize *Use the Reading Skills taught in this module to complete the activity below.*

Carter also experienced disaster in the Middle East. The United States had supported the pro-American shah, or king, of Iran since the 1950s. Many Iranians resented the shah's reform efforts. They also disliked the country's shift from a traditional and agricultural society to a more urban and industrial one. The government severely punished its opponents and controlled all political participation. Many members of the opposition supported the views of Islamic spiritual leader Ruhollah Khomeini. Khomeini had been forced to leave the country because of his criticisms of the shah's policies.

In 1979 Khomeini's supporters drove the shah out of Iran. A month later, Khomeini took control of the government. On November 4, a group of Iranian students attacked the U.S. embassy in Tehran, the capital of Iran, seizing about 90 American hostages. The Iran hostage crisis lasted for more than a year.

10. Summarize the beginning of the Iran hostage crisis in three sentences.

Social Studies Skills

Determine the Strength of an Argument *Use the Social Studies Skills taught in this module to answer the question about the selection below.*

In this module you have read about the Supreme Court case *United States* v. *Nixon*. Nixon argued that executive privilege, a president's right to keep information secret for reasons of national security, protected him from having to give up tapes of his official conversations.

11. In your opinion, how strong was Nixon's argument?

Focus on Writing

12. **Write a Historical Novel** Suppose you have decided to write a historical novel set during the 1970s through the 1990s. You want your story to bring one or more of the major events of this time period to life for readers. Choose a subject that you would like to focus on in your novel. Think about the main events you will describe and the main characters your story will include. Then write the first page of your novel. Be sure to describe where and when your story is taking place. Since this is a novel, you should feel free to write dialogue for historical figures who appear in your story.

Module 16

The Twenty-First Century

★

Essential Question

How is the United States different today than in 1776?

About the Photo: Young people like these are helping to shape the future of the United States.

Explore ONLINE!

VIDEOS, including...

• Election 2008

• 9/11 Watershed Event

• Fighting the War on Terrorism

• Condoleezza Rice

• Computers

☑ Document-Based Investigations

☑ Graphic Organizers

☑ Interactive Games

☑ Image with Hotspots: The Global Automobile Industry

☑ Interactive Map: World Life Expectancy, 1990–2013

☑ Image Carousel: Factors in Climate Change

In this module you will read about the amazing events that have changed our world in recent years. You will also learn about the War on Terror and the development of new technologies.

What You Will Learn ...

Timeline of Events 1995–2015

▶ Explore ONLINE!

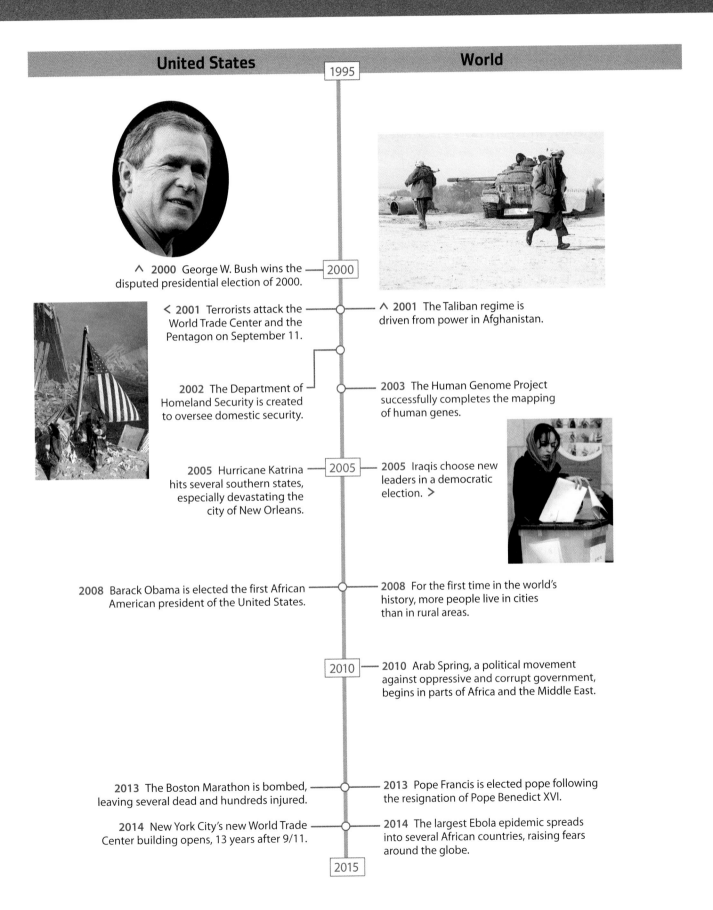

United States

World

1995

∧ **2000** George W. Bush wins the disputed presidential election of 2000.

2000

< **2001** Terrorists attack the World Trade Center and the Pentagon on September 11.

∧ **2001** The Taliban regime is driven from power in Afghanistan.

2002 The Department of Homeland Security is created to oversee domestic security.

2003 The Human Genome Project successfully completes the mapping of human genes.

2005 Hurricane Katrina hits several southern states, especially devastating the city of New Orleans.

2005

2005 Iraqis choose new leaders in a democratic election. >

2008 Barack Obama is elected the first African American president of the United States.

2008 For the first time in the world's history, more people live in cities than in rural areas.

2010

2010 Arab Spring, a political movement against oppressive and corrupt government, begins in parts of Africa and the Middle East.

2013 The Boston Marathon is bombed, leaving several dead and hundreds injured.

2013 Pope Francis is elected pope following the resignation of Pope Benedict XVI.

2014 New York City's new World Trade Center building opens, 13 years after 9/11.

2014 The largest Ebola epidemic spreads into several African countries, raising fears around the globe.

2015

Reading Social Studies

Economics, Politics

In this module you will read about the most recent presidents and their administrations. You will learn about the changing role the United States has gained in the global economy and global politics. You will also read about September 11, 2001, and learn how that tragedy helped shape the world you live in today.

Predict

Often when you are reading, predicting what might come next can help you understand what is happening in the story of history.

Understand Predicting Predicting what may come next in the logical progression of a story relies on understanding what has happened in the past. You have learned many different responses to crises that have occurred throughout U.S. history. You can use this knowledge to predict what may come in the future.

Notice how one reader uses information from the past to predict what may happen in the future.

> The war in Iraq caused fierce debate at home. After months of searching, no weapons of mass destruction were uncovered. No concrete ties between Saddam and al Qaeda could be proven either. Critics began to accuse the Bush administration of exaggerating the danger Saddam posed to the United States. The continuing violence between Iraqi insurgents and U.S. soldiers led many Americans to call for an end to the war.

After reading this section, one reader thought:

> I have read about other wars in which the American public was divided over the action the country should take. In the War of 1812, there was a convention of delegates opposed to the war. In the 1960s and 1970s, many citizens publicly protested the Vietnam War. What happened in these past wars that might happen in the Iraq War? I predict that this war will not end with a clear victory because the American people do not fully support it.

You Try It!

The following passage is from the module you are getting ready to read. As you read the passage, look for the facts that can help you predict what might happen in the future.

> The Internet was first developed in 1969 by scientists at the U.S. Department of Defense. Early computer networks were used mainly by government and university researchers. Then in the 1990s, computer programmers developed the World Wide Web, enabling people to access information from computers around the world. Internet use exploded in the 1990s. Computers and the Internet made it easier and faster for people at home, work, and school to access and share information. This important development was known as the Information Revolution.

After you read the passage, answer the following questions.

1. What other revolutions have you read about in the study of American history, and how have they affected American society?

2. Is the Information Revolution similar to any other revolution you have read about?

3. How might the Information Revolution affect American society in the future?

As you read Module 16, use the information given to predict what may happen in American society in the next ten years.

Key Terms and People

Lesson 1
Al Gore
George W. Bush
World Trade Center
Pentagon
al Qaeda
Osama bin Laden
weapons of mass destruction
service economy
globalization

Lesson 2
Department of Homeland Security
USA PATRIOT Act
Condoleezza Rice
Nancy Pelosi
Barack Obama
Patient Protection and Affordable Care Act

Lesson 3
Internet
Information Revolution
AIDS
ozone layer
global warming
Medicare
Social Security

Challenges for a New Millennium

The Big Idea
George W. Bush and the United States responded to terrorist attacks and a changing economy.

Main Ideas

- George W. Bush won the disputed 2000 presidential election.

- Americans debated the future of the War on Terror that began after terrorists attacked the United States.

- The American economy and job market rapidly changed and affected domestic policy.

Key Terms and People

Al Gore
George W. Bush
World Trade Center
Pentagon
al Qaeda
Osama bin Laden
weapons of mass destruction
service economy
globalization

If YOU were there . . .

It is the December after the presidential election between George W. Bush and Al Gore. For weeks, people have been talking about whether the votes can be recounted by hand. The race was too close to call on election night, and now the candidates are involved in a court case that will decide who the next president will be.

How would you solve the problem of recounting votes?

The 2000 Presidential Election

The United States was at peace and enjoying economic prosperity as the 2000 presidential election neared. The Democrats chose **Al Gore**, who had served as Bill Clinton's vice president, as their nominee. The Republican candidate was Texas governor **George W. Bush**, the son of former president George H. W. Bush.

Campaign Issues One major campaign issue was how to use the federal budget surplus, which totaled nearly $100 billion in 1999. Gore said he would put more money into education and health care, and use some of the surplus to pay off a part of the national debt. Bush promised to return the money to taxpayers through tax cuts. Bush and Gore also debated the role that the United States—now the world's only superpower—should play in global affairs. Campaign polls showed that the race was very close.

On election night, the voting in some states was so close that no winner could be declared right away. It was so close in Florida that the votes had to be recounted. A machine recount found that Bush had received a few hundred more votes than Gore. But Gore supporters wanted the votes in four counties to be counted by hand. They argued that this would ensure all votes were counted. The Bush campaign challenged this in court.

George W. Bush 1946–

George W. Bush was born in Connecticut and grew up mainly in Texas. His family has a long history in politics. His grandfather was a U.S. senator. His father served as president from 1989 to 1993. Bush was a member of the National Guard during the Vietnam War. Then he attended Harvard Business School. He was unsuccessful when he ran for Congress in 1978. He started several oil businesses in Texas. He also became part owner of the Texas Rangers baseball team. He was elected governor of Texas in 1994 and 1998. In 2000 he defeated Al Gore in one of the closest presidential races in American history.

Sequence
What did George W. Bush do before he was elected president?

After several weeks of suspense, the Supreme Court ruled. The Supreme Court said that the manual recounts could not ensure that all votes would be counted the same way. They ordered the recount to stop. Florida's 25 electoral votes went to Bush, making him the winner of the election. He was the first president in more than 100 years to win the electoral vote but lose the popular vote.

Bush's Early Days in Office The disputed election, however, caused lingering bitterness between Democrats and Republicans. Republicans held a small majority in the House of Representatives, while the Senate was split 50–50. When votes in the Senate are tied, the vice president casts the tie-breaking vote. This gave Vice President Dick Cheney an important role in helping to pass Republican legislation.

Bush appointed General Colin Powell to the key position of secretary of state. Powell became the first African American to hold this office. Bush carried through with his campaign promise to cut taxes. Six months after taking office, he signed into law a $1.35 trillion tax-cut plan. He also signed an education reform plan called No Child Left Behind. This created a national set of standards for every student and every school to meet. It also raised funding for schools.

Reading Check
Analyze Information
What was unusual about the outcome of the 2000 presidential election?

Fighting Terrorism

Despite many plans for educational and economic reform, President Bush was soon faced with the challenge of confronting terrorism. His administration became focused on developing a foreign policy to protect Americans from the growing threat of terrorist attacks after the events of September 11, 2001.

September 11, 2001 On September 11, 2001, terrorists took control of four commercial airliners. The hijackers used them as weapons to attack sites in Washington, DC, and New York City. They flew an airplane into each of the two towers of the **World Trade Center**, an important business center in New York City. The resulting fires caused the buildings, which had been the tallest in the nation, to crumble to the ground with many people inside. Another airplane was flown into the **Pentagon**, the headquarters of the Department of Defense located outside of Washington, DC. A fourth airplane crashed in a Pennsylvania field. About 3,000 people were killed in the attacks. These included the airplane passengers, workers and visitors in the World Trade Center and the Pentagon, and rescue workers aiding the victims.

The tragedy brought Americans together. The nation received support from foreign leaders and citizens. One French newspaper's headline read, "WE ARE ALL AMERICANS." President Bush promised to find and punish those responsible for the attacks.

United States officials determined that the hijackers were members of a fundamentalist Islamic terrorist group in Afghanistan called **al Qaeda**, or "the Base." The group was based in Afghanistan and was led by a wealthy Saudi Arabian exile, **Osama bin Laden**. The Taliban was an extreme Islamic group that ruled the country. After Taliban leaders refused to turn over bin Laden, the United States took military action. In October 2001 the United States attacked Afghanistan. It drove the Taliban from power but failed to find and capture bin Laden. The United States then began helping Afghanistan to rebuild and establish a democratic government.

War in Iraq After the attack on Afghanistan, attention turned to Iraq. President Bush argued that Saddam Hussein, the dictator of Iraq, posed an immediate threat to U.S. security. When the Persian Gulf War ended in 1991, Saddam had agreed to give up Iraq's **weapons of mass destruction**. These are chemical, biological, or nuclear weapons that can kill thousands. However, Saddam failed to fully cooperate with UN weapons inspectors.

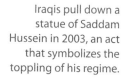

Iraqis pull down a statue of Saddam Hussein in 2003, an act that symbolizes the toppling of his regime.

Leaders from France, Germany, and Russia argued that the UN inspectors should be given more time to search for weapons. President Bush and British prime minister Tony Blair disagreed. They said Iraq should be forced to comply with the weapons ban. On March 20, 2003, the United States and a coalition of allies launched a ground attack on Iraq. Saddam's government collapsed, and Saddam was eventually captured.

As in Afghanistan, U.S. officials began working with Iraqis to establish a democratic government. Violence continued, however. U.S. soldiers and Iraqis who were working to rebuild the country were attacked. Iraqi voters elected new government leaders and approved a new constitution in 2005. In 2006 an Iraqi court sentenced Saddam to death. He was executed a short time later. Deep divisions among Iraqis remained an issue, however, threatening the stability of the new government.

Reading Check
Summarize What led to the war in Iraq?

The New Global Economy

In addition to the issues the nation faced overseas, the Bush administration and later the administration of President Barack Obama confronted a variety of domestic problems. These challenges ranged from unemployment to the national debt.

In public opinion polls taken in 2010, Americans listed economic recovery and unemployment among the most important challenges facing the United States. Other major concerns included health insurance reform, terrorism, and immigration. The growing national debt was another key concern. After several years of surpluses, the government began running a deficit again in 2002. Slow economic growth, the cost of the war in Iraq, and tax cuts all contributed to the rising budget imbalance. Beginning with the 2010 budget, the deficit was expected to fall from previous years, but remain high as a percentage of Gross Domestic Product (GDP). The GDP is the value of all goods and services produced in a country each year.

Financial Crises Affect Americans The American economy has experienced important ups and downs in recent years. During the 1990s the stock market boomed, and unemployment fell to its lowest level in 30 years. Much of this economic growth was powered by Internet companies and other high-tech firms. When some high-tech firms failed to earn profits, their stocks lost value. Many went out of business. Unemployment began rising again. Large investment firms suffered huge losses due to their investments in risky mortgages. Amid controversy, the federal government provided money to help these firms recover.

Changes in American Industry In recent years, many traditional industries have declined in importance to the U.S. economy. Many textile companies, for example, have closed mills. They've shifted their operations to countries where labor is less expensive. There has also been an increased use of computer-driven robots to make manufactured goods. This has often eliminated many jobs. This is part of a larger trend in which the percentage of Americans working in manufacturing has steadily fallen. The U.S. economy has moved toward becoming a **service economy**. This

Financial Crisis

Slowing home sales and failed investments led to an economic downturn. The federal government helped with payments to several banks and manufacturing firms.

means that most people have jobs providing services, such as medical care or entertainment, rather than producing goods.

By the end of the 1990s, about 75 percent of American workers were employed in jobs in the service industry. By 2010 this number had risen to above 80 percent and keeps rising. Health care, computer engineering, and education are expected to be among the fastest-growing fields. Such predictions are based partly on population trends. As the number of older Americans increases, for example, so will the need for nurses and other health-care professionals.

Globalization and the U.S. Economy Another ongoing change in our modern economy is the process of **globalization**—growing connections among economies and cultures all over the world. Multinational corporations, or companies that do business in more than one country, play a large part in globalization. For example, you can find American fast-food restaurants in Russia and Japanese car factories in the United States. Increasing international trade has also contributed to globalization. The use of computerized manufacturing processes has sped up and increased productivity. This has improved the standard of living in many countries, providing more international trade opportunities. In 1995 more than 120 nations joined to form the World Trade Organization (WTO). The WTO's goal is to promote international trade by removing political and economic trade barriers between nations.

At the start of the twenty-first century, the global economy began to slow down. In 2001 the economies of more than a dozen countries were in recession. Many other countries reported lower growth rates. Foreign investment to developing countries declined, damaging their economies. The U.S. economy also weakened.

By 2004 both U.S. and world economies began to recover. However, several major banking firms collapsed and began a global financial crisis in late 2007. Even financially secure banks cut back on their lending. This meant that many businesses could not get the money to invest in new inventory. They could not hire new employees and sometimes had trouble paying their existing workers. The stock market dipped. Unemployment rose quickly. The United States was in an economic recession.

To pull the country out of the recession, the U.S. government passed legislation intended to boost investment in the public and private sectors. Approved by President Bush in 2008, the Troubled Asset Relief Program committed $475 billion to stabilize the U.S. banking and automobile industries. Later, President Obama signed into law the American Recovery and Reinvestment Act of 2009. This program distributed over $8 billion in funds to individuals through tax credits and programs such as Medicaid, food stamps, and unemployment benefits. ARRA also awarded grants and loans for government contracts to American businesses. These actions added jobs, increased GDP, and reduced unemployment in 2009. A slow economic recovery began.

Summary and Preview Terrorism became a major national and international concern after the events of September 11, 2001. At the same time, globalization had a profound effect on the U.S. economy. In the next lesson you will learn about other foreign and domestic policies and issues facing Americans today.

Reading Check
Identify Cause and Effect
What economic trend led to the creation of the World Trade Organization?

Lesson 1 Assessment

Review Ideas, Terms, and People

1. a. Describe What was the outcome of the 2000 presidential election?

b. Explain How did George W. Bush promise to use the government surplus?

c. Elaborate How do you think the election of 2000 shows the importance of voting?

2. a. Identify What is al Qaeda?

b. Explain Why did the United States enter into the war with Iraq?

c. Predict What do you think the future holds for the war on terror?

3. a. Recall How has the American economy changed in the past several decades?

b. Explain What caused government deficits to rise in the early 2000s?

c. Draw Conclusions How do you think globalization has changed the U.S. economy?

Critical Thinking

4. Identify Cause and Effect In this lesson you learned about the major events of George W. Bush's presidency. Create a cause-and-effect graphic organizer similar to the one below to describe events of the presidency of George W. Bush.

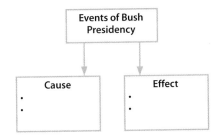

Domestic and Foreign Policy Issues

The Big Idea

Presidents George W. Bush and Barack Obama led the country through many domestic and foreign challenges.

Main Ideas

- The nation faced difficult challenges during President Bush's second term.

- Barack Obama became the first African American president of the United States.

- The Obama administration worked toward economic recovery and ending the Iraq War.

- Donald J. Trump won the 2016 presidential election.

Key Terms and People

Department of Homeland Security
USA PATRIOT Act
Condoleezza Rice
Nancy Pelosi
Barack Obama
Patient Protection and Affordable Care Act

If YOU were there . . .

The Department of Homeland Security has just been established to protect the United States from foreign and domestic threats. You are part of the department's leadership.

What do you think should be done first to safeguard the country?

George W. Bush

After the events of 9/11, President Bush declared that the United States was waging a War on Terror. The **Department of Homeland Security** was established in 2002 to manage the actions. The department was to analyze threats; guard the nation's borders, seaports, and airports; search for terrorists in the United States; and coordinate the country's response to terrorist attacks.

USA PATRIOT Act Responding to 9/11, Congress quickly passed the **USA PATRIOT Act** in late 2001 to give the government power to search and conduct electronic surveillance of suspected terrorists. This law gave the government expanded powers to protect the nation. It allowed the government to
- detain foreigners suspected of terrorism for a week without charging them with a crime,
- tap all phones used by suspects and monitor their email and Internet use,
- make search warrants valid across states,
- order U.S. banks to investigate sources of large foreign accounts, and
- prosecute terrorist crimes without any time restrictions.

Some people have questioned whether the USA PATRIOT Act is constitutional. Critics complained that it gave law enforcement too much power and posed a threat to basic American freedoms. To address these complaints, Congress

Timeline: 9/11 and Beyond

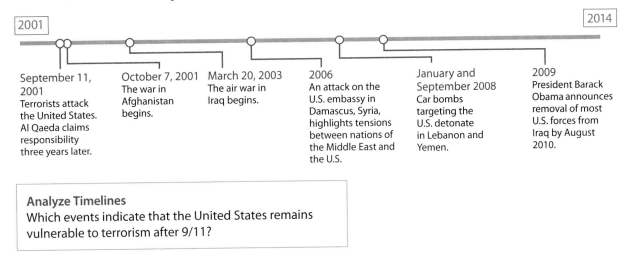

2001
2014

September 11, 2001
Terrorists attack the United States. Al Qaeda claims responsibility three years later.

October 7, 2001
The war in Afghanistan begins.

March 20, 2003
The air war in Iraq begins.

2006
An attack on the U.S. embassy in Damascus, Syria, highlights tensions between nations of the Middle East and the U.S.

January and September 2008
Car bombs targeting the U.S. detonate in Lebanon and Yemen.

2009
President Barack Obama announces removal of most U.S. forces from Iraq by August 2010.

Analyze Timelines
Which events indicate that the United States remains vulnerable to terrorism after 9/11?

let some provisions of the law expire after a set period of time. Since then, some of the provisions have been extended for security purposes.

In response to 9/11, many states have also passed legislation specifying how and when electronic surveillance can be used by the government to monitor people. The debate over the constitutionality of many of these laws continues.

Debating the Iraq War The war in Iraq caused fierce debate at home. After months of searching, no weapons of mass destruction were uncovered. No concrete ties between Saddam Hussein and al Qaeda could be proven either. Critics began to accuse the Bush administration of exaggerating the danger that Saddam posed to the United States. The continuing violence between Iraqi insurgents and U.S. soldiers led many Americans to call for an end to the war. Meanwhile, growing concerns that Iraq's neighbor, Iran, was working to develop nuclear weapons caused additional tensions in the region.

Administration Changes George Bush was re-elected in the 2004 presidential election. Afterwards, Secretary of State Colin Powell resigned. Bush appointed **Condoleezza Rice** as his replacement. She became the first African American woman to hold the office. Bush's other new cabinet appointees included Alberto Gonzales, the first Hispanic attorney general.

In late 2005 Bush nominated two new Supreme Court justices, John Roberts and Samuel Alito. The Senate investigated each thoroughly before approving them. With the confirmation of Bush's nominees, the Court began making more conservative rulings.

Due to public discontent with his policies in the Middle East, President Bush lost much of his support among voters. Democrats gained a majority in both houses of Congress in the 2006 midterm elections. The new Congress elected **Nancy Pelosi** the first female Speaker of the House of Representatives. In response to the outcome of the election, Secretary of

Defense Donald Rumsfeld resigned and a new secretary, Robert Gates, was appointed. The newly elected Congress began calling for a plan to withdraw from Iraq.

Second-term Issues Bush's administration faced much criticism for its response to the natural disasters of hurricanes Katrina and Rita. Hurricane Katrina flooded many parts of the Gulf Coast and the city of New Orleans. Local, state, and federal governments were criticized for their inadequate response to the crisis. The director of the Federal Emergency Management Agency (FEMA) stepped down amid criticism. As victims tried to rebuild their towns and cities, Hurricane Rita struck a second blow to the region. The combined effects of the two storms caused many residents to permanently leave the Gulf Coast area.

President Bush became less popular as the Iraq War continued and the U.S. economy weakened. The financial markets collapsed in the fall of 2008, causing an economic recession. At this point, more than two-thirds of Americans disapproved of Bush administration policies.

Reading Check
Analyze Information What issues did Bush face in his second term?

Barack Obama

In the 2008 presidential election, Americans voted for a change by electing Democrat **Barack Obama**, a U.S. senator from Illinois. In defeating Republican senator John McCain of Arizona, Obama made history as the first African American to be elected president of the United States. Obama went on to be re-elected to the presidency in 2012.

Economic Recovery Soon after taking office, Obama pushed through an economic stimulus package in an effort to end the recession brought on by the crash of the financial markets in 2008. The $787 billion stimulus package law was intended to create 3.5 million American jobs within two

---

BIOGRAPHY

Barack Obama 1961–

In 2008 Barack Obama became the first African American president of the United States. Obama worked as a lawyer and community organizer in Chicago before entering politics. He won his first race for the Illinois State Senate in 1996 and was re-elected in 1998. He lost a 2000 bid for a seat in the U.S. House of Representatives. He was elected to the U.S. Senate in 2004. Obama came to national attention with his keynote address at the 2004 Democratic National Convention. He became the Democratic Party nominee for president four years later. In 2009 Obama won the Nobel Peace Prize, the fourth American president to win this honor.

Summarize
What political offices has Barack Obama held?

Speech on Health Care Reform

"In 2009 President Obama worked with members of Congress to create a health care reform plan, which became the basis for the Patient Protection and Affordable Care Act. His proposals were controversial, especially among Republicans. On September 9 Obama addressed a joint session of Congress to firm up support for the plan."

Analyze Historical Sources
According to Obama, how will the plan help those who already have insurance?

There are now more than 30 million American citizens who cannot get coverage. In just a two-year period, one in every three Americans goes without health care coverage at some point. And every day, 14,000 Americans lose their coverage. In other words, it can happen to anyone. . . .

Now is the time to deliver on health care. The plan I'm announcing tonight would meet three basic goals. It will provide more security and stability to those who have health insurance. It will provide insurance for those who don't. And it will slow the growth of health care costs for our families, our businesses, and our government. It's a plan that asks everyone to take responsibility for meeting this challenge—not just government, not just insurance companies, but everybody including employers and individuals. And it's a plan that incorporates ideas from senators and congressmen, from Democrats and Republicans—and yes, from some of my opponents in both the primary and general election.

years. By the end of 2009, the Federal Reserve reported that there were some signs that a slow economic recovery had begun.

Health Care Reform President Obama also tackled health care reform. A major issue facing the country was that many Americans did not have health insurance and were suffering for it. Some 17.4 percent of non-elderly Americans were uninsured in 2008. About 8 million of those were children.

In 2010 President Obama signed the **Patient Protection and Affordable Care Act** (PPACA) into law. The law aimed to make health care affordable to all Americans. It also specified that most Americans were required to get some level of health insurance. Beginning in 2013, uninsured Americans could buy health insurance plans set up in accordance with the PPACA. However, many people criticized aspects of Obama's health care reform. For instance, whether or not the government could mandate that citizens obtain health insurance is hotly debated.

Issues with health care reform combined with continuing high unemployment rates made some voters unhappy. Many Americans did not see any economic improvement in their lives. This discontent led to Republicans gaining a majority in the U.S. House of Representatives in the 2010 midterm elections.

Though Iraq held free elections in 2005, American forces remained in the country through 2010 to help keep the peace.

War and Terrorism The Obama administration made specific plans to end combat operations in both Iraq and Afghanistan. In 2010 Operation Iraqi Freedom ended seven years after it began, with a withdrawal of combat troops. About 50,000 troops remained for smaller missions and to train Iraqi soldiers until the end of 2011. However, military operations in Afghanistan increased. Obama announced in 2009 that an additional 30,000 troops would be sent to Afghanistan to keep the Taliban from gaining ground. These soldiers joined about 70,000 already there.

Efforts to combat terrorism continued. In 2011 U.S. Special Forces tracked down and killed terrorist Osama bin Laden in Pakistan. This was a huge blow against al Qaeda. A terrorist group known as the Islamic State, or ISIS, gained strength and became a threat in 2014. ISIS quickly captured large areas of territory in Iraq and Syria. The Obama administration responded with military airstrikes against ISIS with the help of other allied countries. The United States also sent several thousand troops to Iraq to help train Iraqi forces.

Gun Violence Domestically, gun violence in schools and elsewhere was a growing problem that challenged presidents Clinton, Bush, and Obama. School shootings and other mass shootings happened in the United States about 67 times between 1996 and 2014. It became a top priority to Americans to stop gun violence everywhere. But how to solve the problem has been debated over and over again with differing opinions.

In 2010 the Supreme Court ruled that the Second Amendment's right to bear arms applies to local and state gun control laws. The Court held that the right to self-defense is fundamental to American civil liberties. This meant that laws banning handguns at state and local levels were unconstitutional. In 2013 President Obama responded to the killing of 20 first-graders in Newtown, Connecticut, with proposals to tighten federal gun-control laws. His plan included background checks for gun sales, an assault weapons ban, limiting ammunition magazine capacity, and other measures. The gun control debate is ongoing.

The 2016 Presidential Election

In 2016, as President Obama entered his final year in office, campaigns for the 2016 presidential election heated up. The election turned out to be one of the most surprising in U.S. history. The Democrats nominated former First Lady and Secretary of State Hillary Clinton as their candidate. The Republicans chose New York businessman and real estate developer Donald Trump.

Before Election Day, political surveys called polls predicted that Clinton would win. However, on November 8, 2016, Trump won the election. He secured 306 electoral votes, well over the 270 electoral votes needed to become President. However, he lost the popular vote to Clinton by nearly 3 million votes. On January 20, 2017, Donald Trump was sworn in as the 45th president of the United States.

Reading Check
Analyze
How was the election of President Barack Obama a first for the United States?

Reading Check
Identify
Who were the candidates for president in the 2016 election?

Surrounded by supporters and family, President-elect Donald Trump delivered his acceptance speech in New York on November 9, 2016.

Summary and Preview The new millennium brought many foreign and domestic challenges for our country's leaders. These challenges have been hotly debated by many Americans. In the next lesson you will learn about technological advances and population changes in the United States today.

Lesson 2 Assessment

Review Ideas, Terms, and People

1. **a. Describe** What power was given to the government by the USA PATRIOT Act?

   b. Explain How did the war in Iraq become a source of strong debate?

   c. Recall Who is Condoleezza Rice?

   d. Interpret Based on Bush's choices for Supreme Court justice nominees, was his administration more politically liberal or conservative?

2. **a. Describe** What was the purpose of Obama's economic stimulus package?

   b. Explain What was the major issue that health care reform was designed to solve?

   c. Interpret Why do you think Obama at first reduced the amount of troops in Iraq rather than withdrawing all troops at one time?

   d. Recall What 2010 ruling did the U.S. Supreme Court make regarding the Second Amendment's right to bear arms?

3. **a. Identify** How many electoral votes does a presidential candidate need to become president?

   b. Summarize Why was the outcome of the 2016 election a surprise to voters?

Critical Thinking

4. **Categorize** In this lesson you learned about the foreign and domestic issues faced by presidents Bush and Obama. Create a table similar to the one below to categorize the presidential policies and actions taken by both presidents.

	International Issues	Domestic Issues
President Bush	• •	• •
President Obama	• •	• •

Rapid Changes

The Big Idea

The United States continues to grow and change as we move ahead in the twenty-first century.

Main Ideas

- Technological advances continue to solve everyday problems.

- The American population is aging and becoming more diverse than ever before.

Key Terms and People

Internet
Information Revolution
AIDS
ozone layer
global warming
Medicare
Social Security

If YOU were there . . .

You are a student studying American history. You have read about the dramatic impact that inventions, new industries, political changes, and wars have had on daily life over the years. In your own life, you have seen how much things can change in just a few years. Now picture yourself living in the United States 50 years from now.

What will be different about life in America?

Technology Moves Forward

As you have seen throughout this book, technological changes and new inventions have dramatic effects on life in the United States and around the world. This continues to be true of our lives today. Just think about all the ways you use technology every day.

One of the technologies that has changed everyday life is the **Internet**. This is a global system of computer networks that allows people anywhere in the world to communicate and share information. The Internet was first developed in 1969 by scientists at the U.S. Department of Defense. Early computer networks were used mainly by government and university researchers. Then in the 1990s, computer programmers developed the World Wide Web, enabling people to access information from computers around the world.

Internet use exploded in the 1990s. Computers and the Internet made it easier and faster for people at home, work, and school to access and share information. This important development was known as the **Information Revolution**.

The communication networks made possible by the Internet made economic interdependence among nations increase tremendously. Excitement about the Internet and the Information Revolution helped fuel the economic boom of the 1990s. Although not all Internet companies succeeded, the Internet has changed the way we find information and communicate with each other. Internet use continues to grow

New Technology Advances in computing power and wireless devices have changed the way people across the world communicate. Social networking has become an important part of everyday life for many Americans.

rapidly around the world today. Many companies capitalize on technological innovations by developing products for personal use. Consumers now want the most current technology in cell phones, laptop computers and tablets, and other personal electronic devices. It is a huge industry.

Cyberbullying A downside of the technological innovations now available to people is cyberbullying. Bullying is harassing a person with threats, lies, or embarrassment of some kind. Bullies intentionally try to hurt their victims. Cyberbullying is a type of bullying that is done online using cell phone text messages and voicemails or computer emails and instant messages. Cyberbullies can be people that one has met in person. They can also be online acquaintances or even strangers. Most often, cyberbullies know their targets.

The following types of cyberbullying are crimes in some states, but not in all:

- threats of violence
- a hate crime (harassment based on race, color, national origin, gender, disability, or religion)
- sexually explicit messages or photos
- stalking
- images of someone in a place where that person would expect privacy

The best defenses against this growing problem are to never give out personal information (such as passwords), to not respond to any threatening messages, to not send embarrassing pictures, and to be as polite as possible in messages. Police should be notified if there are state or local cyberbullying laws that apply. A cyberbullying instance that includes a hate crime may break federal civil rights laws.

Medical Advances Technology is also helping with new medical research. For example, researchers have made important breakthroughs in understanding connections between genetics and illness. In 2003 scientists completed the Human Genome Project. This identified more than 30,000 genes in human DNA. This information could be used to find treatments for a wide range of diseases, including cancer.

Improved technology has made medical diagnoses more successful as well. Magnetic resonance imaging (MRI), for example, produces cross-sectional images of any part of the body. As advances are made, the MRI procedure becomes faster, cheaper, and more widely available. Medical researchers foresee using tiny "nanosensors" about 50,000 times thinner than the width of a human hair to find tumors. They predict using "nanobots" to repair tissues and even genes.

Another ongoing challenge for medical researchers is fighting acquired immune deficiency syndrome (AIDS). **AIDS** is caused by the human immunodeficiency virus (HIV). It effectively shuts down the body's immune system. This makes it more likely that people with AIDS will contract other illnesses and die. As of 2015, as many as 36 million people worldwide had died from AIDS. Scientists have developed drugs that help control HIV. But they have not yet found a cure. Public health officials advocate abstinence and "safer sex" practices to help prevent the spread of HIV. In 2002 leaders from around the world founded the Global Fund to Fight AIDS, Tuberculosis, and Malaria. The Global Fund provides money to treat these deadly diseases and search for cures.

Environmental Damage and Protection Scientists are also searching for ways to help protect the environment. Because environmental quality affects every nation, international solutions are required. In the 1980s, for example, many people became concerned about the condition of the **ozone layer**. This is a thin layer of gas in the upper atmosphere that blocks harmful solar rays. The United States joined with more than 100 other nations

Medical Research
Medical research has improved the lives of millions, as new medicines combat old and new diseases.

Environmental Issues

The nation and the world face the issues of environmental damage and an increase in population.

to ban the use of chemicals that were harming the ozone layer. By 2004 some scientists reported that damage to the ozone layer was slowly being repaired.

Energy consumption in the United States has been increasing along with its population. Today, American transportation remains almost completely dependent on petroleum. In 2014 Americans consumed about 8.8 million barrels of petroleum in the form of gasoline per day. Americans are using more technologies requiring electricity in their homes and workplaces. These technologies include air conditioning, heating, appliances, and electronics. This has increased the use of coal, natural gas, and other energy sources. But while the total energy consumption is going up due to increased population, energy use per household has declined. This is the result of new, more energy-efficient technologies.

Scientists continue to look for ways to reduce American dependence on pollution-producing energy sources. One solution is to cut consumption of raw materials. Objects such as glass and plastic bottles and jars, newspapers, cardboard, and aluminum cans may be recycled. In 2007 recycling saved the energy equivalent of nearly 11 billion gallons of gasoline.

Another environmental issue facing the world is climate change, or **global warming**. Burning fossil fuels such as gasoline and coal releases carbon dioxide into Earth's atmosphere. Many scientists warn that rising levels of carbon dioxide are causing a greenhouse effect. Heat from the sun is trapped in Earth's atmosphere. This could cause temperatures to rise, which could trigger rising sea levels and more severe weather patterns. A 2001 United Nations scientific report predicted that Earth's average temperature could rise between 2 and 10 degrees by 2100. World leaders continue to meet to discuss ways to reduce the effects of global warming.

In October 2015 NASA's Curiosity rover took pictures of itself and sent them back to Earth, becoming one of the first Martian selfies.

Concerns about global warming and high oil prices have encouraged development of new transportation technologies. In 2007 Americans bought record numbers of hybrid cars, which run partially on electricity. Scientists are also developing vehicles that will run entirely on hydrogen and release almost no pollution.

Space Exploration Some scientists take on issues facing our planet. Others look to the challenge of exploring space. In 2004 NASA landed two robotic vehicles on Mars. The rovers began exploring the Martian surface. They sent back images that people could see on NASA's website. In 2009 a probe discovered a significant amount of water on the moon's surface. More unmanned missions are planned.

Although shuttle accidents in 1986 and 2003 killed 14 astronauts, NASA's space shuttle program flew over 100 missions since its initial shuttle launch in 1981. In 2010 President Obama proposed a cut to NASA's budget for *Constellation*, a program that planned to send humans to the moon for the first time since 1972. In 2011 the *Atlantis* crew completed the final mission of NASA's 30-year shuttle program. However, human exploration of space continues on the International Space Station, a space laboratory that has been orbiting Earth and conducting research since 2010.

The Changing American Population

The American population will continue to grow in the twenty-first century. The population is changing and becoming more diverse.

Ethnic Diversity The U.S. Census Bureau reports that our population is more ethnically diverse than ever before. In 2013 the bureau reported that Hispanics made up about 17 percent of the country's total population, making them the country's largest minority group. African Americans made up just over 13 percent of the American population. Asian Americans were about 5 percent.

Not only is American society increasingly diverse. Individual Americans reflect this diversity as well. In the year 2000, the Census Bureau began allowing people to indicate in official surveys that they were of more than one race, and more than 6.8 million Americans did so. In 2008 American voters chose a man of mixed race, Barack Obama, as president for the first time.

These changes are greatly influenced by immigration patterns. Of the more than 40 million foreign-born residents, 53 percent were born in Latin America and 28 percent were born in Asia. Based on these trends, the Census Bureau predicts that the country's non-Hispanic white populations will become a minority by the year 2050. The settlement pattern of most immigrants is that they settle in a U.S. city heavily populated by people of a similar background.

Reasons for immigrating to a country are sometimes referred to as push-pull factors. Push factors are those that cause people to leave their homeland and migrate to another place. An example of a push factor is an

Reading Check
Summarize In what key areas is technology changing modern life?

U.S. Population
The American population
is living longer and is more
ethnically diverse than ever
before.

environmental condition, such as drought or other natural disaster, that turns habitable land into uninhabitable land. Another example of a push factor is a political situation, such as war or the persecution of certain groups of people for ethnic or religious reasons. These and other push factors can motivate people to immigrate to another country in search of a better situation.

Pull factors draw or attract people to another location. Countries with good economic opportunities and high salaries are the destinations for immigrants attracted to those pull factors. Many immigrants to the United States are drawn by economic opportunities. Another example of a pull factor is a favorable climate that attracts immigrants to a country.

Religion Throughout American history, immigrants have added their religious beliefs to the cultural identity of the United States. Most first settlers in the original English colonies were Protestant Christians. Later, immigration increased the numbers of Catholics, Jews, and other religions. Today, immigrants continue to add to our nation's religious diversity. As more immigrants come from Asia and Africa, religions from those world regions have become a part of the American experience.

Currently, about 80 percent of Americans identify themselves as Christians. Among organized religions, the next largest group is Judaism, at about 2 percent of the population. Islam, Buddhism, and Hinduism continue to grow in the United States, although members of each of these faiths make up less than 1 percent of the total U.S. population.

Older Americans The U.S. Census Bureau found in 2010 that Americans were older than ever before. The median age was 37.2—six years older than in 1990. Increased longevity and the aging of the baby-boom generation were the reasons behind the rising median age. On average, Americans live to 78.2 years of age.

This older population places new demands on U.S. programs that provide elder care. These programs need to be reworked because millions of Americans will soon be affected. This includes health care programs such as **Medicare**, which pays medical expenses for senior citizens. The costs of providing Medicare are skyrocketing. By 2010 the costs exceeded $465 billion. The expense will continue to increase as the elderly population increases quickly.

The older population will also drain another U.S. program for the elderly—**Social Security**. It pays benefits to retired Americans. The Social Security system was designed to rely on continued funding from a vast number of younger workers who would contribute taxes to support a small number of retired workers. This worked well when there were many more workers than retirees to support. But in the near future, there will be so many retired people depending on the system that there will not be enough workers to supply the funding needed.

This has led to many debates on how to reform the Social Security and Medicare systems, but no solutions have been decided upon yet. For Social Security, some solutions have been proposed, such as raising deductions for workers, taxing the benefits paid to wealthier Americans, and raising the age at which retirees can collect benefits. The debates are ongoing.

Summary Technological advances are happening quickly to solve problems but sometimes create new issues. The American population is aging and becoming more diverse than ever before. The United States continues to face challenges as well as create opportunities. How would you like to contribute to your country's future?

Reading Check
Draw Conclusions
How might the U.S. population change over the next 100 years?

Lesson 3 Assessment

Review Ideas, Terms, and People

1. **a. Identify** What are some of the world's most recent technological advances?

   b. Explain How did the Internet spark an Information Revolution?

   c. Predict Do you think global warming will affect your life in the future? Why or why not?

2. **a. Describe** Describe the U.S. population today.

   b. Make Inferences Why do you think the Census Bureau started allowing people to mark more than one race?

   c. Elaborate How do you think diversity and shared ideals affect America?

Critical Thinking

3. **Categorize** In this lesson you learned about the changes taking place in the United States. Create a graphic organizer similar to the one below, adding circles as necessary, to describe major technological challenges for the future.

Social Studies Skills

Confront Controversial Issues

Define the Skill

The United States and the world face many challenges in the twenty-first century. People often have different opinions on how to deal with these challenges, which can lead to controversy. Some of the issues discussed in this book remain controversial.

As citizens of a democracy, Americans have a responsibility to confront controversial issues. This includes learning about different issues and why they are controversial. It also involves discussing the issues and forming opinions about them. Part of the democratic system is listening to other people's ideas about how to solve controversial issues and presenting your own ideas in a helpful way. In this way, everyone's ideas can be heard and discussed, so that the best course of action can be followed.

Learn the Skill

To confront controversial issues, it is important to understand them. You can start by identifying them. For example, one controversial issue in the twenty-first century is globalization—the process of economies and cultures becoming more closely connected. Some people think that globalization is a good way to improve the lives of all the world's citizens. Others think that globalization destroys what is unique about individual cultures.

Once the issue has been identified, you can learn more about it. Books, news reports, and articles are good sources of information on controversial issues. They can provide different points of view on an issue. Gathering different opinions about globalization, for example, can help you see why it is controversial. It can also help you determine your own point of view on the issue.

Follow these guidelines to confront other controversial issues.

1. Identify the issue.

2. Learn about the issue. Gather information on the subject from different sources. Determine why the issue is controversial.

3. Figure out your own point of view on the issue.

4. Discuss the issue with others. Because the issue is controversial and may lead to disagreements, it is important to be respectful of differences of opinion.

Practice the Skill

Follow these instructions to confront the controversial issue of how to deal with terrorism.

1. Find at least three articles showing different points of view about dealing with terrorism.

2. Read and take notes on the articles you have found. Based on what you have learned, determine your own point of view.

3. Have a class discussion about dealing with terrorism. Listen to opposing points of view. Share your own ideas and explain how you arrived at your point of view.

Immigration Today

America has always been a nation of immigrants. Today, people from every country move to the United States. In 2012 approximately 13 percent of the U.S. population was foreign born. Many of these people will eventually choose to become naturalized citizens.

Immigration has been a long-standing debate topic in the United States. Some Americans think that immigration should be open to any interested migrant. Others believe that it should be limited for the good of the country. With the threat of global terrorism, U.S. immigration policy is becoming more strict. People from certain countries must register with the Department of Homeland Security.

The issue of immigration has been complicated by illegal immigration. In 2009 the population of illegal immigrants living in the United States was estimated to be about 11 million. The U.S. Congress has been trying to address this problem for decades. It has passed laws attempting to bar illegal entry and limit benefits for illegal immigrants. Some states, such as those along the border between the United States and Mexico, have taken action to stop the illegal entry of people from Mexico and other nations in Central America. For example, Arizona passed a law giving state and local police more authority to enforce federal immigration laws. As of 2015, the debate over immigration and calls for reform continue.

Immigrants from Asia make up about 40 percent of all foreign-born U.S. residents. Chinese and Japanese immigrants have been coming to the United States for generations. Southeast Asians such as the Hmong, Laotians, Vietnamese, and Cambodians are among more recent arrivals.

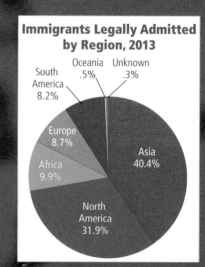

Immigrants Legally Admitted by Region, 2013

- South America 8.2%
- Oceania .5%
- Unknown .3%
- Europe 8.7%
- Africa 9.9%
- Asia 40.4%
- North America 31.9%

Many immigrants from Eastern and Western Europe come to the United States seeking a better life. They accounted for about 9 percent of the immigrants admitted in 2013.

Immigrants from around the world often choose to become naturalized U.S. citizens. The day they take the oath of American citizenship is often a day of celebration, as it was for this mother and daughter from Uganda.

Immigrants arrive in the United States searching for economic, educational, and political opportunities. Immigrants from Mexico and Central America made up about 20 percent of new permanent residents of the United States in 2013.

Interpret Maps

1. **Human-Environment Interaction** From which continent does the largest number of immigrants come?

2. **Movement** How do you think immigration affects U.S. society today?

Module 16 Assessment

Review Vocabulary, Terms, and People

Match the numbered person or term with the correct lettered definition.

1. World Trade Center
2. USA PATRIOT Act
3. Al Gore
4. global warming
5. Social Security
6. service economy
7. AIDS
8. Barack Obama

a. 2000 Democratic presidential candidate
b. the rise in average temperatures around the world
c. program that pays benefits to retired Americans
d. buildings attacked on September 11, 2001
e. deadly disease that shuts down the body's immune system
f. first African American president of the United States
g. in this situation, most jobs involve providing services rather than producing goods
h. gave the U.S. government power to search and conduct electronic surveillance of suspected terrorists

Comprehension and Critical Thinking

Lesson 1

9. a. **Identify** Who was responsible for the September 11, 2001, terrorist attacks on the United States?
   b. **Explain** Why was the 2000 U.S. presidential election controversial?
   c. **Evaluate** What happened in 2007 that contributed to an economic recession?

Lesson 2

10. a. **Evaluate** Do you think the United States was right to go to war with Iraq in 2003? Why?
    b. **Recall** What did the Patient Protection and Affordable Care Act require?
    c. **Identify** What events have made gun violence a current major issue?

Lesson 3

11. a. **Identify** What trend is responsible for increasing diversity in the United States?
    b. **Explain** What is the Information Revolution and how do we depend on it?
    c. **Predict** What aspects of life do you think will be most affected by new technology in the future?

Review Themes

12. **Economics** How have changes in the economy affected American society since 2000?

13. **Politics** How did international politics change over the course of George W. Bush's presidency?

Reading Skills

Predict *Use the Reading Skills taught in this module to answer the questions below.*

14. What might you predict for the future of society in the United States? What about the U.S. economy? How might American politics stay the same or change? What ideas in the module lead you to these conclusions?

Social Studies Skills

Confront Controversial Issues *Use the Social Studies Skills taught in this module to answer the question below.*

15. Name one controversial issue today. What are two different points of view on the issue?

Focus on Writing

16. **Design a Website** The popularity of the Internet dramatically increased in the 1990s, changing the way we communicate and share information. Review what you have learned in this module, and plan a website about America in the late twentieth and early twenty-first century. Decide whether it will be just one page or multiple linked pages. Include information on significant people, events, and ideas, as well as ideas for photos, audio, or video you would like to place on your site. You might also want to provide links to other websites where viewers can find more information. Make sure your links connect to reliable websites, such as government sites or those for newspapers or museums. Finally, choose the website address you would like to use.

References

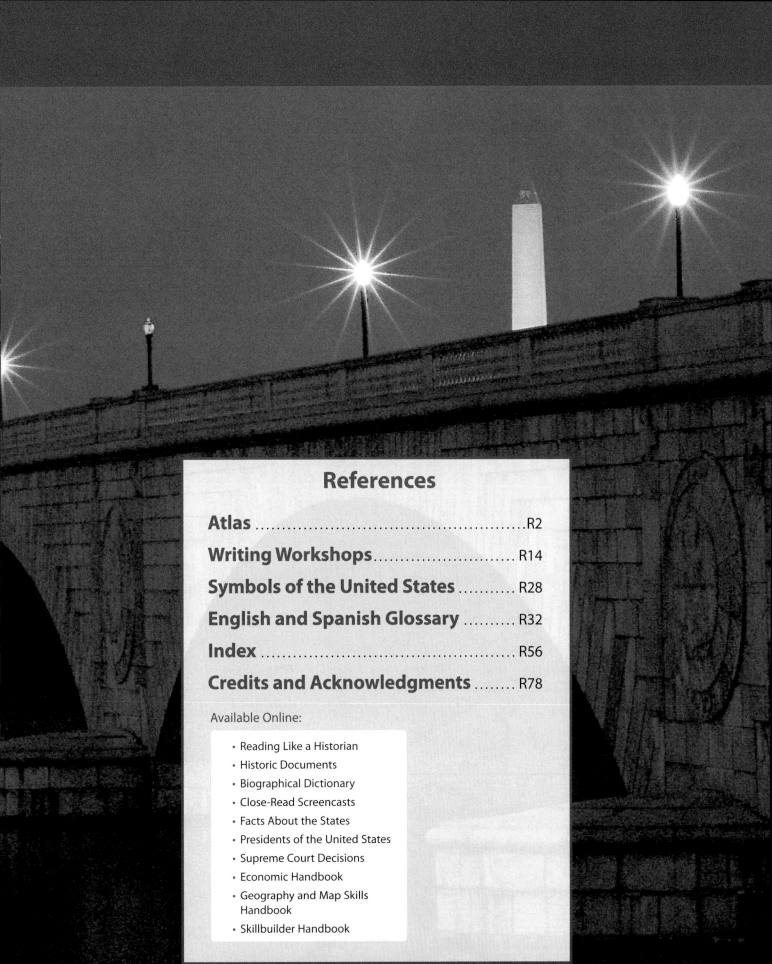

References

Available Online:

- Reading Like a Historian
- Historic Documents
- Biographical Dictionary
- Close-Read Screencasts
- Facts About the States
- Presidents of the United States
- Supreme Court Decisions
- Economic Handbook
- Geography and Map Skills Handbook
- Skillbuilder Handbook

United States: Political

To understand the relative locations of Alaska and Hawaii, as well as the vast distances separating them from the rest of the United States, see the world map.

CANADA

MINNESOTA
Duluth
Superior
Marquette
Sault Ste. Marie
Fargo
Grand Forks

Lake Superior

WISCONSIN
Green Bay
Minneapolis
★ St. Paul
Madison
Milwaukee

MICHIGAN
Lake Michigan
Grand Rapids
Saginaw
Lansing ★
Detroit
Ann Arbor

Lake Huron

IOWA
Sioux Falls
Sioux City
Cedar Rapids
Davenport
Des Moines
Rockford
Chicago
Gary
South Bend
Fort Wayne
Toledo
Peoria

ILLINOIS
Springfield ★

INDIANA
Indianapolis ★
Dayton
Cincinnati

OHIO
Cleveland
Youngstown
Akron
Columbus

Lake Erie

MISSOURI
Kansas City
Kansas City
Jefferson City ★
Topeka ★
St. Louis
East St. Louis
Lake of the Ozarks
Springfield

KENTUCKY
Louisville
Evansville
Frankfort ★
Lexington
Ohio River
Lake Barkley
Kentucky Lake

MICHIGAN

Lake Ontario
Rochester
Syracuse
Buffalo
Albany ★

NEW YORK

Lake Champlain
Burlington
Montpelier ★
Augusta ★

MAINE
Portland

VT
NH
Concord ★
Manchester
Boston ★
Worcester
Providence ★
Cape Cod

MA
Springfield
Hartford ★
CT
RI
New Haven
Bridgeport
Jersey City
Newark
Yonkers
New York City
Long Island
Long Island Sound

Susquehanna River

PENNSYLVANIA
Allentown
Harrisburg ★
Pittsburgh
Philadelphia
Trenton ★
Camden
NJ
Atlantic City

Hudson R.
Connecticut R.

WEST VIRGINIA
Charleston ★
Washington, D.C. ✪
Baltimore
Annapolis ★
MD
DE
Dover ★
Delaware Bay

VIRGINIA
Richmond ★
Newport News
Norfolk
Virginia Beach
Chesapeake

ATLANTIC OCEAN

40°N
70°W
35°N

Greensboro
Durham
Raleigh ★
Winston-Salem
Cape Hatteras

TENNESSEE
Nashville ★
Knoxville
Chattanooga
Memphis

NORTH CAROLINA
Asheville
Charlotte

ARKANSAS
Tulsa
Fayetteville
Little Rock ★
Pine Bluff
Keystone Lake
Lake Texoma

Greenville

SOUTH CAROLINA
Columbia ★
Charleston

Savannah River

MISSISSIPPI
Vicksburg
Jackson ★
Meridian
Huntsville

ALABAMA
Birmingham
Montgomery ★
Columbus

GEORGIA
Atlanta ★
Macon
Savannah
Sea Islands

Chattahoochee R.

✪	National capital
★	State capitals
•	Other cities

0   100   200 Miles
0   100   200 Kilometers

Projection: Albers Equal Area

LOUISIANA
Shreveport
Beaumont
Houston
Galveston
Baton Rouge
New Orleans
Biloxi
Chandeleur Islands
Toledo Bend Reservoir
Red River

Mobile
Pensacola
Tallahassee ★
Jacksonville

FLORIDA
Gainesville
Orlando
Tampa
St. Petersburg
Lake Okeechobee
Cape Canaveral
Fort Myers
Fort Lauderdale
Miami

Cape Sable
Florida Keys
Straits of Florida

Gulf of Mexico

BAHAMAS

25°N
75°W
80°W
85°W
90°W
95°W

N W E S

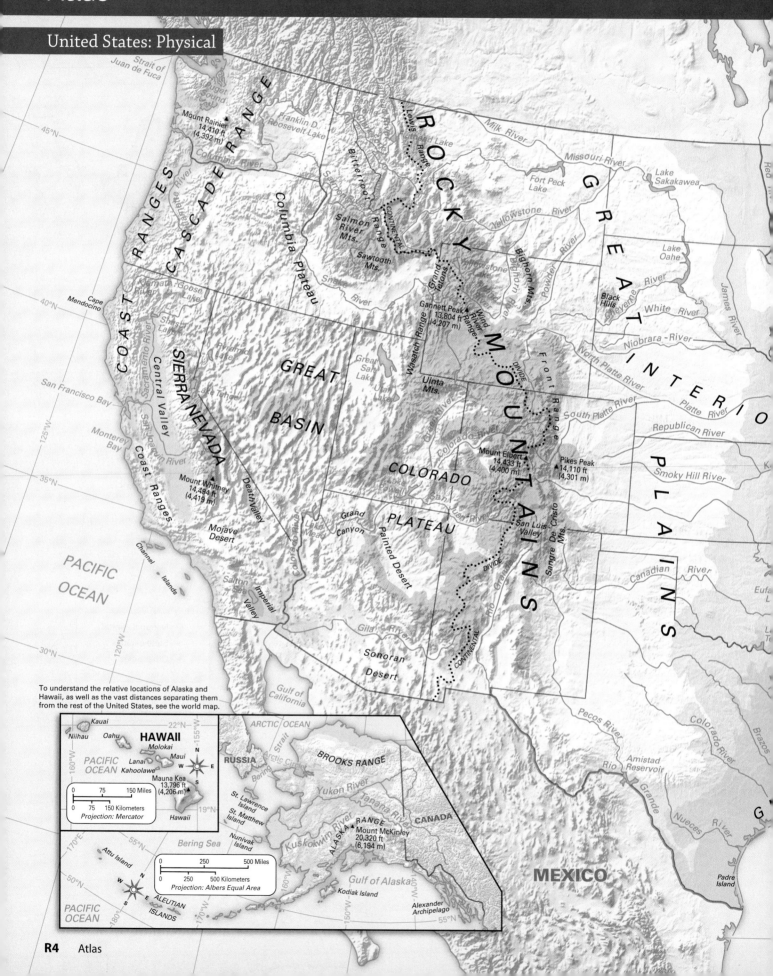

To understand the relative locations of Alaska and Hawaii, as well as the vast distances separating them from the rest of the United States, see the world map.

CANADA

Isle Royale

Mesabi Range

Lake Superior

Minnesota River

Mississippi River

Wisconsin River

Lake Michigan

Lake Huron

St. Lawrence River

St. Lawrence Seaway

Lake Champlain

Longfellow Mts.

Penobscot River

St. John River

Adirondack Mts.

Green Mts.

White Mts.

Connecticut River

Hudson River

Lake Ontario

Cape Cod

Lake Erie

Catskill Mts.

Long Island Sound

Long Island

P L A T E A U

M O U N T A I N S

40°N

Allegheny R.

Susquehanna River

Delaware River

Missouri River

Des Moines River

Illinois River

Wabash River

Scioto River

Delaware Bay

Chesapeake Bay

A L L E G H E N Y

Monongahela R.

Potomac River

ATLANTIC OCEAN

P L A I N S

Ohio River

Kanawha River

James River

A P P A L A C H I A N

70°W

Lake of the Ozarks

OZARK PLATEAU

Cumberland River

Lake Barkley

Cumberland Plateau

Great Smoky Mts.

BLUE RIDGE MOUNTAINS

Roanoke River

Pamlico Sound

Cape Hatteras

35°N

Keystone Lake

Kentucky Lake

P I E D M O N T

Arkansas River

White River

Kentucky River

Tennessee River

Oconee River

Savannah River

Ouachita Mts.

...la ...exoma

Tombigbee River

Coosa River

Chattahoochee River

Altamaha River

Sea Islands

Trinity River

Saline River

Red River

Mississippi River

Pearl River

Alabama R.

C O A S T A L   P L A I N

Okefenokee Swamp

Toledo Bend Reservoir

G U L F

Chandeleur Islands

Mississippi Delta

Cape Canaveral

80°W

F L O R I D A   P E N I N S U L A

ELEVATION

Feet		Meters
13,120		4,000
6,560		2,000
1,640		500
656		200
(Sea level) 0		0 (Sea level)
Below sea level		Below sea level

0   100   200 Miles

0   100   200 Kilometers

Projection: Albers Equal Area

N
W   E
S

Gulf of Mexico

BAHAMAS

25°N

Lake Okeechobee

The Everglades

Cape Sable

Florida Keys

Straits of Florida

75°W

85°W

90°W

95°W

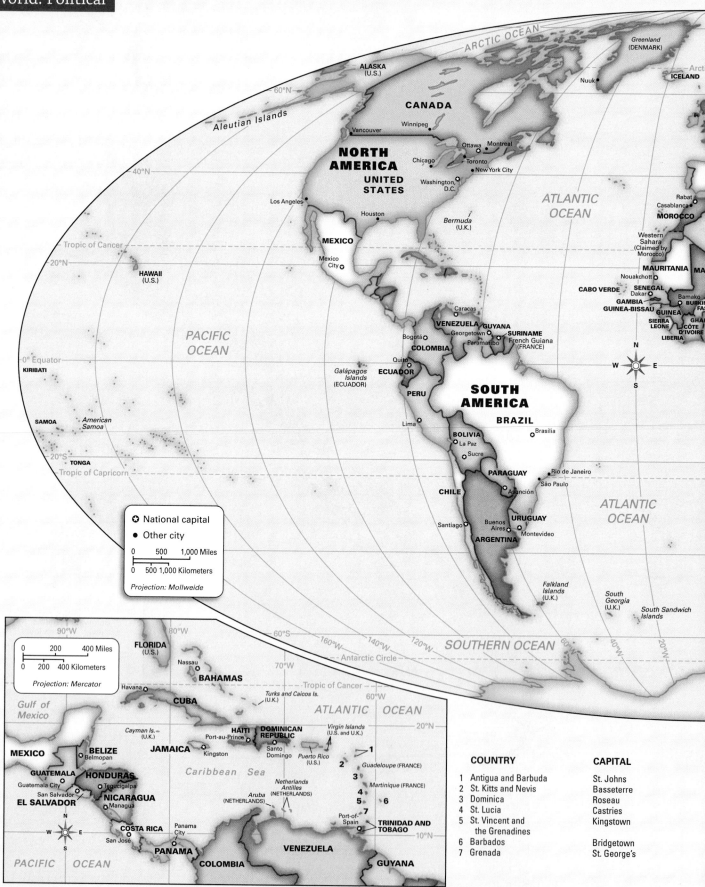

ARCTIC OCEAN

Greenland
(DENMARK)

Arctic

ALASKA
(U.S.)

ICELAND

Nuuk

CANADA

Winnipeg

Vancouver

Ottawa   Montreal

NORTH
AMERICA

Chicago   Toronto
New York City

UNITED
STATES

Washington,
D.C.

Los Angeles

ATLANTIC
OCEAN

Rabat

Houston

Casablanca

MOROCCO

Bermuda
(U.K.)

MEXICO

Tropic of Cancer

Western
Sahara
(Claimed by
Morocco)

Mexico
City

HAWAII
(U.S.)

MAURITANIA   MALI

20°N

Nouakchott

CABO VERDE   SENEGAL

Caracas

Dakar   Bamako   BURKINA

GAMBIA   FASO

VENEZUELA   GUYANA   SURINAME

GUINEA-BISSAU   GUINEA

PACIFIC
OCEAN

Bogotá

Georgetown
Paramaribo   French Guiana
(FRANCE)

SIERRA   GHANA
LEONE   CÔTE
         D'IVOIRE

COLOMBIA

LIBERIA

Quito

N

0° Equator

ECUADOR

KIRIBATI

W   E

Galápagos
Islands
(ECUADOR)

S

PERU

SOUTH
AMERICA

SAMOA

American
Samoa

BRAZIL

Brasília

Lima

BOLIVIA

La Paz

20°S

Sucre

TONGA

Rio de Janeiro

Tropic of Capricorn

PARAGUAY

São Paulo

CHILE

Asunción

ATLANTIC
OCEAN

URUGUAY

Santiago

Buenos
Aires   Montevideo

ARGENTINA

⊛ National capital

• Other city

0   500   1,000 Miles

0   500 1,000 Kilometers

Falkland
Islands
(U.K.)

South
Georgia
(U.K.)

South Sandwich
Islands

Projection: Mollweide

60°S

SOUTHERN OCEAN

Antarctic Circle

90°W

80°W

FLORIDA
(U.S.)

60°W

0   200   400 Miles

Nassau

70°W

0   200   400 Kilometers

Projection: Mercator

BAHAMAS

Tropic of Cancer

Havana

60°W

CUBA

Turks and Caicos Is.
(U.K.)

ATLANTIC   OCEAN

Gulf of
Mexico

20°N

Cayman Is.
(U.K.)

HAITI   DOMINICAN
REPUBLIC

Virgin Islands
(U.S. and U.K.)

1

MEXICO   BELIZE

JAMAICA

Port-au-Prince

Santo

2

Belmopan

Kingston

Domingo   Puerto Rico
(U.S.)

Guadeloupe (FRANCE)

GUATEMALA   HONDURAS

Caribbean   Sea

3

Martinique (FRANCE)

Guatemala City   Tegucigalpa

Netherlands
Antilles
(NETHERLANDS)

4

SAN SALVADOR   NICARAGUA

5   6

EL SALVADOR

Managua

Aruba
(NETHERLANDS)

7

Port-of-

COSTA RICA

Spain   TRINIDAD AND
         TOBAGO

Panama

San José

City

N

10°N

W   E

PANAMA

VENEZUELA

S

PACIFIC   OCEAN

COLOMBIA

GUYANA

COUNTRY	CAPITAL
1 Antigua and Barbuda	St. Johns
2 St. Kitts and Nevis	Basseterre
3 Dominica	Roseau
4 St. Lucia	Castries
5 St. Vincent and the Grenadines	Kingstown
6 Barbados	Bridgetown
7 Grenada	St. George's

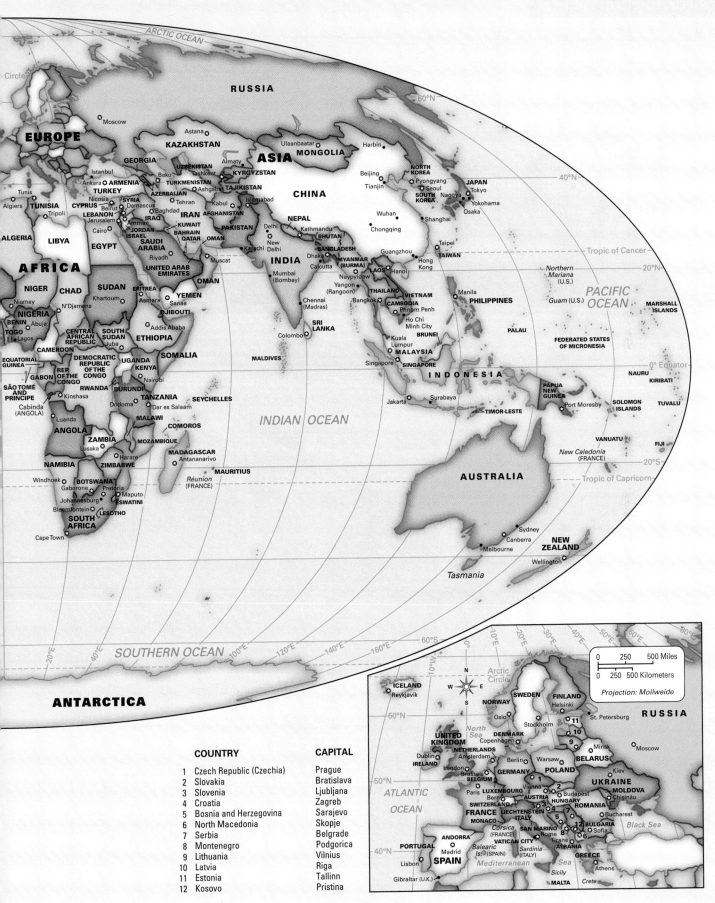

COUNTRY

1. Czech Republic (Czechia)
2. Slovakia
3. Slovenia
4. Croatia
5. Bosnia and Herzegovina
6. North Macedonia
7. Serbia
8. Montenegro
9. Lithuania
10. Latvia
11. Estonia
12. Kosovo

CAPITAL

Prague
Bratislava
Ljubljana
Zagreb
Sarajevo
Skopje
Belgrade
Podgorica
Vilnius
Riga
Tallinn
Pristina

Atlas

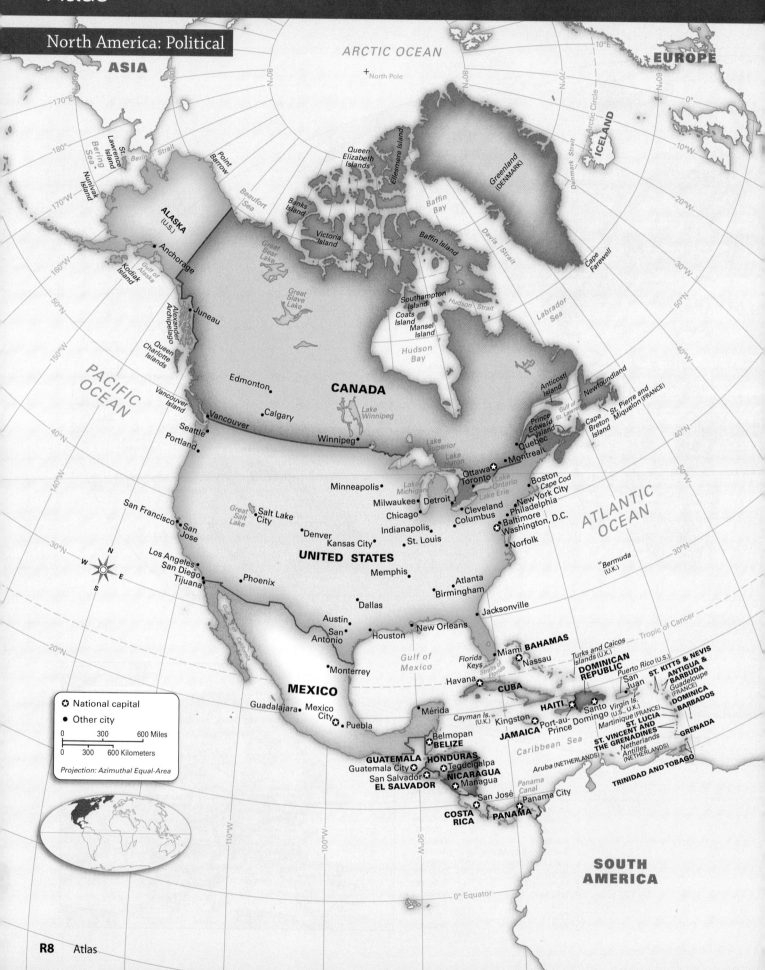

ARCTIC OCEAN

ASIA

EUROPE

+ North Pole

ICELAND

Greenland (DENMARK)

Queen Elizabeth Islands

Ellesmere Island

Beaufort Sea

Banks Island

Baffin Bay

Baffin Island

Denmark Strait

Victoria Island

Cape Farewell

Davis Strait

Great Bear Lake

St. Lawrence Island

Bering Strait

Point Barrow

Nunivak Island

ALASKA (U.S.)

Anchorage

Kodiak Island

Gulf of Alaska

Alexander Archipelago

Juneau

Queen Charlotte Islands

Vancouver Island

Great Slave Lake

Southampton Island

Coats Island

Mansel Island

Hudson Strait

Labrador Sea

Edmonton

CANADA

Lake Winnipeg

Anticosti Island

Newfoundland

Gulf of St. Lawrence

PACIFIC OCEAN

Vancouver

Calgary

Prince Edward Island

Cape Breton Island

St. Pierre and Miquelon (FRANCE)

Seattle

Winnipeg

Lake Superior

Lake Huron

Quebec

Montreal

Portland

Minneapolis

Lake Michigan

Lake Ontario

Ottawa

Toronto

Lake Erie

Boston

Cape Cod

Milwaukee

Detroit

Cleveland

New York City

Philadelphia

ATLANTIC OCEAN

Chicago

Columbus

Baltimore

San Francisco

Great Salt Lake

Salt Lake City

Denver

Indianapolis

St. Louis

Washington, D.C.

Norfolk

San Jose

Kansas City

UNITED STATES

Bermuda (U.K.)

Los Angeles

San Diego

Tijuana

Phoenix

Memphis

Atlanta

Birmingham

Dallas

Jacksonville

Tropic of Cancer

Austin

San Antonio

Houston

New Orleans

Gulf of California

Gulf of Mexico

Florida Keys

Miami

BAHAMAS

Nassau

Turks and Caicos Islands (U.K.)

Monterrey

Havana

Straits of Florida

DOMINICAN REPUBLIC

Puerto Rico (U.S.)

San Juan

ST. KITTS & NEVIS

ANTIGUA & BARBUDA

Guadeloupe (FRANCE)

MEXICO

Guadalajara

Mexico City

CUBA

Cayman Is. (U.K.)

HAITI

Santo Domingo

Virgin Is. (U.S.; U.K.)

DOMINICA

BARBADOS

Mérida

Puebla

Kingston

JAMAICA

Port-au-Prince

Martinique (FRANCE)

ST. LUCIA

Belmopan

BELIZE

Caribbean Sea

ST. VINCENT AND THE GRENADINES

Netherlands Antilles (NETHERLANDS)

GRENADA

GUATEMALA

HONDURAS

Guatemala City

Tegucigalpa

Aruba (NETHERLANDS)

TRINIDAD AND TOBAGO

San Salvador

NICARAGUA

EL SALVADOR

Managua

Panama Canal

COSTA RICA

San José

PANAMA

Panama City

SOUTH AMERICA

0° Equator

Legend

◉ National capital

● Other city

0 — 300 — 600 Miles

0 — 300 — 600 Kilometers

Projection: Azimuthal Equal-Area

South America: Political

CENTRAL
AMERICA

Caribbean Sea

Barranquilla
Cartagena
Caracas

VENEZUELA

Lake
Maracaibo

Georgetown
Paramaribo
GUYANA
Cayenne
SURINAME
French
Guiana
(FRANCE)

Medellín

Bogotá
COLOMBIA
Cali

Malpelo
Island
(COLOMBIA)

ATLANTIC
OCEAN

N
W   E
S

0° Equator

Quito
ECUADOR
Guayaquil

Galápagos
Islands
(ECUADOR)

0° Equator

Belém

PERU

BRAZIL

Recife

Trujillo

10°S

Callao   Lima

PACIFIC
OCEAN

Lake
Titicaca
La Paz
Arequipa

Lake
Poopó
BOLIVIA
Sucre

Salvador

Brasília

Belo Horizonte

10°S

20°S

PARAGUAY

Campinas
São Paulo
Rio de Janeiro

Tropic of Capricorn

San Ambrosio
Island
(CHILE)

San Félix Island
(CHILE)

Asunción

Curitiba

20°S

Tropic of
Capricorn

CHILE

Pôrto Alegre

Juan Fernández
Islands
(CHILE)

Córdoba

Rosario

URUGUAY

30°S

Valparaíso
Santiago

Buenos Aires
Montevideo

ATLANTIC
OCEAN

30°S

ARGENTINA

⊕ National capital
• Other city

0   250   500 Miles
0   250   500 Kilometers

Projection: Azimuthal Equal-Area

40°S

Strait of
Magellan

Falkland
Islands (U.K.)

South Georgia
Island
(U.K.)

50°S

Tierra del
Fuego

Atlas

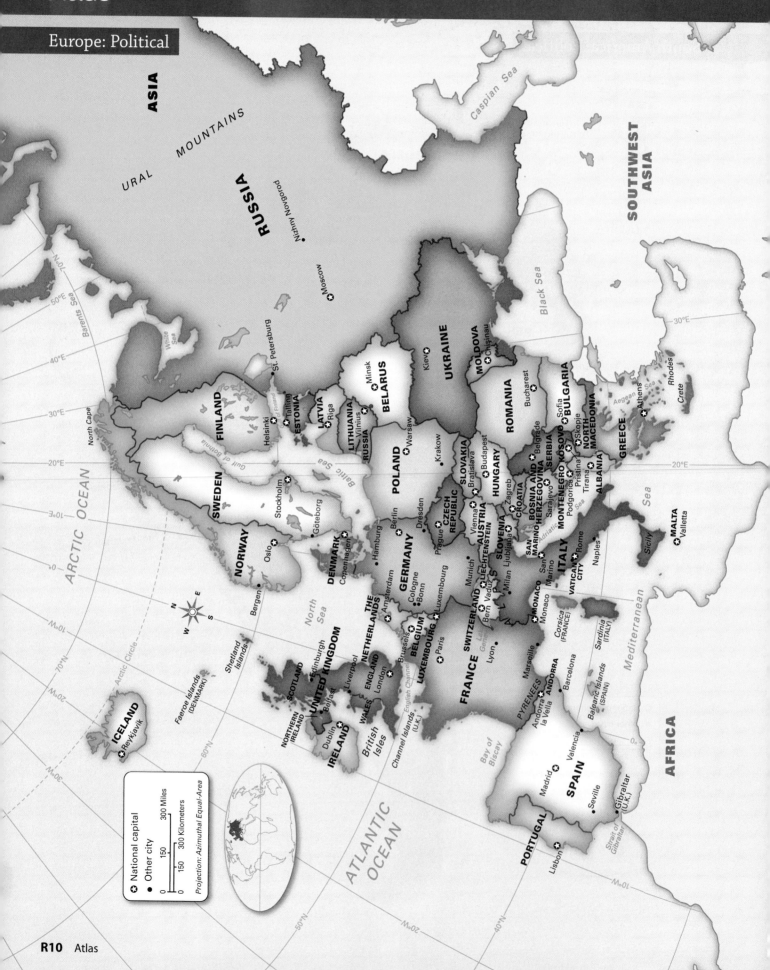

ASIA

URAL MOUNTAINS

RUSSIA

Nizhny Novgorod

Moscow ✪

Caspian Sea

SOUTHWEST ASIA

Barents Sea

White Sea

St. Petersburg

FINLAND

Helsinki ✪

Tallinn
ESTONIA

LATVIA
Riga

LITHUANIA
Vilnius

RUSSIA

Minsk ✪
BELARUS

Warsaw
POLAND

Kraków

UKRAINE

Kiev ✪

MOLDOVA
Chişinău ✪

ROMANIA

Bucharest ✪

Black Sea

Sofia ✪
BULGARIA

NORTH MACEDONIA
Skopje ✪

GREECE

Athens ✪

Aegean Sea

Rhodes

Crete

North Cape

SWEDEN

Stockholm ✪

Göteborg

Gulf of Bothnia

Baltic Sea

NORWAY

Oslo ✪

Bergen

SLOVAKIA
Bratislava

HUNGARY
Budapest ✪

Vienna
AUSTRIA

Zagreb
CROATIA
SLOVENIA
Ljubljana

Belgrade
SERBIA

BOSNIA AND
HERZEGOVINA
Sarajevo

MONTENEGRO
Podgorica

KOSOVO
Pristina

Tirana
ALBANIA

San
Marino
SAN MARINO

ITALY

Rome ✪

VATICAN CITY

Naples

Sicily

MALTA
Valletta ✪

Adriatic Sea

DENMARK
Copenhagen ✪

Hamburg

Berlin
GERMANY

Dresden

Prague
CZECH REPUBLIC

Cologne
Bonn

Munich

LIECHTENSTEIN
Vaduz

Milan

SWITZERLAND
Bern

Geneva

Lyon

Corsica
(FRANCE)

Sardinia
(ITALY)

Mediterranean Sea

ARCTIC OCEAN

N
W E
S

North Sea

Amsterdam
THE NETHERLANDS

Brussels
BELGIUM

LUXEMBOURG
Luxembourg

Paris

FRANCE

MONACO
Monaco

Marseille

ANDORRA
Andorra la Vella

PYRENEES

Barcelona

Balearic Islands
(SPAIN)

AFRICA

Faeroe Islands
(DENMARK)

Shetland Islands

SCOTLAND
Edinburgh

NORTHERN IRELAND
Belfast

IRELAND
Dublin

British Isles

UNITED KINGDOM
Liverpool

WALES

ENGLAND
London

English Channel

Channel Islands
(U.K.)

Bay of Biscay

SPAIN

Madrid ✪

Valencia

Seville

Gibraltar
(U.K.)

Strait of Gibraltar

PORTUGAL

Lisbon ✪

ICELAND
Reykjavik ✪

Arctic Circle

ATLANTIC OCEAN

✪ National capital
• Other city

300 Miles
0 150
0 150 300 Kilometers

Projection: Azimuthal Equal-Area

Atlas

Asia: Political

National capitals
Other cities

750 Miles
750 Kilometers

Projection: Two-Point Equidistant

PACIFIC OCEAN

AUSTRALIA

New Guinea

Arafura Sea

TIMOR-LESTE
Dili

PHILIPPINES
Manila

INDONESIA
Ujung Pandang
Surabaya
Jakarta
Bandung

Celebes Sea
Java Sea

BRUNEI
Bandar Seri Begawan

MALAYSIA
Kuala Lumpur
SINGAPORE
Medan

Aleutian Islands

Bering Sea
Sea of Okhotsk
Sakhalin Island
Kuril Islands (RUSSIA)

JAPAN
Sapporo
Vladivostok
Tokyo
Yokohama
Osaka
Kyoto
Hiroshima
Nagasaki

NORTH KOREA
Pyongyang
SOUTH KOREA
Seoul
Pusan

Ryukyu Islands (JAPAN)

TAIWAN
Taipei

East China Sea
Yellow Sea

Harbin
Fushun
Dalian
Qingdao
Beijing
Shanghai
Nanjing

CHINA
Wuhan
Chongqing
Chengdu

Guangzhou
Hong Kong
Macao
Hainan (CHINA)

South China Sea
Luzon Strait
Tropic of Cancer

VIETNAM
Hanoi
Ho Chi Minh City

LAOS
Vientiane

CAMBODIA
Phnom Penh

THAILAND
Bangkok

MYANMAR (BURMA)
Naypyidaw
Yangon (Rangoon)

Gulf of Thailand

Andaman Sea
Andaman Islands (INDIA)
Nicobar Islands (INDIA)

Yakutsk

Ulaanbaatar
MONGOLIA

Lake Baykal
Irkutsk

RUSSIA

Novosibirsk

Omsk

Yekaterinburg
Chelyabinsk

URAL MOUNTAINS

Moscow

EUROPE
RUSSIA

Astana

KAZAKHSTAN
Aral Sea
Lake Balkhash

Almaty
Bishkek
KYRGYZSTAN
Tashkent
UZBEKISTAN
TAJIKISTAN
Dushanbe

TURKMENISTAN
Ashgabat

Kabul
AFGHANISTAN

Islamabad
Lahore
PAKISTAN
Karachi

NEPAL
Kathmandu

BHUTAN
Thimphu

BANGLADESH
Dhaka

Delhi
New Delhi
Jaipur
Ahmadabad

INDIA

Mumbai (Bombay)
Bangalore

Kolkata (Calcutta)

Chennai (Madras)

SRI LANKA
Colombo

Bay of Bengal

Lakshadweep Islands (INDIA)

Arabian Sea

MALDIVES
Male

INDIAN OCEAN

GEORGIA
Tbilisi
ARMENIA
Yerevan
AZERBAIJAN
Baku

Caspian Sea

Black Sea
Istanbul
Ankara
TURKEY
Izmir
CYPRUS
Nicosia
LEBANON
Beirut
ISRAEL
Tel Aviv
Jerusalem
SYRIA
Damascus
Amman
JORDAN

IRAN
Tehran
Shiraz
Mosul
Baghdad
IRAQ
Basra
KUWAIT
Kuwait City

OMAN
Masqat (Muscat)

UNITED ARAB EMIRATES
Abu Dhabi
Doha
QATAR
BAHRAIN
Manama

SAUDI ARABIA
Riyadh
Mecca
Jidda

YEMEN
Sanaa

Persian Gulf

Socotra (YEMEN)

Gulf of Aden
Red Sea

AFRICA

Mediterranean Sea

Arctic Circle
North Pole

Barents Sea
Kara Sea
Laptev Sea

Africa: Political

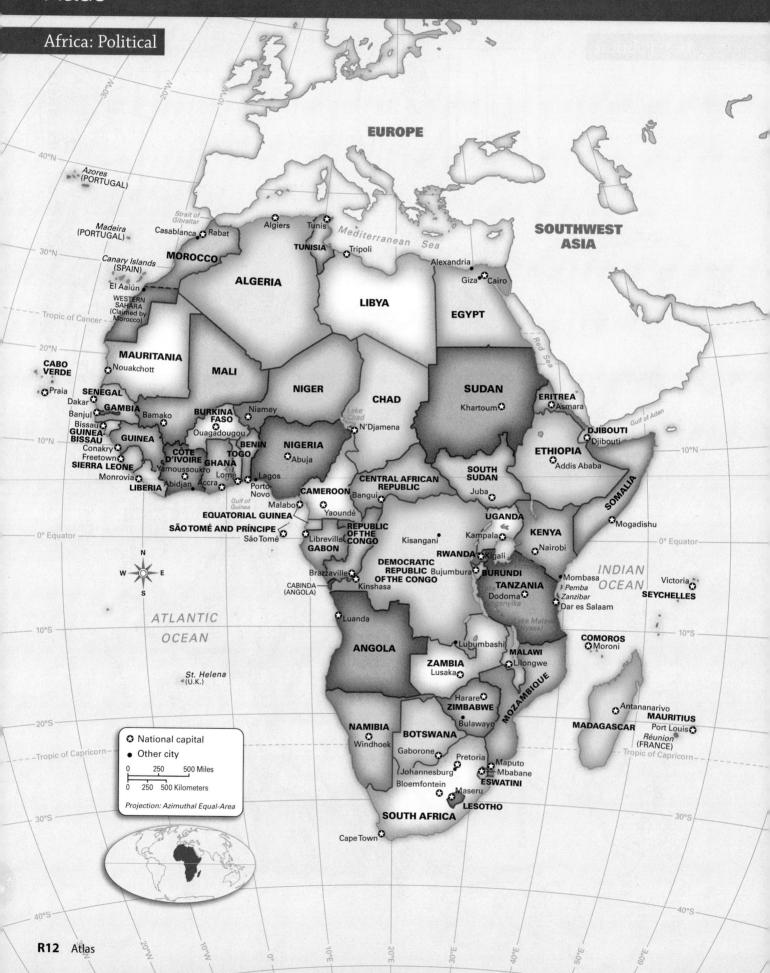

EUROPE

SOUTHWEST ASIA

Mediterranean Sea

Azores
(PORTUGAL)

Madeira
(PORTUGAL)

Strait of
Gibraltar

Casablanca ✪ Rabat

Algiers ✪   ✪ Tunis

TUNISIA

Tripoli ✪

MOROCCO

Canary Islands
(SPAIN)

El Aaiún ✪

WESTERN
SAHARA
(Claimed by
Morocco)

Tropic of Cancer

ALGERIA

LIBYA

EGYPT

Alexandria •

Giza • ✪ Cairo

Red Sea

CABO
VERDE

• Praia

MAURITANIA

✪ Nouakchott

MALI

NIGER

CHAD

SUDAN

Khartoum ✪

ERITREA
✪ Asmara

Gulf of Aden

SENEGAL

Dakar ✪

GAMBIA
Banjul ✪

Bamako ✪

BURKINA
FASO

Niamey ✪

Lake
Chad

N'Djamena ✪

DJIBOUTI
✪ Djibouti

Bissau ✪

GUINEA-
BISSAU

GUINEA

Ouagadougou ✪

BENIN
TOGO

NIGERIA

ETHIOPIA

Addis Ababa ✪

Conakry ✪

GHANA

Abuja ✪

CÔTE
D'IVOIRE

Freetown ✪

SIERRA LEONE

Yamoussoukro ✪

Lomé ✪

Monrovia ✪

LIBERIA

Abidjan ✪
Accra ✪

Porto-
Novo ✪

Lagos •

CAMEROON

CENTRAL AFRICAN
REPUBLIC

SOUTH
SUDAN

SOMALIA

• Mogadishu

Gulf of
Guinea

Malabo ✪

EQUATORIAL GUINEA

Bangui ✪

Juba ✪

SÃO TOMÉ AND PRÍNCIPE

Yaoundé ✪

UGANDA

KENYA

São Tomé ✪

REPUBLIC
OF THE
CONGO

Libreville ✪

GABON

Kisangani •

Kampala ✪

Nairobi ✪

Equator

RWANDA

Kigali ✪

INDIAN
OCEAN

Victoria
✪

SEYCHELLES

Brazzaville ✪

DEMOCRATIC
REPUBLIC
OF THE CONGO

Bujumbura ✪

BURUNDI

• Mombasa

Pemba

CABINDA
(ANGOLA)

Kinshasa ✪

TANZANIA

Dodoma ✪

Zanzibar •

Dar es Salaam •

ATLANTIC
OCEAN

Luanda ✪

Lake
Tanganyika

ANGOLA

• Lubumbashi

Lake Malawi
(Nyasa)

COMOROS
✪ Moroni

St. Helena
(U.K.)

ZAMBIA

Lusaka ✪

MALAWI

Lilongwe ✪

Harare ✪

MOZAMBIQUE

Antananarivo
✪

MAURITIUS

MADAGASCAR

Port Louis ✪

NAMIBIA

ZIMBABWE

• Bulawayo

BOTSWANA

Réunion
(FRANCE)

Tropic of Capricorn

Windhoek ✪

Gaborone ✪

Pretoria ✪

Maputo ✪

Johannesburg •

Mbabane ✪

ESWATINI

Bloemfontein •

Maseru ✪

LESOTHO

SOUTH AFRICA

Cape Town ✪

✪ National capital

• Other city

0   250   500 Miles

0   250   500 Kilometers

Projection: Azimuthal Equal-Area

40°N
30°N
20°N
10°N
0° Equator
10°S
20°S
30°S
40°S

30°W 20°W 10°W 0° 10°E 20°E 30°E 40°E 50°E 60°E

The Pacific: Political

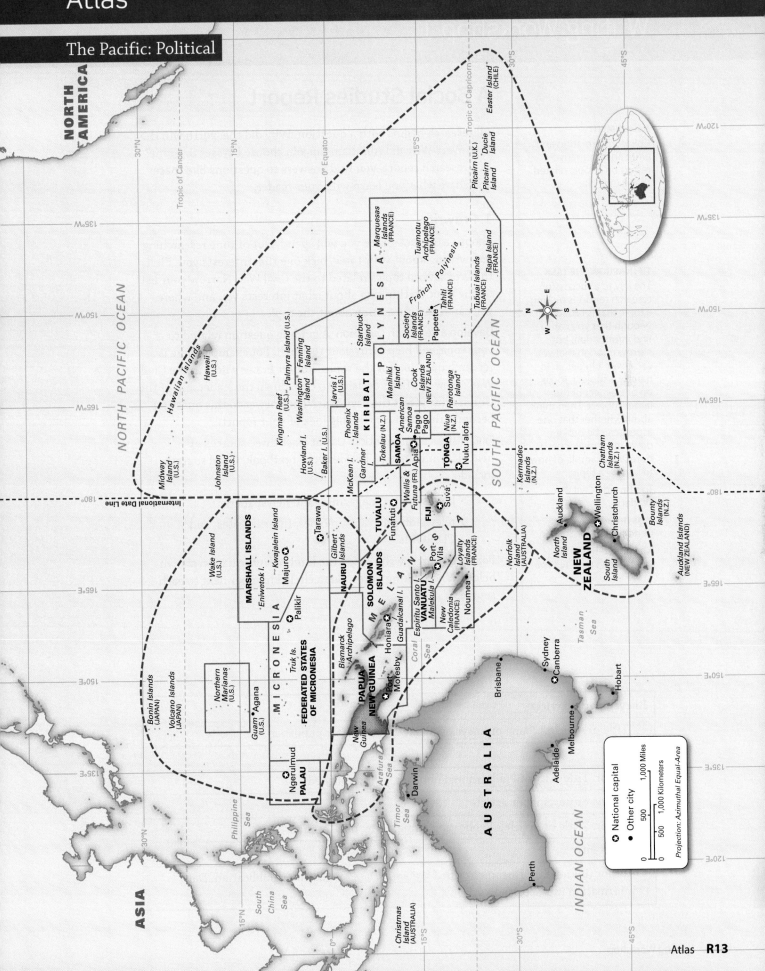

NORTH AMERICA

ASIA

NORTH PACIFIC OCEAN

SOUTH PACIFIC OCEAN

INDIAN OCEAN

Philippine Sea

South China Sea

Coral Sea

Arafura Sea

Timor Sea

Tasman Sea

AUSTRALIA

NEW ZEALAND

PAPUA NEW GUINEA

P O L Y N E S I A

K I R I B A T I

M I C R O N E S I A

M E L A N E S I A

MARSHALL ISLANDS

SOLOMON ISLANDS

TUVALU

VANUATU

FIJI

TONGA

SAMOA

NAURU

PALAU

FEDERATED STATES OF MICRONESIA

International Date Line

Tropic of Cancer

Tropic of Capricorn

0° Equator

Easter Island (CHILE)

Pitcairn (U.K.)
Pitcairn Island
Ducie Island

Marquesas Islands (FRANCE)

Tuamotu Archipelago (FRANCE)

Rapa Island (FRANCE)

French Polynesia

Society Islands (FRANCE)

Tahiti (FRANCE)

Papeete

Tubuai Islands (FRANCE)

Starbuck Island

Manihiki Island

Cook Islands (NEW ZEALAND)

Rarotonga Island

American Samoa
Pago Pago

Niue (N.Z.)

Nuku'alofa

Kingman Reef (U.S.)

Palmyra Island (U.S.)

Fanning Island

Washington Island

Jarvis I. (U.S.)

Phoenix Islands

Howland I. (U.S.)

Baker I. (U.S.)

McKean I.

Gardner I.

Tokelau (N.Z.)

Apia

Wallis & Futuna (FR.)

Suva

Port-Vila

Loyalty Islands (FRANCE)

Noumea

New Caledonia (FRANCE)

Norfolk Island (AUSTRALIA)

Kermadec Islands (N.Z.)

Chatham Islands (N.Z.)

Bounty Islands (N.Z.)

Auckland Islands (NEW ZEALAND)

Auckland

Wellington

Christchurch

North Island

South Island

Espiritu Santo I.

Malekula I.

Hawaiian Islands

Hawaii (U.S.)

Midway Island (U.S.)

Johnston Island (U.S.)

Wake Island (U.S.)

Eniwetok I.

Kwajalein Island

Majuro

Tarawa

Gilbert Islands

Funafuti

Honiara

Guadalcanal I.

Bismarck Archipelago

New Guinea

Port Moresby

Truk Is.

Bonin Islands (JAPAN)

Volcano Islands (JAPAN)

Northern Marianas (U.S.)

Guam (U.S.)
Agana

Palikir

Ngerulmud

Christmas Island (AUSTRALIA)

Darwin

Perth

Adelaide

Melbourne

Hobart

Sydney

Canberra

Brisbane

Legend:
- ✪ National capital
- • Other city

1,000 Miles
500
0

1,000 Kilometers
500
0

Projection: Azimuthal Equal-Area

15°N
30°N
15°S
30°S
45°S

135°W
150°W
165°W
180°
165°E
150°E
135°E
120°E
120°W

A Social Studies Report

All research begins with a question. Why did the North win the Civil War? Why did Abraham Lincoln choose Ulysses S. Grant? In a research report, you find answers to questions like these and share what you learn with your reader.

1. Prewrite

Choose a Subject Since you will spend a lot of time researching and writing about your topic, pick one that interests you. First, think of several topics related to the Civil War. Narrow your list to one topic by thinking about what interests you and where you can find information about the topic.

TIP: NARROW THE TASK
The key to a successful research report is picking a topic that is broad enough that you can find information, but narrow enough that you can cover it in detail. To narrow a subject, focus on one aspect of the larger subject. Then think about whether that one aspect can be broken down into smaller parts. Here's an example of how to narrow a topic:

Too Broad: Civil War Leaders

Less Broad: Civil War Generals

Narrower: Robert E. Lee's Role in the Civil War

Develop a Research Question A guiding question related to your topic will help focus your research. For example, here is a research question for the topic "Robert E. Lee's Role in the Civil War": How did Lee's decision to turn down the leadership of the Union army affect the Civil War? The answer to this question becomes the thesis, or the big idea of your report.

Find Historical Information Use at least three sources of historical information besides your textbook. Good sources include

- books, maps, magazines, and newspapers.
- television programs, movies, Internet sites, and CD-ROMs.

For each source, write down the kinds of information shown below. When taking notes, put a circled number next to each source.

Encyclopedia article
① "Title of Article." <u>Name of Encyclopedia</u>. Edition or year published.
Book
② Author. <u>Title</u>. City of Publication: Publisher, year published.
Magazine or newspaper article
③ Author. "Title of Article." <u>Publication name</u>. Date: page number(s).
Internet site
④ Author (if known). "Document title." <u>Website</u>. Date of electronic publication. Date information was accessed <url>.

TIP: SEE DIFFERENT VIEWPOINTS
Consult a variety of sources, including those with different points of view on the topic. Reading sources with different opinions will give you a more complete picture of your subject. For example, reading articles about Robert E. Lee written by a southern writer as well as a northern writer may give you a more balanced view of Lee.

TIP: RECORD OTHERS' IDEAS
You will be taking three types of notes:

Paraphrases Restatements of all the ideas in your own words

Summaries Brief restatements of only the most important parts

Direct quotations The writer's exact words inside quotation marks

Take Notes As you read the sources, take thorough notes. Take special care to spell names correctly and to record dates and facts accurately. If you use a direct quotation from a source, copy it word for word and enclose it in quotation marks. Along with each note, include the number of its source and its page number.

Organize Your Ideas and Information Informative research reports are usually organized in one of these ways:

- chronological order (the order in which events occurred)
- order of importance
- causes (actions that make something else happen) and effects (results of something else)

Use one of these orders to organize your notes in an outline. Here is a partial outline for a paper on Robert E. Lee.

> The Thesis/Big Idea: Robert E. Lee's decision to decline the leadership of the Union army had serious consequences for the path of the Civil War.
>
> I. Lee's Military Expertise
>   A. Achievements at the U.S. Military Academy
>   B. Achievements during the Mexican War
>
> II. Lee's Personality and Character
>   A. Intelligence and strength
>   B. Honesty and fairness
>   C. Daring and courage
>
> III. Lee's Military Victories
>   A. Battle of Fredericksburg
>   B. Battle of Chancellorsville

2. Write

You can use this framework to help you write your first draft.

A WRITER'S FRAMEWORK

Introduction

- Start with a quote or an interesting historical detail to grab your reader's attention.
- State the main idea of your report.
- Provide any historical background readers need to understand your main idea.

Body

- Present your information under at least three main ideas, using logical order.
- Write at least one paragraph for each of these main ideas.
- Add supporting details, facts, or examples to each paragraph.

Conclusion

- Restate your main idea, using slightly different words.
- Include a general comment about your topic.
- You might comment on how the historical information in your report relates to later historical events.

Study a Model Here is a model of a research report. Study it to see how one student developed a paper. The first and the concluding paragraphs are shown in full. The paragraphs in the body of the paper are summarized.

INTRODUCTORY PARAGRAPH
Attention grabber

Statement of thesis

"I cannot raise my hand against my birthplace, my home, my children." With these words, Robert E. Lee changed the course of the Civil War. Abraham Lincoln had turned to Lee as his first choice for commander of the Union army. However, Lee turned Lincoln down, choosing instead to side with his home state of Virginia and take command of the Confederate army. Lee's decision to turn Lincoln down weakened the North and strengthened the Confederates, turning what might have been an easy victory for the North into a long, costly war.

BODY PARAGRAPHS

In the first part of the body of the report, the student points out that Lee graduated from the U.S. Military Academy at West Point, served in the Mexican War, and was a member of the Union army. She goes on to explain that he would have been a strong leader for the North, and his absence made the North weaker.

In the middle of the report, the writer discusses Lee's personality and character. She includes information about the strength of character he showed while in the military academy and while leading the Confederate army. She discusses and gives examples of his intelligence, his daring, his courage, and his honesty.

In the last part of the body of the report, the student provides examples of Lee leading the outnumbered Confederate army to a series of victories. The student provides details of the battles of Fredericksburg and Chancellorsville and explains how a lesser general than Lee may have lost both battles.

CONCLUDING PARAGRAPH
Summary of main points
Restatement of big idea

Lee's brilliant and resourceful leadership bedeviled a series of Union generals. He won battles that most generals would have lost. If Lee had used these skills to lead the larger and more powerful Union army, the Civil War might have ended in months instead of years.

3. Evaluate and Revise

Evaluate and Revise Your Draft Evaluate your first draft by carefully reading it twice. Ask the questions below to decide which parts of your first draft should be revised.

EVALUATION QUESTIONS FOR AN INFORMATIVE REPORT

- Does the introduction attract the readers' interest and state the big idea/thesis of your report?
- Does the body have at least three paragraphs that develop your big idea? Is the main idea in each paragraph clearly stated?
- Have you included enough information to support each of your main ideas? Are all facts, details, and examples accurate? Are all of them clearly related to the main ideas they support?

- Is the report clearly organized? Does it use chronological order, order of importance, or cause and effect?
- Does the conclusion restate the big idea of your report? Does it end with a general comment about the importance or significance of your topic?
- Have you included at least three sources in the bibliography? Have you included all the sources you used and not any you did not use?

4. Proofread and Publish

Proofread To improve your report before sharing it, check the following:

- The spelling and capitalization of all proper names for people, places, things, and events.
- Punctuation marks around any direct quotation.
- Your list of sources (Works Cited or Bibliography) against a guide to writing research papers. Make sure you follow the examples in the guide when punctuating and capitalizing your source listings.

Publish Choose one or more of these ideas to publish your report:

- Share your report with your classmates by turning it into an informative speech.
- Submit your report to an online discussion group that focuses on the Civil War and ask for feedback.
- With your classmates, create a magazine that includes reports on several different topics or post the reports on your school website.

5. Practice and Apply

Use the steps and strategies outlined in this workshop to research and write an informative report on the Civil War.

Persuasion and History

You have probably heard people disagree about current political events—perhaps a new law or a government leader. People also disagree about events of the past. When we disagree about historical events, those of the past or those of the present, we can use persuasive arguments to convince others to agree with our opinion.

ASSIGNMENT
Write a persuasive essay either for or against one of these statements.

1. New laws should have limited immigration in the late 1800s.

2. The government should have done more to improve conditions in tenements.

1. Prewrite

State Your Opinion Persuasion starts with an opinion or a position on a topic. Choose one of the statements in the assignment and decide on your opinion, either for or against. Write your opinion in a statement: it will be the big idea of your persuasive paper. For example, here is an opinion statement about the first topic:

> *The government should not have limited immigration in the late 1800s.*

Build and Organize a Logical Argument A strong persuasive essay includes a logical argument, sound reasoning, and proof in support of an opinion. Reasons tell why you have an opinion. Proof, or evidence, includes facts, examples, or expert opinions.

Opinion: *Reformers' work improved Americans' lives.*

Reason: *Reforms improved life in cities.*

Evidence: *Lawrence Veiller influenced the passage of the 1901 New York State Tenement House Act.*

Persuasive writing is usually organized by order of importance.

TIP: USE ORDER OF IMPORTANCE
How do you know whether to start or end with your most important or most convincing reason? If you are worried about getting your readers to read your entire paper, you might try to catch their attention by starting with the most convincing reason. If you are concerned that your readers remember one point after they finish reading, you may want to place that point, or reason, at the end of your paper.

2. Write

Follow the framework below to help you write a first draft.

A WRITER'S FRAMEWORK

Introduction

- Start with an interesting opener, such as a quotation or a surprising fact.
- Include your opinion statement, or big idea, for the paper.

Body

- Present one reason and its supporting evidence in each body paragraph.
- Address your reasons by order of importance.

Conclusion

- Restate your opinion in different words.
- Summarize your reasons.
- Make a connection to a current event.

3. Evaluate and Revise

Evaluate Use these questions to discover ways to improve your draft.

> ### EVALUATION QUESTIONS FOR A PERSUASIVE ESSAY
>
> - Does your introduction include a clear statement of your opinion on the topic?
> - Do you present your reasons by order of importance in the body paragraphs?
> - Do you provide at least three reasons to support your opinion?
> - Do you include facts, examples, or expert opinions to support each reason?
> - Do you restate your opinion in different words in your conclusion?
> - Does your conclusion include a summary of the reasons that support your opinion?

TIP: FACT VS. OPINION
Knowing the difference between a fact and an opinion is important for both writers and readers of persuasive essays.

- Facts are statements that can be proven true or false. *Jane Addams founded Hull House in 1889.*

- Opinions are statements of personal belief and cannot be proven. *Jane Addams was the greatest American woman of her time.*

Revise Your essay will be more forceful if you write in the active voice.

> **Passive voice:** *New parks were designed by Frederick Law Olmsted.*
>
> **Active voice:** *Frederick Law Olmsted designed new parks.*

Active voice is more forceful, and often clearer, because it makes a stronger connection between the action and the actor. However, we may use passive voice because we do not know, or do not want to say, who the actor is or was.

> **Example:** *New parks were designed in the late 1800s.*

4. Proofread and Publish

Proofread If you are writing your paper on a computer, you should use the spell-check feature to look for spelling errors. However, the spell-check feature will not help much if you have used the wrong word. Here are some examples to look for: *their/ they're, its/it's, accept/except, affect/effect, advice/advise, altar/alter, capitol/capital.* When you spot one of these words in your paper, check your dictionary to make sure you have used the correct word.

Publish Share your essay with a classmate who took an opinion opposed to yours. Review each other's reasons. Can one of you persuade the other?

5. Practice and Apply

Use the steps and strategies in this workshop to write a persuasive essay.

Writing Workshop 3

Analyzing a Primary Source

ASSIGNMENT
Find a primary source from World War I and write an analysis of it.

Primary sources are often the best sources of information available to historians. Primary sources provide answers to questions about the past. They also provide a unique point of view from the past. Analyzing a primary source allows you to share that information.

1. Prewrite

TIP: USE THE INTERNET
If you find a primary source on the Internet, make sure it is accurate. You should be able to identify the person or institution that runs the website and make sure that person or institution is trustworthy. The website should include basic information about the source, such as its author, when it was written, and where it first appeared. University and library websites are excellent places to find primary sources.

Locate Primary Sources Many primary sources are available in libraries and on the Internet. Letters, diaries, autobiographies, memoirs, newspaper articles, public speeches, and legal documents are good examples of primary sources.

Read the Primary Source Take notes on these questions to better understand the document.

Who wrote the document?

What kind of document is it?

When was it written? Where did it originally appear?

What was the author's point of view? What was his or her experience during the war?

Why did the author write the document?

As you read the primary source, take notes on these questions.

Why is the document important? The answer to this question will be the main idea of your essay.

What questions about World War I does it answer? Answering this question will help you write your body paragraphs.

2. Write

You can use this framework to help you write your first draft.

A WRITER'S FRAMEWORK

Introduction
- Introduce your primary source and its main purpose.
- Introduce the author of the source and include the date it was written.
- State your main idea, explaining why this source is important.

Body
- Explain how the source answers at least two questions about World War I.
- Include examples from the document.

Conclusion
- Summarize the information in the source.
- Restate why the document is important for historians.

3. Evaluate and Revise

Evaluate Use these questions to discover ways to improve your paper.

EVALUATION QUESTIONS FOR ANALYZING A PRIMARY SOURCE

- Do you introduce your primary source with its main purpose?
- Do you introduce the author of the source and the document's date?
- Do you state a main idea, explaining why this source is important?
- Do you explain how the source answers at least two questions about World War I?
- Do you include examples from the document?
- Do you summarize the information in the source?

Revise Make sure each paragraph has a topic sentence at the beginning. Then check the information in the paragraph. It should all relate to the topic sentence. If it does not, there are several ways to fix the paragraph. First, you can remove unrelated information. If the information is related but not clearly explained, add a more detailed explanation. You can also change the topic sentence to include all the information in the paragraph.

4. Proofread and Publish

Proofread Reread your paper carefully to make sure all the verbs are in the same tense. The past tense is usually best for history writing. Summaries of primary sources should also be in the past tense. A direct quotation from a primary source, however, should remain in its original tense.

Publish Share your paper with a classmate. Read each other's papers. Then write a one-paragraph summary of the new information you each learned.

5. Practice and Apply

Use the steps and strategies in this workshop to analyze your primary source.

TIP: USE PRONOUNS EFFECTIVELY
Use pronouns such as *he, she,* and *it* to replace frequently used nouns and proper nouns. This will help you vary your sentences. Make sure that the person or thing to which each pronoun refers is clear. If it is not, repeat the original noun or name.

EXAMPLE
Woodrow Wilson proposed a peace plan called the Fourteen Points. He wanted to make sure the postwar peace would last.

A Descriptive Essay

Write an essay describing either Hoovervilles or the Dust Bowl during the Great Depression.

TIP: USE VISUAL IMAGES
Look at visual images such as photographs from the 1930s. What do they show about Hoovervilles or the Dust Bowl and the people who lived there? Use this information in your description.

Vivid descriptions of a place and time can help us understand history. Primary sources often provide such descriptions from one person's point of view. Historians provide a different point of view in descriptions based on many primary and secondary sources.

1. Prewrite

Get Started Descriptive essays depend on details that will help the reader create a mental picture. The quotes in Module 26 about the Dust Bowl are examples of vivid descriptions. The passage from *The Grapes of Wrath* is another good example. For your description, review the text on the Great Depression and look in the encyclopedia and other sources. Collect as many details as you can about Hoovervilles or the Dust Bowl. Try to find details that involve all of the five senses (sight, sound, smell, touch, and taste). Good description depends on strong details.

Organize Information Make one generalization that sums up all your details. This will be your main idea. Then organize the details and examples you have found into two, three, or four categories. These will become the body paragraphs of the essay. All of these categories should support the main idea.

For example, the main idea of an essay could be that the name *Dust Bowl* was an accurate description of the area. One detail might be that the gritty dirt often became caught in people's skin, hair, and clothing. This detail could fit into the category of people in the Dust Bowl.

2. Write

You can use this framework to help you write your first draft.

A WRITER'S FRAMEWORK

Introduction

- Make a generalization about your topic.
- List the categories that will be included in the body paragraphs.

Body

- Separate details into paragraphs by category.
- Use vivid details that involve the five senses.
- Use details from different sources.

Conclusion

- Summarize your information.
- Explain how your topic is related to larger issues.

3. Evaluate and Revise

Evaluate Use these questions to discover ways to improve your essay.

TIP: SHOW, DON'T TELL
Writers are often advised, "Show, don't tell." This phrase means that writers should use strong words, details, and examples to make a point. Choose vivid, clear examples for your description. They should not need much explanation.

Revise When you revise your essay, make examples and details as specific as possible. This will make your description more vivid.

> **General:** *People built flimsy houses in Hoovervilles.*
>
> **Specific:** *In Hoovervilles, people built shelters out of scraps of lumber, tin, and cardboard.*

4. Proofread and Publish

Proofread Check your sentences for fragments and run-ons. A fragment is an incomplete sentence. Adding a subject or a verb can often make a fragment into a complete sentence. A run-on has too many subjects and verbs for one sentence. It usually needs to be broken into two or more separate sentences.

Publish Share your essay with one or more classmates. Make illustrations based on the descriptions in each other's essays.

5. Practice and Apply

Use the steps and strategies in this workshop to write your descriptive essay.

A News Article

ASSIGNMENT
Write a news article about the anniversary of either (1) the Nuremberg trials, (2) the Supreme Court's *Brown* v. *Board of Education* decision, or (3) the opening of the Vietnam Veterans Memorial.

You have probably read many news articles in newspapers, magazines, or online. News articles keep people informed about events in their communities, the nation, and the world. Sometimes they also remind people about important events from the past.

1. Prewrite

Consider Purpose and Audience Remember that you are writing for people who have a choice about what to read. Your story must keep readers interested. How will you relate the topic of your story to their lives or emotions? At the same time, your story should give people information they need. In order to share information effectively, you must choose the most important details to include in your article.

TIP: BRAINSTORM
Brainstorm ways to interest people in the topic of your article. Take a few minutes to review what you know about the topic. Then write down as many questions, interesting points, and examples as you can.

Write a Compelling Article Make your article vivid and compelling by including

- a short headline showing what the article is about.
- a "hook"—an interesting fact or detail—to get the reader's attention at the beginning of the article.
- clear descriptions of people and events.
- specific examples and quotations.
- reasons why the event is important.

2. Write

You can use this framework to help you write the first draft of your article.

A WRITER'S FRAMEWORK

Introduction

- Grab your reader's attention with a strong headline.
- Begin with a striking detail or quotation for a hook.
- Introduce the event and its importance to people today.

Body

- Describe what happened, who was involved, and where, when, and why the event took place.
- Explain the significance of the event.
- Use details to connect the event to readers' lives or emotions.

Conclusion

- Finish any incomplete thoughts.
- End with a quotation or example that sums up the main point of the article.

3. Evaluate and Revise

Evaluate Use these questions to discover ways to improve your news article.

EVALUATION QUESTIONS FOR A NEWS ARTICLE

- Do you begin with a strong headline and hook?
- Do you introduce the event and its importance to people today?
- Do you describe what happened, who was involved, and where, when, and why the event took place?

- Do you explain the significance of the event?
- Do you use details to connect the event to readers' lives or emotions?
- Do you end with a quotation or example that sums up the main point of the article?

Revise Newspapers and magazines often have limited space. News articles must express a sharply focused idea briefly. To make sure that your article does this, read each sentence carefully. Each sentence should

- be clear and to the point.
- contain no unnecessary words or phrases.
- use only precise words. Eliminate words such as *very* unless they add meaning to the sentence.

4. Proofread and Publish

Proofread Read your essay aloud to catch any mistakes in your spelling or grammar. If something looks or sounds wrong, mark it. Come back to it later to correct the mistake. This is also a good strategy for identifying and fixing awkward sentences.

Publish Exchange articles with a classmate who wrote about a different topic. Did you learn from your classmate's article? Did you find it interesting? Put together a class newspaper that includes all the articles and headlines. Add pictures and display the newspaper on a bulletin board.

5. Practice and Apply

Use the steps and strategies in this workshop to write your news article.

TIP: USE VIVID WRITING
Make sentences more interesting by using vivid words and images. Use strong words that help readers create a mental picture.

An Oral History

Oral histories can provide excellent sources of information about events in the recent past. An oral history is a report based on an interview with a person who experienced or remembers a historical event. Oral histories preserve personal experiences and memories for future generations.

1. Prewrite

Get Started Think about all the events you read about in this unit. Which ones interested you the most? Which ones do you think made the strongest impression on people at the time? Choose one as your subject.

Write Questions

- Focus on finding out how the person you are interviewing experienced the event you chose.
- Write at least ten questions.

Conduct an Interview

- Find an adult family member or friend to interview who remembers participating in or reacting to the event.
- Come prepared with your questions, paper, and something to write with.
- Take notes on the answers. Indicate direct quotations with quotation marks.
- Ask follow-up questions, even if you did not prepare them in advance.

2. Write

You can use this framework, along with your interview notes, to help you write your first draft.

A WRITER'S FRAMEWORK

Introduction

- Grab your reader's attention with an interesting quote from your interview.
- Introduce the event you chose and why it was important.
- Explain how the event affected the person you interviewed.

Body

- Describe the memories and experiences of the person you interviewed about the event.
- Summarize what you learned from the interview.
- Use quotes from the interview.

Conclusion

- Make a generalization about how people reacted to the event.
- Draw conclusions about how people's reactions to the event affected history.

3. Evaluate and Revise

Evaluate Use these questions to discover ways to improve your oral history.

EVALUATION QUESTIONS FOR AN ORAL HISTORY

- Do you introduce the event and the person you interviewed in the first paragraph?
- Do you focus on the event from a personal point of view?
- Do you describe the memories and experiences of the person you interviewed about the event?

- Do you summarize what you learned and use quotes from the interview?
- Do you make generalizations and draw conclusions about people's reactions to the event?

Revise When you revise your oral history, you may need to add background information. Check the material you have included from your interview. If anything is unclear, add more details about the event or time period. Make sure to explain clearly the connections between the personal experience and the event.

4. Proofread and Publish

Proofread In your oral history, you have been using quotations from the person you interviewed. Check the punctuation marks around these direct quotations. Also, check the spelling and capitalization of all proper names, such as the name of the person you interviewed.

Publish Share your oral history with classmates who wrote about the same event. How were the experiences of the people you interviewed similar and different? Share your oral history with the class. The person you interviewed would probably also like to see the finished project.

5. Practice and Apply

Use the steps and strategies in this workshop to write your oral history.

TIP: USE QUOTATIONS EFFECTIVELY

Quotations from your interview will make your oral history more interesting. Introduce quotations with a phrase or a sentence that makes it clear what they are about. Always identify the person who is quoted.

EXAMPLE

Simon remembered taking part in a demonstration in Washington, DC, the night before President Nixon resigned. "There were thousands of people in Lafayette Park across from the White House," Simon recalled.

TIP: USE ELLIPSES

To make a quotation shorter, you can delete some words and replace them with an ellipsis (the symbol ". . ."). Make sure the quotation still makes sense after you do this.

EXAMPLE

Original quotation:
"On the morning of September 11, I woke up, brushed my teeth, ate breakfast, and did everything like any other day."

Quotation with ellipsis:
"On the morning of September 11, I . . . did everything like any other day."

The American flag is a symbol of the nation. It is recognized instantly, whether as a big banner waving in the wind or a tiny emblem worn on a lapel. The flag is so important that it is a major theme of the national anthem, "The Star-Spangled Banner." One of the most popular names for the flag is the Stars and Stripes. It is also known as Old Glory.

The Meaning of the Flag

The American flag has 13 stripes—7 red and 6 white. In the upper-left corner of the flag is the union—50 white five-pointed stars against a blue background.

The 13 stripes stand for the original 13 American states, and the 50 stars represent the states of the nation today. According to the U.S. Department of State, the colors of the flag also are symbolic:

Red stands for courage.

White symbolizes purity.

Blue is the color of vigilance, perseverance, and justice.

Displaying the Flag

It is customary not to display the American flag in bad weather. It is also customary for the flag to be displayed outdoors only from sunrise to sunset, except on certain occasions. In a few special places, however, the flag is always flown day and night. When flown at night, the flag should be illuminated.

Near a speaker's platform, the flag should occupy the place of honor at the speaker's right. When carried in a parade with other flags, the American flag should be on the marching right or in front at the center. When flying with the flags of the 50 states, the national flag must be at the center and the highest point. In a group of national flags, all should be of equal size and all should be flown from staffs, or flagpoles, of equal height.

The flag should never touch the ground or the floor. It should not be marked with any insignia, pictures, or words. Nor should it be used in any disrespectful way—as an advertising decoration, for instance. The flag should never be dipped to honor any person or thing.

Saluting the Flag

The United States, like other countries, has a flag code, or rules for displaying and honoring the flag. For example, all those present should stand at attention facing the flag and salute it when it is being raised or lowered or when it is carried past them in a parade or procession. A man wearing a hat should take it off and hold it with his right hand over his heart. All women and hatless men should stand with their right hands over their hearts to show their respect for the flag. The flag should also receive these honors during the playing of the national anthem and the reciting of the Pledge of Allegiance.

The Pledge of Allegiance

The Pledge of Allegiance was written in 1892 by Massachusetts magazine (*Youth's Companion*) editor Francis Bellamy. (Congress added the words "under God" in 1954.)

> *I pledge allegiance to the flag of the United States of America and to the republic for which it stands, one nation under God, indivisible, with liberty and justice for all.*

Civilians should say the Pledge of Allegiance with their right hands placed over their hearts. People in the armed forces give the military salute. By saying the Pledge of Allegiance, we promise loyalty ("pledge allegiance") to the United States and its ideals.

"The Star-Spangled Banner"

"The Star-Spangled Banner" is the national anthem of the United States. It was written by Francis Scott Key during the War of 1812. While being detained by the British aboard a ship on September 13–14, 1814, Key watched the British bombardment of Fort McHenry at Baltimore. The attack lasted 25 hours. The smoke was so thick that Key could not tell who had won. When the air cleared, Key saw the American flag that was still flying over the fort. "The Star-Spangled Banner" is sung to music written by British composer John Stafford Smith. In 1931 Congress designated "The Star-Spangled Banner" as the national anthem.

I

Oh, say, can you see, by the dawn's early light,
What so proudly we hailed at the twilight's last gleaming,
Whose broad stripes and bright stars through the perilous fight, O'er the ramparts we watched were so gallantly streaming? And the rockets' red glare, the bombs bursting in air, Gave proof through the night that our flag was still there. Oh, say, does that star-spangled banner yet wave O'er the land of the free, and the home of the brave?

II

On the shore, dimly seen through the mists of the deep,
Where the foe's haughty host in dread silence reposes,
What is that which the breeze, o'er the towering steep,
As it fitfully blows, half conceals, half discloses?
Now it catches the gleam of the morning's first beam,
In full glory reflected, now shines on the stream.
'Tis the star-spangled banner; oh, long may it wave
O'er the land of the free, and the home of the brave!

III

And where is that band who so vauntingly swore
That the havoc of war and the battle's confusion
A home and a country should leave us no more?
Their blood has washed out their foul footsteps' pollution.
No refuge could save the hireling and slave
From the terror of flight, or the gloom of the grave:
And the star-spangled banner in triumph doth wave
O'er the land of the free, and the home of the brave!

IV

Oh! thus be it ever when freemen shall stand
Between their loved homes and the war's desolation!
Blest with victory and peace, may the heaven-rescued land
Praise the Power that hath made and preserved us a nation!
Then conquer we must, for our cause it is just,
And this be our motto: "In God is our trust!"
And the star-spangled banner in triumph shall wave,
O'er the land of the free, and the home of the brave!

Sheet music to the national anthem

"America the Beautiful"

One of the most beloved songs celebrating our nation is "America, the Beautiful." Katharine Lee Bates first wrote the lyrics to the song in 1893 after visiting Colorado. The version of the song we know today is set to music by Samuel A. Ward. The first and last stanzas of "America, the Beautiful" are shown below.

> O beautiful for spacious skies,
> For amber waves of grain,
> For purple mountain majesties
> Above the fruited plain!
> America! America!
> God shed his grace on thee
> And crown thy good with brotherhood
> From sea to shining sea!

> O beautiful for patriot dream
> That sees beyond the years
> Thine alabaster cities gleam
> Undimmed by human tears!
> America! America!
> God shed his grace on thee
> And crown thy good with brotherhood
> From sea to shining sea!

Mount Rushmore

Mount Rushmore, located in the Black Hills of South Dakota, is the world's largest sculpture. Known as the "Shrine of Democracy," it features the heads of four of the nation's greatest presidents—George Washington, Thomas Jefferson, Theodore Roosevelt, and Abraham Lincoln.

The original idea to carve massive figures into the mountainside came from South Dakota historian Doane Robinson. He thought that a giant sculpture of notable people in the history of the West would draw thousands of tourists to the Black Hills. Robinson chose sculptor Gutzon Borglum, who had worked on similar projects, to do the work. Borglum wanted to change the focus of the sculpture. He suggested that it should show four presidents who had played a major role in the country's development.

- George Washington—the commander of the Continental army during the American Revolution and the nation's first president
- Thomas Jefferson—the author of the Declaration of Independence who, as president, expanded the nation with the Louisiana Purchase
- Theodore Roosevelt—the president who oversaw the nation's rise to a world power
- Abraham Lincoln—the president who preserved the Union during the Civil War

After exploring the Black Hills, Borglum chose Mount Rushmore as the best site for the sculpture, and work began in 1927. A team of workers first used dynamite to blast away the rock. Then they used jackhammers to create facial features. Finally, they planed the surfaces smooth with hand tools.

Borglum's death in 1941 soon brought work on the sculpture to an end. During the 14 years of the project, his team had blasted some 450,000 tons of rock from the mountainside and created a monument of majestic proportions.

- The presidents' heads are some 60 feet high—about the distance from the pitcher's mound to home plate on a major league baseball diamond.
- The presidents' noses measure about 20 feet long.
- The presidents' eyes are 11 feet wide.
- The presidents' mouths are about 18 feet wide.

The 1927 Act of Congress that provided the initial funds for Borglum's sculpture declared Mount Rushmore a national memorial. Since the late 1930s, the National Park Service has managed the Mount Rushmore National Memorial, which hosts some 3 million visitors each year.

George Washington, Thomas Jefferson, Theodore Roosevelt, and Abraham Lincoln look down from the heights of Mount Rushmore.

James Montgomery Flagg's Uncle Sam proved to be a powerful recruiting tool.

Uncle Sam

One of the most recognizable symbols of the United States government is the character known as Uncle Sam. The origins of this symbol go back to the early 1800s. Samuel Wilson, a merchant from New York State, provided food for the army during the War of 1812. He marked the barrels of food "U.S." to indicate that they were government property. Over time, however, many soldiers began saying that the food was provided by "Uncle Sam."

During the mid-1800s, Uncle Sam began to take on a very distinct and recognizable appearance. This was largely due to the work of Thomas Nast, a cartoonist for the magazine *Harper's Weekly*. In his cartoons, Nast portrayed Sam as a tall, thin man with chin whiskers wearing a top hat, frock coat, and striped pants. Over the years, other artists adopted Nast's image of Uncle Sam, adding such features as a stars and stripes waistcoat.

Perhaps the most famous image of Uncle Sam was produced by artist James Montgomery Flagg during World War I. Originally drawn for a magazine cover warning Americans to be prepared for war, it was quickly adopted by the U.S. Army as a recruiting poster. More than 4 million copies of the poster were produced during 1917 and 1918. It was considered such a powerful recruiting tool that it was also used in the early years of World War II.

Flagg's stern-faced, finger-pointing Uncle Sam was a long way from Samuel Wilson, the food merchant from New York. Wilson, however, was not forgotten. In 1961 Congress recognized him as the origin of "America's national symbol of Uncle Sam."

Political Party Symbols

The symbols of the two major U.S. political parties—the Democratic donkey and the Republican elephant—are recognizable to many Americans. Both symbols have a colorful origin.

The use of the donkey as a symbol for Democrats dates to the presidential election of 1828. Supporters of John Quincy Adams declared that Democrat Andrew Jackson, Adams's opponent, was like a donkey—slow and not very bright. Jackson seized on this charge. He used the donkey on his campaign posters, noting that it was a simple, loyal, and hard-working animal. However, this image did not gain popularity until the mid-1800s—again through the work of Thomas Nast.

In his cartoons, Nast often used a donkey to represent supporters of the Democratic Party. In an 1874 cartoon, Nast showed the donkey, dressed in a lion skin, terrorizing other animals in a zoo. The elephant in the cartoon was labeled "The Republican Vote." In very short order, the two animals became the political party symbols.

This 1874 Thomas Nast cartoon is the first use of the Democratic donkey and the Republican elephant together.

Today, these animals remain the symbols of the two political parties. Images of the donkey and the elephant are used in campaign materials, usually decorated with stars and stripes.

Phonetic Respelling and Pronunciation Guide

Many of the key terms in this textbook have been respelled to help you pronounce them. The letter combinations used in the respelling throughout the narrative are explained in the following phonetic respelling and pronunciation guide. The guide is adapted from *Merriam-Webster's Collegiate Dictionary, 11th Edition; Merriam-Webster's Geographical Dictionary;* and *Merriam-Webster's Biographical Dictionary.*

MARK	AS IN	RESPELLING	EXAMPLE
a	alphabet	a	*AL-fuh-bet
ā	Asia	ay	AY-zhuh
ä	cart, top	ah	KAHRT, TAHP
e	let, ten	e	LET, TEN
ē	even, leaf	ee	EE-vuhn, LEEF
i	it, tip, British	i	IT, TIP, BRIT-ish
ī	site, buy, Ohio	y	SYT, BY, oh-HY-oh
	iris	eye	EYE-ris
k	card	k	KAHRD
ō	over, rainbow	oh	OH-vuhr, RAYN-boh
ù	book, wood	ooh	BOOHK, WOOHD
ò	all, orchid	aw	AWL, AWR-kid
òi	foil, coin	oy	FOYL, KOYN
aù	out	ow	OWT
ə	cup, butter	uh	KUHP, BUHT-uhr
ü	rule, food	oo	ROOL, FOOD
yü	few	yoo	FYOO
zh	vision	zh	VIZH-uhn

*A syllable printed in small capital letters receives heavier emphasis than the other syllable(s) in a word.

A

abolition movement a campaign to end slavery (p. 26)
movimiento abolicionista una campaña para poner fin a la esclavitud (pág. 26)

affirmative action an active effort to improve the employment or educational opportunities of members of minority groups and women (p. 466)
acción afirmativa iniciativas para mejorar las oportunidades laborales o educativas de las minorías y de las mujeres (pág. 466)

AIDS Acquired Immunodeficiency Syndrome, a disease that affects the immune system, making patients vulnerable to infections (p. 504)
SIDA síndrome de inmunodeficiencia adquirida; enfermedad que afecta al sistema inmunológico y hace que los pacientes sean vulnerables a infecciones (pág. 504)

Alien and Sedition Acts (1798) laws passed by a Federalist-dominated Congress aimed at protecting the government from treasonous ideas, actions, and people (p. 18)
Leyes de Extranjeros y Sedición (1798) leyes aprobadas por un Congreso mayormente federalist para proteger al gobierno de la influencia de ideas, acciones y personas desleales (pág. 18)

Allied powers a group of nations that allied to fight the Central powers in World War I, and those countries in opposition to the Axis powers in World War II (pp. 255, 340)
potencias aliadas grupo de naciones que se aliaron para luchar contra las potencias centrales en la Primera Guerra Mundial, y los países que se oponían a las potencias del Eje en la Segunda Guerra Mundial (pág. 255, 340)

al Qaeda the name of the terrorist organization headed by Osama bin Laden and responsible for the September 11, 2001, attacks (p. 492)

al-Qaeda nombre de la organización terrorista encabezada por Osama bin Laden, responsable de los ataques del 11 de septiembre de 2001 (pág. 492)

American Expeditionary Force the U.S. military forces sent to Europe during World War I and led by General John J. Pershing (p. 265)
Fuerza Expedicionaria Estadounidense fuerzas armadas de Estados Unidos bajo el mando del general John J. Pershing que fueron enviadas a Europa en la Primera Guerra Mundial (pág. 265)

American Federation of Labor (AFL) an organization that united skilled workers into national unions for specific industries (p. 162)
Federación Americana del Trabajo (AFL, por sus siglas en inglés) organización que unió a obreros especializados en sindicatos nacionales para industrias específicas (pág. 162)

American Indian Movement (AIM) a civil rights group organized to promote the interests of Native Americans (p. 449)
Movimiento de los Indígenas Americanos (AIM, por sus siglas en inglés) agrupación a favor de los derechos civiles que promueve los intereses de los indígenas norteamericanos (pág. 449)

Antifederalists people who opposed ratification of the Constitution (p. 13)
antifederalistas personas que se oponían a la aprobación de la Constitución (pág. 13)

Anti-Imperialist League a group of citizens opposed to imperialism and, specifically, to the peace treaty that gave the United States control of Cuba, Guam, Puerto Rico, and the Philippines (p. 235)
Liga Antiimperialista grupo de ciudadanos que se oponían al imperialismo y, más específicamente, al tratado de paz que daba a Estados Unidos el control de Cuba, Guam, Puerto Rico y Filipinas (pág. 235)

apartheid a system of segregation practiced in South Africa (p. 469)
apartheid sistema de segregación practicado en Sudáfrica (pág. 469)

appeasement the policy of giving into the demands of a nation in order to avoid war (p. 340)

apacigua miento contemporizacióno política de ceder ante las exigencias de una nación para evitar la Guerra (pág. 340)

Appomattox Courthouse the location where General Robert E. Lee was forced to surrender, thus ending the Civil War (p. 75)
Appomattox Courthouse poblado de Virginia donde el general Robert E. Lee fue obligado a rendirse, dando fi n a la Guerra Civil (pág. 75)

armistice a truce or cease-fire agreement between warring nations (p. 270)
armisticio tregua o acuerdo de cese del fuego entre dos naciones en guerra (pág. 270)

arms race a growth in weapons based on the number of weapons an enemy country has (p. 388)
carrera armamentística aumento de armamentos según la cantidad de armas que tiene un país enemigo (pág. 388)

Articles of Confederation (1777) the document that created the first central government for the United States; was replaced by the Constitution in 1789 (p. 12)
Artículos de Confederación (1777) documento que creó el primer gobierno central en Estados Unidos; fue reemplazado por la Constitución en 1789 (pág. 12)

assimilate to give up traditional ways in favor of mainstream practices (p. 135)
asimilar renunciar a las formas tradicionales en favor de las prácticas generales (pág. 135)

assimilation a process of adopting American beliefs and aspects of American culture (p. 185)
asimilación un proceso de adopción de creencias y aspectos de la cultura americana (pág. 185)

atomic bomb a weapon that receives its explosive power from the splitting of atoms (p. 366)
bomba atómica arma cuyo poder explosivo es generado por la división de átomos (pág. 366)

Axis powers the coalition of nations in World War II that included Germany, Italy, and Japan (p. 340)
potencias del Eje coalición de naciones de la Segunda Guerra Mundial formada por Alemania, Italia y Japón (pág. 340)

B

baby boom a sharp increase in the number of American births during the 1950s and 1960s (p. 390)
boom de la natalidad gran aumento en la cantidad de nacimientos en Estados Unidos durante las décadas de 1950 y 1960 (pág. 390)

Bataan Death March a forced march of American and Filipino soldiers captured by the Japanese along the Bataan Peninsula (p. 357)
marcha de la muerte de Bataán marcha forzada en la península de Bataán de soldados estadounidenses y filipinos capturados por los japoneses (pág. 357)

Battle of Antietam (1862) a Union victory in the Civil War that marked the bloodiest single-day battle in U.S. military history (p. 51)
batalla de Antieta (1862) victoria del ejército de la Unión durante la Guerra Civil en la batalla de un solo día más sangrienta de la historia militar de Estados Unidos (pág. 51)

Battle of El Alamein (1942) a turning point in World War II, in which Allied forces defeated the Afrika Korps of Germany (p. 352)
batalla del El Alamein (1942) momento decisivo en la Segunda Guerra Mundial, en el que las fuerzas aliadas derrotaron al *Afrika Korps* de Alemania (pág. 352)

Battle of Gettysburg (1863) a Union Civil War victory that turned the tide against the Confederates at Gettysburg, Pennsylvania (p. 70)
batalla de Gettysburg (1863) victoria del ejército de la Unión durante la Guerra Civil que cambió el curso de la guerra en contra de los confederados en Gettysburg, Pensilvania (pág. 70)

Battle of Leyte Gulf (1944) the largest naval battle in history, during which the American fleet destroyed most of the Japanese fleet (p. 359)
batalla del golfo de Leyte (1944) la mayor batalla naval de la historia, durante la cual la flota estadounidense destruyó la mayor parte de la flota japonesa (pág. 359)

Battle of Midway (1942) battle of World War II that ended the Japanese advance in the Pacific (p. 358)
batalla de Midway (1942) batalla de la Segunda Guerra Mundial que puso fin al avance de los japoneses en el Pacífico (pág. 358)

Battle of Shiloh (1862) a Civil War battle in Tennessee in which the Union army gained greater control over the Mississippi River valley (p. 54)
batalla de Shiloh (1862) batalla de la Guerra Civil en Tennessee en la que el ejército de la Unión adquirió mayor control sobre el valle del río Mississippi (pág. 54)

Battle of Stalingrad (1942–1943) a major turning point in World War II; Soviet forces defeated Nazi forces after which the Nazis never recovered (p. 354)
batalla de Stalingrado (1942–1943) momento decisivo de la Segunda Guerra Mundial; las fuerzas soviéticas vencieron a las fuerzas nazis, que nunca más se recuperaron (pág. 354)

Battle of the Bulge (1944–1945) the last German advance of World War II, which was stopped by Allied forces (p. 364)
batalla del Bulge (1944–1945) último avance alemán de la Segunda Guerra Mundial, que fue detenido por las fuerzas aliadas (pág. 364)

Battle of the Coral Sea (1942) the first strategic defeat of the Japanese Imperial Navy by American forces during World War II (p. 358)
batalla del mar del Coral (1942) primera derrota estratégica de la armada imperial japonesa ante las fuerzas estadounidenses en la Segunda Guerra Mundial (pág. 358)

Battle of the Little Big Horn (1876) "Custer's Last Stand"; battle between U.S. soldiers, led by George Armstrong Custer, and Sioux warriors, led by Crazy Horse and Sitting Bull, that resulted in the worst defeat for the U.S. Army in the West (p. 133)
batalla de Little Big Horn (1876) última batalla del general Custer; esta batalla entre las tropas de George Armstrong Custer y los guerreros siux al mando de Caballo Loco y Toro Sentado produjo la mayor derrota del ejército estadounidense en el Oeste (pág. 133)

beats young people, many of whom were writers and artists, who discussed their dissatisfaction with the American society of the 1950s (p. 394)
beatniks jóvenes, en su mayoría escritores y artistas, que debatían acerca de su descontento con la sociedad estadounidense de la década de 1950 (pág. 394)

benevolent society an aid organization formed by immigrant communities (p. 175)
sociedad de benefi cencia organización de ayuda formada por comunidades de inmigrantes (pág. 175)

Berlin Wall a barrier of concrete and barbed wire between Communist East Berlin and West Berlin (p. 404)
Muro de Berlín barrera de concreto y alambre de púas que separaba la Berlín oriental comunista de la Berlín occidental (pág. 404)

Bessemer process a process developed in the 1850s that led to faster, cheaper steel production (p. 150)
proceso de Bessemer proceso de producción de acero más económico y rápido, desarrollado en la década de 1850 (pág. 150)

Black Codes laws passed in the southern states during Reconstruction that greatly limited the freedom and rights of African Americans (p. 90)
Códigos Negros decretos aprobados en los estados sureños en la época de la Reconstrucción que limitaron en gran medida la libertad y los derechos de los afroamericanos (pág. 90)

Black Power a social movement that called for African American power and independence (p. 444)
Black Power (Poder Negro) movimiento social que exigía el poder y la independencia de los afroamericanos (pág. 444)

Black Tuesday October 29, 1929, one of the largest U.S. stock market drops (p. 311)
martes negro 29 de octubre de 1929, una de las mayores caídas de la bolsa de valores de Estados Unidos (pág. 311)

Bonus Army a group of World War I veterans that demanded their bonus payments early (p. 314)
Bonus Army grupo de veteranos de la Primera Guerra Mundial que exigía el pago de sus bonos por adelantado (pág. 314)

boomtown a Western community that grew quickly because of the mining boom and often disappeared when the boom ended (p. 123)
pueblo de rápido crecimiento comunidad del Oeste que se desarrolló con gran rapidez debido a la fiebre del oro, pero que desapareció cuando la fiebre terminó (pág. 123)

border states Delaware, Kentucky, Maryland, and Missouri; slave states that lay between the North and the South and did not join the Confederacy during the Civil War (p. 42)
estados fronterizos Delaware, Kentucky, Maryland y Missouri; estados esclavistas ubicados entre el Norte y el Sur y que no se unieron a la Confederación durante la Guerra Civil (pág. 42)

Boxer Rebellion (1900) a siege of a foreign settlement in Beijing by Chinese nationalists who were angry at foreign involvement in China (p. 280)
rebelión de los boxers (1900) asedio a un asentamiento extranjero en Beijing por parte de un grupo de nacionalistas chinos que estaban enojados por la participación extranjera en China (pág. 280)

brinkmanship the Cold War foreign policy designed to "get to the verge without getting into the war" (p. 389)
política arriesgada política exterior durante la Guerra Fría diseñada para "llegar al borde de la guerra sin llegar a la guerra" (pág. 389)

Brown v. Board of Education (1954) Supreme Court decision that ended segregation in public schools (p. 433)
Brown* contra *la Junta Educativa (1954) decisión de la Corte Suprema que puso fin a la segregación en las escuelas públicas (pág. 433)

buffalo soldiers African American soldiers who served in the cavalry during the wars for the west (p. 131)
soldados búfalo soldados afroamericanos que sirvieron en la caballería durante las guerras del oeste (pág. 131)

business cycle the rhythm in which an economy expands and contracts its production (p. 313)
ciclo económico ritmo al que la producción de una economía se expande y se contrae (pág. 313)

buying on margin the process of purchasing stock with credit, hoping to sell at a high enough price to pay the loan and make a profit (p. 310)
compra a crédito proceso de comprar acciones con préstamos, con la esperanza de venderlas a un precio suficientemente alto para pagar el préstamo y obtener una ganancia (pág. 310)

C

Camp David Accords (1978) an agreement between the heads of Israel and Egypt that began peace process in the Middle East (p. 470)
Acuerdos de Camp David (1978) acuerdo entre los líderes de Israel y Egipto que dio inicio a un proceso de paz en el Medio Oriente (pág. 470)

capitalism an economic system in which private businesses run most industries (p. 207)
capitalismo sistema económico en el que las empresas privadas controlan la mayoría de las industrias (pág. 207)

cattle drive a long journey on which cowboys herded cattle to northern markets or better grazing lands (p. 124)
arreo de ganado viaje largo en el que los vaqueros arreaban ganado para llevarlo a los mercados del Norte o a mejores pastos (pág. 124)

Cattle Kingdom an area of the Great Plains on which many ranchers raised cattle in the late 1800s (p. 124)
Reino del Ganado área de las Grandes Planicies en la que muchos rancheros criaban ganado a fi nales de siglo XIX (pág. 124)

Central powers the coalition of nations in World War I that included the German, Austrio-Hungary, and Ottoman empires (p. 255)
Potencias Centrales coalición de naciones de la Primera Guerra Mundial formada por los imperios alemán, austrohúngaro y otomano (pág. 255)

Chinese Exclusion Act (1882) a law passed by Congress that banned Chinese from immigrating to the United States for 10 years (p. 176)
Ley de Exclusión de Chinos (1882) ley aprobada por el Congreso que prohibió la inmigración de chinos a Estados Unidos por 10 años (pág. 176)

Chisholm Trail a trail from San Antonio, Texas, to Abilene, Kansas, established by Jesse Chisholm in the late 1860s for cattle drives (p. 124)
Camino de Chisholm camino creado por Jesse Chisholm a finales de la década de 1860 que iba desde San Antonio, Texas hasta Abilene, Kansas, para arreos de ganado (pág. 124)

Civil Rights Act of 1866 a law that gave African Americans legal rights equal to those of white Americans (p. 92)
Ley de Derechos Civiles de 1866 ley que dio a los afroamericanos los mismos derechos legales que tenían los estadounidenses blancos (pág. 92)

Civil Rights Act of 1964 a law that ended discrimination based on race or gender (p. 442)
Ley de Derechos Civiles de 1964 ley que puso fin a la discriminación en base a la raza o al sexo (pág. 442)

Cold War a period of hostility between Western powers and Communist powers (p. 379)
Guerra Fría período de hostilidades entre las potencias de Occidente y las potencias comunistas (pág. 379)

collective bargaining a technique used by labor unions in which workers act collectively to change working conditions or wages (p. 161)
negociación colectiva método empleado por los sindicatos en el que los trabajadores actúan colectivamente para cambiar las condiciones laborales o los salarios (pág. 161)

Communists people who believe in communism, or the political system in which all resources are shared equally (p. 266)
comunistas personas que creen en el comunismo, es decir, el sistema político en el que los recursos se distribuyen a todos por igual (pág. 266)

Compromise of 1850 Henry Clay's proposed agreement that allowed California to enter the Union as a free state and divided the rest of the Mexican Cession into two territories where slavery would be decided by popular sovereignty (p. 29)
Compromiso de 1850 acuerdo propuesto por Henry Clay en que se permitía a California entrar en la Unión como estado libre y se proponía la division del resto del territorio de la Cesión Mexicana en dos partes donde la esclavitud sería reglamentada por soberanía popular (pág. 29)

Compromise of 1877 an agreement to settle the disputed presidential election of 1876; Democrats agreed to accept Republican Rutherford B. Hayes as president in return for the removal of federal troops from the South (p. 100)

Compromiso de 1877 acuerdo en el que se resolvieron las disputadas elecciones presidenciales de 1876; los demócratas aceptaron al republican Rutherford B. Hayes como presidente a cambio del retiro de las tropas federales del Sur (pág. 100)

Comstock Lode Nevada gold and silver mine discovered by Henry Comstock in 1859 (p. 122)
veta de Comstock mina de oro y plata descubierta en Nevada por Henry Comstock en 1859 (pág. 122)

Confederate States of America the nation formed by the southern states when they seceded from the Union; also known as the Confederacy (p. 31)
Estados Confederados de América nación formada por los estados del Sur cuando se separaron de la Unión; también conocida como Confederación (pág. 31)

Congress of Industrial Organizations (CIO) a union that organized workers according to industry, not by skill (p. 322)
Congreso de Organizaciones Industriales (CIO, por sus siglas en inglés) sindicato que organizó a los trabajadores según la industria y no el nivel de especialización (pag. 322)

conservation the planned management of natural resources to prevent their destruction (p. 216)
conservación administración planifi cada de los recursos naturales para evitar su destrucción (pág. 216)

containment a foreign policy that attempts to stop the spread of communism without ending it in the countries in which it already exists (p. 379)
contención política exterior que intenta detener el avance del comunismo sin eliminarlo en los países en los que ya existe (pág. 379)

contraband an escaped slave who joined the Union army during the Civil War (p. 63)
contrabando esclavo que escapó y se unió al ejército de la Unión durante la Guerra Civil (pág. 63)

Constitutional Convention (1787) a meeting held in Philadelphia at which delegates from the states wrote the Constitution (p. 13)

Convención Constitucional (1787) reunión en Filadelfia en la que delegados de los estados redactaron la Constitución (pág. 13))

Copperheads a group of northern Democrats who opposed abolition and sympathized with the South during the Civil War (p. 65)
copperheads grupo de demócratas del Norte que se oponían a la abolición de la esclavitud y simpatizaban con las creencias sureñas durante la Guerra Civil (pág. 65)

corporation a business that sells portions of ownership called stock shares (p. 156)
corporación compañía que vende algunas partes en forma de acciones (pág. 156)

cotton diplomacy Confederate efforts to use the importance of southern cotton to Britain's textile industry to persuade the British to support the Confederacy in the Civil War (p. 44)
diplomacia del algodón esfuerzos de la Confederación por aprovechar la importancia del algodón del Sur en la industria textil británica para convencer a Gran Bretaña de apoyar a la Confederación en la Guerra Civil (pág. 44)

Cuban missile crisis a threat to national security that occurred when the Soviet Union placed nuclear missiles in Cuba (p. 404)
crisis de los misiles de Cuba amenaza a la seguridad nacional que ocurrió cuando la Unión Soviética colocó misiles nucleares en Cuba (pág. 404)

D

Dawes General Allotment Act (1887) legislation passed by Congress that split up Indian reservation lands among individual Indians and promised them citizenship (p. 135)
Ley de Adjudicación General de Dawes (1887) ley aprobada por el Congreso que dividía el terreno de las reservas indígenas entre sus habitantes y les prometía la ciudadanía (pág. 135)

D-Day (1944) an invasion of Nazi-occupied France by Allied forces (p. 354)
día D (1944) invasión de las fuerzas aliadas en Francia, ocupada por los nazis (pág. 354)

Declaration of Independence (1776) the document written to declare the colonies free from British rule (p. 11)
Declaración de Independencia (1776) document redactado para declarar la independencia de las colonias del dominio británico (pág. 11)

deficit the amount by which a government's spending exceeds its revenue (p. 473)
déficit cantidad en la que los gastos del gobierno superan sus ingresos (pág. 473)

deflation a decrease in money supply and overall lower prices (p. 140)
deflación reducción de la disponibilidad del dinero y baja general en los precios (pág. 140)

Department of Homeland Security a federal agency set up in 2001 to coordinate national efforts to combat terrorism (p. 496)
Departamento de Seguridad Nacional una agencia federal creada en 2001 para coordinar los esfuerzos nacionales de lucha contra el terrorismo (pág. 496)

department store giant retail shop (p. 180)
tiendas por departamentos grandes comercios de venta al público (pág. 180)

détente a period of closer diplomatic relations between the United States and the Communist powers of China and the Soviet Union (p. 460)
distensión período de relaciones diplomáticas más estrechas entre Estados Unidos y las potencias comunistas de China y la Unión Soviética (pág. 460)

Disabled in Action (DIA) a group organized to promote the interests of people with disabilities (p. 450)
Discapacitados en Acción (DIA, por sus siglas en inglés) grupo organizado para promover los intereses de personas con discapacidades (pág. 450)

dollar diplomacy trying to influence foreign governments through economic, not military intervention (p. 245)
diplomacia del dólar modelo político que trata de influir en los gobiernos extranjeros a través del uso de su poder económico y no por la intervención militar (pág. 245)

domino theory the idea that Communism would spread rapidly throughout Southeast Asia (p. 407)
teoría del efecto dominó idea de que el comunismo se extendería rápidamente por el sureste de Asia (pág. 407)

doves opponents of the Vietnam War (p. 413)
palomas opositores a la guerra de Vietnam (pág. 413)

dry farming a method of farming used by Plains farmers in the 1890s that shifted focus from water-dependent crops to more hardy crops (p. 138)
agricultura de secano método de cultivo que usaban los agricultores de las Planicies en la década de 1890 que provocó un cambio de los cultivos que dependían del agua a otros más resistentes (pág. 138)

Dust Bowl an area of the United States that suffered a severe drought during the 1930s (p. 324)
Dust Bowl área de Estados Unidos que sufrió una grave sequía en la década de 1930 (pág. 324)

E

Eighteenth Amendment (1919) a constitutional amendment that outlawed the production and sale of alcoholic beverages in the United States; repealed in 1933 (p. 210)
Decimoctava Enmienda (1919) enmienda constitucional que prohibió la producción y venta de bebidas alcohólicas en Estados Unidos; revocada en 1933 (pág. 210)

emancipation freeing of the slaves (p. 60)
emancipación liberación de los esclavos (pág. 60)

Emancipation Proclamation (1862) an order issued by President Abraham Lincoln freeing the slaves in areas rebelling against the Union; took effect January 1, 1863 (p. 61)
Proclamación de Emancipación (1862) orden emitida por el presidente Abraham Lincoln para liberar a los esclavos en las áreas que se rebelaban contra la Unión; entró en vigor el primero de enero de 1863 (pág. 61)

Enforcement Acts (1870-1871) laws passed by Congress that made it a crime to interfere with elections or deny citizens equal protection under the law (p. 99)
Actos de ejecución (1870-1871) leyes aprobadas por el Congreso que determinaron

que era un crimen interferir con las elecciones o negar a los ciudadanos la igualdad ante la ley (pág. 99)

Equal Rights Amendment (ERA) a proposed amendment to the Constitution that would provide equal rights to women (p. 448)
Enmienda por la Igualdad de Derechos (ERA, por sus siglas en inglés) enmienda constitucional propuesta que otorgaría la igualdad de derechos a la mujer (pág. 448)

Erie Canal the canal that runs from Albany to Buffalo, New York; completed in 1825 (p. 19)
canal de Erie canal que va de Albany a Buffalo, Nueva York; completado en 1825 (pág. 19)

escalation increased involvement in the Vietnam War (p. 411)
escalada mayor participación en la guerra de Vietnam (pág. 411)

Exodusters African Americans who settled western lands in the late 1800s (p. 137)
Exodusters afroamericanos que se establecieron en el Oeste a fi nales del siglo XIX (pág. 137)

expatriates citizens who leave their country to live elsewhere (p. 301)
expatriados ciudadanos que abandonan su país para vivir en otro lugar (pág. 301)

F

Fair Deal President Truman's legislative plan for the nation that included antilynching laws (p. 383)
Fair Deal plan legislativo para la nación propuesto por el presidente Truman que incluía leyes en contra de los linchamientos (pág. 383)

fascism a political system in which the state or government is seen as more important than the individual (p. 338)
fascismo sistema político en el que se considera que el estado o gobierno es más importante que las personas (pág. 338)

federalism U.S. system of government in which power is distributed between a central government and individual states (p. 14)

federalismo sistema de gobierno de Estados Unidos en el que el poder se divide entre una autoridad central y estados individuales (pág. 14)

Federalists people who supported ratification of the Constitution (p. 13)
federalistas personas que apoyaban la ratificación de la Constitución (pág. 13)

Fifteenth Amendment (1870) a constitutional amendment that gave African American men the right to vote (p. 96)
Decimoquinta Enmienda (1870) enmienda constitucional que daba a los hombres afroamericanos el derecho al voto (pág. 96)

54th Massachusetts Infantry African American Civil War regiment that captured Fort Wagner in South Carolina (p. 63)
54to Batallón de Infantería de Massachusetts regimiento afroamericano de la Guerra Civil que tomó el fuerte Wagner en Carolina del Sur (pág. 63)

fireside chats radio programs in which Franklin Roosevelt explained his plan for recovery from the Great Depression (p. 318)
charlas junto a la chimenea programas de radio en los cuales Franklin Roosevelt explicaba su plan para que el país se recuperara de la Gran Depresión (pág. 318)

First Battle of Bull Run (1861) the first major battle of the Civil War, resulting in a Confederate victory; showed that the Civil War would not be won easily (p. 48)
primera batalla de Bull Run (1861) primera batalla importante de la Guerra Civil, en la cual ganó el ejército confederado; demostró que la guerra no se ganaría fácilmente (pág. 48)

flappers young women who challenged traditional ideas of womanhood in the 1920s (p. 291)
flappers mujeres jóvenes que desafi aron las ideas tradicionales sobre la condición de la mujer en la década de 1920 (pág. 291)

Fort Sumter a federal outpost in Charleston, South Carolina, that was attacked by the Confederates in April 1861, sparking the Civil War (p. 40)
fuerte Sumter puesto de avanzada federal en Charleston, Carolina del Sur, cuyo ataque por parte de los confederados en abril de 1861 dio origen a la Guerra Civil (pág. 40)

English and Spanish Glossary　**R39**

English and Spanish Glossary

Fourteenth Amendment (1866) a constitutional amendment giving full rights of citizenship to all people born or naturalized in the United States, except for American Indians (p. 92)
Decimocuarta Enmienda (1866) enmienda constitucional que otorgaba derechos totales de ciudadanía a todas las personas nacidas en Estados Unidos o naturalizadas estadounidenses, con excepción de los indígenas americanos (pág. 92)

Freedmen's Bureau an agency established by Congress in 1865 to help poor people throughout the South (p. 87)
Oficina de los Libertos ofi cina creada por el Congreso en 1865 para ayudar a los pobres del Sur del país (pág. 87)

Freedom Rides a series of integrated bus rides through the South (p. 440)
Viajes de la Libertad serie de viajes en autobús por el Sur en los que se integraban las razas (pág. 440)

Free-Soil Party a political party formed in 1848 by antislavery northerners who left the Whig and Democratic parties because neither addressed the slavery issue (pp. 29, 63)
Partido Tierra Libre partido político formado en 1848 por abolicionistas de los estados del Norte que habían abandonado el Partido Whig y el Partido Demócrata porque ninguno de los dos partidos tenía una postura sobre la esclavitud (pág. 29, 63)

frontier an undeveloped area (p. 122)
frontera área que no está siendo utilizada por el ser humano (pág. 122)

Fugitive Slave Act (1850) a law that made it a crime to help runaway slaves; allowed for the arrest of escaped slaves in areas where slavery was illegal, and required their return to slaveholders (p. 30)
Ley de Esclavos Fugitivos (1850) ley que hacía que ayudar a un esclavo a escapar de su amo fuera un delito; permitía la captura de esclavos fugitivos en zonas donde la esclavitud era ilegal para devolverlos a sus dueños (pág. 30)

fundamentalism a religious belief characterized by a literal interpretation of the Bible (p. 294)
fundamentalismo creencia religiosa caracterizada por una interpretación literal de la Biblia (pág. 294)

G

genocide the complete destruction of a racial or ethnic minority (p. 365)
genocidio destrucción total de una minoría racial o étnica (pág. 365)

Gettysburg Address (1863) a speech given by Abraham Lincoln in which he praised the bravery of Union soldiers and renewed his commitment to winning the Civil War (p. 72)
Discurso de Gettysburg (1863) discurso de Abraham Lincoln en el que alababa la valentía de las tropas de la Unión y renovaba su compromiso de triunfar en la Guerra Civil (pág. 72)

Ghost Dance a religious movement among Native Americans that spread across the Plains in the 1880s (p. 134)
Danza de los Espíritus movimiento religioso de los indígenas norteamericanos que se extendió por la región de las Planicies en la década de 1880 (pág. 134)

GI Bill of Rights (1944) a law that offered veterans money for school, houses, farms, and businesses (p. 381)
Declaración de Derechos de los Soldados (1944) ley que ofrecía a los veteranos de guerra dinero para su educación, vivienda, granjas y negocios (pág. 381)

globalization the process in which the United States is becoming more interdependent with other nations (p. 494)
globalización proceso por el cual Estados Unidos empieza a tener más interdependencia con otras naciones (pág. 494)

global warming an environmental crisis in which the average temperature of the Earth is rising due to pollution (p. 505)
calentamiento global crisis del medio ambiente por la cual está aumentando la temperatura promedio de la Tierra debido a la contaminación (pág. 505)

Great Awakening a religious movement that became widespread in the American colonies in the 1730s and 1740s (p. 10)
Gran Despertar movimiento religioso que tuvo gran popularidad en las colonias norteamericanas en las décadas de 1730 y 1740 (pág. 10)

Great Depression a severe economic crisis that lasted for the entire decade of the 1930s (p. 313)
Gran Depresión grave crisis económica que duró toda la década de 1930 (pág. 313)

Great Migration a period of African American movement from the South to the North (p. 295)
Gran Migración período en que los afroamericanos del Sur se fueron a ciudades del Norte (pág. 295)

Great Society President Lyndon Johnson's legislative plan that included civil rights laws (p. 443)
Gran Sociedad plan legislativo del presidente Lyndon Johnson que incluía leyes a favor de los derechos civiles (pág. 443)

H

habeas corpus the constitutional protection against unlawful imprisonment (p. 65)
hábeas corpus protección constitucional contra el encarcelamiento ilegal (pág. 65)

Harlem Renaissance a period of artistic achievement during the 1920s (p. 300)
Renacimiento de Harlem período de logros artísticos durante la década de 1920 (pág. 300)

hawks supporters of the Vietnam War (p. 414)
halcones partidarios de la guerra de Vietnam (pág. 414)

Haymarket Riot a riot that broke out at Haymarket Square in Chicago over the deaths of two strikers (p. 162)
Revuelta de Haymarket revuelta que se originó en la Plaza Haymarket de Chicago por la muerte de dos huelguistas (pág. 162)

hippies young people who rebelled against the mainstream culture of the 1960s (p. 419)
hippies jóvenes que se rebelaron contra la cultura convencional en la década de 1960 (pág. 419)

Ho Chi Minh Trail a series of jungle paths that allowed Communist forces to travel from North Vietnam to South Vietnam (p. 411)
Camino de Ho Chi Minh serie de caminos por la selva que permitía a las fuerzas comunistas ir desde Vietnam del Norte hacia Vietnam del Sur (pág. 411)

Holocaust a program of mass murder in which the Nazis tried to kill all Jews (p. 364)
Holocausto programa de asesinato en masa ideado por los nazis para exterminar a todos los judíos (pág. 364)

Homestead Act (1862) a law passed by Congress to encourage settlement in the West by giving government-owned land to small farmers (p. 136)
Ley de Heredad (1862) ley aprobada por el Congreso para fomentar la colonización del Oeste mediante la cesión de tierras del gobierno a pequeños agricultores (pág. 136)

Homestead strike (1892) a labor-union strike at Andrew Carnegie's Homestead Steel factory in Pennsylvania that erupted in violence between strikers and private detectives (p. 163)
huelga de Homestead (1892) huelga sindical en la fábrica de acero Homestead de Andrew Carnegie en Pensilvania, que produjo violencia entre huelguistas y detectives privados (pág. 163)

horizontal integration owning all the businesses in a certain field (p. 158)
integración horizontal posesión de todas las empresas en un campo específico (pág. 158)

Hull House a settlement house founded by Jane Addams and Ellen Gates Starr in 1889 (p. 185)
Casa Hull casa de asistencia a la comunidad fundada por Jane Addams y Ellen Gates Starr en 1889 (pág. 185)

human rights the basic rights of all people (p. 469)
derechos humanos derechos fundamentales de todas las personas (pág. 469)

hydrogen bomb a thermonuclear weapon that gets its power from splitting a hydrogen atom (p. 388)
bomba de hidrógeno arma termonuclear cuya potencia es generada por la división de un átomo de hidrógeno (pág. 388)

I

impeachment the process used by a legislative body to bring charges of wrongdoing against a public official (p. 94)
juicio político proceso por el cual un cuerpo legislativo presenta cargos en contra de un funcionario público (pág. 94)

English and Spanish Glossary

imperialism the practice of extending a nation's power by gaining territories for a colonial empire (p. 226)

imperialismo práctica en la que una nación amplía su poder adquiriendo territorios para un imperio colonial (pág. 226)

Industrial Workers of the World (IWW) a union founded in 1905 by socialists and union leaders that included workers not welcomed in the AFL (p. 208)

Trabajadores Industriales del Mundo (IWW, por sus siglas en inglés) sindicato fundado en 1905 por socialistas y líderes sindicales que incluía a los trabajadores que no admitía la Federación Americana del Trabajo (pág. 208)

Information Revolution an increase in the ability to share information between people and locations brought about by the Internet (p. 502)

Revolución de la Información aumento de la capacidad de compartir información entre personas y lugares producido por Internet (pág. 502)

initiative a method of allowing voters to propose a new law if enough signatures are collected on a petition (p. 200)

iniciativa método que permite a los votantes proponer una nueva ley si consiguen suficientes firmas para una petición (pág. 200)

Internet a global system of computers that allows people across the world to communicate (p. 502)

Internet sistema global de computadoras que permite la comunicación entre personas de todo el mundo (pág. 502)

internment the imprisonment of Japanese Americans in special camps during World War II (p. 349)

internamiento encarcelamiento de japonesesamericanos en campos especiales durante la Segunda Guerra Mundial (pág. 349)

Iran-Contra affair a scandal during the Reagan administration in which government officials were accused of selling weapons to Iran and passing the profits to a revolutionary group known as the Contras (p. 476)

asunto Irán-Contras escándalo durante el gobierno de Reagan en el cual funcionarios del gobierno fueron acusados de vender armas a Irán y de entregar las ganancias a un grupo revolucionario conocido como los contras (pág. 476)

Iran hostage crisis a crisis in which Americans were taken hostage by militants in Iran and held for over a year (p. 471)

crisis de los rehenes de Irán crisis en la cual varios estadounidenses fueron tomados como rehenes por militantes iraníes durante más de un año (pág. 471)

ironclad a warship that is heavily armored with iron (p. 52)

acorazado buque de guerra fuertemente protegido con hierro (pág. 52)

island-hopping the strategy used by U.S. forces in the Pacific during World War II that involved taking only strategically important islands (p. 359)

saltar de isla en isla estrategia de las fuerzas de Estados Unidos en el Pacífico durante la Segunda Guerra Mundial que consistía en tomar sólo las islas importantes desde el punto de vista estratégico (pág. 359)

isolationism a national policy of avoiding involvement in other countries' affairs (p. 226)

aislacionismo política nacional de evitar involucrarse en los asuntos de otras naciones (pág. 226)

J

Jacksonian Democracy an expansion of voting rights during the popular Andrew Jackson administration (p. 20)

democracia jacksoniana ampliación del derecho al voto durante el popular gobierno del president Andrew Jackson (pág. 20)

Jamestown the first colony in the U.S.; set up in 1607 along the James River in Virginia (p. 8)

Jamestown primera colonia en territorio estadounidense; fundada en 1607 a orillas del río James en Virginia (pág. 8)

Jazz Age a name for the decade of the 1920s based on the popularity of jazz music (p. 299)

Era del Jazz nombre que se le dio a la década de 1920 por la popularidad de la música de jazz (pág. 299)

Jim Crow law a law that enforced segregation in the southern states (p. 101)

ley de Jim Crow ley que imponía la segregación en los estados del Sur (pág. 101)

K

kamikaze Japanese pilots who flew suicide missions during World War II (p. 362)
kamikaze piloto japonés que volaba en misiones suicidas durante la Segunda Guerra Mundial (pág. 362)

Kellogg-Briand Pact an agreement between nations proposing peaceful solutions to conflicts, signed after World War I (p. 286)
Pacto Kellogg-Briand acuerdo fi rmado entre naciones luego de la Primera Guerra Mundial que proponía soluciones pacíficas a los conflictos (pág. 286)

Knights of Labor secret society that became the first truly national labor union in the United States (p. 161)
Caballeros del Trabajo sociedad secreta que se convirtió en el primer sindicato verdaderamente nacional en Estados Unidos (pág. 161)

Ku Klux Klan a secret society created by white southerners in 1866 that used terror and violence to keep African Americans from obtaining their civil rights (p. 99)
Ku Klux Klan sociedad secreta creada en 1866 por blancos del Sur que usaba el terror y la violencia para impedir que los afroamericanos obtuvieran derechos civiles (pág. 99)

L

League of Nations a coalition of governments designed to find peaceful solutions to disagreements, proposed by Woodrow Wilson (p. 273)
Liga de las Naciones coalición de gobiernos propuesta por Woodrow Wilson y diseñada para buscar soluciones pacíficas a los desacuerdos (pág. 273)

Lend-Lease Act (1941) a law giving Franklin Roosevelt the power to sell, transfer, exchange, or lease military equipment to any country to help it defend itself against the Axis powers (p. 342)
Ley de Préstamo y Arriendo (1941) ley que dio a Franklin Roosevelt el poder de vender, transferir, intercambiar o arrendar equipo militar a cualquier país para la defensa contra las potencias del Eje (pág. 342)

Lewis and Clark expedition an expedition led by Meriwether Lewis and William Clark that began in 1804 to explore the Louisiana Purchase (pp. 18, 114)
expedición de Lewis y Clark expedición encabezada por Meriwether Lewis y William Clark que empezó en 1804 para explorar la Compra de Luisiana (pág. 18, 114)

Liberty bonds loans to the government that aided its ability to prepare for World War I (p. 261)
bonos de la Libertad préstamos hechos al gobierno que le permitieron prepararse para la Primera Guerra Mundial (pág. 261)

Little Rock Nine a group of nine African American students who began the integration of the Little Rock, Arkansas, public school system (p. 433)
los nueve de Little Rock grupo de nueve estudiantes afroamericanos que empezaron la integración del sistema de escuelas públicas de Little Rock, Arkansas (pág. 433)

Long Walk (1864) a 300-mile march made by Navajo captives to a reservation in Bosque Redondo, New Mexico, that led to the deaths of hundreds of Navajo (p. 133)
Larga Marcha (1864) caminata de 300 millas que hizo un grupo de prisioneros navajos hasta una reserva indígena en Bosque Redondo, Nuevo México, en la que murieron cientos de ellos (pág. 133)

Lost Generation the generation of young people who fought in World War I and eventually became disillusioned with the promise of American society (p. 301)
generación perdida generación de jóvenes que lucharon en la Primera Guerra Mundial y terminaron desilusionados con las promesas de la sociedad estadounidense (pág. 301)

Louisiana Purchase (1803) the purchase of French land between the Mississippi River and the Rocky Mountains that doubled the size of the United States (pp. 18, 114)
Compra de Luisiana (1803) adquisición del territorio francés localizado entre el río Mississippi y las montañas Rocallosas que duplicó el tamaño de Estados Unidos (pág. 18, 114)

Lusitania a passenger ship bombed by Germany (p. 259)
Lusitania barco de pasajeros bombardeado por Alemania (pág. 259)

English and Spanish Glossary

M

Manhattan Project the U.S. effort to build an atomic bomb (p. 366)
Proyecto Manhattan plan de Estados Unidos de fabricar una bomba atómica (pág. 366)

manifest destiny a belief shared by many Americans in the mid-1800s that the United States should expand across the continent to the Pacific Ocean (p. 23)
destino manifiesto creencia de muchos ciudadanos estadounidenses a mediados del siglo XIX de que Estados Unidos debía expandirse por todo el continente hasta el océano Pacífico (pág. 23)

March on Washington a huge demonstration organized by Martin Luther King Jr. to protest racial discrimination (p. 442)
Marcha en Washington manifestación enorme organizada por Martin Luther King, Jr. en protesta por la discriminación racial (pág. 442)

Marshall Plan the idea that the U.S. could help rebuild wartorn Europe with loans and other economic aid (p. 379)
Plan Marshall idea de que Estados Unidos podía contribuir con préstamos y otros tipos de ayuda económica a la reconstrucción de la Europa devastada por la guerra (pág. 379)

Massacre at Wounded Knee (1890) the U.S. Army's killing of approximately 150 Sioux at Wounded Knee Creek in South Dakota; ended U.S.-Indian wars on the Plains (p. 133)
masacre de Wounded Knee (1890) matanza de aproximadamente 150 indios siux en Wounded Knee Creek, Dakota del Sur; dio por terminadas las guerras entre estadounidenses e indígenas en las Planicies (pág. 133)

mass culture leisure and cultural activities shared by many people (p. 180)
cultura de masas actividades culturales y del tiempo libre que les gustan a muchas personas (pág. 180)

mass transit public transportation (p. 179)
transporte colectivo transporte público (pág. 179)

Medicare a federal program, established in 1965, that provides hospital insurance and low-cost medical insurance to Americans aged 65 and over (p. 508)

Medicare un programa federal, establecido en 1965, que ofrece seguro de hospital y seguro médico de bajo costo para los estadounidenses de 65 años y mayores (pág. 508)

Mexican Revolution a revolution led by Francisco Madero in 1910 that eventually forced the Mexican dictator Díaz to resign (p. 245)
Revolución Mexicana revolución iniciada en 1910 por Francisco Madero, que finalmente obligó al dictador mexicano Díaz a renunciar (pág. 245)

militarism an increase in the importance of the military of a country (p. 255)
militarismo aumento de la importancia del ejército de un país (pág. 255)

Missouri Compromise (1820) an agreement proposed by Henry Clay that allowed Missouri to enter the Union as a slave state and Maine to enter as a free state and outlawed slavery in any territories or states north of 36°30′ latitude (p. 20)
Compromiso de Missouri (1820) acuerdo propuesto por Henry Clay en el que se aceptaba a Missouri en la Unión como estado esclavista y a Maine como estado libre, además de prohibir la esclavitud en los territorios o estados al norte del paralelo 36°30′ (pág. 20)

mobilize to prepare for war (p. 255)
mobilizarse prepararse para la guerra (pág. 255)

Model T Henry Ford's automobile designed with the average American in mind (p. 286)
modelo T automóvil de Henry Ford diseñado para el estadounidense promedio (pág. 286)

monopoly a complete control over the entire supply of goods or a service in a particular market (p. 158)
monopolio control absoluto de toda la oferta de bienes o de un servicio en un mercado en particular (pág. 158)

Monroe Doctrine (1823) President James Monroe's statement forbidding further colonization in the Americas and declaring that any attempt by a foreign country to colonize would be considered an act of hostility (p. 19)
Doctrina Monroe (1823) declaración hecha por el presidente James Monroe en la que se prohibía la colonización adicional de las Américas y se declaraba que cualquier intento

de colonización por parte de otro país se consideraría un acto hostil (pág. 19)

Montgomery bus boycott a boycott of the Montgomery, Alabama, public bus system to protest its policy of segregation (p. 436)
boicot a los autobuses de Montgomery boicot al sistema público de autobuses de Montgomery, Alabama, en protesta por su política de segregación (pág. 436)

Mormon a member of the Church of Jesus Christ of Latter-day Saints (p. 118)
mormón miembro de la Iglesia de Jesucristo de los Santos de los Últimos Días (pág. 118)

Morrill Act (1862) a federal law passed by Congress that gave land to western states to encourage them to build colleges (p. 136)
Ley de Morrill (1862) ley federal aprobada por el Congreso que otorgaba tierras a los estados del Oeste para fomentar la construcción de universidades (pág. 136)

mountain men men hired by eastern companies to trap animals for fur in the Rocky Mountains and other western regions of the United States (p. 116)
montañeses hombres contratados por compañías del este para atrapar animales y obtener sus pieles en las montañas Rocallosas y en otras regiones del oeste de Estados Unidos (pág. 116)

moving assembly line an innovation of Henry Ford's that dramatically reduced the cost of production (p. 286)
cadena de montaje móvil innovación de Henry Ford que redujo signifi cativamente el costo de producción (pág. 286)

muckrakers a term coined for journalists who "raked up" and exposed corruption and problems of society (p. 197)
muckrakers término acuñado para nombrar a los periodistas que se dedicaban a investigar y exponer la corrupción y los problemas de la sociedad (pág. 197)

N

National American Woman Suffrage Association (NAWSA) an organization founded by Elizabeth Cady Stanton and Susan B. Anthony in 1890 to obtain women's right to vote (p. 210)
Asociación Nacional Americana para el Sufragio Femenino (NAWSA, por sus siglas en inglés) organización fundada en 1890 por Elizabeth Cady Stanton y Susan B. Anthony para obtener el derecho al voto de las mujeres (pág. 210)

National Association for the Advancement of Colored People (NAACP) an organization founded in 1909 by W.E.B. Du Bois and other reformers to bring attention to racial inequality (p. 213)
Asociación Nacional para el Progreso de la Gente de Color (NAACP, por sus siglas en inglés) organización fundada en 1909 por W.E.B. Du Bois y otros reformadores para llamar la atención sobre la desigualdad racial (pág. 213)

National Grange a social and educational organization for farmers (p. 140)
National Grange organización social y educativa para los agricultores (pág. 140)

National Organization for Women (NOW) a group that organized to promote the interests of women (p. 447)
Organización Nacional de la Mujer (NOW, por sus siglas en inglés) grupo organizado para promover los intereses de la mujer (pág. 447)

National War Labor Board a government agency organized to help settle disputes between workers and employers in war industries (p. 263)
Junta Nacional del Trabajo en Tiempos de Guerra agencia del gobierno destinada a resolver disputas entre trabajadores y empleadores en las industrias relacionadas con la guerra (pág. 263)

Nazis the National Socialist Party of Germany, headed by Adolf Hitler (p. 339)
nazis Partido Nacional de Alemania liderado por Adolf Hitler (pág. 339)

New Deal Franklin Roosevelt's legislative plan to end the Great Depression that included dramatic reforms of government agencies and powers (p. 317)
New Deal (Nuveo Trato) plan legislativo de Franklin Roosevelt para poner fin a la Gran Depresión; incluía profundas reformas en las agencias y poderes del gobierno (pág. 317)

English and Spanish Glossary

new immigrant a term often used for an immigrant who arrived in the United States beginning in the 1880s (p. 172)
nuevo inmigrante término empleado a menudo para referirse a los inmigrantes que llegaron a Estados Unidos a partir de la década de 1880 (pág. 172)

Nineteenth Amendment (1920) a constitutional amendment that gave women the vote (p. 211)
Decimonovena Enmienda (1920) enmienda constitucional que dio a la mujer el derecho al voto (pág. 211)

North American Free Trade Agreement (NAFTA) a treaty that eliminated trade barriers between Canada, the United States, and Mexico (p. 480)
Tratado de Libre Comercio de América del Norte (TLCAN o NAFTA) tratado que eliminó las barreras comerciales entre Canadá, Estados Unidos y México (pág. 480)

North Atlantic Treaty Organization (NATO) an alliance of Western powers (p. 380)
Organización del Tratado del Atlántico Norte (OTAN) alianza de potencias occidentales (pág. 380)

Nuremberg trials the war crimes trials of Nazi leaders (p. 377)
juicios de Nuremberg juicios de los crímenes de guerra de los líderes Nazis (pág. 377)

O

old immigrant a term often used for an immigrant who arrived in the United States before the 1880s (p. 172)
antiguo inmigrante término empleado con frecuencia para referirse a los inmigrantes que llegaron a Estados Unidos antes de la década de 1880 (pág. 172)

Open Door Policy a policy established by the United States in 1899 to promote equal access for all nations to trade in China (p. 230)
política de puertas abiertas política establecida por Estados Unidos en 1899 para promover el acceso igualitario de todas las naciones al comercio con China (pág. 230)

Operation Desert Storm the military effort to free Kuwait from Saddam Hussein's invasion (p. 478)
Operación Tormenta del Desierto acción militar para liberar a Kuwait de la invasión de Saddam Hussein (pág. 478)

Oregon Trail a 2,000-mile trail stretching through the Great Plains from western Missouri to the Oregon Territory (pp. 23, 117)
Camino de Oregón ruta de 2,000 millas que cruzaba las Grandes Planicies desde el oeste de Missouri hasta el Territorio de Oregón (pág. 23, 117)

Organization of Petroleum Exporting Countries (OPEC) an alliance of oil rich countries that coordinates oil policies (p. 459)
Organización de Países Exportadores de Petróleo (OPEP) alianza de países ricos en petróleo que coordina las políticas petroleras (pág. 459)

ozone layer a level of the Earth's atmosphere that is being depleted by pollution (p. 504)
capa de ozono nivel de la atmósfera de la Tierra que se está desgastando debido a la contaminación (pág. 504)

P

Paleo-Indians the first Americans who crossed from Asia into North America sometime between 38,000 and 10,000 BC (p. 6)
paleoindígenas primeros habitantes de América que cruzaron de Asia a América del Norte entre 38,000 y 10,000 a. C. (pág. 6)

Panama Canal an artificial waterway across the Isthmus of Panama; completed by the United States in 1914 (p. 241)
canal de Panamá canal artificial que atraviesa el istmo de Panamá; Estados Unidos completó su construcción en 1914 (pág. 241)

patent an exclusive right to make or sell an invention (p. 153)
patente derecho exclusivo para fabricar o vender un invento (pág. 153)

Patient Protection and Affordable Care Act (PPACA) a law, passed in 2010, that required that health coverage be available to all Americans; it also specified that all individuals were required to get some level of health coverage (p. 499)

Ley de Protección al Paciente y Cuidado de Salud Asequible (PPACA) una ley, aprobada en 2010, que requiere que la cobertura de salud esté disponible para todos los estadounidenses; también especifica que todos los individuos deben tener un cierto nivel de cobertura de salud (pág. 499)

Patriots American colonists who fought for independence from Great Britain during the Revolutionary War (p. 11)
patriotas colonos que lucharon para independizarse de Gran Bretaña durante la Guerra de Independencia estadounidense (pág. 11)

Peace Corps a nonmilitary aid program introduced by John Kennedy (p. 402)
Cuerpos de Paz programa de ayuda no military introducido por John Kennedy (pág. 402)

Pearl Harbor a harbor in Hawaii that serves as the base of the U.S. Pacific fleet and was bombed in 1941 by Japan (p. 343)
Pearl Harbor puerto de Hawai que es la base de la flota del Pacífico de Estados Unidos; fue bombardeado por Japón en 1941 (pág. 343)

Pentagon the headquarters of the U.S. military, located outside of Washington, DC (p. 492)
Pentágono sede central del ejército de Estados Unidos, ubicado en las afueras de Washington, DC (pág. 492)

Pickett's Charge (1863) a failed Confederate attack during the Civil War led by General George Pickett at the Battle of Gettysburg (p. 71)
ataque de Pickett (1863) ataque fallido del ejército confederado, al mando del general George Pickett, en la batalla de Gettysburg durante la Guerra Civil (pág. 71)

Platt Amendment a part of the Cuban constitution drafted under the supervision of the United States that limited Cuba's right to make treaties, gave the U.S. the right to intervene in Cuban affairs, and required Cuba to sell or lease land to the U.S. (p. 236)
Enmienda Platt parte de la constitución cubana redactada bajo la supervisión de Estados Unidos que limitaba el derecho de Cuba a fi rmar tratados, le daba a Estados Unidos el derecho de intervenir en los asuntos cubanos y le exigía a Cuba vender o arrendar tierras a Estados Unidos (pág. 236)

Plessy v. *Ferguson* (1896) U.S. Supreme Court case that established the "separate-but-equal" doctrine for public facilities (p. 101)
Plessy contra *Ferguson* (1896) caso en el que la Corte Suprema de Estados Unidos estableció la doctrina de "separados pero iguales" en los lugares públicos (pág. 101)

political machine a powerful organization that influenced city and county politics in the late 1800s (p. 194)
maquinaria política organización poderosa que influía en la política municipal y del condado a finales del siglo XIX (pág. 194)

poll tax a special tax that a person had to pay in order to vote (p. 101)
impuesto electoral impuesto especial que tenía que pagar una persona para poder votar (pág. 101)

Pony Express a system of messengers that carried mail between relay stations on a route 2,000 miles long in 1860 and 1861 (p. 125)
Pony Express sistema de mensajeros que llevaban el correo entre estaciones de relevo a lo largo de una ruta de 2,000 millas en 1860 y 1861 (pág. 125)

Populist Party a political party formed in 1892 that supported free coinage of silver, work reforms, immigration restrictions, and government ownership of railroads and telegraph and telephone systems (p. 141)
Partido Populista partido político formado en 1892 que apoyaba la libre producción de monedas de plata, reformas laborales y restricciones de la inmigración, además de asignar al gobierno la propiedad de los sistemas ferroviario, telegráfico y telefónico (pág. 141)

Progressives a group of reformers who worked to improve social and political problems in the late 1800s (p. 197)
progresistas grupo de reformistas que trabajaron para resolver problemas sociales y políticos a finales del siglo XIX (pág. 197)

Progressive Party a short-lived political party that attempted to institute social reforms (p. 217)
Partido Progresista partido político de poca duración que intentó establecer reformas sociales (pág. 217)

Pullman strike (1894) a railroad strike that ended when President Grover Cleveland sent in federal troops (p. 164)

huelga de Pullman (1894) huelga del ferrocarril que terminó cuando el presidente Grover Cleveland envió a tropas federales (pág. 164)

Pure Food and Drug Act (1906) a law that set regulatory standards for industries involved in preparing food (p. 216)
Ley de Alimentos y Medicamentos Puros (1906) ley que estableció normas regulatorias para las industrias de preparación de productos alimenticios (pág. 216)

Puritans Protestants who wanted to reform the Church of England (p. 8)
puritanos protestantes que querían reformar la Iglesia anglicana (pág. 8)

R

Radical Republicans members of Congress who felt that southern states needed to make great social changes before they could be readmitted to the Union (p. 92)
republicanos radicales miembros del Congreso convencidos de que los estados del Sur necesitaban hacer grandes cambios sociales antes de volver a ser admitidos en la Unión (pág. 92)

realpolitik a foreign policy in which U.S. interests are put over ethical or principled concerns (p. 460)
realpolitik política exterior según la cual los intereses de Estados Unidos están por encima de los asuntos éticos o de principios (pág. 460)

recall a vote to remove an official from office (p. 199)
destitución votación para sacar a un funcionario de su cargo (pág. 199)

Reconstruction (1865–1877) the period following the Civil War during which the U.S. government worked to reunite the nation and to rebuild the southern states (p. 84)
Reconstrucción (1865–1877) período posterior a la Guerra Civil en el que el gobierno de Estados Unidos trabajó por reunifi car de la nación y reconstruir los estados del Sur (pág. 84)

Reconstruction Acts (1867–1868) the laws that put the southern states under U.S.

military control and required them to draft new constitutions upholding the Fourteenth Amendment (p. 93)
Leyes de Reconstrucción (1867–1868) leyes que declaraban a los estados del Sur territorio sujeto al control militar estadounidense y los obligaban a reformar sus constituciones de manera que defendieran la Decimocuarta Enmienda (pág. 93)

Red Scare a widespread fear of communism and Communists (p. 292)
Terror Rojo miedo ampliamente difundido al comunismo y los comunistas (pág. 292)

referendum a procedure that allows voters to approve or reject a law already proposed or passed by government (p. 200)
referéndum proceso que permite a los votantes aprobar o rechazar una ley previamente propuesta o aprobada por el gobierno (pág. 200)

reparations financial payments by the loser of a war (p. 274)
indemnizaciones compensación económica pagada por el bando que es vencido en la guerra (pág. 274)

reservations federal lands set aside for American Indians (p. 130)
reservas territorios federales reservados para los indígenas norteamericanos (pág. 130)

Roosevelt Corollary (1904) Theodore Roosevelt's addition to the Monroe Doctrine warning nations in the Americas that if they didn't pay their debts, the United States would get involved (p. 244)
Corolario de Roosevelt (1904) agregado del presidente Theodore Roosevelt a la Doctrina Monroe advirtiendo a las naciones de América que si no pagaban sus deudas, el gobierno de Estados Unidos intervendría (pág. 244)

S

sanctions economic restrictions placed on a country in an attempt to change its policy decisions (p. 469)
sanciones restricciones económicas aplicadas a un país en un intento de cambiar sus políticas (pág. 469)

Santa Fe Trail an important trade trail west from Independence, Missouri, to Santa Fe, New Mexico (p. 127)
Camino de Santa Fe importante ruta comercial que va desde Independence, Missouri, hasta Santa Fe, Nuevo México (pág. 127)

Scopes trial a trial in which John Scopes was accused of teaching evolution illegally (p. 295)
juicio de Scopes juicio en el cual John Scopes fue acusado de enseñar ilegalmente la teoría de la evolución (pág. 295)

search-and-destroy missions the strategy used in the Vietnam War in which enemy targets were located and attacked (p. 412)
misiones de búsqueda y destrucción estrategia de localización y ataque de objetivos enemigos usada en la guerra de Vietnam (pág. 412)

Second Battle of Bull Run (1862) a Civil War battle in which the Confederate army forced most of the Union army out of Virginia (p. 49)
segunda batalla de Bull Run (1862) batalla de la Guerra Civil en la que el ejército confederado obligó a gran parte del ejército de la Unión a abandoner Virginia (pág. 49)

Second Industrial Revolution a period of rapid growth in manufacturing and industry in the late 1800s (p. 150)
Segunda Revolución Industrial período de gran crecimiento en la manufactura y en la industria a finales del siglo XIX (pág. 150)

segregation the forced separation of people of different races in public places (p. 101)
segregación separación obligada de personas de diferentes razas en lugares públicos (pág. 101)

Selective Service Act (1917) a law that allowed the president to draft soldiers in times of war (p. 261)
Ley de Servicio Selectivo (1917) ley que permitía al presidente reclutar soldados en épocas de Guerra (pág. 261)

service economy an economy in which most jobs involve providing services instead of producing goods (p. 493)

economía de servicios economía en la cual la mayoría de los trabajos consisten en ofrecer un servicio en lugar de producir bienes (pág. 493)

settlement houses neighborhood centers staffed by professionals and volunteers for education, recreation, and social activities in poor areas (p. 184)
organizaciones de servicio a la comunidad centros comunitarios atendidos por profesionales y voluntarios para ofrecer educación, recreación y actividades sociales en zonas pobres (pág. 184)

Seven Days' Battles (1862) a series of Civil War battles in which Confederate army successes forced the Union army to retreat from Richmond, Virginia, the Confederate capital (p. 49)
batallas de los Siete Días (1862) serie de batallas de la Guerra Civil en las que las victorias del ejército confederado obligaron a las tropas de la Unión a retirarse de Richmond, Virginia, la capital confederada (pág. 49)

Seventeenth Amendment (1913) a constitutional amendment allowing American voters to directly elect U.S. senators (p. 199)
Decimoséptima Enmienda (1913) enmienda constitucional que permite a los votantes estadounidenses elegir directamente a los senadores de Estados Unidos (pág. 199)

sharecropping a system used on southern farms after the Civil War in which farmers worked land owned by someone else in return for a small portion of the crops (p. 102)
cultivo de aparceros sistemausado en las granjas sureñas después de la Guerra Civil en el que los agricultores trabajaban las tierras de otra persona a cambio de una pequeña porción de la cosecha (pág. 102)

Shays's Rebellion (1786–87) an uprising of Massachusetts's farmers, led by Daniel Shays, to protest high taxes, heavy debt, and farm foreclosures (p. 13)
Rebelión de Shays (1786–87) rebelión de agricultores de Massachusetts, encabezados por Daniel Shays, para protestar por los altos impuestos, las grandes deudas y el embargo de las granjas (pág. 13)

English and Spanish Glossary

Sherman Antitrust Act (1890) a law that made it illegal to create monopolies or trusts that restrained free trade (p. 159)
Ley Antimonopolio de Sherman (1890) ley que prohibía la creación de monopolios o consorcios que restringieran el libre comercio (pág. 159)

Siege of Vicksburg (1863) the Union army's six-week blockade of Vicksburg that led the city to surrender during the Civil War (p. 55)
Sitio de Vicksburg (1863) bloqueo de seis semanas realizado por el ejército de la Unión en Vicksburg para forzar la rendición de esa ciudad durante la Guerra Civil (pág. 55)

sit-down strike a strike in which workers stay at their work stations so that strikebreakers cannot replace them (p. 322)
huelga de brazos caídos huelga en la cual los trabajadores permanecen en el lugar de trabajo para que los rompehuelgas no los puedan reemplazar (pág. 322)

sit-in a form of protest in which African Americans sat at segregated lunch counters and requested service (p. 437)
sentada forma de protesta de los afroamericanos; se sentaban en los comedores que practicaban la segregación racial y pedían que les sirvieran (pág. 437)

Sixteenth Amendment (1913) an amendment to the Constitution that allows personal income to be taxed (p. 217)
Decimosexta Enmienda (1913) enmienda constitucional que permite los impuestos sobre los ingresos personales (pág. 217)

social Darwinism a view of society based on Charles Darwin's scientific theory of natural selection (p. 158)
darwinismo social visión de la sociedad basada en la teoría científi ca de la selección natural de Charles Darwin (pág. 158)

socialism economic system in which the government owns and operates a country's means of production (p. 208)
socialismo sistema económico en el que el gobierno controla y maneja los medios de producción de un país (pág. 208)

Social Security a program for providing pension benefits for many Americans aged 65 and older (p. 508)

Seguridad Social un programa para proporcionar prestaciones de jubilación para muchos estadounidenses de 65 años y mayores (pág. 508)

Social Security Act (1935) a law that instituted the pension plan Social Security (p. 321)
Ley del Seguro Social (1935) ley que estableció el plan de pensiones del Seguro Social (pág. 321)

sodbusters the name given to Plains farmers who worked hard to break up the region's tough sod (p. 138)
sodbusters nombre dado a los agricultores de las Planicies que se esforzaron mucho para trabajar el duro terreno de la región (pág. 138)

sphere of influence an area where foreign countries control trade or natural resources of another nation or area (p. 230)
esfera de influencia nación o lugar cuyos recursos naturales y comercio son controlados por otro país (pág. 230)

Sputnik the first artificial satellite, launched by the Soviet Union in 1957 (p. 388)
Sputnik primer satélite artificial, lanzado por la Unión Soviética en 1957 (pág. 388)

stagflation a term describing a slowing economy mixed with high unemployment (p. 459)
estagflación término que describe una economía que disminuye su ritmo, acompañado de un desempleo alto (pág. 459)

stalemate a situation in which neither side can win a victory (p. 256)
punto muerto situación en la cual ninguna de las partes puede alcanzar la victoria (pág. 256)

standard time the system set up by the railroad companies that divided the country into four time zones (p. 128)
hora estándar el sistema establecido por las compañías de ferrocarriles que dividieron al país en cuatro zonas de tiempo (pág. 128)

steerage the area on a ship in the lower levels where the steering mechanisms were located and where cramped quarters were provided for people who could only afford cheap passage (p. 173)
tercera clase nivel inferior un barco en el que se encontraban los mecanismos del timón y se ofrecían habitaciones reducidas para las personas que solo podían comprar un pasaje barato (pág. 173)

Strategic Arms Limitation Talks (SALT) negotiations between the United States and the Soviet Union designed to limit nuclear weapons (p. 460)
Tratados de Limitación de Armas Estratégicas (SALT, por sus siglas en inglés) negociaciones entre Estados Unidos y la Unión Soviética diseñadas para limitar el número de armas nucleares (pág. 460)

Student Nonviolent Coordinating Committee (SNCC) a group organized to promote civil rights for African Americans through nonviolent protests (p. 438)
Comité Coordinador Estudiantil No Violento (SNCC, por sus siglas en inglés) grupo organizado para promover los derechos civiles de los afroamericanos con protestas no violentas (pág. 438)

Students for a Democratic Society (SDS) a group organized to protest U.S. involvement in the Vietnam War (p. 418)
Estudiantes por una Sociedad Democrática (SDS, por sus siglas en inglés) grupo organizado para protestar por la participación de Estados Unidos en la guerra de Vietnam (pág. 418)

suburb a neighborhood outside of a downtown area (p. 180)
suburbio vecindario en las afueras de una ciudad (pág. 180)

Sun Belt the southern area of the United States from Florida to California that experienced an increase in population during the 1970s (p. 390)
Sun Belt área del sur de Estados Unidos, desde Florida hasta California, en la que hubo un aumento de la población durante la década de 1970 (pág. 390)

superpower powerful countries that influence events in their regions of the world (p. 378)
superpotencia países poderosos que influyen en los acontecimientos en sus regiones del mundo (pág. 378)

supply-side economics economic theory that focuses on influencing the supply of labor and goods; it usually involves sharp tax cuts (p. 472)
economía de la oferta teoría económica que pretende influenciar la oferta de mano de obra y de bienes; por lo general, implica grandes reducciones de impuestos (pág. 472)

sweatshops hot, stuffy workshops in which workers prepare materials for low wages (p. 175)
fábricas explotadoras talleres calurosos y con el aire cargado en los cuales los trabajadores preparan materiales por salarios reducidos (pág. 175)

T

talkie a film that includes sound (p. 299)
película sonora película que incluye sonido (pág. 299)

Teapot Dome scandal a scandal under the Harding adminstration in which government offi cials were accused of taking bribes to allow oil to be mined from federal lands (p. 285)
escándalo de Teapot Dome escándalo durante el gobierno de Harding en el que se acusó a funcionarios del gobierno de aceptar sobornos para permitir que se usaran tierras federales para extraer petróleo (pág. 285)

Teller Amendment (1898) a congressional resolution stating that the U.S. had no interest in taking control of Cuba (p. 233)
Enmienda Teller (1898) resolución del Congreso en la que Estados Unidos declaró que no tenía intención de tomar el control de Cuba (pág. 233)

temperance movement a social reform effort begun in the mid-1800s to encourage people to drink less alcohol (p. 27)
movimiento de abstinencia movimiento de reforma social iniciado a mediados del siglo XIX para promover el que las personas bebieran menos alcohol (pág. 27)

Tennessee Valley Authority (TVA) a governmental agency designed to bring jobs and electricity to rural areas of the Tennessee River valley (p. 319)
Autoridad del Valle del Tennessee (TVA, por sus siglas en inglés) agencia del gobierno destinada a proveer empleos y energía eléctrica a las áreas rurales del valle del río Tennessee (pág. 319)

Ten Percent Plan President Abraham Lincoln's plan for Reconstruction; once 10 percent of voters in a former Confederate state took a U.S. loyalty oath, they could form a new state government and be readmitted to the Union (p. 85)

Plan del Diez por Ciento plan de Reconstrucción del presidente Abraham Lincoln; si el 10 por ciento de los votantes de un estado que había sido confederado juraba lealtad a la nación, podían formar un Nuevo gobierno y ser readmitidos en la Unión (pág. 85)

terrorism the systematic use of fear or terror to gain goals (p. 482)
terrorismo uso sistemático del miedo o el terror para alcanzar objetivos (pág. 482)

Tet Offensive (1968) a series of attacks by Vietcong forces that proved to many Americans the Vietnam War was not being won (p. 413)
ofensiva del Tet (1968) serie de ataques de las fuerzas del Vietcong que demostró a muchos estadounidenses que no estaban ganando la Guerra de Vietnam (pág. 413)

Thirteenth Amendment (1865) a constitutional amendment that outlawed slavery (p. 85)
Decimotercera Enmienda (1865) enmienda constitucional que prohibió la esclavitud (pág. 85)

38th Parallel the boundary between North and South Korea before the Korean War (p. 384)
paralelo 38 límite entre Corea del Sur Corea del Norte antes de la Guerra de Corea (pág. 384)

Three-Fifths Compromise (1787) an agreement worked out at the Constitutional Convention stating that only three-fifths of the slaves in a state would count when determining a state's population for representation in the lower house of Congress (pp. 13)
Compromiso de las Tres Quintas Partes (1787) acuerdo negociado durante la Convención Constitucional en el que se estableció que solamente tres quintas de los esclavos en un estado contarían para al determiner la representación de ese estado en la cámara baja del Congreso (pág. 13)

Tonkin Gulf Resolution (1964) gave President Johnson the power to send combat troops to Vietnam (p. 410)
Resolución del Golfo de Tonkin (1964) otorgó al presidente Johnson la autoridad de enviar tropas de combate a Vietnam (pág. 410)

totalitarianism a form of government in which every aspect of citizens' lives are controlled by the government (p. 338)

totalitarismo forma de gobierno en la cual todos los aspectos de la vida de los ciudadanos están bajo el control del gobierno (pág. 338)

total war a type of war in which an army destroys its opponent's ability to fight by targeting civilian and economic as well as military resources (p. 74)
guerra total tipo de guerra en la que un ejército destruye la capacidad de lucha de su oponente mediante ataques a la población civil y a la economía así como a los recursos militares (pág. 74)

Trail of Tears (1838–39) an 800-mile forced march made by the Cherokee from their homeland in Georgia to Indian Territory; resulted in the deaths of almost one-fourth of the Cherokee people (p. 22)
Ruta de las Lágrimas (1838–39) marcha forzada de 800 millas que hicieron los cheroquíes desde su territorio natal en Georgia hasta el Territorio Indígena, y en la que perdió la vida casi una cuarta parte del pueblo cheroquí (pág. 22)

transcontinental railroad a railroad system that crossed the continental United States; construction began in 1863 (p. 126)
tren transcontinental línea que cruzaba Estados Unidos de un extremo a otro; su construcción se inició en 1863 (pág. 126)

Treaty of Fort Laramie (1851) a treaty signed in Wyoming by the United States and northern Plains nations (p. 130)
Tratado del Fuerte Laramie (1851) tratado firmado en Wyoming por Estados Unidos y las naciones indígenas de las Planicies del norte (pág. 130)

Treaty of Medicine Lodge (1867) an agreement between the U.S. government and southern Plains Indians in which the Indians agreed to move onto reservations (p. 131)
Tratado de Medicine Lodge (1867) acuerdo entre el gobierno de Estados Unidos y los indígenas de las Planicies del sur en el que los indígenas aceptaron irse a las reservas (pág. 131)

Treaty of Paris of 1783 a peace agreement that officially ended the Revolutionary War and established British recognition of the independence of the United States (p. 11)
Tratado de París de 1783 acuerdo de paz que oficialmente dio por terminada la Guerra

de Independencia estadounidense y en el que Gran Bretaña reconocía la independencia de Estados Unidos (pág. 11)

Treaty of Versailles (1919) brought an end to World War I, but was never ratified by the United States (p. 275)
Tratado de Versalles (1919) puso fin a la Primera Guerra Mundial, pero Estados Unidos nunca lo ratificó (pág. 275)

trench warfare a new kind of warfare in World War I that involved troops digging and fighting from deep trenches (p. 256)
guerra de trincheras nuevo tipo de guerra utilizado en la Primera Guerra Mundial en el cual las tropas cavaban trincheras profundas y luchaban desde ellas (pág. 256)

Triangle Shirtwaist Fire a factory fire that killed 146 workers trapped in the building; led to new safety standard laws (p. 207)
incendio de Triangle Shirtwaist incendio de una fábrica en el que murieron 146 trabajadores atrapados en el edificio; este suceso obligó a crear nuevas leyes de seguridad (pág. 207)

Truman Doctrine a policy attempting to contain the spread of communism, beginning with military aid to the monarchies of Turkey and Greece (p. 379)
Doctrina Truman política que intentaba contener el avance del comunismo, ofreciendo inicialmente ayuda militar a las monarquías de Turquía y Grecia (pág. 379)

trust a number of companies legally grouped under a single board of directors (p. 158)
consorcio varias compañías agrupadas legalmente bajo el mando de una sola junta directiva (pág. 158)

Tuskegee Airmen a group of African American pilots who flew missions in World War I; they were the first African American military pilots (p. 347)
Aviadores de Tuskegee grupo de pilotos afroamericanos que volaron en misiones de la Primera Guerra Mundial; fueron los primeros pilotos afroamericanos del ejército (pág. 347)

Twenty-First Amendment (1933) an amendment to the Constitution that ended Prohibition (p. 294)

Vigésimoprimera Enmienda (1933) enmienda constitucional que puso fin a la Ley Seca (pág. 294)

Twenty-Sixth Amendment (1971) an amendment to the Constitution that lowered the voting age to 18 (p. 421)
Vigésimosexta Enmienda (1971) enmienda constitucional que redujo la edad mínima para votar a 18 años (pág. 421)

U

U-boats German submarines or "untersee boats" (p. 258)
U-boats submarinos alemanes o "barcos untersee" (pág. 258)

United Farm Workers a group organized to promote the interests of migrant farm workers, it eventually led to the Chicano movement (p. 447)
Trabajadores Agrícolas Unidos grupo organizado para promover los intereses de los trabajadores agrícolas migratorios; con el tiempo, dio origen al movimiento chicano (pág. 447)

United Nations an alliance of nations that attempts to end disputes between countries peacefully (p. 377)
Naciones Unidas alianza de naciones que intent resolver de manera pacífica las disputas entre los países (pág. 377)

urban renewal a governmental program that attempted to rid innercities of slums and replace them with lowand middle-income housing (p. 392)
renovación urbana programa gubernamental que intentó eliminar las barriadas de los centros urbanos y reemplazarlos con viviendas para personas de recursos bajos y medios (pág. 392)

USA PATRIOT Act (2001) a law that makes it easier for federal law enforcement agencies to collect information on suspected terrorists (p. 496)
Ley Patriota de EE.UU (2001) una ley que le facilita a las agencias federales recolectar información sobre los terroristas sospechosos (pág. 496)

English and Spanish Glossary

V

vertical integration the business practice of owning all of the businesses involved in each step of a manufacturing process (p. 157)
integración vertical práctica empresarial de poseer todas las empresas que participan en cada paso de un proceso de manufactura (pág. 157)

Vietcong the South Vietnam forces that were supported by North Vietnamese Communists (p. 408)
Vietcong fuerzas de Vietnam del Sur apoyadas por los comunistas de Vietnam del Norte (pág. 408)

Vietnamization a policy introduced in an attempt to leave the Vietnam War, in which Vietnamese forces would take over the fighting (p. 420)
vietnamización política introducida en un intento de salir de la guerra de Vietnam, según la cual las fuerzas vietnamitas se harían cargo de la lucha (pág. 420)

Vietnam Veterans Memorial a war memorial in Washington, DC, dedicated to the veterans of Vietnam (p. 423)
Monumento a los Veteranos de Vietnam monument conmemorativo de la guerra en Washington, DC dedicado a los veteranos de Vietnam (pág. 423)

Voting Rights Act of 1965 provided new powers to the federal government to protect African Americans' voting rights (p. 443)
Ley de Derecho al Voto de 1965 dio nueva autoridad al gobierno federal para proteger el derecho al voto de los afroamericanos (pág. 443)

W

War Powers Act (1973) a law that requires a president to get Congressional approval before sending troops into combat (p. 423)
Ley de Poderes de Guerra (1973) ley que requiere la aprobación del Congreso para que el presidente pueda enviar tropas a la guerra (pág. 423)

War Production Board a government agency set up to oversee production of war materials during World War II (p. 345)
Junta de Producción de Guerra agencia creada por el gobierno para supervisar la producción de materiales de guerra durante la Segunda Guerra Mundial (pág. 345)

Warren Court a Supreme Court headed by Chief Justice Earl Warren that issued many rulings that extended individual rights and freedoms (p. 449)
Corte Warren Corte Suprema presidida por el Magistrado Earl Warren que emitió muchas resoluciones que extendían los derechos y las libertades individuales (pág. 449)

Watergate a scandal in which President Nixon resigned over accusations of illegal activity (p. 461)
Watergate escándalo que provocó la renuncia del presidente Nixon por acusaciones de actividades ilegales (pág. 461)

weapons of mass destruction chemical, biological, or nuclear weapons that can kill thousands (p. 492)
armas de destrucción masiva armas químicas, biológicas o nucleares que pueden matar a miles de personas (pág. 492)

Wilderness Campaign (1864) a series of battles between Union and Confederate forces in northern and central Virginia that delayed the Union capture of Richmond (p. 73)
Campaña de Wilderness (1864) serie de batallas entre la Unión y los confederados en el norte y el centro de Virginia que retrasaron la captura de Richmond por parte de la Unión (pág. 73)

workers' compensation laws laws that guarantee a portion of lost wages to workers who are injured on the job (p. 207)
leyes de compensación laboral leyes que garantizan una parte de los salarios caídos a los trabajadores que se lesionan en el trabajo (pág. 207)

World Trade Center a building complex in New York City that was destroyed by a terrorist attack on September 11, 2001
Las Torres Gemelas unos rascacielos en la Ciudad de Nueva York que fueron destruidos por un acto terrorista el 11 de septiembre, 2001

Y

Yalta Conference a meeting between the leaders of the Allied powers that resulted in a plan for peace after World War II (p. 376)
Conferencia de Yalta reunión de los líderes de las fuerzas aliadas que produjo un plan de paz después de la Segunda Guerra Mundial (pág. 376)

yellow journalism the reporting of exaggerated stories in newspapers to increase sales (p. 232)
prensa amarillista publicación de noticias exageradas en los periódicos para aumentar las ventas (pág. 232)

Z

Zimmermann note a telegram from Germany to Mexico offering Mexico a return of territory in exchange for declaring war on the United States (p. 260)
telegrama Zimmermann telegrama de Alemania a México en el cual se ofrecía a México una devolución de territorios si le declaraba la guerra a Estados Unidos (pág. 260)

zoot-suit riots a series of riots during which Mexican Americans were attacked by whites (p. 348)
disturbios *zoot-suit* serie de disturbios durante los cuales personas de raza blanca atacaron a mexicanoamericanos (pág. 348)

Index

Index

Index

Index

life, 184–186; mass culture, 180–181; mass transit, 179–180; Mexican, 214; neighborhoods of, 173–175; 1900 to 1920, 239p; opposition to, 176–177; quotas on, 292–293; skyscraper building, 179; timeline for 1870 to 1910, 169; in twenty-first century, 506–507, 510c, 510m–511m; urban growth in 1900, 178–179; urban problems, 182–184; work of, 175–176; World War I and, 262

impeachment: of Andrew Johnson, 81, 94–95; of Bill Clinton, 481; of Richard Nixon, 463

imperialism, 226–227, 238m

implementation: of assembly line, 154; of government programs, 314; of school desegregation, 433

implications of Geraldine Ferraro nomination, 474

incentives, 285

Inca, 6, 7. *See also* Native Americans

indentured servants, in English colonies, 8, 9

Indian Citizenship Act, 297

Indian Citizenship Act of 1968, 297

Indian Civil Rights Act of 1968, 449

Indian National Congress of 1885, 223p

Indian Removal Act (1830), 22. *See also* Trail of Tears

Indian reservations, 130, 134–135

Indians, Plains, 129–133; *See* Native Americans

Indian treaties, individuals, rights for, 449–450. *See also* Bill of Rights

industrial age, 146–167; big business dominance, 156–159; cost-and-benefit analysis, 165; Second Industrial Revolution, 150–155; timeline for 1870 to 1900, 147; workers in, 160–164

Industrial Workers of the World (IWW), 208

industrialization, in the North, 24f; interchangeable parts, 24; mass production, 24; steam power, 24; steamboats, 24; steam-power trains, 24; telegraph, 24

influence, spheres of, 230

Influence of Sea Power upon History, The (Mahan), 227

influenza epidemic, after World War I, 272–273

information, identifying, 82

Information Revolution, 502–503

initiatives, 200

innovation, 52, 300

Inouye, Daniel, 350

interchangeable parts, 24, 154. *See also* Whitney, Eli; Industrialization

Intermediate-Rand Nuclear Forces (INF) Treaty, 474f, 476

International Ladies Garment Workers Union (ILGWU), 207

International Military Tribunal, 377

International Space Station (ISS), 506

Internet, 502–503

internment of Japanese Americans in World War II, 349p, 349–350

interstate commerce: Interstate Commerce Act of 1887, 140; Interstate Commerce Commission, 140

inventions: airplane, 152f; automobile, 152f; barbed wire, 125; Bessemer steel making process, 152f; 153–154, 393; dam and reservoir construction, 152f; Edison's "invention factory" in Menlo Park, 152–153; elevator safety brake, 152f; Ferris wheel, 152f; ice cream cones, 181; Internet, 502–503; lightbulbs, 147, 152f; Linotype, 180; machine engine oiling, 152f; at Paris Exposition of

1900, 239f; sonar, 351–352; telegraph, 125; telephone, 152f, 153; *See also* technology

investing in corporations, 156–157, 157p

Invisible Man (Ellison), 394

Iran-Contra affair (1986), 476

Iran hostage crisis (1981), 455p, 470p, 470–471

Iraq, war in, 492–493, 497

ironclad warships, in Civil War, 52, 59f

iron curtain, 379

Iron Triangle assault, in Vietnam War, 398p

Irving, Washington, 19

Islamic State (ISIS) terrorist group, 500

island hopping strategy, in World War II, 359

isolationism, in U.S., 226

Israel, 373p, 378

ISS (International Space Station), 506

Italy: immigrants from, 173–174, 174p; totalitarianism in, 338; in World War II, 341, 352–353

Iwo Jima, battle of, 361p, 361–362

IWW (Industrial Workers of the World), 208

J

Jackson, Andrew, 20, 21f, 22

Jackson, Helen Hunt, 135

Jackson, Robert H., 377

Jackson, Thomas "Stonewall," 48–49, 69

Jacksonian Democracy, 20. *See also* Jackson, Andrew

Jamestown, 3, 8, *See also* Virginia

Japan: atomic bomb and, 366p, 366–367; Meiji Restoration in, 223; Pearl Harbor attacked by (1941), 343m, 343–344, 344p; totalitarianism in, 340; U.S. trade with, 229–230; World War II in Pacific against, 357–362

Japanese Americans, internment of in World War II, 349p, 349–350

Index

Index

Index

Index

Index

in, 226–227; influence of, 238*m*–239*m*; Japan, trade with, 229–230; Latin America policy, 243–244; Panama Canal, 240–242; Spanish American War, 232–237; timeline for 1867 to 1920, 223

United States* v. *Nixon (1974), 462*f*

urban areas: decay of, 467; reform of services in, 198; renewal of, 392

Urban League, 213

USA PATRIOT Act of 2001, 496

U.S. Capitol grounds, 181

U.S. Census Bureau, 142, 506–507

U.S. Department of Agriculture, 140

U.S. Department of Defense, 502

U.S. Department of Homeland Security, 487, 496

U.S. Department of Housing and Urban Development (HUD), 444

U.S. Environmental Protection Agency (EPA), 467

U.S. Forest Service, 216–217

U.S. Sanitary Commission, 45

USS *Maine* (warship), 233, 233*p*

USS *Monitor* Center, 52

U.S. Supreme Court: *Brown* v. *Board of Education* (1954), 429*p*, 433, 434*f*; *Bush* v. *Gore election of 2000,* 491; child labor laws and, 204; Civil Rights Act of 1875 declared unconstitutional by, 101; election of 1876 decided by, 100; *Escobedo* v. *Illinois* (1964), 449; *Guinn* v. *United States* (1915), 213; *Korematsu* v. *United States* (1944), 349; *Lochner* v. *New York* (1897), 207; *Miranda* v. *Arizona* (1966), 449; *Muller* v. *Oregon* (1908), 207; National Industrial Recovery Act (NIRA) declared unconstitutional by, 321; New Deal programs declared unconstitutional by, 323; Nixon and, 458; O'Connor, Sandra Day as

first woman on, 473*f*; *Plessy* v. *Ferguson* (1896), 101–102, 433, 434*f*; on railroad regulation, 140; *Roe* v. *Wade* (1973), 465; *Schenck* v. *United States* (1919), 262*f*; on Second Amendment, 500–501; segregation on public transportation ruled illegal by, 436, 440; *Tinker* v. *Des Moines Independent Community School District* (1969), 449; *United States* v. *Nixon* (1974), 462*f*;

V

Vallandigham, Clement L., 65

Valley Forge, 10

values, rejection of traditional, 418

Van Vorst, Marie, 203

Vanzetti, Bartolomeo, 292, 292*p*

vaqueros (Mexican cowboys), 124

Vassar College, 209

Vegh, Moritz, 365

Veiller, Lawrence, 184

Verdun, battle of, in World War I, 257

Versailles Treaty (World War I), 251, 275–276

vertical integration, in steel industry, 157

Vicksburg, siege of, in Civil War, 55–56, 58*m*–59*m*

Vietcong, 407

Vietnamization strategy, 420

Vietnam Veterans Memorial, 423–424, 424*p*

Vietnam War years, 398–427; antiwar protests, 418–419; conflict in, 406–409; election of 1968, 419–420; hawks and doves in, 413–415; Johnson commitment, 410–411; Kennedy and communism, 402–406; in 1968, 414*m*; Nixon and, 420–421; oral history, 425; Tet Offensive, 413; timeline for 1960 to 1975, 399; U.S. soldiers in, 407*p*, 411–413; Vietcong tunnels, 416*p*–417*p*; Vietnam War end, 399*p*, 421–424

Villa, Francisco "Pancho," 246

Virginia Statute for Religious Freedom (1786), 16

Virginia: slave rebellion in, 3; colonies in, 8; Civil War in, 47–50, 48*m. See also* colonies

visualization, understanding through, 374

visual resources skills, 277

Volstead Act, 293

voting rights: 27, of African Americans, 95*p*, 101–102; to 18-year-olds in Twenty-sixth Amendment to Constitution, 421; expansion of, 199–200; to women in Nineteenth Amendment to Constitution, 103–104, 209–211

Voting Rights Act of 1965, 443

Voting Rights Act of 1975, 447

W

WAAC (Women's Auxiliary Army Corps), 346

Wade, Benjamin, 85, 95

Wade-Davis bill, 85

wage earners, 178

Wagner, Robert F., 322

Wagner Act (National Labor Relations Act), 322

wagon trains, 108*p. See also* westward expansion

Wallace, George, 420

War Industries Board (WIB), 261

War Powers Act of 1973, 423

War Production Board (WPB), in World War II, 345

Warren, Earl, 449

Warsaw Pact of 1955, 373, 380

Washington and Lee University, 49*f*

Washington, Booker T., 211, 212*f*

Washington, DC: in *Brown* v. *Board of Education* (1954), 433; Civil War isolation of, 42; "Hooverville" in (1932), 314; Lincoln assassinated in, 88; September 11, 2001 attacks on, 492; Vietnam Veterans Memorial in, 423*f*; Watergate scandal in, 461

Index

For permission to reproduce copyrighted material, grateful acknowledgment is made to the following sources:

Excerpt from *The Grapes of Wrath* by John Steinbeck. Text copyright 1939 and renewed © 1967 by John Steinbeck. Reprinted by permission of Viking Penguin, a division of Penguin Group (USA) Inc., and Penguin Books Ltd.

Excerpt from *Night* by Elie Wiesel. Text copyright © 1972, 1985 by Elie Wiesel. English translation copyright © 2006 by Marion Wiesel. Originally published as *La Nuit* by Les Editions de Minuit. Text copyright © 1958 by Les Editions de Minuit. Reprinted by permission of Farrar Straus and Giroux, Georges Borchardt, Inc. for Les Editions de Minuit and Recorded Books.

Excerpt from "Now I Lay Me Down to Sleep" by Diana Dwan Poole, from *Chicken Soup for the Veteran's Soul* by Jack Canfield, Mark Victor Hansen, and Sidney R. Slagter. Copyright © by Diana Dwan Poole. Reprinted by permission of The Permissions Company.

Excerpt from "Interview with Todd B. Walton" from The Library of Congress *Veterans History Project*. Reprinted by permission of the Library of Congress.

 Art and Photography Credits

Video reference screens © 2010 A&E Television Networks, LLC. All rights reserved.

Cover: *Cannon* Malcolm MacGregor/Getty Images; *paper texture* Tolga Tezcan/Getty Images

Front Matter: *Transcontinental railroad* ©Bettmann/Corbis; *Migrant Mother photograph* Library of Congress Prints and Photographs Division, Washington, D.C. [LC-DIG-fsa-8b29516]; *Dust Bowl* NOAA George E. Marsh Album; *crowd holding American flags* ©Moodboard/Superstock.

Prologue: *Signing the Declaration of Independence* ©Bettmann/Corbis; *Tax Stamp Act 1765* ©Everett Collection Inc./Superstock; *Declaration of Independence* The Granger Collection, NYC; *Christopher Columbus* by Sebastiano del Piombo (1485–1547 Italian), Metropolitan Museum of Art, New York City/Superstock, Inc.; *The Trail of Tears* by Robert Ottokar Lindneux (1871–1970 American), Woolaroc Museum, Bartlesville, Oklahoma, USA/Superstock; *Boston Massacre engraving* Peter Newark's American Pictures; *John Rutledge* ©North Wind Picture Archives/Alamy; *Gouverneur Morris* ©Bridgeman Images; *George Washington* ©Museum of the City of New York/Corbis; *first cabinet* The Granger Collection, NYC; *Mayflower reconstruction* ©Bettmann/Corbis; *Thomas Jefferson* ©Bettmann/Corbis; *U.S. Constitution* National Archives (London); *signing Magna Carta* ©Bettmann/Corbis; *King William & Queen Mary* ©Michael Nicholson/Corbis; *John Locke* ©Archivo Iconografico, S.A./Corbis; *John Adams* ©RMN-Grand Palais/Art Resource, NY; *Thomas Jefferson* Stock Montage/Getty Images; *Eli Whitney* ©The Picture Art Collection/Alamy; *block-making machine* Library of Congress Prints and Photographs Division, Washington, D.C. [LC-USZ62-110389]; *transformer manufacturing* Library of Congress Prints and Photographs Division, Washington, D.C. [LC-use6-d-002859]; *steamboats at dock* Library of Congress Prints and Photographs Division, Washington, D.C. [LC-D401-19395]; *cotton gin* ©Bettmann/Corbis; *slave cabins* Library of Congress Prints and Photographs Division, Washington D.C. [LC-USZ62-16178]; *Frederick Douglass* ©Corbis; *Sojourner Truth* Courtesy of the Massachusetts Historical Society; *Family Temperance Pledge* Getty Images; *Henry Clay addressing U.S. Senate* Picture Research Consultants, Inc.; *Abraham Lincoln* Library of Congress Prints and Photographs Division, Washington, D.C. [LC-DIG-ppmsca-19204].

Module 1: *Drum corps* National Museum of American History, Smithsonian Institution Photographic Service; *Emancipation Proclamation* ©Superstock; *Archduke Maximilian* ©Hulton-Deutsch Collection/Corbis; *surrender at Appomattox* ©Superstock; *Pennsylvania Sharp Shooters poster* ©Don Troiani/Corbis; *Stonewall Jackson, Bull Run, Aug. 17, 1861* Library of Congress Prints and Photographs Division, Washington, D.C. [LC-USZC2-1784]; *Antietam Battlefield* Courtesy of the National Park Service; *Scott's Great Snake* Library of Congress Geography and Map Division, Washington, D.C. [Digital ID # g3701 scw0011000]; *Vicksburg* ©North Wind Picture Archives/Alamy; *ironclad* Naval Historical Center; *Company E, 4th U.S. Colored Infantry* Library of Congress, Prints and Photographs Division, Washington, D.C. [LC-DIG-cwpb-04294]; *recruitment poster* ©History and Art Collection/Alamy; *Copperheads political cartoon* Library of Congress Prints and Photographs Division, Washington, D.C. [LC-USZ62-132934]; *infantry family* ©Bettmann/Corbis; *Clara Barton* ©Niday Picture Library/Alamy; *Lincoln at Gettysburg* Library of Congress Prints and Photographs Division, Washington, D.C. [LC-DIG-ppmsca-19926]; *Copperheads cartoon* The Granger Collection, NYC; *Lincoln cartoon* ©Hulton Archive/Getty Images.

Module 2: *Charleston ruins* Still Picture Records Section, Special Media Archives Services Division (NWCS-S), National Archives [111-B-744]; *Lincoln assassination* ©Getty Images; *Johnson impeachment ticket* The Granger Collection, NYC; *Hiram Revels* ©Pictorial Press Ltd/Alamy; *Suez Canal* ©Michael Maslan Historic Photographs/Corbis; *Richmond refugees* Library of Congress Prints and Photographs Division, Washington, D.C. [LC-B817-7617]; *African American couple* ©Corbis Historical/Getty Images; *Freedmen's Bureau school* ©Corbis; *Andrew Johnson* Library of Congress Prints and Photographs Division, Washington, D.C. [LC-BH83-171]; *Thaddeus Stevens* ©Corbis; *first vote illustration* ©North Wind Picture Archives—All rights reserved; *Ku Klux Klan member* ©Bettmann/Corbis; *visit from Ku Klux Klan* The Granger Collection, NYC; *For the Sunny South* Library of Congress Prints and Photographs Division, Washington, D.C. [LC-USZC2-1058]; *Henry Grady* ©Bettmann/Corbis; *Atlanta, Georgia 1887* ©Sarin Images/Granger.

Module 3: *Wagon train* ©James L. Amos/Corbis; *sunrise over mountain* ©Alan Majchrowicz/Getty Images; *Toussaint L'Ouverture* The Granger Collection, NYC; *transcontinental railroad marker* Southern Pacific Lines/Courtesy of Picture Research Consultants, Inc.; *Sitting Bull* ©Corbis; *Commodore Perry* Library of Congress Prints and Photographs Division, Washington, D.C. [LC-USZC4-1307]; *Louis Pasteur* ©Gianni Dagli Orti/Shutterstock; *Orient Express poster* The Granger Collection, NYC; *Jim Beckwourth* ©Bettmann/Corbis; *Mormon trek* Used by permission, Utah State Historical Society; *Pacific Ocean seacoast* ©Joseph Sohm-Visions of America/Corbis; *American trapper* ©Bettmann/Getty Images; *Daniel Boone Escorting Pioneers, 1775* George Caleb Bingham (1811–1879/American) Washington University Gallery of Art, St. Louis, Missouri, USA ©SuperStock; *Mississippi River* ©Ron Chapple Stock/Alamy Images; *hydraulic mining* The Granger Collection, NYC; *California cornucopia* ©Collection of the New-York Historical Society, USA/The Bridgeman Art Library; *Nat Love* Library of Congress Prints and Photographs Division, Washington D.C. [LC-USZ62-46841]; *Wyatt Earp* ©Bettmann/Corbis; *Pony Express stamp* ©Science History Images/Alamy; *transcontinental railroad* ©Bettmann/Corbis; *Buffalo Hunt* by Charles Ferdinand Wimar, photo ©Superstock; *Retreat of Reno's Command* ©The Stapleton Collection/Corbis; *Battle of Little Big Horn, Custer's Last Stand,* Lithograph by Kurz & Allison, 1899. ©Bettmann/Getty Images; *Geronimo* Christie's Images/Corbis; *Sarah Winnemucca* The Granger Collection, NYC; *sod house family* Western History Collections, University of Oklahoma; *African American family* The Granger Collection, NYC; *Laura Ingalls Wilder* The Granger Collection, NYC; *Farmer's Alliance songbook* Elias Carr Papers, East Carolina Manuscript Collection; *Guthrie, Oklahoma* ©Corbis.

Module 4: *Cable cars in San Francisco* Picture Research Consultants, Inc.; *Alexander Graham Bell* ©Bettmann/Corbis; *AFL lapel pin* George Meany Memorial Archives; *Eiffel Tower* ©Bettmann/Corbis; *Pierre and Marie Curie* Archives Larousse, Paris, France/Bridgeman Art Library; *steel mill* Library of Congress Prints and Photographs Division, Washington, D.C. [LC-D401-10924LC]; *Duryea car* ©Hulton Archive/Getty Images; *Wright brothers* Library of Congress Prints and Photographs Division, Washington,

D.C. [LC-USZ62-6166-A]; *John Patterson* Montgomery County Historical Society; *Richmond, California, plant* ©Corbis; *Standard Oil certificate* ©INTERFOTO/Alamy; *Rockefeller cartoon* ©Snark/Art Resource, NY; *New York City sweatshop* ©Hulton Deutsch/Corbis Historical/Getty Images; *Pullman strike* ©North Wind Picture Archives.

Module 5: *Immigrants arrive on Ellis Island* ©Bettmann/Corbis; *Statue of Liberty* ©Joseph Sohm/Visions of America/Corbis; *Ferris wheel* ©Corbis; *Nobel Prize* ©Ted Spiegel/Corbis; *Italian immigrants* ©Everett Historical/Shutterstock; *Mexican immigrants* Shades of L.A. Archives/Los Angeles Public Library; *Swedish immigrants* Col. Ernest Swanson Papers, Swenson Swedish Immigration Research Center, Augustana College, Rock Island, IL; *Asian immigrants* National Archives, #90-G-152-2038; *Italian immigrants* ©Corbis; *Vietnamese American celebration* ©A. Ramey/PhotoEdit; *Chicago* ©Chronicle/Alamy; *map of Central Park* ©Collection of The New-York Historical Society; *Central Park* ©David Ball/Corbis; *tenement building* The Granger Collection, NYC; *Hull House children* ©Wallace Kirkland/Getty Images.

Module 6: *Suffrage parade* ©Bettmann/Corbis; *James Garfield pitcher* Collection of Janice L. and David J. Frent; *Titanic poster* The Granger Collection, NYC; *women voting* Library of Congress Prints and Photographs Division, Washington, D.C. [LC-USZ62-75334]; *Boss Tweed cartoon* The Granger Collection, NYC; *Gilded Age Presidents (all)* Picture Research Consultants, Inc.; *NYC sweatshop* ©Bettmann/Corbis; *Jacob Riis* Library of Congress Prints and Photographs Division, Washington, D.C. [LC-USZ62-5511]; *The Jungle* Library of Congress Prints and Photographs Division, Washington, D.C. [LC-DIG-ppmsca-13488]; *child laborers* Library of Congress Prints and Photographs Division, Washington, D.C. [LC-DIG-nclc-01441]; *Triangle Shirtwaist Fire* ©Science History Images/Alamy; *bakery workers* ©ullstein bild/Getty Images; *suffragette protest* ©Bettmann/Getty Images; *Niagara Movement* Library of Congress Prints and Photographs Division, Washington, D.C. [LC-DIG-ppmsca-37818]; *Theodore Roosevelt and John Muir* ©Bettmann/Corbis.

Module 7: *Panama Canal* ©Danny Lehman/Corbis; *Denali National Park* ©Charles Sleicher/AG Pix; *Indian National Congress* ©The Picture Art Collection/Alamy; *buffalo soldier* Denver Public Library, Western History Collection; *Queen Liliuokalani* ©Douglas Peebles/Corbis; *Perry arrives in Japan* National Portrait Gallery, Smithsonian Institution/Art Resource, NY; *Boxer Rebellion* Trustees of The British Library; *New York World newspaper* ©Bettmann/Corbis; *sunken USS Maine* ©Bettmann/Corbis; *Maine explosion* Picture Research Consultants, Inc.; *Battle of San Juan Hill* Library of Congress Prints and Photographs Division, Washington, D.C. [LC-DIG-pga-01889]; *Capture of*

Emilio Aguinaldo The Print Collector/Getty Images; *U.S. Marines in China* ©Bettmann/Corbis; *William Jennings Bryan* ©Bettmann/Corbis; *immigrants arriving in New York City* ©Bettmann/Corbis; *Paris Exposition* ©Bettmann/Corbis; *Gatun Locks* Library of Congress Prints and Photographs Division, Washington, D.C. [Digital ID# pan6a24297]; *Big Stick cartoon* The Granger Collection, NYC; *Pancho Villa* Library of Congress Prints and Photographs Division, Washington, D.C. [LC-DIGggbain-15609].

Module 8: *Soldiers in trench* ©Bettmann/Corbis; *Uncle Sam recruitment poster* Library of Congress Prints and Photographs Division, Washington, D.C. [LC-USZC4-3859]; *Lusitania poster* ©Everett Collection, Inc./Alamy; *gas mask* Collection of Colonel Stuart S. Corning/Courtesy of Picture Research Consultants, Inc.; *Archduke Francis Ferdinand assassination* The Granger Collection, NYC; *British machine gun* ©Universal History Archive/Getty Images; *German U-boat* ©Corbis; *Lusitania sinks* ©SuperStock; *Supreme Court* ©Jurgen Vogt/The Image Bank/Getty Images; *Red Cross volunteers* ©Underwood & Underwood/Corbis; *Teamwork Wins poster* ©K.J.Historical/Corbis; *soldier and gas mask* Houghton Mifflin Harcourt; *Harlem Hellfighters* ©Hulton Archive/Getty Images; *Somme, France, cemetery* ©Michael St. Maur Sheil/Corbis; *War Garden Commission poster* Library of Congress Prints and Photographs Division, Washington, D.C. [LC-USZC4-10671]; *U.S. Bonds poster* Library of Congress Prints and Photographs Division, Washington, D.C. [LC-USZC4-9850].

Module 9: *The Great White Way*, Times Square, 1925 (oil on canvas), Thain, Howard A. (1891–1959)/©Collection of the New-York Historical Society, USA/Bridgeman Images; *Harding campaign button* ©Lance Schriner/Houghton Mifflin Harcourt; *King Tut sarcophagus* ©Egyptian National Museum, Cairo, Egypt/SuperStock; *The Sun Also Rises* The Granger Collection, NYC; *Emperor Hirohito* ©Bettmann/Corbis; *Empire State Building* ©Photo 12/Alamy; *Model T assembly line* ©Bettmann/Getty Images; *Model T* ©Science & Society Picture Library/Getty Images; *Herbert Hoover and Al Smith campaign posters* Janice L. and David J. Frent Collection of Political Americana; *women's college ceremony* Library of Congress Prints and Photographs Division, Washington, D.C. [LC-USZ62-133870]; *Bessie Coleman* ©Bettmann/Corbis; *Life Magazine cover* The Granger Collection, NYC; *Sacco and Vanzetti protest* Library of Congress Prints and Photographs Division, Washington, D.C. [LC-USZ62-136881]; *prohibitionist destroying barrel* ©Bettmann/Corbis; *Jacob Lawrence painting* The Phillips Collection, Washington, D.C.; *Charles Lindbergh* ©New York Daily News Archive/Getty Images; *baseball team* ©NewsCom; *Babe Ruth* ©Bettmann/Corbis; *Louis Armstrong* ©Hulton Archive/Getty Images; *Georgia O'Keeffe* ©Georgia O'Keeffe Museum, Santa Fe/Art Resource.

Module 10: *Car for sale* ©Bettmann/Corbis; *Variety front page* The Granger Collection, NYC; *Roosevelt campaign button* Janice L. and David J. Frent Collection of Political Americana; *Adolf Hitler* ©Bettmann/Corbis; *Wizard of Oz ruby slippers* ©MGM/Kobal/Shutterstock; *Black Tuesday* ©Bettmann/Corbis; *unemployed man with sign* ©Archive Holdings Inc/Getty Images; *Blame It on Hoover cartoon* ©The Granger Collection, NYC; *family listening to radio* ©Bettmann/Corbis; *Eleanor Roosevelt* ©Fotosearch/Getty Images; *two young men working* Library of Congress Prints and Photographs Division, Washington, D.C. [LC-DIG-fsa-8b36006]; *NYA teen girl working* Library of Congress Prints and Photographs Division, Washington, D.C. [LC-DIG-fsa-8d12548]; *Dust Bowl* NOAA George E. Marsh Album; *Migrant Mother photograph* Library of Congress Prints and Photographs Division, Washington, D.C. [LC-DIG-fsa-8b29516]; *Marian Anderson* ©Thomas D. McAvoy/The Life Picture Collection/Getty Images; *Stowaway movie poster* ©Swim Ink 2 LLC/Corbis; *The Grapes of Wrath* The Granger Collection, NYC.

Module 11: *Landing craft in Philippines* ©Corbis; *aircraft at Pearl Harbor* Library of Congress Prints and Photographs Division, Washington, D.C. [LC-DIGfsac-1a35398]; *Enigma machine* AKG-Images, London; *mushroom cloud* ©Hulton Archive/Getty Images; *Hideki Tojo* ©MPI/Getty Images; *Hitler saluting crowd* ©Hugo Jaeger/Timepix/Time Life Pictures/Getty Images; *bombed London street* ©Corbis; *Pearl Harbor attack* ©Corbis; *Standard Oil truck* Library of Congress Prints and Photographs Division, Washington, D.C. [LC-USF34-10032-C]; *Rosie the Riveter poster* Picture Research Consultants, Inc.; *Victory Garden poster* Library of Congress Prints and Photographs Division, Washington, D.C. [LC-USZC4-4436]; *Tuskegee Airmen* ©Everett Collection, Inc./Alamy; *segregated water fountains* ©Bettmann/Corbis; *Lozano family* Shades of L.A. Archives/Los Angeles Public Library; *Japanese internment camp* ©Seattle Post-Intelligencer Collection, Museum of History and Industry/Corbis; *German U-boats* ©Universal History Archive/Shutterstock; *Allied and Axis leaders (all)* ©Bettmann/Corbis; *WWII tanks* ©Corbis; *WWII plane* Library of Congress Prints and Photographs Division, Washington, D.C. [LC-DIG-fsac-1a35398]; *D-Day American soldiers* ©Keystone/Getty Images; *Navajo code talkers* National Archives (NARA); *raising the American flag at Iwo Jima* ©Superstock; *kamikaze pilots* ©Hulton-Deutsch Collection/Corbis; *Battle of the Bulge* ©Corbis; *Buchenwald* ©H. Miller/Hulton Archive/Getty Images; *Hiroshima ruins* ©Bettmann/Corbis; *Auschwitz (barbed wire)* ©R H Productions/Getty Images.

Module 12: *Duck-and-cover drill* ©Bettmann/Corbis; *Grace Hopper and compiler* ©Bettmann/Corbis; *Israeli flag* ©Carl & Ann Purcell/Corbis; *Fats Domino* ©Hulton Archive/Getty Images;